DATE DUE			

GAYLORD M-2   PRINTED IN U.S.A.

BRITAIN, RUSSIA, AND THE ARMED NEUTRALITY OF 1780

BRITAIN, RUSSIA, AND THE ARMED NEUTRALITY OF 1780

Sir James Harris's
Mission to St Petersburg
during the American Revolution

ISABEL DE MADARIAGA

with a foreword by
Samuel Flagg Bemis

HOLLIS & CARTER

LONDON

© by Yale University 1962
Printed in the United States of America for
HOLLIS & CARTER LTD
10 Earlham Street, London W C 2
by the Vail-Ballou Press, Inc., Binghamton, N.Y.
First published in Great Britain 1962

To

S. de M. and C. H. M. A.
without whom this book would
certainly not have been written
by me

Foreword

THE diplomatic history of the war for American independence affords a good illustration of the evolution of this particular discipline from rudimentary unilateral presentation to finished multiarchival historiography internationally shared by historical scholarship. Scholars have studied the archives, both official and private, of the different countries involved as belligerents, or as uneasy neutrals, during that war which we can now look back upon as almost a world war, at least of the Western world. But there has been one conspicuous gap in the literature of the subject: the relations between Great Britain and Russia, which in turn impinge upon the policies of the Netherlands, the Scandinavian countries, and Austria. Conspicuous in this network of interests were the diplomacy of the Armed Neutrality of 1780 and the proposals for mediation—Russian, Austrian, and Austro-Russian—which in turn had their effect on the calculations of the American peace commissioners at Paris. In the present contribution, Isabel de Madariaga (Mrs. Leonard Schapiro) has applied her historical talents and linguistic gifts to fill a gap with what may be considered a definitive study.

Hitherto for a number of reasons I have declined to write forewords to books by colleagues, friends, and former students. In this instance I am departing from my rule because I think it desirable to introduce to the current of American historical scholarship this very important work which lends such dignity, sophistication, and grace to the study of a subject so important to American students. Was not the greatest diplomatic victory in the history of the United States won at the outset in the treaty of peace and independence of 1782–83?

SAMUEL FLAGG BEMIS

Preface

THE PURPOSE of this study is to fill a gap in the diplomatic history of the period of the American War of Independence. At first sight it might not seem that Anglo-Russian relations were of particular importance at a time when Britain was deeply involved in war with the United States, France, Spain, and eventually with the United Provinces of the Netherlands. Two factors, however, brought Russia into the very centre of the picture. One was the British need for naval support which led the British government to seek repeatedly a Russian alliance and the loan of part of the Russian fleet. The other was the launching by Russia in 1780 of the League of Armed Neutrality which cut right across Britain's policy of economic warfare and in time led to the fourth Anglo-Dutch war.

My main object has been to study Anglo-Russian relations. But they cannot be studied in isolation. Inevitably I have been led to examine the policy of the other European great powers in order to establish the background and thus to assess the influences which swayed Britain and Russia. I have therefore had to devote some attention to the War of the Bavarian Succession and its impact on Anglo-Russian relations. Again, Russian leadership of the Armed Neutrality extended the diplomacy of the period over almost the whole of Europe and rendered necessary some study of British and Bourbon relations with the neutral powers. The fact also that during the war a change took place in the very foundations of Russian foreign policy—from a Prussian to an Austrian orientation—rendered essential the examination of both British and Russian relations with these two powers.

The Armed Neutrality played a major part in Anglo-Russian relations, and I have therefore devoted considerable space to its origins and development. Broadly speaking there have been two schools of thought about it. The Russian and to a great extent the French and German historians have praised it as a significant departure in the international law of the sea, even if by the end of the century its principles had been abandoned. French historians have additionally stressed its diplomatic importance, seeing in it the triumph of Vergennes's policy of isolating Britain. Historians in the Anglo-Saxon lands, while appreciating that the Neutral League increased Britain's difficulties, have tended to write if off as the product of the Empress's vanity, diplomatically to some extent effective, legally unsound, and economically of no real importance —an "armed nullity" in fact. Neither of these schools of thought has attempted to fit the Neutral League into the general pattern of Russian policy, political and economic. To them it sprang, like Minerva, fully armed from the Empress Catherine's brain, and conception and gestation have been equally neglected.

Leaving aside questions of national prejudice which have contributed to confuse the issue, attention also has been diverted from the Armed Neutrality itself in the effort to decide who was responsible for launching it—the Empress of Russia or her foreign minister, Count N. I. Panin. The question of the Empress's personal role, the extent to which she knew what she was doing, has indeed roused passionate controversy.

It is my contention that the Armed Neutrality was not a policy suddenly embarked on by the Empress in a fit of vanity or pique. Rather, it was the result of a slowly maturing interest in the problems of neutral trade, in the relations of both belligerent sides with the neutrals, and above all in the vexed question of British relations with the United Provinces, the biggest carriers of Russian exports after Britain. I have therefore devoted a good deal of attention to the development of Anglo-Dutch tension, probably the most important single factor that enabled Russia to launch the Neutral League. I have also attempted, though only briefly, to sketch in the economic background to Russian policy. I have of course had to take a position on the question of the Empress's personal role, since whether she understood what she was doing or not is of vital importance to the interpretation of the diplomacy of this period.

In order to introduce some coherence into the bewildering

variety of problems which arose in Anglo-Russian relations in these five years, I have found it convenient to present this study as a history of the mission of Sir James Harris to St. Petersburg. Harris arrived in Russia just before France recognized America and left when the final peace was about to be signed. His presence gives a certain continuity to the British view of Russia, since both under North and under the Whig government which followed Russia was seen almost entirely through his eyes.

Surveying the whole period of Harris's mission, it is possible to distinguish three broad phases in Anglo-Russian relations. The first phase extends from the recognition of America by France at the beginning of 1778 to the convention of Ainalikawak and the peace of Teschen in May 1779. British foreign policy was dominated by the needs of war—the necessity to secure allies and naval reinforcements and the effort to starve her enemies of naval stores—with all the consequences that this policy entailed. Much more important for Russia, however, was the situation in the Holy Roman Empire, where the unexpected death of the Elector of Bavaria in the last days of 1777 precipitated a crisis that threatened to embroil Russia in war as Prussia's ally. At no point were Russian and British interests able to meet, and by the end of the crisis, in May 1779, Russia had already begun to show a tentative interest in the protection of neutral trade.

The second phase in Anglo-Russian relations lasts from the pacification of the continent in May 1779 until the fall of the North administration in March 1782. It is dominated on the one hand by Russian efforts to be invited to mediate between the belligerents and on the other by the foundation of the Armed Neutrality and the many problems to which it gave rise, such as the Anglo-Dutch war, the joint mediation by Russia and Austria between the belligerents, and the Russian mediation between Britain and the United Provinces. Throughout this period the main lines of British policy continued almost unchanged: to secure an alliance (at the price even of Minorca), to prosecute her policy of economic warfare, and to ward off Russian displeasure at her treatment of neutral trade. Russia, meanwhile, freed largely by the diplomacy of Vergennes from the threat of war, embarked on ambitious measures of trade protection which had the effect of

frustrating Britain's economic warfare. At the same time she secretly abandoned her old ally, Prussia, in favour of Austria, and,
when the death of Maria Theresa in November 1780 cleared the
way, she prepared herself for expansion at the expense of the Ottoman Porte.

The third phase extends from the fall of North to the peace of
Versailles in September 1783. It is characterized by an immediate
relaxation of the tension that had been building up between Britain
and Russia over the problems arising out of the Armed Neutrality.
With the advent of the Whigs, British policy changed from waging
the best possible war to making the best possible peace. Simultaneously Russian attention was diverted from the war in the West
by the outbreak of revolt in the Crimea.

The detailed domestic history of Britain and the actual conduct
of the war in America impinged but little on the diplomatic relations between Britain and Russia. I have therefore touched upon
them only slightly and when necessary. As regards the actual process
by which foreign policy was determined in Britain, the documents
available do not allow one to elaborate much. Minutes of cabinet
meetings, when they exist, record decisions but not the preceding
debates. Wherever possible I have endeavoured to show the process
of thought by which decisions were reached. Since the negotiations
took place mainly in St. Petersburg, the analysis of the formation
of Russian foreign policy inevitably takes up more space. Moreover,
owing to the peculiar conditions prevailing in Russia and the important part which court intrigue played in Harris's mission, I have
found it essential to attempt to penetrate behind the smooth surface
of diplomatic documents to the power struggle beneath. There
were, of course, no public debates on foreign policy in Russia nor
did the press do more than echo official statements and attitudes.
The realities therefore have to be sought in the Empress's own
policies, her correspondence, the letters of her public servants, and
the dispatches of the foreign envoys. By itself, not one of these
sources is sufficient, and experience has now taught me to rely but
rarely on the unsupported word of an eighteenth-century diplomat.
If in the result I have seemed to devote more attention to Russia
than to Britain, it is because British foreign policy is already better
known and because, in spite of the handicap of a virulent parlia-

mentary opposition, it was not at this time the object of the intrigues of the foreign envoys in Britain.

However conscientious the research, one must always be prepared to have one's conclusions invalidated by future discoveries. Where it is possible, as in the case of Britain, to study the development of foreign relations week by week in instructions and dispatches, the picture can be reconstructed fairly faithfully. It has not been possible to present the same detailed analysis of Russian policy, for at vital points in the story the printed documents are silent. I have extended my search for Russian material as widely as I could, and, where I have not been able to find a Russian source to document my interpretation of Russian policy, I have endeavoured to fill the gap from British, French, Prussian, Dutch, Austrian, or Scandinavian sources. I can only hope that Russian documents made available in the future will not radically alter my interpretation of the major issues.

ACKNOWLEDGEMENTS

This book is based on a study which was submitted to the University of London and for which the author was awarded the degree of Doctor of Philosophy in July 1959. It owes much to the kind assistance of numerous people.

I would like in the first place to thank the Earl of Malmesbury who most generously placed at my disposal some of the private papers of Sir James Harris. I also wish to thank the Warden and Fellows of Merton College who kindly allowed me to consult the Harris Papers deposited there. My thanks are also due to the staff of the British Museum and the Public Record Office for their assistance over many years, as well as to the officials of the Archives des Affaires Étrangères and of the Bibliothèque Nationale in Paris. I have also been privileged over the years to use the many facilities and resources of the Institute of Historical Research in the University of London. It is with pleasure that I record here my gratitude to Dr. Georgette Donchin and to the Librarian and staff of the Library of the School of Slavonic and East European Studies in the University of London for their friendly and courteous help. I am also grateful to Miss N. Kerling who translated documents from the Dutch for me, to Mr. W. Slottman who kindly provided me with transcripts from the Haus- Hof- und Staatsarchiv in Vienna and to Miss A. Font for her help with the index.

Professor S. F. Bemis and Professor D. B. Horn both kindly gave me the benefit of their advice which I gratefully acknowledge. To Professor G. J. Renier I owe more than I can express, both for his infectious enthusiasm in the pursuit of historical understanding and for his devastating criticism and intolerance of slovenly thought. I also wish to record my most grateful thanks to Dr. Ragnhild Hatton for her wise guidance, expert advice, and constant support and help. Finally I must record the great debt I owe to my husband, Leonard Schapiro, for his advice, criticism, and unfailing encouragement, and above all for the exemplary patience he has shown in sharing his home for so long with Sir James Harris and Prince Potemkin.

ISABEL DE MADARIAGA

Highgate, 1961

Contents

Abbreviations

Short titles have been used in footnotes for works listed in the Bibliography. The following abbreviations have also been used.

AKV—Arkhiv knyazya Vorontsova

AMON—Archives ou correspondance inédite de la Maison d'Orange-Nassau

Bancroft-Circourt—Circourt, A. de, *Histoire de l'action commune de la France et de l'Amérique pour l'indépendance des États Unis* (translation of the *History of the United States* by G. Bancroft)

BDI—British Diplomatic Instructions

CP Russie—Correspondance Politique, Russie (Archives des Affaires Étrangères)

DNB—Dictionary of National Biography

HMC—Historical Manuscripts Commission

MD—Malmesbury, Earl of, ed., *Diaries and Correspondence of James Harris, First Earl of Malmesbury*

Morskoy Sbornik—O vooruzhennom morskom neytralitete, ed. P. A. Obolensky, in *Morskoy Sbornik*

PKFG—Politische Korrespondenz Friedrichs des Grossen

PSZ—Polnoye sobraniye zakonov

Recueil—Recueil des instructions données aux ambassadeurs de France

Sbornik—Sbornik imperatorskago russkago istoricheskago obshchestva

Note. All single dates throughout the book are in new style, unless otherwise stated; quotations from Harris's dispatches and Russian documents are given in both old and new styles, a difference of 11 days in the 18th century. In quotations, all italics are in the original unless otherwise stated. The system of transliteration of cyrillic used by the *Slavonic and East European Review*, published by the University of London, has been followed, with slight modifications. The 18th-century spelling of Russian names has been used in two cases, namely Galitzin and Markov (instead of Golitsyn and Morkov), since the constant change from one form of spelling to another might have proved confusing.

BRITAIN, RUSSIA, AND THE ARMED NEUTRALITY OF 1780

1. Introduction

In September 1776, much to the regret of King Frederick II of Prussia, the thirty-year-old English minister and envoy plenipotentiary who had been at his court for five years was recalled to Britain. James Harris had started on a diplomatic career at a young age and his rise had been rapid. He was twenty-one when he received his first appointment in 1767 as secretary of embassy under Sir James Grey in Madrid. In 1770 he was acting chargé d'affaires when relations between Britain and Spain almost reached breaking point over the disputed Falkland Islands. Harris conducted himself with skill and firmness and was much praised for the apparent foresight which made him linger for a while some twenty miles from Madrid instead of departing for England during the crisis. That his purpose in lingering was amorous rather than diplomatic did not affect the issue,[1] and Harris was duly rewarded when a year later he was appointed minister to the court of Berlin. His handsome presence and social talents earned him the favour of the Prussian monarch, who even took steps to have him reappointed to Berlin. "Au reste je regretterai toujours le chevalier Harris," wrote Frederick to his representative in London, Count Maltzahn, lamenting Harris's final departure. "Je l'ai toujours estimé pour son fonds de probité et de droiture . . . on aura bien de la peine à lui trouver un digne successeur et qui me fut aussi agréable . . ."[2] Little did Frederick II—or for that matter Harris—foresee the battle which they were soon to wage on paper, for Harris was appointed to the post of envoy plenipotentiary at the court of Fred-

1. Fernan Nuñez, *Vida de Carlos III, 1,* 232–33. Fernan Nuñez, "Aris," and the lady spent many happy evenings together during the month which Harris passed in quasi-exile north of Madrid.
2. 8 October 1776. Bancroft-Circourt, *3,* 201.

erick's ally, Catherine II of Russia, which had been vacant since
the departure of Sir Robert Gunning in 1775.

The importance of Russia in the network of British foreign relations had been gradually increasing throughout the eighteenth
century, though economic rather than political issues tended still
to dominate Anglo-Russian relations. The main bond between
the two countries was the lucrative trade in Russian raw materials:
pitch, hemp, tar, sail cloth, ships' timber, and above all the unique
Riga masts, which were imported into Britain in large quantities.
Russian imports from Britain were on a much smaller scale; hence
Russia maintained a favourable balance of trade, a factor to which
much importance was attached. British merchants in Russia enjoyed considerable advantages over their competitors from other
nations, not only because of the superior British organization and
greater credit facilities, but also by reason of the exceptional privileges granted to them in commercial treaties. The latest of these
dated from 1766 and was due to expire in 1786; it ensured the legal
status of British merchants in Russia, reduced the tariffs on British
goods, and enabled British exporters and importers to pay customs
dues in local currency—a most valuable concession.

But the favoured position of the British merchants was beginning to be felt as a burden in Russia. Moreover, it did not correspond to the theoretical ideas of the Empress and her advisers on
trade. When negotiating the treaty of 1766, the Russians had already made some efforts to claim for themselves a reciprocity which,
in view of the limited foreign trade in Russian ships, was of little
practical value. But their attitude bore witness to a trend which
was to grow stronger as the century advanced.[3]

Though the commercial links between Britain and Russia were
close, and on the whole harmonious, efforts to achieve a parallel
political alliance had failed in the preceding years. The treaty of
1742 had lapsed a long time before. This treaty enshrined the principle that Britain would not come to Russia's assistance in the event
of a war with the Porte, nor would Russia be called on to defend

3. See Gerhardt, *England und der Aufstieg Russlands,* pp. 44–45, 125 ff.; F. de
Martens, *Recueil, 9,* 203 ff. and 242; see also Rahbek Schmidt, "The Treaty of Commerce between Great Britain and Russia, 1766"; Reddaway, "Macartney in Russia
1765–1767"; Spencer, "Lord Sandwich, Russian Masts and American Independence."

Britain's American possessions or to take part in a war outside Europe.[4] The treaty of 1742 had eventually been superseded by the treaty of St. Petersburg of 1755 which bound Russia to create a diversion in the event of a Prussian attack on Hanover.[5] The treaty promptly became a dead letter when Britain signed the treaty of Westminster with Frederick II, and Russia took part in the Seven Years' War as the ally of Austria. But relations between Britain and Russia were not broken off during the war, their respective envoys remained at their posts, and trade continued.

At the end of the Seven Years' War, and with the accession of Catherine II, the opportunity arose of establishing Anglo-Russian relations on a fresh basis. Negotiations for an alliance were carried on throughout the 1760s, but it soon became clear that neither side was willing to pay the price required by the other. The renewal of the treaty of 1742, with some modifications, would have suited Great Britain.[6] But the negotiations foundered on the so-called "Turkish clause"—the exclusion of the *casus foederis* of a Turkish war from the treaty—and on England's reluctance to support Russian policy actively in Poland and Sweden. Catherine was striving to emancipate Russia from the role of auxiliary of one of the great powers, which she had played so far, and to establish her treaty relations on the basis of a real reciprocity of interests. She refused to commit herself to the British system of opposition to France and whichever German power might at the time be allied to her, unless Britain committed herself to support Russian aims.

Thus when the Russo-Turkish war broke out in 1768, Russia fought alone. In the early stages of the war, Britain followed a dual policy. She endeavoured in Constantinople to secure for herself the post of mediator between the warring nations, and she facilitated by every means the transfer of the Russian fleet from the Baltic to the Mediterranean. Russia appreciated the services to her fleet, but preferred to do without the mediation. In the end British policy achieved nothing. The Turks did not have much confidence in the neutrality of a power which had enabled the fleet of their enemy

4. F. de Martens, *Recueil, 9,* 112; cf. Sir Richard Lodge, "The First Anglo-Russian Treaty, 1739–1742."

5. F. de Martens, *Recueil, 9,* 191.

6. Ibid., 217; cf. also SP 103/63 for British policy in these negotiations.

to appear in the Levant and which had strenuously prevented any interposition at sea on their behalf by France; Britain thus lost what influence she had with the Porte. Russian victories stiffened the attitude of the Empress Catherine, and her refusal to allow Britain to set limits to her ambition irritated British statesmen and led them to reconsider their attitude to Russian expansion at the expense of Turkey. Britain now showed herself reluctant to assist the Russian fleet in the Mediterranean with stores and port facilities. She now also opposed the permanent acquisition by Russia of a base in the Mediterranean—the annexation of an island in the Archipelago had been contemplated by the Empress as one of the rewards of her victories. All ideas of an alliance between the two powers faded away completely, and Catherine eventually brought her war against Turkey to a successful conclusion and signed in 1774, without the participation of any other power, the peace treaty of Kutschuk-Kainardji, which established Russia on the Black Sea.[7] Several of its provisions were capable of sowing the seeds of future disputes, notably the setting up of the Khanate of the Crimea as an independent kingdom, subordinate to the Sultan only in religious matters.[8] Neither Russia nor the Porte believed in or intended to respect the complete independence of the Khanate of Crimea, and the ink was no sooner dry on the treaty than a struggle for influence began. In 1777, three years after the peace treaty, matters had come to such a pass that a fresh outbreak of hostilities was both feared and expected.

The abortive negotiations for a treaty with Britain made a lasting impression in Russia. The Empress resented Russia's being treated as a kind of eastern Portugal, a power which could be used by Britain but could not claim equality of status. Not even British assistance to the Russian fleet during the war and British containment of France during this critical period were sufficient to soothe her ruffled feelings. But in spite of the failure to reach an agreement, British statesmen continued to trust in the obvious community of commercial interests between the two powers as a sufficiently strong link to withstand all the stresses and strains of European

7. See Anderson, "Great Britain and the Russo-Turkish War of 1768–1774."
8. For the text of the treaty see Druzhinina, *Kyuchuk-kaynardzhiyskiy mir 1774 goda,* p. 349.

diplomacy, and they still saw Russia primarily as an auxiliary out-post of the anti-Bourbon powers.

The main pillar of Russian foreign policy during the first eight-een years of Catherine's reign was the so-called "Northern system," founded on the treaty of alliance with Prussia of 1764. This treaty had originally been entered into with a view to joint action by Prussia and Russia in the imminent crisis over the succession to the throne in Poland at the death of Augustus III, Elector of Saxony and King of Poland. The "Northern system" extended the benefits of the Russo-Prussian treaty to Denmark-Norway, whose relations with Russia had been satisfactorily solved by the "Mageskifte" treaty of 1767.[9] Russia had originally envisaged the extension of the Northern system to include Britain and a Sweden purged of anti-Russian elements. But Frederick II scoffed at the thought of Britain. "Son roi est l'homme du monde le plus faible qui change ses ministres comme il change ses chemises," [10] he declared, and vowed that Russia and Prussia needed the help of no other power. But though Frederick II needed no other power, he needed Russia very badly, and he used the opportunity of the first Russo-Turkish war to extort a renewal of the treaty of alliance with Russia, extending its validity to 1780; in 1777, the treaty was again secretly renewed, this time until 1788.[11] Thus the Northern system never had any very concrete reality outside the treaties with Prussia and Denmark, but it provided a certain stability in Eastern Europe and effectively neutralized Austria.

With France, Russia entertained friendly relations, which masked a deep suspicion. France was not only the traditional pa-tron of Turkey but also Russia's rival in the control of Sweden. Since the *coup d'état* of 1772 by which Gustavus III had achieved absolute authority in Sweden, his every move was watched in Rus-sia, and his reliance on French funds for the maintenance of his authority gave point to Russian distrust of France. Russia's rela-tions with other powers were mainly governed by considerations of trade. The Dutch Republic came second to Britain in the im-

---

9. See F. de Martens, *Recueil, 6*, 11. See also *Danske Tractater*, p. 229 and definitive treaty of 1773, p. 322; treaty of alliance of 1773, p. 365.
10. F. de Martens, *Recueil, 6*, 40.
11. Ibid., 48 ff. and 100 ff.

portant export trade from Russia, and the commercial relations between the two countries had a long tradition behind them. Spain was considered politically as the shadow of France, but in pursuance of Catherine's intensive drive to increase her commerce direct trade on a very small scale had already begun between Spain and Russia, a Russian consul had been appointed in Cadiz, and at least one Spanish house existed in Russia.[12] Portugal and the minor Mediterranean states were of interest to Russia only in so far as trade relations could be developed, and to the extent that they might provide bases for the Russian fleet when and if it should visit the Mediterranean.

On the surface, Russian relations with Britain in the 1770s were perfectly friendly, as can be seen from the instructions to the newly appointed Russian envoy to the court of the Two Sicilies on 18/29 February 1777: "We have a commercial treaty with the court of London, and over and above that we have everywhere almost the same state interests. Therefore we may both firmly rely on our mutual friendship, even though the previous alliance between us has not been renewed, owing to various difficulties which have prevented an agreement." [13] Unofficial attitudes were of a mixed kind. There was still resentment at Britain's unwillingness to concede anything to the Russian point of view in foreign policy, coupled with admiration for British arrogance, wealth, power, and naval strength. In Russian naval circles pro-British feeling reigned supreme, from the ex-commander in chief of the Russian fleet in the Mediterranean, Aleksey Orlov, to Samuel Greig, the British senior admiral in Russian service. Here and there, however, feelings were entertained that Britain was perhaps too powerful at sea since the Peace of Paris of 1763, and that it would do no harm to the balance of power if she were humbled.[14] A certain amount of *Schaden-*

12. See Ulyanitsky, *Russkiye konsul'stva za granitsey v XVIII v.* for an account of the development of Catherine's consular system throughout Europe; cf. Corberon, *Journal Intime, 2* 195–96.

13. *Sbornik, 145,* 357.

14. See for instance the Russian Foreign Minister to Count Ivan Chernyshev, then ambassador to the court of St. James, on 2/13 January 1769: "The English Ministry . . . on the other hand cannot fail to realize that its one interest, supremacy at sea over one and all, is not such an attribute as to attach the whole North to them alone; moreover, speaking objectively, is not this great domination in the opinion

freude crept into comments on Britain's difficulties with her rebellious American colonies. Both King and government were regarded with patronizing disdain for having allowed the American revolt to develop to such proportions. Though no crowned head approved of the revolt in theory, in practice sympathy tended to go to the American David against the British Goliath. And no power, certainly not Russia, feared for its own future as the result of eventual American independence.

The actual government of the country also came under fire. The Whig accusations that the King intended to establish royal absolutism found a ready echo among enlightened despots abroad. Even more damaging was the evident instability of the North administration. The changeable character of British foreign policy, which was determined not by the sovereign but by the party in power in Parliament, rendered Britain suspect in Russian eyes. The history of the Peace of Utrecht and Frederick II's diatribes against the Peace of Paris confirmed this distrust.

The American rebellion indeed caused Britain to suffer a somewhat painful diplomatic rebuff. In June 1775, shortly after the first encounter between British troops and American militia at Concord, the British government thought it advisable to discover whether Russian troops might be put at Britain's disposal. The first overture made by Britain was unofficial, but Sir Robert Gunning, in August 1775, reported that he had received a very satisfactory answer. In September 1775, the secretary of state, Lord Suffolk, who had understood that the Empress had offered her help, instructed Gunning to apply for the loan of 20,000 Russian troops to be sent to Canada. He was not to insult the Russians by proposing to pay a subsidy for the use of the troops, unless the Russians demanded one, but was of course to offer to pay all expenses. The Russian response to this formal request came as a great disappointment. In a letter to George III, Catherine explained that she had believed the previous overture to refer to the possibility of a war with Spain, but the number and the destination of the succours required of her were such that she could not comply with the British

---

of these same northern powers a matter which does not concern them, or is even harmful to them, particularly if all continental interests are excluded from the system of the English court." (*Sbornik*, 87, 300).

request. Moreover, the Empress asked, what would be the consequences for the dignity of both Britain and Russia "de cette jonc-
tion de nos forces simplement pour calmer une rebellion qui n'est
appuyée d'aucune puissance étrangère?" Might not other powers
be induced to interfere in the American rebellion if Russian troops
appeared on the American continent and might this not lead to a
European war? [15]

These might have been the Empress's official reasons. But Gunning suggested that she was moved also by other considerations,
notably the "erroneous opinion" she entertained "that the measures which His Majesty's ministers have adopted and are pursuing
are far from having the approbation of the nation in general." [16]
Already at this early date Catherine had no sympathy with the
King's methods of handling his rebellious subjects, and in August
1775 she herself had proposed to Gunning not to concentrate on
one single way of putting an end to the revolt, but to try them all—
a broad hint in favour of conciliation.[17] "Que dites-vous," she wrote
in a private letter on 5/16 September 1776, "de ces colonies qui
disent adieu à jamais à l'Angleterre; n'y a-t-il pas là de quoi ranger
tout le monde du côté de l'opposition?" [18]

The situation of Britain was indeed growing more and more difficult. The King was determined to pursue a strong policy which
would compel the Americans to return to their allegiance. The war
was viewed with mixed feelings by the population. While loyal ad-
dresses poured in upon the King, the Whigs conducted a vigorous
opposition in both Houses of Parliament, led by Burke and Fox in
the Commons and by Shelburne, Rockingham, and the fading
ghost of the great Chatham in the Lords. Moreover, the ministers
in whom the King placed his trust did not command universal confidence. Lord North, the First Lord of the Treasury, was too easy-
going a man for the crisis through which Britain was passing; he
was not strong enough either to impose himself on the King or to
resign. Lord George Germain was dogged in the public repute
by his failure to live up to his military duties at the battle of Min-

15. See *Sbornik*, *19*, 463–506, for Sir Robert Gunning's correspondence dealing
with this episode.
16. Ibid., 503, Gunning to Suffolk, 26 September/7 October 1775.
17. Ibid., 488, Gunning to Suffolk, 31 August/11 September 1775.
18. *Sbornik*, *27*, 118, to Madame Bielke.

den, and he proved himself an incompetent military strategist now that he was directing the war in America from London. Suffolk and Weymouth, the secretaries of state for the North and South, were mediocrities, and the former was in addition a victim to gout. The Earl of Sandwich, as First Lord of the Admiralty, though diligent, tolerated corrupt practices in the administration of the navy which undermined its efficiency and rendered his own position liable to the most violent parliamentary attacks. Though the opposition might not yet command many votes in the House, it was vocal and vigorous enough to force the administration to spend valuable time on parliamentary manoeuvres. More dangerous still for Britain, it presented to Europe the spectacle of a country divided against itself, and in the debates on foreign policy it provided other countries with forceful arguments against the government.

The Peace of Paris which concluded the Seven Years' War had left Britain at the very peak of her strength and influence, and confidence in her own powers had led her to view continental alliances as unnecessary hindrances to her freedom of action in emergencies. But when war with America came it was clear to all that Britain's traditional enemy, France, would not hesitate to profit from her difficulties. France, and for that matter Spain, still smarted under the defeats inflicted on them under the leadership of the Great Commoner, and as early as 1775 Vergennes, the French foreign minister, made secret contacts with the rebellious Americans. These contacts developed into extensive financial assistance supplied through bogus trading firms and used mainly for the purchase of armaments. France also allowed the numerous American privateers, which began to prey on British shipping, to use French ports as bases where they fitted themselves out and to which they brought their prizes. When the British ambassador, Lord Stormont, protested, Vergennes agreed to take measures to prevent American abuse of French neutrality, but in fact matters went on much as before. No decision was taken at that time by France to intervene openly in favour of the Americans, for Vergennes was too cautious to commit France to a war until he was certain that the rebellion was sufficiently serious and widespread to cause a substantial diversion of British strength. Moreover he had to be sure that no possibility of compromise existed, and that the prospect of

Britain at war with France might not rally the American rebels to the mother country and lead them to join forces in order to fall upon the surviving French colonial empire in the West Indies.

Unlike Britain, France had fortified her European status by means of two important treaties. She was linked to Spain by the Family Compact of the Bourbon Houses, a defensive alliance which bound Spain to come to France's aid in the event of attack. Though Spain was generally regarded as a mere shadow of France, she was repeatedly able, under the firm rule of Charles III and his exceptionally able minister, Count Floridablanca, to assert her own point of view against her powerful neighbour. The crisis of 1770 over the Falkland Islands, in which France had not supported Spanish pretensions to the extent Spain demanded, had strengthened Spanish determination not to subordinate her policy to that of France. On the question of the American rebellion, Spain was far more reserved than France. Though she might welcome the prospect of weakening Britain, the example of the American colonies was not one she wished to see followed by her own overseas dominions. Moreover her main territorial demands were European, not American. Apart from the recovery of West Florida, ceded to Britain in 1763, the *terra irredenta* of Spain were Minorca and above all Gibraltar.[19] Therefore, before France could commit herself finally to supporting the American rebels and embarking on a war with Britain, Spain had to be persuaded that the advantages she would obtain would outweigh the risks involved.

In addition to the Family Compact, France was bound to Austria by the treaty of 1756, which had been one of the factors leading to the Seven Years' War. The treaty was by no means universally approved of in France, and there were many who felt that while Austria derived all the advantages France bore all the burden.[20] Yet in 1777, though sympathies might have worn thin between the

19. For Spanish policy in the early years of the American War of Independence, see Yela Utrilla, *España ante la independencia de los Estados Unidos;* on Gibraltar in Spanish policy, see Conn, *Gibraltar in British Diplomacy in the Eighteenth Century.*

20. See notably the arguments for and against the Austrian alliance examined by Ségur in *Politique de tous les cabinets de l'Europe.* Vergennes believed that as long as Maria Theresa was alive the alliance on the whole was beneficial to France. (See his mémoire of 1774, Ségur, 3, 158).

Austrians and the French, the treaty was still valid and had not been replaced by any alternative system. Frederick II of Prussia had, it is true, been wooing France for some time, but all he had achieved was the improvement of his own relations with that power. The lasting enmity which the King of Prussia harboured towards his late ally, Britain, was sufficient guarantee that he would not be found fighting at Britain's side, unless the safety of his own state demanded it. While Europe remained quiet, a *rapprochement* between Britain and Prussia was unlikely.

Whatever secret hopes Maria Theresa might have entertained of recovering the lands which Frederick II had seized from her, there was little likelihood that she would take any active steps to fulfill that aim. The Empress was getting old and wished to end her days in peace. As long as Prussia was Russia's ally, there was little that Austria could do. But Austria entertained the hope of weaning Russia from the Prussian alliance and of eventually recreating the bonds that had united the two courts during the early part of the Seven Years' War.[21] The main problem which beset the Empress, however, was the divergence of view between herself and her son, the Emperor Joseph II, who believed in a more active policy and harboured extensive designs for rationalizing the heterogeneous Austrian dominions by territorial readjustments. The plan to round off the German base by annexing Bavaria, possibly in exchange for the Austrian Netherlands, was one means by which Joseph contemplated giving greater cohesion to his realm. The Elector of Bavaria had no direct heir; the succession was due to pass to the Elector Palatine and after him to the Duke of Zweibrücken. Much attention was therefore paid to the health of the Elector of Bavaria, a man of some fifty years of age who might be expected in the normal course of events to live for many more years.

Of the remaining European powers, Portugal was a British satellite, Sweden a French one. Denmark was strongly under Russian influence, though Frederick II also carried much weight there. Count Bernstorff, the chief minister, a man of outstanding abilities,

---

21. See Arneth, *Maria Theresias letzte Regierungszeit*, and the full text of the secret supplement to the instructions of 18 April 1777 to Count Joseph Kaunitz-Rietberg, Austrian envoy to Russia, printed by Winter, "Grundlinien der Österreichischen Russlandspolitik am Ende des 18 Jahrhunderts."

was concerned with the defence of Danish trade and the promotion
of Danish economic development. His personal inclinations were
towards Britain, and this in no way clashed with the prevailing Russian orientation of Danish policy. The United Provinces of the
Netherlands had entered on a period of decline. Political passions,
the desire for profits, and suspicion of the military power which
the Stadholder might command all combined to render the rich
merchants hostile to the House of Orange. The anglophile Stadholder was a well-meaning but irresolute man, unable to stand up
to the so-called Patriot party, and the country was torn by faction.
Amsterdam was the main centre of the patriots; the Stadholder
commanded a following in the more agricultural provinces and
among the nobility. The Netherlands were linked by several important treaties with Britain. Of primary importance were the
treaty of alliance of 1678 and the Marine Treaty of 1674.[22] Though
the alliance between the Netherlands and Britain was regarded as
traditional in both countries, under the impact of the American
rebellion Dutch merchants were beginning to feel it a burden. The
prospect of a vast new market opening up to their ships, if once
America threw her ports open to world trade and ceased to be an
exclusively British preserve, attracted the Dutch merchants and induced them to replace British ships in the trade with America.
Dutch and to a less extent Danish ships sailed from Europe and
either went direct to American ports to load and unload or trans-
shipped their cargoes at St. Eustatius, the great Dutch free port in
the Caribbean, or in the Danish island of Ste. Croix. In May 1776
Britain forbade all trade with American ports, whereupon British
ships, either of the Royal Navy or privateers or sometimes little
better than pirates, acting without a commission, preyed on the
Dutch and Danish ships and brought them into the British West

22. See Chalmers, *Collection of Treaties* p. 177 for the text of the Marine Treaty;
the text of the treaty of 1678 is in Jenkinson, *A Collection of all the Treaties of
Peace, Alliance and Commerce between Great Britain and other Powers,* p. 211.
It will be observed that in dispatches the secretaries of state and the envoys usually
refer to the Anglo-Dutch treaty of 1668 and not to that of 1678, which was the
treaty actually in operation, but when the time came for Britain to claim Dutch
succours the treaty of 1678 was invoked. (See the British request to the States General, 22 July 1779, in *Annual Register,* 1779, p. 428.)

Indian islands, on the grounds that they were trading with American ports or that since their cargo was colonial produce the presumption was that they had loaded at an American port. The admiralty courts in the West Indies were not distinguished either for speed or for incorruptibility,[23] and there were constant disputes between the Dutch, the Danes, and the British on the validity of these captures. Feeling among the merchant communities of Europe began to run high, though as yet these disputes were entirely confined to American waters. Naturally enough the sympathies of the merchants tended to go to the Americans rather than to Britain.

Russia, whither James Harris was about to direct his steps, was still in many ways a mystery to most Englishmen. British envoys at the court of St. Petersburg knew no Russian, seldom left the Europeanized capital, moved in the narrow social circle of the court and the diplomatic world, and had no contact whatsoever with native Russian life. They had little understanding of the mechanism of the Russian administration and rarely penetrated very far behind the scenes.

In 1777 the Empress Catherine II was in the sixteenth year of her reign. Now forty-eight years of age, she was a woman of handsome and majestic appearance, great determination, strong nerves, and hiding under a very feminine behaviour a very masculine temperament. Largely self-educated, she had a good practical intelligence, though not profound, considerable diplomatic skill, much shrewdness and penetration, and great charm. Though she had made unremitting efforts from an early age to adapt and assimilate herself completely to her new country, she retained certain very German qualities, *Gemütlichkeit*, a somewhat heavy-handed humour, a certain cosiness about her domestic life. She was generous to a fault to her favourites and not at all vindictive towards those in disgrace. The Russian court was conducted with magnif-

23. See the two volumes by Pares, *War and Trade in the West Indies* and *Colonial Blockade and Neutral Rights,* for descriptions of the workings of admiralty courts in the West Indies and in Minorca at a slightly earlier period. In these small communities, too many of the people connected with the courts, including sometimes even the judges themselves, had a share in the ventures of the privateers to make them reliable judges of prize cases.

icence and decorum, but it suffered somewhat from the moral example set by the Empress herself with her procession of lovers. Of
these only two, until then, had commanded the Empress's lasting
affection, namely Prince G. G. Orlov, and Prince G. A. Potemkin.
The former had been the Empress's lover for some twelve years,
but he had never really exercised the political power which might
have been his for the asking. After his dismissal in 1772 his importance lay in his connexion with his younger brother Aleksey,
the victor in the naval battle of Tschesme in 1770. The Orlov faction (there were five brothers) was still considered worth wooing—
in the hope that the brothers might return to power—by the foreign diplomats who failed to realize precisely where lay the source
of such power as they had ever comanded. Prince Grigory Alek-
sandrovich Potemkin had occupied the post of favourite in 1774
and had withdrawn in 1776 from the private apartments of the
Empress. But to the surprise of all those who foretold his fall, he
maintained not only his official posts but also his sway over the
Empress. About ten years younger than Catherine, Potemkin was
a man of unusual intelligence, boundless imagination, and remarkable cunning. He was well-read, particularly in the classics of the
Orthodox Church, and had a remarkable capacity for acquiring
knowledge without visible effort. Arrogant and intolerant, he
alienated the powerful magnates about the court, but he could be
kind and even considerate to the poor and the lowly. As a statesman
he was bold and imaginative, but his work was marred by a tem-
peramental incapacity to see anything through to the end, an inability to concentrate on details, and a reluctance to distinguish between his private fortune and the financial resources of the state.
His knowledge of Europe was scanty; he had only once been abroad,
on an official visit to Sweden, but he knew his own country and
understood his own people. At Catherine's side he dominated the
Russian scene from his first appearance as favourite in 1774 to his
death in 1791.[24]

From the date of Potemkin's withdrawal in 1776 until the appearance on the scene of Platon Zubov in 1789, the personalities
who exercised the active functions of favourites were mostly negli-

24. For the theory that he was married to Catherine (plausible though unproved),
see Soloveytchik, *Potemkin*.

gible.[25] Usually chosen by Potemkin himself, they spent the time allotted to them in their gilded cages and then withdrew to live in the country on the rewards of their office. Their only impact on public business occurred when the Empress was due for a change. Then the rival factions produced their candidates and manoeuvred to have them chosen; Catherine herself was in a state of agitation and turned to Potemkin for support; public affairs were in suspense and the court disorganized until Potemkin's candidate was accepted and life returned to normal.

Court life was brilliant and well-organized. The Empress held court days; there were theatrical performances and private parties of pleasure to which the foreign envoys were often invited. The Empress herself did not discuss foreign affairs with the foreign envoys, but they had frequent occasion to meet and converse with her, and those in her favour were invited to be her partners at cards. There was therefore every opportunity for an able, witty, and attractive man to acquire a prominent position in Catherine's intimate circle, but these personal relations by no means reflected Russia's political alignments.

The government of Russia consisted of the Senate, the various "colleges," and the unofficial Council of State.[26] The Senate was an administrative body, charged with many miscellaneous functions, including the supervision and registration of laws and general coordination of all government activity. The colleges were really executive departments, each governed by a board under the chairmanship of the president of the college. The Council of State was an *ad hoc* body of selected advisers set up by Catherine, and its composition varied at different periods of her reign. Of the colleges, those which signified most to the foreign envoys were the colleges of foreign affairs, of commerce, of the admiralty, and of war. The college of foreign affairs was ruled over by Count Nikita Ivanovich Panin, who had presided over Russian foreign policy almost since the accession of Catherine. He was not personally a favourite with the Empress, but she valued his experience. He had

25. During Harris's stay the post was occupied successively by Zorich, Korsakov, and Lanskoy. They played no part in his mission at all.

26. For a useful, if biassed, sketch of the Russian administration see Baranovich et al, *Ocherki istorii SSSR, period feodalizma, Rossiya vo vtoroy polovine XVIII v.,* pp. 284–90.

been governor of the young Grand Duke Paul, the heir to the throne, and had remained extremely attached to his pupil, who returned his affection and relied on Panin to support him against his mother, with whom his relations were anything but close. Panin was the creator of the so-called "Northern system," to which he remained wedded; he was devoted to Frederick II and on friendly terms with the Prussian envoys at the Russian court. The foreign envoys mostly concur in describing Panin as a lazy voluptuary, though the French chargé d'affaires, the Chevalier de Corberon, considered him to be "le matois le plus rusé et d'autant plus dangereux qu'il a une de ces figures de candeur et de bonhommie auxquelles on se trompe." [27] Panin maintained a firm hold on foreign affairs, however, and all business was conducted through him or through his deputy, the vice-chancellor, I. A. Osterman. The reputedly francophile Count Ivan Chernyshev presided over the college of the admiralty. The college of commerce came under A. R. Vorontsov, who admired England but held that Russia should pursue her own path.[28] Potemkin exercised supervision over the college of war and in addition concerned himself with the conduct of relations with the Porte and with the development of Russia's southern provinces. He was at this time promoting the development of the port of Kherson on the Black Sea and actively interested in making use of Russia's right, acquired by the treaty of Kutschuk-Kainardji, to send merchant ships through the Dardanelles and to extend trade relations between south Russia and the Mediterranean countries.

Beneath this seemingly ordered division of duties into well established executive departments, a constant struggle was in progress for power and influence over the Empress with whom final decision in all fields lay. The main battle in foreign affairs was waged between Potemkin and Panin. Potemkin had little if any following among the great nobles and magnates, who were alienated by his arrogance and by his omnipotence. His strength lay in his ascendancy over the Empress's affections and to a certain extent over her

27. Corberon, *Journal Intime*, 2, 239, 6 July 1780.
28. See in Dohm, *Denkwürdigkeiten*, 2, 21, Mémoire remis à S. A. R. Monseigneur le Prince de Prusse le 23 Août à Narva lors de son voyage à la cour de Russie (by Goertz).

mind. Those who hated Potemkin would pin their hopes on Panin; others might still entertain the illusion of achieving something through the Orlov brothers. At a lower level, younger government servants made their fortunes by attaching themselves now to one person, now to another. The divisions at court were not, however, concerned so much with policy as with personalities, so that in spite of all changes of personnel a certain consistent line of policy always emerged. There was also one constant factor on the scene, the Empress herself, whose remarkable strength of mind revealed itself in the steady way in which she pursued her aims in spite of and through the warring factions around her.

Though Harris had been appointed to the court of St. Petersburg in 1776, he did not start on his long journey until the autumn of 1777. He had occupied the time in making arrangements for his marriage, and difficulties over the marriage settlement prevented him from procuring enough ready money for the journey.[29] His instructions were drafted by Suffolk, the secretary of state for the North, on 3 October 1777. Suffolk envisaged no fresh departures in British policy towards Russia and certainly had no intention of forming an alliance with her. But he nevertheless referred in his instructions to the negotiation carried on intermittently for the preceding fifteen years to renew the treaty of 1742, which "though for the present it is interrupted, yet it may be hereafter revived." Harris was ordered to receive any proposals made to him in Russia to revive the alliance and to transmit them "for our consideration." [30] There was nothing here to warn him of the great battle he was destined to wage in Russia. He was also in general terms ordered to preserve and develop harmony between the two courts, to carry out the usual duties of an envoy, and to keep an eye on any possible activities of the Americans. When at last Harris set out for his distant post, he was accompanied by his newly wedded and very young wife and by his sister, so, as he wrote, "I trust we shall enjoy English domestick happiness in the midst of Russian barbarity." [31] After a long and difficult journey, driving at times along the shores

29. Add. MSS. 34.414, Auckland Papers, f. 109, Harris to Eden, 17 August 1777.
30. SP 91/101, draft instructions for James Harris.
31. Add. MSS. 34.414, Auckland Papers, f. 109, Harris to Eden 17 August 1777.

of the Baltic with one wheel of his carriage in the sand and the other
in the sea and suffering the total loss of the wardrobe of the two
ladies, James Harris arrived at last on 26 December 1777 in St.
Petersburg.[32]

32. Harris to Eden, 3 December 1777, *MD, 1*, 156; the same to the same, 5/16
January 1778, ibid., 161; SP 91/101, Oakes to Eden, No. 70, 19/30 December 1777.

2. The War of the Bavarian Succession

BARELY had James Harris arrived in Russia when the pressure of events in Europe and America compelled the British government to reconsider its foreign policy. The surrender of General Burgoyne to the American army at Saratoga and the fear that England would be driven by this blow to seek reconciliation with her colonies removed Vergennes's last doubts about recognizing the United States and giving them effective aid. On 6 February 1778, treaties of friendship and commerce and of defensive alliance were signed between France and the United States of America. No official notification of the French recognition of the United States was made to Britain until March 1778, but reports of British secret agents in Paris showed Suffolk which way the wind was blowing and convinced the British government of the need to consolidate Britain's position against the day when the repression of the American revolt might involve her in a major European war.

In his search for possible allies, two factors attracted Suffolk's attention to Russia. In the first place, during the past year he had been receiving constant reports of strained Russian relations with the Porte, caused by Turkish support for intrigues against the Khan of Crimea, the Russian protected puppet imposed at the peace of Kutschuk-Kainardji. The Russians were preparing for military operations in the Crimea which might lead to war with Turkey. Suffolk may actually have believed, and certainly thought it politic to suggest, that Turkey was being actively egged on by France.[1] The ultimate enemy for both England and Russia was thus the same—France. The other factor which entered into Suffolk's calculations was the existence of a fairly powerful Russian navy. In

1. See *BDI*, 7, Pt. 4, p. 173, Suffolk to Stormont, 26 December 1777.

previous wars with France, Britain had been able to draw upon the resources of the North American continent for privateers, transports, merchant ships, and supplies. Now, faced with the prospect of war with France, and uncertain as to the eventual conduct of Spain, Britain had also to enforce her prohibition of trade with the rebellious colonies, to maintain the flow of troops and supplies to North America, and at the same time to ensure the defence of the West Indian islands and of India. The calls on Britain's naval power were greater than they had ever been; her resources were relatively smaller.

These considerations led the English cabinet at the beginning of 1778 to try to draw Russia into a closer connexion with Britain. In a long dispatch of 9 January 1778, Suffolk outlined to Harris the position as he saw it. The European situation, he wrote, had altered materially since Harris's departure from England. Rebel successes and the French-inspired intrigues of the Turks against Russia seemed to suggest that now was a suitable moment "to discover how far there is any practicable disposition in the Empress of Russia and her ministers towards forming an offensive and defensive alliance with Great Britain." [2]

The alliance Suffolk had in view was to be primarily European in its scope, and the object, as he put it, was to counterbalance the Family Compact of the House of Bourbon. If possible Harris was to secure some "beneficial stipulations" with regard to the American colonies, but the treaty would still be welcome if it provided that Russian succours were not to be used outside Europe and excluded any special guarantee of England's American possessions. But though it was the possibility of war with the Porte supported by France which had drawn Suffolk's attention to the desirability of Russia as an ally, Harris was told that British assistance to Russia in a war with Turkey was to be kept out of the treaty. At most Harris might take the point *ad referendum,* though there was small chance of its being agreed to; a subsidy however would be an "eligible alternative." [3]

In a private letter to Harris of the same date, 9 January 1778, Suffolk revealed how much importance he attached to the task laid on the British envoy:

2. SP 91/102, Suffolk to Harris, No. 1, 9 January 1778 (*MD, 1,* 157 ff.).
3. Ibid.

I have sent you a very nice and important commission. I hope it is clearly and accurately expressed. *The Thing is wished,* and you will acquire great credit if you bring it to bear. A good sum of money would be well employ'd if by any private manoeuvre of that sort a treaty to our mind could be obtained; and you may consider yourself empower'd to have recourse to these means if the point is to be effected by them . . . Be active, accurate and discreet! The moment requires decision and dispatch . . .

In the same letter Suffolk hinted at Britain's delicate relations with the two German powers. Frederick II showed no inclination to sympathize with Britain in her present difficulties, yet in some way Prussian goodwill would have to be won if the projected Anglo-Russian alliance was to be achieved.[4] But it was premature to try to win Prussia to take an active part in the alliance. Moreover, as Suffolk wrote, "entre nous they are very civil to us at Vienna. I don't mean to say *coming,* but this is a reason why at first our alliance should stop with Russia." [5] Britain did not want to be put in the position of having to choose between the Germanic powers in spite of her knowledge of the treaty linking Austria and France.

This was the only indication Harris was given at the time of British policy towards the Holy Roman Empire. Indeed Suffolk, in his instructions, omitted any reference to the most important event which had happened in Germany for some time. On 30 December 1777, the Elector of Bavaria had unexpectedly died. The news had reached England by the time Suffolk signed his instructions to Harris, and certainly the Secretary of State was aware that the death of the Elector might have repercussions beyond the Empire.[6] But it does not seem to have occurred to him that it was a point on which Harris needed any guidance or even that it concerned Russia at all.[7]

4. Harris Papers, Suffolk to Harris, 9 January 1778: "I fear the King of Prussia will be a stumbling block in our way."

5. Ibid.

6. A courier had been sent by Morton Eden, British resident in Bavaria, announcing the illness of the Elector on 28 December 1777 (SP 81/113, Eden to Suffolk, No. 1, 1 January 1778), and Suffolk refers to his unexpected demise in a dispatch to Elliot in Berlin of 9 January 1778 (SP 90/102, Suffolk to Elliot, No. 1).

7. The question of Bavaria is not mentioned at all in Suffolk's dispatches to Harris until April 1778.

Suffolk's instructions did not reach St. Petersburg until 3 February 1778. Meanwhile Harris spent his time studying his new surroundings and his new colleagues. He was immediately struck by what appeared to him to be the great extent of Prussian influence, which he knew very well to be hostile to Great Britain. Russia's major preoccupation at the time was of course the possibility of war with the Porte, and in fact Russian troops were already engaged in the Crimea in an attempt to restore the Khan's authority over his rebellious subjects. News of the death of the Elector of Bavaria reached Petersburg by the end of January 1778 and caused a sensation. Moreover the Emperor Joseph acted with great promptitude. He brought pressure to bear on the new Elector, and by virtue of a secret treaty concluded between himself and the Elector on 3 January 1778 he compelled the cession of part of Bavaria; on 16 January he occupied the ceded area with his troops.[8] The Russians did not fail to see that these sudden moves might lead to conflicts within the Empire in which Russia, as Prussia's ally, might well find herself involved.

In spite of this new turn in the European political scene, Harris determined to act at once on his instructions, though he embarked on his commission in no optimistic frame of mind. He was too new to the post to have formed any useful connexions or to have established any channels for secret information, and he therefore broached the subject with the obvious person, Count Panin. On the very day he received his instructions he aroused Panin in the middle of his afternoon nap and proceeded to sound him on the lines suggested by Suffolk. Startled out of his postprandial routine, Panin seemed both surprised and displeased at the British initiative, but he asked Harris to submit detailed proposals. This Harris refused to do until he knew more of the views of the Russian court. On the following Sunday, 8 February 1778, Panin conveyed to Harris in a long interview that, though Catherine admitted the basic unity of the commercial and political interests of the two countries and would not oppose the projected alliance, she never-

8. The history of the War of the Bavarian Succession can be traced in Reimann, *Geschichte des Bairischen Erbfolgkrieges;* Unzer, *Der Friede von Teschen;* and Oursel, *La diplomatie française sous Louis XVI: Succession de Bavière et paix de Teschen.* The Russian documents are in *Sbornik,* 65. See particularly Oursel, *La diplomatie française,* p. 57.

theless insisted that, "on devroit nécessairement se régler par les circonstances, sans la parfaite connoissance desquelles, elle ne pouvoit entrer dans un plus grand détail." There was, the Empress agreed, "beaucoup de parité entre les positions actuelles des deux cours," but the troubles which threatened her were not yet "assez demêlés" for her to see where they might lead. Moreover, since Harris's instructions had been drafted, the death of the Elector of Bavaria had opened the door to disturbances in the Empire which might have unforeseen consequences. The Empress therefore asked to be given a clear statement of Great Britain's views on the European situation and of the "system" Great Britain built upon these views; she also invited Great Britain to submit a draft of a defensive alliance only, since the word "offensive" was repugnant to her feelings.

Thus far the minister had spoken in the name of the Empress. But Panin left Harris under no illusions as to his own views. Russia might indeed be involved "dans une crise fâcheuse" on her southern borders, but, said Panin, England and Russia might serve each other better "dans les suites de la crise que pendant la crise même." Though Panin declared categorically that Russia was free to enter into any engagements, a reference to the Northern system and to himself as its creator conveyed clearly to Harris that Russian ties with Prussia could not be ignored.[9]

The initial reaction in Russia to Britain's tentative approach was thus not very cordial. The Empress clearly did not regard Suffolk's rather simple analysis of the state of Europe, with France cast for the part of universal disturber, as a sufficiently solid demonstration of common Anglo-Russian interests and a sufficient ground on which to build an alliance. In any case she was probably already informed of French efforts in Constantinople to moderate the warlike ardour of the Turks.[10] Moreover, as Harris in his first opening had made no reference to events in the Empire, Catherine was perfectly justified in postponing any serious consideration of British offers until the attitude to be adopted by all the great powers with

9. SP 91/102, Harris to Suffolk, No. 10, 26 January/6 February 1778 (*MD, 1,* 163), No. 11, 30 January/10 February (*MD, 1,* 165), No. 12, 30 January/10 February 1778 (*MD, 1,* 169). The agreed text in French is printed in *MD, 1,* 167.

10. See *Recueil, 9,* 337, Vergennes to Corberon, 28 December 1777; see also CP Russie, *101,* Vergennes to Corberon, 25 February 1778.

regard to the Bavarian succession became clearer. The situation was still everywhere extremely fluid. There were three potential centres of war: the Near East, where hostilities might break out between Russia and the Porte; the Holy Roman Empire, where war between Prussia and Austria was a possibility if not a probability; and the western world, where war threatened between France and Britain. It remained to be seen whether all these potential quarrels would fuse into one and involve the whole of Europe or whether, in some instances, a reconciliation could be achieved or the war localized. From the Russian point of view a Turkish war presented the major threat; second only to that came the danger of becoming involved in a German war as the ally of Prussia. The war between France and Britain concerned Russia least. If the Porte received no outside support, Russia could reasonably hope to solve her Turkish problems alone. At present France appeared to be urging moderation on the Porte; thus there appeared to be no reason why Russia should bind herself to espouse the British cause in an eventual conflict with France. If hostilities broke out in the Empire, however, and France supported Austria, Russia might be drawn in on the Prussian side, and Britain's attitude to the conflict might acquire considerable importance. The door was therefore not entirely closed on the British proposals: Britain was invited to submit a more detailed statement of policy and even the draft of a treaty.

Some time necessarily passed before Suffolk heard of the fate of Harris's initial *démarches*,[11] and in the first months of 1778 the policy to be pursued by the powers in connexion with the American war and the Bavarian succession gradually took shape. In spite of the Franco-Austrian alliance, France viewed with misgiving the accession of strength which the acquisition of parts of Bavaria would give to the Hapsburgs. Other German powers, notably Saxony, had various claims on the Bavarian succession, and opinion in the Empire could always be mobilized against any increase in the Hapsburg dominions. But the Emperor's main opponent was Frederick II of Prussia, who lived in constant fear of Austrian desire for revenge for the rape of Silesia. For some time Frederick had been wooing

11. The post between London and St. Petersburg normally took between 20 and 30 days, according to the state of the weather and the roads; couriers who travelled night and day could do the journey in as little as 17 days.

France and he now saw an opportunity to drive a wedge between the two allies. On 30 January 1778, he appealed to France, as a guarantor of the treaties of Westphalia, not to support Austrian aggression. The Emperor's invasion of Bavaria led Frederick in turn to mobilize his army. Joseph thereupon called on France for assistance in accordance with the treaty of 1756. Vergennes had now to choose whether to support Austria, and thus almost inevitably bring about a European war in which the Anglo-French quarrel would be submerged, or to limit the war as much as possible and concentrate French resources against Britain. By 6 February 1778, when the Franco-American treaties were signed, it was clear that Vergennes had chosen the latter course.[12] On 21 February 1778 he wrote to the French ambassador in Vienna, Breteuil, informing him that France did not admit the *casus foederis* of the Austrian alliance to exist in the present situation and would not support Austria.[13] Vergennes was in fact determined to prevent the outbreak of war in Germany. His decision was communicated only to Austria however, and Frederick still remained in doubt and anxious for all the Russian support he could obtain.[14]

Though news of the French decision to recognize the United States of America reached England early, the corollary, the determination to preserve peace in Germany, does not seem to have been appreciated. So absorbed was Suffolk in the more immediate problems of British relations with America, France, and Russia that he does not seem to have understood at the time the implications of the Emperor Joseph's actions for the balance of power in central Europe. On 13 March 1778 the French ambassador in London informed the British government of the treaties signed with America.[15] Lord Stormont, the British ambassador in Paris, was thereupon ordered to ask for his passports, and the breach between the two powers became public. On 21 March Suffolk wrote to Harris, telling him to ask for an audience of the Empress at which he might express the King's indignation at France's conduct. He now assumed that there was no further need for Britain to explain her "system";

12. Flassan, *Histoire*, 7, 187, mémoire of Vergennes to the King, 2 February 1778.

13. Unzer, *Der Friede*, pp. 55–56; Oursel, *La diplomatie française*, pp. 130–31; Doniol, *Histoire*, 3, 120, Vergennes to Montmorin, 27 March 1778.

14. Oursel, *La diplomatie française*, pp. 140–43; Unzer, *Der Friede*, pp. 128 ff.

15. See *Annual Register*, 1778, p. 299.

what British conduct must be was obvious from the behaviour of
France.[16] Suffolk had thus failed to understand that what the Empress was waiting to learn was Britain's attitude to the complex
situation developing in the Empire.

Meanwhile Harris had been endeavouring to penetrate further
into the secrets of the Russian court. From the beginning he was
pessimistic as to the outcome of his negotiations. "I cannot but have
my doubts of their willingness here to conclude *any treaty at all
with us,*" he wrote on 2/13 February 1778 to Suffolk.[17] He then
proceeded in his flamboyant style to castigate the blindness of the
Russian statesmen, hoping that they would one day repent the loss
of the opportunity that their "weakness and vanity" had allowed
to pass. At the same time Harris attempted, for the benefit of his
principals, an assessment of the sympathies of the leading servants
of Catherine. However he had not been long enough at the Russian
court to fathom the main trends of opinion with any accuracy. His
portrait of the Russian scene at this time is interesting but not accurate, and he himself was later to change many of his opinions.
Panin he believed at first was anti-French; Catherine's remaining
ministers he condemned altogether as "thorough paced Frenchmen,
and the most satisfactory part of their character to me is their de-
bauchery, their levity and the little precision of their ideas." [18]
Above all he remained struck with what he believed to be the over-
whelming influence exercised by Frederick II.[19] Yet it is very doubtful if the evidence for this Prussian influence came actually from
the Russian court. Panin, it is true, had acknowledged himself the
creator of the Northern system and had hinted at Russia's treaty
connexions in that quarter. He had also declared, however, that
Russia was free to enter into other engagements. The principal
source of the rumours of powerful Prussian influence in Russia was
in fact the court of Berlin, and Frederick II was careful to sub-
stantiate these rumours by attributing to his advice any step taken
by the Russian court. It is more than likely that Harris fell into
Frederick's trap, for he was in constant personal correspondence

16. SP 91/102, Suffolk to Harris, No. 12, 20 March 1778.

17. SP 91/102, Harris to Suffolk, unnumbered, most private, 2/13 February 1778.

18. SP 91/102, Harris to Suffolk, No. 13, 2/13 February 1778.

19. See *MD, 1,* passim, for references to Prussian influence and in particular
Harris to Sir Joseph Yorke at The Hague, *MD, 1,* 174, 2/13 February 1778.

with the British envoy in Berlin, Hugh Elliot, and with the latter's secretary, Robert Liston.[20]

In his endeavours to prepare the ground for a favourable reception of future British proposals, Harris left no stone unturned "to recall this court to a sense of its real interests, by discovering to them the impending dangers that surround them, and which, if they have not recourse to their natural ally, will shake, if not crush, the very foundations of their empire." [21] But Panin was aware that France was having considerable difficulty in inducing Spain to follow her American policy,[22] and he knew that France had no intention of encouraging the Turks. In fact Vergennes had already delicately suggested that the French ambassador in Constantinople might use his influence and his good offices to bring about a reconciliation between Russia and the Porte. Catherine was not at this time inclined to accept French mediation; she had no reason to trust French disinterestedness in this sphere. Nevertheless she kept the idea alive and it was eventually to bear fruit.[23] Moreover to Russia the main trouble centre in the West was the Empire, and Austria was the potential enemy, not France. Panin warned Harris that Russia's conduct would be governed by German affairs and in particular by the existing treaty with Prussia.[24] He refused to be drawn into discussions of French policy or of what Harris called "nearer interests." But he expressed the greatest anxiety to know what policy would be followed by England "in this conjuncture," which he described as "the most critical one . . . Europe ever was in since the Thirty Years' War." [25]

Harris's emphasis on Prussian influence in Russia impressed

20. See for instance Harris Papers, Elliot to Harris, 16 April 1778, in which Elliot states that there would be no Anglo-Russian alliance without Prussian consent, whatever Panin might say.

21. SP 91/102, Harris to Suffolk, No. 18, 13/24 February 1778 (MD, 1, 176).

22. SP 91/102, Harris to Suffolk, No. 14, 2/13 February 1778; Vergennes's difficulties in securing the Spanish alliance can be traced in Doniol, Histoire, 3, passim. See also Bemis, Hussey-Cumberland Mission.

23. See Unzer, Der Friede, p. 167; see also Zinkeisen, Geschichte des osmanischen Reiches, 6, 184.

24. SP 91/102, Harris to Suffolk, No. 20, 20 February/3 March 1778; but see Unzer, Der Friede, pp. 128 ff. for Russian reluctance to come to the aid of Prussia while war with Turkey threatened.

25. SP 91/102, Harris to Suffolk, No. 23, separate, 6/17 March 1778.

Suffolk, for it came at a time when Frederick, uncertain as yet of the future alignment in Germany, was veering somewhat closer to England. The issue on which the two powers drew together was the safety of Hanover. Were France to support Austria, Frederick could bring England over to his side by guaranteeing the defence of Hanover. Should England stand aloof, he could occupy it and justify himself with the argument of self-defence.[26] Until the situation became clearer, Frederick could, at little cost to himself, maintain England in a friendly frame of mind by hinting, as he did, that Prussia would be willing to use its influence in St. Petersburg in support of the proposed British alliance.[27]

Encouraged by the news from Prussia, Suffolk proceeded to prepare fresh instructions for Harris and accompanied them with the draft of a treaty. Britain's main object was, he now wrote, to "obtain a Russian fleet as early as possible," to act in conjunction with the British fleet in Europe against France and Spain in the event of war with the two Bourbon powers.[28] But in his instructions Suffolk still assumed that Russian interest in events in the Empire reflected merely the ascendancy of Prussia over the Empress and Panin. He did not grasp that Russia feared she might be involved as a principal in the impending war in Germany and that the Empress's desire to be informed of Britain's attitude was not dictated by Prussia but arose out of Russia's own situation and treaty connexions. "The system of this court" wrote Suffolk to Harris on 7 April 1778, "is what it evidently ought to be and must be, to resist the ambitious designs of the House of Bourbon and to connect itself with the other powers which may be inclined to the same sentiment." Russia, he believed, must view the situation in the same light, since France was stirring up trouble in Turkey, "on the principle of finding employment for all other countries during their dispute with this." On the Bavarian dispute he remarked that "the Russian Minister cannot give a much stronger proof of the preponderance of Prussian influence at Petersburg than appear'd in his anxiety to learn His Majesty's sentiments upon the events which the Elector of Bavaria's death has produced." However, in

26. See SP 90/102, Elliot to Suffolk, private, 28 March 1778.
27. SP 90/102, Elliot to Suffolk, No. 21, 28 March 1778.
28. SP 91/102, Suffolk to Harris, No. 14, 7 April 1778.

order to satisfy Russia in a matter "foreign to our negotiation," Harris was authorized to state that the King would adhere to the laws of the Empire and that Britain's policy would depend on France's actions. Suffolk further expressed regret that Panin should think such explanations necessary "because it implies more reluctance than is pleasant towards the great object." [29]

On the same day Suffolk sent fresh instructions to Elliot in Berlin. Reading too much into Elliot's reports of possible Prussian support for the Anglo-Russian alliance,[30] Suffolk now suggested that, should Harris's negotiations succeed, the alliance might be extended to include Prussia, in which case England would be prepared to grant a subsidy for the defence of Hanover. Moreover Elliot was given full details of the proposals Harris was instructed to make in Russia and was told to use his discretion in communicating them to Frederick II in the hope that he would promote the alliance.[31]

Harris received his new instructions on 17/28 April 1778. Always prompt in execution he sent the draft treaty to Panin at once, together with the text of a separate article that Suffolk had sent him, by which Russia was to bind herself to send a number of ships to be agreed to the assistance of England should that power be "menacé d'être attaqué ou troublé dans ses royaumes, provinces, états ou possessions." [32] These texts were accompanied by a Note for the Empress, who was spending Easter at her country residence at Tsarskoye Selo, in which Harris outlined England's motives for seeking the alliance and her attitude towards events in Germany, in accordance with Suffolk's statement. The King, moreover, would now give up any request for Russian assistance in America, but no concession could be made on the "Turkish clause," for, as Harris explained, "des considérations de commerce seules portent le roi

29. SP 91/102, Suffolk to Harris, No. 13, 7 April 1778.

30. Fortescue, *Correspondence of King George III, 4,* 98, Lord North to the King, 6 April 1778, "the King of Prussia seems desirous of forwarding our treaty with Russia provided he meets with assistance . . ." See also SP 91/102, Suffolk to Harris, No. 17, 7 April 1778: "You will see that His Prussian Majesty seems to be desirous to be connected again with this country, and not unwilling to promote the renewal of our treaty of alliance with the Empress of Russia, on which a respectable Northern system may be founded."

31. SP 90/102, Suffolk to Elliot, No. 11, 7 April 1778; No. 8, 7 April 1778.

32. SP 91/102, text of article séparé, included in Suffolk to Harris, No. 13, 7 April 1778.

à ne pas admettre le *casus foederis* d'une guerre avec les turcs." [33]

This key sentence in Harris's written Note referred to the English Levant trade. This once flourishing trade had entered a period of decline and had been overtaken by the French Levant trade. But England's refusal to grant Russia the Turkish *casus foederis* had in the past been founded on the need to preserve Turkey's goodwill for British merchants, and this same condition turned up automatically in all projects for an Anglo-Russian alliance regardless of the actual importance of the Levant trade to the British economy.[34] Legend dies hard however, and the draft treaty sent to Harris was in fact the same as the one his predecessors had failed to make palatable to Russia before. Suffolk appears to have hoped that Russia would grant now, out of friendliness to a hard-pressed Britain, what she had refused in the past.

The first rumours that Harris heard of the reception of his proposals were not encouraging. On 5 May 1778 he discovered that the Empress had sent for all the papers concerned with the abortive negotiations conducted by his predecessors [35]—an ominous sign. On 20 May 1778 he spent the day at Panin's country house, and there, between dinner and supper, he was taken aside and told that his mission had failed.[36] The next day Panin formally communicated to Harris the Empress's reasons for refusing to ally herself with Britain. As Catherine put it, she had on her accession appreciated "qu'il ne convenoit point à son Empire de se lier accéssoirement à tel ou tel système, sous des conditions subsidiaires, qui ne forment que des liens aussi passagers que le moment d'intérêt qui les a dictés, mais qu'il devait apprécier son intérêt essentiel d'après sa position et en faire la base de ses alliances." What Catherine meant was that there was no reason for Russia to attach herself and her

33. SP 91/102, Harris to Suffolk, Enclosure A in No. 42, 11/22 May 1778.

34. See for instance the figures of the total amount spent abroad by England in the period 1700 to 1780, broken down betwen the Levant, the East Indies, and Russia, viz.: £4,500,000 in the Levant, £42,500,000 in the East Indies, and £25,000,000 in Russia. Quoted in Reading, *The Anglo-Russian Commercial Treaty of 1734*, p. 296. Wood, however, in *A History of the Levant Company*, points out (p. 159) that the Levant trade enjoyed a short-lived boom in 1775–77, a factor which may have contributed to stiffen British reluctance to defend Russia against Turkey.

35. SP 91/102, Harris to Suffolk, No. 38, 24 April/5 May 1778.

36. SP 91/102, Harris to Suffolk, No. 40, 4/15 May 1778; No. 42, 11/22 May 1778 (*MD, 1*, 190).

Northern system to Britain on account of Britain's quarrel with the House of Bourbon. Moreover, the reply continued, the Porte was Russia's main enemy; against Turkey alone did Russia need alliances, and she could not renounce British help against a powerful enemy on the very eve of a war. There was no parallel between the American colonies and Turkey. The alternative of a subsidy instead of the Turkish *casus foederis* was no longer acceptable now that danger actually threatened. As regards Germany, Russia had alliances with the foremost courts and could not allow her policy to depend on that of France.[37]

To sweeten the pill, Panin assured Harris that the Empress's predilection for England continued unchanged and that as soon as she saw an opening she would embrace Britain's alliance with eagerness. Harris argued his case as strongly as he dared, but the interview with Panin left him under the impression that Russia would not consent to an alliance on any terms, for the proposal was turned down without any inquiry as to the extent of Harris's powers to negotiate on the basis of the draft. However, he consoled himself with the reflection that Britain had been a great nation before Russia even existed and "that the time will probably come when they will stand in much greater need of us than we ever can of them." [38]

It is more than probable that, by adhering to the traditional policy of refusing aid to Russia against Turkey, Suffolk had given the Empress the pretext she needed to reject Britain's offer. But a second and equally important reason for Russia's refusal must be sought elsewhere. The situation in Germany was still not at all clear, but by the end of April it was known that Austria could not

37. SP 91/102, Harris to Suffolk, No. 42, 11/22 May 1778, Enclosure B, Note said by Panin to have been corrected by the Empress herself. The Russian historian and lawyer, F. de Martens, prints in his *Recueil, 9,* 319, a document which he does not date, but attributes to 1781. This document contains Catherine's comments on a British offer of alliance, and it seems to me to belong rather to 1778. Catherine comments adversely on Britain's refusal to grant succours against Turkey and the Tartars; she implies that Britain expected Russia to send troops and ships to America even though such a demand was not openly made. She remarks that she is supposed to supply fourteen ships, whereas Britain will only supply twelve. She concludes: "Je crois que nous devons éviter d'être entrainés dans des guerres quelconques qui ne nous regardent pas, parce qu'il n'est pas agréable d'être à la queue de personne, comme nous en avons fait la triste preuve ci-devant, en égard à la cour de Vienne."

38. SP 91/102, Harris to Suffolk, No. 42, 11/22 May 1778 (*MD, 1,* 190).

count on French military support in the event of a Prussian attack on the Hapsburg lands.[39] There was therefore a fair chance that the war in Germany might be localized, when and if it broke out. Though war with the Porte was reputed to be desired by Potemkin,[40] no one in Russia wished to be drawn into war in Germany. The diplomatic possibilities of this somewhat complex situation did not escape the Empress's shrewd eye. From the beginning Panin had emphasized to Count Solms, the Prussian envoy, that Russia could not support Prussia actively while war with Turkey seemed imminent.[41] He even insisted that Russia must remain on friendly terms with Austria in order to induce her not to encourage the Turks in warlike measures. In their efforts to conciliate Russia, not only France but Prussia and Austria too brought pressure to bear on the Porte in favour of moderation. At the end of April the Austrian chancellor, Prince Kaunitz, laid before Catherine a full account of all the Austrian negotiations with Berlin up to 1 April 1778 and assured her that Austria had no intention of attacking Prussia.[42] Such evidence of Austrian deference was bound to be pleasing to Catherine, for there had always existed a certain rivalry and mutual disapproval between the two great ladies of Europe.

39. See Oursel, *La diplomatie français,* pp. 140–43; Flassan, *Histoire,* 7, 195–97.

40. Unzer, *Der Friede,* pp. 128 ff., using the dispatches of Solms, the Prussian envoy, from St. Petersburg, suggests that there was a war party in Russia headed by Potemkin and Field Marshal Rumyantsev, and a peace party headed by Panin. For Prussia, who wanted to free Russian hands for a war against Austria, the victory of the peace party was all-important, and Solms attached great importance to the influence which Potemkin or Panin exercised over the Empress. Already at this early date Solms feared that Panin's influence was declining, and to this factor he attributed the lack of support which Russia gave to Prussia. Panin was certainly kept to a great extent in ignorance of Russian policy towards the Porte, which was conducted by the Empress, Potemkin, and Rumyantsev.

41. Ibid., p. 137, p. 150.

42. Ibid., pp. 131 ff., p. 159. According to Harris the Empress-Queen wrote a personal letter to Catherine, setting out her own conduct and that of Prussia and inviting Catherine to decide which was the aggressor. Maria Theresa then bewailed the fact that at her age, when she should be preparing for the next world, she found herself on the eve of war, and she pressed Catherine, as a Christian and as a ruler, to use her influence with the King of Prussia to make him desist from his impossible demands. (See SP 91/102, Harris to Suffolk, No. 37, 24 April/5 May 1778, *MD, 1,* 189.) This letter is quoted from Harris's summary (as printed in von Raumer, *Beiträge zur neueren Geschichte aus dem britischen und französischen Reichsarchive,* 3, Pt. 5, p. 334) by Reimann in *Geschichte des Bairischen Erbfolgkrieges,* p. 95; but as it is not quoted by either Unzer or Oursel and is not mentioned in Arneth, *Maria Theresias letzte Regierungszeit,* its existence cannot entirely be assumed.

Maria Theresa was the older, and undoubtedly the more virtuous, though the less entertaining of the two. She disapproved of Catherine's private life and probably shared her son's haughty view of the upstart German princess on the Russian throne, "la princesse de Zerbst catherinisée," as he later called her.[43]

While Russia was thus appealed to on all sides to exercise a moderating influence in Germany, the Turkish problem appeared to take a turn for the worse. A warlike mood prevailed in Turkish councils during the month of April.[44] Hence Russia preferred for the time being to leave the German powers in doubt as to her future course of action in the Bavarian quarrel.[45] In this situation the essential community of interests between Russia and France began to make itself felt. France desired peace on the continent in order to concentrate on the now inevitable maritime war against Britain. Russia preferred a Turkish war to a German war, but faced with the prospect of both she preferred to fight neither. France actively, Russia passively, were working to prevent the outbreak of a general European war.

In these circumstances it is not surprising that Russia should have refused to bind herself to act with Britain against the one power whose policy at that time coincided with her own. Why should Russia enter into an alliance directly aimed at France, one that would moreover deprive her of a substantial part of her fleet should war in fact break out with the Porte? Indeed, the British terms could not have been very impressive from the Russian point of view. Catherine and Panin may well have interpreted this offer as further evidence of Britain's tendency to regard Russia as a minor and dependent power instead of treating her as an equal, and they may have harboured genuine resentment at the idea that the Russian fleet, which had so recently won its laurels in the first Turkish war, should be handed over to Britain like a body of hired German mercenaries.

There is one further factor that must be considered because

43. Arneth, *Maria Theresias letzte Regierungszeit, 4*, 670, quotes Maria Theresa on the "Abneigung und Abscheu die ein Charakter wie derjenige der Kaiserin von Russland mir immer entflösst." For Joseph's opinion, see Arneth, *Joseph II und Katharina*, p. 277, note, Joseph to Kaunitz, 9 August 1786.

44. Zinkeisen, *Geschichte des osmanischen Reiches, 6*, 197; Unzer, *Der Friede*, p. 170 (Solms to Frederick of 24 April 1778).

45. Ibid., p. 176.

it may possibly have influenced Catherine's decision. Towards the
end of April, Harris appears to have heard rumours of cabinet
changes from his friends in England. On 10/21 April 1778 he wrote
to Suffolk to inquire whether there was any truth in them. Suffolk
replied in May that the rumours were untrue and attributed
Harris's question to newspaper gossip collected by the Russian
envoy, Musin Pushkin, in London and forwarded by him.[46] It was
quite true, however, that towards the end of March 1778 North
had made an effort to retire, and negotiations had been undertaken
with Chatham and Shelburne for a new cabinet to be formed. The
plan was frustrated by the obstinacy of the King, and in any case
on 7 April Chatham suffered a stroke from which he was not to
recover.[47] Musin Pushkin doubtless did forward newspaper gossip
to his court, and Catherine may have been strengthened in her
decision not to conclude an alliance with a government that was
likely to fall. She had but a poor opinion of the North administration, and the King's appeal to the nation to observe a "public fast
and humiliation" and to pray for its sins on the occasion of the
American revolt aroused her to philosophic ire. On 25 April 1778
she wrote to her correspondent Madame Bielke:

> Pour vos amis, les Anglais, on peut leur dire ce que Molière
> fait tant répéter à George Dandin: "George Dandin, tu l'as
> bien voulu." Ces gens-là font toujours ce dont personne ne
> s'avise; il y a 15 ans qu'ils sont partis du pied gauche. Lorsque
> toute l'Europe était attentive à voir les mesures de vigueur
> qu'ils allaient prendre, que vont-ils faire? Ils publient un
> jour de jeûne: le beau moyen de relever le courage d'une na-
> tion! A présent ils prônent partout leur faiblesse.[48]

These are not the terms one uses about a prospective ally.

The hopes that Suffolk had placed in Prussian intervention on
Britain's behalf in St. Petersburg proved completely vain. Frederick
II had flirted with Britain only as long as he remained uncertain of

46. SP 91/102, Harris to Suffolk, No. 32, 10/21 April 1778; SP 91/102, Suffolk to
Harris, No. 19, 19 May 1778.

47. See Lecky, *History of England*, *4*, 454–58; Ritcheson, *British Politics*, pp. 250 ff.

48. *Sbornik*, *27*, 146. For George III's appeal to the nation of January 1778, see
The Gentleman's Magazine, 1778, p. 15. See also Catherine to Grimm, 8/19 June
1778, in *Sbornik*, *23*, 93.

France. By the beginning of May he had received assurances that France did not admit the *casus foederis* to exist with regard to Austria, and at once the temper of the Prussian court changed. Indeed Elliot thought it wiser not to act on his instructions, and in his talks with the Prussian ministers he did not touch on the subject of the Anglo-Russian treaty, let alone the offer of a subsidy to Prussia to defend Hanover. It was clearly in Frederick's interest now to flatter and follow France.[49] But Elliot's reports contributed to strengthen the prevailing British impression that Prussia exercised a despotic influence over St. Petersburg. On 19 May 1778, before Harris had received his final reply from Panin, Elliot wrote to Suffolk warning him that Harris would receive no explicit answer from Russia until the affairs of the Empire were decided and that various pretexts would be found to delay matters until Frederick II had expressed his final approval or disapproval of the projected alliance. It is unlikely that Frederick in fact exercised any direct influence on the Russian decision; he probably did not have time to do so. But the impression remained with Suffolk, Elliot, and Harris that Russia was acting under Prussian direction.[50]

For the time being Suffolk interpreted the Russian refusal of a defensive alliance as a Russian rejection of a British favour. Though the turn of events might in time reopen the negotiation, for the moment it must be considered at an end, wrote Suffolk to Harris on 16 June 1778, and "any steps taken to revive it on the part of Russia must be taken *ad referendum* unless they entirely coincide with the projet and separate article already in your possession." [51]

Meanwhile England and France drifted into open war. The withdrawal of ambassadors had been the signal in both countries for warlike preparations. On 17 June 1778 there occurred a fight at sea between the French frigate *Belle Poule* and HMS *Arethusa*, an

49. SP 90/102, Elliot to Suffolk, No. 30, 4 May 1778.

50. SP 90/102, Elliot to Suffolk, No. 33, 19 May 1778; copy sent to Harris (in Harris Papers); No. 36, 5 June 1778; Frederick, wrote Elliot, "will keep Russia in his own hands, to be bestowed according to his interest or inclination" as long as matters remained unsettled in the Empire. See Unzer, *Der Friede*, pp. 128 ff. for Frederick's disappointment with the lack of support from Russia.

51. SP 91/102, Suffolk to Harris, No. 21, 16 June 1778.

incident immediately seized on by both sides to prove that the other was the aggressor.[52] Though no formal declaration of war was issued by either side, it was now openly recognized that a state of war existed. A fortnight later war broke out in the Holy Roman Empire when Prussian troops invaded Bohemia.

These events naturally had their repercussions in St. Petersburg. Panin had indeed from the start attempted to soften the bad impression left by Russia's abrupt refusal to negotiate with England at all. Less than a week after Catherine's negative reply had been comunicated to Harris in May, Panin reopened the matter in conversation with him. He expressed in general terms the Empress's wish for an alliance with England, but he dwelt also on the difficulties: the present uncertain state of affairs in Europe and England's reluctance to admit the *casus foederis* in the case of war with the Porte. He felt that England was clinging unreasonably to the terms of the Anglo-Russian alliance of 1742, from which the Turkish *casus foederis* had been excluded. Harris attributed this new, softened tone to bad news from the Crimea, but the cause of Panin's friendlier attitude was mainly to be found in the tense state of affairs in Germany. Though an alliance with England was not for the moment advantageous on English terms, Russia had no wish to alienate Britain when war between Austria and Prussia appeared imminent. Panin expressed anxiety with regard to the neutrality of the Electorate of Hanover and hinted at Danish and Prussian support to preserve it. On several occasions the Russian minister lamented to Harris that England had so little connexion with the continent. But though he seemed more willing to entertain the idea of an English alliance, Panin still put forward the "Turkish clause" as the main stumbling block.[53]

As time passed Harris began to doubt whether the Russian rejection of the English overtures was as decisive as he had at first

52. The account of the captain of the *Belle Poule* is printed in Doniol, *Histoire, 3,* ch. 4, p. 163. According to W. Laird Clowes, *The Royal Navy. A History from the Earliest Times to the Present, 4,* 13 ff. Britain was technically the aggressor, but "though Keppel [the British admiral] was not, probably, over particular, the behaviour of the *Licorne* and *Belle Poule* was so unfriendly as to justify his proceedings."

53. SP 91/102, Harris to Suffolk, No. 44, 16/27 May 1778; No. 48, 5/16 June 1778.

thought.[54] In the middle of July 1778 he wrote to Suffolk that it seemed to him that proposals for reviving the negotiations might be expected from Russia in the not very distant future.[55] The outbreak of war between Prussia and Austria had in fact led Panin to encourage Harris's hopes more openly. At the end of July 1778, Panin forecast a general European war, "and then he did not doubt but that the courts of London and Petersburg would very soon understand each other and conclude the alliance so long in agitation, 'for,' said he, 'we must be friends, and the smaller obstacles will yield to the greater reasons of state—necessity.' " Harris replied politely, in accordance with his instructions, that England would always pay attention to Russian proposals, and did not pursue the matter. But he felt sufficiently encouraged by the Russian reception of the news of the *Belle Poule–Arethusa* incident and by the personal favour which the Empress constantly showed him to believe "they begin to feel they have rated themselves too high and us too low." And, he added, "I am convinced the only way of bringing the alliance to bear in the manner we wish, is to make them feel they want it, and that we can do without." [56]

Harris's cool reception of Panin's conciliatory words met with Suffolk's perfect approval. He hoped that Panin's concern at England's lack of continental connexions showed an "inclination in him to promote the Northern system, which the situation of affairs at Petersburg may soon render an object of greater utility to Russia than it seems lately to have been considered." But it was for the Empress to make the first move, he emphasized in July 1778.[57] A month later, Suffolk again expressed the hope that Russia might soon see the offers made by England "in their true light," and welcome the opportunity of defending the liberties of Europe in alliance with England and "appearing with credit as a maritime

54. SP 91/102, Harris to Suffolk, No. 51, 15/26 June 1778.

55. SP 91/102, Harris to Suffolk, No. 54, 3/14 July 1778.

56. SP 91/102, Harris to Suffolk, No. 56, 17/28 July 1778; see also Unzer, *Der Friede*, p. 187, Panin to the Prussian envoy Solms: "Warten Sie nur ein Weilchen, dann machen wir mit; es ist unmöglich dass wenn zwei Grossmächte wie Preussen und Oesterreich im Kriege sind, wir aus dem Spiele bleiben" (in Solms to Frederick, 30 June 1778).

57. SP 91/102, Suffolk to Harris, No. 25, 17 July 1778.

power." "But," added Suffolk, "everything seems to be in so uncertain and capricious a state at Petersburg that till an overture
is actually made, I shall not rely much upon appearances. And after
what has passed lately, that overture must come from thence." [58]

The uncertainty and capriciousness which Suffolk attributed to
St. Petersburg was not merely a reflection on Catherine's diplomacy.
Harris had also kept his principal fully informed about social and
political life in the Russian capital. Closer acquaintance with the
Russian scene had not raised his opinion either of Russia or of
Russian statesmen. In the government, confusion and imperfection
reigned; the army was in decay, the navy defective. The political
system was inconstant and languid, such as "must ultimately reduce
this immense mass of power to that state of Asiatic insignificancy
from which it so lately emerged." [59] On 3/14 July 1778 Harris,
echoing the court gossip current among the fallen Orlov faction,
warned Suffolk that "the situation of this country becomes every
day more extraordinary and a total relaxation in the sovereign
authority and the unlimited powers in the hands of a man like
Potemkin, may soon make it very alarming . . ." [60] At the end of
July he availed himself of the opportunity to send a letter by a
private hand in which he expressed himself very frankly on the
many shortcomings of Russia. Of Catherine his impression was
that she had

> a masculine force of mind, obstinacy in adhering to a plan and
> intrepidity in the execution of it; but she wants the more manly
> virtues of deliberation, forbearance in prosperity and accuracy
> of judgment; while she possesses in a high degree the weak-
> nesses vulgarly attributed to her sex: love of flattery, and its
> inseparable companion, vanity; an inattention to unpleasant
> though salutary advice, and a propensity to voluptuousness,
> which leads her into excesses that would debase a female char-
> acter in any sphere of life.[61]

58. SP 91/102, Suffolk to Harris, No. 27, 28 August 1778.
59. Private letter from Harris to Sir Joseph Yorke at The Hague, *MD, 1,* 186,
1/12 May 1778.
60. SP 91/102, Harris to Suffolk, No. 54, 3/14 July 1778.
61. SP 91/102, Harris to Suffolk, unnumbered letter, 20/31 July 1778, *MD, 1,*
203.

It was easy to blame Catherine for many feminine and some un-feminine weaknesses, but it was dangerous not to see that she was above all a consummate actress who used her very weaknesses to conceal her singular strength of purpose. In other fields Harris was also critical: the Empress's internal policy was characterized by a "mistaken lenity," [62] the conduct of foreign affairs suffered from the laziness and inattention of Panin, the Russian representatives abroad received no instructions, and "what is worse he suffers them to transmit to him intelligence that would disgrace the most mercenary gazetteer." Harris almost begs Suffolk's pardon for having to fill his dispatches with "a repetition of the same indecorous scenes which cast such a cloud over the splendour of this empire," but he still entertained the hope that the Empress's good sense "and a reflection on the consequences of the disgraceful life she leads, will reclaim her before national distress . . . makes her tenure of her crown precarious." [63]

The picture painted by Harris of the Russian court is remarkable because it conveys little that could be useful to Suffolk and much that was really misleading. He made no effort to analyse the objective realities of Russian policy, derived from her geographical situation, her resources, and her treaties; and in his concentration on the system of favouritism, Harris failed to see the many stable factors in the Empress's government which, in spite of much inefficiency and corruption, enabled Russia to play such a prominent part in the late eighteenth century.

Nevertheless, though Russia might seem such an undesirable ally, the alarming situation in the Empire, which continued throughout the summer, encouraged Harris's hopes that a Russo-British alliance might yet be achieved. It was true that the actual military operations on the Bohemian border revealed no great inclination on the part of either Austria or Prussia to pursue the war with energy. And in spite of these operations, secret negotiations initiated by the Empress-Queen behind the back of the Emperor continued between Austria and Prussia. But towards the end

62. Ibid. How superficial was Harris's understanding of Russia is revealed by his comments on the Pugachev rising which he attributes to the "specious pretext of the cruelty" of the landowners. He shows neither understanding of nor sympathy for the position of the serfs.

63. SP 91/102, Harris to Suffolk, No. 59, 26 July/7 August 1778.

of August 1778, Frederick II abruptly broke off all further talks. Meanwhile France, on 22 July 1778, had offered her good offices to the belligerents. As long as the secret talks continued the French offer was premature, and it was not taken up. Russia, in turn, refused to commit herself to assist Frederick while there was hope that an agreement might be reached directly between the parties. But the final breakdown of the talks spurred all sides to fresh activity. Frederick appealed again to Russia for some demonstration of support; he no longer expected armed assistance, but he proposed that some declaration of Russian intentions might be made to Austria. Soon after, he indicated to Vergennes that he would accept French mediation provided Russia were associated with France. Kaunitz, hearing that Prussia was amenable to Franco-Russian mediation, hastened to secure Russian goodwill for Austria by dispatching a courier on 27 September 1778 to St. Petersburg declaring Austrian willingness to accept a Franco-Russian mediation.[64]

Meanwhile the Turkish crisis had also taken a turn for the better. Though war had nearly broken out in August, an outbreak of plague in the Turkish fleet, the loss of seven ships in a storm, and the unreliable temper of the army somewhat reduced the war fever of the Turks. In August 1778 France offered her formal mediation to the Porte. By mid-September the Turks gave up all hope of conducting military operations during the current campaigning season, and a change of Grand Vizier brought a more moderate party to the fore.[65] Faced with these changed circumstances in the south, the Russian Empress felt herself free to appear with *éclat* on the German scene. Urged forward by Frederick's request for some demonstration of support and unwilling to lose the opportunity provided by the French offer of mediation and Prussia's conditional acceptance, she decided to force matters into the open and to grant Prussia strong diplomatic support. On 22 September/2 October 1778 a declaration was dispatched to Vienna in which Catherine called on Austria to reconcile herself with Prussia; otherwise Russia would no longer be able to see with indifference the progress of an unjust war and would be compelled in her own interests to intervene. Copies of the Empress's declaration were sent to London,

64. See Unzer, *Der Friede*, p. 188 ff. for an account of the diplomacy of this period of the Bavarian war.

65. Zinkeisen, *Geschichte des osmanischen Reiches*, 6, 208 ff.

Versailles, Copenhagen, and Stockholm in order to mobilize diplomatic support for the pressure which Russia hoped to bring to bear on Austria.[66]

What Russia hoped to achieve with the declaration, and how it would affect Britain, emerges from Harris's dispatches. Panin did not hesitate to tell him about it in advance and to discuss with him its implications for England. Both Austria and France would now have to show their hands, said Panin. "If," added he, "they declare openly in favour of their pretensions on the Bavarian succession, you may depend on having powerful and useful allies on the continent. If not, you need have no apprehensions for the Electorate of Hanover, but be able to direct your whole force towards the defence of that part of the British dominions, which the court of Versailles seems to be most the desirous to wrest from you." If a general war ensued, it would be desirable, said Panin, "that those powers who are united by their inclinations and interest, should be able also to unite their forces against one common enemy." If France decided to support Austria, then "a very natural system of alliance opens itself, providing your court should think it advisable to take a share in continental affairs." And if not, declared Panin, Britain would have to deal with France "on an element alone, where you hitherto have always had, and are still so likely to maintain a superiority."[67]

In his conversation with Harris with regard to German affairs, Panin was quite frank. It was perfectly clear that if the Empress's bold stroke failed and war followed, then inevitably Europe would divide into two camps—France, Austria, and Turkey against England, Prussia, and Russia. Panin was equally outspoken on what

66. Unzer, *Der Friede*, pp. 188 ff. Catherine's declaration is printed in *Sbornik, 65*, 15; see *Sbornik, 20, 376* for Catherine's letter to Frederick II of 1/12 October 1778, explaining her policy to him.

67. SP 91/102, Harris to Suffolk, No. 75, 21 September/2 October 1778; No. 77, 23 September/4 October 1778. This last dispatch was written *en clair* and sent to London by a Russian courier. In accordance with the practice of the times it was meant not only for Suffolk but also for Panin. A dispatch sent *en clair* by a Russian courier would inevitably be read by the Russian authorities; a dispatch sent through the post would also be examined and if possible deciphered. This led to an elaborate technique by which certain portions of a dispatch were deliberately left *en clair* in order to mislead the unauthorized reader as to its real content. On the examination of letters by the Russian post office in this period see Brückner, "Vskrytiye chuzhikh pisem' i depesh pri Yekaterine II"; see also Beer and Fiedler, *Joseph II und Graf Ludwig Cobenzl, 1*, 81, 97 for Cobenzl's description of the operation of Catherine's *cabinet noir*, in his dispatches of 13 and 20 December 1780.

would ensue if war did not break out: England, he had stated, would be considered quite able to deal alone with a maritime war with France.

Meanwhile Suffolk was trying to dispel a further cloud which had arisen on England's horizon. On 11 October 1778 a note had been received from the court of Spain, inviting both belligerents to inform the King of Spain of their respective terms for a pacification which he would then willingly set in motion, provided certain outstanding disputes between England and Spain were solved at the same time.[68] The Spanish note contained an ominous suggestion that unless the mediation succeeded and unless Spanish demands were satisfied, Spain would be compelled by circumstances to take part in the war. Ever since the news of the signing of the Franco-American treaty, Spain had been hinting to England that her neutrality in the forthcoming war could be secured by concessions, the principal one being the return of Gibraltar to Spain. The British government had temporized and endeavoured to buy Spanish neutrality with fair words. Words, however, would satisfy Spain no longer.

It was natural that Suffolk should immediately have interpreted the Spanish offer of mediation as a move towards finding a pretext for taking part in the war at France's side.[69] If Britain had felt the need of naval assistance from Russia against France alone, how much more dangerous was her situation now that there was a prospect of united action by the Bourbon fleets, which together outnumbered the Royal Navy and which were both in reasonably good condition at that time. Harris's dispatches from St. Petersburg had seemed recently to indicate a greater inclination on the part of Russia to unite with Britain. Therefore, in spite of Suffolk's previous determination to leave all initiative for the renewal of the negotiations to the Russians, he decided to put forward fresh proposals of alliance in the renewed hope of procuring naval assistance. For Harris's benefit, Suffolk analysed the situation created by the Spanish concealed threat and endeavoured to find the point at which English and Russian interests met, "for, if the fleets of France and Spain should ever be masters of the sea," he wrote on 27 October

68. Conn, *Gibralter in British Diplomacy*, pp. 180 ff.
69. SP 91/102, Suffolk to Harris, No. 31, most confidential, 27 October 1778.

1778, "there is an end of the naval power of Russia; she must from that moment bid adieu to her marine." Suffolk's reasoning here however did not take into account the fact that the Russians knew that their navy could not be used outside the Baltic and the North Sea except with the tacit permission of one or other of the maritime powers, France or England. France had, it is true, shown hostility in the past to the display of Russian naval power in the Mediterranean, but dependence on Britain might prove unreliable in the future.

In making these new proposals of alliance, "with more hopes of success than heretofore," Suffolk was prepared to make some concessions to Russia, on paper at least. Very reluctantly, he authorized Harris to give up the Turkish clause, but this concession was hedged about with many restrictions. Harris was to conceal his power to do so "till you are morally certain the alliance cannot be brought about without this concession," in order to avoid the "mischievous consequences" of the concession being bruited abroad, "which would be all pure loss if the negotiation fails." In fact Suffolk even harboured the hope that the Empress might be so forcibly struck and alarmed by Britain's situation that she would conclude the alliance and lend her ships "without demanding this inconvenient sacrifice." The main difficulty lay however in the fact that while Suffolk was prepared to give up the Turkish clause in writing, he wanted at the same time to insert into the treaty some security against "the King's being called upon to *perform his engagements in a manner incompatible with his present situation*" (Suffolk's italics). Britain, for instance, in the event of a Russian war with Turkey, would not be able to send a British fleet to the Archipelago, for such a fleet would be as lost to Britain as the Empress's would be to her were it sent out of Europe. He therefore proposed that the two parties should agree that Russian ships would not be used outside Europe, nor those of Britain east of Malta. This, argued Suffolk, was not the same as the Turkish clause; it was only making an exception of one method of assisting Russia in the event of a Turkish war. Other means remained, such as a subsidy or the proposed joint activity of the Russian and British fleets in the Mediterranean west of Malta, which could preserve navigation in that sea for Russia against France and Spain and "perhaps may in the course of events lead to some establishment in it which would be of the utmost importance to Russia." [70]

To sum up: though Britain now agreed to the Turkish *casus foederis,* assistance to Russia in the event of a Turkish war would be limited to a subsidy; and Russia, on the ratification of the treaty, was to lend a squadron to Britain for use in the war against France, on the understanding that should war break out with Turkey, Russia could expect no naval assistance from Britain against Turkey and the Turkish islands east of Malta. Suffolk even expressed the hope that the Empress might not entertain the idea of sending her fleet into the Mediterranean at all as it was an expensive operation, in which case a war against Turkey would have to be fought exclusively by Russian troops on land, with the aid of a British subsidy. As the Turkish clause was not insisted on, Suffolk expected all to be plain sailing. His only reservations came from the "indolence, dissipation and disgraceful scenes" which Harris saw so much of, which rendered all prospect of an alliance with Russia so hazardous and exposed the best concerted measures to caprice. But in Britain's present situation she could not afford to choose her allies, and Harris was therefore urged to "be active, be successful and expect reward!" [71]

A few days later Suffolk received Harris's dispatches of 2 and 4 October 1778, with the British envoy's account of the Russian declaration to Austria and Panin's outspoken analysis of the future alignment of the powers should Austria refuse to submit to what appeared to be a Russian ultimatum. Suffolk welcomed the Russian declaration, which he hoped might, in the event of war in Germany, lead to the formation of that "Northern system which has so long been the object of his [Panin's] wishes." Even so, however, as he warned Harris on 3 November 1778, Britain was in no position to take an active part in continental affairs. If Panin's reference to British interest in the continent meant "that the King should support an army in Germany or send British troops thither, I must

---

70. SP 91/102, Suffolk to Harris, Nos. 32–34, 27 October 1778. Suffolk also proposed suggesting to Panin that Russia should borrow some ships from the Danish navy.

71. SP 91/102, Suffolk to Harris, No. 33, 27 October 1778. For the projet de traité sent to Harris see SP 103/63.

explicitly tell you our present situation will admit of doing neither the one nor the other. But if a proper subsidy properly bestowed would be understood as taking a sufficient share in continental affairs to promote and establish a respectable alliance, you may encourage the idea." A subsidy in Germany, wrote Suffolk, might be regarded by the Empress as equivalent to the Turkish clause and, as Harris knew how much Great Britain wanted to avoid this engagement, he was to exert every endeavour to obtain the treaty on the basis of a German subsidy instead of the Turkish *casus foederis*, and Russia was in addition to bind herself to the defence of the Electorate of Hanover.[72]

In the space of a few days Suffolk had thus shifted the ground on which he proposed to build an alliance from a possible Russo-Turkish war to a possible war between Russia and Austria. But in either case, he stressed, Britain would be unable to do more than provide a subsidy in exchange for the use of the greater portion of the Russian fleet and could offer neither troops nor ships to assist the Russians in what might develop for them into a war on two fronts. However, by the time these new instructions reached Harris in Russia, the situation in the Holy Roman Empire had begun to change for the better.

A fortnight after Catherine dispatched her declaration to Vienna, Count Joseph Kaunitz, the Austrian envoy, communicated to Panin Austrian willingness to accept Franco-Russian mediation in the conflict with Prussia.[73] The Austrian courier bearing this news had crossed the Russian courier carrying Catherine's ultimatum to Austria, and it still remained to be seen how Austria would react to the strong terms in which the Russian Empress had expressed herself. But Austrian willingness to consent to a mediation showed that there was some chance of avoiding or postponing a recourse to arms, and Catherine did not hesitate to accept the proffered olive branch. On 10/21 October 1778 she sent instructions to her ambassadors in Paris and Vienna and to the headquarters of Frederick II, declaring her agreement to undertake the role of mediator in the

72. SP 91/102, Suffolk to Harris, No. 37, 3 November 1778; Suffolk again however urged that "an immediate naval assistance is, in the present hour, the hinge upon which everything must turn."

73. Unzer, *Der Friede*, p. 211.

conflict.[74] At the same time Russia proposed that France should be entrusted with the task of drawing up a plan of accommodation.[75]

Harris, who had now been some eight months at the Russian court, had already established for himself a fairly efficient, and not inexpensive, network of agents who supplied him with information.[76] By the middle of October he was able to inform Suffolk of the Austrian appeal to Russian good offices.[77] But he was horrified to hear that Russia had placed the initiative for a settlement in French hands. He was only too well aware that a joint mediation, particularly a successful one, heralded that *rapprochement* between France and Russia which it was his task to prevent. He wrote at once to Suffolk to warn him of this new "inconsistent" and "unwise" policy which was being pursued by Russia.[78]

Suffolk's letters of 27 October 1778, instructing Harris to reopen negotiations for a Russian alliance with Britain and at the same time to communicate the Spanish offer of mediation and the British reply, reached Harris by 20 November. Suffolk's additional instructions of 3 November proposing a subsidy for the defence of the Electorate of Hanover reached him only on 6 December. Austria had still not replied to the Russian declaration of 22 September/2 October, but tension in the Empire was dying down while the agreement of all the parties was secured to the joint mediation of France and Russia. Clearly Suffolk's proposal of a subsidy to Russia in the event of war with Austria was out of date. Unfortunately for Britain, the very enemy against whom she wished to direct the alliance was now acting formally with Russia to promote peace in Germany and was also employed in reconciling Russia and the Porte. It was an inopportune moment to launch proposals for an alliance against France, as Harris was well aware. But this did not deter him from making the attempt.

74. Oursel, *La diplomatie française*, p. 279; Unzer, *Der Friede*, p. 212. For the text of Catherine's instructions see *Sbornik*, *65*, 24.

75. See *Sbornik*, *65*, 24–25 for Panin's instructions to Baryatinsky of 10/21 October 1778.

76. See my article, "The Use of British Secret Funds at St. Petersburg, 1777–1782."

77. SP 91/102, Harris to Suffolk, No. 62, 5/16 October 1778.

78. SP 91/102, Harris to Suffolk, No. 84, 12/23 October 1778; No. 85, 16/27 October.

Panin's reaction to the fresh British approach was inauspicious from the start. He refused to regard the Spanish offer of mediation as a plot concerted with France,[79] and when Harris proceeded to sound him on the prospects of a closer connexion between Britain and Russia, he was not encouraging; he assured Harris of Catherine's regard for England but pointed out that as she was deeply engaged in terminating the German quarrel she could not enter into engagements against a court with which she was acting as joint mediatrix.[80] Harris expressed no surprise at Panin's negative attitude. But instead of attaching weight to the fairly valid objections Panin had put forward, he attributed his failure to impress the Russian minister to the influence exercised on the latter by Frederick II. He had gradually allowed himself to believe that Panin was completely dominated by Frederick II and that any negotiation which he conducted through him was bound to fail; he no longer trusted Panin to repeat accurately to the Empress what he had been told by the foreign envoys. He determined therefore to seek a fresh channel, and in the first place approached Aleksey Orlov, "an honest and cordial friend," as Harris described him. Orlov approved the idea of an English alliance and used the opportunity to further the personal animosity of the Orlov faction against Panin by confirming Harris in the view that Panin was not to be trusted to repeat verbal communications accurately to the Empress. Orlov himself had no influence at the time and declined to intervene on Harris's behalf, but he gave him momentous advice which was to make Harris's career in St. Petersburg dramatic and varied and enable him to attain a prestige in Russia granted to few foreign envoys. "Speak to Potemkin," Orlov told Harris. "He is all powerful." If he were indifferent, Harris should win him with

79. SP 91/102, Harris to Suffolk, No. 91, 12/23 November 1778, No. 93, 16/27 November, and No. 103, 20/31 December 1778; for the Spanish side see Danvila, *Historia 5*, 10–38. It is clear from Bemis, *Diplomacy of the American Revolution*, pp. 75 ff. that the Spanish offers of mediation were as distasteful to France as they were to England. Spain was willing to sell her neutrality to England for Gibraltar and Minorca. But if this failed she hoped, by negotiating with England, to frighten France into promising to secure these *desiderata* for her in exchange for her participation in the war. See also Conn, *Gibraltar in British Diplomacy*, pp. 180 ff.

80. SP 91/102, Harris to Suffolk, No. 93, 16/27 November 1778 (*MD, 1*, 216); No. 103, 20/31 December 1778.

flattery; if he favoured England's cause, he might turn against it if he felt slighted.[81]

So far Harris had had no business dealings with the powerful favourite, and his acquaintance with him extended only to the common courtesies of court life. He knew that Potemkin took no direct part in the conduct of foreign affairs except in so far as they concerned the Porte. The extent of his secret influence was difficult to gauge, though it was widely assumed that he had inspired Catherine's ultimatum to Austria.[82] Harris had no very high opinion of the Prince, largely because he derived his information from Orlov who hated him.[83] To Potemkin, however, he now turned, and believing him accessible to flattery he endeavoured to adapt his language to what he assumed was the character of the man: interposition on England's behalf at Madrid and Versailles, declared Harris, would raise the glory of Catherine's reign to its highest pitch, and those who shared her confidence would share her glory. He then explained for the Prince's benefit England's position and her wishes in respect of the alliance, knowing, as he said, that nothing could be done for England without the Prince's knowledge and approbation. But at this stage Potemkin would not commit himself and merely replied that he would not oppose the Empress in anything she undertook in England's favour. However Harris soon heard "from undoubted authority" that Potemkin had repeated their conversation word for word to the Empress that same evening, and on the next day Catherine treated Harris with great affability. Beyond providing the assurance that Potemkin could be trusted to repeat to Catherine what he had been told, Harris's new channel of approach had availed him nothing.[84]

The negotiation itself Harris had of course to carry on through

81. SP 91/102, Harris to Suffolk, No. 103, 20/31 December 1778. Aleksey Orlov had only recently returned to court, and his arrival had been welcomed by Harris, who believed that Orlov was the only man who could "preserve or rather restore the honour and dignity of the Empire." See SP 91/102, Harris to Suffolk, No. 81, 5/16 October 1778 (*MD, 1,* 213).

82. CP Russie, *101,* Corberon to Vergennes, 9 October 1778: "on dit ici que M. Potemkin est le principal ressort des ces nouveaux mouvements"; cf. Unzer, *Der Friede,* pp. 209–10 for Joseph Kaunitz's view.

83. See Harris's remarkable account in SP 91/102, No. 81, 5/16 October 1778 (*MD, 1,* 213).

84. SP 91/102, Harris to Suffolk, No. 103, 20/31 December 1778.

normal channels. Panin's attitude in their repeated conversations was so negative, and Harris was so convinced of his untrustworthiness, that he determined to set down the gist of his instructions on paper in the certainty that a written memorial would be read by the Empress.[85] He supported his memorial in long arguments with Panin, but the latter still insisted that Russia could take no decision until a reply was received from the court of Vienna to Catherine's ultimatum of 22 September/2 October 1778. For though Russia and France had agreed to mediate, and their mediation had been accepted by both Prussia and Austria, neither of these latter powers had consented to submit its peace terms to the mediators, and there still existed the fear in Russia that Austria might take offence at the tone of the Russian declaration and the mediation might therefore never materialize.[86]

During the next few days, Harris still hoped that his memorial, combined with whatever pressure Potemkin or Orlov might bring to bear on the Empress, would achieve something. But his hopes were dashed when the Austrian answer finally arrived on 12 December 1778. It was couched in terms so flattering to the Empress that all thought of English concerns was swept away, wrote Harris. This was what the Empress and Panin had been waiting for before deciding finally what course to adopt with regard to England. As long as any doubts remained of Austrian willingness to be reasonable, the door to England must be kept open in case of a general war. It could now be gently closed.[87]

85. SP 91/102, Harris to Suffolk, No. 103, 20/31 December 1778, Enclosure A. On the Empress's methods of work see a letter from A. A. Bezborodko to A. R. Vorontsov of 3/14 June 1780. The Empress approved the drafts of all dispatches to Russian envoys abroad, and she saw dispatches from her envoys in full and not merely in summaries prepared for her. (*Sbornik, 26,* 370, *Letters of A. A. Bezborodko to A. R. Vorontsov,* at 372)

86. SP 91/102, Harris to Suffolk, No. 103, 20/31 December 1778; Unzer, *Der Friede,* p. 248.

87. SP 91/102, Harris to Suffolk, No. 103, 20/31 December 1778. The Austrian reply had been delayed partly owing to the absence of Joseph from Vienna, partly because Kaunitz wished to know the Russian reaction to his request for a Franco-Russian mediation, sent on 27 September, before committing himself. The Austrian reply is dated 14/25 November 1778, and is printed in *Sbornik, 65,* 88 (incorrectly dated, according to Unzer). Catherine may also have been influenced by the arrival on 7 December of a dispatch of 6 November from Vergennes to Corberon expressing French pleasure at the prospect of acting with Russia in the mediation, ibid., 229.

Still, the Russians were in no hurry, and it was not until 30
December 1778 that Harris received his final answer at the hands of
Panin. In a long memorandum, couched in very friendly terms,
Panin stressed the Empress's friendship towards England which was
not only "une affection habituelle" but also "un principe invari-
able de sa politique." But her own situation prevented her from
acting as her feelings would direct. Her commitments with regard
to the Porte, to Germany, and now to France were too many, and
Great Britain must recognize that Russia would be spreading and
multiplying her efforts too far were she to undertake naval assistance to Great Britain. So clear was this in Russian eyes that the
Empress did not fear "que la confiance en son amitié et en ses
sentiments puisse en souffrir quelque atteinte." The concluding
paragraphs of the memorandum sounded a more ominous note,
for it went on to put forward an *insinuation amicale* to Great
Britain, urging her to be more moderate in her treatment of neutral
shipping on the high seas,[88] always a sore subject in a maritime war.
And, in the last paragraph, the Empress pointed out that the joint
mediation with France in the German conflict might lead to increased confidence between the two countries and that in this case
the Empress would not hesitate to insinuate to France her desire
to see harmony restored between France and England. Panin, speaking for himself (a purely conventional distinction intended to
shield the Empress from a rebuff), amplified the point. The mediation, he said, might provide the Empress with the opportunity to
speak to France on the war with England, and "if by her influence,
the Empress should be fortunate enough, to procure us a permanent
and honourable peace, he did not doubt but we should prefer it
to the most glorious war." Panin even went so far as to ask to be
informed of England's terms for a pacification, in order not to
advance any views which might in the event be contrary to British
plans.[89]

Though Harris had been convinced from the beginning that his
negotiations were bound to fail, he was nevertheless discouraged
both by the finality of the Russian reply and by the hint it con-

88. For developments in the war at sea, see next chapter.
89. SP 91/102, Harris to Suffolk, No. 103, 20/31 December 1778, Enclosure C;
No. 105, 20/31 December 1778.

tained that the matters in discussion between the two countries were now to be extended to include such subjects as neutral trade and Russian mediation between France and England. He attributed the Russian refusal, wrongly in this case, to Prussian influence. A *rapprochement* between France and Russia was however a favourite object of Frederick II, and Harris dreaded that the joint mediation in Germany would increase French influence in St. Petersburg. The French would flatter Catherine and humour her weaknesses; the national character of both French and Russians was so alike in their "levity" and "profligacy" that French influence would find plenty of support around the throne, and he lamented that "we, who are too great either to flatter or court," did not receive the share of attention which was Britain's due.[90] Moreover, Harris believed that as long as Panin remained in office there would be no hope of achieving an Anglo-Russian alliance. The hint of a desire to mediate he regarded with the deepest suspicion. Such proposals arose more from "the exalted notions of their own power than from any sincere and cordial desire of serving us," and should Russia be charged with making a peace she could not be relied upon to procure suitable terms. Russians were so puffed up with vanity "that they no longer consider themselves on the same level with the rest of Europe." [91] In one last lament Harris bewailed the fact that he stood alone, with no one to help or advise him and no one on whom he could rely, and that he had to do "with a set of men, ignorant of, or indifferent to the interests of their own country, and on whose understanding truth and common sense never can operate." [92]

Much of Harris's outburst must be disregarded as the effect of failure on his proud and mercurial temperament. Nevertheless it was, to say the least, unfortunate that failure led him to berate the Russian statesmen rather than to analyse objectively the causes of the Russian refusal of England's offers. Though Prussian influence would undoubtedly be used against a Russian alliance with Britain, it was not on this occasion a decisive factor—indeed it is doubtful if there was any opportunity for it to be exercised. The clue to

90. SP 91/102, Harris to Suffolk, No. 106, 20/31 December 1778.
91. SP 91/102, Harris to Suffolk, No. 108, 20/31 December 1778.
92. SP 91/102, Harris to Suffolk, No. 106, 20/31 December 1778.

Catherine's decision lies in the highly deferential Austrian attitude to the Russian ultimatum and in the reduction of tension in Germany. Harris indeed saw that this was so. "Had the mediation in Germany not taken place; or had the court of Vienna talked in a higher style, some hopes might still have remained of bringing the business to a favourable issue," he wrote to Suffolk in December.[93] Though Russian relations with the Porte were still tense, the joint mediation with France was in the nature of a guarantee that French efforts to restrain the Turks were sincere. In relation to Turkey the English alliance was of little use to Russia, since Harris, in accordance with his instructions, had concealed his power to waive the Turkish clause. Yet even had the Empress known of it, it is doubtful whether it would have influenced her, for she was studying the English offer in the light of German affairs. As long as peace or war was in the balance, the possibility of English help (and the Empress did not know that it would amount only to a subsidy) could not be neglected. Once the mediation was well and truly launched, the Empress hesitated no longer.[94]

Even in the eighteenth century it was not within the bounds of customary diplomacy to bind oneself by a defensive treaty with one party to a war while acting as co-mediator in a separate conflict with the other party. Naturally enough Catherine considered first the interests of Russia. She had no object to gain from a general European war. The French policy of preventing a conflict in Germany suited Russia far better than the British implicit, if not explicit, intention of embroiling Russia in a European war.

Thus, under the impact of the war in America and the impending war with France, Britain slowly moved out of the splendid isolation which had characterized her policy since the Peace of Paris of 1763. Nevertheless, Suffolk's approach to Russia was still conditioned by a number of traditional assumptions, notably the existence of a

93. SP 91/102, Harris to Suffolk, No. 108, 20/31 December 1778.

94. Suffolk, remembering the rumours of government changes in Britain forwarded by Musin Pushkin which might have prejudiced Catherine against an English alliance in May 1778, warned Harris in October that he would "hear no more of such stuff," and stressed government stability. (SP 91/102, Suffolk to Harris, No. 33, 27 October 1778.) But some scathing comments in a letter from the Empress's secretary, A. A. Bezborodko, to Field Marshal Rumyantsev on 2/13 December 1778 show that the stability of such an administration was no merit in Russian eyes. (See Maykov, *Pis'ma A. A. Bezborodka*, p. 31.)

"natural alliance" between the two powers, in which Russia played the part of a British auxiliary against the common and principal enemy of both—France. In spite of the rebuff suffered by Gunning in 1775, the British offers put forward by Suffolk still made no concessions to Russia's own political requirements. More surprising, however, was Suffolk's inability to perceive that Russian interest in events in Germany was not merely the result of Prussian influence at the Russian court and that the balance of power in the Holy Roman Empire was of considerably greater importance to Russia than the conflict between Britain and France. The only proposal to Russia which took account of the fact that she might be compelled to draw the sword in Germany, the offer in October–December 1778 of a subsidy in exchange for the defence of Hanover, came in any case too late, when the Franco-Russian mediation had already been launched. At no stage either did Suffolk reveal any awareness that in the event of the war spreading in Europe, Britain herself, by then already at war with France, would probably again be in her traditional position of siding with whichever of the German powers opposed France. The flickering *rapprochement* with Prussia in April 1778 was conditioned mainly by the hope that Prussia would persuade Russia to join in the war against France at sea. Never was Britain's lack of continental connexions more noticeable than now, when British diplomacy appeared powerless to take the initiative anywhere in Europe.[95] Peace in Germany and in the Near East was in French hands, and Russia followed in France's wake. With the shadow of a hostile Spain looming on the horizon, Britain found herself quite alone.

Russia meanwhile was careful not to forfeit any chance of alliance with Britain until she was certain she would not need it. Her policy was mainly governed by the need to keep the two areas of conflict— the Empire and the Porte—separate and by the need to solve the

95. Suffolk's only positive suggestion in relation to Russo-Turkish relations was to propose to the Empress that Russian troops should evacuate the Crimea in order to put Turkey in the wrong and on condition that no Turkish troops should be admitted into the Crimea either. But, he added, if this should cause too great a disadvantage to Russia in the event of a war or if such a proposal might be misunderstood, Harris could drop the idea. He should in any case not speak to Panin about it, but only to the Empress herself or to G. Orlov. Harris never acted on this suggestion (SP 91/102, Suffolk to Harris, unnumbered, most secret, 9 January 1778).

conflict peacefully if a war on two fronts was to be avoided. French policy coincided with that of Russia, and a *rapprochement* was effected which was to last until the fall of the North administration. By now the main lines of Russian policy towards the Franco-British conflict were indeed beginning to emerge, though this was not perceived in Britain. Having tasted the pleasures of peacemaking, Catherine was finding it easy and attractive to move from the position of a potential ally to that of a potential mediator, who must remain neutral in the interests of such an exalted task. But neutrality does not mean inactivity, and Catherine was now about to profit from the dissatisfaction of the neutral maritime states with the conduct of the war at sea and to press forward with her diplomatic offensive in Europe.

3. The War at Sea

Since the outbreak of hostilities between Britain and America, Dutch, Danish, French, and other ships had been endeavouring to evade the British prohibition of trade with American ports.[1] British warships and privateers based on the West Indian islands in turn engaged with alacrity in enforcing the prohibition of trade and pounced on any neutral which came their way, whether with good reason or with none. In the circumstances it was not surprising that friction arose between the neutrals on the one hand and Britain on the other. British envoys were instructed to bring pressure to bear at neutral capitals for the stricter observation of the proclamations against contraband trade with the British colonies which many countries had issued;[2] and the Danish and Dutch envoys in London bombarded Suffolk with protests at the "highhanded" treatment meted out to their ships by British commanders and admiralty courts. Long and acrimonious disputes rumbled on for years, complicated by the time taken to receive reports from distant islands and the impossibility of trusting any of the evidence put forward by either side.[3]

Until the spring of 1778 these incidents had been mainly limited

1. Statutes at Large, 16 George III, C. 5, 2 May 1776; for instructions to privateers of the same date see Hennings, *Sammlung*, p. 19.

2. See Bemis, *Diplomacy of the American Revolution*, p. 115, on the prohibitions issued by Denmark, the United Provinces, and Portugal; cf. Gorman, *America and Belgium*, p. 130, for the prohibition of the export of munitions from the Austrian Netherlands.

3. See Bemis, *Diplomacy of the American Revolution*, pp. 123 ff.; Edler, *The Dutch Republic and the American Revolution*, pp. 25 ff.; de Germiny, *Les Brigandages Maritimes de L'Angleterre*, 3, 7 ff.; see also Public Record Office, Foreign Entry Books, passim for the years 1776–78 for correspondence about the alleged illegal detention of ships by British privateers and about the contraband trade carried on with the Americans by Danes and Dutch.

to West Indian waters. But immediately after the combat of the *Arethusa* and the *Belle Poule* in June 1778, which definitely marked the outbreak of hostilities between Britain and France, both belligerents took steps to organize the war at sea. An Order in Council of 5 August 1778 authorized letters of marque to be issued to British privateers for the seizure of French ships and French property on board neutral ships. No reference was made in these Instructions to Privateers to any treaty rights which a neutral might have to transport non-contraband goods to an enemy port in time of war, nor was any definition of contraband given for the guidance of the privateers. Disputes arising over the rights of neutrals were, it must be assumed, to be settled by the admiralty courts.[4]

France announced her policy in an Ordonnance de la Marine of 24 June 1778, which re-enacted the provisions of a previous ordonnance of 1681.[5] This ordonnance was particularly severe on neutrals, and proclaimed the doctrine that enemy goods on board a neutral ship contaminated the ship and rendered it and the cargo good prize. In France too no respect whatsoever was paid to the treaty rights which neutrals might have secured for themselves, and all could expect equally harsh treatment. But Vergennes soon had second thoughts on the subject: France was too dependent on neutral shipping for her supplies, particularly of the essential naval stores from the Baltic. Barely a month after the proclamation of the first ordonnance, a fresh Ordonnance de la Marine was issued on 26 July 1778, which upheld the doctrine of "free ships, free goods," thus allowing neutrals to carry enemy property and to trade with enemy ports except in contraband of war; the definition of contraband remained unchanged from the previous ordonnance and did not include naval stores.[6] By proclaiming more favourable terms for the neutrals Vergennes hoped to achieve two objects: the first was to encourage neutrals to continue to supply France with the sinews of war; the second was to sow dissension between Great Britain and the neutrals and to make the latter gravitate towards French political leadership. The new ordonnance bore quite dis-

4. Hennings, *Sammlung*, p. 44.
5. G. F. de Martens, *Recueil*, *3*, 117. For the ordonnance of 1681 see *Traité des prises, ou principes de la jurisprudence françoise*, p. xvii.
6. G. F. de Martens, *Recueil*, *4*, 198; Hennings, *Sammlung*, p. 139.

tinctly the character of a concession, since, in a final paragraph, France reserved the right to alter her principles if within six months Britain did not observe a similar system.

The new French ordonnance was naturally enough welcomed by the neutral trading nations. But in Britain, both the principles proclaimed in the ordonnance and the method employed, a unilateral declaration, drew strong protests. "I am astonished," wrote Suffolk to Sir Joseph Yorke at The Hague on 13 October 1778, "that the neutral powers, so far from regarding the *Reglemens* . . . as an attention, or a favour, have not expressed the highest indignation at them. For, in this declaration, the Law of Nations, and all treaties whatsoever are totally set aside. Stat pro ratione voluntas. His Most Christian Majesty, freeing himself entirely from all sorts of restrictions, tells the world what his arbitrary pleasure is, what he will do . . ." [7]

The whole question of the rights of neutral trade and shipping during a war was an extremely complex one and had given rise to innumerable disputes which were usually ultimately settled by the strongest power enforcing its interpretation of the rights of a belligerent. But there did exist a body of international law of the sea which had grown up over the centuries by a combination of custom and treaties. The fourteenth-century code of maritime law, the Consullat del Mar, proclaimed the principle that enemy goods on a neutral ship were good prize and the corollary that neutral goods on an enemy ship were free. At various times between the fourteenth and sixteenth centuries these principles had been modified, mostly in the direction of greater harshness towards the neutrals. With the growth of the great merchant navies of the late seventeenth century the maritime states sought protection for their trade in the much more favourable principle, "free ships, free goods, unfree ships, unfree goods." This principle had the advantage of securing the ship from condemnation (unless it were carrying contraband), and it also considerably simplified court proceedings, since only the nationality of the ship had to be enquired into. It was therefore incorporated into a number of treaties between individual states in the seventeenth century. But in spite of the benefits which they might derive as neutrals from these more

7. SP 84/562, Suffolk to Yorke, 13 October 1778, unnumbered, most confidential.

moderate principles, most European powers when they were at war continued to proclaim the harsher doctrine that the flag did not cover the cargo. Even existing treaties between a belligerent and a neutral were by no means always observed, though occasionally a belligerent might condescend to do so as a special mark of favour towards a friendly neutral; political and economic necessity might also sometimes induce a belligerent to adopt a more moderate attitude. In general, the doctrine "free ships, free goods" corresponded to the interests of the small powers with large merchant fleets, such as Denmark and Holland, which in the event of a European war would endeavour to remain neutral; for political and economic reasons it might also at times suit the interests of France and Spain, two nations which had insufficient merchant shipping of their own and might welcome the opportunity of using neutral shipping to supplement their needs. One power, however, stood out against any improvement in the security of neutral navigation, and that was Britain.[8]

The position of Britain was in this respect unique. At the end of the eighteenth century she was the only one of the powers equipped with both a fighting navy and a merchant fleet sufficient for her needs. Britain therefore had no reason to be tender to neutral shipping, and it was in her interests to adhere to a system which enabled her to seize enemy property wherever she found it.[9] The legal arguments used to support the British position were that the law of the sea was founded on the Consullat del Mar and that the doctrine "free ships, free goods" was a privilege having its origin only in treaties. Where no commercial treaty existed between Britain and a neutral specifically establishing the neutral right to carry enemy goods, then captured enemy property must

8. For the general history of neutral rights at sea see Kulsrud, *Maritime Neutrality to 1780;* Jessup and Deak, *Neutrality, its History, Economics and Law;* the best analytic account of the problems of 1776–83 is by Bergbohm, *Die bewaffnete Neutralität, 1780–1783.* Katchenowsky, *Prize Law,* is a useful survey, see pp. 51 ff. for the 18th century.

9. Britain had trifled with the principle "free ships, free goods" at the end of the 17th century, and it was incorporated for instance into the treaty of 1665 with Spain (Chalmers, *Collection of Treaties, 2, 5,* Articles XXII and XXVI). It was also incorporated in the treaty of Utrecht with France (ibid., *1,* 390, Article XVII) presumably because neither Britain nor France would be neutral in a war in which either was involved.

be adjudicated according to the rules of the Consullat.[10] Many arguments in defence of the British position could be drawn from the writings of a number of famous jurists, notably Grotius, Heineccius, Bynkershoek, and Pufendorf. The opposing view, favoured by the neutrals, had also been ably championed by the Dane, M. Hübner, for instance, and the Swiss, E. Vattel.[11] It received additional support when it was incorporated in the treaty of commerce between France and the newly formed United States of America, and it was perhaps also more in consonance with the liberal climate of opinion of the Enlightenment.[12] On legal argument alone, the issue could not be decided. Each side would put forward its claims; diplomacy and armed force would tilt the scale.

The definition of contraband was a further source of friction between neutrals and belligerents, for it was neither universal nor precise. In some treaties, all "munitions of war" were treated as contraband; in others, soldiers, food, money, ships, sails, and tackle were listed; in others, only manufactured weapons. By the beginning of the eighteenth century, provisions were generally accounted as non-contraband, and in many cases naval stores as well, notably in the treaty of Utrecht.[13] Here again the interests

10. Katchenowsky, *Prize Law*, p. 54; British reply to the Prussian commissioners at the time of the Silesian loan dispute, p. 55. See also Satow, *The Silesian Loan and Frederick the Great*, pp. 73 ff. and particularly p. 88, note.

11. For the extremely complex history of the principle "free ships, free goods," see the works quoted in note 8. See particularly the brief survey in Bergbohm, *Die bewaffnete Neutralität*, pp. 34–40, and the bibliography of the subject he gives in p. 34, n. 1; see also Scott, *Armed Neutralities*, pp. 1–272, for extracts from the leading publicists of the age, for and against. For a view strongly in favour of the British position, see Piggott and Omond, *Documentary History of the Armed Neutralities*, Introduction. The contemporary English standpoint is also expounded by Jenkinson in the Introduction to his *Collection of All the Treaties of Peace, Alliance and Commerce between Great Britain and other Powers . . . To which is prefixed a Discourse on the Conduct of the Government of Great Britain in respect to Neutral Nations* (1785).

12. In the period from 1650 to 1780, 36 treaties were concluded on the principle "free ships, free goods," while only 15 followed the principles of the Consullat del Mar. See Matzen, *Forelaesninger over den Positive Folkeret*, quoted in Scott, *Armed Neutralities*, p. 163. For the Franco-American treaty, see G. F. de Martens, *Recueil, Supplément 3*, 587, Articles 13, 14, 23, 24.

13. Bergbohm, *Die bewaffnete Neutralität*, p. 40, a short general account of the history of contraband. See Article XX of the treaty of Utrecht.

of France and Spain, on the one hand, and Britain, on the other, diverged. The former powers, relying on neutral carriers, desired a narrow definition of contraband to enable them to receive supplies of raw materials useful both in peace and war. Britain attempted to enforce a very wide conception of contraband in order to prevent these very raw materials from being delivered to her enemies. The interpretation of the contraband clauses in treaties by the admiralty courts gave rise to constant disputes. Some powers (e.g. Russia and Denmark) considered that only those articles actually mentioned by name in the relative article of a treaty were contraband. The British position was that such listed items were definitely contraband, but the fact that a particular item did not figure on the list did not preclude its being regarded as contraband if it could be used for war.[14]

In a maritime war the main objects of contention were naval stores, namely ships' timber, masts, sail cloth, pitch, tar, hemp, and cordage. In the British view, naval stores, though also used for peaceful purposes, were the raw materials of a fighting navy and could therefore legitimately be condemned as contraband.[15] The area from which most of these supplies were drawn was the Baltic, and Britain's relations with the principal producers—Russia, Denmark, and Sweden—were governed by commercial treaties. In the treaties with Denmark and Sweden naval stores were not specifically named as contraband, but the drafting of the relevant articles was in each case sufficiently general for the British courts to interpret them in the British sense.[16] Judging by the bare text

14. See for instance the judgement of Sir Henry Penrice in the case of the *Med Guds Hielpe*, of 1745, reaffirmed in 1750: "Pitch and tar are not enumerated in the 11th article of the Swedish treaty but I rather think those enumerated were mentioned rather for example than by way of exclusion and that there are other contraband goods than what are mentioned in that article." Quoted in Roscoe, ed., *Reports of [English] Prize Cases*, p. 1.

15. See for instance the notorious judgement of Sir James Marriott in the case of the Dutch ship *Vryheit*, of 2 December 1778, quoted in Roscoe, *Reports*, p. 12; Hennings, *Sammlung*, p. 42.

16. For the Anglo-Swedish treaty of 1666, see Dumont, *Corps universel, 6*, Pt. 3, p. 83; contraband is defined as including "all other things necessary for warlike use." For the Anglo-Danish treaty of 1670, see ibid., 7, Pt. 1, p. 132; Article 3 lists some contraband items, though not naval stores, but includes the words "ou autres choses nécéssaires pour l'usage de la guerre."

of the Anglo-Russian treaty of 1766, the Russians were entitled, according to Articles X and XI, to follow the principle "free ships, free goods" and to carry naval stores to the enemies of Britain during a war.[17] But recent research has shown that there was some confusion in Britain over the legal status of the Russian trade. This may perhaps be imputed to Sir James Marriott, the advocate general, whose interpretation of the law remained constantly subordinated to his patriotism.[18] In the negotiations for the renewal of the commercial treaty in 1766, Marriott, Sandwich, the secretary of state concerned, and Macartney, the British envoy in Russia, were all under the impression that by renewing the relevant clauses of the treaty of 1734 Russia would be deprived of the privilege of "free ships, free goods," and that "we are now the judges of what shall be esteemed munitions." Yet a British prize judge had ruled in 1747 that Article XI of the treaty of 1734 entitled Russia to carry naval stores to the enemy, and the House of Lords had upheld this ruling.[19] The divergence of opinion on the interpretation of these important clauses in the treaty of 1766 was to be the cause of great dissension between Britain and Russia, even though the Russian merchant navy was virtually nonexistent at the outbreak of the Anglo-French war.

The Marine Treaty of 1674 between England and Holland was also to prove the source of constant friction between the two countries. This treaty entitled the Dutch to the benefit of the principle "free ships, free goods" and allowed them to carry on coastal trade from one enemy port to another and to act as carriers of goods

17. See F. de Martens, *Recueil, 9, 242,* Articles X and XI. Article X states that the subjects of the two parties "shall be at liberty to go, come, and trade freely with the States with which one or the other of the parties shall at this or at any future period be engaged in war provided they do not carry warlike stores to the enemy"; Article XI lists a number of contraband items which were liable to condemnation, though not naval stores, and then continues "but neither the ships nor passengers, nor the other merchandises found at the same time, shall be detained or hindered from prosecuting their voyage."

18. According to Marriott, "The Law of Nations, *which is the usage of nations* . . . has varied as any one maritime power has possessed the ascendant and *given the law* to others," quoted by Spencer, in "Lord Sandwich, Russian Masts and American Independence," at p. 120. See also Roscoe, *History of the English Prize Court,* pp. 56–57, on Marriott's incapacity to state legal propositions clearly.

19. See Spencer, "Lord Sandwich," pp. 117 ff.

from any country to enemy ports. Naval stores were specifically described as non-contraband.[20]

France was also bound by commercial treaties with some of the Baltic powers. But since the French ordonnance of July 1778 provided more favourable terms than the treaties, the powers concerned were quite content not to invoke their treaty rights. Nevertheless, France, as already noted, reserved to herself the right to revert to her old system should Great Britain refuse to modify her principles.[21]

Even before the outbreak of war with France, it was clear that in the event of war spreading to Europe there would be trouble with the neutrals. Sir Joseph Yorke, the British envoy at The Hague, was instructed to make an attempt to negotiate a modification of the Marine Treaty of 1674 which conferred such awkward privileges on the Dutch.[22] On 14 April 1778 Suffolk wrote to Yorke that "we can never permit the subjects of the Republick to become the carriers of our enemies and the old claim of free ships free goods can never be admitted . . ."[23]

Acting on this principle, privateers and the Royal Navy started operations in European waters; many Dutch, Danish, Swedish, and Prussian ships were seized indiscriminately and on most varied pretexts and started their long journey through the admiralty courts. During the summer the neutral outcry mounted ever higher, and there was some justification for these protests, for there had been no declaration of war to notify the beginning of hostilities to traders.[24] The merchants of Amsterdam in particular were loud in their complaints, and on 18 September the States of Holland decided to arm thirty-two ships in defence of their

20. Chalmers, *Collection of Treaties, 1*, 177. Articles 2 and 3 deal with contraband; Article 3 states that naval stores may be carried to enemy ports. Article 8 proclaims the doctrine "free ships, free goods."

21. For the Franco-Swedish treaty of 1741 see de Clercq, *Recueil des traités de France, 1*, 44; for the Franco-Danish treaty of 1742, see p. 46.

22. Bemis, *Diplomacy of the American Revolution*, p. 139.

23. SP 84/561, Suffolk to Yorke, No. 6, 14 April 1778.

24. Between 21 July and 23 September 1778, complaints were made to Suffolk by the Dutch envoy, Welderen; the Swede, Nolcken; the Dane, Dreyer; and the Prussian, Maltzahn, in respect of 22 ships detained by British cruisers and privateers. (See Foreign Entry Book, SP 104/236.)

trade.[25] Meanwhile the Dutch envoy to Great Britain, Count Welderen, presented on 28 September 1778 a memorandum recapitulating the Dutch grievances and demanding the release of captured Dutch ships.[26]

The British government showed considerable moderation in its attitude to all these complaints. A number of Dutch ships were released, and orders were given to detain only those carrying "naval stores or other contraband." [27] Meanwhile Suffolk, who had been prevented by his health from paying "a more early attention to this material business," [28] was revolving various plans to pacify the neutrals. There were really two separate problems: that of the Dutch, invoking their rights under the treaty of 1674, and that of the other neutrals whose claim to "free ships, free goods" Britain did not recognize. Suffolk's confidant was Sir Joseph Yorke, though Yorke was not perhaps the ideal adviser in these matters. He had been at The Hague since 1751 and had made it a matter of principle to adopt an attitude of systematic arrogance towards the merchant republic and towards the Prince of Orange. He often wrote of, and presumably thought of, the Dutch as boorish money-grubbers, and had thus indirectly rendered easier the task of the more supple French envoy, the Duc de la Vauguyon, of extending French influence among the wealthy regents of Holland.[29]

As far as the Dutch were concerned, Suffolk's problem was to get "rid of the schackles of the commercial treaty, at least with regard to naval and warlike stores, without a breach." The treaty of alliance of 1668 "makes the performing any hostile act what-

25. Fauchille, *La diplomatie française*, p. 78.

26. SP 84/561, Yorke to Suffolk, No. 63, 1 September 1778; SP 84/562, Welderen to Suffolk, 28 September 1778.

27. SP 84/562, Suffolk to Yorke, No. 22, 8 September 1778, and Suffolk to the Lords of the Admiralty, 29 September 1778.

28. SP 84/562, Suffolk to Yorke, unnumbered, 29 September 1778; Suffolk now had leisure to devote himself to the problem for until the King returned from the West country "it is impossible to receive His Majesty's final pleasure and collect enough of his servants together to give matters a proper sanction." (Unnumbered, quite private, 29 September 1778.)

29. See e.g. Yorke to Harris, 18 September 1779: "I speak not of the degenerate Dutch, they are worse than nothing . . ." (Harris Papers)

soever against the King of Great Britain and his subjects either
by sea or land a casus foederis." [30] If the Dutch were to insist on
their rights under the treaty of 1674, then Britain could demand
hers under the treaty of 1668. But the trouble was that Britain
did not want to invoke the treaty and demand active succours
from the Dutch, knowing full well that in the present state of the
Dutch defences, active assistance would be more of a liability than
a benevolent neutrality. In the circumstances, however, Suffolk
considered that the Dutch were not entitled to an exact observation of the Marine Treaty. As regards the other neutrals, the
British position was that none of them enjoyed by treaty the right
to carry enemy goods and that in any case naval stores were contraband. At this stage Suffolk hoped to negotiate a compromise
agreement with the Dutch by which they would give up the right
to carry naval stores. To all the neutrals, he intended to propose
that Britain would agree to release captured ships, purchasing the
cargoes if owned by neutrals and condemning them if enemy-
owned. In both cases the neutral shipper was to receive freight,
and in the former costs as well.[31] British policy was to be declared
in a memorial to be issued far and wide. Suffolk enclosed a draft
to Yorke, inviting him to "criticise, correct, detract or add to it—
and when you have done so, if you will put it into French (which
will be but a small trouble to you) it will make its appearance
with much grace and many favourable circumstances." [32]

While Yorke was engaged in sounding the Dutch, Suffolk began
to have second thoughts about his plan.[33] On 13 October 1778, in
a long dispatch to Yorke, he expressed his doubts whether the
mode of procedure they had been discussing could in fact be
adopted:

> No sovereign, in the plenitude even of despotic power, can
> prescribe any other rule for his conduct, in these matters, than

30. Cf. references in n. 28. For the Anglo-Dutch treaty of 1668, see Dumont, *Corps
universel*, 7, Pt. 1, p. 66, Article I.

31. SP 84/562, Draft of a memorial enclosed in Yorke to Suffolk, unnumbered,
most private, 6 October 1778. Suffolk's own draft is not there, but I quote from the
text which Yorke had been working on.

32. SP 84/562, Suffolk to Yorke, unnumbered, 29 September 1778, quite private.

33. SP 84/562, Yorke to Suffolk, unnumbered, most private, 6 October 1778.

the general law of nations, and the stipulations of particular treaties, where they exist. He has, under these authorities, a right upon a point in question, or he has not a right. If he has not, no arbitrary declaration can give him one. And it seems to me very nice and problematical, how far an acquiescence in the Declaration we have been thinking of . . . may be relied upon or expected. It is a public act of state declaratory of what? Of the King's resolution not to adhere to a treaty subsisting between him and the country it is addressed to! . . . Now upon much reflection I fear the step we have been thinking of for His Majesty will stand upon no better foundation of right, than the reglemens of the French King.[34]

If, as Suffolk now thought, the issuing of a unilateral declaration was "too irregular" and "unbecoming an English monarch" some other means must be found to secure the substance of what Britain desired.[35] The British attitude was moderate: "We are willing," wrote Suffolk, "that the Dutch subject, owner, or carrier, of naval stores, should be no loser." In the case of a Dutch owner, Britain would offer to purchase the cargo at a just evaluation; in the case of a carrier, to pay the freight when the cargo belonged to the enemy; in both cases, to pay the expenses incurred by capture.[36]

The solution Suffolk found to this dilemma was a typical compromise. The idea of a declaration was abandoned, and instead a circular was sent out to British envoys and residents at the principal neutral capitals, and a separate memorandum was delivered to Count Welderen, the Dutch envoy, on 19 October 1778 in reply to the Dutch memorial of 28 September 1778. In his reply to the Dutch, Suffolk stated that in view of the suddenness of the outbreak of hostilities, Britain would buy cargoes of naval stores on Dutch ships already seized, without distinguishing between enemy and neutral property. For the future, Yorke was to be instructed to enter into negotiations with the Dutch to settle the treatment of naval stores belonging to the enemy, either by re-

34. SP 84/562, Suffolk to Yorke, unnumbered, 13 October 1778, most confidential.
35. SP 84/562, Suffolk to Yorke, unnumbered, most private, 13 October 1778.
36. SP 84/562, Suffolk to Yorke, unnumbered, most confidential, 13 October 1778.

vising the Marine Treaty or by negotiating a new one. "But, if that is impracticable," wrote Suffolk, "they must give us credit for our good intentions, and trust to what will probably be the equitable decisions of the Court of Admiralty." [37]

The circular to the neutrals was a good deal stiffer. Suffolk stated that British practice with regard to neutral trade was governed by the general law of nations or the stipulations of treaties where they exist "according to the manner in which they have been constantly understood." He pointed out that no treaty existed between Britain and any of these neutrals which authorized the covering of enemy goods.[38] However, as a concession, cargoes of naval stores which were neutral property in neutral ships detained before 10 November 1778 would also be purchased at a fair valuation in view of the lack of notice of the existence of a state of war. After 10 November 1778, naval stores would be condemned as contraband, enemy property would be condemned, and ships would have to go before the admiralty courts to prove the nature of their cargoes.[39] From a letter to the Lords of the Admiralty of 19 October 1778, the policy now to be followed by Britain emerges more clearly. Suffolk invited the noble lords to give directions to the Commissioners of the Navy Board "to purchase all naval stores taken on board of neutral ships fit for His Majesty's service that are or may be condemned as lawful prize in the courts of admiralty, or which by order of the court shall be decreed to be restored to the claimants upon condition that the same shall be sold for the King's use, His Majesty paying all expences of legal proceedings the freight and incident charges upon a fair valuation . . ." [40]

37. SP 84/562, Suffolk to Welderen, 19 October 1778; Suffolk to Yorke, unnumbered, 20 October 1778. Suffolk's Note to Welderen was to a great extent modelled on the draft declaration as amended by Yorke.

38. Foreign Entry Book, SP 104/236, Circular to Elliot (Berlin), Wroughton (Sweden), Delaval (Copenhagen) 20 October 1778; to Mathias (Bremen, Hamburg, and Lübeck), 23 October 1778, enclosing copies of letters of 19 October 1778 to Maltzahn, Nolcken, and Dreyer.

39. See for example SP 90/102, Suffolk to Elliot, 19 October 1778, copy of Suffolk to Maltzahn. Suffolk rather unconvincingly attacks the French *règlement*, "où la sévérité insidieuse et extrême est égale à la subtilité de l'équivoque dans les termes." But it did allow "free ships, free goods," which was what the neutrals cared about!

40. Foreign Entry Book, SP 104/236, Suffolk to the Lords of the Admiralty, 19 October 1778.

Suffolk had hesitated to issue a declaration because a one-sided proclamation that a treaty was to be overruled was unworthy of "the just character of His present Majesty" and might be a "dangerous instrument in the hands of our enemies." [41] But neither he nor his advisers appreciated that in setting up a new category of cargo, neither innocent nor guilty, which would be returned to the claimants only on condition it was sold to the Navy Board, he was doing precisely what he criticized the French king for doing: he was overruling existing treaties and establishing a system of pre-emptive purchase which was bound to dislocate trade and cause dissatisfaction.[42]

That Britain should make any concession at all, such as the decision to purchase cargoes seized before 10 November 1778, was regarded by the neutrals as a sign of weakness and encouraged them to contest the decisions of the admiralty courts and to seek redress through diplomatic channels. In practice most countries accepted the jurisdiction of admiralty courts. But when a neutral state was powerful enough or had a very strong case, a revision of the sentence could be procured by diplomatic pressure or ships might be released as an act of grace.[43] The official British reply to diplomatic protests was invariably that it was against the British constitution to release ships except after trial and sentence before an admiralty court judge.[44] This was in itself an excellent principle designed to avoid piracy on the high seas or the payment of ransom to unscrupulous privateers. By making it illegal to release ships except on sentence, privateers were encouraged to bring their captures in to port, and a sufficiently large number was condemned to make privateering a lucrative profession. Some

41. SP 84/562, Suffolk to Yorke, unnumbered, 13 October 1778, most confidential.

42. Statutes at Large, *13*, 1778, 19 George III, c. 67. An Act was passed enabling the Commissioners of the Navy Board to purchase cargoes of naval stores on neutral ships "which may in many cases be expedient without proceeding to the condemnation thereof." The Act was necessary since such purchases might contravene the Navigation Acts.

43. See for instance the Anglo-Prussian dispute over ships in Satow, *The Silesian Loan.*

44. See for instance SP 75/135, Suffolk to Delaval, No. 23, 27 November 1778: Count Bernstorff must see the "impropriety and even impossibility of entering into a discussion on the judicial proceedings of a court of law in any other manner than by an appeal to the superior one of the King in Council. This has been invariably the rule, and the constitution of this country will not admit of any other."

control could also be exercised over the excesses of privateers, and
by the infliction of penalties (the costs of the action and damages)
they were restrained from bringing in genuinely innocent ships.

The neutrals, however, still had various grounds for complaint.
First of all, when the decisions of the courts depended, as they
often did, on the interpretation of clauses in treaties, the sovereigns of neutral states frequently contested the right of English
judges to be sole interpreters of treaties and the law. Secondly, the
admiralty courts could and did receive instructions from the secretaries of state on the interpretation of treaties, instructions which
needless to say were in accordance with the needs of British foreign policy at the time.[45] Thirdly it was not in fact the case that
ships could not be released until sentenced by a court. Ships
seized by the Royal Navy were frequently released without trial,
and in some cases those taken by privateers were similarly treated.[46]

Apart from bringing pressure to bear through diplomatic channels, neutral maritime powers had in the past sought to protect
their trade by joint naval action, notably during the war of the
League of Augsburg [47] and during the Seven Years' War. The nations concerned were Sweden, Denmark, and in the eighteenth century Russia also; their purpose was in part to close the Baltic to
belligerent ships and privateers and in part to protect neutral
shipping in the North Sea.[48] It was not surprising, therefore, that

45. See for instance Adm. 1/3886, Sir James Marriott to the Lords of the Admiralty,
31 July 1780: "The direction and meaning of the court of Admiralty from the beginning of hostilities have been always agreeable to the tenour of the Act of Parliament and to the terms of His Majesty's Declaration that the stores should be purchased." Marriott here shows that a declaration by Suffolk in the name of the government, and an Act of Parliament (19 George III, c. 67) is regarded by him as
overriding existing treaties.

46. For an example of the release of ships seized by the Navy, without going
before the courts see Ch. 6, n. 46; for an example of the release of a ship taken by
a privateer, see Ch. 15, n. 42.

47. Katchenowsky, Prize Law, p. 49. For the convention between Denmark and
Sweden see Dumont, Corps universel, 7, Pt. 2, p. 235. See also Clark, The Dutch
Alliance and the War Against French Trade, 1688–1697.

48. Katchenowsky, Prize Law, p. 60. See also Kulsrud, Maritime Neutrality, and
Taube, "Le statut juridique de la mer baltique jusqu'au début du XIXe siècle,"
p. 469. See G. F. de Martens, Recueil, Supplément, 3, 36–41 for the convention concluded between Russia and Sweden on 20 March 1759, and p. 42 for the act of accession of Denmark; by Article 1 of the convention neutral ships would be able to
trade freely with non-blockaded Prussian ports except in contraband of war (Russia
was at war with Prussia).

even before the outbreak of war with Britain, Vergennes should have suggested some kind of joint action on the part of France, Spain, and the United Provinces to protect trade.[49] But his suggestion was premature. The publication of the second French ordonnance, with its promise of vast profits if only Britain could be made to follow similar principles did spur the Dutch on to secure for themselves the full application of the stipulations of the Marine Treaty of 1674. It did not however inspire them to take collective action, for if these privileges could be observed for the Dutch alone, their carrying trade, which was no longer in its prime, could again outstrip all its rivals.

Until the summer of 1778 the powers interested in defending the rights of neutrals had been the United Provinces, Sweden, Denmark, and Prussia. The intervention of Russia was to change the whole situation. Russia was a great land power with a small navy and a still smaller merchant fleet. She had in the past taken an active part in endeavouring to close the Baltic to belligerent ships, but her interests did not extend beyond the area. It was the type of cargo around which the present dispute centred that brought Russia into the picture, for she was the great supplier of naval stores of all kinds.[50] A maritime war would inevitably increase the demand for these Russian products. France had long relied on Russia for her naval stores. England too depended on Riga masts for her ships. The trade in naval stores was mostly organized by English factors in Russia. Through them French agents in various disguises, or undisguised, were purchasing large quantities of hemp and flax which were loaded in Danish, Swedish, or Dutch bottoms. Information as to ships and cargo was then duly passed by the English factors to the British consul in St. Petersburg and thence to the Admiralty in England, which organized their interception. There was a small amount of direct trade in French bottoms, and Tuscan and Genoese ships occasionally appeared in Russian ports. Direct trade with Spain had also been inaugurated in Catherine's reign, and in August 1778 two Spanish frigates arrived at Cronstadt, the first ever to enter

49. Fauchille, *La diplomatie française*, p. 38.

50. For a very brief survey of Russian foreign trade in the latter half of the 18th century, see Baranovich et al, *Ocherki istorii SSSR—Period feodalizma—Rossiya vo vtoroy polovine XVIII v.*, pp. 126 ff.

the Baltic.[51] The number of Russian houses dealing in naval stores was small and mostly concentrated in the old Livonian towns such as Riga and Reval, and not many merchants used their own ships. By the time the cargo of naval stores had been loaded on board ship, the Russian producer had received his money so that only the shipper suffered if the ships were seized.

One element, however, was essential for the continued smooth progress of this highly satisfactory trade: a safe access to Russian ports for ships arriving to take up their cargoes. Russian attention was forcibly drawn to the war at sea by the appearance in August 1778 in the North Sea of an American privateer, the *General Mifflin*[52] of Boston, which took an English ship, the *Good Intent*, off the North Cape and sank it, after having already seized and sent into port seven other ships. Catherine's indignation was aroused at this impertinent interference with Russian trade. "Je suis fâchée, mais très fâchée," she wrote to her confidant Grimm on 11/22 August 1778. Unlike "frère G., on ne me joue point impunément sur le nez." She began at once to explore the idea of joint action by the Baltic powers.[53] Her first approach was naturally enough to her ally Denmark, and on 17/28 August 1778 Sacken, the Russian envoy to the court of Denmark, was instructed to sound Bernstorff's views. It was too late to send a squadron to northern waters in the current year, but the Empress proposed, in view of the depredations of American corsairs, that Russia and Denmark should each arm a small detachment to cruise off their coasts in spring 1779.[54]

51. For British supplies of timber, see Albion, *Forests and Sea Power*, pp. 44, 141, 147–48; for the position in Russia see SP 91/102, Harris to Suffolk, No. 61, 7/18 August 1778.

52. Bemis, *Diplomacy of the American Revolution*, p. 151 states that the ship was known to be an American privateer but was not otherwise identified. In the reports of Consul Shairp it is named as the *General Mifflin*, a privateer with a distinguished record of captures brought into French ports on the Atlantic. See SP 91/102, Shairp to Suffolk enclosing a letter from the captain of the *Good Intent* to a merchant in Archangel, 22 August/2 September 1778.

53. See *Pis'ma i zapiski imperatritsy Yekateriny vtoroy k grafu Nikite Ivanovichu Paninu*, in *Chteniya v imperatorskom obshchestve istorii i drevnostey rossiyskikh* (Moscow, 1863), 2, Pt. 2, p. 109, Catherine to Panin, n.d.; Catherine to Grimm, 11/22 August in *Sbornik, 23*, 95—"frère G." is of course George III.

54. *Morskoy Sbornik, 43* (September 1859), Pt. 3, p. 30. Documents concerning the Armed Neutrality of 1780, No. 1, Projet de lettre du comte Panin à M. Sacken

A few days after the dispatch of the courier to Copenhagen, Panin authorized Harris to inform his court "ministerially" that though the ships captured by the American privateer were not Russian, since it was the Russian trade alone that was being interfered with, Russia had invited Denmark to take joint action; he expressed his conviction that the Russian proposal would be adopted.[55]

Neither the plan as it stood nor the manner in which it was communicated to Harris was likely to arouse apprehension in Britain. In fact when Suffolk heard of it, it barely detained his attention, so absorbed was he in the far more serious problem of circumventing the Marine Treaty with Holland. But unbeknown to the British statesman, the Danes were harbouring more ambitious ideas. Bernstorff, quite independently, had already toyed with the idea of trade protection, and on 25 August 1778 he had instructed the Danish envoy in Stockholm to sound Sweden informally as to the possibility of concerted action by Sweden, Holland, and Denmark.[56] Moreover, on 27 August 1778, Vergennes had instructed La Vauguyon to remind the Dutch that unless they compelled Great Britain to respect French goods on Dutch ships, France would have to take reprisals. A similar communication was addressed by France to Sweden and Denmark.[57] French pressure, coupled with the genuine Danish grievances, led Bernstorff to endeavour to use the Russian opening to secure Russian support for a plan designed to force Britain to show more respect for neutral trade. In his reply to Sacken, dated 18/29 September 1778, the Danish minister put forward proposals for a convention between Russia and Denmark, to be communicated to the belligerents except for its secret articles. The public part of the convention should express the resolution of the two powers to arm

à Copenhague, approved by the Empress 16/27 August 1778; dispatched by courier 17/28 August 1778.

55. SP 91/102, Harris to Suffolk, No. 66, 24 August/4 September 1778; No. 67, 24 August/4 September 1778. Fauchille's description (pp. 216–18) of Harris complaining of the activities of the *General Mifflin* to Panin and Potemkin and persuading the Empress to propose her naval patrol is quite unsupported by Harris's own dispatches.

56. Quoted from Boye, *De vaebnede Neutralitetsforbund et avsnit av Folkerettens Historie,* in Scott, *Armed Neutralities* at p. 48.

57. Fauchille, *La diplomatie française,* p. 75, p. 210.

squadrons to protect their own and their ally's ships; the convention should last for the duration of the war and should not be limited to certain seas, though the Baltic and the North Sea should be specially named; the carrying of contraband should be forbidden to the subjects of the two powers, and the decision as to what constituted contraband should be in accordance with their respective treaties with the belligerents; alternatively those articles should be considered contraband "que ces puissances regardaient comme telles en general vis-à-vis de toutes les autres puissance neutres de l'Europe, conformément au droit des gens universel et avoué comme tel." The convention should be communicated to the belligerents with a declaration that the signatories intended to observe a strict neutrality. The secret articles, according to Bernstorff's plan, should provide that each power should arm a squadron of six warships and four frigates to cruise from the Elbe to Schagen or Archangel; the squadrons should cruise separately and only join forces in case of need, and they were to be ordered to convoy merchant ships from eight to ten leagues offshore to their port of destination in Russia or Denmark–Norway. Finally Bernstorff proposed that Russia should use all her influence in Great Britain "pour porter cette nation à des principles équitables conformes à ses traités avec nous et au droit des gens sur la nature des prises et sur l'inviolabilité du pavillon neutre."

In explanation of his effort to use the projected convention as a means of forcing Britain to adopt more favourable principles, Bernstorff dwelt on the many protests which Danes, Swedes, and Dutch had all made against British policy, and he called attention to the fact that France had only granted six months in which to secure a change of heart in Britain. The Empress of Russia alone, he declared, "en joignant [ses instances] comme une puissance également neutre et interessée, pourra décider ce différend, le plus important et le plus décisif de tous pour le commerce d'exportation des produits du Nord." Bernstorff then proceeded to lay down the main points of a charter for safe navigation for neutrals, and he expressed the hope that the Empress would agree to bring pressure to bear in London to secure their adoption:

> Tout ce qu'on demande à l'Angleterre se peut réduire à cinq points si évidents et si équitables . . . :

1) Que les vaisseaux neutres puissent naviguer librement de port en port et sur les côtes des nations en guerre.

2) Que les effets appartenant aux sujets des dites puissances en guerre doivent être libres sur les vaisseaux neutres, à l'exception des marchandises de contrebande.

3) Que celles-ci doivent être également fixées: et que par conséquent l'Angleterre n'étende sous aucun pretexte cette dénomination plus loin que la France le fait actuellement (à quoi les articles 19 et 20 du traité d'Utrecht de 1713, ainsi que nos anciens traités avec la France et l'Angleterre pourroient servir d'explication).

4) Qu'il faut déterminer ce qui caractérise un port bloqué, dénomination qu'on ne peut accorder qu'à celui, où il y a par la disposition de la puissance qui l'attaque avec des vaisseaux arrêtés et suffisament proches, un danger évident d'entrer.

5) Que ces principes soyent rendus publics pour servir de règle manifeste, comme aux armateurs, décidant sans autre procédure et forme de procès.

These rules, explained Bernstorff, if adopted by England, would render neutral navigation almost entirely safe. Even the Americans, in their declaration of 9 May 1778, had adopted satisfactory rules, "et il n'y a que les Anglois qui par un intérêt surement très mal entendu balancent encore; la gloire de les déterminer paroit reservée à Sa Majesté l'Impératrice." [58]

The turn which Bernstorff had given to the Empress's proposal was clearly aimed at Britain and Britain alone. The Anglo-Danish treaty of 1670, as interpreted by Denmark, allowed the Danes to claim the same privileges as the Dutch under the treaty of 1674, but

58. *Morskoy Sbornik, 43, 44,* No. 2, Sacken to Panin, 18/29 September 1778 enclosing a note by Bernstorff to Sacken of 28 September 1778. Bernstorff was influenced in the principles he set out by the Danish writer M. Hübner, author of *De la saisie des bâtiments neutres,* published in 1759. Hübner had been sent to London at the beginning of the Seven Years' War to argue the Danish case against British detention of Danish ships. (See Katchenowsky, *Prize Law,* p. 60; Boye, *De vaebnede Neutralitetsforbund,* pp. 51–52.) For the American declaration of 9 May 1778 see G.F. de Martens, *Recueil, 3,* 17.

this reading of the treaty had always been contested by Britain. Towards the end of September 1778 Bernstorff instructed Dreyer, the Danish envoy at the court of St. James, to reopen the vexed question of the interpretation of the treaty. He received the usual answer, "that the claim Mr. de Dreyer makes is not founded in the tenour of the treaty and that it has never been admitted. Usage must be considered as the true explication of treaties and, particularly, in those of old date." [59]

The Danish reply to the Russian overture reached St. Petersburg on 21 October 1778, and its repercussions were immediately felt by Harris who, however, judging by the tenor of his dispatches, did not discover the details of Bernstorff's plan. But in an "occasional conversation" with Harris, on 22 October, Panin stressed the close links between Russia and Denmark. He commented on Denmark's favourable disposition towards Britain, but expressed his sorrow that Britain "had stopped some of their vessels; and hoped, that for the trifling advantage which could arise from such seizures, we should not run the risk of altering sentiments, from which we might reap so essential a benefit." [60] Not only in St. Petersburg but in Copenhagen also Russian diplomacy reacted at once to Bernstorff's appeal for Russian support, and Sacken urged on his British colleague that the Empress would see with pleasure Danish trade treated with indulgence and "even some partiality." [61]

Other powers as well now began to feel that it was worth-while to bring in Russia as a defender of neutral trade. The Dutch resident in St. Petersburg, Swart, was active in working up the French chargé d'affaires and tried to get him to speak to Panin. Corberon was too cautious to act without instructions, but he took the opportunity to paint in glowing colours the moderate conduct of France towards the neutrals. Panin replied that complaints against British conduct were reaching him from all quarters, "et qu'il falloit bien que cette puissance changeât de ton et mit de l'eau dans son vin." But he did not pursue the matter of collective ac-

59. SP 75/134, Suffolk to Delaval, No. 20, 6 October 1778; cf. also Marriott's judgement in the case of *Les Quatre Frères*, Minot, *Decisions of the High Court of Admiralty*, p. 171.

60. SP 91/102, Harris to Suffolk, No. 84, 12/23 October 1778.

61. SP 75/134, Delaval to Suffolk, No. 42, 21 November 1778.

tion by the Northern powers, and he left Corberon under the impression that Russia would never agree to join Sweden, Holland, and Denmark since the British hold on Russian trade was so strong.[62] Action jointly with Sweden had not formed part of Catherine's original plan, but Bernstorff had already approached the Swedes in August, and early in October Denmark made a formal proposal to Sweden to conclude a convention on the model of that concluded in 1759.[63] Swedish reaction was at first cautious; Sweden still hoped that London would respond to friendly representations.[64] However, Britain's circular of 19 October to the neutrals proved so unsatisfactory that Sweden and Denmark both protested,[65] and Vergennes, in turn, on 5 November 1778 again warned Sweden and Denmark that if Britain did not change her system France would have to take reprisals.[66] On 22 November 1778 for the first time Vergennes himself took up the idea that Russia should lead the maritime neutrals. In a dispatch to Corberon he suggested that Russia should make common cause with Sweden, Denmark, Holland, and Prussia to force Britain to change her system: "Peut-être M. le comte de Panin, qui sent toute l'injustice de l'Angleterre, pourroit-il engager sa souveraine à faire une démarche publique dans ce but," wrote the French minister.[67] On 19 December 1778, the Swedish envoy in St. Petersburg made a formal proposal to Russia to join with Sweden in arming a fleet to defend the trade of the North, and declared his conviction that Denmark would also join.[68]

Meanwhile the reports of the Russian envoy in England tended

62. CP Russie, *101*, Corberon to Vergennes, No. 42, 27 October 1778. On 17 September Vergennes for the first time suggested to his diplomatic representatives in Stockholm and Copenhagen, but not in Russia, that they should take some measures for trade protection. See Fauchille, *La diplomatie française*, p. 210.

63. D'Albedyhll, *Recueil*, p. 15. D'Albedyhll was secretary at the Swedish legation in St. Petersburg.

64. See D'Albedyhll, *Recueil*, p. 16; Fauchille, *La diplomatie française*, pp. 222–23.

65. Fauchille, *La diplomatie française*, p. 225.

66. "La lenteur et la mollesse des representations à Londres ont enhardi le gouvernment britannique à faire une réponse presque entièrement négative qui renverse toutes les lois de la mer." (Vergennes to d'Usson (Sweden) and Caillard (Denmark) quoted by Fauchille, p. 225–26.)

67. CP Russie, *101*, Vergennes to Corberon, No. 27, 22 November 1778.

68. SP 91/102, Harris to Suffolk, No. 102, 11/22 December 1778 (*MD, 1*, 219); Fauchille, *La diplomatie française*, p. 228.

if anything to exacerbate matters. In describing the activities of British privateers, such words as "cupidity," "avidity," "arrogance," "uncontrolled violence" flowed from his pen.[69] Indeed, when Suffolk sent Harris copies of the circular to the neutrals of 19 October 1778, for the information of the Russian court, he warned him that Musin Pushkin had "talked in a very unkind and improper manner" to the envoys of other neutral courts, and he feared that his reports to the Empress would show the same bias.[70] Shortly afterwards, Musin Pushkin had occasion to complain of the detention by Britain of the first Russian ship to come in the way of the British patrols. The *Jonge Prins* of Riga, Russian owned, with a cargo of hemp and flax of doubtful ownership, shipped to various French importers in Nantes, had been brought into Dover on 10 October. The Russian consul, A. Baxter, acting through the envoy, demanded its release.[71]

When the Swedish proposal was made in December, Russia had not yet replied to Bernstorff's plan of September. But the reaction of Denmark to Russia's first overture, the Swedish proposals, the mounting pressure of the neutrals, French diplomatic activity, and the British circular of 19 October 1778 forced the Russian government to take stock of the situation and reach some kind of decision. A general examination of the problems of neutral trade as they affected Russia was made at the same time as the Russian government considered the British offer of alliance. Two days after Harris was given the Russian reply to his proposals, on 22 December 1778/2 January 1779, the Empress approved a memorandum by Count Panin setting out his views on the policy to be followed by Russia in the matter of neutral trade. As Panin saw it, the problems facing Denmark and Russia were quite different. The Danes wished to protect not only their coasts but their ships

69. Bil'basov, "Rossiya i Angliya v XVIII veke," at p. 17, Musin Pushkin to Panin, 1778, n.d.

70. SP 91/102, Suffolk to Harris, No. 35, 27 October 1778.

71. SP 91/102, Musin Pushkin to Suffolk, 27 November 1778, enclosing a memorial by the consul. The British attitude to the Anglo-Russian treaty emerges from a written note by Fraser to Suffolk: "*Probably* as the cargo consists of hemp and flax bound to a French port it may be deemed naval stores and be ordered to be sold, but if the property appears to be as claimed [namely Russian] the produce will be paid to the claimant," (ibid., note endorsed shown to Baxter by Oakes (the former chargé d'affaires) at dinner yesterday, undated).

trading anywhere on the high seas; hence Bernstorff's plan aimed at extorting from Britain an acknowledgement of the principle "free ships, free goods." In contrast Russia had few ships and needed only to protect her coasts, so as to ensure a free access to ships coming to take up their cargo. A convention on the lines suggested by Bernstorff seemed to him useless and possibly even harmful. There were even stronger objections to common action with Sweden. The Swedes were "utterly devoted to France," and Panin feared that should the Russian and Swedish fleets appear together on the seas the Swedes might deliberately seek a quarrel with a British warship or privateer and drag the Russians in with them. A further consideration which weighed heavily with Panin was the position of Britain. The decline of Britain could not be seen with indifference by Russia, not only because of trade relations but for reasons of high policy. It was necessary to keep within bounds the preponderance of the Bourbon Houses since Russian influence was the result of the natural rivalry between the other first-class powers. Panin recommended therefore that the Empress should adhere to her original resolution and confine herself to sending out a squadron which would politely request privateers of all nations to withdraw from seas leading only to Russian ports. The Danes could be invited to act in a similar way. As for Sweden's proposal, Panin thought it would be unwise to decline it too abruptly. Russia could however communicate to Sweden the Empress's plan of a joint declaration with Denmark to the courts of St. James and Versailles to explain the reason for their armaments and invite Sweden to issue a similar declaration and send out a squadron of her own, which should treat all ships with equal impartiality.[72]

Several points emerge from this statement of policy. In the first place, Russia did not consider her own interests sufficiently bound up with those of the maritime neutrals to induce her to take part in a general defence of neutral trade or of the principles on which neutrals desired to see their trade secured. Secondly, a major obstacle to the re-creation of the Baltic unity of 1759 lay in Russian doubts about Sweden's good faith. Finally, Panin, in spite of his

72. *Morskoy Sbornik, 43, 53,* No. 3, Mneniye grafa Panina o merakh dlya prikrytiya torgovli v severnom more na 1779.

opposition to an alliance with Britain, had no wish to see her power too far reduced. Though the question was not mentioned in Panin's report, it is also probable that the Empress and Panin were unwilling to embark on ambitious measures of trade protection on the lines proposed by Bernstorff when the Turkish and Bavarian conflicts were only just beginning to show signs of a peaceful outcome. The issue of maritime trade, however important, was still a marginal one for Russia.[73] But, though Russia was not yet prepared to place herself at the head of the neutrals, the general outcry against Britain, coupled probably with pressure from Denmark, did lead her to urge Britain strongly to adopt more moderate principles. Hence when Russia refused the British proposals for an alliance, she linked this refusal with an *insinuation amicale* on the treatment of neutral trade.

Harris does not appear to have paid much attention to the growing Russian interest in problems of neutral trade. He may have been misled by the fact that the Russian project originated with the appearance of an American privateer and could therefore be regarded as a gesture friendly to Britain. Panin's hint in October that Denmark was dissatisfied with British treatment of her ships appears however to have been the precursor of a number of talks between Harris and the foreign minister on the subject, but Harris did not think these of sufficient importance to mention them in his dispatches at the time.[74] Sometime in November 1778 he had communicated to Panin Lord Suffolk's circular of 19 October on the treatment of neutral ships, which had not been addressed directly to the Russian court. It was apparently well received, and as Harris wrote later, as "it was evident to me, no

73. It is likely that Panin persuaded the Empress against the policy of trade protection, judging from a cryptic reference in a letter from Bezborodko to Rumyantsev, of 26 February/8 March 1780, Maykov, *Pis'ma A. A. Bezborodka*, p. 58, in which he suggests that the "immobility of the ministry wasted a whole year."

74. But Corberon believed that Harris had persuaded Russia to suggest measures of trade protection to Denmark (CP Russie, *101*, No. 42, to Vergennes, 27 October 1778). It seems that neither Harris nor Corberon could credit Russia with any initiative in the matter. Cf. SP 91/102, Harris to Suffolk, No. 101, 7/18 December 1778. "I am sorry to say that, in discoursing with me on our detention of neutral ships, we have never agreed in our opinions: he [Panin] is totally ignorant of all commercial matters and receives ideas on these subjects from persons who are very far from being our well-wishers."

disadvantage could accrue to the trade of this country, I did not
expect to hear any more about it." [75] In spite of his efficient information service, Harris never heard of the principles which
Bernstorff hoped to persuade Russia to enforce—or if he did, he
never mentioned them in his reports to Suffolk. But in one of the
many conversations Harris and Panin conducted during the negotiations for the British alliance, Panin raised the subject of British
treatment of neutral trade very forcibly. He pointed out that Denmark, Sweden, and Holland [76] had all solicited the Empress to join
with them in making representations to Britain on this subject;
that though the Empress had no desire to injure Britain, she
could not regard the activity of British privateers in the north with
indifference; and that she hoped that Britain might give more
precision to her "vague and uncertain definition" of naval and
warlike stores. The Empress was not satisfied, he declared, with
the British circular of 19 October 1778 and had asked him to draft
a memorial which, to spare Harris's feelings, was to be delivered
to Suffolk through the Russian envoy in London. Harris expressed
himself hurt and surprised to hear such language from Russia and
argued that his feelings would suffer much more if the memorial
were delivered in London and not through him. On 29 December
Panin told Harris that the Empress had acceded to his request to
withdraw the representation in London; at the same time he informed Harris officially of the Swedish proposal for a convention

75. Not until his No. 104 of 20/31 December 1778 did Harris refer specifically
to the Russian reaction to the British declaration of 19 October 1778. (*MD, 1,* 220).

76. In the published Russian documents there is no reference to a Dutch request
for Russian help in defence of trade. But Swart, the Dutch resident, had spoken
to Corberon on the subject, and it is more than likely that he also spoke if not
to Panin himself then to other members of the college of foreign affairs. Swart
was only a resident, and did not mix in the *grand monde* on the same footing
as envoys and chargés d'affaires. Bergbohm, *Die bewaffnete Neutralität,* p. 117,
quoting Weydemeyer, *Dvor i zamechatel'nyye lyudi v Rossii,* p. 198, says that the
Hanse towns also appealed to the Empress for protection of their trade. Weydemeyer gives no reference for this statement, and I have found no evidence of such
an appeal in the printed documents I have consulted. But it is not unlikely, since
a Russian consul, St. Paul, was appointed as consul-general by the Empress in
November/December 1778 to Lübeck, Hamburg, and Bremen, thus creating a
more direct link between these towns and Russia. (See Aleksandrenko, *Russkiye
diplomaticheskiye agenty, 1,* 194, circular rescript to Musin Pushkin, 22 November/3
December 1778.)

and of the Russian determination "never to submit to see a Swedish fleet join that of France." [77]

Harris had therefore secured a minor victory in persuading the Empress to withdraw her ministerial representation in London, and he was reassured by Panin's attitude to the Swedish proposals. The next day, however, Harris was handed not only the formal Russian rejection of Britain's offer of alliance but also the strongly worded *insinuation* on the subject of neutral trade, which replaced the representation in London. The Empress took her stand not upon law but upon expediency. She refused to enter into "le droit de part et d'autre" but pointed out that the neutrals appeared to regard the British circular of 19 October 1778 as the enunciation of "un droit nouveau" with reference to the preemptive purchasing of naval stores on board captured neutrals. Though far from desiring to enter any "concert équivoque à l'égard de la Grande Bretagne," Catherine could not be indifferent to the neutral viewpoint. British policy might indeed lead to a scarcity of naval stores in France, but this would not decide the issue of the war. Was it worth-while to antagonize the neutrals by clinging to a definition of contraband which they did not accept? Was it worth driving them into organizing convoys for their merchant ships, a system which might lead to unpleasant incidents? And the Empress concluded, in a phrase which is a gem of diplomatic hypocrisy, that if only Britain would attend to the imperial remonstrance and thus change the attitude of the neutrals towards her, Russia would have served British interests better than "si elle faisoit agir dix ou douze vaisseaux pour sa défense." [78]

In view of the casualness of Harris's previous references to Russian interest in neutral shipping, the terms of the *insinuation amicale* must have come to him as a very unpleasant surprise. Russian championship of the neutrals, coupled with joint Franco-Russian action in the dispute between Austria and Prussia, seemed to reveal an ominous shift in Russian policy from benevolent neutrality to strict impartiality. Harris's somewhat superficial analysis of Russian motives attributed his failure to secure the alliance

77. SP 91/102, Harris to Suffolk, No. 104, 20/31 December 1778; No. 103, 20/31 December 1778.

78. SP 91/102, Harris to Suffolk, Enclosure C in No. 103, 20/31 December 1778.

to Prussian influence and the Russian policy on neutral trade either to "the inconsistency and relaxation which reign throughout every part of this government" or more simply to Russian ignorance of international law.[79] But Panin, without being in any sense actively anti-British, was simply seeking Russia's best interests by playing on the embarrassments of other powers in order to secure and retain for Russia a commanding position in the balance of power.

During the first few months of 1779 complete confusion reigned among the powers as to what plan was finally going to emerge from the North. Acting on Vergennes's instructions of 22 November 1778, Corberon had pressed on Panin that Russia alone could force Britain, "par des conseils d'amitié," to change her tune. Panin had blamed the British government and had spoken of its system as absurd. He told Corberon that the Empress had ordered strong representations to be made in London.[80] Vergennes in turn continued to urge Corberon to persuade Russia to take the lead in defence of the neutrals, with particular reference to the Swedish plan, of which he was fully informed.[81] In London, Suffolk took fright at rumours which reached him of this same Swedish plan and, on 5 January 1779, he wrote to warn Harris. He was horrified at the thought that instead of a declaration by Russia that she intended to protect her coasts, a plan was afoot for a full-scale convention between the three Baltic powers, "which can have no other object than the supplying of His Majesty's enemies with naval stores . . ." He instructed Harris to find out at once whether the Empress really approved of such a plan.[82] Harris promptly tackled Panin who replied, in accordance with the memorandum on Russian policy of 22 December 1778/2 January 1779, that Russia would not consent to a coalition of the kind feared by Suffolk but that she was determined to defend her trade in the

79. SP 91/102, Harris to Suffolk, No. 102, 11/22 December (*MD, I,* 219).

80. CP Russie, *101,* Corberon to Vergennes, No. 54, 29 December 1778. Fauchille (*La diplomatie française,* p. 250) states that Panin had deceived the Empress and that no representation on neutral shipping was made in London. In fact of course a strong protest was delivered by Russia, but directly to Harris and not through Musin Pushkin.

81. CP Russie, *101,* No. 30, Vergennes to Corberon, 27 December 1778.

82. SP 91/103, Suffolk to Harris, No. 1, 5 January 1779.

North Sea, had invited Denmark to join her, and intended to
extend the invitation to Sweden. Harris regarded this reply as
unsatisfactory, and warned Suffolk that he would withhold judgement until he could obtain a sight of the instructions to be given
to the commander of the Russian cruising squadron.[83]

Denmark and Sweden were equally in the dark as to Russian
intentions. Not until mid-February 1779 did Panin finally deliver
himself of a reply to Bernstorff's letter of 18/29 September and the
Swedish proposals of 19 December 1778.[84] Meanwhile Bernstorff
had put off replying to Sweden in the hope of obtaining a reply
from Russia. He used the interval to increase the pressure on
Britain to extort an acknowledgement of the Danish right to "free
ships, free goods," and a definition of what constituted contraband.[85] The Russian replies to Sweden and Denmark were identical. The Empress turned down the idea of a convention on the
grounds that it might arouse too much suspicion among the belligerents and might give rise to incidents which would force one or
other of the contracting parties to abandon its neutrality. To avoid
these drawbacks and yet protect her trade, the Empress proposed
using her small squadron to protect "toute navigation étrangère
sans exception" in the North Sea. She invited both countries to
arm squadrons for the same purpose and to issue a declaration to
the belligerents explaining the purpose of their armaments. In the
enclosed draft of her declaration, the Empress invited the belligerents to instruct their privateers and warships not to cruise or
pursue vessels into those areas where navigation was no longer
doubtful "mais uniquement destinée pour le commerce des trois
couronnes." [86] No specific limits were laid down for the area to be

83. SP 91/103, Harris to Suffolk, No. 8, 1/12 February 1779; No. 9, 1/12 February
1779 (MD, I, 229).

84. Russia had postponed a reply to these proposals by referring Sweden to the
Russian protest to London, which the Empress hoped would achieve some results.
See D'Albedyhll, Recueil, p. 17.

85. Bernstorff eventually issued his own definition, in explanation of Article 16
of the Anglo-Danish treaty of 1670, in which provisions and naval stores were explicitly stated not to be contraband (SP 75/134, No. 46, 19 December 1778; see also
Hennings, Sammlung, p. 5).

86. Morskoy Sbornik, 43, No. 4, Note pour Mr. d'Ahlefeld, approved by the
Empress on 8/19 January 1779, handed to the Danish envoy only on 2/13 February
1779; No. 10, Note pour Baron Nolcken, delivered to him on 12/23 February.
See also D'Albedyhll, Recueil, p. 46.

patrolled, which thus did not correspond with any of the accepted definitions of territorial waters; the Empress's patrol might therefore well be regarded as infringing the principle of the freedom of the seas.[87]

The Russian reply to his plan for a convention came as a disappointment to Bernstorff. He took exception to the suggestion of protecting "toute navigation étrangère sans exception," for he had intended to extend protection only to the ships of the contracting parties.[88] Bernstorff knew that the trade in naval stores from the north was to a very large extent in British ships, which would thus be protected from attack by French privateers. The Russian plan amounted therefore to a concession to Britain at a time when Bernstorff was hoping to use general neutral discontent to force Britain to acknowledge more favourable maritime principles. On 19 March 1779, Bernstorff gave his considered reply. To his previous arguments he added new ones. In the first place Russia was not hampered by her treaties with the belligerents, but Denmark was bound to observe her existing treaties. Though she could defend her own ships, she was not justified in turning away all privateers. Denmark's trade was also much more vulnerable than that of Russia to reprisals by the belligerents. Moreover, he pointed out, Russia would have to cruise only from the North Cape to Archangel; Denmark had to protect the much more difficult coastline from the North Cape to the Elbe, which would strain her resources to the uttermost and might leave her West Indian islands denuded of protection. Finally, and this may have been Bernstorff's most serious objection, France would regard this measure as directed against her and her allies, and could justifiably accuse Denmark of unneutral behaviour. Britain would have all the benefit.[89] Denmark therefore refused to enter fully into the

87. The extent of territorial waters was not yet clearly defined at this time. For a full discussion of this problem in the 18th century, see Fulton, *Sovereignty of the Sea*, Sec. II, Ch. 1, pp. 537–75. In talks with Corberon, Panin implied that Russian protection would be granted to ships of all nations only within territorial waters (Fauchille, *La diplomatie française*, pp. 258–59). It is not clear what definition of territorial waters Panin had in mind.

88. *Morskoy Sbornik, 43*, No. 7, p. 60, Chekalevsky (acting Russian chargé d'affaires) to Panin, 2/13 March 1779.

89. *Morskoy Sbornik, 43*, No. 9, p. 63, Bernstorff to d'Ahlefeld, 19 March 1779. See also Eggers, *Denkwürdigkeiten*, Pt. 2, p. 81, Note de l'Envoyé de Dannemarc remise au Ministre de Russie . . . en 1779.

Empress's plan without the protection of a formal convention; though Bernstorff agreed to arm a squadron and to patrol Danish coasts in order to defend Danish and Russian shipping against privateers, no Danish proclamation was issued to the belligerent states, and Danish protection was not extended to ships of all nations.[90] Bernstorff's reply reveals the extent to which Denmark and Russia were acting at cross purposes. The Danish minister wished to procure more favourable terms for trade in general and to protect Danish ships from seizure and condemnation of their cargoes. Russia was not interested in principles but wished to ensure safe access for shipping of all nations to her ports where they would pick up their cargoes. The maritime power and the land power stood in a different relation to the belligerents.

Sweden too reacted unfavourably to the half-hearted Russian plan. Attacks on the Swedish flag occurred mainly outside the Baltic and therefore well away from the Swedish coasts.[91] Dissatisfied with the Russian plan for a limited coastal patrol, the King of Sweden replied on 18 March 1779 that though he would join with Russia in making a declaration to the belligerents he intended in accordance with his previous proposals to supply convoys for Swedish merchant ships.[92] The decision to use convoys went far beyond anything the Empress was contemplating. Convoys could cause endless disputes between neutrals and belligerents, for an incident involving warships had far more serious repercussions than one involving merely merchant vessels. In discussing the news with Harris, Panin expressed himself strongly opposed to a measure he regarded as premature, violent, and likely to lead to un-

90. It is evident from the tenor of the Note de l'Envoyé de Dannemarc quoted in note 89 that Denmark refused to enter into the Russian plan, and that therefore no declaration was issued. Bergbohm, *Die bewaffnete Neutralität*, p. 98, note, assumes that it must have been issued, but for some reason has not been printed, and is surprised that the replies of France and Britain have not been printed either. But I have found no trace of a Danish declaration in State Papers Denmark. According to Morton Eden, Bernstorff received the Russian declaration with indifference, "coldly observing that it was advantageous to England" (SP 75/135, Eden to Weymouth, No. 12, 29 May 1779). See also Fauchille, *La diplomatie française*, p. 241, using the reports of the French chargé d'affaires in Copenhagen.

91. D'Albedyhll, *Recueil*, p. 17.

92. D'Albedyhll, *Recueil*, p. 52; *Morskoy Sbornik*, *43*, No. 11, p. 67, 18 March 1779 (possibly 18/29 March).

pleasant consequences. He asked Harris not to consider "this hasty step of Sweden, either as authorised by, or undertaken with the knowledge of Russia; . . . his court and that of Copenhagen acted on a very different principle, and in the small armament they were fitting out had no other view than that of preventing the northern coasts of their dominions from being molested by privateers." [93] The official Russian reply to Sweden's communication was somewhat milder in tone. On 9/20 April 1779, the Empress accepted Sweden's decision to institute convoys for Swedish ships but declared that Russia could not enter into such measures as their respective problems were quite different. Russia had already made representations at the court of St. James on the treatment of neutral ships, and the Empress hoped that London would adopt more satisfactory principles. If however the dispute continued, then Russia would agree to consult with Sweden and make further joint representations.[94]

There is no doubt that Panin was at this time perfectly sincere in his opposition to the Swedish plan for convoys and to the Danish plan for extensive trade protection. But the subtle distinction between the protection of ships and the protection of coasts was not appreciated by Harris. When on 1 March 1779 Panin read to Harris the draft of the Empress's declaration to be made to the belligerent courts, Harris did not grasp its implications. He was alarmed to hear that in spite of the Swedish intention of arming convoys Russia was still prepared to act with Sweden on her more limited plan. Harris remained completely unconvinced by the Russian disclaimers of any hostile intention and expressed his hope to Panin that the northern powers might not have allowed themselves to be imposed upon by the "specious and insidious language of the court of France." Panin, according to Harris, "spared no professions" to convince him of the contrary, "but as they were void of argument, and wanted proofs, I could not listen to them with that attention he required." The English diplomat ended the interview on a somewhat threatening note by suggesting that if Danish and Swedish ships were to be cruising in the Baltic, Britain could not remain unarmed in the area, and the Baltic being thus

93. SP 91/103, Harris to Suffolk, No. 13, 19 February/2 March 1779.
94. *Morskoy Sbornik, 43*, No. 13, p. 74. Note for Baron Nolcken, 9/20 April 1779.

filled with warships great confusion might ensue.[95] Harris was in fact blinded as to Russia's true intentions by his suspicion of Panin, whose position as guardian of Russian interests he could not understand when once these appeared to him to be divorced from British interests. He was also hampered by his own ignorance in matters of trade and maritime law, which prevented him from grasping that the declaration read to him by Panin contained nothing to injure vital British interests, however much any attempt to organize trade protection might be traditionally distasteful to Britain.

Harris's reports, and rumours from other capitals interested in sowing dissension between Britain and Russia, were quite sufficient to arouse anxiety in London. On 30 March 1779 Lord Weymouth,[96] acting as secretary of state for the North after gout had forced Suffolk to withdraw from the scene, wrote to Harris urging him to lose no opportunity to convince Panin of the lenity of the admiralty courts and of the attention shown by Britain to neutral shipping. "And," added Weymouth optimistically, "at a proper and seasonable moment, when you shall find Mr. Panin convinced of these truths," Harris was to persuade the Empress that the best proof of friendship she could give to England was to decline entering into any measures aimed at protecting the transport of naval stores to France.[97]

The seasonable moment when Harris should find Panin "convinced of these truths" never came; he continued to warn his principals of the possibility of Russian duplicity and directed his attention to securing a view of the instructions to be given to the commander of the Russian cruising squadron—a task not in itself very difficult in a country where the senior admiral was a Scotsman.[98] On 5/16 March 1779 he was able to report that they con-

95. SP 91/103, Harris to Suffolk, No. 13, 19 February/2 March 1779.

96. Lord Weymouth had been secretary of state for the Southern Department in 1768–70, and again from 1775. According to the *DNB*, he was reputed to be ambitious, unreliable, and lazy.

97. SP 91/103, Weymouth to Harris, No. 9, 30 March 1779.

98. Admiral Samuel Greig had been in Russian service since 1764 and had distinguished himself at the battle of Tschesme. He was on far more friendly terms with Harris than official dispatches reveal. Among the Harris Papers there are several letters from Greig to Harris; they are not particularly interesting but they

formed to what Panin had told him, but as the commander concerned continued for a while to dawdle in the capital Harris began
to think that the idea of a convention between the three Baltic
powers, in which he still believed in spite of Panin's denials, had at
last been dropped.[99] In the meantime Weymouth expressed a qualified satisfaction on hearing of the instructions to the commander
of the squadron. As long as the Russian ships continued within the
bounds prescribed, he thought there would be little danger of any
difficulties arising. "At the same time," he wrote on 13 April 1779,
"I cannot help expressing my wishes, that Her Imperial Majesty
had not adopted this measure, as there is no answering for what
may happen where the indiscretion of an officer may bring on
disagreeable discussions." [100]

Finally, on 22 April 1779, the Empress's declaration of her intention to institute a patrol of her coasts in the North Sea to keep
away privateers was delivered to Lord Weymouth by the Russian
envoy, Musin Pushkin. The British Secretary of State made a
formal and polite reply, expressing the desire of His Majesty to
prevent as far as possible the least interruption to the lawful commerce of the three Northern powers and stressing that all precautions were taken to avoid seizures in the territorial waters of
friendly states.[101] Indeed, after all the recent alarms, Britain had
much to be grateful for. After having been urged in the Empress's

---

show that it was through Greig that Harris maintained his contacts with Aleksey
Orlov. Greig's disposition was known in Britain. See for instance SP 91/102, Suffolk
to Harris, No. 5, 3 February 1778: "Admiral Greig is very loyally and zealously
disposed towards this country and deserves your particular regard and civilities."
Greig also corresponded with the First Lord of the Admiralty, Lord Sandwich.
(See *Sandwich Papers*, passim.)

99. SP 91/103, Harris to Suffolk, No. 17, 5/16 March 1779. The instructions were,
according to Harris: "to cruize from the North Cape to Swiatoi, and Archangel; to
stop all armed vessels of any nation whatsoever which appear, to signify to them,
that they must not remain in that district, and if they refuse, to force them to obey.
The Danes on the other side are to protect the trade from the North Cape to
Stade." There were not, thought Harris, any secret instructions. Rear Admiral
Khmetevsky, the commander of the squadron, asked for some additional instructions,
but these have not been published (*Arkhiv gosudarstvennogo soveta*, 2, 171).

100. SP 91/103, Weymouth to Harris, No. 10, 13 April 1779.

101. SP 91/103, Weymouth to Harris, No. 13, 30 April 1779, enclosing the text
of Musin Pushkin's declaration of 22 April 1779; No. 19, 16 July 1779, enclosing the
text of the reply to Musin Pushkin.

insinuation amicale of December 1778/January 1779 to pay more attention to neutral rights, British merchant ships were now going to enjoy the privilege of being protected from attack by French or American privateers for a distance of some leagues from the Russian coasts.

Vergennes meanwhile continued to place great hopes in the possible association of the Northern powers. He urged Corberon to encourage Russia to persevere in uniting Sweden and Denmark "pour mettre les Anglois à la raison" and refused to believe in the existence of a plan for Russia and Denmark to arm ships to protect British trade to Archangel from attacks by American privateers.[102] His hopes were not altogether unwarranted. Panin had strongly condemned British treatment of the neutrals to Corberon, and this was only one aspect of what seemed to be a growing *rapprochement* between France and Russia. Their common action as mediators between Austria and Prussia was having its effect; negotiations were on foot to draw up a plan of pacification to be submitted to a congress of the powers, and the congress in fact met for the first time at Teschen on 11 March 1779. In a different sphere France was showing her goodwill by smoothing the way for a Russo-Turkish agreement—though the Russians were well aware that France was inspired purely by self-interest.[103]

Thus Corberon was thunderstruck when he heard of the terms of the Russian declaration. "Toutes les protestations que le comte Panin m'a faites, les paroles qu'il m'a données sont annulées par les effets. . . . La cour de Petersbourg vient de donner une déclaration à la Suède et au Dannemark . . . louche et insidieuse qui . . . tend à engager les deux puissances à servir indirectement la cause britannique," he wrote to Vergennes. Corberon saw at once what Harris had failed to see, that if Russia was merely protecting navigation off her own coasts she was protecting the British trade to Archangel. The unilateral closing of parts of the North Sea to privateers was moreover contrary to the principle of the freedom of the seas, and Corberon commented angrily: "Il paroit que la Russie emprunte le langage révoltant de la cour de Londres et qu'elle vou-

102. CP Russie, *102*, Vergennes to Corberon, No. 1, 4 February 1779.
103. Maykov, *Pis'ma A. A. Bezborodka*, p. 35, Bezborodko to Rumyantsev, 28 December 1778/7 January 1779.

droit tendre à son même système en établissant son empire sur les
mers du Nord." [104]

The Russian declaration was delivered to Vergennes by Prince
Baryatinsky, Russian ambassador to the court of France, on 6 April
1779.[105] Vergennes promptly condemned the declaration as bad
diplomacy, bad economics, and bad maritime law. The Empress's
plan was weighted in favour of Britain, said the French minister.
Had Russia intended to protect her own trade, France would have
approved, but now Russia was protecting British trade. Moreover
the extent of the coastal patrol was an infringement of the principle of the freedom of the seas. Vergennes warned Baryatinsky
that if a French ship should pursue an enemy ship in the open
sea, Baltic or North, the Russian squadron had no right to come
to the defence of the enemy ship, and that the French ship had a
right to take its prize into a Russian port. Turning to the economic argument, Vergennes protested that it was in Russia's interest for as many ships as possible to be seized, since Britain was
in perpetual need of naval stores and would have to return for
more.[106]

But though Vergennes expressed himself so forcibly in this interview with the Russian ambassador, it would have been undip-
lomatic to treat Russia officially to such strong language. The
French reply, dated 16 April 1779, was much more moderate in
tone though quite firm in refusing even to understand the implications in maritime law of the Russian declaration. The King of
France, ran the answer, while stressing his conviction that the
Empress had no intention "de donner aucune atteinte au droit
incontestable que toutes les nations ont de naviguer librement

104. CP Russie, *102*, Corberon to Vergennes, No. 10, 9 March 1779.

105. CP Russie, *102*, Vergennes to Corberon, No. 6, 10 April 1779. The instruction
from Panin to Baryatinsky is dated 28 February/11 March 1779, and a copy (perhaps an intercept) is in the French archives at p. 129.

106. Solov'yev, *Istoriya Rossii, 6*, tom. 29, appendix, col. 11683; see also F. de
Martens, *Recueil, 13–14*, France, p. 152, quoting from Baryatinsky's dispatch of
28 March/8 April 1779. It is curious that Martens, in his comments, does not
realize why Vergennes was dissatisfied with the Empress's decision to patrol her
coasts. He contrasts Vergennes's reception of Baryatinsky's communication of 6
April with his welcome for the declaration of the Armed Neutrality (see Ch. 7).
For a lawyer, his inability to distinguish between the two types of commerce protection is to say the least peculiar.

dans toutes les mers qui ne sont pas fermées," would as a further proof of friendship for Russia give orders to his ships "qui pourront être dans le cas de se porter dans la mer du nord, de s'abstenir de commettre aucune hostilité à la vue des côtes, des ports et des rades de l'Empire de Russie, et cela sous peine de punitions exemplaires." [107] Thus France, while not accepting the Empress's right to lay down the law, agreed to abide by the Empress's request to refrain from hostilities within a certain distance of her coasts.

So seriously however did Vergennes view the disadvantages to France of the Russian coastal patrol that he attempted to mobilize Prussia on his side, in the hope that Catherine might listen to the remonstrances of her ally.[108] The violence of French reaction probably came as a disagreeable surprise in St. Petersburg. But events elsewhere came to the assistance of France, and one of Vergennes's carefully laid plans matured at the right time. On 8/19 April 1779 news arrived in St. Petersburg of the signature of the convention of Ainalikawak between Russia and the Porte, which put an end for the time being to the disputes between the two powers on the interpretation of the treaty of Kutschuk-Kainardji. The discreet but active assistance of the French ambassador to the Porte was acknowledged in Russia and produced a certain goodwill towards France. As Corberon described Panin's attitude on the occasion: "son coeur étoit ouvert et nageoit de joie." [109] Therefore, in spite of rumours that several of Catherine's advisers were much displeased at the tone of Vergennes's interview with Baryatinsky (rumours which Harris sedulously spread), Panin declared himself satisfied with the French reply.[110] Russia armed her small squadron and patrolled the area between the North Cape

107. Fauchille, La diplomatie française, p. 269.

108. See e.g. Vergennes to Pons, French envoy to Frederick II, 8 April 1779; see also Pons to Vergennes, 17 April 1779, quoting Frederick II as saying: "Je me ferai un plaisir à faire retracter les intentions de l'impératrice" (Fauchille, La diplomatie française, p. 267).

109. Fauchille, p. 271. For the text of the Convention of Ainalikawak, signed on 10 March 1779, see G. F. de Martens, Recueil, Supplément, 3, 653.

110. SP 91/103, Harris to Weymouth, No. 28, 3/24 May 1779; No. 33, 31 May/11 June 1779.

and Archangel; the French conformed to their intention of avoiding disputes, and no untoward incidents occurred.[111]

Logically enough it was Britain rather than France who kept the issue alive. Soon after he received the Russian declaration from Musin Pushkin, Weymouth warned Harris of rumours of activity by French warships and privateers in the North Sea. Should Russia not drive them away, he declared, Britain would have to send a squadron to protect her trade in those waters. Panin however denied any knowledge of French ships in that neighbourhood and repeated again the Empress's decision to patrol only between the North Cape and Archangel. But Britain's haste to make the most of the protection promised by Russia probably served to show him very effectively how well-grounded Vergennes's complaints had been.[112]

The first attempt by Russia to undertake trade protection satisfied no one in the end. Bernstorff's intention had been to use the threat of a Northern coalition to force Britain to modify her treatment of Danish ships; Sweden was dissatisfied because the Russian plan offered no protection to Swedish ships on the high seas.[113] In Britain, Russia's policy had aroused much anxiety. Both Weymouth and Harris at first suspected in it a Franco-Swedish intrigue. The Russian declaration, when it came, proved innocuous; in fact some advantage for Britain might even have been derived from it. Nevertheless, Weymouth would have been much happier had it never been made at all. All forms of trade protection were not only suspect but unnecessary in British eyes, since neutrals were expected to rely on the equity and moderation of the admiralty courts, and any dispute could be resolved in Britain's favour by the overriding argument of self-defence. Moreover

111. See Anderson, *Naval Wars in the Baltic during the Sailing-Ship Epoch, 1522–1850*, p. 236, for an account of the armament of the Russian squadron of 2 battleships and 2 frigates from Reval, which were joined in the North Sea by a similar force from Archangel.

112. SP 91/103, Weymouth to Harris, No. 13, 30 April 1779; No. 14, 14 May 1779; Harris to Weymouth, No. 33, 31 May/11 June 1779; No. 35, 7/18 June 1779.

113. Denmark armed a larger squadron than Russia—10 battleships and 6 frigates. Only 5 battleships and 4 frigates left the Sound. Sweden armed 10 battleships and 6 frigates, and sent all but 4 battleships into the North Sea (Anderson, *Naval Wars*, p. 236).

Weymouth genuinely feared that France or Sweden might deliberately provoke incidents of a nature to irritate the susceptible
Russians, such as challenging capture in areas patrolled by Russia.

Vergennes at the time had welcomed the first rumours of a
concert between the Northern powers. When, however, he discovered how prejudicial to France the Empress's declaration was,
he became convinced that the whole plan had been inspired by
Harris, an opinion which Frederick II shared.[114] How far this was
from the truth can be seen from Harris's own dispatches and the
opinion of Weymouth quoted above.

Two features of this diplomatic interlude were to have consequences for the future. In the first place the inability of Harris
or Weymouth to distinguish the different motives that inspired
the policies of the three Northern courts, and the mental confusion
which the whole episode engendered, explain in great part the
lack of suspicion with which Britain viewed subsequent moves in
the development of Russian policy towards neutral trade.[115] Secondly, the strong French objections underlined the difficulties
which Bernstorff had already pointed out of a partial plan for
trade protection. A piecemeal approach to the problem left all the
interested powers in a weak position and laid them open to reprisals from one or other belligerent without the certainty that
collective action would immediately follow. Only a convention, as
the Danish statesman had foreseen, could give enough cohesion to

114. See e.g. Doniol, *Histoire*, *3*, 783–84; Fauchille, *La diplomatie française*, pp.
236, 256. Both Doniol and Fauchille accept Vergennes's opinion as correct. Fauchille
goes so far as to say that Harris had seduced Panin and "par Potemkin il s'était
emparé de Catherine." Fauchille also assumes that the award of the Order of the
Bath to Harris in March 1779 was a reward from his government for having procured the Russian declaration. But as is evident from *MD*, *1*, 218, the award was
decided on in December 1778, but at the request of the King the order was conferred
on Harris by Catherine herself in March 1779 (SP 91/103, Harris to Suffolk, 15/26
March 1779).

115. It is only fair to Harris to point out that he did warn Weymouth that the
Russians had "such imperfect notions of trade" and were so willing to listen to
the complaints of neutrals that he would never be able to convince them either
of the equity of British proceedings or of the British view that Russian trade
would profit rather than lose by the condemnation of naval stores. He would be
raising false hopes, he argued, if he did not point out that Russia might "take
some unpleasant share in these discussions" particularly after peace should be
achieved in Germany. (SP 91/103, Harris to Weymouth, No. 26, 23 April/4 May
1779).

the movement to impress itself on the powers at war. Though at that time Russia did not wish to commit herself by treaty obligations to the protection of neutral trade nor to the consideration of the principles which should govern it, yet, as Catherine advanced her diplomatic offensive further into Europe there lay to her hand the tempting possibility of assuming the leadership of the discontented neutrals.

the probable ... ...

4. Harris's Personal Diplomacy

By the end of 1778, the double direction that Russian foreign policy would take during the Anglo-French war was already beginning to be discernible. The Empress had shown her interest in problems of neutral trade, though before Europe was pacified it was dangerous for Russia to embark on ambitious plans of trade protection, and she was influenced by Panin's counsels of moderation. European opinion was however misled as to Russian ideas in the matter of trade, when it was seen that the institution of naval patrols by Russia in March 1779 in the result favoured Britain. In this respect, Russia appeared to have shown herself the traditional friend of Britain. The second direction in which Russian foreign policy was to evolve was also foreshadowed at the end of 1778. Engaged as Russia now was with France in mediating between Austria and Prussia, it was a natural step for her to offer to use her situation to bring about a reconciliation between Britain and France.[1]

The first power to offer to mediate between the belligerents had been Spain, in October 1778. Early in December 1778, Panin had dropped his first hint, and at the end of the month, when the Russian minister rejected Britain's offer of alliance, he had invited Harris to communicate to him Britain's probable peace terms. Harris at this stage merely referred Panin to the British reply to Spain, which he had communicated to Russia in November 1778, and which stated that no discussion could take place until France had withdrawn from America, though Britain was willing to discuss outstanding problems with Spain.[2]

1. Maykov, Pis'ma A. A. Bezborodka, p. 37, Bezborodko to Rumyantsev, 18/29 January 1779.
2. SP 91/102, Harris to Suffolk, No. 101, 7/18 December 1778; No. 105, 20/31 December 1778. For the British reply to Spain see Conn, Gibraltar in British Diplomacy, p. 185.

Harris by no means welcomed this new development. He was persuaded that no good could come of a Russian mediation between Britain and France. The failure of his negotiations for the alliance had had a very depressing effect on his mercurial temperament, and he viewed the Russian scene with a jaundiced eye. He could not find a good word either for Russian policy or Russian statesmen, and the Empress did not escape his strictures. She no longer possessed the force of mind or the "systematick perseverance" that distinguished her previously, wrote the disgruntled envoy. Her life was becoming more and more dissipated, her society was "often collected from the lowest degrees of her court," her health was affected by the life she led, "and the reflections, she necessarily must make whenever she allows herself calmly to consider the effects of her present conduct, must necessarily contribute to impair it." [3] Harris was no puritan and this diatribe must be attributed to his galling sense of failure.

Harris's first reports of Panin's tentative and unofficial overtures for a Russian mediation between Britain and France drew no reply whatsoever from London. Harris himself took them lightly. "Count Panin often talks of putting an end to the war between us and France," he wrote to Suffolk on 8/19 February 1779, "but I doubt whether he has ever thought seriously on the subject, or reduced his ideas to any system." [4] Towards the end of February 1779, Panin once more hinted at Russia's desire to mediate and suggested that after peace had been restored an alliance between Britain and Russia might more easily be considered.[5] Harris again gave a non-committal reply, and this time his report home drew some response. Weymouth approved his language and belatedly instructed him to answer such overtures by referring Panin to the King's reply to Spain, as Harris had already done. The point of Panin's last words was not lost on Weymouth. There was now little reason to expect Russia to espouse England's cause, he thought, but he too did not regard the suggestion of mediation as seriously intended.[6]

3. SP 91/102, Harris to Suffolk, No. 106, 20/31 December 1778; SP 91/103, No. 2, 11/22 January 1779.
4. SP 91/103, Harris to Suffolk, No. 10.
5. SP 91/103, Harris to Suffolk, No. 12, 15/26 February 1779.
6. SP 91/103, Weymouth to Harris, No. 9, 30 March 1779.

Harris was less than ever inclined to trust Russia when he saw the undoubted *rapprochement* between Russia and France brought about by the convention of Ainalikawak and still more by the success of their joint efforts to pacify Germany. The Congress of Teschen had opened on 11 March 1779, and for the time being Russian attention was concentrated almost exclusively on the Holy Roman Empire. Harris saw truly where British interests lay: "I see nothing likely to restore this country to us in the shape we wish but a continuation of war," he wrote to Weymouth in April 1779.[7] And in a later, more confidential, unburdening of himself to the under-secretary, W. Fraser, he wrote: "Our affairs go on finely, yet I dread the effect this general tranquillity in which we are not included, may produce." Peace in Germany, Harris believed, would put an end to any immediate prospects of obtaining Russian assistance, but should there be war the Russians "will be of course our allies." [8]

By the beginning of May, Panin knew that sufficient progress had been made in the Congress of Teschen to warrant pressing forward with his plan to mediate between Britain and France. On 2 May 1779, he expressed to the French chargé d'affaires Russia's willingness to "rendre la pareille" to France for her services in promoting the convention of Ainalikawak,[9] and he inquired eagerly what answer Harris had received from London to the Russian request for the British peace terms. Harris again referred Panin to the British reply to Spain and came away from his interview convinced that Russia would now extend no favours to Britain which were not also extended to France.[10]

The Peace of Teschen was signed on 13 May 1779. The continent was pacified at last, and the prospect for Britain of winning one of the continental powers to take part in the war against France receded, as Harris had foreseen, into the distance. The powers settled down to watch the duel between Britain and France, which by wearing them both down could not but tend to the

7. SP 91/103, Harris to Weymouth, No. 25, 16/27 April 1779.

8. SP 91/103, private, Harris to W. Fraser, 23 May/3 June 1779; Harris to Weymouth, No. 23, 5/16 April 1779 (*MD, 1*, 229).

9. CP Russie, *102*, Corberon to Vergennes, No. 18, 3 May 1779.

10. SP 91/103, Harris to Weymouth, No. 30, 23 May/3 June 1779, describing an interview earlier in the month.

advantage of the others. At the same time Russia recovered her full liberty of action and found herself, with increased prestige as the guarantor of the German constitution, enabled to devote her undivided attention to the maritime war. Towards the end of May, Panin again urged on Harris that Britain should confide her peace terms to Russia, and he implied that Catherine could be trusted to watch over British interests since she disapproved of French recognition of the Americans as a blow to monarchical solidarity. These fair words were however qualified by Panin's assertion that the Empress had equal obligations to Britain and to France, to the former for her conduct during the previous war with the Porte, to the latter for her assistance in procuring the convention of Ainalikawak. She therefore stood "in a degree of the most perfect impartiality between the one and the other" and would endeavour to satisfy the "dignity, the honour and the interests of each." A similar overture, added Panin, was to be made by Russia in Versailles. Harris, who still harboured hopes of more active Russian support for Britain, declared that only an "active interposition" on Britain's behalf could procure the sort of peace she could accept. By this he meant an ultimatum threatening France, similar to the menacing declaration Russia had made to Austria in September/October 1778 over the Bavarian dispute. Panin utterly refused to consider such a step, which might "replunge Europe into that state of general disorder, from which it had so lately, and so miraculously escaped," and which would ill requite France for her recent services. No formal offer of mediation was as yet made by Russia, but an agreed version of this conversation was drawn up, which should have left no doubt in London that Panin was speaking in the name of the Empress and not simply in his own.[11]

In Vienna also, soon after the signature of the Peace of Teschen, a hint had been dropped that Austria would welcome the opportunity to reconcile the belligerents.[12] But current developments in Western Europe were combining to render nugatory both the Russian and the Austrian plans. Ever since Spain had first pro-

---

11. Ibid., and enclosure, Paper A, in French.

12. SP 80/221, Keith to Weymouth, separate unnumbered, 19 May 1779. Kaunitz proposed Austria's good offices, acting with any other power Britain might choose to name.

posed her mediation in October 1778, desultory negotiations had
been pursued between London and Madrid. Spanish policy aimed
at drawing them out at least until the spring of 1779, in order to
put pressure on France to guarantee the Spanish desiderata, Gibraltar and Minorca, as the price of Spanish participation in the
war; also, spring was the proper season to launch a naval campaign
and in particular to organize the junction of the French and Spanish fleets on which high hopes could justifiably be placed. Therefore while concerted plans for naval operations were being discussed between France and Spain, the latter still insisted on her
freedom of action and proposed a long truce to the belligerents.
Spanish procrastination at last drove France to agree to the Spanish
terms, and on 12 April 1779 the treaty of Aranjuez was signed
setting out the terms of Spain's entry into the war.[13] The Spanish
proposal for a truce was rejected by Britain on 4 May 1779, thus
giving the signal for the coming into operation of the treaty of
Aranjuez, but the breach between the two countries was deliberately delayed by Spain in order to give time for the junction of the
French and Spanish fleets. Finally, on 16 June the Spanish ambassador in Britain, Count Almodóvar, asked for his passports.[14]

Harris was not officially informed of the course of negotiations
with Spain, but on 18 June Weymouth told him that they had
been carried on ever since the autumn and had now culminated
in a breach between the two countries.[15] But the breach with
Spain led at first to no change in British policy towards Russia.
Harris was still to stress the mutual advantages of an alliance to
both Britain and Russia, rather than the benefit Britain would
derive from an ally.[16] Either from inattention, or because he
genuinely believed it unimportant, Weymouth did not trouble to
give any reply to Harris's report at the end of May of Panin's
renewed offer of the Empress's good offices. The news reached him
on 23 June, but not one line, whether of approval of Harris's

13. For these negotiations see Doniol, *Histoire, 3,* Chs. 9, 10, 11, 13 passim.
Danvila, *Historia, 1,* 343 ff.; *5,* 11 ff.

14. Doniol, *Histoire, 3,* Ch. 13, pp. 790–94. See also p. 777. For Almodóvar's communication to Weymouth of 16 June 1779, see *Annual Register,* 1779, p. 359; for
Weymouth's answer of 13 July 1779, see p. 386.

15. SP 91/103, Weymouth to Harris, unnumbered, 18 June 1779.

16. SP 91/103, Weymouth to Harris, No. 18, 2 July 1779.

conduct or of instruction for the future, ever reached Harris on the subject. The offer of Austrian good offices, equally ill-timed, was treated with far greater courtesy. When Weymouth wrote to Keith at the end of July, he declared that Britain would readily accept the offices of the Empress Queen if, in the new conditions of the Spanish war, they could still be employed with any hope of success.[17]

Vergennes in his turn had no intention of being diverted from his war against Britain by the Russian and Austrian desire to appear with credit on the European stage as peacemakers. France clearly could not give up the war just when she expected an accession of strength.[18] The offer of the Empress Queen was refused on the excuse that France could not accept it after the failure of the good offices of the King of Spain. The emergence of Spain as a belligerent also gave Vergennes the pretext he needed for postponing consideration of the Russian offer of mediation without hurting the Empress's susceptibilities. French acceptance was made conditional on offers from Britain being made through Russia and on the agreement of the Spanish court being obtained, an event which Vergennes knew to be unlikely.[19] For the time being the chances of mediation were slender, but the idea remained dormant, not dead.

The tenor of Harris's conferences with Panin in the early part of 1779, their fruitless conversations on the vexed topic of neutral rights, and Panin's refusal to endorse any measures openly hostile to France all contributed to confirm Harris in his opinion that the Russian minister was irrevocably opposed to Britain. He continued therefore to cultivate the friendship of Potemkin, whom he now credited with "a very superior understanding, a clear head and quick conception," in the hope that through him he might be able to influence the Empress.[20] Potemkin's influence might moreover become a more important factor, for the Prince was beginning to take a wider interest in Russia's foreign relations. As Harris discovered, both the Empress and the favourite were now turning

17. SP 90/221, Weymouth to Keith, No. 9, 16 July 1779.
18. Doniol, *Histoire*, *3*, Ch. 13, p. 777, Vergennes to Montmorin, 29 May 1779.
19. Doniol, *Histoire*, *3*, Ch. 13, p. 795, Montmorin to Vergennes, 20 June 1779.
20. SP 91/103, Harris to Weymouth, No. 31, 23 May/3 June 1779, *MD*, *1*, 232.

their minds to the realization of the so-called "Greek project,"
namely the overthrow of the Ottoman Empire and the setting up
of an orthodox Christian empire with its capital in Constantinople
and Catherine's grandson Constantine on the throne. Beneath
these somewhat chimerical plans lay the more concrete ambition
of extending Russian territory on the Black Sea.[21] Such a policy
could not be carried out without careful diplomatic preparation,
and the Prince was gradually being drawn into closer relations
with all the principal foreign envoys. It was to him rather than to
Panin that the Empress turned, for Panin frowned on the plan as
a whole and may well have foreseen that it would have a disrupt-
ing effect on the Northern system he had built up. The growing
interest of the Prince in foreign affairs intensified the existing
rivalry between the two men. Panin owed his position at court to
years of solid work on behalf of Russia and Catherine. Potemkin
owed his power to the passion he had once aroused in Catherine.
Though his talents had enabled him to preserve his ascendancy
when once the idyll was over, in the eyes of many his power was
tainted at the source and his position an anomaly. The arrogant
Potemkin took few pains to conciliate his many enemies and relied
—as it turned out, rightly—on the continued friendship, confidence, and affection of Catherine. By temperament too he seems
to have shared her sympathy for Great Britain. As Harris wrote:
"I do not find that Prince Potemkin is Prussian; neither, from his
conversation, is he French." He determined therefore to use him

21. Harris first mentioned the Empress's Eastern project in SP 91/103, No. 31,
of 23 May/3 June 1779, *MD, 1,* 232 (wrongly dated). In a private letter of the
same date Harris stressed the importance of these Eastern projects, which he described as the "reigning idea (and it carries away all others)." Harris saw that this
new interest might have important repercussions on Russian foreign policy and
wrote home "with a view of hinting to your Lordship that, if His Majesty should
stand in indispensable need of assistance from this quarter, the only means of obtaining it is, by encouraging this romantic idea. She is so warmly bent on it, that
such a conduct, dexterously managed, would give us the firmest hold of this court;
and as its execution, whenever seriously planned, would instantly appear impracticable, we need not be apprehensive of having engaged ourselves too far in an
unpleasant transaction." (*MD, 1,* 237) Weymouth's reaction was to inquire if the
Eastern project was likely to interfere with British trade, and he told Harris to
confine himself to general expressions of British inclination to promote Russian
aims, in the certainty that these could not conflict with those of England (SP
91/103, No. 21, 27 July 1779).

as a channel of communication and through him to undermine Panin's credit with the Empress which he suspected was already on the wane.[22]

Corberon had no reason to complain of Panin's attitude to France now that Vergennes had decided to refrain from protesting against Russia's one-sided plan for the protection of merchant shipping off her coasts. But he too thought it advisable to cultivate Potemkin. Through a somewhat disreputable French hanger-on of the Prince, the Chevalier de la Teyssonière, he was introduced to his private circle and soon thought he had good grounds to congratulate himself on his success. The Prince tranquilly sat back and allowed himself to be wooed by both sides, and convinced both Harris and Corberon that he had been won over to their respective and contradictory opinions.[23]

Panin's reaction to the news of the breach between Britain and Spain strengthened Harris's conviction of his deep-rooted enmity. "Vous vous etes attirè vos malheurs vous-memes, ils vous accableront; vous brusquez les puissances neutres; chaque jour vous donne des nouveaux ennemis, il vous faut la paix à tout prix et vous devez faire des cessions considérables pour l'obtenir" said Panin according to Harris's later report, and the Russian minister refused to pass any judgement on Spain's behaviour.[24] Catherine showed very different feelings. She expressed her indignation at Spain and "praised the spirited address of Parliament." [25] This difference in their words led Harris to believe that there was a difference in their policy, and though he lacked any fresh and precise instructions he determined to cultivate the faint gleam of hope

22. SP 91/103, Harris to Weymouth, No. 31, 23 May/3 June 1779 (*MD, 1,* 232). In this dispatch Harris gives a general survey of the Russian court for Weymouth's information. But he reveals here the prejudices of his main informants at court, the Orlov faction. The court was depraved and immoral, wrote Harris, and there was no hope of redeeming Catherine from her public and private vices.

23. See e.g. CP Russie, *102,* Corberon to Vergennes, No. 18, 3 May 1779: "je suis parvenu à être presque de son intimité"; No. 20, 5 May 1779: "Le Prince Potemkin est à nous, j'en ai journellement des preuves . . ."

24. SP 91/104, Harris to Stormont, unnumbered, private, 15/26 February 1780. Harris did not report these words at the time to Weymouth in his No. 37, 21 June/2 July 1779 (SP 91/103), because, he said, he did not wish to create bad feeling between Britain and Russia, and he did not believe Panin's words to correspond to the views of the Empress.

25. SP 91/103, Harris to Weymouth, No. 40, 2/13 July 1779.

to which the Empress's conduct gave rise. The personal favour he
enjoyed at court assisted him in his task. He was often in the
Empress's company, he was invited to her card table, he walked
with her in the park of her summer residence at Tsarskoye Selo.[26]
On 12 July 1779 Harris was present at a theatrical performance at
the palace at Peterhof. Between the acts the Empress approached
him "and seemed to take a much greater share in our concerns,
and to see them in a very different light, from what her Minister
wishes to make me believe she does." Harris took the opportunity
to enlarge on Britain's solitary position and expressed the hope
that she would not be abandoned by the only great power able to
counteract the league of her enemies. The Empress replied: "I
always was, and always shall be, the firm friend of England . . .
The hostile measures, that court [Spain] has adopted, give me great
concern; but your resources and national spirit are great; and be
assured that nothing can be sincerer than my friendship for
England." [27]

Catherine's words were undoubtedly more encouraging than
anything Harris ever reported Count Panin as saying. But it is
probable that Harris read more into them than the Empress actually meant. There was no real divergence of views on policy
between the Empress and Panin at this stage, however different
the words they might choose to use. Very revealing is the text of
the instructions drawn up on 15/26 July 1779 for I. M. Simolin,
who had been appointed to replace the inefficient Musin Pushkin
in London. Simolin was told that though times had changed since
the previous abortive negotiations for an Anglo-Russian treaty in
1769, there could still "be no question of an alliance." Russia's
obligations to France since Ainalikawak and Teschen were frankly
acknowledged, and Simolin was instructed to show "not the slightest prejudice against France," to avoid any signs of participation
in the victories or defeats of the belligerents, but to stress Russia's
interest in seeing the end of the war between Britain, France,
and Spain. At the same time Simolin was to maintain the friendly
tone normal in intercourse between Britain and Russia and

26. See e.g. SP 91/103, Harris to Weymouth, No. 31, 23 May/3 June 1779; No.
47, 7/18 August 1779 (*MD, 1,* 243).

27. SP 91/103, Harris to Weymouth, No. 42, 5/16 July 1779 (*MD, 1,* 240).

founded on their commercial connexion and their mutual interest in keeping peace in the north.[28] This instruction was presumably drafted under Panin's eye, but there is no doubt that it was seen and approved by Catherine, who, if she had wished, could have expressed warmer feelings towards England.

Harris however was determined to take advantage of the divergence he thought he saw between Panin and his imperial mistress. The outbreak of war with Spain meant for him that Russian assistance was more necessary than ever. Lacking any precise instructions from London, he decided nonetheless to embark on a course of his own, original both in its aims and in its tactics, which if it had succeeded might indeed have changed the course of the war. He had already thrown off casually to Panin the idea that the Empress should intervene between Britain and France as an armed mediator, and Panin had refused even to contemplate such a plan. Harris now proposed to persuade the Empress herself to act towards France, on Britain's behalf, the part she had acted towards Austria on Prussia's behalf, in the recent conflict in the Empire. He wished to draw her into making a declaration to the Bourbon powers urging them to desist from the war, but a declaration backed by an imposing armament.[29]

The first step in this plan was to procure a private interview with the Empress. Harris therefore intensified his siege of the favourite through whom alone such a favour could be obtained. At the beginning Harris confined himself to painting in glowing colours the glory of the role Potemkin would play if he could only induce the Empress to "stand forth" and put an end to the war.[30] He followed this up somewhat naively by sending through the common post an *en clair* dispatch to London in which he indulged in the most fulsome flattery of the powerful minister, rightly surmising that it would be read in the Russian chancellery.[31] Little by little

28. Aleksandrenko, *Russkiye diplomaticheskiye agenty*, 2, 195.

29. See *MD, 1,* 242, Harris to Morton Eden in Copenhagen, where he speaks of the difficulty and delicacy of his task, "particularly as I am without a single instruction from home," and declares his determination to go forward "without dreading either a disavowal or disgrace."

30. SP 91/103, Harris to Weymouth, No. 56, 9/20 September 1779 (*MD, 1,* 245).

31. SP 91/103, Harris to Weymouth, No. 43, 9/20 July 1779. "The superiority of his genius; the facility with which he comprehends the most intricate affairs; and

Harris, in private confabulation with the Prince, unfolded to him the full details of his plan for a declaration to Madrid and Versailles backed by a naval armament. Potemkin, though doubtful that such a policy would gain the support of Panin, agreed to persuade the Empress to receive Harris, and it is fair to surmise that Harris's project was fully discussed by the Empress and the favourite before the actual interview took place.[32]

On 2 August 1779 Harris was at last admitted to a private audience with the Empress. Inspired by the Empress's kind reception, he explained that "from the ambition of France, and from the simplicity of Spain, joined to a kind of apathy with which the rest of Europe seemed to regard our concerns, we found ourselves waging a very unequal war." He stressed the danger for Russia implicit in the diminution of British preponderance and appealed to her for some proof of Russian friendship.

Catherine came to the point at once and asked Harris if he had any concrete proposals to make. Harris was here on difficult ground, for his last instructions were to wait until Russia renewed proposals for an alliance. He declared however that if the Empress was now disposed to listen to such proposals he could take it upon himself to renew them. But he thought such proposals did not "come up to the urgency of the moment" and brought forward his own plan of the "spirited declaration" to the courts of Madrid and Versailles, backed by a naval armament.

The Empress expressed the strongest desire to assist Britain, both from political motives and from personal inclination. But she saw at once that Harris's plan threatened to plunge Russia into war. She had, said Catherine (as reported by Harris), "the highest opinion of our national strength and spirit, and did not doubt that we should still overmatch the French and Spaniards." The Empress then touched on the far more delicate subject of the American war, "lamented our not having been able to stop it in the beginning, and hinted at the possibility of restoring peace, by

---

the great and liberal principles on which he forms every part of his conduct, joined to the activity of which is capable in carrying his councils into execution, justly entitle him to that great share of confidence and favour his Sovereign so judiciously places in him. He certainly is, in every sense of the word, the first man in this great Empire." Frederick II could hardly do better at flattery.

32. SP 91/103, Harris to Weymouth, No. 56, 9/26 September 1779 (*MD, I,* 245).

renouncing our struggle with our Colonies." When Harris asked her whether, in Britain's place, she would consent to peace on such terms, she replied, with great vehemence: "J'aimerai mieux perdre la tête." When Harris pressed the Empress further, she asked what reason Russia had to interfere in a quarrel foreign to her own concerns "on a subject I am not supposed to understand, and with courts at such a distance from me?" Harris endeavoured to argue that Russian intervention would lead to a restoration of tranquillity, that Russia was too great to see any great events with indifference, and that "the concerns of Europe were now the concerns of Russia." And he added the double-edged compliment: "If Peter the Great could see the navy he had created, now become considerable enough, not only to unite itself to that of England, but to assist it in maintaining the superiority of the sea, he would confess himself not the greatest sovereign Russia had." Catherine accepted the compliment and assured Harris that she wished England well, but although he had removed some objections to his plan, other very powerful ones remained. She asked him therefore to send in his views in writing and, after a conversation lasting more than an hour, dismissed him.[33]

The day after his interview with Catherine, on 3 August 1779, Harris delivered to Potemkin a memorial for the Empress, in which he recapitulated his arguments of the previous day.[34] The following day he was present at a small private party attended by the Empress. Catherine took the opportunity to tell him that she had been much struck by his arguments. "Depuis notre conversation je n'ai fait que rêver à vos affaires; ma tête fermente; et si je puis trouver les moyens, vous verrez l'empressement avec lequel je vous servirai," she declared. Harris had every reason to feel encouraged, but he believed he must expect opposition to his policy from Panin, and he was confirmed in this belief by Potemkin. The Prince in fact advised him to find out beforehand what arguments

---

33. Ibid. Contrast Harris's account with the garbled story given by Goertz (later Prussian envoy at St. Petersburg), in *Mémoire ou précis historique sur la Neutralité Armée et son origine, suivie de pièces justificatives*. Goertz (p. 22) says that in exchange for the Turkish *casus foederis*, the Empress proposed an alliance and an armed mediation.

34. SP 91/103, Harris to Weymouth, Paper A, enclosed in No. 56, 9/20 September 1779.

Panin was likely to use and prepare himself to counter them.[35]

The Empress had been sufficiently affected by Harris's persistence to call for a full-scale examination of Russian policy towards the Anglo-French war, and accordingly, on 11 August 1779, the members of the Russian college of foreign affairs met to consider the problem. Their deliberations were embodied in a long report presented to the Empress.

From this report it is clear that Panin and his colleagues felt that Britain was sufficiently strong to withstand her enemies without substantial diminution of her power. Though the joint Bourbon fleets would outnumber the British fleet, their maritime ascendancy would be only temporary, and the chances of an invasion of Britain were rated low. Turning to the internal state of Great Britain, Catherine's advisers were more pessimistic. The government was not such as to inspire confidence abroad; its members showed merely their anxiety to keep in power and subordinated the welfare of the state to their private views. By neglecting continental powers, the ministry had lost the influence abroad which Britain had previously shared with France, and Britain was maintaining her system of isolation in the faith that guineas would purchase allies or mercenaries as required. But the great powers could not be counted on a level with the "small German courts, accustomed to put a price on the blood of their subjects and sell them for cash," though, the report added, Britain seemed to have regarded Russia in this light whenever the question of renewing the Anglo-Russian treaty had been considered.

The same indifference to other powers had led Britain to alienate the neutrals in the present war. The United Provinces, Sweden, and Denmark had all taken steps to protect their trade, but Britain changed neither her principles nor her behaviour, and this could only proceed from an "arrogant" conviction that her forces were sufficient to outweigh those of her enemies. Unless Britain suffered repeated defeats, which had not happened so far and was unlikely, there was little prospect of the Bourbon Houses achieving a significant rise at her expense. There was therefore no need for Russia to take any special measures for the future, "all the more as the return of England to the situation she was in before the war of

35. SP 91/103, Harris to Weymouth, No. 56, 9/20 September 1779.

1755 would make her feel the necessity of the friendship and alliance of Russia more than she did after the peace of 1763 confirmed her decisive supremacy at sea, for then she began to show intractability in all her negotiations with us." Moreover the recent improvement of France's attitude towards Russia deserved some return. The way should be prepared for Russia to appear as a mediator by preserving a strict impartiality; in fact "all the benefit would be for England, both for reasons of trade and because of the development of events." As for relations with other powers, above all the Northern system must be preserved. Prussia and Denmark were the naval and military sentinels of Russia; Prussia would not welcome direct or indirect assistance to Britain, and it was in the interests of all the neutrals, particularly the Dutch, that some balance should be maintained between Britain and France. In conclusion the report expressed the view that England stood in no particular danger from the entry of Spain into the war, and was not likely to be brought low. If unforeseen events occurred the position could be reconsidered and steps could be taken to restore the balance between the belligerents.[36]

The report of the college of foreign affairs reveals the extent to which Panin had moved away from any idea of benevolent neutrality towards Britain. There was no desire to have France replace Britain. The commercial ties between Britain and Russia were too strong to warrant an overthrow of the traditional policy of friendship. But it was considered unwise for Russia to become too dependent on a very strong Britain, and the dominant position Britain had secured at the Peace of Paris in 1763 was felt to put all the other powers at a disadvantage. The derogatory references to the North administration merely echo what Catherine herself had frequently written to her correspondents. Indeed, though the Empress might declare that she herself would prefer to lose her head rather than consent to peace on French terms, she saw no reason why George III should not in fact submit to the loss of the American colonies. She had from the beginning foreseen that they would break away completely,[37] and she had no reason

36. *AKV*, *34*, 388 ff.
37. See Catherine to Madame Bielke, 30 June/11 July 1775, *Sbornik*, 27, 44. See also *AKV*, *28*, 82, Catherine to Simon Vorontsov, 28 February/11 March 1789 in

to fear any harmful repercussions from American independence.[38] Faith in Britain's basic strength, coupled with contempt for her government, led Russia to view with indifference the outcome of the American war. From the Russian point of view, therefore, the policy Panin proposed, though not adventurous, was sensible.

It remained to be seen how far the Empress would be influenced by such considerations, and to this Harris at once directed his attention. Bearing in mind Potemkin's warning that he should prepare himself to answer whatever arguments Panin might use against his proposals, he improvised a manoeuvre that went even further. "By employing various means unnecessary to repeat to your Lordship," Harris obtained an abstract of the report of the college of foreign affairs. In a second memorial to the Empress he set himself to correct the impression Panin had given that Britain was to blame for the failure of past negotiations for an alliance. At the same time he painted a tragic picture of Britain, facing her enemies single-handed, and contrasted it with the Seven Years' War when Britain faced the same enemies but with a powerful ally, Prussia, and the American forces at her disposal.[39] This memorial Harris delivered to the Empress through Potemkin at about the same time as the report of the foreign department was expected to reach her. Meanwhile he embarked with enthusiasm on the political education of Potemkin and spent many hours describ-

which Catherine, speaking it is true long after the event, implies that in her interview with Harris she had had the misfortune of predicting "ce qu'il en arriverait des affaires d'Amérique . . ."

38. A British argument that the loss of the American colonies would harm the Russian export trade in naval stores, since they would now be free to export goods rivalling Russian produce, was rejected by the Russians. On the contrary, Russia would benefit from American independence, since Britain would cease to encourage the Americans with special bounties to produce naval stores. See *AKV*, *34*, 388; Albion, *Forests and Sea Power*, pp. 40 ff.; Gerhardt, *England und der Aufstieg Russlands*, pp. 50 ff.; Aleksandrenko, *Russkiye diplomaticheskiye agenty*, *2*, p. 112, Musin Pushkin to Panin 23 May/3 June 1766.

39. SP 91/103, Harris to Weymouth, No. 56, 9/20 September 1779, Enclosure, Paper B, probably dated 16/27 August, delivered to Potemkin on 17/28 August 1779. In the accompanying dispatch No. 56 Harris gives a short summary of the report of the secret department of the college of foreign affairs, mentioning the report's reference to Prussia and to the desirability of the return of Britain to her situation at the peace of Aix-la-Chapelle; he does not refer to the Russian criticisms of the British government and of the British attitude to neutral trade.

ing how the initiative in proposing closer connexions had always come from Britain. He blamed Panin freely for giving the impression that Britain could expect no help from Russia and went so far as to hint that Panin was corrupt. "A Russian minister, who could attempt to mislead his sovereign so egregiously, as to advance, that it was equally the interest of the court of Petersburg, to keep well with France, as with England, must, either be very unequal to the duties of his post, or else, . . . he acted in it, from principles I would not allow myself to imagine," said Harris to the Prince. Past services rendered by Britain during the first Turkish war were duly touched on and glorified. Potemkin expressed himself willing to use Harris's arguments in discussion with the Empress, but he hinted to Harris that though he himself took no account of such things, Britain was constantly being accused of "fierté" and "froideur" in the conduct of her relations with Russia, and the Empress was inclined to believe these charges. He personally could do nothing to forward a decision as the Empress had declared her intention of asking the advice of her Council of State, "and till then would certainly not be influenced in her opinion by the advice of anybody." [40] By his negligence however the Prince allowed Harris's opponents a chance to state their case. The Chevalier de la Teyssonière procured a copy of Harris's second memorial and handed it to Corberon, and the latter, who was now frequently received in the Prince's intimate circle, lost no opportunity to counter Harris's arguments.[41] Panin in turn urged on the Empress the need to observe strict impartiality if a Russian mediation was ever to be accepted and stressed the lack of government stability in Britain and Harris's lack of instructions.[42]

40. SP 91/103, Harris to Weymouth, No. 56, 9/20 September 1779.
41. CP Russie, *103*, Corberon to Vergennes, No. 35, 3 September 1779; unnumbered, 9 September 1779. In a garbled form this story eventually reached the public. It was said that Harris had written a paper refuting the principles of the Neutral League, to be delivered to the Empress by Potemkin. The Prince's pocket was picked by "one of his low mistresses" in the pay of Panin, and Panin prepared a counter-statement and defeated Harris. "The whole anecdote is an invention," writes the editor of the *Malmesbury Diaries,* and is echoed by Bergbohm, *Die bewaffnete Neutralität,* p. 112, note. But de la Teyssonière was probably not above picking the Prince's pocket, and the origin of the story which appeared in the gazettes in 1781 must be traced to this episode (*MD, 1,* 390, note).
42. SP 91/103, Harris to Weymouth, No. 56 9/20 September 1779.

As September advanced Harris felt that he must obtain some kind of an answer to communicate to his principals, who had been left in complete ignorance of the policy he was pursuing. Throughout the summer he had confined himself to mysterious hints that he "had been forced to deviate from the common track in which business is carried on." [43] But the Empress had deferred calling her Council of State until mid-September. She had invited the members to submit their opinion in writing, and Harris's memorial was also debated, Potemkin supporting his arguments and Panin opposing them.[44] According to Panin's own account of this meeting, Harris had been very nearly successful in his aims. But after Panin had spoken, "on a trouvé mes raisons si convaincantes que tout le conseil s'est réuni avec moi." Panin had privately reinforced his views with the Empress, using arguments he had not wished to put in writing, and he had convinced her. Describing his triumph to the Prussian envoy, the Russian minister could not resist a most patronizing tone: "M. Harris est un jeune ministre, sage à la vérité, mais entreprenant. Il fait son devoir. Il voudrait quelque chose, et il sent qu'il ne saurait le faire avec moi . . . M. Harris . . . a raison de s'adresser à d'autres moins instruits. Mais ne vous inquiétez pas: malgré les apparences brillantes des autres, je réponds de soutenir mon système." And he added: "[M. Harris] n'a surement pas d'ordre de sa cour de faire ce qu'il fait; mais prévoyant que le besoin pourrait exister, il voudrait tout préparer, pour pouvoir dire: voilà une cour que je vous offre." [45] This was a remarkably shrewd exposition of the policy that Harris had been following during the summer.

No formal reply was made to Harris's memorial, since it was an unofficial document delivered personally to Potemkin and had never been shown by the British envoy to Panin.[46] But on 17 Sep-

43. SP 91/103, Harris to Weymouth, No. 44, 16/27 July 1779.

44. There is no Russian source available for the meeting of the Council of State; the present account is reconstructed from Bancroft-Circourt, *3*, 227, Goertz to Frederick, 13/24 September 1779; CP Russie, *103*, Corberon to Vergennes, No. 40, 5 October 1779; No. 49, 2 November 1779. Presumably the report of the college of foreign affairs (see pp. 108–09) formed the groundwork of the debate.

45. Bancroft-Circourt, *3*, 227.

46. The innocent Corberon, delighted with his ingenuity in securing a copy of Harris's memorial, saw Panin early in October, and assuming the Russian minister to be ignorant of Harris's manoeuvres told him of the gist of Harris's

tember Harris procured a private interview with the favourite at which he was informed that he had failed to move the Empress. He bewailed the fact that in spite of her friendship for England she had been influenced by persons "of an inferior capacity" and "much less weight" than the Prince to leave Britain to wage an unequal battle for a further year. Potemkin, apparently unmoved by the hint that Panin's influence had carried more weight than his own, assured Harris that the Empress desired to be helpful. It was too late to undertake any action in the present campaigning season, but he advised Harris not to hurry the Empress and to leave her to work out her own plans. Thus ended Harris's first effort at mobilizing Russian support through Potemkin alone, behind the back of the minister for foreign affairs.[47]

Harris gives his own reasons for the Empress's refusal to adopt his policy, and these are worth examining because British policy towards Russia was formulated on the basis of his reports. As Harris put it, the Empress, "diffident perhaps of Prince Potemkin's experience in foreign affairs, and not sufficiently relying on her own superiour judgement and parts" thought it necessary to consult her advisers and thus gave time to the opposition party to work on her. Harris accused Panin of having procured from the King of Prussia some ostensible dispatches, intended to be shown to the Empress, in which Frederick II stressed the ease with which France and Spain might be separated and his certainty that after the present campaign France would apply for Russian mediation. But Harris did not believe that the influence of Panin and of Frederick's ostensible dispatches had by themselves been enough to sway Catherine. The real cause of his failure was lack of stability on the part of Prince Potemkin. He believed that Frederick, "ever fertile in resources," had indirectly hinted to Potemkin his willingness to help him on to the throne of the Duchy of Curland [48] and

---

memorial to Potemkin. With a straight face Panin assured him: "Je sais tout et rien ne se fera." (CP Russie, *103*, to Vergennes, No. 40, 5 October 1779).

47. SP 91/103, Harris to Weymouth, No. 56, 9/20 September 1779.

48. The Duchy of Curland was at the time occupied by Pierre Biren, son of the Empress Anna Ioannovna's hated favourite. Catherine II had replaced the elder Biren on the throne in 1762, and Curland was to all intents and purposes completely dependent on Russia, though technically an independent duchy under Polish suzerainty.

that he had even suggested that a marriage with one of the sisters of the Grand Duchess Maria Feodorovna, wife of the Grand Duke Paul and a princess of Württemberg, was not impossible. And, thought Harris, "such is his ambition, that his penetration and cunning, great as it is, is instantly blinded whenever he perceives any hopes of gratifying his predominant passion." [49]

How far was Harris justified in his conclusions? From the correspondence between Frederick II and his minister in St. Petersburg, Count Solms, it is clear that Frederick II was already somewhat anxious at the decline of his influence in Russia which the independence of Russian policy in the Bavarian war had revealed to him. Though Frederick's long-term aim was to bring about an alliance between Prussia, Russia, and France, the Franco-Austrian alliance was for the time being an insuperable bar. The principal object of Prussia at the moment was to persuade the Empress not to remove the Russian garrison from Poland,[50] and a subsidiary one was the possibility that eventually France might be brought to agree to joint mediation by Russia and Prussia between the Bourbon powers and Britain. Solms never mentioned Harris's interview with the Empress and possibly never found out about it. In a letter to Solms of 14 August 1779 Frederick II did assert roundly that Britain "n'éprouve que le sort qu'elle a bien mérité, et la balance de l'Europe ne sera surement point agitée quand même elle perdrait parci parlà quelques îles dans l'autre partie du monde." He spoke of Britain in terms reminiscent of one of the allegedly ostensible dispatches Harris accused Panin of procuring.

49. SP 91/103, Harris to Weymouth, No. 57, 9/20 September 1779. Corberon, on the other hand, heard that Harris had been granted a credit of £36,000, of which 100,000 roubles, he reported, had been paid to Potemkin to buy his support. This was quite untrue (see my article, "The Use of British Secret Funds in St. Petersburg, 1777–1782"). It is however quoted as a fact by Fauchille, *La diplomatie française*, pp. 292–93.

50. Russian troops had remained in Poland since the first Turkish war and the first partition. Considerations of expense led Catherine to desire their withdrawal, but neither Potemkin nor Panin approved of the measure, the former because of the necessity of keeping Poland quiet in the event of war with Turkey; the latter, echoing Frederick's own anxiety, out of fear that recent Austrian troop movements indicated Austrian intentions to stir up trouble in Poland. Panin was very peevish about the whole matter as "le borgne" (his flattering nickname for Potemkin) kept him in ignorance as to his intentions. See *PKFG, 43*, 206 ff. Frederick II to Solms, 5 August 1779, 21 August 1779; p. 224, Solms to Frederick, 6 August 1779.

But Frederick's vigorous denunciation of Britain came in response to a conversation Solms had had with Harris before the latter's interview with the Empress and therefore had nothing to do either with Panin or with his efforts to work against Harris's proposed policy.[51] Solms was on the point of departure from St. Petersburg and in fact left at the end of August 1779. He was replaced by Count Johann Eustache von Goertz, who had already played a discreet but important part in the diplomacy of the Bavarian succession.[52] Frederick's instructions to Goertz are relevant to the determination of whether Harris was right in thinking that Potemkin had failed him and had allowed himself to be seduced by the mirage of Prussian support for aims which were generally imputed to him. The new Prussian envoy was instructed to sound Russia on the possibility of a triple alliance between Prussia, Russia, and the Ottoman Porte—a further stage in Frederick's policy of isolating Austria. To further any of his aims Frederick II was willing to assist Potemkin to obtain either Curland or Poland for himself. There is no evidence that Frederick so much as contemplated at the time that Russia might be drawn into the war on Britain's side, and Goertz's instructions to dangle Curland and Poland before the Prince's eyes were intended to influence the favourite to approve of a *rapprochement* between Russia and France and of the projected alliance between Russia, Prussia, and the Porte.[53] Moreover Goertz only arrived in St. Petersburg on 16 September 1779,[54] the day before Harris received his final reply from Potemkin. Goertz had no time to exercise the influence on the favourite ascribed to him by the British envoy.

It is impossible on the evidence available to assess whether the unpredictable Potemkin was likely to be swayed by the King of Prussia's bribes in the manner suggested by Harris. From the con-

51. *PKFG, 43*, 218, referring to Solms's dispatch of 30 July 1779 reporting his talk with Harris.

52. Johann Eustache, Count Goertz had been in the service of the court of Weimar; in 1778 he was employed by Frederick II on a delicate mission to the Duke of Zweibrücken, in connection with the Bavarian war, and, remaining in Prussian service, he was transferred as envoy to St. Petersburg in 1779.

53. For Frederick's instructions to Goertz, see *PKFG, 43*, 172, 15 July 1779; cf. also 284, Frederick II to the chargé d'affaires, Huttel, 28 September 1779; Goertz, *Historische und Politische Denkwürdigkeiten*, p. 123.

54. SP 91/103, Harris to Weymouth, No. 59, 9/20 September 1779 (*MD, 1*, 260).

flicting reports about him, no very clear picture of his political
system at the time emerges, other than an automatic opposition
to Panin, whatever the issue. Judging from Harris's account, he
undoubtedly encouraged the British envoy to hope. But how far
was he guided by the belief that it was in Russia's interest to support Britain against France? And how far was his main motive
to wean Catherine from the Prussian alliance and the minister
responsible for it, namely Panin? Potemkin was nothing if not
skilful in his handling of human beings, and his relationship with
Corberon at the time when he was also assisting Harris provides a
valuable commentary on his methods. Throughout the spring and
summer the Prince had often invited the visits of the spritely young
Frenchman, and had shown "une forte inclination particulière
pour la France dont il aime le climat" (he had never been there).[55]
Their conversation had frequently touched on the Prince's plans
to extend direct commerce with France through the Black Sea
and on the possibility of a commercial treaty with France, a plan
which Corberon had done his best to further ever since he had
arrived in Russia.[56] Most revealing, however, is Corberon's account of a tête-à-tête dinner with the Prince on 10 September 1779,
when the Prince had declared "que le système des Anglois étoit in-
explicable et qu'on ne pouvoit l'attribuer qu'au but que sembloit
avoir George III d'étendre son pouvoir sur sa nation." [57] When
Corberon expatiated on the friendly relations between France
and Russia and even hinted at the possibility of an alliance, the
Prince "m'a fait un signe d'approbation et avec un sourire de la
confiance il m'a répondu 'vous avez bien raison; mais l'Autriche,
l'Autriche.' " [58] One might well ask, "qui trompe-t-on ici." Clearly

55. CP Russie, *102*, Corberon to Vergennes, No. 18, 18 May 1779. On 6 August,
Potemkin sent for Corberon, and in a private talk with him left him with the
impression that "il veut nous servir" (No. 32, 10 August 1779). This was four days
after Harris's audience with the Empress which the Prince had arranged.

56. See *Journal Intime, 2,* passim for Corberon's repeated attempts to further a
treaty of commerce between Russia and France.

57. Whig attacks on the North administration profoundly influenced those enlightened despots, Frederick II and Catherine II. See also Frederick to his niece,
the Princess of Orange, 7 February 1780, on the principles of the British government: "sotte vanité, ignorance des intérêts et des forces des puissance de l'Europe,
orgueil de porter seuls le trident de Neptune et ce projet d'établir le despotisme
royal sur les ruines de la liberté anglaise." (*PKFG, 44,* 67).

58. CP Russie, *103*, Corberon to Vergennes, No. 36, 10 September 1779.

Potemkin was not the friend of Britain Harris believed him to be. Neither, as his actions were to show, was he devoted to France.[59] His attitude is probably best understood in the light of the Greek project. He would forward the interests of any power likely to assist its realization, and he would oppose the conservative policy of Panin. So far the Greek project was still in the realm of speculation, and there was no need for Potemkin to take any decisive stand on issues of foreign policy. But rivalry with Panin for control over its conduct was a real and present issue, and from this date the struggle between the two men became ever fiercer.

In the final analysis the purely personal motives put forward by Harris to explain his failure to persuade the Empress to put a stop to hostilities by an armed mediation are too superficial to account for Catherine's decision. Harris chose to portray himself as defeated by Prussian intrigues, but the Empress was more concerned with objective realities. An armed mediation would involve Russia in expensive military and naval preparations, and she would lose all the benefits of the recent *rapprochement* with France.[60] However warm Catherine's personal sympathy for Britain, it did not extend to George III or the North administration. Her condemnation to Harris in July of Spain's intervention in the war should be compared with what she was writing a little later to her confidant Baron Grimm: "Was soll man mit die [sic] Leute machen, stolz im Glücke, Advocaten im Unglücke, schnacken wenn zu thun Zeit ist; halbe Worte und halbe Werke machen nicht Dinge, die ganz gethan sein müssten." [61] The conclusion Catherine drew from Britain's difficulties was that they should render her "plus traitable." [62] It is very probable that she relied on Panin's sober and

---

59. There was a certain naïveté about Corberon, which he would most energetically have disclaimed. But how else can one account for the idea he entertained that Panin was friendly not only to Britain but to Harris (CP Russie, *103*, to Vergennes, No. 32, 10 August 1779). Corberon too read more into Potemkin's pretty speeches than they meant, but he may also have been misled by de la Teyssonière, who plays a peculiar role in the Prince's entourage.

60. See for instance Catherine to Grimm, 14/25 July 1779, "Vous savez comme je pense sur tous ceux qui occupent les premières places depuis le règne bienheureux de Louis XVI" (*Sbornik, 23*, 152). This remark was of course intended for French ears, but the *rapprochement* was nevertheless real.

61. *Sbornik, 23*, 146, Catherine to Grimm, 1/12 July 1779.

62. Ibid., 147, the same to the same, 5/16 July 1779.

experienced judgement and that the report of the college of foreign affairs met with her approval. As her faithful echo and private secretary Bezborodko wrote on 11/22 September 1779: "It does not appear that political matters in Europe interest us very specially as yet. The expectation that Britain, by her own resources, can hold out against the two principal Bourbon Houses is the reason why we are for the time being putting off any question of undertaking any special obligations towards England, who is making very powerful efforts in that direction. Thus we pay Britain back for the lack of confidence she showed to us during the negotiations of Count Chernyshev." [63] Britain offered only the dangers of armed championship. The level-headed Vergennes contented himself with Russia's neutrality and made no effort to detach Russia from her traditional British friendship.[64] There was no inducement for Russia to choose the former course and precipitate herself into a quite unnecessary war.[65]

But Harris did not penetrate sufficiently into the complexities of Russian policy to discern the factors by which it was governed. Convinced that he had been defeated by Prussian flattery and Prussian bribery, he thought in terms of more flattery and bigger bribes. As he wrote to Weymouth in September 1779: "Both the Sovereign and the Favorite may be led to do anything by well-timed and adroit flattery; and to this alone the King of Prussia owes his amazing influence here. A conduct formed on these principles, from a National Character like ours . . . would, undoubtedly, prepare her [the Empress] to receive any proposals His Maj-

63. Maykov, *Pis'ma A. A. Bezborodka*, p. 44, to Rumyantsev.

64. CP Russie, *102*, Vergennes to Corberon, No. 8, 16 May 1779: "Il ne s'agit pas pour nous de rompre ses liaisons avec l'Angleterre pour l'attirer entièrement de notre côté. Nous ne voulons pas la convaincre qu'elle doit nous traiter comme la nation favorite mais seulement qu'elle a tout à gagner à nous regarder comme lui voulant point de mal et pouvant lui faire du bien." See also No. 11, 3 July 1889; No. 25, 23 September 1779.

65. See also Panin to Goertz, "Je sens fort bien que, par mécontentement contre le ministère britannique actuel, les autres puissances ne doivent pas laisser écraser l'Angleterre, mais elle en est encore loin. Il est bon . . . qu'elle soit ramenée à cet état de puissance où elle était avant la dernière guerre. Il n'est pas mal qu'elle perde quelque chose. Il ne faut pas croire que tout ce qu'elle perdra fera une augmentation de puissance pour la France: cela se partagera entre l'Espagne et toutes les puissances commerçantes . . ." (Bancroft-Circourt, *3*, 227, Goertz to Frederick, 13/24 September 1779).

esty might think proper to make." [66] Harris had been acting throughout on his own initiative and without instructions [67] (as Panin had surmised), and it was perhaps in order to ward off a reprimand that he insisted in his dispatches that "H.I.M. would at once have adopted the measure I proposed" had it not been for the intrigues of his enemies. In the circumstances he thought himself justified in putting forward suggestions to his principals of the best means to persuade the Empress by the following spring to be no longer "an indifferent spectator." [68]

At the same time as he sent Weymouth his long account of his personal diplomacy during the summer, he outlined his plan for the future, the product, as he put it, of mature reflection, close study of the Russian court, and an anticipation of the Empress's wishes. He proposed that the King should write to the Empress in his own hand; this, he thought, would give her infinite pleasure, particularly if the King referred to the "great part" Catherine acted in Europe. The King should offer a general alliance to go hand in hand with naval assistance; England should give up the Turkish clause and assure Russia that she would rather owe peace to Catherine than to anyone else. The King's letter should also refer to the terms on which Britain would be willing to make peace, in order to counteract the intrigues of the pro-French party in St. Petersburg who were always alleging that France was more willing to take Russia into her confidence than Britain. The letter to the Empress should be accompanied by an "ostensible dispatch" addressed to himself and containing a "panegyrick" on Prince Potemkin, preferably in French as Harris credited the Prince with sufficient cunning to cast doubt on the oral translation of a document he could not read. [69] In view of the urgency of the matter,

66. SP 91/103, Harris to Weymouth, No. 58, separate and secret, 9/20 September 1779.
67. The only instructions Harris received throughout the summer were: "You have at different times received such ample instructions for your conduct and are so fully informed of His Majesty's wishes to form an alliance with the court of Russia that it is unnecessary for me to enlarge upon it at present." (Weymouth to Harris, No. 23, 13 August 1779). Harris received them in September, long after he had embarked on his individual negotiation.
68. SP 91/103, Harris to Weymouth, No. 58, 9/20 September 1779.
69. Ibid.

Harris sent his dispatches by his own servant, having no courier at his disposal.

Some months later Harris said that the idea of a personal letter from George III to the Empress had been suggested to him by Potemkin.[70] It is possible that the whole proposal to renew the offer of alliance, submitting British peace terms at the same time, was also discussed with Potemkin. At any rate it is evident that Harris let himself be guided to some extent by the Prince. He was thus allowing the initiative of deciding the form which British relations with Russia should take to pass out of his own hands into those of one of the leading Russian statesmen, who had so far done little to justify the faith Harris placed in him.

70. SP 91/104, Harris to Stormont, No. 13, 15/26 February 1780 (*MD, 1,* 282).

5. The Third Attempt to Win Russia

THE SUMMER OF 1779 had not been a happy one in Britain. A prolonged government crisis had followed the resignation and subsequent death of Lord Suffolk.[1] Lord Weymouth continued for the time being to carry out the duties of secretary of state for the North as well as those of his own department. Suffering from government weakness at the centre and diplomatic isolation, the mistress of the seas had in addition experienced the painful humiliation of watching the joint French and Spanish fleets parade up and down the Channel almost unchallenged. Although this demonstration of Bourbon naval power had not led to the expected invasion of Britain [2] it did impress on the government ever more strongly the need for naval reinforcements. In March 1779, tentative efforts had been made to secure some help from Denmark, but these had led to nothing.[3] The impossibility of procuring assistance anywhere else, the visible proof of Britain's naval inferiority, the need to strengthen the government's influence, and Catherine's sympathy over the Spanish intervention in the war caused Weymouth in the autumn to take up again the idea of a Russian alliance in spite of the previous decision to wait for an opening

1. For the government crisis in England, see Butterfield, *George III, Lord North and the People*, passim.

2. See for instance a letter from Plymouth to James Harris senior of 17 August 1779: "The consternation amongst all ranks is not to be expressed; many families have already removed and others are removing." (Malmesbury, *Series of Letters of the First Earl of Malmesbury, his family and friends, from 1745 to 1820, 1,* 422.)

3. Morton Eden had been sent to Copenhagen to replace Delaval in March 1779, with instructions to attempt to secure the use of some Danish warships in exchange for a subsidy and the defence of the Danish West and East Indian possessions. See SP 75/135, Weymouth to Morton Eden, 2 March 1779 (separate instructions) and Eden to Weymouth, No. 6, 24 April 1779.

from the Russian side.[4] He had as yet no information about the independent policy Harris was pursuing, but in mid-September 1779 he urged Harris to spare no efforts to incline the Empress to that alliance which in any case he believed her to desire. "Till our fleet shall have recovered the decided superiority over our enemies, we must remain in a state of constant anxiety," he explained.[5] But he made no suggestions as to how Harris was to proceed in his negotiations; he merely referred him to past instructions, without realizing that Suffolk's latest offers had been founded on the possibility of Russia being drawn into the War of the Bavarian Succession.

Weymouth's instructions reached St. Petersburg on 5 October 1779, but for once Harris felt justified in not acting on them immediately and resolved to wait for a reply to the account of his personal diplomacy during the summer, which he had sent off by his servant on 9/20 September. Meanwhile he regarded St. Petersburg as a battlefield with France, Prussia, and Britain gaining or losing ground according to the skill of their representatives and the extent of the influence of their respective partisans, Potemkin and Panin. If he were to believe Panin, he wrote, he would abandon every hope of success. "He admits neither of our being in a position to stand in need of the alliance of this country, nor, even if we were, that it would be sound policy to assist us." Potemkin, meantime, still assured him that Catherine was favourably disposed towards Britain.[6] Harris was of course aware of the rivalry between Panin and Potemkin, but he was misled by his belief, in many ways natural to an English diplomat, that its main object was a difference of policy towards Britain. It was however a personal struggle for power between Panin and Potemkin centring on the future Greek project. The first victim of this gradual reorientation of Russian foreign policy was in fact Prussia. Frederick's object of securing an alliance between Prussia, Russia, and the Porte cut right across the ideas that the Empress and Potemkin were

4. See e.g. SP 91/103, Weymouth to Harris, No. 24, 7 September 1779; No. 26, 14 September 1779; cf. Fortescue, *Correspondence of King George III*, *4*, 455, the King to North, 11 October 1779: "such an event would give great credit to administration."

5. SP 91/103, Weymouth to Harris, No. 24, 14 September 1779.

6. SP 91/103, Harris to Weymouth, No. 63, 1/12 October 1779.

entertaining of an ultimate overthrow of the Ottoman Empire. Panin knew enough of the Empress's projects to realize that if he supported a plan to ally Russia with the Porte he would only undermine his own influence with her. Goertz's overtures met with scant response and were soon turned down.[7]

Meantime in London the long-delayed appointment of a new secretary of state for the North was at last made and a firmer hand than Weymouth's, that of Lord Stormont, ex-ambassador to Vienna and Paris, took charge of the negotiations with Russia.[8] Harris's account of his interview with the Empress and his subsequent attempt to induce her to launch an armed mediation had reached London by 15 October 1779. His individual initiative drew neither blame nor praise from his new chief. But Stormont must have been impressed by Harris's account of his activities and by his arguments, for in view of the urgent need of naval reinforcements, which Weymouth had already stressed, he decided to adopt the policy Harris had proposed. Stormont himself would have preferred a full-scale alliance between Britain and Russia, but, judging by Harris's dispatches, a declaration backed by a naval armament appeared to be more in line with Catherine's own wishes, "and in a negotiation where we have so many difficulties to contend with, we must drive the nail that will go." If therefore Catherine still seemed to incline towards an armed mediation, Harris was to pursue that line, wrote Stormont. If she seemed to prefer an alliance he was authorized to use his full powers. The

7. See *PKFG, 43, 313,* Goertz to Frederick, 1 October 1779. For Catherine's reasons for refusing to enter into Frederick's views see a memorandum by Bezborodko of 18/29 September 1779, F. de Martens, *Recueil, 6,* 120. Strangely enough, Frederick's envoys at the Russian court did not think it necessary to inform their master about the Empress's oriental project. Goertz mentions it for the first time on 26 December 1780 (*PKFG, 45,* 171). Frederick therefore lacked information about one essential element in Russian policy.

8. "We shall see what the new secretary does, he is used to foreign affairs and ought to enter more feelingly into a foreign minister's affairs than a home bred one," wrote Harris on 9/20 November 1779 to his sister Gertrude. He was not only referring to his diplomatic activity, but to his hopes of being granted some financial assistance, for the expenses, both private and for intelligence purposes, of his post were such as to make him wish to give it up (Merton Papers). Stormont did in fact intercede for Harris with the King, who allowed him to draw £3,000 of secret service money for his personal use (see my article, "The Use of British Secret Funds at St. Petersburg, 1777–1782."

treaty was to be "unclogged with any restrictions" provided that the present war with France and Spain was expressly declared to be the *casus foederis*. On that condition and that condition only, Harris was empowered to conclude the treaty and to waive the Turkish clause; he was also authorized to give up the now out-of-date restriction which Suffolk had originally placed on the use of the British fleet in the Eastern Mediterranean. The power to waive the Turkish clause was however still to be kept secret by Harris until he was morally certain of achieving the alliance and securing the use of the Russian fleet as soon as the weather permitted.

Symptomatic of the extent to which London had been impressed by the picture of a Catherine only too anxious to "stand forth" and withheld from doing so by the sinister influence of France and Prussia is Stormont's further suggestion: if the Empress, he wrote, "from a peculiar turn of mind, and from that heroism of sentiment which she loves to display, and which, often affects the mode of her proceedings, should chuse to promise the succours we desire, before any treaty is entered into, wishing that it may appear that this assistance is spontaneous, granted upon great reasons of policy and not in consequence of a formal engagement: if this should be Her Imperial Majesty's wish there can be no objection to the complying with it." In that case the treaty, instead of stipulating for succours, must recite the voluntary engagement of the Empress to grant assistance and make sure that they would be available for the present war with France and Spain or with either of these powers.[9]

In accordance with Harris's suggestions, Stormont enclosed a personal letter from George III, which the King had very reluctantly agreed to write to the Empress and which Harris was instructed to deliver in person or through Potemkin. Should Harris find that the Empress's sentiments had changed, he was authorized not to deliver the letter at all. But the letter was not couched in the terms Harris had suggested in his dispatches. It did not contain any request for an alliance nor did it specify the terms on which the

9. SP 91/103, Stormont to Harris, No. 40, 5 November 1779. The numbering of these dispatches is misleading. Weymouth's last of 1 October 1779 is numbered 29. It is followed by Stormont's first, numbered 30, his second and third, numbered 40 and 41, and then the numbering returns to 32.

King would make peace. It merely stated in general, in highly flattering phrases, the King's hope that the Empress would not remain an idle spectator of the upsetting of the European balance.[10] In addition Stormont provided Harris with an ostensible dispatch to be shown to Potemkin, in which he spoke of the "knowledge, sagacity and penetration" of the Prince, "which no artifice can mislead," of the great role he could now act, by which he would "secure to himself a place in the records of fame, by the side of his Sovereign, *et sera à jamais associé à sa gloire*." But, as Stormont explained, since it was known that the British diplomats corresponded in their own language, he could not write in French without showing his hand too clearly. He therefore composed his "spontaneous" tribute to the Prince in English, with an occasional flourish in French, and wrote it in his own hand.[11]

It is evident from Stormont's instructions that the British government was being guided by Harris's dispatches in the formulation of its new policy towards Russia. The method of personal flattery was to be used to persuade the Empress to subscribe to a course which might lead her to take an active part in the war and would certainly lead her into the expense of the mobilization of part of her forces. In exchange she was to be offered British assistance in the event of a war with Turkey. The immediate advantages were all on Britain's side; but this was counterbalanced in British opinion by the view that it was not in Russia's interest to see British naval supremacy reduced and the command of the Mediterranean devolve upon the Bourbon powers—France was after all the traditional ally of the Turk. That the question of whether or not to assist Britain had now become involved in a struggle for power within the Russian court was accepted by both Stormont and Harris. It was taken for granted that success or failure would depend on whether Panin or Potemkin exercised most influence over the Empress. But there was one notable omission in Stormont's instructions. In spite of Panin's frequent requests, in spite of Harris's recommendation that the King's letter

10. SP 91/103, Stormont to Harris, No. 30, 5 November 1779. See Fortescue, *Correspondence of King George III, 4*, 471, 1 and 4 November 1779, Stormont to the King. For the King's letter, see *MD, 1*, 264.

11. SP 91/103, unnumbered, secret, Stormont to Harris, 5 November 1779; cf. No. 30 of the same date.

should outline the terms on which Britain would make peace, this aspect of Anglo-Russian negotiation was entirely ignored by the Secretary of State. British reticence on this subject in fact meant that the Empress was to be invited to launch an armed mediation without knowing anything of the terms she was expected to enforce. The omission may have arisen on Stormont's part because he believed the Empress to be so anxious to "stand forth" on Britain's behalf that the armed mediation was only a subterfuge to give her a valid pretext. But it does reveal, more clearly than words could do, that the ultimate purpose of Britain was to draw Russia into the war in some form or other, on her behalf, and that even the "armed mediation" was to be but the preliminary to direct participation in hostilities.

Stormont's instructions reached Harris on 3 December 1779. According to his previous practice, his normal twice-weekly dispatches contained only brief hints about the progress he was making, until at last on 26 February 1780 he felt himself sufficiently advanced to send back an English courier. With a short word of praise for Stormont's clear instructions "so perfectly consonant to what I had conceived to be the wishes and sentiments of this court," Harris embarked on an account of his negotiation. The very day his servant returned, on 3 December 1779, he communicated to Potemkin the British proposals for an alliance. The Prince expressed his own approval of the projected alliance, assured Harris that he would support it, and advised him to lose no time in mentioning the matter to Panin, with whom it was necessary to keep up appearances; he in turn would let Harris know what the Empress herself thought of the overtures.[12]

Panin meantime had not failed to observe the arrival of Harris's messenger; he too had his particular friend among the foreign envoys at the Russian court, and he unbosomed himself to Count Goertz, the Prussian envoy. "Et si avec tout l'Angleterre nous entraîne?" he exclaimed to him. Though he had no special animosity towards England, declared Panin, he feared that she wished to draw the whole of Europe into war "pour rétablir dans cette confusion ses propres affaires." France would call on Austria for assistance, and the Emperor would seize the opportunity to fall on Russia and Prussia. When Goertz endeavoured to reassure Panin,

12. SP 91/104, Harris to Stormont, No. 11, 15/26 February 1780 (MD, 1, 270).

the Russian minister exclaimed, "je ne pourrai probablement rien, je suis vieux, on le sent et on parait trouver mes avis vieux." From others in Panin's confidence Goertz heard "combien ce ministre est outré contre les intrigues du sieur Harris avec le favori." Three days passed, and Harris, who had visited Potemkin the very day his courier arrived, had still not called on Panin. Such visible proof of the loss of his own influence, coupled with genuine fear for Russia if she should become entangled in the maritime war, led him to speak more and more openly to Goertz. His animosity was directed not only towards Harris but against the North administration "qui voyait ses têtes en peril ne balancerait pas de mettre l'Europe en combustion . . . il ne voudrait plus être ministre si ce malheur avait lieu." [13]

Thus, when Harris at last visited Panin on 7 December 1779 the latter had already worked himself up to a high degree of indignation. Panin moreover was already beginning to feel the first symptoms of an illness which was to keep him in the background for some time. But he concealed his real feelings from Harris and was as usual "very profuse in his assurances of regard." Harris, according to his account, believed that Panin had "no reason as yet to think I had withdrawn my confidence." He therefore summoned the Russian minister to put into practice "his avowed friendly feelings as I brought proposals which could not fail to meet his entire approbation in every point." Here Harris cannot be acquitted of prevarication. He must have known that his constant visits to Potemkin and the dispatch of couriers of which Panin was told nothing could not pass unperceived. But if his policy of working through Potemkin only was to be accepted in London, it was essential to show that Panin had no grounds for hostility, that he had always been treated with proper courtesy, and that only native perversity and allegiance to Prussia led him to combat Harris's plans.

In this atmosphere of mutual distrust and dissimulation Harris unfolded himself. In this initial stage he took up first the project of an alliance which Stormont had regarded as more desirable. In

13. *PKFG*, *43*, 443, Goertz to Frederick, 7 December; CP Russie, *103*, Corberon to Vergennes, No. 55, 7 December 1779, No. 56, 10 December 1779. Harris however wrote that Panin had been unable to receive him any earlier. (SP 91/104, No. 11, 15/26 February 1780, *MD*, *1*, 270).

a memorial for the Empress, he stressed that whereas Britain wanted peace on proper terms, the Bourbon powers, judging by the state of their armaments, were minded to pursue the war. Britain could not hold out alone, he wrote, and "l'Impératrice seule peut imposer la loi"; Britain would be satisfied to leave her interests in Russian hands if Russia could procure peace. But as it was unlikely that the Bourbons would give up their warlike designs, Britain hoped that the Empress would use "la force que Dieu lui a confiée" and by her representations stop the war. Should the Empress agree, he proposed entering immediately on negotiations for a defensive alliance, without any restrictions. Such an alliance, added Harris, was so much in conformity with Panin's principles that he was sure it would meet no obstacle from him and that he would support it.[14]

In fact, of course, such an alliance was not in the least in conformity with Panin's principles, as Harris well knew. On 8 or 9 December 1779, Panin forwarded Harris's memorial to the Empress with his comments. To Goertz he outlined the objections he had put forward to Harris's proposals: the danger that Russia would be drawn into the war and that the system he had built up over the last twenty years would be totally overthrown. Though when he spoke to Goertz on 10 December Panin did not yet know Catherine's decision, he still hoped that he would be able to "parer le coup," though he added, "j'ignore quelles espérances le prince Potemkin donne au sieur Harris." [15] Harris's constant attendance on the Prince drove Panin still further in pursuit of his private vendetta, and he did not hesitate to betray Harris to Goertz. He read to the Prussian envoy the text of Harris's memorial to the Empress and let him know that Britain had at last consented to grant the Turkish *casus foederis*. Meanwhile the Grand Duke, having been informed of Harris's proposals, called on Panin and begged him to stand fast; indeed he even tackled his mother on the subject.[16]

14. SP 91/104, Harris to Stormont, No. 11, 15/26 February 1780; Enclosure, Paper A, 26 November/7 December 1779. In proposing an alliance without any restrictions Harris was already revealing his power to waive the Turkish clause.
15. *PKFG, 43*, 450, Goertz to Frederick, 10 December 1779.
16. Bancroft-Circourt, *3*, 229, Goertz to Frederick, 3/14 December 1779.

Harris, who had his own very effective channels of information,[17] discovered at once that Panin had forwarded his memorial with adverse comments to the Empress. He immediately called on Potemkin, who anticipated the cause of Harris's visit by declaring to him that he had already seen Panin's recommendation to the Empress, and, though he himself condemned it, he feared that the Empress might be influenced by Panin's arguments. Harris inquired what could have caused the Empress to change her mind. Illness, was the Prince's answer, the illness of the Empress's young favourite, Lanskoy,[18] which absorbed all her attention and left her no energy for matters of state. His own influence, added the Prince, was suspended; he was out of favour for having advised the Empress to get rid of her favourite before he died in her arms. Harris declared himself equally "confounded and surprised" by what he heard. Could the Empress prefer "the doctrines of a person weakened by age and infirmities . . . [Panin] to the spirited advice she received from him [Potemkin]?" Potemkin was proving in the eyes of Europe that he had only the exterior marks of favour but no power. Believing the Prince to be roused and piqued by his words, Harris took from his pocket "your Lordship's private letter, and, after translating it to him, I observed, that testimonies of regard like these, were due only to the greatest man; that these were not the studied and interested compliments of an antichamber, but sentiments of high esteem arising from conviction, the more honorable, as they came gratuitously from one of the best judges of real merit." Fired by these expressions of "spontaneous" praise, Potemkin declared that before he slept he would have a trial of skill, "whether there was in the Empire any influence more powerful than his." [19]

But though Harris did not know it, and was not to know for

17. In the six months ending in November 1779, Harris had spent nearly £1,450 in bribing petty officials. See my article, "The Use of British Secret Funds at St. Petersburg, 1777-1782."

18. A. D. Lanskoy, aged 22, became favourite in October 1779; he was unassuming and played no part in politics. He died in office in 1784, leaving his imperial mistress disconsolate.

19. SP 91/104, Harris to Stormont, No. 11, 15/26 February 1780. This somewhat piquant passage has been omitted from the text published in the *Malmesbury Diaries, 1,* 270.

some time, the Empress had already reached a decision. On 14 December Panin confided to Goertz that the Empress had approved his arguments and that the British offers were to be refused, though as Goertz remarked, "il faut voir . . . si le Prince Potemkin ne voudra employer tout son crédit à se venger de cette espèce de défaite." [20] So far nothing had been said officially to Harris by Panin, though the British envoy must have surmised that the Empress's decision had already been taken and that it was negative. Goertz remarked that he seemed "très consterné et abattu." [21] But before Panin received Harris, the Russian minister fell so dangerously ill that his life was even despaired of. Harris spared no effort in the period of grace furnished him by Panin's illness to influence the Empress to change her mind. On 29 December he had a further interview with Potemkin who declared that he had taken every opportunity to enforce Harris's arguments with the Empress, and that she was "most thoroughly English in her wishes and tenets." Yet, he said, the Empress was held back from positive action by the insinuations of Britain's enemies that she was playing a double game: that Britain was negotiating with Vienna and that she was endeavouring to separate Russia from her allies and to surprise her into a war. Harris expressed his disappointment at this reply. The accusation of playing a double game, and of intriguing with Vienna, was "too contemptible to be dwelt upon, since our national character alone, was sufficient to destroy so idle a charge." And he gave vent to his indignation that any of Catherine's advisers could so forget his dignity, be so unacquainted with the resources of Russia, so lacking in confidence in Catherine's fame, as to believe that any intervention of hers would not immediately intimidate Britain's enemies into suing for peace, but "would (as if it came from the Republic of Lucca or S. Marino) only serve to animate and excite them to prolong the war." [22]

Potemkin, who had several times tried to interrupt the irate Harris, told him at last to address these reproaches to Panin, not to himself. He revived Harris's hopes by telling him that the Empress

20. Bancroft-Circourt, *3*, 229, Goertz to Frederick, 3/14 December 1779.
21. Ibid., 230, Goertz to Frederick, 10/21 December 1779.
22. SP 91/104, Harris to Stormont, No. 11, 15/26 February 1780. *MD, 1,* at p. 274 prints an incorrect date for this meeting, which took place on 18 December 1779, Old Style.

had asked for a further memorial, "expressive of your notions and instructions," and he hoped thus to be able to mollify the reply prepared by Panin. Harris promptly set to and produced another memorial in which he pointed out that the consequence of a French victory would be a total derangement of the equilibrium of Europe and a complete revolution in its commerce. To Russia alone would go the glory if Britain were saved; she alone was in a position to restore the balance between the belligerents; she who led in all alliances she formed.[23]

This was the last of Harris's efforts in the old year. The next day he fell so ill with jaundice—an illness that gave rise to much malicious comment [24]—that he was obliged to keep to his house for three weeks. Nothing was lost thereby, owing to the general standstill at court while Lanskoy's life hung in the balance. Harris employed the intervening time in keeping Potemkin regularly informed of all news from England and "writing him short notes, to keep up his good disposition, which I all along have and still do believe to be perfectly sincere." [25] But in spite of Harris's deployment of diplomatic activity and the energy of Potemkin's remonstrances with the Empress (if one may trust his account of them to Harris), Panin had already won the day. Owing to Panin's own illness the official communication of the Empress's reply to Harris was delayed, though Panin was not too unwell to receive Goertz and read to him the Empress's reply to Harris before he communi-

23. SP 91/104, Paper B, undated, but by inference of 30 December 1779, enclosed in No. 11 of 15/26 February 1780.

24. See e.g. Bancroft-Circourt, 3, 231, Goertz to Frederick, 20/31 December 1779.

25. SP 91/104, Harris to Stormont, No. 11, 15/26 February 1780. The Harris Papers include a rough draft of one of these notes which gives a good idea of the terms on which Harris stood with Potemkin: "Mon Prince, Me sentant toujours trop faible pour sortir je me vois obligé de me servir de cette voye pour souhaiter à Votre Altesse les Bonnes Fêtes. N'aient jusqu'à présent aucune réponse à la note que j'ai donné à Monsieur le Comte de Panin j'ose me flatter mon Prince que votre crédit nous obtiendra à la fin une plus favorable que celle que vous m'avez dit que ce ministre avoit eu ordre de me remettre: La Russie peut tout; Votre Altesse peut tout en Russie; le sort de l'Angleterre, peut-être celui de l'Europe depends de vous; si vous employez Mon Prince, la grande considération dont vous jouissez auprès de votre souveraine à la déterminer [a few words crossed out] à une démarche si conforme à ses sentiments à ses interêts mêmes, la reconnoissance que vous (obtenez) dans le moment ne scaura être égale que la gloire que (l'avenir) vous sera reservé dans l'avenir." (Dated 25 December 1779, presumably O.S.)

cated it to the British envoy.[26] The illness of Harris himself prevented any communication between him and Panin for some three weeks. It was not until 20 January 1780 that their decisive interview took place, and Panin read to Harris the Empress's reply to the British request for an alliance:

> L'impératrice aime la paix [ran the Empress's answer] . . .
> Sa Majesté Impériale se tient convaincue que les démarches
> que la cour de Londres lui propose pour l'accélerer, produiront, à coup sûr un effet tout à fait contraire, vû, qu'une proposition de paix, ou une médiation offerte, sans aucune condition conciliante, mais appuyée, au contraire, de démonstrations, doivent nécéssairement produire un effet directement opposé au sentimens de l'Impératrice pour le Roi et sa nation, et ne sauroit manquer de provoquer les ennemis de la Grande Bretagne à une extension indéterminée de la guerre, en y enveloppant tout le continent de l'Europe.

The proper time to conclude alliances, added the Empress, was not in the middle of a war, and particularly a war the cause of which had never been regarded as a *casus foederis* in previous Anglo-Russian alliances, since it arose outside the European possessions of the two parties. In her final paragraph the Empress again hinted at her desire to be entrusted with the task of mediating between the belligerents.[27]

Harris did not accept this reply from Panin without some endeavour to argue on its assumptions. He drew a comparison with the Empress's intervention in the War of the Bavarian Succession, and turning Catherine's own words against her he called it "une médiation offerte sans aucune condition conciliante mais appuyée au contraire de démonstrations." But Panin refused to be drawn into argument. He dwelt instead on the Empress's earnest desire to reconcile the belligerents and entreated Harris to "furnish the

26. Bancroft-Circourt, *3*, 231, Goertz to Frederick, 20/31 December 1779: Panin read the reply "telle qu'il la remettra, laquelle il lui aurait déjà remise si ce ministre d'Angleterre n'avait pris la jaunisse."

27. SP 91/104, Paper C, enclosed in No. 11, Harris to Stormont, 15/26 February 1780, *MD, 1,* 280. Panin had stressed that the Russian reply was in the Empress's own words. But he told Goertz that he had dictated it himself (*PKFG, 44,* 1, Goertz to Frederick, 17 December 1779).

Empress with materials, which would justify her interference between us and our enemies." [28] Panin could afford to rest content
with his victory, and indeed Goertz doubted that "à moins de grands
évènements ce ministre revienne encore à vouloir mettre sur le
tapis une pareille négociation." [29]

Harris however still did not think that all was lost and did not
yet write to Stormont. Illness now struck down Potemkin, who was
unable to receive Harris until 29 January 1780. The bed-ridden
Prince immediately confirmed Harris even further in his view that
there was a fundamental difference of outlook between the Empress and Panin. He read the official reply which Panin had dictated
to Harris (and which one can fairly assume he had already seen)
and declared: "Such will ever be the language of indolent and
torpid ministers; cold professions, false logick and narrow views.
I can assure you . . . the Empress's feelings are very ill represented, and I recognise in this abstract nothing she would own
but the last paragraph. It is true, from a timidity contrary to her
general character, and arising from the impulse of the day, she
refuses your propositions; but she never meant to do it in a cold
style, and you must consider what you have shown me are produc-
tions of Count Panin pour le decorum seulement." [30]

In spite of Potemkin's assurances, Harris was bound to take
Panin's reply as official and to forward it as such to his court. Yet
Potemkin's words encouraged him to take up again the alternative
policy of an armed mediation by Russia without an alliance. Aware
that fear of being drawn into the war was the main deterrent preventing Catherine from "standing forth," he totally reversed the
picture of the relative situations of Britain and the Bourbon powers
that he had previously painted. It is a tribute to his versatility that
he was able to produce equally ingenious arguments in defence of
France's weakness as he had previously used to convince Catherine
of France's strength. Instead of dwelling on Britain's isolation and
inability to stand up to the united Bourbon powers, he now urged
that Britain had repulsed her two enemies so effectively as to make

28. SP 91/104, Harris to Stormont, No. 11, 15/26 February 1780.
29. Bancroft-Circourt, 3, 232, Goertz to Frederick, 27 December 1779/7 January
1780.
30. SP 91/104, Harris to Stormont, No. 11, 15/26 February 1780.

them doubt their own security when Britain went over to the offensive. Britain had won the last two campaigns; [31] France and Spain must dread a third. In such circumstances the end of the war depended on Catherine's intervention: "by refusing it . . . she becomes, in a manner, responsible for the disorder which the continuation of the war might produce in the general system, since every impartial thinking mind must allow, that an immediate cessation, not a prolongation, of hostilities must necessarily follow so powerful an interposition." He therefore suggested to Potemkin that if Catherine really dreaded drawing the sword, it would be very easy to "find terms for a declaration, which would impress very sufficiently the mind of our enemies with Her Imperial Majesty's sentiments, without committing her dignity, and without engaging her to take an active part in our quarrel." [32]

Potemkin appeared to think it worth-while to present to the Empress Harris's new arguments in favour of a declaration to France and Spain and asked him to incorporate them in a memorial which he could use to rekindle her ambition and her inclination for England. Harris immediately complied and now depicted France as "plus ou moins degoûtée de la guerre." It was France who threatened to spread the conflict, for if she failed she would endeavour to embroil the whole of Europe.[33] As a final proof of the fate in store for Europe if Bourbon supremacy were ever achieved, he adduced the recent detention by Spain of a number of neutral ships suspected of attempting to run the blockade of Gibraltar. The whole question of the treatment of neutral ships was a delicate one for a British envoy to raise in Russia, but Potemkin's reaction when he read Harris's memorial must have seemed to justify the latter. "Par Dieu, vous la tenez," exclaimed the Prince, "the Empress ab-

31. Since France entered the war the situation was roughly as follows: Britain had improved her situation slightly in America and had won in India. France had on balance been successful in the West Indies; the Franco-Spanish fleet had failed to invade Britain, an attack on Jersey had been beaten off, and Rodney had captured a Spanish convoy, defeated the Spanish admiral Juan de Lángara off Cape St. Vincent, and relieved Gibraltar.

32. SP 91/104, Harris to Stormont, No. 11, 15/26 February 1780.

33. SP 91/104, Paper D, enclosed in No. 11 of 15/26 February 1780. Undated, but by inference of 30 January 1780.

horrs the Inquisition, and never will suffer its precepts to be exercised on the seas. If what you advance is confirmed by our letters from Spain, you may depend on it, we shall be no longer inactive." [34]

But the negotiation was now at an end. Catherine was beginning to harbour other plans. Harris's last memorial only served in a manner to return the ball to the Russian court by leaving Catherine under the impression that in spite of her present refusal England still relied on Russian friendship and goodwill.

Tribute must be paid to the energy with which Harris pursued his aims. He was undoubtedly led by Potemkin to think even in September 1779 that a formal proposal of alliance stood more chance than it did. His own mistake lay in interpreting Catherine's general expressions of goodwill towards the British people as a desire for a closer political connexion between the two courts. His misfortune lay in accepting Potemkin's explanations of Catherine's behaviour and his advice on how to proceed. The fate of George III's letter to Catherine shows to what extent Harris was misled in supposing that a personal appeal to her vanity could move her. To begin with it played no part in the negotiation at all. Though, according to Harris, Potemkin often asked for it, Harris does not seem to have thought that an opportune moment for its delivery arose during the course of the negotiations. He did not surrender to Potemkin's importunities until some time after he had received his final and negative reply at the end of January. Shortly afterwards, on 14 February, Harris was present at a small private supper party attended by the Empress. Catherine took him aside and spoke to him in the most cordial manner: *"Vous m'avez donné des insomnies,"* she declared. "The several papers you have given in to Prince Potemkin . . . have made me revolve in my mind every kind of means by which I could assist you. I would do everything to serve you, except involving myself in the war." When Harris endeavoured to argue with her, Catherine silenced him with the remark: "Je sais déjà tout ce que vous pouvez me dire; cela a déjà fait assez d'impression sur moi, *si j'étois plus jeune, je serois peut-être moins sage."* And she indicated to Harris that she would reply

34. SP 91/104, No. 11, 15/26 February (*MD, 1,* 270).

shortly to the King's letter offering her services to reconcile the belligerents.[35] Indeed, the very next day Catherine's reply was handed by Potemkin to Harris. In it she stressed again her desire for peace and her willingness to mediate. "Mes vues ont toujours été pacifiques," wrote the Empress. "Depuis peu seulement sortie d'un état de guerre pénible malgrès les succès, à peine la Russie goûte-t-elle encore les douceurs de la paix . . ." Catherine then went on to suggest that Britain's enemies: "souhaitent autant qu'elle même le retour de la pacification. Si j'y puis contribuer," she added, "ou lui être utile, je la prie d'être intimement persuadé que personne ne s'y employera avec plus d'empressement que . . . Caterine." [36] Neither the King's letter, therefore, nor Stormont's tribute of flattery to Potemkin served any noticeable purpose.

It appears in fact that Catherine's mind was made up almost at once to refuse the offer of alliance. She saw, as Panin had seen, that the implicit purpose of the alliance was to draw her into the war. In no other way could the Russian fleet be made available for Britain, and that was the primary purpose of effecting the alliance at all. Throughout the month of December rumours flew about St. Petersburg, but long before Harris received his final reply, Frederick II, Vergennes, and even Joseph and Maria Theresa had been set at ease as to Russia's intentions.[37] Harris was the last to know, and the various delays caused by the illness of all the participants only served to prolong the agony.

Harris's vigorous offensive on Britain's behalf was not however without its consequences at the Russian court. The pro-Prussian party was up in arms against him, and even the Grand Duke "ne cache pas son mécontentement de ses menées." [38] Panin, whose relations with Harris had been steadily deteriorating throughout 1779, now really became the bitter enemy Harris had long believed him

35. SP 91/104, Harris to Stormont, No. 13, 15/26 February 1780. (*MD, 1,* 282)

36. SP 91/104, enclosure in Harris to Stormont, No. 13, 15/26 February 1780, dated 3 February (O.S.) and said to be written in Catherine's own hand.

37. See above, note 26; on 17 December 1779 Corberon told Vergennes of an interview with Panin in which the Russian minister had declared that the Empress would follow his advice (CP Russie, *103,* No. 57). See also Wiener Staatsarchiv, Seddeler (Austrian chargé d'affaires) to Kaunitz, 14 January 1780. Harris, it will be remembered, was only given his reply on 20 January 1780.

38. Bancroft-Circourt, *3,* 232, Goertz to Frederick, 27 December 1779/7 January 1780.

to be. He was led to the extreme length of betraying the Empress
by revealing all Harris's *démarches* to Goertz. His motives were
probably mixed as in most human activity. He may genuinely have
feared for Russia if she became involved in the maritime war, the
policy which he believed Potemkin to be advocating. Entangled
with his fears however was his fierce hatred for the Prince and the
bitter prospect of his own loss of influence and the decline of that
of Prussia. His own waning importance was a deep humiliation,
particularly as he saw that he might even lose control of relations
with Prussia, the bulwark of his position. He had already advised
Goertz to cultivate Potemkin—as things were he would not take
offence—in connexion with Frederick's plan for a convention com-
plementing the existing treaty between Russia and Prussia.[39] He
probably did not yet realize the extent to which Frederick and
Goertz regarded him at this time as a broken reed. The news of
Britain's offer of alliance had horrified Frederick, and he had
blamed Goertz for having failed to win over Potemkin. The appointment to Russia in the autumn of a new Austrian ambassador,
Count Ludwig Cobenzl, whom Frederick believed to be pro-British,
had already considerably alarmed him. An alliance between Russia
and Britain would, he thought, open the door to an Austro-Russian
entente. A great sigh of relief went up from Potsdam at the news
of Harris's failure, but the conclusion Frederick drew from these
events was that Goertz must devote himself to cultivating Potemkin,
the "maitre ressort de toute la machine," and, taking a leaf out of
Harris's book, Frederick authorized Goertz to write "panegyricks"
of the Prince, even in his *billets* to his friends in St. Petersburg.[40]
A somewhat piquant correspondence followed between the King
and the envoy on the best manner of winning the unpredictable
favourite. Both agreed that it would be unwise for Goertz "de
s'abandonner à lui seul en lui faisant bassement la cour" (probably

39. *PKFG, 43,* 443, Goertz to Frederick, 7 December 1779. Frederick had thought
up this convention, based on a reciprocal guarantee of Russian and Prussian territory when the Empress refused the triple alliance with the Porte (See ibid., 334,
Frederick to Goertz, 26 October 1779, and passim).

40. *PKFG, 43,* 444, Frederick to Goertz, 21 December 1779; p. 451, 25 December
1779. Frederick's instructions were in part no doubt due to the fact that Panin
was gravely ill, and in the event of his death it was rumoured that Potemkin
might succeed to his influence, if not to his post, in foreign affairs.

a malicious reference to Harris's performance); and the parsimonious Frederick was probably relieved to hear that bribing the Prince's hangers-on would be a waste of money as they exercised no influence over his mind. To win the Prince's confidence, Goertz would have to cultivate his tastes, but unfortunately, as he explained to Frederick, "sa grande passion c'est le grec et les rites d'église. Malheureusement, j'ignore le premier et suis encore plus neuf dans les cérémonies religieuses." Frederick the rationalist expressed surprise that such interests should have survived years of imperial favour at the Russian court. But, he told Goertz, "quel qu'il soit, il ne faut pas s'y arrêter; la prudence vent qu'on prenne les hommes tels qu'on les trouve . . ." [41] Neither Greek syntax nor church ceremonial were therefore to be neglected by the Prussian envoy in his efforts to win the confidence of the Prince. Frederick II was always a hard taskmaster.

In obedience to his sovereign's instructions, and with the tacit permission of Panin, Goertz did approach Potemkin on the subject of the proposed convention. This interview, which took place on 24 December 1779, when the Prince was apparently occupied in furthering Harris's plans, is extremely revealing of the technique of the favourite in his relations with foreign diplomats. The same scene might have been enacted with Harris. The Prince skilfully placed the blame on Panin and his underlings for the lack of success Goertz had met with in securing Prussian objects; he convinced Goertz, and through him Frederick II, that he and the Empress approved of Frederick's proposed convention and that Panin, out of laziness, had allowed the matter to slide. He succeeded too in implanting in the mind of the Prussian envoy his favourite notion that the Empress and Panin did not see eye to eye.[42] Though Goertz and his master never quite felt that confidence in Potemkin which they justifiably had in Panin, on the whole and for the time being they trusted his assertions of friendship. And Potemkin won a further round in his struggle with Panin, who now ceased to be the sole minister with whom Goertz communicated.

41. *PKFG, 44,* 35, Goertz to Frederick, 4 January 1780; Frederick to Goertz, 18 January 1780; p. 43, Goertz to Frederick, 7 January 1780; Frederick to Goertz, 22 January 1780.

42. *PKFG, 44,* 13, Goertz to Frederick, 24 December 1779; p. 14, Frederick to Goertz, 8 January 1780.

Bearing in mind this evidence of Potemkin's methods, it is plain that his support of Harris was more apparent than real. In part he was doubtless guided by the desire to show the Empress that Panin had forfeited the confidence of Britain and was thus unfit for his post. But there is another aspect to Potemkin which one can never ignore. More than any mortal he enjoyed the full confidence of Catherine, and this warrants the assumption that, in his many conferences with Harris, Potemkin was to some extent acting in a manner preconcerted with his Imperial mistress. Catherine and Potemkin represented the friends of Britain while Panin was left the ungracious role of the obstructor.[43] Not only did the Empress promise to distribute a thousand roubles to the poor of St. Petersburg should Rodney defeat the Spanish fleet; she openly rejoiced at the news of the victory of the English Admiral off Cape St. Vincent and told Harris, at a ball at which they were both present, that it was given in his and Rodney's honour.[44] How could Harris suspect that not long before the Empress had asked Goertz "d'un ton ironique si je ne savais pas ce qui pouvait avoir donné la jaunisse au sieur Harris, s'il avait eu lieu de se fâcher, et s'il était si colère?" [45] The duplicity of the Russian court was beyond Harris's penetration.[46] Potemkin encouraged him far too openly; Panin violently opposed him and betrayed him to Prussia and to France. But Catherine's own manner and the Prince's real personal liking for Harris served to keep hope alive in Britain; it ensured that Russia would continue to be wooed even if she were never won.

43. This was notably the opinion of Vergennes. "Il y a peut-être," he wrote to Corberon on 30 January 1780, "dans la manière dont M. le Pce Potemkin se conduit vis-à-vis de M. Harris plus d'adresse que de penchant pour l'Angleterre. Je ne serois pas étonné que ce ne fut par sistème que tandis que M. le cte Panin est ouvertement pour la paix le favory se montre moins éloigné de la guerre et que l'impce placée entre ces deux personnages ne dirigeât leurs mouvements pour être mieux instruite et se ménager les moyens d'être tôt ou tard chargée de la médiation." And he added a warning which might well have applied to Harris: "Au reste, M. c'est aux actes qu'on doit se rapporter pour juger les dispositions de Catherine II" (CP Russie, *104*, No. 2).

44. SP 91/104, Harris to Stormont, No. 13, 2/13 February 1780 (*MD, 1*, 282); No. 17, 21 February/3 March 1780 (*MD, 1*, 283).

45. Bancroft-Circourt, *3*, 232, Goertz to Frederick, 7 January 1780 (not quoted in *PKFG*).

46. SP 91/104, Harris to Stormont, No. 17, 21 February/3 March 1780 (*MD, 1*, 283).

6. The League of Armed Neutrality (1)

WHEN THE Empress Catherine refused Britain's offer of alliance in January 1780 and turned down the proposal to appear as an armed mediator on Britain's behalf, she was already tentatively feeling her way towards a fresh departure in Russian foreign policy. No very clear pattern emerges from the available documents, for Catherine was above all a brilliant opportunist. But an analysis of developments in two fields—the efforts of Russia to be invited to mediate between Britain and the Bourbons and the treatment of neutral trade by the belligerents—enables one to determine the elements from which Catherine eventually constructed the most notable improvisation of the war, namely the League of Armed Neutrality.

Ever since May 1779, Panin had been pressing on Harris and Corberon the Russian desire to be entrusted with a mediation between Britain and the Bourbons. Absorbed in their hopes and plans for a Russian alliance or an armed mediation, Harris and Stormont (and Weymouth before him) had tended to ignore these overtures. The more skilful Vergennes, though he felt no enthusiasm for the Russian offers, was quite willing to keep the Empress out of mischief by carrying on desultory discussions.[1] Accordingly the subject had been debated at intervals throughout the spring and summer of 1779 by Panin and Corberon, and Panin informed the French chargé d'affaires that a similar overture had been made to Britain, who had deigned to make no answer. Indeed Corberon, who favoured a Russian mediation, was sufficiently impressed to

1. See Vergennes to Montmorin, 21 September 1779: both Catherine and Maria Theresa "ont l'ambition de la médiation, il faut les amuser le plus longtemps possible avec ce hochet, sans cependant le leur abandonner entièrement" (quoted in Doniol, *Histoire, 4*, 432–33). Cf. CP Russie, *103*, Vergennes to Corberon, No. 22, 9 September; No. 34, 4 December 1779.

warn Vergennes at the end of October 1779 that Catherine thought of nothing but of becoming mediator, or rather "arbiter," in the conflict between Britain and the Bourbons.[2] Potemkin too assured Corberon of Russian willingness to mediate and expressed astonishment to the young Frenchman that Britain had ignored the Russian offers.[3]

Harris's renewal in December of the British proposals for an alliance had enabled Catherine and Panin to press once again Russian claims to be entrusted with restoring peace between Britain and the Bourbons. These same proposals were used by Panin to bring further pressure to bear on France to accept Russian mediation. Without as yet betraying the details of the British offer, Panin on 10 December 1779 warned Corberon that the best way of foiling all British intrigues was to make peace. Corberon took the warning sufficiently seriously to propose to Vergennes that some overture should be made to Russia by France. The Empress, he wrote, was so "romanesque" that she might easily be induced to "faire une démarche pareille à celle qui eût lieu de sa part à la cour de Vienne"—a policy of which the dangers for France were only too evident. Corberon had no concrete information at this stage of what Harris was proposing to Russia, and his reference to a possible Russian armed mediation evidently reflects the use Panin had made of the proposals put forward by Harris.[4]

Potemkin also sent for Corberon in mid-December. At a time when he was believed by Harris to be persuading the Empress to accept Britain's proposals, he was also stressing to Corberon that Britain urgently desired peace: it was unfortunate, the Prince explained, that France did not. Now was the time when both powers should "songer à s'accomoder," he declared to Corberon.[5] This conversation, when repeated by Corberon to Panin, so infuriated the Russian minister that he broke the faith he owed to Harris and revealed to Corberon the full nature of Britain's proposals as he interpreted them. Britain did not want peace, said Panin, and had on the contrary attempted to engage Russia to

2. CP Russie, *103*, Corberon to Vergennes, No. 48, 26 October 1779.
3. CP Russie, *103*, Corberon to Vergennes, No. 49, 2 November 1779.
4. CP Russie, *103*, Corberon to Vergennes, No. 56, 10 December 1779.
5. CP Russie, *103*, Corberon to Vergennes, No. 57, 17 December 1779.

enter the war. The Empress had refused to entertain such extravagant ideas, but, Panin urged again, France should submit her conditions for peace. Once Britain too had been asked for her peace terms, she would no longer have a pretext to request help from Russia.[6]

That the Empress really wished to achieve the position of mediator between Britain and France is confirmed by the attitude of Potemkin to Corberon. In January 1780 Panin caused inquiries to be made of the Dutch resident regarding the armistice of 1609 between Spain and the seven United Provinces—seeing in the Dutch revolt a precedent for the revolt of the thirteen colonies.[7] But that Panin was carrying on his policy without communicating fully with Catherine is suggested by his request to Corberon, early in February 1780, not to discuss the mediation with anyone, not even the vice-chancellor, Osterman. He, Panin, would not, he said, even mention the subject as yet to the Empress.[8] Indeed, peculiar conditions prevailed at that time in the Russian court. Panin had not seen the Empress throughout January and February, whether because of his illness or that of Lanskoy, and relations between the sovereign and her minister had been exacerbated by a tactless reference in a German newspaper to the influence Panin exercised over the Empress.[9]

Meanwhile, during the spring and summer of 1779 the war at sea had continued to rumble in the background. Increasing pres-

6. These Russian overtures were also discussed at the time by Vergennes with Spain. (See CP Russie, *103*, Corberon to Vergennes, No. 57, 17 December 1779; *104*, Vergennes to Corberon, No. 1, 13 January 1780; No. 2, 30 January 1780.) See later, Ch. 9, p. 223.

7. Wiener Staatsarchiv, Seddeler to Kaunitz, 14 January 1780; this idea was suggested by Vergennes (CP Russie, *103*, Vergennes to Corberon, No. 34, 4 December 1779); Panin had already asked Corberon for details of the Spanish proposal of October 1778 (Ibid., *103*, Corberon to Vergennes, No. 31, 6 August 1779).

8. CP Russie, *104*, Corberon to Vergennes, No. 7, 12 February 1780.

9. The *Courier du Bas Rhin* contained a report that Russia had been about to help Britain with 60,000 troops, but that Panin had written such an impressive memorandum opposing this policy that he had persuaded the Empress and her Council to remain neutral. This report irritated the Empress when she saw it, and Panin who suffered under her displeasure put it about that Harris had been responsible for sending the information to the gazette. (CP Russie, *104*, Corberon to Vergennes, No. 12, 29 February 1780; PKFG, *44*, 102, Goertz to Frederick, 15 February 1780).

sure was being put by both belligerents on the neutrals. On 1 March 1779 France had suspended the favourable *règlement* of July 1778, and Dutch shipping was no longer able to carry enemy goods without fear of capture and condemnation. But in order to keep agitation in the Dutch Republic alive, and probably also in order to ensure the continuation of supplies to France, the towns of Amsterdam and Haarlem were exempted from this suspension, and their ships were treated as though the *règlement* of 1778 was still valid.[10] The special treatment accorded to Amsterdam had its effect on the other Dutch ports, and pressure in favour of granting convoys to all ships, even those carrying naval stores, increased. In April 1779, Britain announced that all vessels carrying naval stores would be detained even if sailing in convoy.[11] The intervention of Spain in the war gave Britain a fresh pretext to demand from the Dutch either the succours provided for in the treaty of 1678 or the surrender of their naval privileges. On 22 July 1779, Yorke presented to the States General a formal demand for the recognition of the *casus foederis* of the alliance.[12] Throughout the summer the Dutch dawdled and delayed without taking any decision. Active French diplomacy finally gave the victory to the Patriot party, and on 8 November 1779 the States General agreed that two merchant fleets should sail under convoy; ships carrying hemp, iron, pitch, or tar would enjoy protection, but not ships carrying timber.[13]

Denmark too had taken the opportunity offered by Britain's need to press for a more favourable treatment of Danish shipping. The British overture for a loan of Danish ships in March 1779

10. See Fauchille, *La diplomatie française*, Ch. 4, Sections i and ii, and Edler, *The Dutch Republic and the American Revolution*, pp. 120 ff. for Anglo-Dutch relations at this period.

11. C. de Martens, *Nouvelles causes célèbres du droit des gens, I*, 149, Yorke to the States General, 9 April 1779.

12. *Annual Register*, 1779, p. 428. Britain did not actually want Dutch assistance, but now that Spain had attacked her she could use the demand for the *casus foederis* of the treaty of 1678 as a means of forcing the Dutch to give way on "free ships, free goods." See notably Yorke to Harris, 18 September 1779: "when I demanded the succours which I neither wanted nor wish'd, I only meant to embarrass our enemies and to stop the career of their intrigues. This to a certain degree has been achieved for hitherto no convoy has ventured to stir." (Harris Papers).

13. See Fauchille, *La diplomatie française*, pp. 175–76; Edler, *The Dutch Republic and the American Revolution*, pp. 129–30.

opened the door to an endless series of arguments between the new British envoy, Morton Eden, and Bernstorff over the detention by Britain of Danish ships and the steadfast British refusal to define contraband.[14] The entrance of Spain into the war only made Bernstorff insist still more strongly on securing for Denmark at least that advantage which he claimed was hers by treaty, namely the right to carry salted provisions, the produce of Denmark, to enemy countries. On 20 July 1779 the Danish envoy presented a memorial to Weymouth, demanding the application of the Anglo-Danish treaty of 1670 to the Danish prizes in British ports, and raised the question of the freedom of salted provisions.[15] On the advice of Sir James Marriott,[16] Weymouth still insisted that according to ancient custom provisions were contraband, but he gave in to the extent of declaring that in future privateers would not seize Danish ships so laden. But Bernstorff was not seeking such a backdoor concession; he wanted the principle of the non-contraband nature of one of Denmark's principal exports to be proclaimed publicly, preferably by an admiralty court decision. In the fond hope that an alliance with Denmark might still be achieved, Weymouth was driven in August 1779 to propose negotiating such alterations to the Anglo-Danish treaty of 1670 as might be "regarded as mutually beneficial," but Eden found the atmosphere so inauspicious that he warned Weymouth against entertaining any hopes of naval assistance from Denmark.[17] More-

---

14. SP 75/135, Eden to Weymouth, No. 5, 15 April 1779; No. 13, 1 June 1779; No. 22, 27 July 1779 etc.

15. SP 75/135, Dreyer to Weymouth, 20 July 1779.

16. The advice of Sir James Marriott is worth quoting because it reveals the attitude of mind of the admiralty judge; "Why are problematical questions to be kept up for ye sake of what is called *sporting* a cause" wrote Marriott to Weymouth. "The present relative position of all ye maritime powers in Europe is such, and the *possible* questions of ye law of nations are so refined, and capable of multiplication ad infinitum that it is ye wisdom of every government to keep as many questions of this sort at rest as possible; but if any unhappy misunderstanding or spirit should raise them: there can be but one plain rule to decide them
Salus suprema lex."
However justifiable Marriott's stand in Britain's emergency it was not an argument likely to convince Bernstorff. See SP 75/135, Marriott to Weymouth, 29 July 1779; Weymouth to Dreyer, 5 August 1779.

17. SP 75/135, Weymouth to Eden, No. 13, 27 August 1779; Eden to Weymouth, No. 29, 11 September 1779, and particularly No. 34, 9 October 1779.

over, acting in the spirit of the Russo-Danish treaty of alliance and of the more recent exchange of views between Russia and Denmark and the decision to patrol the North Sea, Bernstorff did not hesitate to seek the diplomatic support of Russia in his quarrel with Britain.[18]

But Britain was by no means the only offender. The Spanish instruction of 1 July 1779 on the conduct of the war at sea was harsher towards neutral trade than that of Britain. It proclaimed the doctrine of "enemy ships, enemy goods," thus rendering neutral goods on board an enemy ship liable to condemnation; and in addition it declared good prize enemy goods on board a neutral. The definition of contraband was very wide, and it included naval stores. Moreover Spain had declared a blockade of Gibraltar, thus opening the way to a constant series of bickerings with the neutral trading powers.[19] Any ship sailing a little too near the middle of the Straits was immediately suspected of blockade running with the prospect of obtaining a very good price for the cargo. Spanish suspicions were more often justified than was ever admitted by the neutral traders,[20] but there is no doubt that Spanish procedure was harsh and arbitrary. Danish and Dutch protests led Vergennes to fear that all his careful nursing of neutral trade would be wasted.

After the institution in spring 1779 of the Russian naval patrol of the North Sea, which had proved from Britain's point of view so innocuous, Harris had eventually come to think that "this court will not give us any very serious trouble on these subjects." [21] He was unduly optimistic. In the ensuing months the Russian at-

18. Dreyer was active in working up the Russian envoy in London, Musin Pushkin, who presumably reported adversely to Panin on the working of the admiralty courts. Weymouth sent copies of Dreyer's memorials and of his replies to Harris so that he could counter Danish complaints in Russia. (See SP 91/103, Weymouth to Harris, No. 22, 6 August 1779; cf. also Aleksandrenko, *Diplomaticheskiye agenty*, 2, 195, instructions to I. M. Simolin, July 1779).

19. Danvila, *Historia, 5,* 82, ordonnance of 1 July 1779 and circular issued on 10 July 1779.

20. At the request of General Eliott, the governor of Gibraltar, Yorke endeavoured to enlist the help of Dutch ship-owners in running the blockade. (SP 84/566, Yorke to Weymouth, No. 81, 24 September 1779). The Spanish in turn complained to the Dutch that their ships carried double passports and hid British goods from Spanish privateers, while revealing Spanish goods to British privateers.

21. SP 91/103, Harris to Weymouth, No. 32, 23 May/3 June 1779.

titude towards British seizures at sea sharpened perceptively. Unfortunately the subject was not confined to sterile arguments on abstract principles between Panin and Harris. For at the request of Denmark, Panin severely criticized British condemnation of salted provisions on board Danish ships.[22] "I am sorry to say," wrote Harris, "that the Russian Minister's ears are always more open to these kinds of complaints, than to any assurances I can make him on the legality of our conduct and uprightness of our intentions relative to neutral ships." But again Harris made the mistake of assuming that Panin was acting not on the Empress's instructions in passing on these complaints but on those of Frederick II [23] —a quite unwarrantable assumption. As the summer advanced the arguments between Harris and Panin became ever more acrimonious. "I can gain no point in talking to Count Panin on the subject of neutral ships," wrote Harris on 28 August/8 September 1779. "Ignorant to a degree of all commercial matters, and partial to every argument which militates against us, I neither can persuade or convince him, that we are regulated in our present conduct by as much equity as the situation of a nation in war will admit of." Panin, who stood on the comfortable ground of the sanctity of treaties, blamed England without reserve and accused her of treating her friends with "levity, indifference and harshness." He took credit to himself for having restrained Denmark from instituting convoys when Sweden had done so, but he would "no longer attempt to influence them on this point, unless we became more moderate towards their ships." Harris replied with gusto that Britain relied on her national character, and those who thought the moment of danger was the time to wrest from her privileges she had long enjoyed "knew but little of the spirit and genius of the English nation." [24] Such arguments were not likely to incline Panin to look favourably on an alliance with England.

From the moment the war spread to European waters the Empress had shown an active interest in the protection of trade with Russia. At the same time as she instituted the naval patrol of the coasts, in March 1779, the first complaint against the detention by

22. SP 91/103, Harris to Weymouth, No. 37, 2 July 1779.
23. SP 91/103, Harris to Weymouth, No. 49, 9/20 August 1779.
24. SP 91/103, Harris to Weymouth, No. 53, 28 August/8 September 1779.

Britain of Russian property on board a Dutch ship was delivered to Harris. The *Henrietta and Johanna,* chartered by two Russian merchants of Vyborg and loaded on their account with timber, pitch, and iron bars for Bordeaux and Cádiz, had been held at Yarmouth. The owners had appealed to the Empress who found their complaint justified under the Anglo-Russian treaty.[25] A further protest was delivered to Weymouth by the Russian envoy in London on 30 September 1779 against the forced sale of the cargo of the Russian ship, *Jonge Prins* of Riga, which had been detained in 1778.[26] Immersed as they were in the major problems of the war, the interruption of the trifling Russian trade did not detain the attention of either Weymouth or Stormont for very long. Harris was instructed on 5 November 1779 to reply directly to Panin and to explain that the cargo had been sold to the Navy Board, who were authorized to pay freight, expenses, and the price of the cargo to anyone legally authorized to receive the money.[27] Meanwhile the Russian merchants of Riga submitted a memorial for the Empress to the president of the Russian college of commerce complaining of the treatment meted out by Britain to Russian ships.[28] With his usual resourcefulness, Harris obtained a copy of the memorial which he annotated in the margin with

25. SP 91/103, Harris to Suffolk, No. 18, 8/19 March 1779. The *Henrietta and Johanna* had called at Yarmouth for water and, according to a note handed by Panin to Harris, had been detained on the frivolous pretext that the cargo was on French account. The British version of this incident was that the master was one Blakey, a British subject; the ship was "principally his"; the oath by which he had acquired a Dutch pass was probably fraudulent, and the ship made out for Cádiz "in order to cheat the cruizers" (Spain was not yet at war). The divergence of opinion on matters of fact is typical of the problems raised by the seizure of neutral ships (SP 91/103, Weymouth to Harris, No. 11, 20 April 1779; Note of 19 April 1779 from Philip Crespigny, Doctors' Commons, to Weymouth).

26. SP 91/103, Musin Pushkin to Weymouth, 30 September 1779. The ship had been released in February 1779, with freight and costs, on condition the cargo was sold to the Navy Board in accordance with the British declaration of October 1778. The Russian memorial complained of the delay in giving judgement and alleged that the cargo was sold at less than the market price, a loss which should not be inflicted on the Russian owners.

27. SP 91/103, Stormont to Harris, enclosure with No. 40, 5 November 1779.

28. A copy of the memorial is enclosed in SP 91/103, Harris to Weymouth, No. 60, 17/28 September 1779. It dealt with the *Jonge Prins* and complained that the ship had been so badly cared for it had to be sold in Holland, that the owners had been made to pay costs, and that they had had to sue the privateer which took it.

copious extracts from Blackstone's *Commentaries on the Laws of England* "as the Empress studies Blackstone constantly"; he then forwarded this document through Potemkin to the Empress, and through the favourite he heard that the Empress had refused to take the matter seriously. But he feared that since Count Panin "is continually talking to her of our arrogance at sea," Catherine would be both hurt and displeased should any interruption of the Russian trade occur. For the first time, though not the last, Harris proposed to the Secretary of State that in view of the trifling nature of the Russian trade British warships should let Russian ships pass unmolested, but at the time he drew no reply.[29] In spite of Potemkin's assurances that the Empress attached but little importance to the matter, Catherine reacted energetically in defence of her trade. On 8/19 November 1779 a rescript was dispatched by courier to the new Russian envoy in London, I. M. Simolin. In her instructions, the Empress expressed no surprise at the "insolence," "insubordination," and "cupidity" of the English privateers; the main burden of her complaint was directed at the slowness of the admiralty courts in redressing the injuries to the Russian flag. "We do not believe however," she wrote, "that this partial behaviour of the British courts is the result of orders given to them by the government," and in that hope she ordered Simolin to make strong representations in favour of her merchants.[30]

Simolin, who had arrived in London on 10 October 1779, had previously occupied the post of envoy at the Swedish court and had been a dependent of Panin. He had now transferred his allegiance to Potemkin, and his appointment was welcomed by Harris. He showed far greater capacity than Musin Pushkin and was if anything more favourably inclined to Britain than to France.[31]

29. SP 91/103, Harris to Weymouth, No. 60, 17/28 September 1779.

30. Aleksandrenko, *Russkiye diplomaticheskiye agenty*, 2, 200, Rescript to Simolin, 8/19 November 1779. It is possible that the protest was originally to be made through Harris: see *Morskoy Sbornik*, *43* (September 1859), p. 78, No. 15, Projet d'une note pour M. Harris, 6/17 November 1779. There is no record of this note having been delivered to Harris.

31. SP 91/103, Harris to Weymouth, No. 59, 9/20 September 1779 (*MD, 1,* 260): "Mr. Simolin's dispatches are superior to those of his predecessors; they are more intelligible, more accurate and infinitely more impartial" (SP 91/103, Harris to Stormont, No. 75, 20 November/1 December 1779).

In accordance with his instructions on 17 December 1779 he complained to Stormont that Russian ships, laden with "marchandises non prohibées" had been taken into British ports "contre les engagemens d'un traité solennel" and demanded in the name of the Empress prompt and complete satisfaction for the owners; punishment of the privateers who had illegally laid hands on the Russian flag and on Russian property; the speeding up of court procedure; and finally orders to be given to the Royal Navy and to privateers not to "arrêter la navigation et le commerce des sujets de l'Impératrice soit dans leurs propres vaisseaux, soit dans les bâtimens neutres." He concluded with the hope that Stormont would procure him a satisfactory answer and that the King would issue fresh orders to the Navy and to privateers "de se conduire dorénavant à l'égard des bâtimens russes et autres neutres, chargés de propriétés russes, suivant les principes et la lettre des engagemens, qui subsistent entre les deux nations." [32] Stormont, in the belief that Harris had already cleared up the matter with Panin in response to the memorial delivered on 30 September by Musin Pushkin, did not take much trouble over his reply. On 19 December 1779 he saw Simolin and assured him of the King's friendship for Russia and of his resolution always to fulfil the terms of the treaty. Both the orders given to privateers and the decisions of the admiralty court were based on the treaty, he declared, and he referred Simolin to the reply he expected Harris to have made already in Russia in response to his own dispatch of 5 November.[33] Stormont was in fact quibbling, since a decision by the admiralty court to release ship and cargo provided the cargo were sold to the Navy Board was not in accordance with the Anglo-Russian treaty. On the other hand the Russian request also went beyond the bounds of the treaty. Russia had the right to claim the benefit of the principle "free ships, free goods" for her own vessels. But in that case Russian property loaded on board a neutral ship was not entitled to more protection than the neutral concerned could claim under existing treaties or international law. Stormont, however, did not pay much attention to the Russian protest; he wrote

32. SP 91/103, Mémoire by Simolin to Lord Stormont, 17 December 1779.
33. SP 91/103, Stormont to Simolin, 19 December 1779.

to Harris to inform him of what had passed and told him to use the same arguments as before to Panin; no new ones were necessary.[34]

When he received Stormont's instructions Harris was still suffering from jaundice and unable to go out. He too attached little importance to the Russian complaints. For one thing the subject had not formed part of his discussions with Potemkin but had been raised only by Panin. He therefore argued that the defence of Russian shipping and neutral trade in general was not the Empress's policy but that of her minister.[35] Since he was unable to visit Panin, Harris dispatched a written memorial on 11 January 1780, blandly repeating the usual British arguments: Britain, he declared, would always fulfil the terms of the Anglo-Russian treaty, and her conduct had invariably been governed by principles of moderation and equity, "en autant qu'on puisse le faire dans les désordres inséparables d'un état de guerre." These same principles, he added, had been followed in the case of the two ships mentioned in the Russian memorial; the admiralty courts had already pronounced judgement in both cases, "et quand votre excellence sera instruit de la sentence elle ne trouvera plus occasion de plainte ni de réparation à exiger." Britain thus continued to abide by her policy of bringing Russian ships in to port and putting them through the machinery of the admiralty courts.[36]

34. SP 91/103, Stormont to Harris, No. 33, 17 December 1779.

35. See e.g. SP 91/104, Harris to Stormont, No. 91, 31 December/11 January: "I have reason to believe [her] sentiments are infinitely more moderate on these subjects than those of her minister, who, I flatter myself . . . will desist from pursuing a point, which he never can gain, and which, if obtained, would be of very immaterial advantage to Russia."

36. SP 91/104, Note to Count Panin, enclosed in Harris to Stormont, No. 90, 31 December 1779/11 January 1780 (MD, 1, 269). In this letter Harris used the phrase: l'Impératrice peut être assurée, que la navigation de ses sujets ne sera jamais interrompue ou arrêtée par les vaisseaux de la Grande Bretagne." The Editor of the Malmesbury Diaries, who in any case printed only the first half of Harris's Note, misunderstood its meaning and added, as his own comment: "The following is another sop given to the Empress . . . and we suspended our right of searching Russian ships." This phrase of the Editor's, taken in conjunction with the truncated text printed in MD, 1, 269, has led many authors to repeat that Britain gave up her right to search Russian ships (e.g. Bemis, Diplomacy of the American Revolution, p. 150; Fauchille, La diplomatie française, p. 306; Bergbohm, Die bewaffnete Neutralität, p. 117). The full text of the letter shows that no such concession was made or intended. Nor did Harris have any instructions to

The Empress's interest in neutral trade had thus shown itself fairly constantly since December 1778, when the first Russian protest was lodged against Britain's declaration of 19 October 1778 which set aside Russian and Dutch treaty rights in favour of the pre-emptive purchase of naval stores. It had been kept alive by the Danish request for diplomatic support in Britain against the detention of Danish ships. The Empress was also presumably informed of the lengthy and acrimonious dispute between Britain and the United Provinces, and it is likely that the reports she received from the pro-French envoy at The Hague, Prince D. A. Galitzin,[37] were sympathetic to the Dutch complaints. She had herself been induced to send a strong protest to Britain on 19 November 1779 against the treatment of Russian ships and Russian property on board a Dutch ship. As long as war threatened in the Empire or with the Porte, Russian policy had been cautious. The Empress had confined herself in March 1779 simply to the protection of ships approaching the Russian coasts. By the autumn of 1779 the situation had changed. Peace had been restored on the continent, and the way was open for Russia to pursue a bolder policy with regard to the maritime war. To secure the position of mediator between France and Britain would increase considerably Russian influence in Europe, and France, after the recent *rap-*

---

give up the right of search which was not in dispute. Harris had indeed in September 1779 proposed that Russian shipping should be allowed to pass unmolested (SP 91/103, to Weymouth, No. 60, 17/28 September); he drew no reply at the time. When Stormont at last answered him on this matter on 11 April 1780, he wrote: "The giving orders not to visit any Russian ship is a thing utterly impossible, as that would be such evident partiality as every other friendly power would have reason to resent" (SP 91/104, No. 19). The British contention that to stop a ship, search it, and if necessary bring it before an admiralty court did not constitute an illegitimate interruption of neutral trade remained unchanged in theory and in practice. What is more, Harris's letter was never interpreted at the time in the manner which subsequent commentators have followed. The note printed in *Morskoy Sbornik, 43,* 79, No. 16, dated simply 1780, belongs to 22 December 1780/2 January 1781, and is therefore wrongly placed in this series of documents.

37. "Did Prince Galitzin pay any attention to me or shew any desire to be connected with me, I should never have declined it," wrote Sir Joseph Yorke to Harris on 21 March 1780, "but he is all French, little and polite and I have no apparatus for electricity, nor any ambition to have my name inrolled as a natural philosopher" (Harris Papers). Galitzin had been ambassador to France (1763) and had made contacts with the French salons. He was appointed to The Hague in 1773.

prochement with Russia, had at least received the Russian overtures politely. Britain, the traditional friend, was insistently demanding an alliance or at the very least an armed mediation on
her behalf. The neutrals saw their chance of securing safer navigation in wartime, but they needed the leadership and protection
of a great power. At some stage in the course of the autumn, the
Empress evidently took up the idea of constructing out of these
various elements a project to impose her good offices on the belligerents by means of an armed mediation concerted with the
neutral states.

By the end of November 1779 the Anglo-Dutch dispute had
reached a critical point when a large convoy began to gather in the
Texel. Britain refused to be impressed by this demonstration of
Dutch firmness and determined to organize the interception of the
Dutch convoy by a squadron of the Royal Navy. It was probably
this exacerbation of Anglo-Dutch relations that led the Empress
to explore the possibility of a joint Russian-Dutch *démarche* in
the form of an armed mediation. The first evidence of such an intention on her part comes from the Prussian envoy at The Hague,
Thulemeier, writing to Frederick II on 7 January 1780. According
to Thulemeier, Yorke's boasts of the Russian Empress's friendship
for England were not confirmed by the langauge held by Galitzin.
The Russian ambassador had apparently hinted to Thulemeier
"qu'il seroit à desirer que les Etats Généraux missent trente
vaisseaux en mer; qu'il leur conviendroit alors de réclamer la
médiation de V.M. et de l'Impératrice sa souveraine, et que cette
Princesse, en renforçant l'escadre hollandaise de 20 vaisseaux de
guerre pourroit pacifier les troubles subsistants entre la France at
l'Angleterre." Thulemeier replied briefly to these hints that neutrality was the best policy for the Dutch. He was uncertain whether
Galitzin was acting on instructions from his court or simply out
of sympathy with the Patriot faction.[38]

Early in 1780 Galitzin came further into the open. On 27 January he had an interview with the Prince of Orange in which he
endeavoured to enlist the Prince's interest in joining with Russia
in measures for the protection of neutral trade, leading to the

38. Fruin and Colenbrander, *Depêches van Thulemeier, 1763–1788*, p. 224.

offer of a mediation backed by force.[39] The initial response of
the Prince of Orange was somewhat negative, but he agreed to
think over the proposal. On 31 January Galitzin renewed his overtures, this time in more detail. He again urged that the Dutch Republic should enter into negotiations with his court in order to
offer a joint mediation to the belligerents. Russia, he declared,
could supply twenty or twenty-five ships. Holland should arm
twenty ships in addition to the thirty the armament of which had
already been ordered for convoy duty, thus raising to seventy the
number of ships the mediating powers could control. Galitzin assured the Prince of Orange that Russia had no intention of espous-
ing the British side. At the request of the Stadholder, he explained
the peace terms which it would be the task of the mediating powers
to enforce: first, the independence of the American colonies would
have to be recognized, since there could be no peace in Europe
as long as Britain entertained a hope of their recovery; and secondly
Britain would have to recognize the rights of neutral trade at sea.
The Russian envoy however left himself open to misinterpretation
on two counts: he made it clear that he was speaking from himself
and that his purpose was to engage the Dutch to make overtures
to Russia. The Empress was therefore in no way committed by
anything he said. And he informed the Prince that "since four
days ago," he was assured that France approved the plan, and
though he also declared himself convinced that Britain would
welcome such a mediation he nevertheless left the Prince under
the impression that he was acting under French inspiration, even
direction, and without the orders of his court.[40]

Galitzin's proposals were startling enough for the Prince of
Orange. And they came at a time when the United Provinces faced
a grave crisis in its relations with Britain, for the Dutch convoy,
which had sailed on 27 December 1779, was intercepted on 29

39. *AMON*, 2, 140, Prince of Orange to Grand Pensionary van Bleiswijk, 27 January 1780; "eene mediatie te offereeren gewapender hand," the prince quoted
Galitzin as saying.

40. Ibid., 145, the same to the same, 31 January 1780. The French ambassador
in The Hague however first mentions Galitzin's activities to Vergennes on 8 or
11 February 1780; Galitzin apparently spoke to him on 3 February. (See Fauchille,
La diplomatie française, pp. 192 ff.)

December by a squadron of the Royal Navy. The Dutch commander refused to allow his convoy to be visited, shots were exchanged, and eleven Dutch ships were brought into British ports.[41] Meanwhile opinion in Britain was moving towards the unilateral suspension of what Stormont called the "murtherous treaty" of 1674, if the Dutch did not agree to grant succours or give up their privileges,[42] and on 28 January 1780 Yorke was instructed to deliver a verbal declaration to that effect to the States General.[43] The Russian overtures therefore offered the United Provinces the hope of support were they to resist British pressure. Nevertheless the Dutch reaction to this overture was extremely slow and cautious. The Prince regarded the union of the United Provinces with the Northern courts for the protection of trade as desirable, but he feared taking any step which might give Britain grounds to declare war.[44] The Grand Pensionary, when these proposals were communicated to him, considered that the idea of mediation should be kept subordinate to the principal aim of trade protection. For the time being no formal reply was given to Galitzin. The Dutch constitution demanded that lengthy consultations should first take place with the leading regents, and Galitzin himself was advised to sound the opinion of the principal burghers of Amsterdam.[45]

Meanwhile in St. Petersburg, the Empress's interest in maritime trade was kept alive by a whole series of events. In December 1779 a Swedish warship convoying a number of merchantmen was stopped by the Royal Navy and brought into the Downs.[46]

41. SP 84/569, enclosure in Sandwich to Stormont, 7 January 1780. For the fate of the ships in the High Court of Admiralty see Edler, *The Dutch Republic and the American Revolution*, p. 132.

42. SP 84/569, Stormont to Yorke, 11 January 1780.

43. SP 84/569, Minute of a meeting at Lord North's, 27 January 1780; Stormont to Yorke, No. 6, 28 January 1780 enclosing project of a verbal declaration. Received by Yorke by 4 February 1780 (printed in C. de Martens, *Nouvelles causes célèbres du droit des gens, 1*, 162).

44. *AMON, 2*, 148, Prince of Orange to van Bleiswijk, 27 January 1780.

45. Ibid., 148, van Bleiswijk to Prince of Orange, 1 February 1780; Prince of Orange to van Bleiswijk, 18 February 1780.

46. Adm. 1/663, Admiral Drake, C-in-C, the Downs, to Philip Stephens, under secretary of the Admiralty, 5 December 1779. In order to avoid an incident Britain offered to purchase the full value of the cargoes, with freight and demurrage,

Towards the end of January or early in February news reached Russia of the British attack on the Dutch convoy. Harris realized that in the present state of Russian opinion Britain's action might be unfavourably looked upon, but in a dispatch of 24 January/4 February 1780 he expressed the hope that Catherine at least would approve Britain's stand.[47] A few days later he was much encouraged to hear that the Empress had called Britain's behaviour "spirited and decisive . . . and she will not easily alter her opinion on this article." [48] This however did not represent the view current for instance in Vienna, where it was believed that the Empress was "exceedingly nettled" on hearing the news of the British attack on the Dutch convoy.[49]

Towards the end of January, the Danish chargé d'affaires received orders to seek Russian support for Danish complaints about the treatment of neutral ships by Spain.[50] Harris, still convalescing from his attack of jaundice, had at first been cheered to hear that the Empress was annoyed with Spain and had expressed her indignation in the strongest terms: "I hope," he wrote on 3/14 January 1780, "when I get abroad, to reap some advantage from this disposition." [51] A few days later he confirmed that the Empress appeared determined to make strong representations in Madrid in view of the many complaints that were reaching her. Since his residence in Russia, Harris wrote, he had never seen the Empress so aroused by any event as by this interruption of neutral trade by Spain, "a sentiment which I flatter myself, I have in some degree

---

without the ships going before the admiralty court. "No difficulty will arise from the court of Admiralty," wrote Stormont to the King, on 14 December 1779. "Sir James Marriott is clearly of opinion that the purchase violates no rule of the Admiralty Court" (Fortescue, *Correspondence of King George III, 4,* 519). This procedure saved the expense attending a long demurrage and avoided "all complaints from the court of Sweden upon points which we can never give up, but which are of disagreeable discussion" as Stormont put it.

47. SP 91/104, Harris to Stormont, No. 7, 24 January/4 February 1780.
48. SP 91/104, Harris to Stormont, No. 9, 31 January/12 February 1780.
49. Sir Robert Keith to Harris, 1 April 1780 (Harris Papers); cf. Fauchille, *La diplomatie française,* p. 192, for Swart's report to the States General that the Empress was shocked by Britain's attack. But these two reports probably echo Panin's views; Harris echoes Potemkin's.
50. CP Russie, *104,* Corberon to Vergennes, No. 4, 28 January 1780.
51. SP 91/104, Harris to Stormont, No. 1.

contributed to promote." [52] But there were dangers which Harris seems not to have suspected, in fanning the Empress's anger at interference with neutral trade, even by a Bourbon power.

The news that the Spaniards had laid hands on a ship chartered by a Russian firm proved to be the last straw where Catherine was concerned. The *Concordia,* loaded with corn for Marseilles, Genoa, and Leghorn, had been stopped and brought into Cádiz. On 30 January (or 11 February) 1780, a strongly worded rescript was sent to S. S. Zinovyev, the Russian envoy in Madrid. He was to ask immediately for the release of all ships detained in Cádiz on which there were cargoes belonging to Russian subjects; if Spain pleaded self-defence, Zinovyev should demand compensation and should point out that when Britain used that same argument she always paid. In addition the envoys from other neutral courts in Madrid were to be informed of his *démarche.*[53] Not content with this protest in Madrid, the Empress ordered a memorial in the same terms to be delivered to Normandez, the Spanish chargé d'affaires in St. Petersburg. The memorial also demanded compensation for the forced sale of cargoes and the lifting of an order alleged to have been made by Spain to bring into Cádiz all ships attempting to enter the Mediterranean. It ended with a stiff rebuke to Spain for thus stifling the nascent Russian-Spanish trade.[54]

By the middle of February 1780, the Empress evidently felt that the time was ripe for some *démarche d'éclat* on her part. Both Britain and Spain were oppressing the neutrals, who appeared to be looking to Russia to champion their interests. A Russian ship and Russian property on a Dutch ship had been detained by Brit-

52. SP 91/104, Harris to Stormont, No. 4, 17/28 January 1780; CP Russie, *104,* Corberon to Vergennes, No. 4, 28 January 1780.

53. *Morskoy Sbornik, 43,* 83, No. 18. The rescript is dated 19/30 January 1780 in *Morskoy Sbornik,* but both Harris and Corberon imply that it was dated 30 January/11 February. (See SP 91/104, No. 11, 15/26 February; CP Russie, *104,* Corberon to Vergennes, No. 6, 10 February 1780).

54. *Morskoy Sbornik, 43,* 80, No. 17. There was in fact no such Spanish order, but Spanish practice may have led the neutrals to believe in its existence. Spain had however threatened to stop all Dutch ships unless the Dutch secured observation of the treaty of 1674 from Britain: see memorandum of 15 November 1779 by Floridablanca to the Dutch resident in Madrid, copy enclosed in SP 84/566, Yorke to Weymouth, 8 December 1779.

ain, and Russian property had been detained by Spain.[55] Though she could not yet have heard the result of Galitzin's overtures of 27 January 1780 at The Hague, she was probably sufficiently aware of feeling in the United Provinces to count on some cooperation from the Dutch in her plans. At any rate, some time in February, perhaps earlier, Catherine determined to put herself at the head of the neutrals, to defend their rights vis-à-vis the belligerents and to define what those rights were. The first indication of her intentions came in a letter of 2/13 February 1780 to her confidant Baron Grimm: "Mon bon ami," Catherine wrote, "un de ces jours vous entendrez dire que certaine déclaration a été déclarée et vous direz que c'est du volcanique . . ." But the Empress gave no indication of what her declaration was to contain, beyond the suggestion that it referred to maritime affairs and was intended for both belligerent sides. In her own inimitable style, her letter continued:

> . . . ma il n'y avait plus moyen de faire autrement, denn die Teutschen hassen nichts so als wenn die Leute ihnen auf die Nase spielen wollen . . . Le confrère Charles [the King of Spain] échauffe nos oreilles dans ce moment; je vous prie de nous prêter la vôtre pour écouter ce que nous allons lui dire et à d'autres aussi, denn das ist eben so raisonnable wie die Projekte des Abts von St. Pierre.

In addition, Catherine gave Grimm a hint that proves she had already determined to mobilize her fleet: "il y aura au printemps et pendant l'été des vaisseaux russes à Livourne . . ."[56]

Spain now played straight into Catherine's hands. Scarcely had the Empress's memorial complaining about the seizure of the *Concordia* been delivered to the Spanish chargé d'affaires when news arrived in St. Petersburg on 17 February of a fresh Spanish

---

55. The only complaint made against France occurred in July 1779: see CP Russie, *103*, Vergennes to Sartine, 3 July 1779, enclosing memoir from Baryatinsky reclaiming Russian property seized on board a Danish or English ship (the nationality to be determined by the admiralty court) belonging to Sidnev, James & Co., Russian merchants in Constantinople (a half-English firm).

56. See *Sbornik, 23*, 171, Catherine to Grimm. The Abbé de St. Pierre was an 18th century utopist, author of a "projet de la paix perpetuelle," which was eventually translated into Russian.

offence. The *St. Nicholas* of St. Petersburg, a Russian ship, loaded with corn for Málaga and Leghorn, had been seized and taken into Cádiz; the cargo had been sold without allowing the captain to defend his ship and without even showing the nationality of the ship at the time, in spite of the protests of the Russian consul.[57] This time Russia herself had been directly injured by Spain. The Empress now decided that the moment had come. Without consulting either the Council of State or Count Panin, on 8/19 February 1780 she drafted with her own hand an *ukaz* to the college of the admiralty ordering the immediate armament of a squadron of fifteen ships of the line and five frigates.[58] The order was kept secret not only from Panin but from all the foreign envoys with the exception of Harris. He heard of it in characteristic fashion three days later, on 22 February, from Potemkin, who "with an impetuous joy, perfectly analogous to his character" heartily congratulated Harris on the Russian armament and told him that though the squadron "will be supposed to protect the Russian trade, *envers et contre tous,* they are meant to chastise the Spaniards, whose insolence and arbitrary conduct the Empress cannot put up with." Harris however was unconvinced; he did not see how this measure would benefit Britain. Either out of sheer ignorance or as part of a plan to deceive Britain for the time being as to Russia's policy, Potemkin continued to urge the advantages of Russia's naval armament for Britain. "It is entirely owing to what you have advanced," he declared. "Count Panin would have kept the whole from her." The decision flowed spontaneously from the Empress, and Harris's enemies would not dare oppose it; and the Prince added: "Your nation may consider themselves as having twenty ships added to their fleet; for though, perhaps, we shall not operate with you, we certainly shall direct the attention of as many of those of your enemies." Harris still doubted and demurred for he saw in this move nothing more than a renewal of the measures of trade protection which had been agreed on among the three Northern courts the previous winter. Potemkin thereupon, "al-

57. Bergbohm, *Die bewaffnete Neutralität,* p. 122; SP 91/104, Harris to Stormont, No. 11, 15/26 February 1780 (*MD, 1,* 270).

58. *Morskoy Sbornik, 43,* 88, appended to No. 19, the Empress to Count Panin, 14/25 February 1780.

most out of humour" with Harris, told him that he had given him the good news at Catherine's express request as she knew it would give him pleasure and that "beside myself, you are, at this moment, the only person acquainted with her design." [59]

How utterly misleading Potemkin's assurances were can be seen from the further development of the Empress's policy. Six days after she had ordered the armament of her squadron, on 14/25 February 1780, the Empress approved an instruction to Count Panin, prepared under her orders by her secretary Bezborodko, in which she communicated to her foreign minister the purpose for which she had mobilized part of her fleet. By this time the Empress must have been informed of the results of Galitzin's preliminary talks in The Hague. In his discussions with the Prince of Orange, Galitzin had dwelt mainly on the idea of an armed mediation as a means of securing safe navigation and had not emphasized the question of trade protection by itself. It is possible that his reports stressed Dutch preference for the latter policy rather than the former, and that the Empress was influenced by his accounts to abandon the idea of an armed mediation in favour of an ambitious measure of trade protection designed to enforce certain principles. According to her own account, the Empress was induced to adopt the idea of clarifying maritime law by the news of the British threat to suspend the Anglo-Dutch treaty and to reduce the Dutch to the status of unprivileged neutrals.[60] Assuming Galitzin to have been promptly informed of Yorke's threat, the news could have reached Catherine by 22 or 23 February.[61] At

59. SP 91/104, Harris to Stormont, No. 11, 15/26 February 1780 (*MD, 1*, 270).

60. Catherine's rescript to Simolin of 13/24 January 1781 (quoted in F. de Martens, *Recueil, 9*, 313/14). Here the Empress states: "Quand enfin la cour de Londres se décida à déclarer à la république de Hollande qu'elle se voyait obligée de suspendre pour un certain temps tous les engagements qu'elle avait pris à son égard, et de les remplacer exclusivement par les droits généraux à tous les peuples, cette déclaration dut provoquer naturellement un sentiment de méfiance générale et une incertitude encore plus grande au sujet de la navigation et le commerce des neutres. C'est alors que nous nous mîmes à réfléchir aux moyens de prevenir pour les temps futurs toute espèce de malentendus et d'ennuis pouvant provenir de paroles mal définies . . ."

61. Galitzin's dispatches have not been published, but assuming that he wrote home on 4 or 5 February 1780, his reports would have been received by 22 or 23 February. It took roughly eighteen days for a courier to travel between The Hague and St. Petersburg, but the journey could be done in 15 days.

any rate the main object of the Empress's instruction to Panin was to order him to invite the neutral states to join with Russia in making a declaration to the belligerents of the principles governing free trade and contraband; and to invite the neutral states to unite with Russia, by means of a convention, to enforce these principles with their fleets. For Panin's information, a copy of the Empress's *ukaz* to the admiralty, ordering the armament of her fleet, was attached to Bezborodko's memorandum. She explained in addition that she proposed sending two warships and two frigates to patrol the North Sea as in 1779 and ordered her minister to invite Sweden and Denmark to do the same. Panin was instructed to discuss the new Russian policy with the foreign envoys at the Russian court and to communicate it to Russian envoys abroad, both at neutral and belligerent courts.[62]

On the same day, 14/25 February 1780, Catherine dispatched a personal rescript to Galitzin at The Hague informing him of the armament of her fleet and of its purpose. She now instructed him to sound the Dutch on what they were prepared to do to defend their trade against both belligerents and on their willingness to join with Russia in making a declaration on free trade and the definition of contraband, but without committing her name in any way.[63] The Russian envoy at The Hague was therefore at that

62. *Morskoy Sbornik*, *43*, 88, No. 19, Catherine to Panin, 14/25 February 1780.

63. *Morskoy Sbornik*, *43*, 335, No. 21. It is unfortunate that the Editor of the documents published in the *Morskoy Sbornik* did not print any extracts from the Russian correspondence with the United Provinces earlier than this personal rescript of the Empress to Galitzin. Examination of these dispatches would prove or disprove once and for all the contention of contemporaries that Galitzin was acting without instructions when he first spoke to the Prince of Orange in January (see pp. 215 ff.) and also in March. (See Fruin and Colenbrander, *Depêches van Thulemeier, 1763–1788*, p. 227, Thulemeier to Frederick II, 10 March 1780: "On est persuadé d'un autre côté qu'elles [les démarches de Galitzin] n'ont été dictées que par le zèle de ce ministre sans qu'il y ait été autorisé par les ordres de sa souveraine.") It is of course untrue that Galitzin was acting without instructions in March, since we have the Empress's rescript to him of 14/25 February 1780. Moreover the fact that he was the only foreign envoy to whom she wrote at this stage of her policy seems to indicate that she had already been in communication with him on related matters and that she now wished to sound Dutch opinion on a different policy than that which she had previously proposed. Otherwise how to account for this priority given over Denmark, the Empress's ally, and her partner in the measures of trade protection in 1779? It is to say the least

time the only Russian minister abroad to be given any inkling of the Empress's plan directly by herself.

The news that Catherine had ordered the armament of part of the fleet did not long remain a secret and caused a sensation in the capital.[64] Incredible confusion reigned in the diplomatic corps as to the purpose of the squadron. Harris, who had every reason to be satisfied with what Potemkin had told him, struck his French colleague as looking remarkably gloomy the day after his interview with the Prince.[65] Corberon, whose suspicions had been aroused by Harris's repeated visits to the Prince, had procured, with Panin's permission, an interview for himself with Potemkin, in which the Prince kept silent about the Russian armament but again repeated that Britain wanted peace. Corberon took the bull by the horns and declared to Potemkin that he was being deceived by Harris and that British policy was simply to change a particular into a general war. Somewhat tactlessly he informed Potemkin that he had seen Harris's memorandum of 16/27 August 1779, which he declared to be a tissue of lies. At Potemkin's request he handed him a memorial in reply to that of Harris, and Potemkin "avec beaucoup de grace et de gaieté" assured him that the Empress's one desire was to restore peace between the belligerents.[66] Corberon went away reassured and communicated his impression to his Prussian colleague.[67] When a few days later Corberon heard of the order to arm the squadron, he kept his head and did not take alarm. Through the pro-French faction at court he heard of the Empress's intention to form a league to protect trade, and he was soon completely tranquillized by receiving indirectly a message

---

extremely unlikely that Galitzin would have embarked on proposing an armed mediation to the Dutch without instructions—but it is not unlikely that his instructions told him to do so "as from himself." It will be observed that the instructions of 14/25 February 1780 also caution Galitzin not to commit the Empress's name.

64. SP 91/104, Harris to Stormont, No. 11, 15/26 February 1780 (*MD, I,* 270).

65. CP Russie, *104,* Corberon to Vergennes, No. 12, 29 February 1780.

66. CP Russie, *104,* Corberon to Vergennes, No. 10, 25 February 1780. Harris's account of this interview between Corberon and the Prince, as told him by Potemkin presumably, is a travesty of what Corberon describes, and is in SP 91/104, Harris to Stormont, No. 21, 10/21 March 1780 (*MD, I,* 288). See also Ch. 4, pp. 110 ff.

67. *PKFG, 44,* 128, Goertz to Frederick II, 29 February 1780.

from the Empress that France had nothing to fear and that Panin would shortly be speaking to him on the subject.[68] Goertz too was somewhat nonplussed at the news of the armament. The current rumour was that the Empress was incensed at the behaviour of Spain, and the armament had been ordered in consequence. It appeared therefore to be an anti-Bourbon move. The fact that Osterman, the vice-chancellor, disclaimed any knowledge of the Empress's decision and asserted that she had herself "minuté l'ordre sans le concours du ministère" made it all the more mysterious.[69]

The behaviour of Count Panin only served to increase the general bewilderment. Most of the foreign envoys were aware that he had not seen the Empress for some two months. Few however realized how strained were their relations. Panin did not trust any of his subordinates to act as an intermediary between himself and the Empress, and though the two may have corresponded this certainly did not replace the confidential discussion of matters of state.[70] Panin was not consulted by the Empress when she ordered the arming of the fleet. It is more than likely that she did not consult him either when she instructed Galitzin to sound Dutch opinion on a possible armed mediation. Panin was therefore thunderstruck when he received through Bezborodko the Empress's written orders to organize a league of neutrals. He believed at first sight that this new policy represented an anti-Bourbon move and a complete victory for Harris and Potemkin. Spanish seizures had after all been specifically mentioned by the Empress, in her instructions to him, as the immediate cause of her decision. Goertz, who saw him at the time, described the scene thus:

68. CP Russie, *104*, Corberon to Vergennes, No. 12, 29 February 1780; No. 13, 3 March 1780.

69. *PKFG, 44*, p. 128, Goertz to Frederick II, 29 February 1780.

70. The evidence that Panin and the Empress had not met comes from many quarters. See e.g. CP Russie, *104*, Corberon to Vergennes, No. 10, 25 February 1780; *PKFG, 44*, 84, Goertz to Frederick II, 4 February 1780: "Le comte Panin n'a pas vu sa souveraine depuis quelques mois, et il n'y a pas d'apparence qu'il puisse sortir de sitôt. Il ne charge personne de lui parler d'affaires, et ainsi elles se font toujours d'un jour à l'autre, sans qu'on sache trop comment." The fact that Catherine sent her instructions to Panin in writing through Bezborodko is further confirmation.

Je trouvai ensuite le comte Panin dans un état véritablement touchant . . . Le comte Panin, accablé physiquement et moralement, me dit avec beaucoup d'émotion qu'il me priait de ne point me laisser alarmer ni entrainer; qu'effectivement le ministre d'Angleterre venait de nouveau de faire un rude assaut; qu'il avait trouvé moyen pour un objet qui n'était qu'une misère d'aigrir sa souveraine, de la porter même à une démarche d'éclat; que nonobstant cette démarche il m'assurait que c'était toujours avec le principe de conserver la neutralité.

Should Spain, said Panin to Goertz, react in a moderate way, then

cette démarche que le ministre d'Angleterre avait malicieuse-ment occasionnée, devait tourner contre lui-même . . . que le tout était une trâme noire et méchante, que jusqu'à présent il avait cru que le sieur Harris entendait son métier, mais qu'il agissait comme un garçon; qu'il ne le considérait que comme un déséspéré qui se permettait tout . . . et qui n'était nulle-ment autorisé par sa cour.[71]

Seldom perhaps has a minister expressed himself more bitterly about one of the envoys accredited to his court, and that to the envoy of a power by no means friendly. But Panin's outburst is extremely revealing of the extent to which he was out of touch with the thoughts of the Empress and with Harris's own views. He believed that Harris had procured the armament of the fleet and the decision to organize the league of neutrals. Yet Harris had played no part in the Empress's decision, except perhaps by his encouragement of Russian resentment against Spain, and he had not at first welcomed the news of the armament of the fleet, sus-pecting that it would be used only for commerce protection.

The violence of Panin's reaction and his unguarded language led the foreign envoys in St. Petersburg to believe that in fact the Empress's new plan was directed primarily against the Bourbon

71. *PKFG, 44,* 128, Goertz to Frederick II, 29 February 1780; see also CP Russie, *104,* Corberon to Vergennes, No. 12, 29 February 1780: "[Harris] n'agissoit pas en ministre mais en homme sans principes, sans droiture, sans délicatesse et avec une méchanceté atroce."

powers. Harris soon shared this opinion. He was able to report to
Stormont the Empress's intention of embarking on measures of
trade protection on the very day after the Empress sent her orders
to Panin. But as he understood it, the Empress intended to invite
the neutral courts to join with her in protecting trade "against
the arbitrary proceedings of Spain." And, he added, "If this disposition holds and no means are found by his Prussian Majesty, to
give it another turn, the most pleasing consequences may arise
from it." He coupled these optimistic interpretations however with
a warning against possible evil consequences of intrigue at the
Russian court. Nevertheless, the general tone of his dispatch was
hopeful. The Empress had already compared Britain's conduct
favourably with that of other powers, and he urged on Stormont
the absolute necessity for Britain to avoid giving a shadow of
complaint in the treatment of Russian ships. If this conduct was
followed he expressed the belief "that the whole armament would
sooner or later be at our disposal." Most significant are however
the concluding words of Harris's dispatch: "These my Lord are
not my own sentiments alone, they belong to Prince Potemkin." [72]
Encouraged by the Prince's words, Harris worked hard to prevent
the Empress from changing her mind. Having heard rumours that
Panin, "more Prussian than ever," was preparing a memorial for
the Empress opposing the measure, he in turn took "every step
. . . to prevent its effect, and as it militates directly against the
Empress's own opinion . . . I trust it will make no impression, nor
interrupt the continuation of an armament which must at least employ the attention of our enemies . . ." [73] On 7 March 1780 he
wrote to his colleague in Copenhagen, Morton Eden, a letter of
qualified optimism as "the whole is the Empress's own act and deed,
without the advice or even approbation of Count Panin . . . It
is considered here as a strong measure in our favour, and occasions
reports which I wish were true . . . If Spain under these circumstances should give a haughty answer, and we, as I have strongly
urged, pay particular attention to those few ships carrying the Russian flag, it is certain the present armament may end in a junction
with ours; but this is more to be wished than expected." On the

72. SP 91/104, Harris to Stormont, No. 15, 15/26 February 1780.
73. SP 91/104, Harris to Stormont, No. 16, 21 February/3 March 1780.

same day Harris wrote to Stormont, urging in very strong terms that Britain should if necessary depart from the general rule and let the Russian merchantmen pass by unmolested, at the same time assuring the Empress that Britain relied too much on Russian friendship to suppose that Russian ships would ever carry contraband.[74]

While Harris was thus doing his best to further the Empress's policy, Panin began to have second thoughts. When Goertz saw him again at the beginning of March, he found the minister "occupé à donner une tournure à cette affaire . . . qu'il espérait toujours que tout cet éclat qu'on engageait sa souveraine à faire pour un si mince objet, en profitant d'un moment d'humeur, pourrait se tourner contre l'Angleterre . . . qu' . . . il pourrait naturellement en résulter une chose à l'execution de laquelle aucune puissance jusqu'à présent n'avait pu se permettre de penser, quoique tous l'eussent cru nécéssaire: c'était d'établir et de fixer un droit public pour les puissances neutres dans une guerre maritime: que c'était le moment d'en venir là." [75] Panin had in fact been persuaded by those who knew more of the Empress's intentions that a league of neutral powers, though ostensibly provoked by Spain's behaviour, might serve equally well against Britain.[76] But he now proceeded to make use of the plan in order to rehabilitate himself, by taking the credit for the idea of laying down the principles of neutral navigation and allowing the majority of the foreign envoys to believe that this was a modification of her original plan which he hoped to persuade the Empress to accept.[77] He did not hesitate to confide in Goertz that he hoped "par là . . . porter un coup sensible à l'Angleterre par cette même démarche à laquelle les intrigues de son ministre avaient donné naissance." On 7 March 1780 Panin told Goertz that he had submitted his draft to the Empress, and if she approved it, as he expected she would, "les principes établis pour cette espèce de droit public maritime seront

74. Harris to Morton Eden, 25 February/7 March 1780, *MD, 1*, 285; SP 91/104, Harris to Stormont, No. 17 (duplicate) 25 February/7 March 1780 (*MD, 1*, 284).
75. *PKFG, 44*, 134, Goertz to Frederick II, 3 March 1780.
76. According to Catherine herself, it was P. Bakunin, a member of the college of foreign affairs, who persuaded Panin of the advantages of the policy devised by the Empress. See A. V. Khrapovitsky, *Dnevnik 1782–1793*, ed. N. Barsukov, p. 485.
77. *PKFG, 44*, 134, Goertz to Frederick II, 3 March 1780.

moins agréables à l'Angleterre qu'à toute autre puissance." [78]

On 9 March 1780 preparations for Catherine's diplomatic offensive were complete. On that day she approved the declaration of neutral rights to be issued to the belligerents, which the neutral powers were to be invited to enforce under her leadership. In dispatches to her representatives in Sweden and Denmark she proposed that joint action should be taken by the three courts to protect neutral trade in the North Sea, as had been undertaken in 1779; and in addition she proposed, in terms which reflected the Danish plan of September 1778, the making of a joint declaration of neutral rights of which she enclosed a draft: it was composed of five articles, the second of which proclaimed the principle, "free ships, free goods." [79] Copies of the declaration were sent to the Russian envoys at the belligerent courts with instructions to present them to the respective foreign ministers and explain the necessity, which the Empress felt, of protecting the Russian flag.[80] A third set of instructions was issued to the Russian envoys at the neutral courts of Lisbon and The Hague, instructing them to communicate the Russian *démarche* to their courts and to invite them to join in proclaiming and enforcing the same principles.[81] A special rescript was in addition sent to Zinovyev in Madrid, instructing him to demand the release of the Russian ship *St. Nicholas* and to point out, in case of delay, that the Russian fleet would be sent "where honour, utility and necessity require." [82]

78. *PKFG, 44,* 145, Goertz to Frederick II, 7 March 1780.

79. *Morskoy Sbornik, 43,* 338, No. 23, rescript to Sacken, signed by Catherine, approved 27 February/9 March 1780; p. 342, No. 24, *ukaz* to Rückman, signed by Panin and Osterman, 28 February/10 March 1780. For a further analysis of the declaration see Ch. 7.

80. *Morskoy Sbornik, 43,* 345, No. 25, Draft rescript to Paris, London, and Madrid, dated 27 February/9 March 1780. A copy of the declaration of 28 February/11 March 1779 on the coastal patrol in the North Sea in that year was also enclosed in the rescript of Zinovyev. Spain had not been a belligerent at that time and had therefore not been notified.

81. *Morskoy Sbornik, 43,* 350, No. 27, Draft rescript to Lisbon and The Hague, approved by the Empress on 27 February/9 March 1780.

82. *Morskoy Sbornik, 43,* No. 28, p. 353, enclosing a copy of the memorial previously delivered to Normandez. Copies of both these documents were sent to Baryatinsky in No. 26, p. 349, with orders to invite France to urge Spain to see reason. A circular explaining the armament of the fleet and enclosing a copy of the declaration of principles was issued by Panin and Osterman on 28 February/10 March 1780 to Russian representatives in Mitau, Danzig, Berlin, Hamburg, Dresden,

It was now time for Panin to inform the various foreign envoys in St. Petersburg of this latest departure in Russian foreign policy. The couriers, bearing the Empress's impressive series of instructions, were to leave on 10 March 1780.[83] The first to be officially notified was needless to say Count Goertz, who on 10 March 1780 was able to congratulate Frederick II on the good news that the Empress had approved what he believed to be Panin's plan. It only remained for Spain to give a satisfactory reply to the Empress's representations, he wrote, and then "tout retombera sur le ministre d'Angleterre dont il [Panin] ne peut assez blâmer la conduite et il se flatte que lui et le ministère britannique se repentiront de s'être permis de pareilles intrigues." [84] Frederick was delighted with the news and proceeded at once to take the credit for what he believed to be a signal defeat of Britain at the Russian court.[85]

The idea that he had been successful in countering a British plot was also conveyed by Panin to the Chevalier de Corberon. In a dispatch which was evidently intended to be read by Panin since it was written *en clair* and sent by a Russian courier, Corberon lavished praise on the way this "sage et respectable ministre" had defeated "les projets monstrueux enfantés par l'Angleterre." Three times, "du fond de sa chambre, Panin a arrêté par ses objections fortes le conseil déjà entrainé," wrote Corberon. Panin had told him his plans in confidence, he added, and had conveyed to him his earnest desire that Spain should satisfy the Empress. "Par ce moyen, a-t-il insinué," continued Corberon, "l'Angleterre certainement subira l'humiliation qu'elle mérite." The Chargé d'Affaires knew enough of French policy to welcome the neutral league, and though the official reply to Russia would be made in Versailles, Corberon informed Panin that his government always acted in

---

Warsaw, Regensburg, Vienna, Venice, Naples, and Constantinople (*Morskoy Sbornik*, *43*, 355, No. 29).

83. SP 91/104, Harris to Stormont, No. 18, 3/14 March 1780. The Russian couriers had been delayed so that the envoys of the courts invited to cooperate could send their dispatches by them (*Morskoy Sbornik*, *43*, 356, No. 30).

84. *PKFG*, *44*, 152, Goertz to Frederick II, 10 March 1780.

85. Ibid., 159, Frederick II to Goltz (Paris), 27 March 1780: "Je me félicite d'avoir porté les choses en Russie jusqu'à ce point." It was to Frederick's interest to exaggerate the extent of his influence in St. Petersburg when he was dealing with the court of Versailles.

accordance with the *droit des gens* and would without doubt consider the action of the court of Petersburg as in line with its own principles.[86]

Spain's position was more difficult. Floridablanca had no intention of allowing the neutrals to break the blockade of Gibraltar, but on the other hand the protests of Denmark and Russia had already led him to fear that a league of neutrals against Spain might be formed. A new *règlement* on neutral trade was issued on 13 March 1780, which, however, still maintained the right to condemn enemy goods on board a neutral. The majority of the ships detained in Cádiz were now released, including the Russian ship *St. Nicholas*.[87] When Panin read the declaration to Normandez in St. Petersburg, the Spaniard replied very cautiously and, without entering into the substance of the declaration, merely expressed Spain's intention of satisfying Russian claims.[88]

Meanwhile Galitzin had been pursuing his negotiations with the Dutch. He had dropped a hint to Vauguyon, the French ambassador, to the effect that he was prepared to transmit to the Empress any suggestions made by the States General for the protection of trade. Vauguyon at once arranged for Galitzin to meet the Patriot leaders of Amsterdam. The Russian minister also urged on the Grand Pensionary the necessity of uniting the neutrals in defence of their rights and assured him that his court would listen to any insinuations put forward by the States General. By the end of February, under pressure from Amsterdam and from the Grand Pensionary, the Prince of Orange conveyed to Galitzin that he believed the Republic would be "très disposée à faire une alliance défensive avec l'Impératrice pour protéger le commerce et maintenir la liberté de la navigation." [89] The Empress had presumably

86. CP Russie, *104*, Corberon to Vergennes, No. 14, 10 March 1780; *Morskoy Sbornik*, *43*, 356, No. 30, Protokol po delu o vooruzhennom neytralitete, 5/16 March 1780, dictated by Panin to Bezborodko and read by the Empress on 6/17 March 1780.

87. Fauchille, *La diplomatie française*, p. 330; for the text of the new *règlement*, see G. F. de Martens, *Recueil*, *4*, 268.

88. For Normandez's reply to Floridablanca of 10 March 1780 see Danvila, *Historia*, *5*, 341; for Normandez's reply to Panin see *Morskoy Sbornik*, *43*, 356, No. 30.

89. Fauchille, *La diplomatie française*, pp. 192–94, for Vauguyon's account of Galitzin's conversation with him; *AMON*, *2*, 151, 152, 154, 156, and 159 for Galitzin's negotiations in The Hague, and p. 160, van Bleiswijk to Prince of Orange, enclosing agreed formula for the reply to Galitzin, n.d. but presumably end February 1780.

been sufficiently encouraged by Galitzin's first reports to count on Dutch cooperation. The courier who carried her declaration to the Republic must have crossed the courier who brought to Russia the news of the Dutch agreement to join in measures to protect neutral trade.[90] Swart, the Dutch resident in St. Petersburg, may not yet have known much of what had been taking place in The Hague when Panin read the Russian declaration to him on 10 March 1780. But he knew enough of Dutch policy to express the opinion that the Republic could not but adhere to measures so much in conformity with its interests.[91]

The remaining neutral envoys, the Swede, the Dane, and the Portuguese, all expressed approval of the Empress's declaration.[92] It remained only to discover what Britain thought of it. With complete unscrupulousness Panin had used his position to portray the Empress throughout Europe as the sponsor of a policy aimed against Britain, and in pursuit of his private vendetta against Harris he knew no bounds. Whereas the other powers mainly affected had been given tranquillizing hints from time to time, Harris had been told nothing at all by Panin—and it was Panin, not Potemkin, who was actually drafting the declaration. But Harris began to

90. It is difficult to establish exactly the sequence of events in the United Provinces, since Galitzin's dispatches have not been published. But there is evidence that something was known in St. Petersburg of the Dutch attitude to the Russian plans before 10 March, for on that day Osterman, the vice-chancellor, wrote to Galitzin declaring "la concordance des sentiments de l'impératrice" with those of the Dutch, "et son désir que la négotiation fut conduite avec promptitude." (See Fauchille, *La diplomatie française*, p. 338, n. 3.) There is also evidence from Harris that at about this time news had reached Russia from Holland. Writing on 3/14 March, Harris said that three days previously (11 March) the Dutch resident, Swart, had handed to Panin a "partial and prejudiced account" of British dealings with the Dutch Republic and had signified to Panin that the Dutch were to arm 50 warships to protect trade and proposed to invite Russia to join them (SP 91/104, Harris to Stormont, No. 18). This is not in fact what the Dutch reply amounted to, but the figure of 50 ships had figured in Galitzin's discussions with the Prince of Orange, and it may have been mentioned between Swart and Panin. See also *AMON*, 2, 151, the Prince of Orange to van Bleiswijk, 18 February 1780.

91. *Morskoy Sbornik, 43, 356*, No. 30.

92. Ibid. The Protocol does not mention communication of the Russian project to the Austrian envoy, Cobenzl, but unofficially Cobenzl knew all about it and quoted Panin as saying that the neutrals would be invited to join Russia "und zu dem nämlichen Ende Ihre Flotte auslaufen zu lassen, um laut eigener Worte des Grafen Panins das Wort 'Oberherrschaft zu See' aus dem Dictionnaire Europas gänzlich auszulöschen." (Wiener Staatsarchiv, Cobenzl to Kaunitz, 10 March 1780).

feel uneasy when he heard that the other ministers had been informed of the content of the Russian declaration, and yet no word
had been said to him. Not until 15 March, five days after the other
envoys had been received by Panin, was the declaration formally
read to Harris by the Russian minister. To Harris, of course,
Panin did not pretend that it was the result of his victory over
British intrigues. On the contrary, he assured Harris repeatedly
that "the whole was the Empress's own act and deed" and disclaimed any credit for the idea. Harris, knowing that Stormont
would already have been informed of the declaration by Simolin
since the Russian couriers had left five days before, did not comment on its substance in his dispatch.[93] But it must have been a
very serious blow to him. He must have been aware at once of
the political repercussions of the public appearance on the European stage of Russia as the champion of "free ships, free goods" for
all the neutrals. France and Spain must welcome the Russian declaration, for they depended on neutral shipping for naval stores.
The neutrals were all bound to welcome it. Only Britain, as
Harris well knew, must be expected to oppose it as running counter
both to her needs and her traditions. Thus in the conflict over
neutral rights, Russia, hitherto regarded as the traditional friend
of Britain, appeared to be taking the side of the Bourbons and the
neutrals, for, though technically the Russian declaration was impartial and applied to both belligerent sides equally, its results
would undoubtedly favour Britain's enemies.

This turn in Russian policy was so unexpected that it inevitably
gave rise to the question of who was responsible for the declaration of the Armed Neutrality. Had the Empress understood the
political implications of the policy inaugurated in her name, or
was she the victim of an anti-British court intrigue? The view
which came to be accepted by contemporaries emanated from
Panin—namely that the Empress, when planning the Neutral

93. SP 91/104, Harris to Stormont, No. 20, 6/17 March 1780 (*MD, 1*, 286). Corberon
confirms that Harris was only told of the declaration five days after the other ministers had been informed (CP Russie, *104*, Corberon to Vergennes, No. 15, 21 March
1780). In his account to the Empress of his activities of 5/16 March, Panin omits
to mention the fact that he delayed the communication to Harris and implies that
Harris, Corberon, and Normandez were all informed on the same day (*Morskoy
Sbornik, 43*, 356, No. 30, Protokol . . .)

League, intended to benefit Britain, but her foreign minister skilfully turned the point of the operation against Britain and in
favour of France. According to this version, Panin is assumed to
have deceived Catherine, too ignorant herself to perceive the implications of her declaration, or to have won her over by a judicious
appeal to her vanity to take up a position as legislatrix of the seas.

The intrigues which surrounded the birth of the League of
Armed Neutrality of 1780 make the task of analysing its origin a
complicated one.[94] It is useful therefore to recall that the armament of the fleet came as a complete surprise to Harris; he had not
requested it in any way and was at first doubtful of its advantages
for Britain. He was gradually led, by the assurances of Potemkin,
to hope that Britain would derive profit from it. Meanwhile Panin,
to whom the order to arm the fleet came also as a complete surprise,
was convinced that the Empress had been induced to make this
move by Harris acting through Potemkin.[95] When he was persuaded that the Empress's design to form a league of neutral
powers was not a move in Britain's favour, he covered the blunder
of his initial opposition by implying that he had given a turn to
Catherine's policy which would foil Harris's intrigues. When Harris then discovered what the Empress had put her name to, he
too became convinced that she had been deceived by Panin into
approving principles of maritime law, the implications of which
she did not understand.[96] Thus the long dispute on who was
responsible for the Neutral League, the Empress or Panin, started
on its journey through history. But before determining who was
responsible, it is necessary to analyse the declaration of principles
itself, and to assess its true character and place in Russian history.

94. See Appendix.

95. See e.g. Bancroft-Circourt, *3*, 240, Goertz to Frederick, 28 February/10 March:
"il y a apparence que l'effet de cet armement naval, dont le ministre anglais était
parvenu *à faire prendre la résolution dans un moment d'humeur* qu'il avait fomenté,
pourrait bien tourner contre sa nation." (My italics)

96. See e.g. SP 91/104, Harris to Stormont, No. 51, 15/26 May 1780. In 1782, Harris
could still write to Fox that the Empress had been "egregiously deceived" in the
drawing up of the declaration (FO 65/6, No. 4, 19/30 April 1782 (*MD, 1*, 501)).

7. The League of Armed Neutrality (2)

THE PRINCIPLES which the Empress of Russian put forward in her declaration of 28 February/10 March to the belligerents for the future regulation of the rights of neutral trade at sea were as follows:

1. That neutral vessels may navigate freely from port to port and along the coasts of the nations at war;

2. That the effects belonging to subjects of the said powers at war shall be free on board neutral vessels, with the exception of contraband merchandise;

3. That, as to the specification of the above mentioned merchandise, the Empress holds to what is enumerated in the 10th and 11th articles of her treaty of commerce with Great Britain, extending her obligations to all the powers at war;

4. That to determine what constitutes a blockaded port, this designation shall apply only to a port where the attacking power has stationed its vessels sufficiently near and in such a way as to render access thereto clearly dangerous;

5. That these principles shall serve as a rule for proceedings and judgments as to the legality of prizes.[1]

Of these five principles, all of which were controversial by contemporary canons of international maritime law,[2] two were of

1. Scott, *Armed Neutralities*, p. 273.
2. See Bergbohm, *Die bewaffnete Neutralität*, pp. 30 ff. for a comprehensive discussion of the five principles of the Empress's declaration in relation to contemporary maritime law.

such outstanding importance that the attention of all powers concentrated on them. The second principle put forward as a doctrine of universal application by the future members of the League the old and disputed claim to "free ships, free goods." The third principle, defining the nature of contraband, was controversial on two grounds. In the first place, the Empress simply stated that because a particular list of commodities had been declared to be contraband in the Anglo-Russian treaty of 1766, these, and only these commodities could be regarded as contraband when found in her ships by any belligerent power. In the second place, naval stores did not figure on this list. It is clear from the Empress's communications to Sweden, Denmark, and the Dutch Republic that she intended each power to insist on the application of the contraband clauses of their own respective treaties with the belligerents and not simply to apply the terms of the Anglo-Russian treaty.[3] This, however, was not immediately evident, and there is no doubt that the declaration was regarded at the time as making trade in naval stores safe for all neutrals. Contemporaries did not distinguish the two elements in the League of Armed Neutrality: first, the idea of a union of the neutral powers to protect their rights, and secondly the definition of what these rights were. Though a union of neutral powers would certainly not be welcomed by Britain, it was the inclusion of the principle "free ships, free goods" in the declaration which led European opinion to see in the Russian *démarche* an anti-British demonstration.

There can be no doubt that the idea of forming a league of neutral powers at this particular moment stemmed from Catherine herself. The evidence of the documents and of contemporaries, before Panin had muddied the waters, all points unmistakably to this conclusion. The activities of Galitzin at The Hague in January 1780 show that already then the Empress was thinking of some form of combined action with one at least of the neutrals. Her letter to Grimm of 2/13 February 1780, in which she first mentions a forthcoming declaration, antedates her instructions of 14/25 February to Panin. The fact that she dictated these instructions to her secretary, Bezborodko, confirms the current report that she had not seen Panin for some time. There is also, for what

3. See *Morskoy Sbornik, 43,* 338, No. 23; p. 342, No. 24; and p. 350, No. 27.

it is worth, the Empress's own statement to that effect. Much later, in 1788, commenting on the assertion by Abbé Dénina in his *Essai sur la vie et le règne de Fréderic II* that the idea of a neutral league had originally been conceived by Frederick II in 1744, she wrote in the margin of the book: "Cela n'est pas vrai, la neutralité armée est sortit du cerveau de Catherine II et de nulle autre. Le c-te Bezborodka peut attester cela parce que cette idée partit comme par inspiration de la bouche de cette Impératrice un matin." [4] But the clearest, most convincing proof that the Empress and not Panin thought up the Neutral League is given by Panin himself. His outbursts to Goertz, his violent diatribes against Harris, show how utterly surprised and overwhelmed he was at what he understood to be a victory of the pro-English faction at court. Panin's initial opposition to the Empress's new policy, amply documented by Goertz and even by Harris, is also confirmed by Catherine, for in the same marginal remark to Dénina's book, she continued: "Le c-te Panin n'en vouloit pas entendre parler, parce que ce n'étoit pas lui qui l'avoit imaginé, et on a eu beaucoup de peine à la lui faire comprendre; ce fut Bacounin qui en fut chargé, et enfin il y mis la main." [5] The honour therefore of launching the Neutral League in the winter of 1780 must go to the Empress.

But was the Empress aware of the political significance of the principles which the Neutral League was designed to enforce, and in particular of Article 2? Here Panin was supposed to have triumphed, and there are many accounts of the way in which the elderly statesman was suddenly inspired to safeguard the interests of Russia and save Catherine from the British. [6] How far did these principles, which the Empress did probably leave Panin to draft, serve Russian interests, and did Catherine understand them?

It will have been noticed that the five principles of the Empress's declaration correspond in almost every particular with those suggested in September 1778 by Bernstorff. [7] It is clear therefore that

4. A. V. Khrapovitsky, *Dnevnik 1782–1793*, p. 485.
5. Ibid.
6. See e.g. CP Russie, *104*, Corberon to Vergennes, No. 14, 10 March 1780; *Sbornik*, 26, 329, account by the Marquis of Parelo, chargé d'affaires of the King of the Two Sicilies, written in 1784.
7. See Ch. 3, pp. 74–75.

Panin did not extend the search for a precedent very far afield but simply took over Bernstorff's plan bodily. The formulation of these five points represents at first glance the interests of a nation with a large merchant fleet rather than those of a nation with no fleet worth the name. But there were several good reasons why the principle of "free ships, free goods" corresponded to basic Russian interests. In the first place, the Empress, a child of the enlightenment, had always devoted a good deal of attention to the economic problems facing Russia, notably in the field of foreign trade. Considerable interest was aroused by the economic theories propounded in France and Britain, and, though theory might run far ahead of practice, her reign is marked by a distinctive effort to see these problems in terms of the national interest as a whole, and not merely as methods for raising revenue.[8] Her victory in the first Turkish war had enabled her to wrest from the Porte the right for her ships to trade from the Black Sea to the Mediterranean through the Dardanelles. If she now proclaimed the principle "free ships, free goods" for her merchant fleet, and showed every intention of enforcing it, her subjects might be led by the prospect of certain profit and preferential treatment to venture into this field. Catherine was a realist but also an optimist. As she wrote to her confidant, Baron Grimm, on 14/25 May 1780: "mon commerce est comme mes villes, sur le papier et dans l'imagination; mais défiez vous de cela; tout cela poussera lorsqu'on s'y attendra le moins, comme les champignons." [9] The greater security of trade in Russian-owned ships might also increase the temptation for ships of other nations to take out Russian passes and sail under the Russian flag, thus increasing the total Russian register.[10]

8. Gerhardt, *England und der Aufstieg Russlands*, pp. 125 ff.; Pokrovsky, *Vneshnyaya torgovlya i vneshnyaya torgovaya politika Rossii*, pp. 106 ff.; Firsov, *Pravitel'stvo i obshchestvo v ikh otnosheniyakh k vneshney torgovle Rossii v tsarstvovaniye Imperatritsy Yekateriny II*, pp. 20–85, p. 333.

9. *Sbornik, 23,* 175, Catherine to Grimm, 14/25 May 1780. Catherine is obviously referring to trade with France and Spain, and not to the already flourishing trade with Britain and the United Provinces.

10. This was a not unjustifiable hope, judging by Vergennes's immediate reaction. On 25 April 1780 he wrote to Corberon inviting him to find out from Panin "les ressources que nous pourrions trouver dans la navigation russe pour le transport des provisions maritimes que nous sommes dans le cas de tirer de l'Empire." See CP Russie, *104,* Vergennes to Corberon, No. 11, 25 April 1780.

In the second place, the Empress had always viewed with reserve the great dependence of the Russian export trade on British ships. In her famous "Instruction" to the Legislative Commission of 1767, she had already pointed out the disadvantages of selling to only one customer.[11] In fact Britain by no means held a monopoly of the shipment of Russian export goods. British ships outnumbered all others, particularly in the port of St. Petersburg, but Dutch ships were next in number and outnumbered the British in Riga for instance.[12] In 1778, 5.6 million roubles worth of goods were exported from St. Petersburg in British bottoms, and 5.4 million roubles worth in ships of other nations.[13] Since the outbreak of war British ships could no longer supply the French and Spanish markets. This trade could only be kept alive by neutrals, mainly the Dutch who for instance carried the bulk of the hemp exported from Russia to France.[14] As early as 1776 the British consul in St. Petersburg noted the great extension of direct trade between Russia and France and Spain, mostly in naval stores. In that year 339 British ships had visited St. Petersburg, and 285 other foreign ships.[15] In 1779, the figures were 314 British ships and 379 foreign ships.[16] With such a high proportion of the Russian export trade carried in neutral ships it was not surprising that the Empress should have endeavoured to ensure them safe access to her ports. But more than that was necessary. The 1770s and 1780s were a pe-

11. See Reddaway, *Documents of Catherine the Great*, p. 266, Ch. XIII of the Instruction, Articles 327 and 328; see also Rahbek Schmidt, "The Treaty of Commerce between Great Britain and Russia, 1766," for a study of Catherine's anti-monopolistic policy in trade; cf. also Dmytryshin, "The Economic Content of the 1767 Nakaz of Catherine II" (at p. 6), and Firsov, *Pravitel'stvo*, p. 332.

12. Rahbek Schmidt, "The Treaty of Commerce," pp. 119–20.

13. Figures supplied by Consul Shairp for 1778. Never before, commented the consul, had the amount carried by non-British shipping come so near to that carried in British bottoms. He attributed this change to the number of ships sailing for Elsinore and Amsterdam but in reality destined for French ports, as well as to the increase of direct trade in neutral bottoms to France (SP 91/103, Shairp to Weymouth, 7/18 May 1779).

14. SP 91/102, Consul Shairp to W. Frazer, 19 July 1778.

15. SP 91/101, Consul Shairp to Suffolk, 7/18 February 1777, giving the figures for 1776.

16. SP 91/104, Consul Shairp to Stormont, 15/26 February 1780 (figures for 1779). But though British ships were outnumbered, exports on British ships were higher in value (6,032,602 roubles) than on foreign ships (2,192,956 roubles).

riod of economic expansion in Russia; the nobility took an active part in the exploitation of the natural resources of their estates, and both national and class interests were served by a policy which aimed at encouraging the development of foreign trade by every means. If new markets for Russian produce were to be opened up, the neutrals must be able not only to arrive safely and load up their cargoes; they must be certain of reaching their ultimate destination. Hence the privileged position of the Dutch under the treaty of 1674 was advantageous to Russia, since if they could secure respect for their rights they would be able to supply France and Spain with naval stores.[17] The extension of the principle of "free ships, free goods" to all the neutral trading nations was therefore quite in line with the needs of Russian economic development at that time.

There was a further reason for Russia to take up the principle of "free ships, free goods." It was incorporated in her only commercial treaty, that with Great Britain. It would have been strange indeed had Russia refrained from proclaiming a principle to which she was entitled by treaty with one belligerent and which was now proclaimed for reasons of expediency by the leader of the other belligerent camp. But the doctrine "free ships, free goods" was not being championed by Russia for the first time. Ever since Russia had had a navy, Russian statesmen had been compelled to define their attitude to this problem, and it had been conditioned, as in the case of other powers, by their strength at sea. The Russian fighting fleet was small and inexperienced. Russia could not therefore afford to offend any of the major powers who were in a position to defend their trade. As early as 1719, during the Great Northern War with Sweden, Peter I had declared that he would place no obstacles in the way of neutral navigation to Swedish ports if the Swedes reciprocated in kind and even if they did not.[18] This was due to no kindness to Sweden but to fear of British reprisals if British trade with Sweden were interrupted. In the

17. See e.g. Maykov, *Pis'ma A. A. Bezborodka*, p. 66, Bezborodko to Rumyantsev, 23 April/5 May 1780.

18. For past Russian practice see Taube, "Le statut juridique de la Mer Baltique jusqu'au début du XIX siècle"; *Morskoy Sbornik, 12* (1854), p. 173, "Obozreniye traktatov o morskom torgovom neutralitete" (anon.).

Seven Years' War a convention was concluded between Sweden and Russia, to which Denmark later acceded, which by Article 1 allowed neutrals to trade freely, except in contraband, with the ports of Prussia with whom Russia was at war.[19] During the Russo-Turkish war of 1768–1774, the same caution in the treatment of neutrals was observed. The Russian fleet was too far from its base, and surrounded by too many powers which viewed its presence in the Mediterranean with hostility, to allow Russia to detain ships carrying enemy property in the usual manner.[20] "Free ships, free goods" was therefore not only in conformity with Russian interests at the time; it also belonged to the Russian tradition, by force of circumstance, no doubt. But what Russia had granted to others in the past she saw no reason not to secure for herself now.

The view that the Empress was deceived into approving principles she did not understand must rest on two assumptions: first that she was an ignorant woman, incapable of appreciating the subtleties of maritime international law and the conditions of trade; and secondly that in arming her fleet she intended to benefit Britain but was misled into changing her policy. It is difficult to believe that Catherine, who had trained herself to be a ruler by constant and systematic reading during her years as Grand Duchess; who had studied Blackstone and Montesquieu, Beccaria and Bayle; who read the gazettes; and who was kept informed of the Anglo-Dutch dispute in which these principles were constantly ventilated by her ministers at both courts, could really have failed to understand the legal, political, and economic implications of the principle "free ships, free goods."

There is no evidence other than Harris's reports of Potemkin's pretty speeches that the Empress contemplated the armament of

19. G. F. de Martens, *Recueil, Supplément*, tome 3, pp. 36–41.

20. For instructions to Admiral Orlov, see *Sbornik, 1*, passim. See particularly the rescript of 11/22 August 1769, p. 22; see also rescript to Admiral Spiridov, 19 May 1770, p. 123. It must be added that Russian ships did frequently detain neutral ships, and disputes arising from these detentions had not yet been settled by 1780. The Empress had on the whole endeavoured to give satisfaction, for it was her policy to subordinate her rights as a belligerent to the political situation and to avoid giving any pretext to France or Spain to send squadrons into the Eastern Mediterranean on the excuse of commerce protection.

her fleet as a measure in Britain's favour. Though her manner to
the British envoy was invariably friendly, and she expressed pleasure at the news of British victories, she had shown when she refused the British offer of alliance that she intended to maintain
a strict neutrality. Moreover Catherine had already twice remonstrated with Britain over the treatment of neutral trade, once in
December 1778 and again in November 1779, when Simolin had
protested at the detention of Russian ships and had also demanded
the free passage of Russian goods on board other neutrals,[21] notably a Dutch ship. The Empress had been taken aback by Britain's
attack on the Dutch convoy, and, as Harris later admitted, she
had tactfully protested against such arbitrary behaviour.[22] "Neutrality" was indeed the key word in the League of Armed Neutrality, but there is evidence that the Empress did not intend
that Russian neutrality should even appear to incline towards
Britain. Galitzin said as much to the Prince of Orange. But above
all, that Russia should have approached the United Provinces at
all with a view to concerting common measures of trade protection
is evidence of an orientation in Russian policy which by no stretch
of the imagination could be interpreted as favouring Britain. That
the Empress was planning measures of trade protection against
both belligerent sides emerges from every single reference she
made to her policy before Panin was instructed to carry it out.
In her letter to Grimm of 2/13 February, she writes of a declaration to be made to the King of Spain "et à d'autres aussi." In her
rescript to Galitzin of 14/25 February she instructs him to sound
the Dutch on measures of trade protection against both belligerent
sides. Moreover even Potemkin told Harris, when he first mentioned the armament of the fleet, that it was intended to defend
trade "envers et contre tous." [23] In circles close to the Empress it
was fully understood that the Neutral League would protect di-

21. See Ch. 6, p. 149.
22. On 28 April/9 May 1780 Harris wrote to Keith "that the Empress never
disapproved our conduct with the Dutch, never but in the most gentle manner
accuses us of arbitrary behaviour and her Ministers and not herself have explained
her sentiments to Europe as friendly to France and most hostile to us" (Add. MSS.
35.518, f. 262). Harris does here admit that Catherine had thought the attack
arbitrary.
23. See Ch. 6, pp. 158–59.

rect trade between Russia and the two Bourbon powers and "would enable them to sustain the war." It was also fully appreciated that the League would deprive Britain of her maritime supremacy.[24] Thus the picture of Catherine deceived by Panin into putting her name to a policy which though ostensibly directed against Spain was in fact aimed at Britain will not stand up against an analysis of the events. The Spanish seizures in fact provided Russia with an occasion for appearing impartial. Harris indeed heard later in April a perfectly accurate account of the Empress's reasoning which Panin had given to the Swedish envoy, but he was by then too prejudiced to believe it. When Nolcken had asked Panin why the Russian Empress now proposed to Sweden the very plan she had rejected the previous year when it had been proposed to her, Panin replied "that then [1778–79] England was the only power who had given rise to complaints, and that it would have appeared hostile to her to have adopted at that period such a measure—that now Spain having also caused great interruption to neutral trade, it could be carried into execution without any appearance of partiality." [25]

That the Empress initiated and carried through the whole policy is finally confirmed by her private secretary Bezborodko in a letter of 26 February/8 March 1780, the day before the Empress signed the declaration. According to Bezborodko, Spain had provided the occasion for Catherine to launch her league of neutrals. The declaration itself was "based on the droit des gens, on the rules drawn up for the use of the fleet when it was sent to the archipelago, on the Anglo-Russian commercial treaty and on other sources." And he further described the advantages the Empress expected to draw from her new policy:

> These arrangements are producing a considerable effect on people. There seems to be no doubt that the court of Versailles, wishing to keep us from any connexion with Britain, does not only itself give us no cause to make use of this armament, but will also force the court of Madrid back onto a proper course . . . England will be even more careful not to offend

24. Maykov, *Pis'ma A. A. Bezborodka*, p. 66, Bezborodko to Rumyantsev, 23 April/ 4 May 1780.
25. SP 91/104, Harris to Stormont, No. 36, 17/28 April 1780.

us in the hope of gaining our help should things take a turn against her. The union of the five neutral powers can contribute considerably to stopping the war, and finally this conduct will give rise to a new system in the case of all wars between maritime powers. This achievement must be attributed to the Empress alone, who not only first suggested the idea, but has had to raise the failing spirits of her advisers by her own firmness before she can think of emboldening the councils of her allies, particularly the Portuguese.[26]

These words must carry more weight than the deliberate distortions which were given currency by Panin and Potemkin.

A further candidate for the honour of fathering the League of Armed Neutrality eventually emerged—namely Frederick II. When Harris saw how ill the Neutral League served the interests of his country, he put forward the view that Panin had acted under the inspiration of Frederick II. But the evidence shows that neither Goertz nor Frederick knew anything about the declaration until it was issued. In fact the news of Catherine's naval armament caused Frederick considerable anxiety.[27] Moreover, early in March 1780 the Princess of Orange communicated to her uncle the Dutch reply to Galitzin's overtures. Frederick, not realizing that the initiative had come from Russia, encouraged Holland to concert measures with Sweden and Denmark. "Mais je doute," he wrote, "que l'impératrice de Russie entre facilement dans ce parti; car son commerce n'a rien à risquer, parceque ce sont les marchands anglais qui le font. En second lieu l'Impératrice est si fière que je n'ose vous promettre de réussir, connaissant assez le terrain de Petersbourg pour prévoir toutes les difficultés que vous y trouverez." [28] The only part Frederick played was to enjoin repeatedly on his minister in Paris, Count Goltz, the necessity for France to persuade Spain to use more moderation.[29]

The initiative for forming the Neutral League therefore belongs to the Empress. But the confusing accounts of her policy

26. Maykov, *Pis'ma A. A. Bezborodka*, p. 58.
27. Harris Papers, Liston to Harris, 18 March 1780.
28. *PKFG*, *44*, 126, Princess of Orange to Frederick II, 6 March 1780; p. 127, Frederick II to Princess of Orange, 13 March 1780; cf. also p. 140, Frederick to Thulemeier, 16 March 1780.
29. *PKFG*, *44*, 138, Frederick to Goltz, 16 March 1780.

could not have arisen were it not for one grave weakness in the Russian system. The Empress conceived great ideas, and she read and approved the written documents in which they were expressed. But she could not control the verbal indiscretions of her servants. The rivalry of Panin and Potemkin led them both, in different ways and to a different degree, to betray the Empress. It was his hatred of Potemkin that drove Panin to revenge himself on Harris and Britain and to twist the Neutral League into an anti-British demonstration. Yet the immediate pretext of the Empress's action in arming the fleet had after all been the behaviour of Spain. When Vergennes in April 1780, in order to encourage Russian shipping to trade with French ports, suggested exempting them from the "droit de frêt" and the "droit d'aubaine," the Empress asked that these concessions should be put off until the end of the war, as she did not want to appear partial in her policy.[30]

When Catherine was told that Stormont had expressed astonishment at hearing of the purpose of her armament, which he had thought to have been made on Britain's behalf, she is reported to have exclaimed: "Et à quel titre a-t-on pu le croire? C'est apparement Mr. Harris qui aura forgé ces chimères." [31] It is Potemkin who should bear the blame, though, for his assurances to Harris were quite categoric. Clearly he either deceived Harris deliberately or was himself unaware of the implications of the Empress's plan, notably of the principle "free ships, free goods." At the beginning of May 1780, in one of his unceasing efforts to galvanize the Prince into action, Harris repeated to him "the talk of the town," that he, Potemkin, had been overreached. He expressed his disappointment that Potemkin had not been "kind enough" to show him the declaration before it was issued, when he could "easily have marked out to him the malicious and hostile turn which had been given to it" and prevented the triumph of Potemkin's, and incidentally his own, enemies. Faced with this remarkable suggestion Potemkin replied very mildly. He admitted that he had been "inattentive." He knew the Empress's instruc-

30. CP Russie, *104*, Vergennes to Corberon, No. 11, 25 April, 1780; Corberon to Vergennes, No. 24, 23 May 1780.

31. CP Russie, *104*, Corberon to Vergennes, private letter, 5 May 1780. See also Bezborodko to Rumyantsev, 23 April/4 May 1780, Maykov, *Pis'ma A. A. Bezborodka*, p. 66.

tions to be precise, and he could not suppose that her servants would so distort their original meaning. He confessed himself totally ignorant of all commercial matters, unacquainted with the *droit des gens;* he had therefore only taken a cursory view of the declaration when it was shown to him, and since he had been informed that Panin was to discuss it with the foreign envoys in St. Petersburg he had assumed that Harris had seen it before it was sent off.[32]

It is probably true that Potemkin knew little of commercial law. But he was not ignorant in matters of trade. He was himself actively engaged in promoting trade from the Black Sea, and a brisk export trade in naval stores was conducted from his estates in Belorussia.[33] A man of unusually sharp intelligence, he cannot be acquitted of knowledge of the Empress's plans. But it is just possible that in a grand, careless way he did not stop to think that to put Britain on the same level as Spain in her treatment of neutral ships was a bitter blow to those who had believed in his assurances of Russian friendship. So great, however, was his ascendancy over Harris that he managed to convince the latter not only of his good faith but of his ignorance, and he confirmed Harris in the view that Catherine had been betrayed by ill-intentioned advisers into taking a step which ran counter to her real inclinations. Potemkin's personal predilection for Harris's society was now openly gossiped about at court, and it was even reported that the Empress had taken the Prince to task on the subject. Potemkin had explained "que le personnel de Mr. Harris lui plaisait sans que cela influât en rien sur les affaires et l'opinion qu'il avait adoptée." [34] But there was probably a good deal of truth in the opinion, which the shrewd Vergennes maintained throughout, that the apparent divisions on policy at the Russian court were a mask behind which the Empress could "travailler plus tranquillement au maintien du système de la neutralité." [35]

However much the Empress's policy was misinterpreted at the time owing to the unpredictable behaviour of her underlings, it is clear that the Neutral League and the principles it championed

32. SP 91/105, Harris to Stormont, No. 49, 15/26 May 1780.

33. Dobrynin, *Istinnoye povestvovaniye, Russkaya Starina,* 1871, *4,* 106.

34. CP Russie, *104,* Corberon to Vergennes, No. 16, 1 April 1780.

35. CP Russie, *104,* Vergennes to Corberon, No. 9, 15 April 1780.

were well within the framework of traditional Russian policy, though one must not under-estimate the attraction to Catherine of becoming a law-giver in a field in which Russia had so far played an insignificant part. Such a role would appeal both to Catherine's personal and to her national vanity. The spectacle of Russia leading the united neutrals in defence of their alleged rights against both belligerents, and eventually perhaps forming so coherent a group as to impose their mediation on the powers at war, seems to have been before her at the time. Maybe she under-estimated the complexities of maritime law and tradition, and her policy was not based on a secure foundation of common interests. But she did undoubtedly seize the moment when transitory conditions seemed to unite a number of European powers in order to put herself at their head and give added weight to Russia in the concert of Europe.

The Empress's declaration on neutral trade was immediately welcomed by Vergennes. Catherine's present policy harmonized so well with his own that it was not unnatural that he, and after him his admirers among French historians, should have believed that he had inspired it.[36] The Empress's declaration required France to make no departure from her present attitude towards neutral shipping, and the official French reply, dated 25 April 1780, welcomed the new Russian *démarche* in glowing terms and expressed great satisfaction at the community of views between France and Russia.[37]

Vergennes's main anxiety concerned the attitude Spain might adopt. In St. Petersburg, Versailles, and Berlin much thought was given to the task of inducing the Spaniards to give a polite answer to the Russian declaration.[38] The anxiety was however needless.

36. See e.g. Doniol, *Histoire, 4,* Pt. 5, p. 696; Fauchille, *La diplomatie française,* p. 355.

37. Scott, *Armed Neutralities,* p. 284; Vergennes to Montmorin, 3 April 1780, quoted in Fauchille, *La diplomatie française,* p. 377.

38. See *Morskoy Sbornik, 43,* 356, No. 30, Panin to the Empress, 5/16 March 1780, for Panin's request to Corberon to bring pressure to bear on Madrid; see also Corberon to Vergennes, 29 February 1780, "C'est sur la raideur du Pardo que Sir Harris fonde ses espérances . . ." (Fauchille, *La diplomatie française,* p. 235); see also CP Russie, *104,* Corberon to Vergennes, No. 14, 10 March 1780; Vergennes to Montmorin, 2 March 1780, Fauchille, p. 327; *PKFG, 44,* 152, Goertz to Frederick, 10 March 1780, "Tout va dépendre de la manière dont on répondra à Madrid . . ."

Floridablanca took fright at the idea that the impending League of the North might be directed against Spain, and in a somewhat half-hearted way he was prepared to make concessions to neutral trade. The Spanish reply, dated 18 April 1780, after blaming Britain for Spain's past deviations from strict justice in her conduct towards neutral ships, declared Spain's intention of respecting the neutral flags of all courts "that have consented or shall consent to defend it till His Majesty finds what part the English navy takes, and whether they will, together with their privateers, keep within proper bounds." Neutrals were however warned that the blockade of Gibraltar continued in force, and that the rules established by the Spanish *règlement* of 13 March 1780 must be followed.[39]

It now remained for Russia to gain the adherence of the neutral powers to the plan for a convention, and here difficulties were to arise where they were least expected. Panin, now completely recovered from his illness and rejuvenated by the apparent renewal of the Empress's confidence in him, indulged in an unwonted burst of activity. However, Danish caution and Swedish vanity were to lead to unforeseen delays. The Empress's rescript to Sacken of 27 February/9 March 1780 in which she had put forward Bernstorff's plan of September 1778 as the basis for negotiations with Denmark, clearly shows that she expected Denmark to welcome her new policy. Bernstorff did indeed joyfully accede to her plan, and then proceeded to put forward every possible difficulty, for the Empress had now proposed something very different from his own more limited plan for a convention to safeguard the trade of the Baltic states.

Bernstorff was at this time in a somewhat difficult position. He represented the more moderate element in the Danish Royal Council, and he believed in a neutrality which favoured Britain, as long as Denmark ran no risk of alienating Russia.[40] But his colleagues on the Royal Council had for some time desired to take a stronger line with Britain in view of the persistent seizure of Danish ships.[41] The issue had become acute in the autumn of 1779,

39. Scott, *Armed Neutralities*, p. 279.

40. See Holm, *Om Danmarks*, pp. 74 ff., Bernstorff to the King of Denmark, 17 March 1780, for an exposé of Bernstorff's political ideas.

41. Bernstorff's difficulties were partly due to the fact that several members of the Danish Royal Council and even of the Royal Family were engaged in trade

for in spite of the cold reception granted to previous British overtures Stormont had made a fresh effort in November to secure an
alliance with Denmark, offering a subsidy and the guarantee of
the Danish East and West Indian possessions in exchange for the
assistance of twelve ships of the line.[42] Bernstorff temporized on
these proposals, fully aware that Britain was at the same time seeking the alliance of Russia; meanwhile he put forward the claims
of Denmark to participate in the immunities theoretically allowed
to the Dutch flag and pressed for a revision of the article dealing
with contraband goods in the Anglo-Danish treaty.[43] On 8 February Stormont, who had not yet heard from Harris that Russia
had refused the British proposals for an alliance, wrote to Eden
proposing a triple alliance between Russia, Denmark, and Britain,
with the present war as the *casus foederis,* and suggesting that the
remodelling of the commercial treaty could go *pari passu* with the
drafting of the main treaty.[44]

Fully conversant with the intricacies of the British constitution,
Bernstorff was aware that a ruling of the admiralty court on the
interpretation of the Anglo-Danish treaty was an essential pre-
requisite for settling the status of Danish shipping.[45] But strangely
enough, whenever a Danish ship or Danish property aboard another neutral was captured, the admiralty court found grounds to
release or condemn without a definite reference to the treaty.[46]
Hence Bernstorff's efforts to use the British overture to extort a
recognition of the privileges of Danish navigation. While the British offers were still being discussed by the Danish Council, news
reached Copenhagen of the Russian proposal to form a neutral
league.[47]

---

in provisions, and they naturally objected to British seizures (see SP 75/136, Eden
to Stormont, No. 23, 29 April 1780).

42. SP 75/135, Stormont to Eden, No. 19, 30 November 1779; Harris was not
informed of these proposals.

43. SP 75/136, Eden to Stormont, No. 5, 11 January 1780; No. 6, 15 January 1780.

44. SP 75/136, Stormont to Eden, No. 4, 8 February 1780.

45. SP 75/136, Eden to Stormont, No. 12, 4 March 1780.

46. SP 75/136, Eden to Stormont, No. 21, 15 April 1780; No. 22, 22 April 1780;
No. 23, 29 April 1780, for Danish dissatisfaction at the release of the *Johanna
Elisabeth* without a decision being made by the court of appeal on Danish rights
under the treaty.

47. See Holm, *Om Danmarks,* pp. 70 and 74 ff. for Danish comments on the
British proposals (Bernstorff to the King, 3 March and 17 March 1780). The Russian declaration reached Copenhagen on 26 March (Holm, p. 94).

The Russian proposals went far beyond anything that Bernstorff had ever contemplated, though the principles it proclaimed were those he had himself drafted. It was one thing to extort concessions for Danish trade from Britain; but it was quite another to involve Denmark in the protection of the trade of her privileged commercial rivals, the Dutch. In a dispatch to the Danish envoy in St. Petersburg, Schumacher, Bernstorff expressed the hope that the whole idea might be dropped, at least in respect of Denmark.[48] To Sacken, the Russian envoy in Copenhagen, he spoke more circumspectly. He stressed the disadvantages of a plan which established no clear distinction between Denmark and Sweden in relation to Russia. Denmark was Russia's ally and Sweden was not, and it was important to Bernstorff to maintain the appearance of greater cordiality and intimacy between Russia and Denmark than between Russia and Sweden. In the second place, Bernstorff objected to the invitation to the United Provinces to join the League, on the grounds that they were slow, ill-equipped, and torn by faction. In addition both Sweden and the United Provinces were already involved in disputes over trade with Britain, "qu'il était utile d'avoir ni à partager ni à venger." Assuming that the Russian declaration was in fact a draft which had not yet been delivered to the belligerents, Bernstorff put forward counter-proposals to Russia. He suggested that a declaration should be made as part of a Russo-Danish convention, thus distinguishing Russo-Danish action from that of the other neutrals.[49]

But though he was taken aback by the Russian initiative and spoke of the Empress's declaration to Eden as "a piece of ostentation," Bernstorff nevertheless used the threat of Danish adherence to the Neutral League to secure free trade in the one commodity he was really interested in—salted provisions. Meanwhile the condemnation of a Danish cargo on board a Swedish ship finally decided the Council to demand the remodelling of the Anglo-Danish treaty [50] and to accede to Catherine's proposal to form a neutral

48. Boye, *De vaebnede Neutralitetsforbund et avsnit av Folkerettens Historie*, quoted in Scott, *Armed Neutralities*, p. 46, at p. 56.

49. *Morskoy Sbornik, 43*, 362, Bernstorff to Sacken, 30 March 1780. For Bernstorff's counter-proposals see Holm, *Om Danmarks*, pp. 97–104.

50. See SP 75/136, Stormont to Eden, No. 14, 21 April 1780, explaining the admiralty court's decision in the case of the Swedish ship *Concordia*, with a cargo of salt beef, Danish property, which was condemned; and Eden to Stormont, No.

league.[51] Stormont realized that this was no time for trifling, and
on 30 May 1780 he proposed that instead of the lengthy negotiation for remodelling the treaty, an explanatory article should be
agreed on to replace the existing Article 3 of the treaty of 1670.[52]
He enclosed a project by which the Danes gave up the right to
carry ships' timber in exchange for the freedom to trade in all kinds
of provisions to enemy ports. The vexed question of "free ships,
free goods" was not mooted; the British draft article dealt with
the definition of contraband alone. Bernstorff welcomed the British concession over the non-contraband nature of provisions, but
he still pressed for the recognition of Denmark's right to "free
ships, free goods." His position was all the more delicate in that,
though he desired to maintain Denmark in a halfway position between Russia and Britain, neither the Danish Royal Council nor
Russia agreed with him.

The Danish counter-proposals in fact met with scant sympathy
in Russia. Panin promptly eliminated any suggestion of special
treatment for Denmark on the ground that accession must be made
equally easy for all neutrals. He did however agree to a secret article by which the proposed Russo-Danish convention was to form
an integral part of the treaty of perpetual friendship of 1773, thus
to some extent meeting Bernstorff's objections.[53] But he insisted
that Denmark must make a declaration on the lines of that of the
Empress. Bernstorff was unable to hold out against the majority
of the Council, which saw an opportunity to secure Russian protection for the Danish claim of "free ships, free goods." [54] He therefore carried on negotiations with Russia and Britain simultaneously. A convention with Russia was signed on 9 July 1780 and
Denmark issued a declaration of the principles of neutral trade
and of the intention to enforce them by arming part of the Dan-

29, 13 May 1780 for the Danish decision to ask for the remodelling of the Anglo-
Danish treaty, as a result of the Royal Council's anger at the British decision in
the case of the *Concordia*.

51. SP 75/136, Eden to Stormont, No. 30, 16 May 1780.

52. SP 75/136, Stormont to Eden, No. 19, 30 May 1780.

53. *Morskoy Sbornik, 43,* 378, Panin to Catherine, 23 May/4 June 1780, enclosing
the drafts of the conventions. Scott, *Armed Neutralities,* p. 299, does not print the
text of the secret article, for which see *Morskoy Sbornik, 44,* 155, No. 49.

54. *Morskoy Sbornik, 43,* 384, Panin to Sacken, draft approved by the Empress
on 30 May/11 June 1780; SP 75/136, Eden to Stormont, No. 43, 11 July 1780.

ish navy. It was somewhat more conciliatory in tone than that of the Empress of Russia, but it incorporated all the five principles which Catherine had proclaimed. Article 2, which defined contraband, invoked the third article of the Anglo-Danish treaty of 1670 as governing the issue between Britain and Denmark.[55] It was on this very article that negotiations were at that time proceeding between Bernstorff and Eden. The claim to "free ships, free goods" in paragraph 2 of the Danish declaration was of course combated by Eden in his talks with Bernstorff. But as the Danish minister made it clear that while Denmark would not give up the right she would nevertheless not insist on enforcing it, the negotiations for the modification of the Anglo-Danish treaty continued.[56] The text of the new explanatory article agreed by Stormont was dated 4 July 1780, but in fact Eden received the Danish ratification only on 3 October 1780. Thus, though Denmark was technically a pillar of Catherine's Neutral League, secretly a breach was already being made in the system. Denmark was about to give up the right to carry naval stores in favour of a free and certain trade in the foodstuffs which provided the bulk of Danish exports. Though the claim to "free ships, free goods" remained on paper, it would cease to be a bone of contention in practice.[57]

Swedish reaction was somewhat different. The King of Sweden had already decided to institute convoys to protect his ships, ostensibly against both belligerents, in practice only against Britain. He might be expected to fall in at once with Catherine's new plans. But young and vain, the King did not wish to appear to be acting

55. See Scott, *Armed Neutralities*, p. 297; Articles 26 and 27 of the Danish-French commercial treaty of 1742 were to rule relations with France and were extended to Spain with whom Denmark had no commercial treaty.

56. SP 75/136, Eden to Stormont, No. 43, 11 July 1780.

57. For the text of the explanatory article, see Scott, *Armed Neutralities*, p. 295; because it is dated 4 July 1780, it has been assumed (notably by Fauchille, *La diplomatie française*, pp. 427 ff. whose account is extremely biassed) that the explanatory article was the result of a clever intrigue between Britain and Bernstorff to circumvent Russia before Denmark joined the League. But the negotiations on the article continued for some time after Denmark had signed the Russo-Danish convention, and Bernstorff did not discuss it with the Royal Council until after 18 July 1780. (See SP 75/136, Eden to Stormont, No. 46, 18 July 1780). The idea had in any case been mooted long before the Empress thought of the Neutral League. There was however something underhand in Bernstorff's concealment of the negotiations with Eden from Russia.

solely under Russian impulsion. He therefore requested an explanation in more detail of some of the issues raised by the declaration [58] and in addition put forward the suggestion that Russia
and Sweden should work towards a joint mediation between the
belligerents.[59] However, the Empress and Panin were not going
to be drawn into showing any special favours to Sweden. The
Swedish proposal was swept aside and Panin substituted a separate article, which was also included in the convention with Denmark, by which the signatories bound themselves to cooperate in
achieving peace between the belligerents when the opportunity
should arise.[60] The Russian draft was eventually accepted by the
King of Sweden, and the Swedish declaration was issued on 21 July
1780.[61] The Russo-Swedish convention was signed on 1 August
1780; it was drawn up in the same terms as the Russo-Danish convention, but Article 2 invoked the terms of the Anglo-Swedish
treaty of 1661 to govern the definition of contraband in relation
to Britain.[62]

The three Baltic powers had now agreed to act in unison, though
Denmark's impending treachery was of course not suspected. The
squadrons of the signatories were to act together or separately to
protect the trade of their own or their allies' subjects but in accordance with the treaties that bound each signatory separately
to the belligerents. They were to concert diplomatic action when
it became necessary to demand compensation for damages inflicted
on their subjects and were also to concert measures and unite their
forces in the event of one of the signatories being attacked "in con-

58. Scott, *Armed Neutralities*, p. 278; *Morskoy Sbornik, 43,* 371, No. 36, Rückman
(Russian chargé d'affaires) to Panin, 25 March/5 April 1780.

59. *Morskoy Sbornik, 43,* 378, Panin to Catherine, 23 May/4 June 1780.

60. Scott, *Armed Neutralities*, p. 299 (Article 2 of the separate articles) and p.
311, ditto.

61. Scott, *Armed Neutralities*, p. 307.

62. Scott, *Armed Neutralities*, p. 311. The Franco-Swedish treaty of 1741 did not
deal with contraband, but it granted Sweden the privileges enjoyed by the Hanseatic
towns in France, and the King of Sweden "had nothing to add thereto." With
Spain, Sweden had no treaty and so the principles of the Anglo-Swedish and the
Franco-Swedish treaties were extended to apply to that country too. There were
some minor additions to Article 3 of the separate articles on the facilities to be
offered to the Swedish fleet in Russian ports; otherwise the texts of the separate
articles in the Russo-Danish and Russo-Swedish conventions were identical.

sequence or in contempt" of the convention (Article 8). Though this does not emerge from the text of the treaty, it is clear that such action was intended to be limited in scope. As Panin had stated to the King of Sweden, in reply to his request for an explanation of Russian policy, the united powers would make common cause at sea only "without its being a groundwork for other operations, as these connections are purely maritime, having no other object than naval commerce and navigation." [63] A loop-hole was thus left open for the signatories to escape becoming embroiled in the Anglo-French war.

Apart from these immediate aims, the conventions also laid down certain long-term objects. The principles of neutral navigation therein proclaimed were to be regarded as permanent (Article 9) and efforts were eventually to be made to secure their adoption by the maritime powers in general in all future naval wars (separate Article 5). Neutral nations were to be invited to accede freely to the existing conventions. The whole neutral edifice of the north was finally completed by the accession on 7 September 1780 of Denmark to the Russo-Swedish convention [64] and the accession on 9 September 1780 of Sweden to the Russo-Danish convention.[65]

The Russian approach to Portugal to join the Neutral League met at first with a negative reply. Portugal was too closely bound to Britain to take such a hostile step, and according to rumour too many Portuguese received a share of the lucrative British cap-

63. Scott, *Armed Neutralities*, p. 288. Reply of the Court of Russia to the Request of Sweden for Explanations respecting the Project for an Armed Neutrality, 29 April 1780. See also *AMON*, 5, 213, Thulemeier to Frederick II, 27 June 1780, reporting a remark attributed to Panin that "le traité d'alliance ne pourra être relatif qu'aux insultes que les cours alliées éprouveraient sur mer."

64. Scott, *Armed Neutralities*, p. 321.

65. Ibid., p. 322. Scott, *Armed Neutralities*, p. 290 prints a "Declaration of His Danish Majesty regarding the Neutrality of the Baltic Sea," which he dates 8 May 1781. In fact this declaration belongs to 1781 and has been wrongly dated by G. F. de Martens, *Recueil*, 3, 175, and by Clausen, *Recueil de tous les traités . . . de Danemark, 1766–1794*, p. 138 etc., and quoted as such also by Bergbohm, *Die bewaffnete Neutralität*, p. 281. Eggers, *Denkwürdigkeiten*, p. 138, note, gives the correct date. The first separate articles however of both the Russo-Danish and the Russo-Swedish conventions did express the agreement of the three powers to concert measures to prevent "all hostilities, piracy and acts of violence" in the Baltic.

tures carried out by British ships based on Portuguese ports to wish to abandon their present system.[66] Negotiations with the United Provinces were to prove long and complicated. The Empress's memorandum proposing the formation of the Neutral League had been formally presented to the States General on 3 April 1780.[67] It was followed soon after by the threatened declaration of the court of St. James unilaterally abrogating all treaty privileges set forth in the various Anglo-Dutch treaties and, in particular, suspending the Marine Treaty of 1674.[68] The United Provinces were now regarded by Britain as having forfeited the right to "free ships, free goods." The States General thereupon agreed on 24 April 1780 to undertake negotiations with Russia,[69] but the Dutch resisted Galitzin's pressure to issue immediately a declaration of principles similar to that of Russia. They wished to avoid driving Britain into war, and before issuing a declaration they wished to conclude a defensive alliance with the Northern powers.[70] Such a negotiation was too important, in the opinion of the States General, to be conducted by their resident in Russia, Swart, who, though he had considerable knowledge of backstairs intrigue, had little opportunity to circulate in high society or among the more influential courtiers.[71] The States General therefore de-

66. See Fauchille, *La diplomatie française*, p. 553 for details of the Portuguese reaction to the Russian proposals. According to the *Gazette de la Haye* of 24 March 1780, Commodore Johnstone, commander of the squadron cruising off Lisbon had rented a house in Lisbon to conduct his affairs in greater comfort (Harris Papers, Yorke to Harris, enclosure in 1 April 1780).

67. Scott, *Armed Neutralities*, p. 275.

68. Ibid., p. 277, Declaration of the Court of London to the States General of the Netherlands withdrawing all Treaty Privileges, 17 April 1780.

69. See *Nieuwe Nederlandsche Jaerboeken*, 1780, *1*, 564, for text of the resolution of the States General.

70. See *AMON*, 2, 177, Grand Pensionary to Prince of Orange, 8 April 1780; p. 179, Prince of Orange to Grand Pensionary, 8 April 1780; p. 201, the same to the same, 6 May 1780; and p. 202 for the Grand Pensionary's reply of the same date.

71. See Corberon, *Journal Intime*, 2, 196: "C'est un grand nouvelliste, un peu partial, un peu loup-garou, un peu borné, un peu grossier, un peu honnête, mais qui à la faveur de tous ces un peu et d'une grande routine, n'est pas un homme indifférent. Il a d'ailleurs un grain d'originalité qui me plaît assez, et de très bon vin que j'aime beaucoup. Je vais chez lui comme au café et cela est commode." Harris's grand Whig prejudices render him far more scathing: "The Dutch resident, Swart, is a man neither of birth nor character, totally improper for the post he fills: he is married here, and though his wife has given strong marks of preference

cided to appoint two special envoys who were entrusted with the negotiations and were given instructions not to conclude an alliance
unless they could achieve a Russian guarantee for the Dutch possessions overseas.[72] The tempo of affairs was so slow in the unwieldy
republic that the special envoys did not set out until the summer
and were not due to arrive in St. Petersburg until September 1780.

The first few months of 1780 were thus a period of intense
diplomatic activity in St. Petersburg, and the Empress might well
have felt satisfaction as she surveyed the scene. Russia had launched
an international enterprise which would extend her influence from
Sweden to Portugal. The Empress was universally acclaimed among
the merchant communities and her achievement celebrated in
somewhat limping verse.[73] But she had another profound motive
for self-satisfaction. At the beginning of February 1780 a messenger
had arrived in St. Petersburg from the Russian ambassador in
Vienna, Prince D. M. Galitzin,[74] bringing the news that the Emperor Joseph II had expressed a wish to meet the Empress Catherine in person, on the occasion of journeys which the two sovereigns had both planned shortly to undertake in their respective
dominions.[75] Such a move on the part of the Emperor represented
a great triumph for Catherine, and it was no wonder that "she
reddened with joy when the dispatches were read to her." [76] The

to others of still lower origin than himself, yet these make still part of his house-
hold, and she still governs his house" (SP 91/103, Harris to Weymouth, No. 59, 9/20
September 1779 (*MD, 1,* 260)).

72. For instructions to the Dutch plenipotentiaries see Edler, *Dutch Republic
and American Revolution,* p. 146; Yorke to Harris, 8 July 1780 (Harris Papers).

73. See e.g. Bil'basov, *Istoriya Yekateriny vtoroy,* 2 (*12*), Obzor inostrannykh
sochineniy, No. 365; No. 367:

> Poursuis Auguste impératrice
> Poursuis tous tes nobles projets . . .
> Arbitre, équitable et puissante
> Finis l'esclavage des mers . . .

74. Prince D. M. Galitzin had represented Russia in Vienna since 1762, and is
not to be confused with the envoy of the same surname at The Hague.

75. See Arneth, *Maria Theresias letzte Regierungszeit, 4,* 667–70 for an account
of the Emperor's decision to meet Catherine—taken without consulting Kaunitz.

76. SP 91/104, Harris to Stormont, No. 12, 15/26 February 1780. It is possible
that this news, which reached Russia at the beginning of February, encouraged
Catherine to launch out into the Neutral League, in the full confidence that she
need fear no continental troubles in her rear. But on the whole at this very

initiative had come from the Emperor; it set the seal on the predominant position Russia had acquired in German affairs as a
result of her intervention in the War of the Bavarian Succession.
Strict secrecy surrounded the projected interview at first, but the
news was soon bruited abroad and immediately set all courts spec-
ulating on the possible consequences of this unforeseen event.
The interview was expected to take place early in June, but already London, Versailles, and Berlin were contemplating with
pleasure, anxiety, and fear the prospect opened up by the meeting
of the restless Joseph and the ambitious Catherine.

---

early stage in the development of Russian policy Austrian influence appears to
have been slight.

8. The Impact of the Armed Neutrality on Britain

STORMONT had weathered this difficult period, during which the tension caused by the British detention of neutral ships had mounted ever higher, because of the confidence which Harris's dispatches inspired in him; he felt that whatever Panin might say, the Empress was fundamentally inclined to favour Great Britain. Early in 1780 he still harboured some hopes that he might be able to procure naval support for Britain from Denmark, Russia, or possibly both. Yet both powers had repeatedly protested against British treatment of neutral shipping. It never occurred to Stormont that Russia, with her tiny merchant fleet, would take more than limited action to protect what appeared to be her immediate interests, namely the approach to her coasts. He was reassured too by Harris's reports that the energetic protests of Russia against the detention of Russian ships represented Panin's policy and not that of the Empress.[1] The first faint cloud appeared on this horizon when Sir Joseph Yorke at last began to notice the activities of Galitzin at The Hague. Towards the middle of February 1780 he wrote to Stormont of the desire among the more "violent" of the Dutch to win the support of the Northern powers in their quarrel with Britain—but he did not yet suspect that Russia entered the picture.[2] Stormont was not at the time unduly disturbed; he expected the Dutch to appeal to the Northern powers for support, but trusted that the commercial rivalry between the Scandinavian nations and their Dutch rivals would prevent any concerted action.[3]

1. SP 91/104, Harris to Stormont, No. 91, 31 December 1779/11 January 1780.
2. SP 84/569, Yorke to Stormont, No. 13, 11 February 1780.
3. SP 84/569, Stormont to Yorke, No. 7, 15 February 1780.

Yorke himself seems not to have taken Galitzin's activities seriously when he discovered them,[4] but at last, on 11 March 1780, he thought it worth-while to warn Harris of the use to which the Empress's name was being put. He was convinced that Galitzin had no orders from his court, "but I think it likely he has intrigued through Count Panin to get leave of representing things otherwise than they are: and that somehow the King of Prussia is at the bottom." [5] Once again Panin and Frederick II were cast as the villains of the piece. Stormont was quicker to take alarm. On 7 March 1780 he wrote to Harris to warn him of what he believed to be a Dutch plan to form a league of commerce protection in common with the Northern powers, and he expressed his surprise "that it is not only countenanced but strongly abetted by Prince Galitzin." He urged Harris at once to endeavour to get Galitzin's instructions revoked, if he had any. And if he had none, Harris was to procure a reprimand to the Russian minister for his extraordinary behaviour.[6] Stormont had of course as yet no knowledge of Catherine's plan for a neutral league. The news that the Dutch were planning, apparently on their own initiative, to unite with the Northern powers merely served to determine him to pursue an increasingly rigid policy. In this he acted under the influence of Yorke, who encouraged him in the belief that strong measures would make the Dutch more tractable and who hoped that the plan for a union with the Northern powers would not go beyond mere words.[7]

Harris's habit of reporting on the progress of his diplomatic activity only when he could give a definitive account of the end of a particular phase of it had certain disadvantages for his principals. They were kept in the dark for a long time as to the out-

4. Yorke first mentions the possibility of joint action by the United Provinces and Russia on 22 February 1780 (SP 84/569, No. 16, to Stormont).

5. Harris Papers, 11 March 1780, to Harris. It is interesting to note in view of the theory put forward by Fauchille, that Vauguyon was the guiding spirit in the Dutch intrigue with Galitzin, that according to Yorke, "the French ambassador does not seem to have procured any positive orders relative to the intrigue for applying to Russia but only watches the steps that are taken, and to give account of them . . ." (SP 84/569, Yorke to Stormont, No. 21, 3 March 1780).

6. SP 91/104, Stormont to Harris, No. 11, 7 March 1780.

7. SP 84/569, Yorke to Stormont, No. 14, 15 February 1780; No. 16, 22 February 1780; No. 25, 17 March 1780.

come of his negotiations, though he did drop occasional hints on the difficulties he was meeting. Stormont only heard of the failure of the proposed Russian alliance, which he had set in train as early as November 1779, on 21 March 1780, when an enormous packet from Harris reached him at last.[8] He took the set-back in good part; for the present the idea of an alliance must be dropped. "It is not for the King's dignity to *sollicit* any alliance, how respectable how desirable soever," he wrote to Harris on 11 April 1780. But if a fresh opportunity arose, Harris's instructions still held good. Above all Stormont was impressed by Harris's accounts of the personal favour shown him by the Empress and by the general tone of her expressions of sympathy towards England. Hence he even interpreted the armament of her squadron, news of which reached him in these same dispatches, as a good sign, and he expressed the hope that it would not remain in the Baltic but make an appearance in the Mediterranean to protect trade against the "violence of Spain," "a measure of great dignity for Russia, and of no small advantage to this country . . ." [9] Stormont was also much encouraged with the news Harris had early procured of the impending interview between the Empress and Joseph II. He had been long at the Austrian court and viewed the traditional Anglo-Austrian alliance with nostalgia. "Since the destruction of that system," he wrote hopefully to Harris, "all our foreign politicks have been nothing more than the little expedients of the day." [10] Though too experienced to expect any immediate results from such an interview, he began to hope that, with the help of Russia, Austria might be weaned from France and a breach made in the existing system of alliances on the continent into which Britain might insert herself.

On the whole, therefore, in spite of the evasiveness of Denmark and Russia's refusal to conclude an alliance, Stormont still viewed Britain's prospects with a certain equanimity at the end of March 1780. But all his hopes were shattered when Simolin early in April

8. SP 91/104, Stormont to Harris, No. 14, 24 March 1780.

9. SP 91/104, Stormont to Harris, No. 15, 11 April 1780. This dispatch, though dated and presumably sent on 11 April was drafted earlier, before Stormont had received the news of the Empress's declaration which had reached him on 1 April.

10. SP 91/104, Stormont to Harris, No. 16, 11 April 1780.

presented him with a copy of the Empress's declaration on the principles which were to govern neutral trade. Stormont saw at once that article 2 of the declaration ran completely counter to the policy which Britain had been pursuing with regard to the Dutch Republic.[11] His reaction to the Russian declaration is expressed in five dispatches to Harris, of 11 April 1780, which reveal a mounting crescendo of bewilderment. But though Stormont could not understand the cause of the Russian declaration, he understood only too well the effects it would have. The second article, as he wrote to Harris, "proceeds upon a mistake and lays down as a principle of the law of Nations, *that* which is a manifest variation of that law which some states have agreed to make by particular specifick engagements." It was awkward to enter into discussion of points of substance with a court hitherto regarded as friendly, but "it is absolutely impossible to admit a principle that is in direct contradiction to the uniform decisions of the court of Admiralty, of this country and every other country, from time immemorial." [12] A good face had to be put upon this blow in public, however, and Stormont warned Harris that British official opinion was to be that the declaration had been called for by the conduct of Spain and had been communicated to Britain as a matter of form in order that Russia might keep up the appearance of strict impartiality.[13] But Harris was instructed to attempt to explain through Panin to the Empress "the objections there are to some of the positions in the declaration." He was to take extreme care "not to drop a syllable that can be construed into an acquiescence in the erroneous doctrine which that article [2] endeavours to establish." [14]

A polite but non-committal reply was dispatched to Harris to deliver in Russia. Here the usual British position was set out, namely that British conduct was governed by equity and moderation. It was in accordance with the principles generally acknowl-

11. Fortescue, *Correspondence of King George III*, 5, 38, Stormont to the King, 1 April 1780: "The second article if adhered to would totally destroy all that has been so properly resolved with regard to the Dutch."

12. SP 91/104, the same to the same, No. 17, 11 April 1780.

13. Ibid., the same to the same, No. 21, 11 April 1780. See also *PKFG, 44*, 210, n. 2, Maltzahn to Frederick, 7 April 1780.

14. Ibid., the same to the same, No. 17, 11 April 1780.

edged to be the law of nations and with the tenor of British engagements with other powers, which engagements "have altered this primitive law, by mutual stipulations, proportioned to the will and convenience of the contracting parties." Since the beginning of hostilities, the King had given orders "respecting the flag of Her Imperial Majesty and the commerce of her subjects, agreeable to the law of nations, and the tenor of the engagements stipulated by his treaty of commerce with her, and to which he shall adhere with the most scrupulous exactness," continued the British reply. Should any irregularity occur, the courts of admiralty would redress every hardship in "so equitable a manner, that Her Imperial Majesty shall be perfectly satisfied, and acknowledge a like spirit of justice which she herself possesses." [15] But though this official reply was couched in conciliatory terms, Stormont could not control the unruly tongues of his colleagues. Lord Hillsborough, secretary of state for the South, could not resist a *bon mot* to the effect that the Russian merchant navy would be the best protected of all fleets, as there were at least three warships to every merchant vessel. The remark flew round the diplomatic world in London and found its way into Simolin's dispatches to St. Petersburg. It did Britain no good.[16]

15. See Scott, *Armed Neutralities*, p. 282, for the text of the British reply dated 23 April 1780. See also Fortescue, *Correspondence of King George III, 5,* 38, Stormont to the King, 1 (?) April 1780. Harris saw Panin and delivered it on 24 April/5 May 1780, and the date given by Scott is Old Style. Reading the truncated letter of Harris of 30 December/11 January 1780 (see Ch. 6, pp. 150–51 and note 36). together with the British reply to the Russian declaration, Bergbohm, *Die bewaffnete Neutralität*, p. 144 and note 1, states that Britain clearly intended that Russian ships would in future be judged in the admiralty courts in accordance with paragraph two of the declaration, i.e. they would be entitled to "free ships, free goods." He further states that from then on Russian complaints about the treatment of their ships ceased. On both these points he is incorrect. (See Stormont's instruction to Harris of 11 April 1780 quoted in Ch. 6, note 36, and for Anglo-Russian disputes over shipping see Chapter 15.)

16. Simolin's dispatch of 27 March/7 April 1780 is printed in part in F. de Martens, *Recueil, 9,* 311, but Martens does not quote the offending remark. At the time Harris only heard that Simolin had quoted some remark which had offended the Empress. But later, in August 1782, he explained that it was Hillsborough who had "threatened, and, what was worse *persifflèd* the Russian fleet; and Simolin was forced to put this unguarded and unpleasant *plaisanterie* in his reports, since Lord Hillsborough had repeated it to the Prussian and Dane" (*MD, 1,* 535, Harris to Grantham, 16/27 August 1782). See also on British opinion, *PKFG, 44,* 203, 219, Maltzahn to Frederick, 7, 11, 14 April 1780.

Harris was still waiting to hear what Britain's reaction to the Empress's declaration would be, and perhaps he hoped that some attention would be paid to his urgent prompting that special treatment should be meted out to Russian ships. He appears still to have believed at this time that the declaration had been caused by the behaviour of Spain. As he wrote to Keith on 31 March/11 April, "nothing material is altered in the conduct or sentiments [of this court] since my last letter [of 7 March]. Our adversaries are straining every nerve to place us in the same predicament as Spain, to make it [Russia] act against us, at least to prevent our court reaping any *advantage* from the fleet fitting out here . . ." [17] Meanwhile he turned with alacrity to the task of attacking the activities of Galitzin at The Hague. To talk with Panin was a waste of time, since "his sentiments on neutral trade . . . arise from prejudice, not from conviction . . ." [18] but he waited on Potemkin when he knew he would have the indolent prince at his mercy, namely when the latter was still in bed. Relying on the information he had received from Yorke and Stormont, Harris painted a lurid picture of a Galitzin acting under Prussian and French orders. Potemkin immediately agreed that Galitzin "thought to please Count Panin and received his cue from some subaltern in office devoted to Prussia." He assured Harris that Galitzin was acting without authority but seemed strangely reluctant to undertake to have him reprimanded.[19] His unwillingness or inability to pursue the matter of reprimanding Galitzin, coupled with certain alarming moves by the King of Prussia, led Harris to suspect that "my friend's fidelity has been shaken or his political faith corrupted" by direct offers from Prussia.[20]

Frederick II had in fact shown increasing anxiety as the time approached for the meeting between the Empress and the Emperor Joseph. He did not at first fear that Catherine would be won over

17. Add. MSS. 35.518, f. 218.

18. SP 91/104, Harris to Stormont, No. 27, 24 March/4 April 1780.

19. SP 91/104, Harris to Stormont, No. 28, 24 March/4 April 1780. Harris prepared a memorial for the Empress on Galitzin's alleged crimes (Enclosure in No. 28) but a week later he heard that Potemkin had still not shown it to the Empress (SP 91/104, Harris to Stormont, No. 29, 31 March/11 April 1780 (*MD, 1*, 293)).

20. SP 91/104, Harris to Stormont, unnumbered, 31 March/11 April 1780, *MD, 1*, 292.

by the Emperor; "je me flatte qu'elle est trop ancrée dans son système actuel pour se laisser ébranler," he wrote to Goertz on 4 March 1780. But he trembled for the influence the Emperor might acquire over the unstable Potemkin and ordered Goertz to find out without fail "les moyens qu'on pourrait employer pour mettre le Pce Potemkin à l'abri de tous les traits et artifices dont l'Empereur fera usage." [21] But Goertz, like Harris, failed to plumb the depths of the Prince's cunning. For Potemkin had already taken steps to forestall Goertz and assuage Prussian anxiety. Almost at the same time as the Prince was congratulating Harris on Prussia's complete loss of influence at St. Petersburg, he had lamented to Goertz that he had never been able to manoeuvre his regiment before the greatest soldier in Europe and suggested that perhaps he might be able to display its prowess before Frederick's heir. Could not the Prince of Prussia be made to "faire un petit voyage par ici?" Potemkin proposed to the startled Goertz, and he took care to press on the Prussian envoy that the reply to this invitation should go through him, Potemkin, to the Empress, and not through Panin.[22]

No analysis of Potemkin's motives can ever be conclusive. How far was he acting on the Empress's orders in extending this invitation to the Prince of Prussia? Did she intend to assuage the alarm which she knew Frederick II must feel when he heard of the visit of the Emperor? Or was this Potemkin's own deep-laid plot? It was not beyond Potemkin to surmise that the gauche and unprepossessing Prince of Prussia might deal the death blow to Prussian preponderance in Russia, particularly if the Emperor genuinely succeeded in ingratiating himself with Catherine.

Goertz, considerably taken aback by Potemkin's proposal, suffered a further shock when some two weeks later Panin suggested quite independently that Frederick II should send his nephew on a visit to Russia, as an antidote to the Emperor.[23] Frederick was much embarrassed by these repeated invitations, neither of which

21. *PKFG*, *44*, 109, Frederick to Goertz, 4 March 1780; see also p. 118, 7 March 1780; p. 129, 14 March 1780.

22. *PKFG*, *44*, 134, Goertz to Frederick, 3 March 1780. Potemkin had made his suggestion before Goertz even knew about the visit of the Emperor (Dohm, *Denkwürdigkeiten*, 2, p. xvii).

23. Ibid.

had actually been made in the name of the Empress. Moreover he knew Catherine, and he knew his nephew, and he feared that the latter would not gain from a comparison with the Emperor. But in the circumstances he thought it wiser to agree, and he decided that this was the occasion to bind Potemkin to him.[24] It was therefore Potemkin's invitation which was accepted, and the unfortunate Goertz had to bear the brunt of Panin's anger at the prospect of losing control of relations with Prussia.[25] But Harris was equally alarmed when he discovered what Goertz and the Prince were preparing. He had of course no idea that the invitation to the Prince of Prussia came from Potemkin himself and believed that some great personal advantage had been held out to Potemkin to induce him to support a move he would otherwise have opposed. This shook his so far untroubled faith in the Prince and even led him to propose to his principals the holding out of some gigantic bribe to bind Potemkin forever to Britain's cause. Stormont would not agree to any exceptional expenditure unless it were as a reward for services rendered, such as the actual signature of a treaty, and Harris himself soon felt sufficiently reassured of the Prince's good faith to abandon the idea.[26] But the fact that he should have contemplated bribery on such a scale shows the extent of his dismay at this new development. He feared that if once Potemkin were won over to the Prussian party, all hopes for Britain at St. Petersburg would be at an end.

When, on 30 April 1780, after an uncommonly quick journey by the courier, Stormont's enormous packet of 11 April was delivered to him, Harris was at last able to devote himself to the far more difficult task of endeavouring to persuade the Empress to recede from article 2 of her declaration. On 2 May he waited on the Prince and reminded him that the latter had led him to be-

24. *PKFG, 44*, 136, Frederick to Goertz, 15 March 1780.

25. Ibid., p. 196, Goertz to Frederick, 31 March 1780. "Dès que vous en êtes là avec le Prince Potemkin je ne puis plus rien dire," said Panin to Goertz. And he insisted that his own invitation should be absolutely concealed. Panin's suspicion that Goertz had given himself over to Potemkin led to a coolness between the two men for a while. (Dohm, *Denkwürdigkeiten*, 2, p. xvii.)

26. See my article, "The Use of British Secret Funds at St. Petersburg, 1777–1782." In spite of the rumours current at the time and since that Harris paid large sums of money to Potemkin, it is clear that Potemkin was never the recipient of British subsidies or bribes during Harris's mission.

lieve on 22 February that the Russian armament would prove to be of great assistance to Britain. What, Harris asked, had led the Empress to change her policy? And what could now be done to convince Europe that Catherine was not alienated from Britain? After much pressing, Potemkin consented to transmit a written memorial to the Empress.[27] Harris, ever prompt at dispatching business, immediately prepared not one but two memorials. In the first he attacked the Russian declaration, pointing out that the principle "free ships, free goods" afforded protection to the trade of France and Spain but no corresponding benefit to Britain. His second memorial was devoted to the well-worn subject of Galitzin's unfriendly conduct at The Hague. He was accused of having encouraged the Dutch to rely on Russian assistance in their quarrel with Britain and of having received his orders from the French ambassador.[28]

Having delivered his memorials to Potemkin, Harris went on 5 May 1780 as in duty bound to pay a call on Panin to inform him of the British reception of the Russian refusal of an alliance and to present Britain's reply to the Russian declaration. Relations between the two men were by now extremely bad, though this was naturally concealed beneath the veneer of courtesy which their position and their training exacted of them. Harris was aware of the campaign Panin was conducting against him; the report had reached him that Panin was determined to make him feel "the folly" of his conduct and to disgrace him both in Russia and in England.[29] Harris's own neglect of Panin and his preference for the Prince were now public property.[30] On this occasion he

27. SP 91/104, Harris to Stormont, No. 49, 15/26 May 1780.

28. Ibid., Enclosures A and B. This second memorial was based on information from Yorke: "Count Panin, Mr. de Swart and P. Gallitzin between them have twisted the proposal of the Empress of Russia into a general union . . . and Count Panin is said to have gone so far as to presume to intimate, that if Holland joined the League, Russia would guarantee the treaty of 1674." This, wrote Yorke, had prevented him getting the better of the Dutch amicably. "Mr. de Swart," he added, "says you will be catched in a trap by having this turned against you . . ." (1 April 1780). See also letter of 15 April 1780 on the continuing intimacy between Galitzin and Vauguyon (Harris Papers).

29. SP 91/104, Harris to Stormont, No. 43, 24 April/5 May 1780.

30. The amount of feeling engendered on both sides is illustrated by the following outburst of Harris to the Danish chargé d'affaires, who repeated it to Goertz: " 'La Russie aurait mieux fait de nous déclarer la guerre, et de donner ses misérables

started off with a flourish: "The history of the present century afforded repeated proofs, that the English fought and conquered less for themselves than for the sake of their allies, and to preserve that equilibrium of power, on which the fate all Europe depends." Panin accepted with equanimity, the assurance that Britain was in reality fighting a battle in the interests of the whole of Europe and expressed his polite regret that it had not been possible to achieve an alliance. The two men entered into the real subject of their conversation when Harris read out the British reply to the Russian declaration. Harris was on somewhat delicate ground; he had to convince Panin of Britain's desire to defer to Russia without however admitting that Britain in any way accepted the Russian declaration. Moreover he was aware that Simolin's report from London conveyed a far truer picture of the British reaction to the Empress's policy than was contained in the official British reply. He therefore endeavoured to correct any misapprehensions which Simolin's dispatches might have given rise to, and watered down British abhorrence of the Empress's principles to "doubts" and "uneasiness" such as arise "in private life, when two friends mistake each other." To emphasize his point, Harris delivered to Panin as a "raisonnement amical" the memorial on the Russian declaration which he had already delivered to Potemkin. Panin in turn assured Harris that the declaration was the Empress's own work and that on this occasion he had "officiated merely as the Empress's secretary." And he explained that as he understood the declaration, "each nation ought to abide by their treaties of commerce . . . and that he believed this (though he did not take upon himself to say so) was the whole meaning of the declaration." [31]

But neither Potemkin's nor Panin's doubtless much more re-

---

vaisseaux à la France, que de faire une pareille déclaration; mais l'impératrice est aveuglée par le comte Panin, qui a de la haine contre nous, et qui se fait mener par le roi de Prusse . . . mais, malgré cela, l'Angleterre ne souffrira pas cette association, et plutôt elle déclarerait la guerre à toutes les puissances. J'userai encore de modération, car je sais qu'il en faut ici; mais à la fin ce sera moi qui ferai les déclarations de ma cour, et je saurai bien ce qu'il faudra leur dire.' Cela est bien arrogant et bien anglais," commented Goertz, who promptly repeated the whole to Panin. (Bancroft-Circourt, *3*, 248, Goertz to Frederick, 28 April/9 May 1780).

31. SP 91/105, Harris to Stormont, No. 50, 15/26 May 1780 (*MD*, *1*, 301). The footnote on *MD*, *1*, 302 is incorrect and refers to another of Stormont's voluminous dispatches of 11 April 1780, not to the British reply.

strained representations would move the Empress. On 8 May Harris saw Potemkin again in Tsarskoye Selo, and he was not encouraging. The London gossip which Simolin had forwarded had done its work; the Empress had been hurt and her indignation aroused. Harris's memorial had somewhat soothed the imperial feelings, but the Empress was not disposed to retract from any one of the five points of her declaration nor to make any specific explanation of the motives leading to the armament of the fleet, such as attributing it to Spanish interference with trade in the Straits. But Harris refused to take no for an answer, and succeeded in working up the Prince to the point of making a further effort on his behalf. When he saw Harris again in the evening, the Prince gave him the satisfaction of hearing that the Empress had consented to give a "severe reprimand" to Galitzin and had given orders for a letter to be written to Simolin "more explicit of her intentions than any he had yet received." The five principles however remained unchanged, for, as Potemkin explained, the idea of being an universal legislatrix of the seas "had laid so strongly hold of her imagination, that it resisted all his skill; that it must be left to be destroyed by its own folly." [32]

On his own initiative, or possibly on instructions from the Empress, Potemkin then inquired what would be the reaction in Britain if the Empress were to consider her declaration as made for herself alone and to enforce it no further than regarded the rights of her own subjects and her own flag. It is not quite clear how far-reaching this proposal of Potemkin's was. But unfortunately for Harris, he could not stop to find out. His instructions from London were quite categorical. He was not to enter into any discussion of principles, and in particular of the obnoxious article 2, nor to hint in any way that Britain could ever accept this principle. He could not therefore even discuss the possibility that Britain might accept article 2 for Russia alone, in spite of the

32. SP 91/105, Harris to Stormont, No. 49, 15/26 May 1780. Was Galitzin ever reprimanded? The Russian archives would reveal the answer. Yorke wrote on 10 June 1780 that "Pce Gallitzin . . . is horribly down in the mouth and plainly shows he is not pleased with what he has received." But later on, he reported that Galitzin was the "ecco" of the French ambassador in all he said, "and they play the cards in each others hands; it does not seem by this that the reproof was very severe" (16 September 1780, to Harris, Harris Papers).

paradoxical fact that Russia was entitled to "free ships, free goods" under the terms of the Anglo-Russian treaty of 1766. The one opening which showed some promise of persuading the Empress to change her mind on this vital question was one he could not pursue.

As proof however of the sincerity and loyalty with which he had acted, when Potemkin saw Harris again, on 10 May 1780, he showed him the draft of the *ukaz* to the Russian admiralty setting forth the instructions to be given to the Russian commerce-protecting squadron. According to this *ukaz*, the fleet was to protect Russian merchant ships alone; it was to be divided into three squadrons, one to cruise in the Cattegat, the second in the Channel, and the third off Lisbon. Harris could make no objection to the use of the Russian fleet to protect Russian merchantmen, but he seized at once on one offending point, the stationing of a squadron in the Channel, "where the nation suffers no fleet to cruize on so ambiguous a commission." He begged Potemkin to have the destination of this squadron changed, as it gave the impression that the armament was directed against Great Britain. Potemkin saw the point and acquiesced directly. "Monsieur le comte de Panin a voulu me jouer encore un tour de son métier," was his comment, and he was probably right in interpreting the order to station a squadron in the Channel as a further effort on Panin's part to emphasize the anti-British intention of the Russian armament.

A few days later, on 19 May 1780, the day before he was to escort the Empress to Mogilyev to meet Joseph II, the Prince was able to report that the Channel squadron was now to be sent to the Mediterranean.[33] He then, "with more frankness than he ever spoke to me in his life," wrote Harris, declared himself unable to persuade the Empress to recede from the principles of her declaration. The Empress had even shown displeasure at the liberty he had taken, said Potemkin, and he felt "for the first time in his life, that he had been fairly outwitted." "It cannot, it shall not

33. SP 91/105, Harris to Stormont, No. 49, 15/26 May 1780; cf. *PSZ*, 20, No. 15016, Instructions of the Admiralty College, dated 10/21 May 1780; one squadron was to cruise in the Mediterranean from Gibraltar to Turkish waters, without entering them; the second off Lisbon, from the Channel to Gibraltar; the third from the Sound to the Channel, but without entering the Channel "except in case of extreme necessity."

last," Harris quoted the Prince as saying, "the journey, and its concomitant circumstances will, I hope, turn the arms of those who have given rise to this pernicious doctrine against themselves; and I hope, at our return, to restore my sovereign to you as much your friend as ever. In the meanwhile," continued the Prince, "let me give you some advice; France has already acquiesced in every part of the declaration, and offered, in the most friendly manner, her ports for the Empress's ships . . . let our merchantmen now pass unmolested; they, at most, do not exceed twenty sail; their free passage can do you little harm, but if you stop them, you will lose forever the friendship of the Empress." When Harris tried to put again the British argument and referred to the danger that ships of other nations would conceal their identity under the Russian flag if Russian navigation were to be privileged in this manner, Potemkin swept his arguments aside:

> Her Imperial Majesty would never suffer such a collusion; be assured she means to be equitable, give in to her humours; allow her to be in the right, tho' she is in the wrong, and she will correct herself . . . add to this complaisance for her whims and opinions, a great appearance of confidence, and you still will recover her. Ask her mediation between you and your enemies; tell her as much of your secret as is necessary —acquaint her with the terms on which you wish for an accommodation for America . . . how much you are ready to grant, and they to receive. Affect to have a thorough reliance in her penetration, honour, and friendship, and you may depend, not only of her never betraying you, but be almost certain, that she will begin by being your mediatrix, and if she does not succeed, end by being your ally.

And Potemkin finally desired Harris "very earnestly to write home accurately what he said . . . he would second it with all his influence and zeal." On this long conversation, Harris commented: "I needs must believe Pce Potemkin sincere. He obtains no end in deceiving me." [34]

Harris had of course to balance what he heard from Potemkin against what he heard from Panin, and very different was the

34. SP 91/105, Harris to Stormont, No. 49, 15/26 May 1780.

language held by the latter. He hinted that Britain had not understood the real meaning of the Empress's declaration and that the
British had reacted with too much heat. Echoing Potemkin, though
in stronger terms, he urged on Harris that Britain should treat
neutral shipping with more moderation or at least define contraband goods more precisely. He advised Britain to regulate her
behaviour according to her situation: she now stood alone, and
Panin expressed the fear that if she continued thus to flout neutral
opinion, even her great resources would not enable her to carry
the burden.[35]

It can easily be believed that a conversation conducted on these
lines would contribute nothing to the improvement of relations
between the two men and would certainly not induce Panin to
moderate his opposition to Britain's policy in the councils of the
Empress. But Harris's hopes were somewhat raised when Panin
appeared to confirm what he had already heard from Potemkin,
namely that the Empress did not propose to extend the protection
of her fleet to merchantmen of other nations and that she intended
the relations between neutrals and belligerents to be governed
not by her declaration, but by the tenor of the relevant clauses of
such treaties as might exist already between them.[36] On this somewhat more cheerful note the interview ended. Harris of course
attached no importance to some hints thrown out by Panin that
the League of Neutrals might assist in procuring a peace. In his
opinion it was much more likely to prolong the war.[37]

Before making up his mind finally on the advice he wished to
offer to Stormont about the prospects for Britain at the Russian
court, Harris made one further and very expensive effort to pene-

---

35. SP 91/105, Harris to Stormont, No. 50, 15/26 May 1780 (MD, 1, 301). See
also Joseph II to Maria Theresa, 8 June 1780, "qu'elle [Catherine] est fort contente
de sa declaration et peu des Anglais qui ne veulent l'accepter telle qu'elle est . . ."
(Arneth, Maria Theresia und Joseph II, 3, 250).

36. See PSZ, 20, No. 15016, Instruction from the Admiralty College; no mention
is made of protection to be extended by the Russian fleet to ships of other nations.
On 8/19 May 1780 the Empress issued a code for the guidance of her merchant
navy, setting out the conditions entitling them to the protection of her fleet, basing
herself on the treaty of 1766. Contraband under that treaty would not be entitled
to protection (see PSZ, 20, No. 15014, printed in translation in Scott, Armed Neutralities, p. 291).

37. SP 91/105, Harris to Stormont, No. 50, 15/26 May 1780 (MD, 1, 301).

trate what he regarded as the Russian enigma. He offered the lavish sum of fifteen thousand roubles to a man whom he believed to be in the know and put to him a series of questions on the Empress's motives in launching the Neutral League, on her political views, on those of Panin, and on those of Potemkin.[38] The answers he received confirmed him in the opinion he had already formed of the alignment at the Russian court. His nameless informant told him that the declaration of the principles of neutral navigation and the Neutral League were "the child of the Empress's own brain, occasioned solely by the conduct of Spain"; the Empress from habit inclined towards England but was now determined to observe a perfect neutrality, even though it might prejudice Britain. Potemkin, added Harris's informer, disliked the French and was piqued against the King of Prussia. He had no regular system of politics, but at the moment he was anxious that the visit of the Emperor should prove a success. As for Panin, he had now been completely won over to the French party at court.[39]

With this information, neither novel enough nor penetrating enough to justify his enormous expenditure, Harris had perforce to be content. But he did not query it, for it fitted in too well with his own preconceived ideas of the characters and policies of the three personalities involved. In the end therefore, Harris's analysis of the Russian situation was founded on the opinion that "the declaration was originally resolved and drawn up, without the most remote idea of injuring us; that the Empress even thought she saw our advantage in it; and if her artful ministers and our still more artful enemies, had not combined to give it a turn very different from her meaning, it would have operated strongly in our behalf." By her ignorance of the matter, the Empress had given a handle to her ministers and to those of other courts to "put a construction, and give a sense to her words, she never intended they should convey." The universal adulation which had greeted the Empress's declaration had confirmed her in "the pleasing though preposterous idea" of appearing as the legislatrix of the seas, and she was not to be moved from that position. Panin would not, and Potemkin could not, believed Harris, persuade her on

38. See my article, "The Use of British Secret Funds at St. Petersburg, 1777–1782."
39. SP 91/105, Harris to Stormont, No. 53, 15/26 May 1780.

that subject. Britain could now only accept the Neutral League with as good a grace as possible.

In forwarding his advice to Stormont, Harris had to devote some attention to the tricky problem of the character and influence of the two men he had mainly to deal with. As Harris described them, the one, Panin, "was ever striving to make me believe he was acting less in opposition to our interests and views, than he well knew I suspected him to be; while the other . . . was willing to convince me, that he was promoting them with more influence and weight than he really employed." Some allowance must be made for the insincerity of each. "Count Panin is *determined* to be our enemy; Prince Potemkin is *disposed* to be our friend," but, Harris added rather sourly, he would be more effective if he understood the intrigues of the cabinet as well as those of the court.[40] Nevertheless Potemkin's advice on how to proceed in future seemed to Harris worth following. It coincided with Harris's own observation of the situation, or at least he believed himself to have reached a similar conclusion independently of the Prince. He urged on Stormont the necessity, if Russia was to be won, of making some concession to her in the matter of trade. So completely did Harris misread the Empress's character and Panin's policy that he warned Stormont that if Russian ships were stopped, the Empress was capable, in a gust of passion, of laying an embargo on all British vessels in Russian ports and of annulling the Anglo-Russian commercial treaty. This he believed to be Count Panin's object, and it would be immediately followed by the conclusion of a Franco-Russian treaty. In addition Britain should, he thought, show her confidence in Russia by inviting the Empress's good offices. It is noteworthy that on the repeated occasions when Panin had hinted at the desirability of Britain communicating her peace terms to Russia, Harris had waved him airily aside. The same advice coming now from Potemkin he took very seriously. Mediation was "the easiest bait" for the Empress to swallow.[41]

On 20 May 1780, the Empress, escorted by Potemkin, left the

40. SP 91/105, Harris to Stormont, No. 51, 15/26 May 1780. Part of this dispatch is printed in *MD, 1*, 305, where it has simply been tacked on to the mutilated end of No. 50 of the same date.

41. SP 91/105, Harris to Stormont, No. 49, 15/26 May 1780.

capital for Mogilyev, there to await the Emperor. Meanwhile, Panin in St. Petersburg was putting the finishing touches to the Neutral League. Harris had understood from his last conversation with Panin that the Empress "meant nothing more by her armed Neutrality, than that each nation should protect their respective trade, according to the different treaties and regulations." He was horrified when he heard that conventions were to be drawn up by which the five powers were to agree to stand by each other in support of the declaration.[42] In spite of Potemkin's advice to accept the League as a *fait accompli* he continued to struggle against what appeared to him to be a fresh departure in the policy of trade protection. The absence of Potemkin rendered Harris's communication with the Prince less frequent but not less intimate. At Potemkin's request he corresponded with him. He appealed repeatedly to the Prince's vanity and begged him not to let himself be duped by Panin,[43] whom he accused of acting solely under Prussian orders. "Si vous me refusez votre assistance," wrote Harris, "tout est perdu, le triomphe du Comte Panin est parfait." [44] According to Harris's account, the Prince did make one final appeal to the Empress to abandon her plan, whereupon she lost her temper with him and said "that no one but herself saw the end of what she proposed, and on this occasion declared she would not be checked by any advice whatsoever." The Empress was delighted with the progress Panin was making with the negotiations with Sweden and Denmark and was determined to carry through her policy.[45] The only satisfaction Harris obtained at

42. SP 91/105, Harris to Stormont, No. 59, 19/30 May 1780 (*MD, I*, 311).

43. "De grace, ne le [Panin] permettez pas de jouir plus longtemps de l'idée de vous avoir joué . . ." (undated letter).

44. Letter of 16/27 May 1780, copies of both enclosed in SP 91/105, Harris to Stormont, No. 59, 19/30 May 1780.

45. Potemkin sent Harris a verbal message by a relative of his describing his last effort, and the news was confirmed by "respectable collateral intelligence" (See SP 91/105, Harris to Stormont, No. 69, 9/20 June 1780). This however conflicts with the account of A. A. Bezborodko to A. Vorontsov of 1/11 June 1780. He reported that the Empress was delighted with the progress of her plan, and added "I did not observe that the slightest effort was made from the other side to oppose this." He had been present at a conference at which Panin's drafts had been discussed (see *Sbornik, 26*, 371). It is however possible that an altercation took place between Potemkin and the Empress unbeknown to Bezborodko and that Potemkin had not been present at the conference.

this period was the discovery that the secret orders to the Russian commerce-protecting squadrons (and they did not long remain a secret from Harris) were to avoid anything that might lead to an altercation with the belligerents, and, contrary to the provisions of the conventions, they were not to extend their protection to belligerent property in neutral bottoms but only to Russian vessels and Russian property on neutral vessels.[46] Without waiting for the conclusion of the treaties with Denmark and Sweden, the Russian fleet sailed away from Cronstadt on 21 June 1780.[47]

Harris had thus failed to prevent the formation of the Neutral League. And he now began to see that his position had become somewhat exposed. Thanks to the frankness with which Potemkin had admitted himself worsted in a duel with Panin and to his willingness to be blamed by Harris for having apparently been outwitted, the Prince had completely recovered the confidence of the British envoy. "I should shelter myself under a falsehood," wrote Harris, "if I was to attempt to attribute any part of what happen'd to a duplicity in him." But he also began to see that his present ally, as he believed him to be, might not be forever with him. "He is of a temper ever to be influenced by the impulsion of the moment, to be wrought upon by what strikes his fancy and imagination, without consulting his reason and judgement and is

46. SP 91/105, Harris to Stormont, No. 71, 12/23 June 1780 (*MD, 1,* 318). However the Russian commanders were ordered (Art. 4) not to allow the visit of ships in their convoy, and (Art. 9) to use force if necessary to recapture Russian ships, if innocent, from privateers or warships (cf. *PSZ,* 20, No. 15016). According to Corberon, these orders were only valid until the conventions with Denmark and Sweden were signed. After that the Russian fleet was to protect the ships and goods of the co-signatories of the conventions (CP Russie, *104,* to Vergennes, No. 24, 23 May 1780). According to Harris, Admiral Greig told him that, should the Empress require the fleet to act against Britain, the British officers would resign in a body, and great discontent reigned among them at the prospect of the inglorious service they were to render. (SP 91/105, to Stormont, No. 52, 15/26 May 1780, No. 60, 22 May 12 June, No. 66, 2/13 June 1780). Greig had also protested at the declaration of maritime principles.

47. See Anderson, *Naval Wars in the Baltic during the Sailing-Ship Epoch 1522–1850,* pp. 236 ff. A circular to the belligerents was issued by Russia explaining the purpose of the fleet and requesting facilities for it in their ports; the circular speaks only of protecting Russian ships (SP 91/105, Simolin to Stormont, 11 July 1780). Stormont replied that the Russian fleet would be welcomed as a friendly neutral and that the Russian flag would be treated in accordance with the treaty of 1766 and generally accepted principles of the *droit des gens* (Ibid., projet de réponse verbale, read to Simolin, 11 July 1780).

not of a character to persist long in a uniform predilection, either for the same person or for the same cause . . ." On the other hand Panin, Harris thought, could now be trusted to pursue a course of systematic hatred and vindictiveness against Britain. He now perceived that his own person had become involved in the struggle between Panin and Potemkin, and he foresaw all the disadvantages of the position he had allowed himself to drift into. "With such a friend, and such an enemy I have much to fear and little to hope," he wrote. The slightest incident might lose him the confidence of the Prince, and British interests would then be left to the tender mercies of Panin. For the first time, he now formally proposed to Stormont that he should be recalled and replaced in St. Petersburg by a minister "less obnoxious to Count Panin." [48]

It was not only the delicacy of Harris's position between Panin and Potemkin that rendered him a dangerous minister for Britain in Russia. He had now also become a misleading counsellor. As a result of attaching himself to one party, that of Potemkin, he saw Panin through Potemkin's eyes. He accepted Potemkin's portrayal of Panin as a *"fourbe à système";* he did not see that Potemkin, by exaggerating Panin's evil influence, could account all the better for his own inability to remove the Empress from her chosen path, while still leaving Harris under the impression that he had used all his powers of persuasion. He was misled by the extreme frankness of the Prince, on the principle that a man who will admit to a humiliating defeat cannot possibly be lying. He allowed himself to be convinced that only by following Potemkin's advice could the goodwill of the Empress be preserved, and Potemkin led him on, suggesting fresh concessions to the Empress's whims, which he promised would recover her completely for Britain.

There was of course a bitter struggle for power between Panin

48. SP 91/105 Harris to Stormont, No. 56, secret and private, 15/26 May 1780 (*MD, 1,* 318, wrongly dated 15/26 June 1780). The note on p. 318 of *MD, 1,* is incorrect. Harris asked to be recalled before the signature of any of the conventions implementing the Declaration of the Armed Neutrality. On 9/20 November 1779 he had already written to his sister Gertrude to express his hope that he would not remain much longer in St. Petersburg (Merton Papers) but this was rather a reflection on the incompetent conduct of foreign affairs by Suffolk and Weymouth, and he hoped for better things from Stormont. His galling sense of failure must have been further exacerbated by hearing from Yorke that Swart described him to the Dutch as having been duped by Potemkin, which as Yorke put it "is calling you a fool and him a knave" (Harris Papers, Yorke to Harris, 9 May 1780).

and Potemkin; the Prince was not acting solely in the interests of his imperial mistress, he had his own ends to pursue, and doubtless he found Harris a useful tool. It is difficult to disentangle from the lengthy speeches quoted by Harris where the Prince is pursuing his own particular intrigue and where he is carrying out a plan concerted with the Empress. He probably did serve Harris quite genuinely in stressing the danger of alienating Britain if the Empress wanted to secure the mediation and in obtaining the alteration of the destination of the Russian squadron from the Channel to the Mediterranean. But as far as he was concerned, this particular round with Panin was now over. The second round, the visit of the Emperor, was about to begin, and no British concerns were at stake there. The advice which the Prince gave to Harris to accept the declaration on neutral navigation as a *fait accompli,* to refrain from molesting the Empress's ships, and to seek the Empress's mediation was probably concerted with the Empress. Only thus can one explain the Prince's earnest insistence to Harris that his words should be repeated to London. They represented the policy agreed on between the Empress and himself, and they were entrusted to him to speak rather than to Panin in order to make them more effective when it was clear to both that Panin had forfeited Harris's confidence. Potemkin now controlled Russian relations with Britain; he, and not Panin, was to meet the Emperor, a meeting which might give him control of Russian relations with Austria. He had already made inroads into Panin's hold on Prussian affairs. He might well rest content with both his political influence and the intimate and apparently unshakeable bond which united him to Catherine.

Harris was undoubtedly sincere in his desire to be recalled. He realized that he had failed to discern and prevent a development in Russian policy most injurious to Britain, and, dramatizing the situation to himself, he proposed his recall partly to ward off the disgrace which he believed to be impending.[49] But his request was not entertained for a moment in London. Stormont replied briefly in July that Harris's removal would be "highly prejudicial to the

49. See Yorke to Harris, 10 June 1780, replying to a letter of 16 May: "I am sorry . . . to see that you are dejected and apprehend disgrace . . . Away with such ideas till we have weathered the storm" (Harris Papers).

King's affairs" and would enable his own personal critics to triumph over his failure.[50] He did not enter into the substance of Harris's analysis of his position, in so far as Harris himself had seen it. That these were difficult moments for the fiery envoy is confirmed by the reports of his colleagues: "il court à cheval se promener, il n'est jamais chez lui et paroit se fuire lui-même," wrote Corberon to Vergennes on 6 June 1780.[51]

50. SP 91/105, Stormont to Harris, No. 42, 14 July 1780.
51. CP Russie, *104*, No. 27, 6 June 1780.

9. Imperial Interlude: The Dutch Accession to the Armed Neutrality

MEANWHILE the Empress Catherine and the Emperor Joseph were busily engaged in making the best possible impression on each other in Mogilyev. Both were determined that their meeting should prove a success; hence whatever their real feelings, the accounts which emanated from their imperial majesties concurred in portraying them as delighted. Catherine was in fact pleased with her guest, as she reveals in one of her frequent *billets* to Potemkin;[1] Joseph's real opinions emerge from those letters to his mother which were not sent *en clair* by the Russian post.[2] His purpose in planning the visit had been to restore close and friendly relations with Russia, to do away with the bad impressions left by "Prussian slanders," and to let the Empress see him and judge him for herself; he therefore took great pains to make a good impression. But neither Joseph nor Kaunitz thought that Austria should take the initiative in proposing a closer political connexion.[3] The question of an alliance was not discussed, for Catherine too refused to take the lead. But in the various conversational skirmishes conducted by Joseph and Catherine, the latter dropped embarrassed hints on the suitability of Rome as the capital of the Western Empire and inferred the equal suitability of Constantinople as the capital of the Empire of the East.[4] Potemkin too threw out various remarks about the desirability of

1. *Sbornik*, 27, 182, 9/20 June 1780.

2. Arneth, *Maria Theresia und Joseph II, 3*, passim.

3. Arneth, *Maria Theresias letzte Regierungszeit, 4*, 674–76, for Kaunitz's memoranda on the forthcoming interview, of 23 April 1780; p. 678 for Joseph's own ideas.

4. Arneth, *Maria Theresia und Joseph II, 3*, Joseph to Maria Theresa, p. 250, 8 June 1780; p. 256, 14 June 1780; p. 267, 4 July 1780.

restoring "l'ancienne confiance et intimité" between the two courts but made no suggestion as to the means to adopt. Cobenzl, speaking "from himself" suggested a mutual guarantee of Austrian and Russian possessions, and Potemkin undertook to sound the Empress on these lines.[5] Catherine's reply was cautious for she envisaged Austrian support of Russia as necessary for her plans against Turkey, but she did not want to be drawn into Austria's German policy.[6] During Joseph's visit matters were carried no further, but the seed of a future understanding had been sown.

After a few days spent together in Mogilyev, the Emperor left for Moscow under the somewhat casual escort of Potemkin.[7] At the Empress's invitation he was to rejoin the court at Tsarskoye Selo late in June, and on his arrival at the imperial summer residence the assembled envoys had an opportunity of judging for themselves the impact of his visit.[8] On the whole they seem to have read their own prejudices into the situation. The Marquis de Vérac, the new French envoy, who arrived at the beginning of July to take over from Corberon, had barely had time to feel his ground. Nevertheless he drew the conclusion that the Emperor had not really been very successful in Russia. The more experienced Corberon reached the same conclusion.[9] Harris of course was strongly in favour of the *rapprochement* between Austria and Russia, and probably at the instigation of Potemkin, he wrote *en clair* letters to Keith by Austrian couriers designed to raise Potemkin in Austrian estimation and to portray his ardent attachment to Austria. He was sufficiently encouraged by the Emperor's reception in Russia to report that the King of Prussia's influence had suffered so severely that it must be beyond recovery. Joseph acted the part of the fox with skill and left Harris under the impression that his good wishes were with Britain in the war

5. Ibid., 267, Joseph to Maria Theresa, 4 July 1780; p. 274, 8 July 1780.

6. Ibid., Joseph to Maria Theresa, p. 278, 12 July 1780.

7. Ibid., Joseph to Maria Theresa, p. 262, 28 June 1780: "Le Prince de Potemkin a prit fort ses aises; Je ne l'ai vu que trois fois à Moscou; Il ne m'a rien dit en affaires."

8. See Corberon, *Journal Intime*, 2, 231 ff. passim for his comments on the Emperor's visit.

9. CP Russie, *104*, Vérac to Vergennes, No. 2, 13 July 1780. Corberon, *Journal Intime*, 2, 258. See also SP 91/105, Harris to Stormont, No. 82, 14/25 July 1780 (*MD, 1*, 324).

with France.[10] To Vérac however the Emperor sang a different tune. He assured him that Russian sentiments towards France were such as France might desire. "M. Harris," said Joseph to Vérac, "s'est bien trompé en croyant que ses intrigues ici pourroient avoir du succés. L'Impératrice n'ignore aucunement les moyens qu'il a employés; elle m'en a parlé avec le mépris qu'ils méritent, et c'est un homme qui s'est absolument cassé le col . . ." And he added a warning to Vérac which shows that Joseph was not lacking in perception: "On a grand tort d'imaginer que l'attachement de l'Impératrice pour telle ou telle personne puisse lui faire adopter leurs conseils. Elle s'en est expliquée clairement avec moi, et un moyen sûr de lui déplaire est de paroître avoir cette idée et d'agir en conséquence." [11] At least in one respect however, the Emperor was perfectly honest with Harris. He remarked to him that the Empress was strongly influenced by the opposition in Britain, which was not surprising since the attacks by the Whigs on North's administration supplied Catherine with many sound arguments in favour of her policy of defending neutral trade.[12]

The confusion about Austria's real inclinations at this time was partly due to the prevalent idea that the Emperor was or ought to be dissatisfied with the support he had received from France in the crisis which had been solved by the peace of Teschen. The behaviour of many of the Austrian envoys abroad contributed to strengthen this impression.[13] But the Emperor had no intention of abandoning the French alliance, the crown of Kaunitz's statesmanship. Meanwhile France was rendered uneasy, and Britain was lulled into confiding in the Emperor in the belief that the anti-

10. Add. MSS. 35.518, f. 258, Harris to Keith, 24 April/4 May 1780: Potemkin had expressed the strongest desire to please the Emperor, wrote Harris, and he must be sincere since he regrets the steps he took in the late German dispute "and would willingly repair the evil he had caus'd." See Add. MSS. 35.519 passim for other examples. See SP 91/105, Harris to Stormont, No. 82, 14/25 July 1780 (*MD*, *1*, 324).

11. CP Russie, *104*, Vérac to Vergennes, No. 2, 13 July 1780, and particularly No. 3, 21 July 1780, also quoted in Corberon, *Journal Intime*, 2, 257, note.

12. SP 91/105, Harris to Stormont, No. 82, 14/25 July 1780.

13. Corberon, *Journal Intime*, 2, p. 232. See also CP Russie, *105*, Corberon to Vergennes, unnumbered, 15 October 1780 (report delivered by Corberon on his return to France) in which he declares that Cobenzl was devoted to Harris "dont il est l'espion et l'agent dans les intrigues qui se trament entre celui-ci et le Pce Potemkin."

French gossip current at the Austrian court reflected a new trend in Austrian policy. For Frederick II also this was an anxious time, but he was reasonably reassured by the reports he received from Goertz. The Prussian envoy, who of course received his information from Panin, also reported what Frederick wished to hear, namely that Joseph had "excedé l'impératrice à force de l'obséder et de parler, et qu'il aurait mieux réussi en l'écoutant." [14] Goertz therefore still entertained the hope that the Prince of Prussia's visit might produce some good results for Prussia and restore the balance.

Harris now had two aims in view: to place obstacles in the way of Dutch accession to the Neutral League and to raise Austrian influence at the expense of Prussian as much as lay within his power. Beyond that however, he had reached the conclusion that nothing whatsoever could be done for Britain as long as Count Panin remained in office. "If he was removed a season would not pass without my being able to lead her [the Empress] into any lengths to serve us," he wrote to Stormont on 2/13 June 1780.[15] Without admitting it explicitly to Stormont, he set about intensifying the feud between Panin and Potemkin in the hope that this might lead to the final overthrow of the minister. Three days after Potemkin's return to Tsarskoye Selo, on 20 June/1 July 1780, Harris was able to have a long and private conversation with him of a truly remarkable nature. In the most outspoken manner he reproached the Prince for neglecting to counteract the intrigues of Panin and for failing to listen to his, Harris's, admonitions. He described the pleasure with which he had connected himself and Britain's fate with the Prince and the fortitude with which he had borne the jealousy and animosity of the Empress's other ministers, who envied the favour in which he stood. But the time had now come to ask Potemkin frankly "whether he really meant passively and supinely to allow the new system they were creating to be established, and whilst he forced me, for my own vindication, to represent him to my court as a lukewarm and useless friend, to hold himself out to the rest of Europe as either really enjoying noth-

---

14. *PKFG*, *44*, 426, Goertz to Frederick II, 11 August 1780: "On a vu dans l'Empereur qu'un homme qui flattait bassement."

15. SP 91/105, Harris to Stormont, No. 64, 2/13 June 1780.

ing but the image of the favour of his sovereign, or at best not know-ing how to manage it." Harris then went on to describe the tri-umph of Potemkin's enemies, their surprise and malicious pleas-ure at the idea of having "overreached, duped, and deceived him." Treading on far more delicate ground, Harris apologized for ob-serving "that the duration of an influence like his, depended on its being regularly and vigorously exercised—that if he permitted it to lay dormant, he might lose it irrecoverably." His enemies would spare no pains to overthrow him and would show him no mercy: "he could not doubt his high titles, his honours, his riches would be forced from him the moment Count Panin came into power, and that if he left him his life, it would be to pass it in exile, and his family, that he so affectionately loved, would be reduced to misery and want." Few people, urged Harris, "would be so moderate as not to remove from the presence of his im-perial mistress a person [Panin] who, if he enjoyed his power, would not leave him a day in possession of the smallest of his em-ployments." [16]

Potemkin must have listened with some amusement to Harris's lecture on the duties of a favourite and the proper method of preserving his influence—an art in which he had already proved himself a past master. Could Harris have read the notes which the Empress wrote almost daily to the Prince when they were separated by a few miles, and even when they were under the same roof, he might have been surprised at the extent and the depth of their understanding. "Farewell my friend," wrote Catherine to the Prince on 22 May/3 June 1780, when he had left her to meet the Emperor, "we are very dull without you. I am longing very much to see you again." And a fortnight later, when the Prince was escorting the Emperor to Moscow: "Batin'ka prince . . . without you I am inexpressibly bored. It is a long time since I have seen you . . ." And again, on 11/22 June 1780: "I much want to know, batin'ka, how you are. Mon bon ami, all is empty without you, je suis charmée de vous revoir et je m'en vais ordonner vos quartiers à Tsarskoye Selo." [17] This is not the language used to a political collaborator but that of profound affection and dependence.

16. SP 91/105, Harris to Stormont, No. 76, 23 June/4 July 1780. (*MD, 1*, 320). The most interesting parts of this dispatch have been omitted in the printed version.
17. *Sbornik*, 27, 180, 182, and 183.

Harris's allusion to the family which the Prince so affectionately loved was also a little near the bone. Potemkin had five nieces, who were all ladies in waiting to the Empress; one of them, Alexandra Engelhardt, remained for years on particularly close terms with her imperial mistress. The five ladies were all in turn (or simultaneously) the mistresses of their uncle, and there were recurring tiffs between Catherine and Potemkin when it became urgently necessary to find husbands for them.[18] In spite of Harris's boldness, however, or perhaps because of it, Potemkin listened attentively to Harris's diatribes. But he refused to be drawn into any positive declaration of agreement on the necessity to overthrow Panin. On the subject of his own future, should Count Panin achieve power, a phrase which both men understood to mean the death of the Empress and the accession of the Grand Duke Paul, Potemkin assured Harris that though the matter occupied his thoughts, yet it was a delicate subject and he could not tell Harris all he felt and knew—a tactful way of telling Harris to mind his own business.[19]

Thus Harris's first effort to galvanize the Prince into securing the dismissal of Count Panin failed. In spite of the personal favour he enjoyed with both the Empress and Potemkin, Harris had been unable to exercise any influence over policy. But he did not draw the conclusion which a less prejudiced mind might have drawn, namely that personal factors influenced the Empress comparatively little—a point which the Emperor Joseph had already seized. He confused sympathy with the nation, which the Empress undoubtedly felt, with the desire for a political *rapprochement* with a government she regarded as unstable, which the Empress did not think advisable.[20] And when he failed in his plans, he believed the reason to be the existence of some deeper and more powerful influence than that of Potemkin. He continued to devote immense

18. See Corberon, *Journal Intime*, 2, 372. See also SP 91/102, No. 73, Harris to Suffolk, 14/25 September 1778 (*MD*, *1*, 209).

19. SP 91/105, Harris to Stormont, No. 76, 23 June/4 July 1780. (*MD*, *1*, 320).

20. See Arneth, *Maria Theresia und Joseph II*, *3*, 268, Joseph to Maria Theresa, 2 July 1780: "qu'elle [Catherine] regrette dans son âme la mauvaise situation dans laquelle, à ce qu'elle croit, l'Angleterre se trouve, aimant les Anglais, mais méprisant la faiblesse du Roi et les sottises réitérées de leur ministère, qu'elle croit devoir succomber à ses fâcheuses circonstances, et elle en attend l'issue." Admittedly these are Catherine's views seen through the eyes of Joseph, but Catherine's policy and her letters to Grimm confirm his interpretation (See *Sbornik*, *23*, passim).

energy to the task of spurring the Prince to action. "I am talking to him eternally," he wrote to Stormont on 14/25 July 1780,[21] and to Sir Joseph Yorke he wrote, "Could I cure him of the most unaccountable carelessness and inattention, we should soon triumph. These vices hurt him as much as me; and if he does not bestir himself we shall fall together, though with this difference, that his fall will be somewhat more severe than mine."[22] Nothing reveals more clearly the distorted picture which Harris had now created for himself than this idea that Potemkin's favour and power at court depended on the triumph of a pro-British party over Panin. He assumed that if Panin prevailed in the field of policy, Potemkin must necessarily be dismissed and with him all hopes of a Russo-British connexion. He was incapable of envisaging that British concerns were really marginal to Russia; the fundamental struggle was for a Prussian or an Austrian orientation of Russian policy. The Ottoman Empire was the lodestar to which the Empress's and Potemkin's eyes were now directed with a unity of purpose which bound them so closely together that no disagreements over Britain could impair it for long.

Meanwhile Panin, who was publicly engaged in completing the initial stage of the Neutral League, had been privately pursuing a second element in the Empress's policy which had rather been lost sight of in the flurry caused by her championship of neutral trade—namely bringing the belligerents to a point where an offer to interpose as a mediator could have some chance of success. Vergennes had always paid Russia the compliment of attentively discussing the Russian overtures, but without any intention of allowing a formal offer to be made. The conduct of his ally Spain, however, began to make him view with more favour a possible Russian offer of good offices.

Spain had perfectly clear and limited objectives in the war—Gibraltar and Minorca; moreover she was not committed to fight for the independence of the American provinces. But Floridablanca had not hesitated to pursue secret negotiations with Britain behind France's back. One Thomas Hussey, formerly the chaplain at the Spanish Embassy in London, had, apparently on his own

21. SP 91/105, Harris to Stormont, No. 83, 14/25 July 1780.
22. MD, 1, 325, 14/25 July 1780.

initiative, served as a go-between; he left England in December 1779, saw Floridablanca in January 1780, and returned to report to Lord George Germain, secretary of state for the colonies.[23] When Floridablanca heard through France of the Russian overtures made in December 1779 to Corberon by Panin, he instructed the Spanish chargé d'affaires to reply politely that no mediator would be more welcome to Spain than Russia but to be careful to make no suggestion that Spain desired peace or was actually asking for Russian mediation.[24] And he continued to encourage the direct talks which had been inaugurated by Hussey between Britain and Spain, which caused Vergennes considerable disquiet.[25]

From France's point of view a Russian mediation was more promising than direct talks between Britain and Spain, and probably with this in mind Vergennes decided to place before the Empress the full range of French commitments in America. On 12 February 1780 he wrote to Corberon enclosing a copy of the Franco-American treaty and proposing that a direct approach should be made by Russia to Spain.[26] On 21 March 1780 Corberon reported that Panin advised that the time was not yet ripe for a direct approach to Spain. It was better, thought Panin, to wait and see what kind of reception the Empress's declaration on neutral trade received from the neutrals and from Spain. The formation of the Neutral League might also give more weight to Russian efforts to restore peace.[27]

Harris immediately felt the repercussions of the French communication of the terms of the Franco-American treaty. Some time in mid-March 1780 he had received a message through a third person, who may or may not have been Potemkin, from the Empress. Catherine here expressed the wish that Britain should renew her efforts at conciliation with the Americans as she had reason

23. For the history of these negotiations see Bemis, *Hussey-Cumberland Mission*, passim.

24. See Danvila, *Historia*, *5*, 145–46, Floridablanca to Normandez, 28 January 1780. These instructions of Floridablanca's have been incorrectly interpreted by Bemis, *Hussey-Cumberland Mission*, p. 23, note 16, as expressing a spontaneous desire for peace on the part of Spain.

25. See Bemis, *Hussey-Cumberland Mission*, pp. 62 ff.

26. CP Russie, *104*, Vergennes to Corberon, No. 3, 12 February 1780.

27. CP Russie, *104*, Corberon to Vergennes, No. 15, 21 March 1780; *Morskoy Sbornik*, *43*, 356, No. 30, Panin to the Empress, 5/16 March 1780.

to believe that such an approach would not be rejected. Tell Harris, the Empress was reported to have said, "not from me ministerially, but as from a hearty well-wisher to his country, that I have the strongest grounds for advancing what I say . . ." [28] At this date Catherine still evidently believed that a successful effort might be made to divide the colonies and to restore some at least to their allegiance. Judging by what she soon after said to Joseph II she neither wished nor expected that Britain should recover them all.[29] What reasons she had for believing that the Americans were in a conciliatory mood she did not reveal. But the Franco-American treaty had obviously convinced her of the difficulty of a successful mediation as long as Britain refused to contemplate any alternative but complete American submission and as long as France considered herself bound by treaty to complete American independence. Catherine's message however met with the usual fate of all such overtures on the part of Russia. Stormont could not identify Catherine's source of information on the temper of the American rebels, and he had very painful grounds for believing it to be untrustworthy. He therefore instructed Harris to make again the standard British reply, that the King was invariably disposed to receive "his rebellious subjects into his allegiance, whenever they are disposed to return to their duty and to a constitutional dependance upon this country." [30]

Panin in turn pressed upon Harris early in April 1780 the need for some solution of the American problem, though his suggestions were not to Harris's taste: he "flung out vague and inadmissible plans of pacification, and as he formerly advised us to relinquish our American possessions from necessity, so he now recommended the same measure from their insignificancy." [31] On 5 May 1780, at the same time as he handed Panin the formal British reply to the Empress's declaration of maritime principles, Har-

28. SP 91/104, Harris to Stormont, No. 24, 13/24 March 1780; the footnote on p. 290 of *MD, 1*, is incorrect. When Harris wrote his No. 24, he did know the contents of Corberon's dispatches; and the treaty referred to is that between France and America and not France and Spain.

29. *Arneth, Maria Theresia und Joseph II, 3*, 250, Joseph to Maria Theresa, 8 June 1780: "qu'elle [Catherine] désire que la paix se fasse et qu'une partie des colonies obtiennent la liberté."

30. SP 91/104, Stormont to Harris, No. 28, 25 April 1780.

31. SP 91/104, Harris to Stormont, No. 27, 24 March/4 April 1780.

ris also produced for the first time a formal answer to the Russian
offers of good offices, the last of which had been made on 20 January 1780. In this note Harris stressed that Britain wanted peace
and sought no conquests; she wished only to assert her rights and
to seek reparation for the insult to her honour.[32]

Neither the manner nor the matter of Russian policy at this
time had anything to recommend Russia as a mediator to Britain.
No connexion with Russia was possible, in Stormont's opinion,
while the Empress followed a minister, whose weakness she knew,
into plots engineered by France and Prussia.[33] Logically enough,
Stormont attached more importance to what the Empress did than
to what Potemkin said. Commenting on Harris's long account of
his interview with Potemkin on 19 May 1780, when the Prince had
urged so vehemently that Britain place her trust in Russia, Stormont wrote that Britain was disposed to follow the Prince's advice, but in the present circumstances, "the idea of a mediation
appears quite impossible" and it would probably be declined. Had
the Empress continued to act as at the beginning of the year, then
perhaps the mediation of the two imperial courts might have been
accepted. "But were she now to act as a mediatrix, she would
probably engage in that work with the same disposition she has
shewn of late, to establish what her flatterers call the Liberty of
the Seas . . ."[34] Stormont, who was far from Potemkin's overpowering personality, was also more disposed to doubt his influence. Thus, because he had already determined to reject them,
Stormont did not take seriously the Russian overtures for mediation made by Potemkin and Panin.

Undeterred by Britain's cold reception of his offers to make
peace, Panin continued to explore this avenue with France.[35]

---

32. SP 91/105, Harris to Stormont, No. 50, 15/26 May, Enclosure, Paper D, 22
April/3 May 1780 (*MD, 1*, 301).

33. SP 91/105, Stormont to Harris, No. 39, 14 July 1780.

34. SP 91/105, Stormont to Harris, No. 40, 14 July 1780.

35. See e.g. CP Russie, *104*, Corberon to Vergennes, No. 24, 23 May 1780. Panin
proposed to Corberon that the Americans should issue a declaration of their desire
to be free, to counter British rumours of the desire of many Americans to remain
loyal to the Crown. Apparently he did not regard the Declaration of Independence
as sufficiently explicit of American intentions, and wanted not "merely" a Congress
resolution but a declaration by the nation. On 25 June 1780 Vergennes sent
Corberon a copy of a declaration by the Americans never to give up their inde-

The arrival in June 1780 of the Spanish reply to the Empress's declaration on neutral trade, which showed that for the time being Spain was going to fall in with the Empress's wishes, opened the door to direct conversations between Russia and Spain.[36] A few days later, over the dinner table, Panin, Corberon, and Normandez held a conference to discuss a Russian offer of good offices. Panin implied that the Empress had given him a free hand, and Normandez promptly sent off a courier to his court. Harris's excellent information service supplied him almost immediately with news of what he held to be Panin's unauthorized "tampering with the Bourbon ministers." [37] But Panin's overture to Spain was to lead to unexpected consequences.

The secret and unofficial negotiations between Britain and Spain inaugurated by Thomas Hussey in December 1779 had now borne fruit. Richard Cumberland, a secretary of Lord George Germain, had been sent, unofficially but no longer secretly, to Spain to carry on discussions there. His mission had no chance of success from the start for it was founded on a misconception. Spain intended to negotiate the return of Gibraltar; Cumberland was instructed to negotiate on anything except Gibraltar. Floridablanca nevertheless allowed the negotiations to continue in a leisurely manner as a means of putting pressure on France to be attentive to Spanish military objectives and of keeping hope alive in Britain that Spain and France might yet be separated.[38] He decided to make use of Normandez's report of the Russian offer of good offices to put pressure on Cumberland. Cumberland was therefore told of this Russian overture, which might of course jeopardize the whole success of his mission.[39] But Cumberland's reports, when they reached England in August 1780, alarmed Stormont considerably. He was puzzled as to whether the Empress wished to mediate a general peace or merely a particular peace between

pendence, but it is not clear whether this was the Declaration of 1776 or some other document (ibid., *104*, Vergennes to Corberon, No. 13, 25 June 1780).

36. The Spanish reply, though dated 19 April 1780, was not delivered in Russia until the end of June. See also CP Russie, *104*, Corberon to Vergennes, No. 33, 23 June 1780.

37. SP 91/105, Harris to Stormont, No. 72, 12/23 June 1780.

38. Bemis, *Hussey-Cumberland Mission*, p. 100; Doniol, *Histoire*, *4*, 408–09, Montmorin to Vergennes, 1 September 1780.

39. Bemis, *Hussey-Cumberland Mission*, p. 113, note 22.

Britain and Spain. He could not understand how the Empress, who had been so lately incensed against Spain, should now offer to act on the Spaniards' behalf, particularly as she must have known that direct negotiations between Spain and Britain were already going on.[40] To take such a step and not make a similar overture to Britain was "very extraordinary." Could it have been taken without Potemkin's knowledge? If so, did not this confirm the report of a secret understanding between Panin and Vergennes, behind the back of the Empress?[41]

How completely Harris in September had forgotten his talks with Panin in April and Potemkin in May is revealed by the tenor of his replies. He thought the whole thing was "nothing more than some vague and general expressions of Count Panin which were unauthorized by the Empress . . . Mr. Normandez, either wilfully, or, what I think from my knowledge of him, through simplicity, considered these expressions as amounting to an actual offer . . ."[42] Subsequent inquiries through Potemkin confirmed him in this view. Potemkin expressed surprise at the news and declared "upon his honour that he had not the remotest knowledge" of the matter. He probably knew nothing about the actual conversations which Panin had held with Corberon and Normandez, though he well knew that mediation came within the general lines of the Empress's policy. Intensive inquiry led Harris to affirm categorically that nothing had passed in Count Panin's office on the subject of mediation except the allegedly unauthorized overtures he had already mentioned in his dispatches in June, which, he declared could not amount to more than the expression of a strong desire on the part of the Empress to be invited by the belligerents to settle their differences.[43]

The alarm which this supposed offer of the Empress to mediate between Britain and Spain caused in the breasts of Stormont and Harris must in part be attributed to the complete failure of either ever to take seriously anything that Panin said on the subject. Stormont evidently assumed that all previous Russian offers of

40. SP 91/105, Stormont to Harris, No. 46, 15 August 1780.
41. SP 91/105, Stormont to Harris, No. 47, 22 August 1780.
42. SP 91/106, Harris to Stormont, No. 106, 4/15 September 1780.
43. SP 91/106, Harris to Stormont, No. 110, 11/22 September 1780.

good offices had been finally disposed of by Harris on 5 May 1780.
The rumour which had now reached London from Spain was
merely a clever Spanish move to make use of the opening that
Panin had indeed made for the first time to Spain in June 1780
but which had been repeatedly made to Britain and France earlier.
For the time being however, the Russian overture to the Bourbon
powers led to no immediate results. The Spanish reply, when it
arrived in September 1780, merely stated that Spain would consult
with France and would then reply to the Empress's insinuations.[44]
Meanwhile Cumberland was told that Spain would make no reply
to the Russian offer until Britain had been given an opportunity
to carry the direct Anglo-Spanish negotiation a stage further.[45]
Vergennes in turn, though he did not want a Russian mediation
to materialize, kept the idea alive. He was deeply suspicious of the
separate negotiations being carried on by Cumberland in Spain,
and he saw the possibility of using the Russian opening to force
the winding up of Cumberland's mission. At the same time, as
long as France seemed to welcome the Russian initiative, the Empress would be kept out of British toils.[46]

Meanwhile Panin continued to explore the avenue with the new
French envoy, Vérac—not a very outstanding figure. As Harris
wrote, "he is certainly more a man of society than of business, and
yet with many pleasing accomplishments he has not that turn of
manners or conversation likely to amuse the Empress." Corberon
in his private journal confirms the impression that Vérac was not
likely to strike out a line of his own in opposition to Harris.[47]
The French envoy made no effort to cultivate Potemkin but attached himself firmly to Panin, whom he had no reason to distrust,
and on the whole this served him well. Panin's hatred and distrust
of Harris had grown to such proportions that he did not hesitate
to condemn the English envoy's behaviour loudly to the Bour-

44. CP Russie, *105*, Vérac to Vergennes, No. 12, 8 September 1780.

45. Bemis, *Hussey-Cumberland Mission*, pp. 81 ff. and p. 92; Danvila, *Historia, 5*,
159, note by Floridablanca, undated, but presumably July or August 1780, "que con
la Rusia no se tratará ni responderá sin ver lo que dice su [the British] corte."

46. Doniol, *Histoire, 4*, 464. Vergennes had not been told officially about these
secret negotiations between Britain and Spain until April 1780.

47. SP 91/105, Harris to Stormont, No. 83, 14/25 July 1780; cf. also Corberon,
Journal Intime, 2, 233 et seq.

bons.[48] He did not go so far as to pre-concert with Vérac the replies France should make to Russia in order to please the Empress, as Harris suggested,[49] yet at this period Franco-Russian relations were more friendly and founded on a closer active cooperation than had been the case for a long time. Panin in his interviews with Vérac allowed his imagination to wander over various proposals for bringing the war to an end. He expressed his approval of the independence of America as beneficial to Russia, discussed the Cumberland mission, and urged the appointment of a Spanish ambassador to Russia to take over from the limited Normandez. The impression grew in France that Russia could be relied on to protect French interests.[50]

Meanwhile Harris intensified his efforts to secure the removal of Count Panin from office. Having failed to move Potemkin, he determined to procure a second private interview with the Empress, in which he would be able to reveal to her the alleged duplicity of her minister.[51] His hopes of being granted an audience were not entirely unfounded, for he continued throughout the summer to be treated with notable favour by the Empress. In July she consented to stand godmother to Harris's infant daughter. Early in August, on hearing the news of the British victories in the Carolinas, the Empress took Harris up in her carriage for a two hours' ride, congratulated him on the British victory, and expressed her strong desire for a reconciliation between Britain and America as the first step towards victory over the Bourbons. As they were not alone, however, Harris was unable to use this opportunity to "unmask" Panin.[52]

He continued equally high in the favour of Potemkin, who undoubtedly genuinely liked his company. The Prince introduced Harris to the pleasures of Russian country life and bore him off to spend a week-end at a country house in Finland at which no one else was present but members of his family. The Prince's way of life was singular, commented Harris: "His hours for eating and

48. CP Russie, *105*, Vérac to Vergennes, No. 7, 11 August 1780.

49. SP 91/105, Harris to Stormont, No. 64, 2/13 June 1780.

50. CP Russie, *105*, Vérac to Vergennes, No. 11, 1 September 1780.

51. SP 91/105, Harris to Stormont, No. 80, 7/18 July 1780 (*MD, 1*, 332); No. 89, 28 July/8 August 1780; No. 92, 4/15 August 1780.

52. SP 91/105, Harris to Stormont, No. 87, 21 July/1 August 1780.

sleeping are uncertain, and we were frequently airing in the rain in an open carriage at midnight." Nevertheless Harris was visibly enchanted with the openness and freedom with which the Prince spoke and with his mixture of wit, "levity, learning and humour." [53] In spite of all his precautions Harris undoubtedly felt flattered by the unique favour he enjoyed with the otherwise inaccessible Potemkin. He had travelled a long way from his first impression of the Prince as a mere Pandarus. Potemkin was of course the channel through which Harris hoped to procure his interview with the Empress, and he left the Prince no peace on the subject. "I am labouring eternally to excite my friend to act," he wrote at the beginning of August 1780, "convinced that one vigorous effort from him would overset the whole, and restore the Empress to her natural sentiments and system." [54]

Early in September the Prince of Prussia arrived to pay his respects to the Empress, and the Dutch plenipotentiaries arrived soon afterwards to cement Dutch adherence to the Neutral League. Harris did not fear the visit of the Prussian Prince, who was unlikely to score a personal success after the Emperor. The British envoy worked hard of course to underline the contrast between the Emperor and the gauche Prussian Prince, but even without his efforts the visit was foredoomed to failure. The Empress was tired of Prussia and could scarcely bring herself to be polite to her guest. Though Goertz, in his official dispatches to Frederick II, felt compelled to paint a more favourable picture of Frederick William's reception—he was after all the heir to the Prussian throne—in his later account to the German historian Dohm he confirms that the Empress soon found the Prince's visit wearisome

53. SP 91/105, Harris to Stormont, No. 85, 21 July/1 August 1780 (MD, 1, 326). This dispatch gives an interesting picture of the relations between the two men and confirms the ascendancy which Potemkin had by this time won over Harris. That Potemkin's personal liking for Harris was genuine is further proved by the fact that later in the autumn he invited Harris to accompany him during the winter on a five weeks' tour of some distant provinces. Harris wrote home for permission to absent himself from the capital but Stormont refused it on the grounds that when important negotiations were going on Harris must be at his post. (See SP 91/106, Harris to Stormont, separate and private, No. 117, 22 September/3 October 1780, and Stormont to Harris, No. 63, 3 November 1780).

54. SP 91/105, Harris to Stormont, No. 88, 24 July/4 August 1780.

and took steps to curtail it.[55] Catherine in turn assured Joseph II that the impression he had made had not been effaced by "le gros Gu," as she unkindly described the future king of Prussia.[56]

Meanwhile the arrival of the Dutch plenipotentiaries carried negotiations with the Republic no further. On 8 September they put forward their demand for a Russian guarantee of Dutch possessions as part of the treaty embodying their accession to the Neutral League. If such a guarantee were refused, the ambassadors declared, they had no powers to negotiate but must refer back for instructions.[57] Such a guarantee formed no part of Catherine's plans; the Dutch overseas possessions were far too widespread and far too vulnerable for her to commit Russia to the wildcat idea of defending them, and her purpose in forming the League was strictly limited to common action over incidents that might arise in defence of trade. Three days after they had presented their proposals, Panin informed the Dutch ambassadors that the Empress would not consent to the guarantee but would accept them as neutrals into the convention as already drawn up between the three Baltic states.[58] The negotiation was now back where it had begun.

Harris in his official dispatches attributed the failure of the Dutch to the vigorous representations he had made on the subject to Potemkin and even to Panin.[59] Maybe he believed what he wrote, for he could not see that neither the Empress nor Panin

55. Contrast *PKFG, 44, 473*, Goertz to Frederick, 12 September 1780; p. 478, 15 September 1780; and Dohm, *Denkwürdigkeiten*, 2, xvii ff.; cf. SP 91/106, Harris to Stormont, No. 101, 28 August/8 September 1780 (*MD, 1,* 331); No. 118, 25 September/6 October 1780. The Prince of Prussia profited from Potemkin's temporary absence to cultivate his favourite niece, but the return of the uncle soon put a stop to this trifling. (SP 91/106, Harris to Stormont, No. 122, 29 September/10 October 1780; No. 125, 2/13 October 1780 (*MD, 1,* 336)). See also Corberon, *Journal Intime*, *2,* 334 et seq. for accounts of the reception of the Prince of Prussia, and Maykov, *Pis'ma A. A. Bezborodka*, p. 70, Bezborodko to Rumyantsev, 17/28 October 1780.

56. See *Arneth, Joseph II und Katharina*, p. 11, Catherine to Joseph, October, n.d.

57. SP 91/106, Harris to Stormont, No. 100, 28 August/8 September 1780; CP Russie, *105,* Vérac to Vergennes, No. 13, 12 September 1780. For once the French and the British accounts agree.

58. SP 91/106, Harris to Stormont, No. 103, 1/12 September 1780.

59. "To him [Potemkin] we must impute her rejecting . . . the guaranty . . ." (SP 91/106, Harris to Stormont, No. 103, 1/12 September 1780).

wished to commit Russia to a policy so likely to lead to war. It also never occurred to him that the Dutch demand for a Russian guarantee was greeted with horror by Vergennes [60] and that Vérac immediately set to work to persuade the Dutch plenipotentiaries of the impossibility of securing it.[61]

Not only was the Dutch negotiation thus hanging fire but the Empress was also at this time being plagued by a series of domestic disturbances which may have contributed to her ill-humoured reception of the Prussian Prince. Above all she was tired of the favourite Lanskoy and did not know whether to replace him or not. As usual on these occasions, her relations with Potemkin became strained, as the Prince did not hesitate to give her advice on the choice of a successor. It was a matter of considerable importance to him to have a man in this key position chosen from the lower ranks of the nobility and unable therefore to count on any support from the magnates. The Empress, moreover, was annoyed with one of Potemkin's nieces, who had allowed herself to comment a little too freely on Catherine's amorous propensities, and irritated with the uncle for having made it necessary for another of his nieces to make a strategic if temporary withdrawal from the court. In fact, as Corberon described it, "l'Impératrice est d'une humeur abominable." [62] In addition relations between Panin and Potemkin had become so bad in September that in the course of a meeting of the Council of State they burst into recriminations and mutual accusations of receiving bribes from England and France respectively. The quarrel grew to such proportions that the Empress had to be summoned "pour mettre le holà." [63]

60. CP Russie, *104*, Vergennes to Vérac, No. 1, 30 June 1780, informing Vérac that Vauguyon had been instructed to persuade the Dutch to drop the demand for a guarantee of the Dutch East Indies.

61. *AMON*, 2, 265, Heeckeren (Dutch plenipotentiary) to the Prince of Orange, 14 September 1780. Frederick II also refused to support the Dutch demand for a guarantee in Russia (see *PKFG*, *44*, 431, Frederick to the Princess of Orange, 31 August 1780; p. 456, Princess of Orange to Frederick, 12 September 1780; p. 457, Frederick II to Princess of Orange, 18 September 1780).

62. SP 91/105, Harris to Stormont, No. 94, 14/25 August 1780; see also Corberon, *Journal Intime*, 2, 327, 369 ff.; CP Russie, *105*, Corberon to Vergennes, 15 October 1780 (unnumbered report, on his return to France).

63. Corberon, *Journal Intime*, 2, 370. But the quarrel may have been about the Greek project. See Grigorovich, *Kantsler A. A. Bezborodko, Sbornik*, 26, 221, note 156.

A further blow was in store for Catherine. On 9 October she received the news from her minister in Copenhagen of the agreement which had only just been ratified between Britain and Denmark to modify the Anglo-Danish treaty. Both the Empress and Panin reacted at first very strongly against what they regarded as the duplicity of Bernstorff, and Panin was ordered to express to the Danish envoy, Schumacher, the Empress's disapproval of such double-dealing.[64] Though the Anglo-Danish agreement affected the Neutral League only in that it withdrew the right to carry naval stores to the enemy from one of the signatories, yet implicit in the whole policy of protecting neutral trade there had been an attempt to render the trade in precisely these commodities safe. The public revelation of this hitherto secret agreement led to a crisis in the Danish government and to the fall of Bernstorff at the beginning of November 1780.[65] But the united front of the Baltic powers could not be restored.

The Danish crisis coincided with a new Russian outburst against the British treatment of Russian shipping. The news that two Russian ships had recently been detained and taken into British ports had reached St. Petersburg.[66] In addition a copy of the British instructions to privateers of 1778 had been captured by the

64. SP 91/106, Harris to Stormont, No. 123, 29 September/10 October 1780; No. 134, 20/31 October 1780; CP Russie, *105*, Vérac to Vergennes, No. 17, 20 October 1780; see also Holm, *Om Danmarks*, pp. 133 ff.

65. The fall of Bernstorff was currently attributed to the Empress Catherine, who was said to have complained strongly to the Danish court. The CP Russie reveals however that the Empress decided against making any strong *démarche* to the Danish court such as asking for his removal. But Panin did express strong verbal disapproval to Schumacher and thus provided the anti-Bernstorff party in Denmark, led by the Dowager Queen Juliana, with the pretext they needed to get rid of him. Catherine was furious when she heard that the fall of Bernstorff was generally considered to be her work, and Panin had difficulty in dissuading her from honouring Bernstorff with the Grand Cordon of the Order of St. Andrew as a mark of her refusal to participate in his disgrace. (See *PKFG*, *45*, 126, Goertz to Frederick, 12 December 1780). For Bernstorff's defence see Holm, *Om Danmarks*, p. 154, Mémoire sur les reproches de M. le cte de Panin renfermés dans le rapport de M. Schumacher du 13 octobre 1780, dated 10 November 1780. Fauchille, *La diplomatie française*, p. 445, gives a highly biassed account of this episode, alleging a letter from Catherine to Queen Juliana Maria demanding the removal of Bernstorff. But Shchelkunov in his *Pis'ma imperatritsy Yekateriny II k datskoy koroleve Yuliane Marii* prints no such letter, and its existence must be doubted.

66. SP 91/105, Harris to Stormont, No. 120, 25 September/6 October 1780.

French and had been forwarded to Russia by Vergennes with a suitable commentary. Panin promptly seized on the ammunition supplied him by Vergennes and proceeded to work up the Empress's indignation against Britain.[67] He drafted a memorial in which he was alleged to have described Britain as the "tyrants of the sea" and to have accused her of treating the Neutral League with "derision and contempt." [68] Harris feared that the Empress, "so wrong-headed on this article, so perfectly ignorant of what is customary and just," so "beyond the reach of plain sense and truth" would be capable of going to any lengths.[69] He found Potemkin, though he agreed with all Harris said, unwilling to speak to the Empress.[70] Indeed, annoyed as she already was by the defection of Denmark, Catherine did not hesitate to lodge a strong protest through Simolin in Britain.[71]

But far the most pressing problem at this time from Britain's point of view was to prevent Dutch accession to the Neutral League. If once Dutch ships could claim the protection of the League to enforce their privileges under the treaty of 1674, it might be beyond the power of Britain to prevent naval stores from reaching France and Spain. If their accession appeared to be inevitable, then a pretext must be found to declare war on them which was in every way unconnected with the disputes arising over neutral trade, and if possible war must be declared before the Dutch signed any convention with Russia. Only thus could Britain hope to evade swinging the whole Neutral League round against her in defence of the Dutch Republic, for the signatories were bound to come to the defence of any of them attacked "en haine de la convention." It was imperative to warn the Empress, before she allowed them to join the League, that Britain had already sufficient grounds to declare war on the United Provinces. The difficulty lay in the fact that the Empress might not take the

67. CP Russie, *105*, Vérac to Vergennes, No. 15, 6 October 1780; "[Panin] me dit en riant qu'un chef de pirate ne pourrait guère donner des ordres différents." Cf. Ch. 3, p. 58, and n. 4.

68. SP 91/106, Harris to Stormont, No. 123, 29 September/10 October 1780.

69. SP 91/106, Harris to Stormont, No. 120, 25 September/6 October; No. 123, 29 September/10 October 1780.

70. SP 91/106, Harris to Stormont, No. 134, 6/17 October (*MD, 1*, 337).

71. See Chapter 15.

same view of Dutch ingratitude and might face Britain with a *fait accompli*. At any rate Stormont thought the effort worth-while, and he accordingly instructed Harris on 19 September 1780 to convey to the Empress the British grievances against the United Provinces, such as their failure to comply with the Anglo-Dutch treaty of alliance by which they were bound to grant succours to Britain in the event of attack in Europe; and the unneutral partiality they had shown by supplying the Bourbons with naval stores and by imposing penalties on Dutch merchants attempting to run the blockade of Gibraltar.[72] Normally, wrote Stormont, such a *démarche* should be made through Panin, but as he assumed that Panin would distort what he was told to further his own ends, Harris was to act through Potemkin, while taking care not to give Panin "just cause for complaint." The Empress however must realize that, should the Dutch continue in their present policy, Britain would force a rupture: "Had not we acted with uncommon moderation, there would have been a breach long ago." [73]

The accidents of war now provided Stormont with the pretext he needed to force a breach with the Dutch. On 3 September 1780 a British warship had captured on board a neutral vessel Henry Laurens, former president of the American Congress. Laurens threw his papers overboard, but they were rescued by the British captain, and among them was found the draft of a treaty of commerce between the United States and the United Provinces dated 1778. This draft was the outcome of discussions conducted there between William Lee, who held a roving diplomatic commission from Congress, and one Jean de Neufville, a business man appointed by the pensionary of Amsterdam, van Berckel. Neither of the two men had any powers to negotiate such a treaty, and the draft could not be said to represent the fruit of discussions between responsible and authorized representatives of the Dutch and American governments. The British government, however, chose to regard the draft as evidence of a past intention on the part of the

72. A placart had been issued by the Dutch on 31 December 1779 (see Faucnille, *La diplomatie française*, p. 182) prohibiting the Dutch under pain of a fine from running the blockade of Gibraltar.

73. SP 91/105, Stormont to Harris, Nos. 51 and 52, 19 September 1780.

Dutch to enter into an alliance with the rebellious colonies, and Stormont decided to build his case on this slender foundation.[74] On 13 October he instructed Harris to convey this information to the Empress as further evidence of the double-dealing of the Dutch, in the hope that she would refrain from connecting herself with what he regarded as a minority party, and factious at that, which temporarily dominated the States General.[75] Yorke, on 21 October 1780, conveyed to Harris even more clearly that this discovery was to be the peg on which British action would hang. "The consequences must be very important," he wrote, "and will fully justify any step we may be forced to take with this country, without furnishing a pretext to any neutral power to interfere, as none of them have been consulted upon it, nor can it be wrested into the *casus foederis* of any subsequent agreement." [76]

The States General had not yet met to consider the report of the Dutch plenipotentiaries in Russia and to make up their minds whether to accede to the Neutral League without the Russian guarantee of Dutch possessions. While there was still a chance that they might have second thoughts, Stormont believed that strong measures might serve his purpose. Accordingly Yorke presented on 10 November 1780 what amounted to an ultimatum to the States General. He demanded the disavowal of the conduct of van Berckel and the punishment of the culprit.[77] On 14 November 1780 Stormont wrote to Harris to explain that the Dutch situation had now completely changed. It was no longer a question of endeavouring to persuade the Empress not to receive them into the Neutral League. Harris must now state quite clearly that the present British quarrel with the Republic had nothing to do with the League or with neutral trade. The business now stood on its own ground, and it would require "no laboured colouring

---

74. See Bemis, *Diplomacy of the American Revolution*, pp. 156 ff. for a brief account of this episode. See also *AMON*, 5, 290 ff.; Fortescue, *Correspondence of King George III*, 5, 140, Stormont to the King, 12 October 1780. See also Christie, *The End of North's Ministry, 1780–1782*, pp. 243 ff. for an account of British policy at this stage, and HMC, Knox Papers, p. 271.

75. SP 91/106, Stormont to Harris, No. 58, 13 October 1780.

76. Harris Papers.

77. Christie, *The End of North's Ministry*, p. 246.

to raise the Empress's highest indignation; it will, I am sure, be sufficient to represent it in its native deformity." [78]

Harris accepted at their face value the protestations of Stormont and Yorke and tried to make the Empress and Potemkin see things as he saw them. He prepared a strong memorial, painting the iniquitous conduct of the Dutch, for Potemkin to deliver to the Empress.[79] His hopes were raised by Potemkin's reports that the Empress had determined in any case never to join the Dutch against Britain and that, should her proposals return to her altered from The Hague, she would break off the negotiations.[80] Nevertheless though the Empress disapproved of the behaviour of the regents of Amsterdam, she "does not give it that weight it deserves," explained Potemkin.[81] Harris was at that time hampered in his efforts to influence the Empress by the fact that Potemkin and Catherine were not yet perfectly reconciled. The Empress had been induced, said Potemkin, to believe that he was ignorant in matters of foreign policy and too liable to be influenced by Harris, "without consulting the good of the Empire or her personal glory." [82] Potemkin had therefore been unable or unwilling to help Harris to procure the private interview with the Empress he still desired, and the Prince's value to Harris as an intermediary suffered a temporary decline.[83] When Harris received directly from Yorke a copy of the British ultimatum to the States General of 10 November 1780, he therefore hastened to present it to Panin ministerially, in order if possible to persuade the Russian minister that a breach was impending between Britain and the Dutch on grounds quite unconnected with the Neutral League. But Panin refused to believe that a breach would really take place and chose to interpret the ultimatum as empty words, meant to please and placate the people of Great Britain.[84]

78. SP 91/106, Stormont to Harris, No. 66, 14 November 1780. See also *AMON*, 2, 341, Thulemeier to Frederick II, 1 December 1780.

79. Enclosure in SP 91/106, Harris to Stormont, No. 140, 30 October/10 November 1780.

80. SP 91/106, Harris to Stormont, No. 144, 6/17 November 1780.

81. SP 91/106, Harris to Stormont, No. 146, 17/28 November 1780 (*MD, 1*, 342).

82. Sp 91/106, No. 128, 6/17 October 1780.

83. SP 91/106, Harris to Stormont, No. 137, 23 October/3 November 1780.

84. SP 91/106, Harris to Stormont, No. 139, 13/24 December 1780.

Meanwhile the Patriot party in the Republic secured a decision on 20 November 1780 by the States General to accede to the Neutral League on the Empress's terms.[85] A Dutch courier arrived in St. Petersburg on 4/15 December 1780 bringing full powers to the Dutch plenipotentiaries to sign the convention as proposed by Russia. Harris made one final effort to prevent their accession. Towards the middle of December 1780 he submitted a memorial to the Empress through Potemkin, asserting that the Empress's name was being misused all over Europe and that the Dutch were boasting that Russia would now support them in anything.[86] But in spite of the efforts on his behalf which Harris believed Potemkin to have made,[87] the Empress would not be moved. Panin meanwhile was hastening the negotiations with the plenipotentiaries. "He has deprived himself of the pleasures of society, and has borrowed many hours from his sleep," wrote Harris, "in order to get his papers in readiness to present to the Empress." [88]

Since both the Empress and Panin were determined to complete the association of the neutral powers, and since neither seemed to have envisaged how seriously Dutch accession was viewed in Britain, the negotiations with the Dutch proceeded to the inevitable outcome. On 4 January 1781 the Dutch plenipotentiaries appended their signatures to the convention with Russia and became members of the Neutral League.[89] They did not know it, but they were no longer neutrals. Yet Harris, in spite of this defeat, had other grounds for hope for, in the course of the autumn, he had embarked on a highly secret negotiation through Potemkin which seemed to promise that Russia would be won for Britain at last.

85. Piggott and Omond, *Documentary History of the Armed Neutralities,* p. 247.

86. SP 91/106, Harris to Stormont, No. 157, 13/24 December 1780, Enclosure, Paper A.

87. Harris praised Potemkin's conduct highly on this occasion, but, he wrote, the Prince "found in the mind of his sovereign an opiniative resistance, not to be overcome either by his arguments or by his persuasions." (SP 91/106, Harris to Stormont, No. 157, 13/24 December (*MD, 1,* 348).

88. SP 91/106, Harris to Stormont, No. 156, 8/19 December 1780.

89. Scott, *Armed Neutralities,* p. 346 ff.

10. The Offer of Minorca: Catherine Receives Harris

THOUGH the war against America, France, and Spain had not gone badly for Britain in the course of 1780, the North administration was faced with considerable problems of both domestic and foreign policy. Parliament was dissolved in the summer, and elections in September 1780 returned a fresh House of Commons, which, it was hoped would prove more docile.[1] Abroad no help was to be expected from any European power, and Russia, still regarded by many as Britain's most likely ally, had pursued a bewildering and incomprehensible line of her own which in the long run was bound to injure Britain's interests. The prospect of war with Holland rendered it all the more necessary to secure a European ally, both to provide assistance in the form of ships and to consolidate the position of the government at home by the evidence of some striking success in the foreign field. The only great power with a navy on which Britain might draw was still Russia, and all Harris's dispatches went to show that Russia had not one foreign policy but two: that of the Empress (and Potemkin) and that of Panin. There was still hope that the Empress might see through the intrigues of her foreign minister and follow the real dictates of her heart, namely her sympathy for the British nation.

During the month of October 1780 Stormont therefore launched a new idea. He now proposed to offer Russia some really solid inducement to join in the war against the Bourbons. The idea of bribing Catherine to take part in the war had occurred to Stormont before. Already in May 1780, when the Empress's recent dec-

1. See Christie, *The End of North's Ministry*, pp. 1-45.

239

laration of the principles of the Armed Neutrality had shown
her resolve to keep Russia out of the war, Stormont had put
forward to Harris the idea that Russia should be persuaded to
launch an attack on the Spanish island of Majorca; it was but
poorly defended, a small force could take it, and "the advantage
to Russia of such a port so situated is too obvious to be dwelt
upon." Great Britain, added Stormont, would rejoice at Russia's
acquiring such a footing in the Mediterranean "and would most
heartily assist her in an attack upon Majorca." If the plan were
properly presented to the Empress, Stormont expressed the hope
that she would adopt it, one of his reasons being "that Peter the
Great would at once have caught at the idea." [2] But when Stormont's dispatches arrived in June 1780 the Empress and Potemkin
were away in Mogilyev entertaining the Emperor, and the final
touches were being put to the structure of the Neutral League in
the Baltic. The time was obviously not propitious for such a
proposal, and Harris appears to have used his own judgement and
allowed Stormont's suggestion to drop.[3]

But the idea of purchasing the Russian alliance by some kind
of territorial bribe had taken root in Stormont's mind. He may
also have been influenced in the autumn of 1780 by a rumour that
the Bourbon powers were offering Russia Puerto Rico or Trinidad
as the price of alliance, a rumour which caused him much anxiety
since it came just after the report that Russia had offered to mediate on Spain's behalf.[4] Stormont was still convinced that if only
Russia would espouse the cause of Britain, France and Spain
would be forced to give up the struggle. But he was aware that in
the present temper of the Empress such an aim could not be
achieved "unless we can hold out to the Empress some object
worthy of her ambition." He therefore instructed Harris to find
out, discreetly, if there were any cession of territory Great Britain
could make which was likely to be of use to Catherine in increasing her commercial and naval strength. In exchange, the Empress
would be expected to conclude an alliance with Britain "making
the present war the *casus foederis*" and assisting Britain with all

2. SP 91/104, Stormont to Harris, No. 31, 9 May 1780.
3. SP 91/105, Harris to Stormont, No. 61, 26 May/6 June 1780.
4. SP 91/105, Stormont to Harris, No. 50, 8 September 1780.

her forces (*"totis viribus"*) against France, Spain, and the rebellious colonies until these returned to their allegiance. At this stage Harris was however only to feel his way without committing the government; he was not authorized to make any formal offer whatsoever.[5]

Stormont's instructions reached Harris by the middle of November 1780, and at the first suitable moment the British envoy entered upon his delicate task and broached the subject to Potemkin. Mournfully surveying the spectacle of his country, without allies and abandoned by her friends, he speculated aloud on the necessity Britain would find herself in of making territorial concessions at the peace, and on the advantages of ceding territory voluntarily to one's friends instead of compulsorily to one's enemies. Potemkin seized the point at once: "What can you cede to us?" he exclaimed. Harris, disclaiming any authority to cede anything, directed the Prince's attention successively to America, the East Indies, the Sugar Islands. Potemkin, who knew full well that Russia could not hope to keep possessions in the Caribbean, asked for something nearer home. "You would ruin us if you give us distant colonies," he declared. "You see our ships can scarce get out of the Baltick, how would you have them cross the Atlantick?" His roving fancy then fixed on Minorca which, he asserted, would bind the Empress to Britain forever.[6]

Early in December Potemkin recurred to the subject of Minorca several times. Clearly he was genuinely attracted by the idea of erecting "a column of the Empress's glory" in the middle of the Mediterranean Sea. He visualized a Russian fleet anchored at Mahon, the local population deported, and the island peopled by Greeks. Its value to Russia as a naval base in the war against the

5. SP 91/106, Stormont to Harris, No. 61, 20 October 1780, which had reached Harris by 14 November. The editor of *MD* has wrongly dated this dispatch 28 October (*1*, 345) and therefore assumes that Harris had had the same idea and had acted in anticipation of Stormont's instructions. But bold as he was, Harris would never have embarked on such a dangerous course without instructions.

6. SP 91/106, Harris to Stormont, No. 158, 13/24 December 1780 (*MD*, *1*, 363). Harris waited until he could send a courier to report his discussions in full. Meanwhile, on 24 November/5 December 1780, he wrote briefly that "Prince Potemkin, though he did not directly say so, yesterday, clearly gave me to understand that the only cession which would induce the Empress to become our Ally, was that of Minorca." (SP 91/106, Harris to Stormont, No. 150, *MD*, *1*, 345.)

Porte, which both he and the Empress contemplated as the first step in restoring the Greek empire of the East, was incalculable. But from the very beginning of the discussions between Harris and Potemkin the subject of a possible cession of territory by Britain was seen in a somewhat different light from that in which Stormont had contemplated it. The Secretary of State, in his instructions to Harris, had put forward the idea of a territorial cession as the price of an effective Russian alliance in the present war against France and Spain, and even in America. But Harris, according to his account, never went further than suggesting that such a cession might "rouse [Britain's friends] to activity, and end the contest by rendering it more equal." He even went so far as to express to Potemkin, as his own private opinion, that Britain "ought to gratify her [the Empress] with such a part of them [British possessions] as she chose, if by it we could obtain a lasting peace." Possibly because he realized that if such an offer were accepted it would inevitably drive Russia into the war, Harris refrained from actually demanding Russian assistance in exchange for the cession of Minorca, and Potemkin throughout referred to it as the price of a peace negotiated by the Empress. How much further the two men went in their private discussions Harris's dispatches do not reveal. But Potemkin did urge Harris most insistently to find out from his court whether such a cession was possible, i.e. to have the talks transformed from unofficial into official: "Persuade your ministers to give it [Minorca] us, and we shall give you peace, and then unite ourselves to you by the firmest and most lasting alliance" was the main burden of his advice on how the proposal should be presented by Britain.[7]

From Potemkin's personal point of view Harris's opening came at a very opportune moment, for ever since September his relations with the Empress had remained strained. Catherine herself had not completely recovered from the personal and political crisis she had been through. Lanskoy had pleaded his cause so pitifully that the Empress had not had the heart to dismiss him. Though nothing could really estrange her from Potemkin, and she always missed him if he left the court for as little as a few days, there

7. SP 91/106, Harris to Stormont, No. 158, 13/24 December 1780.

were several fairly severe quarrels between them. It is possible that these quarrels were over differences of policy, but if so they were rendered more serious by purely personal differences. The evident estrangement between the Empress and Potemkin was noticed by the foreign envoys, and there were rumours that the Prince's career was coming to an end.[8] Even Harris was alarmed when at the beginning of November he found Potemkin, "usually a perfect master of his passions," so infuriated at having actually been dismissed by the Empress from her presence that he declared his intention of leaving the court, retiring from his functions, and taking refuge in foreign travel. Harris saw sufficiently clearly to realize that Potemkin would recover his influence, but at the time he had to give up all hopes of securing an audience with the Empress.[9] Catherine, so Potemkin told the British envoy, had repeatedly refused to see Harris, and "sometimes," said he, "when I speak of foreign affairs she lets me remain without any answer, at a stand, and at others replies to me with warmth and displeasure." Harris, whose sense of perspective was somewhat out of focus owing to the warping influence of Potemkin and the hothouse atmosphere of intrigue in which he lived, never failed to point the moral as he saw it to the Prince: "[He] must needs see his cause and ours are now become inseparable; that the safety of the state, besides his honour, nay, his security, was at stake, and that it became him to use every means to prevent the cabal getting head, since, if it did, his fall was not less certain than the rupture with England . . ."[10]

Harris's offer of Minorca, for as such it was clearly interpreted, by providing Potemkin with a foreign policy of his own contributed to restore him to Catherine's confidence. Such an offer was of course in line with the most cherished project of the Empress —and one to which curiously enough few of the foreign envoys at her court attached much importance. Harris had indeed mentioned

8. *PKFG*, *45*, 96, Goertz to Frederick, 24 November 1780; but see also p. 111, note 2 (undated) and p. 120, note 2, 5 December 1780, for Panin's opinion that Potemkin's career was by no means nearing its end.

9. SP 91/106, Harris to Stormont, separate, secret, No. 137, 23 October/3 November 1780.

10. SP 91/106, Harris to Stormont, No. 157, 13/24 December 1780.

the existence of the Greek project to his principals in June 1779, but he never took it seriously.[11] Goertz did not mention it to Frederick II until 26 December 1780; he had known of it before but considered it too extravagant to be worth mentioning.[12] Corberon only mentioned it in passing, in connexion with the birth of the Grand Duke Constantine in 1779.[13] But to Potemkin and Catherine the expansion of Russia at the expense of Turkey was both possible and desirable and had influenced their wish for a *rapprochement* with the Emperor. Minorca would prove an excellent stepping stone for the realization of their dream, and Harris's opening galvanized Potemkin into immediate activity. When Harris refused to dispatch a courier and report their discussions with a view to a formal offer being made by Britain, Potemkin "gave Her Imperial Majesty no rest" until she consented to receive Harris for a second time.[14]

The hope which this renewal of diplomatic activity gave rise to induced Harris to try his fortune again with the Empress by means of a memorial, which he submitted to her towards the middle of December, without going through Count Panin. His main purpose was to turn her aside from admitting the Dutch to the Neutral League, but he took the opportunity of setting out what he thought the Empress ought to know and what he alleged Panin was concealing from her. He described how Catherine's name was being used all over Europe to further a policy which was not hers. France, he declared, boasted everywhere of her influence in Russia; Spain asserted that the Empress had offered her an advantageous mediation; Holland believed that Russia would support her in anything. The King of Prussia had been so bold as to say that he had been invited to accede to the Armed Neutrality; [15] Catherine's name had been used in Denmark to provoke the fall of Bernstorff. "En un mot, on ne rougit pas de com-

11. SP 91/103, Harris to Weymouth, No. 31, 23 May/3 June 1779 (*MD*, *1*, 232. See Ch. 4, pp. 101–02, n. 21).

12. *PKFG*, *45*, 171, Goertz to Frederick, 26 December 1780.

13. CP Russie, *102*, Corberon to Vergennes, No. 21, 14 May 1779.

14. SP 91/106, Harris to Stormont, No. 158, 13/24 December 1780.

15. See Chs. 12, p. 306 and 13, pp. 320 ff. for Prussian accession to the Armed Neutrality.

promettre le nom de Sa Majesté Impériale en toute occasion,"
wrote Harris, and he added that this policy was supported by a
large party in St. Petersburg which sought not only to conceal the
truth from the Empress but to prevent her real sentiments being
known.[16]

How far Catherine relished this bold attack history does not
tell, but at this time she was having her own difficulties with
Panin, which will be discussed later. Yet there were two aspects
of Russian foreign policy on which the Empress and Panin were
in complete agreement.[17] One was the determination to make the
Neutral League as neutral and as effective as possible. The other
was by constant pressure to bring the belligerents to the point of
asking for Russian mediation. Developments in this latter field, of
which Harris thought he was aware, form the background to the
Empress's personal interview with the British envoy and must be
outlined in order to grasp the situation in its full complexity.

Panin's exploratory talks with Vérac on the possibility of putting an end to the war between Britain and the Bourbons had
continued throughout the autumn. On 1 September 1780 he
proposed to Vérac as his own idea that first an armistice should
be declared and then the King of France should ask each American
province separately if it still wanted complete independence. Vergennes seems to have thought the latter suggestion promising; it
offered a face-saving solution for Britain, and the King of France
would be relieved of his treaty obligation to secure complete American independence if a number of provinces stated publicly that
they no longer desired it. At any rate, the discussions were proving
useful enough to be worth pursuing, particularly if Russia should
attempt to introduce the principles of the Neutral League into
the peace. Vergennes accordingly instructed Vérac on 12 October

16. SP 91/106, Harris to Stormont, No. 157, 13/24 December 1780, Enclosure,
Paper A. (See also Ch. 9, p. 238).

17. Though Catherine might not know all that Panin said to Vérac, there is
evidence from many quarters that no written instructions to her envoys abroad
were sent without her previous approval. Written instructions are therefore a
reliable guide to the policy of the Empress herself. Harris also heard that the
Empress read all incoming dispatches in full and told Stormont there was no surer
way of reaching her than speaking to Simolin (see FO 65/1, No. 167, 22 December
1780/2 January 1781).

1780 to urge Panin to press the Empress to mediate, "assaisonée d'une force suffisante." [18]

Meanwhile the picture of Russian policy suffered a further peculiar twist. The various treaties between the three Baltic powers which established the nucleus of the Neutral League were at last, in September 1780, not only signed but ratified. The next step was a formal communication of these treaties to the belligerent courts. Before anything was done about it Harris, by means of secret channels of information, heard a startling piece of news. From an "undoubted authority" he learnt that the Empress had ordered Count Panin, in the last week of October, "to tender to the belligerent powers an offer of her mediation." He was excessively puzzled by this new development and could not imagine by whom the Empress had been induced to take such a step. He knew beyond doubt, so he said, that Panin had been taken by surprise; Potemkin denied all knowledge of the matter, and it really appeared to be a step which the Empress had taken "from her own head, without consulting or previously forewarning any person whatsoever." He was the more puzzled as only a year before the Empress had made it clear that she would mediate only if she were invited to do so and not proffer her unsolicited services. Though shocked and surprised by the news, Harris, inspired by Potemkin, advised that Britain should roundly accept the Empress's offer of mediation and communicate the terms on which peace could be made.[19]

But for once Harris's information service had let him down. He had procured only a garbled version of an instruction concerning an *insinuation verbale* which was to be made by the Russian envoys in Versailles, Madrid, and London when the treaties forming the Neutral League were communicated to these courts. Though it did not contain an offer of mediation, as Harris believed, the *insinuation* did include a strongly worded exhortation to the belligerents to make peace on the grounds of the suffering inflicted on neutrals by the continuation of the war at sea. It was

18. CP Russie, *105*, No. 11, Vérac to Vergennes, 1 September 1780; Vergennes to Vérac, No. 9, 12 October 1780.

19. SP 91/106, Harris to Stormont, No. 131, 13/24 October 1780; No 133, 16/27 October 1780, *MD, 1,* 338.

couched in identical terms to all the belligerents.[20] Thus, when
Potemkin denied to Harris all knowledge of an offer of mediation,
he was speaking the truth, and he had taken the trouble to examine the papers himself.[21] Nevertheless, as Panin had constantly
been pressing on Harris the necessity for Britain to make peace,
the British envoy was at a loss what to believe. What is more,
Panin's approach to the subject was such as to arouse Harris's
utmost indignation. He praised the moderation, prudence, and
good conduct of France in such a manner as to convey his implicit
disapproval of Britain. He pointed out that Britain could now be
matched in a naval war and that "the general disposition of Europe" was averse to British enjoyment of that superiority at sea
"and those pretensions annexed to it" which had been hers in
previous wars. Those who wished Britain well, declared the Russian minister, could not do better than recommend to Britain to
make peace "on terms which might meet the ideas of all belligerent powers," and, to crown the insult, Panin added that though
he had no orders from the Empress to speak on the subject, he had
given his own opinion "merely to shew his regard and esteem." [22]
When Harris rushed off to vent his indignation on Potemkin, the
Prince, with one of his characteristic right about turns, explained
that "it was merely a trick of [Panin's] . . . to engage me [Harris]
to represent the present temper of this court in such a light as to
create a diffidence in the King's mind, in order that His Majesty's
answer to the Empress's offer of mediation might bear the features
of mistrust and doubt." [23] And yet Potemkin knew no offer was
intended at the moment.

20. See Ch. 11 for further discussion.

21. In view of the confusion which arose about this alleged Russian proposal to
mediate, it is useful to record that Potemkin told Harris he had sent for the
relevant papers (SP 91/106, Harris to Stormont, No. 136, 23 October/3 November
1780, MD, 1, 339); and, according to Goertz, Catherine asked Panin to send her the
papers concerning the Neutral League to show them to Potemkin (PKFG, 45, 33,
note, Goertz to Frederick, 24 October 1780); on 31 October Catherine had returned
the papers to Panin "en approuvant entièrement son plan." (ibid.) For the papers,
see Morskoy Sbornik, 44, 157 ff., Nos. 51, 52, 53, 54, and 55.

22. SP 91/106, Harris to Stormont, No. 136, 23 October/3 November 1780; MD, 1,
339.

23. SP 91/106, Harris to Stormont, No. 139, 27 October/7 November 1780. "Your
Friend's reasoning on the subject seems a little too refined," commented Stormont
on 5 December 1780 (ibid., to Harris, No. 68).

Indeed the disadvantages for Harris of quarrelling with Panin were considerable. For in spite of Harris's many assurances to Stormont that he had always avoided a breach with Panin, the social and political campaign they waged on each other had reached new and relentless depths.[24] Though they continued to meet in society and even visited each other, Harris met Panin only once between 27 October and 17 December to discuss business.[25] As a result Harris was out of touch with the day-to-day developments of Russian diplomacy which Potemkin did not trouble his head with. Moreover Panin was undoubtedly revenging himself on Harris by plotting his course with Vérac alone. He communicated to the Empress an account of his talks with Vérac and also the bulk of Vergennes's ideas as expressed in his dispatch of 12 October to Vérac, but he carefully eliminated any suggestion that the ideas of Vergennes were an elaboration of what he himself, Panin, had put forward. This was all done with great secrecy and promises not to allow Potemkin, and therefore Harris, to know anything about it. Catherine, reported Panin to Vérac, was delighted at this show of French amenability to her wishes, but her reply consisted only of vague assurances.[26] She was clearly not yet prepared to commit herself and risk a rebuff. But Panin still asserted to Vérac that he was only waiting for a reply from the British court to proceed further. He expressed the view that the North administration, with a new and presumably well-chosen Parliament behind them, could now safely negotiate for peace without fearing for their heads, and the peace terms which he put forward as his own, or even Catherine's, were such as he thought France was bound to welcome—a long armistice, during which America would be free and would trade freely.[27]

In accordance with his promise to Vérac, Panin concealed from Harris the various solutions for the American deadlock he had

24. See e.g. Panin's confidences to Goertz in *PKFG, 45,* passim; and cf. SP 91/106, Harris to Stormont, No. 129, 6/17 October 1780: "He attacks me with more vengeance and malevolence than I thought could exist in so cold a character, and in my social, as well as in my publick life endeavours to injure me."

25. SP 91/106, Harris to Stormont, No. 159, 13/24 December 1780.

26. CP Russie, *105,* Vérac to Vergennes, No. 20, 14 November 1780. Panin told Vérac that the coolness of Catherine's reply was simulated.

27. Ibid.

discussed with the French envoy. He went further. He concealed from him the existence of the *insinuation verbale* which was to accompany the communication of the conventions of the Neutral League to the belligerent courts,[28] though he had explained to Vérac that if it contained expressions displeasing to France, this was simply because, owing to the circumstances, the same attitude must be adopted towards all the belligerents.[29] Not until 17 December did the subject of mediation come up again between Harris and Panin, but the Russian minister again confined himself to generalities. The tone of the interview was so unpleasant that Harris was convinced that Panin deliberately intended to provoke him into some expression of greater reliance on Potemkin. Any offer of good offices coming from such a tainted source he refused to regard as coming from the Empress.[30]

It was against this background of confusion and rumour, with the Dutch accession to the Neutral League still to come, that Harris was at last granted the long desired private audience with the Empress. It was arranged for 19 December 1780, and the day before Potemkin, after spending some two hours with the Empress, proceeded to advise Harris on what he should say and on how he should behave. He urged Harris to be unreserved, open, and candid; not to appear embarrassed or intimidated (this was scarcely necessary; Harris was clearly not a shy man); to avoid cunning and dissimulation; to flatter the Empress "for what she ought to be, not what she is." He warned Harris not to expect to be able to induce her to break off the Dutch negotiation or to prevent her from completing her plans for the Neutral League. Let Harris, said Potemkin, content himself with destroying its effects, for the Neutral League "was conceived by mistake, perfected by vanity [and] maintained by pride and obstinacy, you well know the hold these passions have on female minds, and if you attempt to slacken you will only tighten the knot." The Prince ended by recommending to Harris that he should make the Empress feel that Britain had full confidence in her, for "it is because she supposes

28. SP 91/106, Harris to Stormont, No. 139, 27 October/7 November 1780. The Russian courier left that night.
29. CP Russie, *105*, Vérac to Vergennes, No. 20, 14 November 1780.
30. SP 91/106, Harris to Stormont, No. 159, 13/24 December 1780.

your nation has not this confidence that she is displeased." If Harris succeeded in making the first step, Potemkin assured him that he would take care of the rest.[31]

It is clear that Potemkin, fired by the idea of the acquisition of Minorca, had overcome the Empress's reluctance to receive Harris. The implications of this unofficial opening must have been discussed between them. Moreover it is more than likely that the two hours Potemkin passed with the Empress the day before Harris's audience were spent on a thorough survey of Russian foreign policy. Potemkin's warnings to accept the Neutral League as a *fait accompli* were undoubtedly based on the knowledge of Catherine's firm decision to adhere to her policy in maritime affairs. It was also good advice from a purely personal point of view: Catherine could not fail to be irritated should Harris challenge her on this issue. But when the Prince spoke to Harris of the hold of vanity over a female mind, of the Empress's weakened intellects and increased passions, he did him a disservice. For Harris tended far too much already to under-estimate her capacity to impose her point of view on her advisers on major issues of policy, however much she might be deceived or kept in ignorance on the day-to-day developments. Potemkin's unchivalrous description of his imperial mistress can be explained in only one way: by lowering Catherine in Harris's estimation, he raised himself and made himself more than ever necessary to the Englishman, more than ever the arbiter of British policy to Russia—and at the same time he could always explain away his failures by his inability to cope with a capricious female.

At 10.30 a. m. on 19 December 1780 Harris was fetched by one of the Empress's attendants and introduced through a back door into her private apartments. Throughout the interview he was in a difficult position. He was hampered by the fact that an envoy cannot speak as freely as a sovereign, and Catherine, both as a ruler and as a woman, took full advantage of her privileged position to order the conversation the way she wanted it. Moreover Harris had really no constructive proposals to make. He believed that the Empress had already offered to mediate between the belligerents,

31. SP 91/106, Harris to Stormont, No. 157, 13/24 December 1780 (*MD, I*, 348).

but, since he had received no fresh instructions from London on this issue and no official communication of the Empress's alleged offer from Panin, there was nothing he could say. The cession of Minorca, though it might hover in the Empress's mind and in his, was still confined to the strictly unofficial sphere and could not be mentioned. All Harris could do therefore was to pursue his original intention of using this opportunity to undermine Count Panin once and for all with the Empress by revealing to her the way in which her name had allegedly been abused to cover his anti-British intrigues all over Europe.

The Empress too had her own ideas of what she intended to extract from Britain as a result of this audience, and whenever Harris directed her attention to Panin's intrigues she brought him back firmly to the point which interested her, namely the necessity of peace. She was not pro-French, she assured him, but if Britain complained of being friendless, it was because she did not wish to have any friends. "Vous êtes si roides, si reservés; vous n'avez point de confiance en moi," she declared, doubtless alluding to the lack of any information on British peace terms to correspond with the friendly confidence shown by Vergennes. When Harris put forward the only British position he was authorized to mention, namely the restoration of conditions as at the Peace of Paris of 1763, the Empress waved him aside: "Vous faites bien d'y prétendre, si vous êtes en force de la [the Peace of Paris] soutenir," was her comment. When Harris declared that Britain had "une confiance aveugle en elle," she replied tartly: "Témoignez le autrement que par des paroles, vous verrez alors combien je suis de vos amis; vous ne faites que me rebuter. Comment voulez vous que je vous veuille du bien?"

Harris thought the time ripe to touch on one of his main objects in the interview, his attack on Panin. If the Empress believed herself to have been rebuffed by Britain, he exclaimed, it was because British conduct had not been represented to her in its true light. "Qui auroit osé me tromper?" demanded Catherine, to which Harris, nothing loath, replied: "Votre Premier Ministre, Madame, le comte Panin; il est le plus dangereux de nos ennemis." He then developed his attack in full scale and accused Panin of plotting to sow discord between Britain and Russia; of being entirely governed by the King of Prussia; of aiming at drawing France and Russia closer together, and of being in a perfect understanding with the French government. The Empress answered with considerable warmth that she would dismiss her minister the moment he deceived her, but she knew him well, and his intrigues had no effect on her. She was not a child, she said, "personne ne m'empêche de faire ce que je veux; je vois clair." When Harris adduced as additional evidence of Panin's perfidy the accusation that he had invited Frederick II to join the Neutral League, Catherine replied haughtily that she would be delighted if he did. "Je soutiendrai mon projet, je le crois salutaire," she declared. Undaunted by the Empress's visible irritation, Harris ventured even further: "On dit, Madame (mais je crains de l'offenser), que c'est le projet des françois, et que le votre étoit très différent." The Empress, really piqued, replied "(avec violence) 'Mensonge atroce!'" The ensuing discussion on the Neutral League was unsatisfactory to both parties. Harris put forward the argument of the damage it did to the British cause by allowing the Bourbons to use their own shipping as troop transports and to rely on neutral shipping for the supply of essential war materials. Catherine defended her trade: "C'est mon enfant que mon commerce, et vous ne voulez pas que je me fâche?" she asked.[32] When Harris continued to argue, she took advantage of her imperial position to close the subject. "Ne parlons plus la dessus, nous nous brouillerons," she exclaimed and brought the talk around to the subject that really interested her. "Faites la paix," she declared.

Harris was not to be side-tracked from his attack on Panin. British lack of confidence had been due to reluctance to work with such a minister, he urged, and should he have to deal further through Count Panin, "il me trahira, ou bien il ne vous rendra que très imparfaitement ce que je lui aurai dit." Submit everything to him in writing, retorted the Empress, he will be unable to change anything, and "s'il me cache la vérité, je le chasse." Pursuing his point, Harris explained that Britain's reserve was due to

32. "When the Empress called her trade her children she might have added that they are in a state of weak and unhealthy infancy," commented Harris (SP 91/106, to Stormont, No. 160, 13/24 December 1780).

the impression that everywhere Russian influence was exercised in a manner hostile to Britain. "En Dannemarc son nom a chassé le premier Ministre; et le roi de Prusse et la France l'employe à leur fantaisie partout." Catherine reacted strongly against these assertions. It was all mere gossip, "c'est une imbécilité que d'ajouter foi à de pareilles absurdités," she exclaimed, and she denied most vehemently having had anything to do with the dismissal of Bernstorff.

Again and again the Empress brought the talk back to the subject of peace: "Faites la paix, je vous l'ai souvent dit." Harris promptly took her up and declared that had the Empress often told him to make peace he would have reported it to his court. Catherine insisted that she had ordered Panin to speak to him on the subject, and Harris, who could not deny that Panin had frequently done so, had to indulge in a little prevarication: "Il m'a bien tenu quelques propos vagues relatifs à une pacification, mais pas au nom de Votre Majesté Impériale, et j'avoue que tout ce qui venoit de lui seul, m'a toujours paru suspect," he replied. "Vous l'entendez au moins de ma part à présent," said the Empress, and she put before Harris in her own name the approach to the problem of America which had been discussed between Panin and Vérac: "faites la paix; traitez avec vos colonies en détail; tâchez de les diviser; leur alliance avec les François tombe alors d'elle-même, et cela leur servira d'échappatoire, car il faut penser aussi que chaque puissance voudroit sauver son honneur." This concern for French honour aroused Harris: "Mais les françois ont lézé notre honneur; faut-il que nous pensions au leur?" he asked. "Quand on veut faire la paix, on commence par oublier le mal qu'on s'est fait réciproquement," replied the Empress, who then proceeded to urge on Harris in very strong terms her own desire to show her goodwill towards Britain and her inability hitherto to act as she would wish. "[Votre ministère] m'ont révolté; ils m'ont empêché de témoigner à votre nation ma bonne volonté; je les ay trouvé en opposition à moi partout; c'est dans leur conduite, pas dans la mienne, qu'il faut chercher le mal passé, et le remède futur." Britain, declared Catherine, could rely on her friendship and her justice, and she insisted that Harris should give full weight to her words when he wrote home. "Si après tout ce que je viens de vous dire, je lui trouve la même indifférence, la même roideur, que sais-je moi, le même ton de supériorité avec moi, je ne me mêle plus de rien." But Catherine was not optimistic; she warned Harris that should she have to judge Britain's behaviour by the past, she expected nothing: "vous continuerez à roidir, vous n'ajouterez pas foi à ce que je dis."

Harris, remembering Potemkin's advice, tried what a little flattery would do, but the Empress did not respond. "Je suis lasse d'être généreuse," she exclaimed, and urged some complaisance towards herself. "Laissez mon commerce en repos et n'arrêtez pas le peu de vaisseaux que j'ai; je vous dis qu'ils sont mes enfans; je voudrai que mes peuples devinssent industrieux; est-ce dans le caractère d'une nation philosophe de s'y opposer?"

The Empress refused to express an opinion on the suitability of a return to the Peace of Paris as Britain's peace terms. But she assured Harris again that never would she be numbered among Britain's enemies, and rose from her seat to indicate the end of the audience. But Harris had not finished. He stressed that their interview could not remain secret and that his enemies would do their best to find out what had been said and to prejudice the Empress against Britain. He begged the Empress to regard all that might pass between the departure and the return of his courier as "non avenu." "Que vous me connoissez mal," exclaimed Catherine, "suis-je un enfant? n'ai'je pas assez dit?" Harris then accepted his dismissal with a few words of flattery and admiration for the day when the Empress would add fresh glory to her reign by giving to her Empire its most useful and natural ally. Catherine also expressed her desire to see that day dawn. But again she repeated her doubts: "je prévois qu'il n'en sera rien, et que je fais inutilement le dernier effort en votre faveur."

This interview between the Empress and the envoy is remarkable in more ways than one. The personalities of the two protagonists emerge vividly, for Harris wrote his account in dialogue form, preserving as far as he could remember them the Empress's own words. In fact he did not do full justice to his own audacity, for presumably to save time and paper he omitted much of what he himself said; he curtailed in particular his description of the harm the Neutral League did to Britain and did not report in full his attack on Panin.[33]

Catherine's attitude, as it emerges from Harris's written record, is perfectly clear on a number of points. In the first place, though she twice spoke of it, in what appears a disparaging manner, as "cette nullité armée," she stood by the policy of the Neutral League and by the maritime principles it was intended to defend.[34] In the second place, the restoration of peace preferably by herself was in the forefront of her policy. Though Minorca was not mentioned, the extent of Britain's need, which Harris's talks with Potemkin had revealed, was too good an opportunity to lose. By the end of the interview, the opening made by Stormont's original idea of an offensive alliance to be guaranteed by the cession of Minorca had been thoroughly exploited by Catherine to put Britain into a position where, without completely alienating her, the government could no longer refuse to take seriously her willingness to be invited to mediate. Catherine left Harris in no doubt on that score; her parting words are clear: "Je vous parle très sérieusement, Monsieur Harris, faites envisager à votre cour, qu'il y va du tout; surtout qu'elle ait de la confiance en moi . . ."[35] In addition Catherine had evidently given up any idea that the whole of America could be recovered and expected Britain to make some concession to France in order to provide some common ground on which negotiations could start.

In the third place, though Catherine had no intention of aligning herself against Britain, she disliked the British government. The accusations of "roideur" and "froideur" and of a "ton de supériorité" were probably the result of accumulated resentment against British neglect of Russian political interests in the past. The "opposition," however, which the Empress declared she met everywhere, could only apply to the Neutral League. For in gen-

33. SP 91/106, Harris to Stormont, No. 157, 13/24 December, printed in full, with minor textual alterations in *MD, I*, 348.

34. This *jeu de mots* by Catherine sounds a little odd in view of her defence of the Neutral League. Bergbohm, *Die bewaffnete Neutralität*, p. 203, note 9 puts forward the ingenious suggestion (also apparently thought of by D'Albedyhll) that the Empress was quoting an English quip, of which Harris might have been in ignorance, and was using the phrase ironically.

35. SP 91/106. Harris to Stormont, No. 157, 13/24 December 1780.

eral the North administration had shown considerable deference to Russia, as compared with the record of previous governments. But the drawbacks of public debates over foreign policy are many, and Catherine tended naturally to identify herself with the loud and often unjust criticisms of the Whigs.

The fourth point that emerges from the written record of Harris's audience is that nowhere did the Empress herself express any desire for an alliance with England. Though she spoke in general terms of the pleasure it would give her to see the two nations allied, it was only in response to Harris's fulsome compliments. It was the language of courtesy, not diplomacy. The Empress did not intend to abandon her neutrality, but she was quite prepared to use her position as the leading neutral power friendly to Britain in the general opinion to force herself on the belligerents as a mediator. Her words would conciliate Britain; her deeds would disarm France.

Harris's boldness in attacking the Neutral League, in spite of Potemkin's warning, was not perhaps very wise. But his audacious offensive against Panin justified itself in the event. The Empress certainly did not react as vigorously as might be expected against these accusations of dishonesty levelled by a foreign envoy against a minister of her choosing. She already had her own reasons for distrusting him, and Harris's reference to the part she was reputed to have played in the fall of Bernstorff visibly vexed her. But Harris went too far in assuming that all he disliked in Russian foreign policy was the result of Panin's independent action behind the back of his sovereign. There is an undertone of irritation in Catherine's words, not at the suggestion that Panin was trying to deceive her but at the implication that he had succeeded.

Harris of course did not content himself with merely sending home an account of his interview. It was both his right and his duty to interpret the scene he had recounted, and it was this interpretation, rather than the Empress's own words, which in fact coloured British policy towards Russia. But Harris's interpretation was not his own unaided work. Immediately after his audience he joined Potemkin, and the two men thrashed the whole matter out at great length, that day and the next. When he wrote home, Harris admitted that he would not have dared to assert thus

SIR JAMES HARRIS
engraved by Caroline Watson
from the portrait by Sir Joshua Reynolds
British Museum

PRINCE G. A. POTEMKIN
by G.-B. Lampi senior

CATHERINE II
by F. S. Rokotov

COUNT N. I. PANIN
by A. Roslin

positively his opinion had he not been confirmed in it by Potemkin. He then summed up his impressions.[36]

The Empress, wrote Harris, was adamant with regard to the Neutral League, but out of pride, which prevented her from retracting, and not, as previously, out of conviction of its utility. She was in fact now convinced both of its unjust consequences to others and of the inconvenience it might bring on herself, and "she only wishes to find a pretext to destroy its effects." If she were not opposed on this issue, she might be quietly led away from it. But she must be humoured. Therefore, recommended Harris (and of course Potemkin), a free passage should be granted to Russian ships, if necessary by means of a private *démarche* known only to Russia.[37] The Empress would then "immediately, and before any advantage can arise to her trade . . . become our warm and zealous friend." [38]

On the subject of peace, Harris again accepted Potemkin's version of the Empress's views rather than her own words to him at his audience. The Empress, said Potemkin, regarded the Peace of Paris as "the most equitable one we could propose." Carried away by his enthusiasm for Minorca, Potemkin gave Harris his word of honour that "if you will, for a while, favour exclusively her ships, or say you will do so, which comes to the same thing; and if you will confess that you cannot place too much confidence in her, you may be certain of her procuring for you, either as mediatrix, or if that fails as ally, the same conditions as those of the Peace of Paris . . . Let your Ministry speak out . . ." [39] Catherine, however, had merely replied "nous verrons" to Harris's suggestion of the Peace of Paris as a basis for negotiating a peace. Nevertheless, under Potemkin's influence Harris urged Stormont to accept the offer of mediation, which he believed the Empress to have made, to communicate Britain's minimum demands for peace, and even to consult her and keep her informed on British plans for conciliating the American colonies. And so impressed was he with Potemkin's interpretation that he declared that the Empress

36. SP 91/106, Harris to Stormont, No. 157, 13/24 December 1780.
37. SP 91/106, Harris to Stormont, No. 162, 13/24 December 1780 (*MD, 1,* 366).
38. SP 91/106, Harris to Stormont, No. 157, 13/24 December 1780.
39. Ibid.

was still inwardly "satisfied that a close alliance with Great Britain, is the most salutary measure she can adopt." [40]

As regards Minorca, Harris had no alternative but to report the Prince's views, for he had been unable personally to ascertain the Empress's own. The day after the interview Potemkin assured Harris that the Empress would fulfill all he had promised and "gave me clearly to understand that she had already caught at it." Harris begged Potemkin to "move with caution" in this matter and to remember that he was "talking from my own head." [41] But by now Stormont's original idea of the cession of a British possession in exchange for armed Russian assistance had disappeared completely. The offer of Minorca, Harris now wrote, though it was to be kept quite apart from the proposed mediation and was to be the price of a future alliance, was nevertheless the crux of the negotiation on which all else depended. [42]

Having thus thoroughly perverted Harris's judgement on the results of his audience, Potemkin proceeded to enmesh the British envoy still further in his toils. He warned him once again to "reflect on the character and sex" of the Empress. Let his government "talk to her passions, to her feelings . . . For God's sake do not be afraid to flatter her . . . She asks for nothing but praise and compliment; give her that and she in return will give you the whole force of her empire." Harris was only too deeply impressed: "These my Lord," he wrote to Stormont, "are the Prince's own words, and they contain the whole secret of this court." [43] But Harris went even further. Convinced by Potemkin that the Empress's powers were declining, that the "false notions" she had received through the "medium of her passions" must be combated "not with the weapons of reason and good sense, but with those the wise ever employ with the weak"; that the Empress was incapable of independent judgement and veered round with every burst of servile flattery, Harris gravely warned Stormont: "If we lose this opportunity, these passions, more powerful than her reason, instead

40. SP 91/106, Harris to Stormont, No. 162, 13/24 December 1780.
41. SP 91/106, Harris to Stormont, No. 158, 13/24 December 1780.
42. SP 91/106, Harris to Stormont, No. 162, 13/24 December 1780.
43. SP 91/106, Harris to Stormont, No. 157, 13/24 December 1780.

of subsiding will increase, and their influence will hurry her into all those excesses we so much apprehend; led blindly by the impulse and encouraged in them by the animosity of our enemies, she will forget her natural interests, her reputation and the welfare of her Empire and be carried to the most dangerous and fatal lengths." [44]

When all allowance is made for the natural flamboyance of Harris's language, this was most misleading advice. The Empress was by no means a cold and passionless woman, but she stands out among her advisers as remarkably level-headed and steady of purpose in the various critical phases of her reign, and particularly in her diplomacy. In fact she compares very well with Potemkin himself in this respect.[45] Harris however portrays her here as a woman who will be driven to disastrous lengths if her every whim is not complied with. It might have dawned on Harris that Potemkin's idea of the kind of flattery suitable to be lavished on his imperial mistress would prove rather expensive for Britain. But by now Harris was completely under Potemkin's sway. Though he continued to regard the Prince's disorderly private life with fastidious distaste and to deplore his unbusinesslike habits, no praise was too high for his acumen and his honesty. Harris's dispatches are full of repeated tributes: "His penetration and acuteness are most extraordinary and . . . he cannot have the most distant view of deceiving me . . . we must most necessarily fall or rise together"; "to him I owe all, and cannot say too much in praise of his activity, his zeal, and the surprising abilities he has shown on this occasion." [46] "Our political opinions never have differed." [47] Harris's extremely long dispatches exude an atmosphere of conspiratorial drama. We are no longer in the presence of an empress, a minister, and an ambassador. Harris and Potemkin have become two paladins about to rescue the heroine from the wicked machinations of her enemies and, having broken the spell which blinded

44. SP 91/106, Harris to Stormont, No. 162, 13/24 December 1780.

45. See for instance the remarkable correspondence between Potemkin and Catherine, when the Prince nearly threw up his command during the second Turkish war. *Sbornik*, 27, 425 ff.

46. SP 91/106, Harris to Stormont, No. 162, 13/24 December 1780.

47. SP 91/106, Harris to Stormont, No. 157, 13/24 December 1780.

her to reality, to restore her to her true friends.[48] Caught up in the dramatic plot of his own creation, Harris never stopped to consider that he might be dancing to Potemkin's tune.

Cold print cannot reproduce exact shades of manner and meaning, and it is possible that Harris had more justification than appears from his report for attributing to the Empress a warm desire for an alliance with Britain. But his account of his audience could not have led Stormont to believe in any such desire had it not been for the accompanying dispatches full of advice and comment inspired by Potemkin. There is a clear divergence between the Empress's words and manner and those of her favourite, and Harris preferred to rely on the latter. The impression Stormont must have derived therefore was that the Empress was only prevented by the flattery and intrigues of the pro-French party from following the course which her real inclinations and national interest demanded, namely an alliance with Britain; were she offered Minorca, she would come forward as a benevolent mediator and if necessary use her armed forces to procure a peace along the lines of the Peace of Paris of 1763. She was tired of the Neutral League but too far committed to retract. If she were offered an easy way out, such as a secret concession to Russian shipping, she would see to it that the League should not be more than a "nullité armée." She was however so ruled by her passions, so impervious to reason, that were her conditions not complied with, she would be capable of going to extreme lengths and perhaps even of causing Britain real injury. Should her wishes be complied with, all would go well. "I think, and I flatter myself, I shall not be single in my opinion," wrote Harris, "that our situation here is mended; is become even an agreeable one, and that it is in our option to make it still more so, by following the path the Empress herself shows us." For "the Empress," read of course Potemkin, who repeatedly pledged his word to Harris that if London came up to what Harris had promised he would see to it that all he had promised in Russia's name would come true.[49]

48. "I tremble lest your ministry should not give you credit for what you write; that they will believe intelligence from other quarters in preference to yours; that this will make them backward and shy" . . . said Potemkin to Harris (SP 91/106, No. 162, 13/24 December 1780).

49. SP 91/106, Harris to Stormont, No. 162, 13/24 December 1780.

Harris had other reasons for viewing the future in a more rosy light. Since the visit of the Emperor, he had observed with pleasure the persistence of the Empress's friendly feelings towards Joseph. Harris still hankered after an alliance between Britain and Austria or, even better, a triple alliance between the two imperial courts and Britain.[50] Certainly the enthusiasm which the Empress had determined to feel for Joseph had remained unabated since his visit, and the two had maintained a fairly frequent correspondence, though they had scarcely touched on political matters of any importance. But the myth of their mutual friendship was by now well established, and it entered into the diplomatic calculations of other powers. Harris was delighted to learn that the Empress had apparently declared to her secretary, Bezborodko, her intention of forming a connexion with the Emperor so close that not even her successor could shake it—a reference to the pro-Prussian proclivities of the Grand Duke Paul.[51] But Harris did not know that the Emperor had already acted. In November 1780 he had authorized Cobenzl to make an informal approach to the Russians to conclude an alliance between the two empires. The diplomatic revolution he had so long desired was about to begin.[52] Not long after the first overture was made by Cobenzl, news reached St. Petersburg of an event of European-wide importance. On 29 November the Empress Maria Theresa died. Speculation was immediately rife on the consequences for Europe, for though Joseph had been Holy Roman Emperor since the death of his father, the realities of power had still been vested in his mother, ruler in her own right of the Hapsburg homelands. Now at last he stepped into his whole inheritance, and statesmen everywhere waited to see what changes the energetic, enterprising, and erratic Joseph would introduce into Austrian policy. The news reached St. Petersburg on 13 December 1780 and precipitated the court into a mourning which seemed exaggerated to those who did not know the secret of the

50. See Harris to Sir Robert Keith, 29 November 1780, *MD, 1*, 343. See also Harris to Stormont, "I think the substituting the interests of Austria here in the room of that of Prussia, must be productive of good consequences, I labour at it with all my force . . ." (SP 91/106, No. 160, 13/24 December 1780).

51. SP 91/106, Harris to Stormont, No. 160, 13/24 December 1780.

52. For the history of this treaty, see my article, "The Secret Austro-Russian Treaty of 1781."

Austrian overture.[53] The Empress at once wrote with her own hand
a letter of sympathetic condolences to the bereaved Joseph.[54] Her
sympathy for the son may have been genuine, but her regret at the
loss of the mother must have been tempered by pleasure at the
political prospects which the removal of Maria Theresa's restrain-
ing hand opened up to her.

The first person to suffer from this new turn of affairs was Panin.
Early in December 1780, before Harris's audience, the Empress had
suddenly rounded on him and accused him of having through the
Prince of Prussia procured the dismissal of Bernstorff. Panin defended himself, declared that he had only followed the Empress's
orders in writing to Denmark, and chalked up another black mark
against Harris for spreading the rumour.[55] Goertz, distressed at his
inability to effect anything for Prussia, had meanwhile cooked up
with Frederick II one of those little diplomatic manoeuvres so
comical when studied in cold print. He had proposed that Frederick should write to him, abusing him for having failed to secure
the confidence of Panin and for being so unsuccessful a servant of
Prussia. Frederick II duly composed a letter full of reproaches to
Goertz, and, armed with this document, the Prussian envoy visited
his Russian friend and begged him to prove that Prussian influence
was not dead at St. Petersburg and to help restore him to the good
graces of his Prussian master. Panin replied pathetically: "Je vous
demande pardon . . . mais je suis depuis hier dans votre cas. J'ai
aussi une souveraine qui m'en veut et on n'aimerait pas mieux
que ma perte." Panin then went on to refer to a possible change of
foreign policy in Russia and declared that if his system went he
would go too.[56] He had been fighting a losing battle for some time
to preserve the Prussian orientation of the Russian court, but the
Emperor's overture for a Russian-Austrian alliance cut the ground
completely from under him. It was not surprising therefore that
the Empress should have allowed Harris to attack Panin with im-

53. SP 91/106, Harris to Stormont, No. 154, 4/15 December 1780.
54. Arneth, *Joseph II und Katharina*, p. 25, Catherine to Joseph, 2/13 December
1780.
55. *PKFG, 45*, 126, Goertz to Frederick, 8 December 1780.
56. *PKFG, 45*, 50, Goertz to Frederick, 7 November 1780; p. 52, Frederick to
Goertz, 21 November 1780 (the "ostensible" rebuke!) and p. 126, Goertz to Frederick,
8 December 1780,

punity in the course of his audience. Panin was opposing her policy of *rapprochement* with Austria, and he was quite lacking in enthusiasm for the Greek project.[57] Only in one respect did the Empress and Panin see eye to eye, and that was the completion of the edifice of the Neutral League.

By the first few days of 1781 Russia found herself in a dominating position in European diplomacy. France was showing every sign of falling in with her plans for an eventual mediation; Britain was wooing her, though still in secret, with the offer of Minorca, to become a benevolent mediator if not openly an ally. She was the leader of a group of neutral states bound to defend their trade, which had only just been joined by the United Provinces, and she was being offered the alliance she most desired, that of Austria. But simultaneous developments as yet unknown in Russia were to complicate the situation to an unexpected extent and reduce Harris's glowing hopes to ashes.

57. *PKFG, 45,* 171, Goertz to Frederick, 26 December 1780.

11. The Austro-Russian Mediation

HARRIS'S DISCOVERY of the Empress's supposed intention to offer her mediation formally to Britain and the Bourbons reached Stormont by 21 November 1780.[1] He was at the time engaged in building up pressure against the Dutch to prevent their accession to the Neutral League, in the full knowledge that if he failed war between Britain and the United Provinces would follow. Britain was diplomatically now almost completely isolated and might, by declaring war on the Dutch, finally alienate the one power—Russia—on whose lasting friendship hopes had so long and so vainly been placed. It was too soon to expect a reply to his suggestion of a territorial cession to Russia and uncertainty about Russia's future course led Stormont to seek for diplomatic support elsewhere. He took up again a policy which he had long favoured, namely the renewal of old ties between Britain and Austria.

The revival of Stormont's interest in Austria followed naturally on the rise of Austrian influence in Russia. To Harris, therefore, Stormont had urged the desirability of some form of alliance between Austria and Russia. There was no scope, he had written in August 1780, for "a great manly policy" until such a connexion had been formed "as every friend to the real interests of Europe must ardently wish to see." [2] In his desire to please Austria and at the same time to bring pressure to bear on the Dutch, Stormont had even thrown out the suggestion, in the summer of 1780, that now was the time for Austria to take up the question of the reopening of the Scheldt. Keith mentioned the matter tentatively to Kaunitz in September, but Kaunitz was not to be drawn and prob-

1. Fortescue, *Correspondence of King George III*, 5, 155, Minute of Cabinet, 21 November 1780.
2. SP 91/105, Stormont to Harris, No. 48, 25 August 1780.

ably formed his own conclusions as to the extent of Britain's need of Austrian support.[3] Meanwhile, though he did not at all deny Austria's connexion with France, Kaunitz gave Keith the impression that Austrian sympathies were with Britain. He assured the British envoy repeatedly that Austrian influence would be used in St. Petersburg to counter the designs of Britain's enemies in that quarter and urged on Keith the necessity for Britain to seize the first favourable opening to make peace on honourable terms.[4]

Panin's frequent references in the past to the Empress's desire to make peace had always been swept aside by Harris and Stormont as not representing her policy but that of her minister. They now both believed implicitly that the information procured by Harris through his undercover agents was accurate and that Catherine was about to offer her formal mediation.[5] Neither Harris nor Stormont could account for what appeared to them to be a sudden decision on the Empress's part, and the first step was to make sure that she was not acting under Prussian or French inspiration. In view of the generally friendly tone adopted by Kaunitz, the cabinet decided on 21 November 1780 to communicate the news of Russia's forthcoming offer to Keith, so that he could discover if the Emperor Joseph was in any way associated with the move.[6]

Meanwhile rumours of an alleged Russian offer of mediation had also reached Vienna. They came from Paris and were merely a reflection of the discussions which Panin had conducted with Vérac, but they of course confirmed what Harris had reported on the basis of his secret information. Early in December, Keith, in accordance with his instructions, sounded Kaunitz about the proposed Russian offer, and hinted at a possible French or Prussian origin. Kaunitz denied that France could have anything to do with the proposed mediation, since Austria would

3. SP 80/223, Stormont to Keith, No. 32, 8 August 1780; Keith to Stormont, No. 79, 6 September 1780. The Scheldt was closed to navigation from the Austrian Netherlands. For the history of this issue see Bindoff, *The Scheldt Question*, notably Ch. 6.

4. SP 80/223, Keith to Stormont, No. 99, 15 November 1780.

5. The same rumour had reached Stormont from Copenhagen (SP 71/136, Eden to Stormont, No. 63, 10 October 1780; No. 64, 14 October 1780) but Eden's information reflected Panin's talks with Vérac and Normandez; it came from Bernstorff and the Bourbon ministers in Denmark.

6. Fortescue, *Correspondence of King George III*, 5, 155, Minute of Cabinet, 21 November 1780; SP 80/223, Stormont to Keith, No. 54, 21 November 1780.

certainly in that case have been informed.[7] It must, Kaunitz believed, have originated either in Petersburg or in Potsdam. Having
thus thoroughly frightened Keith with the spectre of a Russian-
Prussian mediation, Kaunitz reminded the British envoy of the
previous Austrian offer of mediation in 1779, expressing the hope
that if Russia were now actually to offer her mediation, "the King
your master will not forget the former offer of this court." The
Emperor, he added, would not dislike a joint mediation with
Russia but would have no hand in one with Prussia.[8] Kaunitz's
policy at this stage was conditioned not by his belief in a forthcoming offer of mediation from Russia, of which he had not heard
a word from Cobenzl,[9] but by the desire to make sure of Austrian
participation in any measure of international scope and thus ensure Prussia's exclusion.

Meanwhile Stormont, encouraged by Harris, became more and
more firmly convinced that this to him quite unaccountable Russian offer of mediation was to be made. On 1 December he received Harris's dispatch informing him that the couriers bearing
the official Russian communication of the formation of the Neutral
League and the supposed Russian offer of mediation were to have
left for France, Spain, and England on 7 November.[10] The Russian
offer might therefore be made at any moment now. Stormont found
himself quite unable to interpret Russian intentions. Unlike Harris, he occasionally gave the Empress credit for understanding the
policy pursued in her name. Though she might be committed by
her "passions" to support of the Neutral League, "still I doubt
much if she . . . does not see, in its fullest extent the mischief
that must result from it to Great Britain," he had written to Harris
on 14 November 1780. Not only was the League anti-British in its
principles but its main point seemed constantly to be directed
against Britain rather than against Spain who had originally, Stormont believed, been cast for the role of villain. Stormont was led

7. SP 80/223, No. 112, 10 December 1780.
8. Ibid.
9. At the end of December Kaunitz expressed his surprise to Keith that in spite
of the close connexion between Austria and Russia, the Empress had not said a
word to Cobenzl about her intention to offer her mediation. See SP 80/223, Keith
to Stormont, No. 122, 27 December 1780; No. 126, 30 December 1780.
10. SP 91/106, Harris to Stormont, No. 139, 27 October/7 November 1780.

to suspect "that there is some secret arrangement with France, approved by the Empress herself." [11] Panin's language, when on 27 October 1780 he pressed on Harris the urgent necessity of making peace, made the worst possible impression.[12] Yet the Empress and Potemkin continued to make friendly assurances. It was not surprising that in this state of uncertainty as to what was to emerge from Russia, and seeing war with Holland approaching, Stormont should have turned again to Austria. On the day he received Harris's dispatch, Stormont wrote to Keith, informing him that the Russian offer of mediation was not merely a rumour but a certainty and asking him to sound Kaunitz on the possibility of Austrian participation in such a mediation.[13] Unaware that Kaunitz had already staked a claim for Austria, and without waiting for Keith's reply to his instructions of 1 December, Stormont was driven further towards Austria by the pressure of events. On 11 December 1780 the cabinet decided that, in spite of the Franco-Austrian alliance, an effort should be made to secure an alliance between Britain, Austria, and Russia and, if this proved abortive, to notify Austria that if Russia offered her mediation, Britain would ask for that of the Emperor.[14]

In two dispatches of 12 December 1780 Stormont outlined the new British policy to Keith. He realized of course that Austria might not wish for the moment to sever her ties with France and therefore directed Keith to use great caution and address in opening himself to Austria. The desirable aim towards which Keith should work was an alliance of the two imperial courts, Britain, and possibly Denmark; if the present war could be the *casus foederis* of such an alliance "it would be a great point indeed." But even if the present war were excluded, the alliance would be highly beneficial and would have a favourable influence on the course of the war. If however the Emperor were unable, so soon after his accession, to shake off the bonds of France, and no alliance proved possible, then Keith should confine himself to paving the way for one

11. SP 91/106, Stormont to Harris, No 65, 14 November 1780.

12. SP 91/106, Harris to Stormont, No. 136, 23 October/3 November 1780 (*MD, 1,* 339).

13. SP 80/223, Stormont to Keith, No. 59, 1 December 1780.

14. Fortescue, *Correspondence of King George III, 5,* 161, Minute of Cabinet, 11 December 1780.

by weakening the Franco-Austrian alliance as much as possible and impressing on the Emperor the sincerely friendly feelings of Britain.[15] As a further inducement to the Emperor and to assist in the promotion of this desirable union, Stormont, in a "Most Secret" dispatch, proposed a little judicious territorial bribery, in terms similar to those he had used in October to Harris in Russia. "If you can discover any object of ambition," he wrote, "to which the Emperor's views are pointed, any project of his, the execution of which, could be promoted by Great Britain . . . it will be taken immediately into the most serious consideration." He had, he informed Keith, repeatedly sounded the Empress of Russia to know the secret object of her ambition, but there were inevitable difficulties and delays in dealing with that court owing to the impossibility of working, in such delicate matters, through the proper ministerial channels, namely Count Panin. But if the Emperor could propose some plan that suited Catherine, and in which Britain might also join, this might constitute a bond of union between the three courts, and an agreement might be reached directly between the two sovereigns without going through the hands of Panin.[16]

The alliance represented the distant ideal. Stormont's more immediate purpose was to use Austria to paralyse Russia. France, he feared, meant to swing the Neutral League against Britain. The Emperor could assist Britain by opposing French policy in Russia. Believing as he did that the Empress meant to offer her mediation and fearing as he did that such a mediation, with or without the Neutral League, would be turned against Britain by the artfulness and influence of Prussia and France, Stormont informed Keith that Britain intended to apply to Joseph II to take part in the peacemaking when the offer finally materialized. Such joint action might indeed help to build the union between the two imperial courts which the Secretary of State hoped to see.[17]

Stormont's dispatches to Keith reveal the extent of his hopes in Austria and the extent of his fears of what the Russian reaction

15. SP 80/223, Stormont to Keith, No. 62, 12 December 1780; No. 63, most secret, 12 December 1780.

16. SP 80/223, Stormont to Keith, No. 63, most secret, 12 December 1780. "I speak to you of what is wished, not what can be proposed," added Stormont, urging Keith to be very cautious.

17. SP 80/223, Stormont to Keith, No. 62, 12 December 1780.

would be to a British breach with Holland calculated to take place almost at the very moment when the Dutch were about to become the allies of Russia. By 15 December it was clear that the Dutch had no intention of giving in to British pressure, and Stormont, aware that it was essential for the breach with the Republic to take place before they acceded to the Neutral League, wrote to Yorke on 16 December to withdraw immediately to Antwerp. On the same day, 16 December 1780, the long-awaited Russian communication was made [18] and turned out to be quite different from what Stormont had expected. Simolin informed the Secretary of State officially of the establishment of the Neutral League and at the same time delivered himself of the *insinuation verbale* of which Harris had procured a garbled version in October. It was not a direct offer of mediation as Stormont at once realized.[19] Simolin, on behalf of the Empress, explained that the purpose of the conventions establishing the Neutral League was the defence of the rights and privileges to which neutral shipping was entitled. The Empress however expressed a strong desire that the belligerents might quickly find "des moyens raisonnables et supportables pour tous les côtés, pour leur pacification quand même cela seroit en sacrifiant, ou échangeant, quelques cessions de peu de conséquence ou par des condescendances . . ." The war had so far given no decided advantage to either side. In fulfilment of her constantly expressed decision of maintaining a strict neutrality, the Empress refused to pass judgement on the motives, aims, and hopes of the belligerents. She was fully prepared to give proofs of her goodwill, but this ultimately depended on the belligerents themselves. If,

18. Christie, *The End of North's Ministry*, p. 247, quoting Stormont to the King, 15 December 1780; SP 91/106, Stormont to Harris, No. 70, 26 December 1780, enclosing note from Simolin accompanying the delivery of the conventions. The separate articles in the conventions were not communicated. Stormont replied on 26 December 1780 that British conduct was governed by treaties, and, where these did not exist, by the law of nations; the least abuse was corrected by the admiralty courts. (See *Morskoy Sbornik, 44*, 163, No. 54, Rescript to London and Madrid, 19/28 October 1780; SP 91/106, Simolin to Stormont, 16 December 1780, and Stormont to Simolin, 26 December 1780).

19. SP 91/106, Stormont to Harris, No. 71, 26 December 1780: "If the opening for a mediation (for you observe it is not a direct offer) . . ."; see also Lord George Germaine to Under-Secretary Knox, 17 December 1780: "The mediation from Russia is not absolutely offered, but held out in a manner that the not accepting of it would be an affront" (HMC, Misc. Coll., *6*, Papers of H. V. Knox, p. 173).

declared Simolin, the British court did not think the time yet ripe for peace, the Empress's words should not be regarded as pressing her desire to play a part but as an expression of her sincere wish to see an end to a conflict which was causing considerable disturbance to neutral trade. He ended with the assertion that the Empress "met un prix trop haut à ses soins et à ses services en faveur des autres pour aller au devant de qui que ce soit," but she would not refuse these services if they were requested in a friendly manner.[20]

There was much to disturb Stormont in this *insinuation verbale*. It was clearly not a direct offer of mediation, though as Kaunitz later commented it could be regarded as a "tâtonnement embrouillé" in that direction.[21] But there had been, so Stormont thought, no previous soundings on the part of Russia, either to him or to Harris, and he was still "quite in the dark" as to the origins of this Russian *démarche*.[22] He had thus conveniently forgotten the many occasions on which Panin had spoken to Harris, urging the necessity for peace, or, at the least, Stormont still remained convinced that Panin spoke for himself only and that the Empress thought otherwise. Moreover the tone of Simolin's *insinuation verbale* was very disagreeable, with its references to "cessions" and "condescendances," the latter word clearly implying some recognition of France's treaty with America. In spite of these drawbacks, Stormont could if he chose interpret Simolin's words as an offer of mediation, and the issue probably hung in the balance for a few days. The possibility of immobilizing Russia by putting her in the position of a formal mediator must have occurred to Stormont whenever he considered the rapid deterioration of British relations with Holland. Simolin's *insinuation verbale* had been couched in such terms as to confirm

20. SP 91/106, Simolin to Stormont, 16 December 1780, *insinuation verbale*, taken down in writing by Stormont. Compare with *Morskoy Sbornik, 44,* 157, No. 51, Rescript to Simolin (and Zinovyev), 27 October/7 November 1780. Seeing that the Russian courier left on 7 November it is surprising that Simolin did not speak to Stormont before 16 December 1780. But the delay may have been due to the need to concert the communication of the conventions with his Danish and Swedish colleagues. (See *Morskoy Sbornik, 44,* 162, No. 53, Rescript to Sacken in Denmark, 19/28 October 1781; p. 165, No. 55, Rescript to Musin Pushkin in Sweden of the same date. See SP 95/130, Nolcken to Stormont, 18 December 1780, communicating a copy of the convention and Stormont to Wroughton (British envoy in Stockholm) 26 December 1780, Note to be delivered in reply; and SP 75/136, copy of convention communicated by Dreyer (n.d.) and Stormont to Dreyer, 26 December 1780.)

21. FO 7/1, Keith to Stormont, No. 8, 10 January 1781.

22. SP 80/223, Stormont to Keith, No. 67, 26 December 1780.

that the Empress took the Neutral League seriously, and Stormont had to face the possibility that war with Holland might provoke the Empress into taking active measures in defence of the Dutch. He still hoped that some hitch would arise which would enable Russia not to accept the Dutch as members. But the only clear way out of the dilemma for Britain, seeing that the Dutch were determined to join the League, was to declare war and, by forcing them into belligerency, disqualify them for admission into an essentially neutral club.

Two days later, on 18 December, the cabinet decided to issue a manifesto breaking off relations with the Dutch, but publication was deferred until 20 December in order to leave the Dutch time to reply to the last British memorial handed in by Yorke.[23] On 19 December Yorke's dispatches arrived reporting that the States General had refused an immediate reply, and on 20 December Stormont published a manifesto setting out the British grievances against the Dutch Republic, notably the refusal to punish the pensionary of Amsterdam for appending his name to the Laurens treaty. This manifesto, though not an actual declaration of war, notified the world of the withdrawal of the British ambassador from The Hague and of the British intention "to pursue such vigorous measures as the occasion fully justifies, and our dignity and the essential interests of our people require." [24] An Order in Council was issued on 20 December authorizing reprisals against Dutch shipping and property, and on 21 December 1780 instructions were issued to captains of privateers to start rounding up Dutch ships.[25]

On 20 December Stormont also received Keith's dispatch of 10

23. See Christie, *The End of North's Ministry*, p. 247. A meeting of the cabinet had taken place to decide this fateful breach. H. V. Knox, under-secretary of Lord George Germain (secretary of state for the colonies) provides a description of what was probably this meeting: "The Ministers who met were Lord North, the Chancellor, President [Bathurst], three Secretaries, Sandwich and Amherst. The first and third fell asleep as soon as the business was opened—Lord Hillsborough nodded and dropped his hat; Lord Sandwich was overcome at first, but rubbed his eyes and seemed attentive. Lord Amherst kept awake but said nothing. Lord Stormont, the reader of these important papers, the Chancellor and Lord George Germain only gave them consideration, but when the others awoke they approved of what was proposed" (HMC, Misc. Coll., *6*, Papers of H. V. Knox, p. 271).

24. Christie, *The End of North's Ministry*, pp. 247–48; Scott, *Armed Neutralities*, p. 330.

25. Ibid., pp. 334, 335.

December in which the British envoy described Kaunitz's reaction
to the alleged Russian offer of mediation and notably the hint
Kaunitz had given that Austria would take offence if she were left
out of the peace-making.[26] At about the same time the cabinet considered the situation produced by Simolin's *insinuation verbale*
and Keith's report on Austria's attitude.[27] Stormont had already
committed himself very far with Keith in stating the Russian offer
of mediation to be a fact. Though it had not taken the form he
expected, it now suited Stormont to force Russia into an immediate mediation with Austria. The Prussian influence which he
feared lay behind her defence of neutral trade would be neutralized
in a mediation undertaken together with Austria, the Empress
would be prevented from taking any hasty step, and, as Stormont
wrote to Harris, he hoped that "in the course of this business her
affection for Britain would revive." [28]

Accordingly, when Stormont received Simolin again on 23 December 1780, the Secretary of State announced that Britain would
be delighted to make peace as soon as France ceased to be in league
with the rebel Americans. But, added Stormont, Austria, inspired
by the same humanitarian motives as Russia, had in 1779 offered
her good offices to bring about peace. In order to make a suitable
return, the King desired that "la paix puisse se négocier sous la
médiation des deux cours impériales." [29] Simolin's courier, who
left on 26 December, bore dispatches to Harris informing him that
Britain had invited the mediation of the two imperial courts.[30] On
the same day a courier left for Vienna to inform Keith of the contents of the Russian *insinuation verbale* and of the British reply
and instructing him to request the mediation of the Emperor Joseph.[31]

26. SP 80/223, Keith to Stormont, No. 112, 10 December 1780, endorsed received
on 20 December 1780.

27. I have found no record of this meeting and can therefore not date it precisely, but Stormont informed Keith that he had consulted His Majesty's confidential servants and the King before replying (SP 80/223, Stormont to Keith, No. 67,
26 December 1780).

28. SP 91/106, Stormont to Harris, No. 71, 26 December 1780.

29. SP 91/106, Stormont to Simolin, draft reply of verbal answer, sent to Harris
on 26 December 1780.

30. SP 91/106, Stormont to Harris, No. 72 26 December 1780 (endorsed "by a
Russian courier").

31. FO 80/223, Stormont to Keith, No. 67, 26 December 1780.

Stormont's decision to bring about a mediation of the two imperial courts led to considerable confusion in the other capitals of Europe. On 6 January 1781 Keith informed Kaunitz of the British invitation. The Imperial Chancellor was visibly delighted and recommended strict secrecy on the subject while he prepared Austria's next move.[32] On 10 January Kaunitz sent off a series of dispatches to Russia, France, and Spain, explaining that Austria had been invited by Britain to take part with Russia in a mediation and inviting the Bourbon powers to accept Austrian good offices.[33] Had Stormont been allowed access to Kaunitz's inmost thoughts, he would have thought twice about inviting Austrian cooperation, for already at this very early stage Kaunitz refused to take seriously the British condition, the eternal stumbling block to any negotiation, namely that France must first give up her treaty with the Americans. It was in any case useless to expect France to accept a mediation on any such terms. The formula Kaunitz devised to meet these conflicting requirements and to serve as a basis for a *rapprochement* between the belligerents was that "dans tout ce qu'elles pourront se proposer, aucune d'elles ne propose jamais à l'autre, que ce qu'elle croiroit pouvoir accorder, si elle étoit à sa place." It was intended as a rebuke to Britain for her reservations regarding the Americans.[34] The negotiations, Kaunitz suggested, should take place in Vienna under his own eye.[35]

Unlike Stormont and Harris, Vergennes had always treated Panin's talk of peace seriously, and for various reasons he had begun to prepare his mind in summer and autumn 1780 to accept the intervention of another power in the solution of the Anglo-French conflict. In the first place France was now in the throes of a financial crisis that rendered the effective prosecution of the war problematic.[36] The fortunes of war had not reduced Britain to a

32. FO 7/1, Keith to Stormont, No. 8, 10 January 1781.

33. FO 7/1, Keith to Stormont, No. 9, 10 January 1781; Beer and Fiedler, *Joseph II und Graf Ludwig Cobenzl, I,* 108, Kaunitz to Cobenzl, 10 January 1781; Arneth and Flammermont, *Correspondance, I,* 12, Kaunitz to Mercy, mentioned in Joseph to Mercy, 10 January 1781.

34. Beer, *Joseph II, Leopold II, und Kaunitz,* p. 29, Kaunitz to Joseph, 9 January 1781; for Kaunitz's famous formula, see FO 7/1, Kaunitz to Keith, réponse verbale, 9 January 1781; see also Arneth, *Joseph II und Katharina,* p. 33, Joseph II to Catherine, 10 Jan. 1781.

35. FO 7/1, Keith to Stormont, No. 9, 10 January 1781.

36. Doniol, *Histoire, 4,* 488.

point where she must sue for peace; the mediation, or better still, the arbitration of Russia, supported by the Neutral League, might compel Britain to come to terms.[37] In the second place Vergennes continued to be very perturbed at the presence of Richard Cumberland in Spain. Russia, or at any rate Panin, had shown every consideration for French treaty commitments with America, and Vergennes believed that these would be taken into account in any proposals for peace put forward by the Empress.[38] He had no reason to suppose that a divergence of views existed on major issues of policy between the Empress and Panin, whatever their personal relations might be, since in fact the policy which Panin preached, neutrality, was pursued by the Empress and was all that France could desire.

But even though Vergennes was thus preparing himself for the eventual emergence of a mediation, he did not regard the *insinuation verbale* which accompanied the communication of the conventions forming the Neutral League as an offer of Russian good offices. He had been told by Vérac that such an *insinuation* was to be made to the three belligerent courts, but Panin had never suggested to Vérac that it contained an offer of mediation. When the Russian chargé d'affaires, Khotinsky, read the Russian communication to him on 3 December 1780, Vergennes simply considered it as a further step in building up the Neutral League. He answered on 12 December praising the Russian measure as designed to protect the freedom of the seas and referred to the various orders issued in France to ensure that French warships and privateers complied with the rules laid down by the Empress in her declaration. In reply to the *insinuation verbale,* he praised the Empress's attention to "le rétablissement de la tranquilité publique," and added that "il seroit très agréable au Roi de le devoir aux bons offices de Sa Majesté Impériale mais, qu'il étoit difficile de se flatter qu'il pût être prochain tant qu'il n'y auroit pas des ouvertures qui pourroient servir de baze à une négociation." Moreover, Vergennes observed, he could agree to nothing without consulting his allies, and only after having done so could he make a more explicit reply

37. Ibid. 496 et seq., Vergennes to Montmorin, 28 September 1780.

38. Ibid., 506–07, Vergennes to Montmorin, 27 November 1780; and particularly Appendix, p. 518, Vergennes to Montmorin, 18 August 1780.

"aux offices de la cour de Russie." [39] One may judge of his confusion and dismay when on 19 January 1781 Mercy Argenteau, the Austrian ambassador, communicated to him the British acceptance of an alleged Russian offer to mediate and the British invitation to Austria to associate herself with Russia.[40] He was all the more astonished and embarrassed since Kaunitz naturally assumed that the same Russian offer had been made to France,[41] and that France had concealed it from her ally Austria and replied to it secretly, without showing that confidence in Austria which Stormont had so promptly displayed.[42] On the other hand the whole operation must have borne to Vergennes all the signs of a plot hatched between London and Vienna. He had been told that the same *insinuation verbale* was to be made in Versailles as in London; he had

39. CP Russie, *105*, Vergennes to Vérac, No. 17, 28 December 1780, enclosing a note of Khotinsky's communication of the conventions and his reply (printed in Scott, *Armed Neutralities*, p. 329); there is no copy of his reply to the *insinuation verbale*, which was presumably verbal, but its tenor is repeated by Vergennes to Montmorin in a dispatch of 15 December 1780 (printed in Doniol, *Histoire*, *4*, Appendix, p. 523).

40. Arneth and Flammermont, *Correspondance*, *1*, 15, Mercy to Joseph, 21 January 1781. In an ostensible dispatch, intended to be shown to Panin, Vergennes wrote to Vérac: "J'ai peine à croire . . . qu'on s'attendit à Petersbourg que la démarche que M. Simolin avait ordre de faire auprès du Ministère Bque en communiquant la convention entre les puissances du Nord, dut avoit des suites aussi intéressantes que celles dont vous êtes peut-être déjà instruit . . . Le Roy n'a pas pu croire que l'office verbal dont le Sr Chotinski avait accompagné la notte, qu'il avoit ordre de remettre à cette occasion, demandât de la part de Sa Majesté autre chose que la répétition verbale des mêmes assurances, tant de fois articulées en son nom, de la satisfaction bien réelle avec laquelle Sa Majesté verroit l'impératrice de Russie contribuer par sa médiation à terminer la guerre actuelle." (CP Russie, *106*, Vergennes to Vérac, No. 3, 30 January 1781.)

41. Arneth and Flammermont, *Correspondance*, *1*, 11, Kaunitz to Mercy, 5 January 1781: "Je suis très étonné de ce que ni M. de Vergennes, ni M. de Maurepas . . . ne vous ait rien dit dans ces derniers temps de la médiation russe, dont cependant il doit avoir été question, à ce qu'on me suppose de bon lieu."

42. See Kaunitz's dispatch to Mercy of 17 February 1781. Kaunitz had now discovered from Cobenzl that the same *insinuation* had been made to both courts, "mais, ce qu'il y a d'assez singulier, c'est que la réponse de la France à l'insinuation verbale que l'impératrice nous assure avoir été faite à Versailles et à Madrid, parfaitement pareille à celle qu'a faite Simolin à Londres, était déjà arrivée à Petersbourg le 27 janvier dernier, et par conséquent depêchée à Versailles quinze jours au moins avant la communication que vous avez été chargé d'en faire, sans que M. de Vergennes vous en ai dit un mot. Cachotterie inconcevable, dont je ne vois pas la fin, et qui a fait des impressions si défavorables dans l'esprit de l'Empereur, que j'ai eu bien de la peine à les combattre." (Arneth and Flammermont, *Correspondance*, *1*, 23.)

received no offer of mediation, and he now found that Britain had stolen a march on him, had appeared more amenable to Russia's desire to be entrusted with the role of mediator, and had made use of a Russian opening which had not seemed to Vergennes to warrant that construction. Worst of all he found himself saddled with Austria as a mediator instead of the Neutral League. He thoroughly disapproved of Vienna as the place for a peace congress, for he relied on Russia to champion French interests, and he felt, justifiably, that in Vienna any Russian envoy would be dominated by the overpowering Kaunitz.[43]

Vergennes had undoubtedly been outwitted, and he felt it. To cover himself, he assiduously spread the report that the *insinuation* made by Simolin in London had been couched in much stronger terms than that made to him in Versailles by Khotinsky. The communications were, however, identical, as Vérac continued to assure Vergennes,[44] though there was this difference, that Simolin, an experienced diplomat, spoke authoritatively and allowed Stormont to take a written note of a verbal communication; whereas Khotinsky was a chargé d'affaires who did not give Vergennes a written note, and moreover "sa traduction orale n'étoit pas parfaitement intelligible." [45]

Vergennes's distaste for a mediation in which Austria played a part found expression in his dispatches to Vérac. Since Britain had introduced Austria into the picture, he believed that Stormont had grounds to rely on the Emperor for support. France relied on Rus-

---

43. CP Russie, *106*, Vergennes to Vérac, No. 4, 30 January 1781.

44. CP Russie, *106*, Vergennes to Vérac, No. 3, 30 January 1781; FO 7/1, Keith to Stormont, No. 19, 3 February 1781, reporting what Kaunitz had told him of Vergennes's opinion, and No. 21, 7 February 1781. Cf. CP Russie, *106*, Vérac to Vergennes, No. 10, 18 February/1 March 1781.

45. CP Russie, *106*, Vergennes to Vérac, No. 12, 7 April 1781. It may be added that the only difference in the rescripts to Simolin and Khotinsky was that to Simolin the Empress wrote in the first person; Panin wrote of her in the third person to Khotinsky. Doniol's account of this episode (*Histoire, 4,* 486 ff.) is quite unreliable. He accepts Vergennes's version that a different *insinuation verbale* had been made in Versailles and in London, and does not mention Vergennes's dismay at Britain's initiative. Yet he himself prints Vergennes's dispatch of 22 January 1781 to Montmorin (*4,* 524) in which the foreign minister informs Montmorin of the Austrian overture and refers back to the *insinuation verbale* as containing the expression of the Empress's desire to see the end of hostilities "et . . . d'y contribuer sans cependant nous faire une offre directe de sa mediation."

sia: "nous pouvons donc nous flatter que le plénipotentiaire russe s'inclineroit pour nous dans le congrès," he wrote to Vérac on 30 January 1781. And he expressed the hope that Russia too would object to Vienna as the venue of the congress, since the Russian envoy would inevitably be eclipsed by Kaunitz.[46] The Anglo-Austrian initiative had however placed Vergennes in a position where he could not refuse the offer of good offices made to him by Kaunitz on behalf of Austria, and implicitly on behalf of Russia, though Russia had said no word. Moreover Kaunitz did his best to sweeten a pill he knew Vergennes would find difficult to swallow. He communicated to the Austrian envoy in France, Mercy Argenteau, for Vergennes's information, his comments on the British pre-condition, namely that France must abandon the Americans. "Si on veut sérieusement la paix," he had written to Joseph on 9 January 1781, "ce n'est pas par des propositions aussi inadmissibles que l'est celle que l'Angleterre établit pour préalable dans sa réponse que l'on peut se flatter d'y parvenir." [47] These words helped to soothe Vergennes's ruffled feelings and allayed his suspicions of Austria to some degree. He began to feel slightly more confidence in Joseph II,[48] and moreover he was to a certain extent moved by the fear that the breach between Britain and Holland might lead to an extension of the war. An Austro-Russian mediation would at any rate keep these two powers occupied and reduce the dangers of a general European war. Accordingly, on 27 January 1781 Vergennes accepted the Austrian offer, though he made his reply conditional on the agreement of Spain and on the formal consent of Russia to the addition of Austria as a mediator.[49] To Mercy, Ver-

46. CP Russie, *106*, Vergennes to Vérac, No. 4, 30 January 1781.

47. Beer, *Joseph II, Leopold II und Kaunitz*, p. 29, Kaunitz to Joseph, 9 January 1781.

48. Arneth and Flammermont, *Correspondance, 1*, 18, Mercy to Kaunitz, 21 January 1781; Doniol, *Histoire, 4*, Appendix, Vergennes to Montmorin, 22 January 1781.

49. CP Russie, *106*, Vergennes to Vérac, No. 4, 30 January 1781. For the text of the French reply to Kaunitz, see Flassan, *Histoire, 1*, Bk. 7, p. 302, dated 27 January 1781. Here too Vergennes's vexation at having been caught napping is perceptible. The King, he wrote, "aurait prevenu la démarche que l'Angleterre vient de faire," had it not been for his treaty connexion with Spain on the one hand, and, on the other, "si l'office de la cour impériale de Russie avait été rendu aussi explicite à Versailles qu'il parait l'avoir été à Londres." Kaunitz apparently thought this note too sharp to be communicated to the Empress. (Beer, *Joseph II, Leopold II und Kaunitz*, p. 35, Kaunitz to Joseph, 6 February 1781.)

gennes hypocritically expressed his approval of Vienna as the venue
for the congress and his delight that this would enable Kaunitz
himself to play a part in the negotiations.[50]

That the Empress had not regarded her *insinuation verbale* as
an offer of her mediation can also be deduced by the Russian reaction to the new situation. The first news to reach Russia was probably an extremely cautious communication from the Emperor
Joseph to the Empress of the reports reaching Austria, through
Keith, that Russia was expected by Britain shortly to offer her
mediation and that Britain had determined to accept. There was
no mention that Austria too might be invited to participate.[51] The
letter reached Russia on 17 January 1781. On 22 January Kaunitz's
official communication of 10 January reached Cobenzl, informing
him of the British invitation to Austria to join the mediation allegedly offered by Catherine and expressing also Kaunitz's deep
surprise that Cobenzl had not been informed by the Russians of
the overture they were supposed to have made to England.[52] But
here again, as though fearful of offending the Empress, the official
communication was accompanied by a letter from the Emperor
himself, in which he expressed his complete astonishment at finding
himself invited by Britain to join with Russia in making peace. He
clearly feared that Catherine would suspect that the plan had been
concerted between Britain and Austria and wished to guard against
such an interpretation on her part now above all when negotiations
for an alliance between Austria and Russia had begun. In the most
flattering language, he expressed the honour he would feel at being
joined with her in such a task. He took for granted that the *insinuation verbale* made by Simolin to Stormont had in fact been an offer
of mediation and praised it as a masterpiece which left nothing for
him to add.[53]

50. Arneth and Flammermont, *Correspondance, 1,* 18, Mercy to Kaunitz, 21 January 1781. Mercy was not deceived.

51. Arneth, *Joseph II und Katharina,* p. 30, Joseph to Catherine, 1 January 1781.

52. Beer and Fiedler, *Joseph II und Graf Ludwig Cobenzl, 1,* 108, Kaunitz to
Cobenzl, 10 January 1781. "Vous serez, sans doute, encore plus étonné que moi, mon
cher comte, de n'avoir rien sçu et de ne vous être pas même douté de la démarche
que vient de faire en Angleterre la cour ou vous êtes." See also p. 112, Cobenzl to
Joseph, 4 February 1781.

53. Arneth *Joseph II und Katharina,* p. 33, Joseph to Catherine, 10 January 1781.
The Emperor deliberately laid on his flattery with a trowel: see ibid., footnote,

The Russian response to the mediation which Stormont had brought about must be seen through the eyes of Cobenzl, Vérac, and Harris. The Empress, reported Cobenzl to Joseph, was "très aise d'être associée à Votre Majesté pour l'ouvrage de la médiation." [54] Indeed the Empress herself, writing to Joseph on 22 January/2 February 1781, expressed her satisfaction and pleasure at the prospect of engaging with the Emperor in this humanitarian project, though she rated the chance of success low.[55] Panin took a very different line to Cobenzl. Peace, he thought, was not yet possible since the combattants were not yet exhausted. The British proposal and "la manière dont était conçue la réponse donnée à M. de Simolin sur l'article important de l'Amérique servoit de preuve que la cour de Londres n'avoit en vue par cette démarche que de détourner l'attention de l'Impératrice de la neutralité armée, pour lui faire embrasser une chimère qui ne produiroit aucun effet," Panin was reported by Cobenzl to have said.[56]

To Vérac, Panin was even more outspoken. The admission of the Emperor, he declared, was "une chose à laquelle on ne s'étoit pas attendue," though it was impossible to refuse it. The British request for a mediation was only a ruse, he believed, "qu'ils mettent en avant pour endormir la Russie et arrêter l'activité de ses mesures." [57] Indeed Panin correctly interpreted Stormont's pur-

Joseph to Kaunitz of 9 January 1781. On the Austro–Russian negotiations for an alliance, see Ch. 13, pp. 313 ff.

54. Beer and Fiedler, *Joseph II und Graf Ludwig Cobenzl*, *1*, 112, Cobenzl to Joseph, 4 February 1781.

55. Arneth, *Joseph II und Katharina*, p. 38, Catherine to Joseph, 22 January/3 February 1781. In this letter the Empress does speak of a "proposition de médiation que je lui [Britain] ai fait faire tout comme à la France et à l'Espagne, en communiquant à ces puissances la convention des neutres." This is the only Russian source which mentions a Russian offer, but it cannot be regarded as conclusive evidence that an offer was made or even specifically intended at that time, since the actual text of the *insinuation verbale* delivered by Simolin to Stormont does not warrant that construction. On the other hand, the Empress had been told by Joseph that Britain had accepted her "offer" to mediate; she could not very well reply that she had not made one, particularly when she had in fact been bringing pressure on both belligerent sides for some time to be invited to mediate. Her letter to Joseph must be interpreted as acceptance of a *fait accompli*.

56. Beer and Fiedler, *Joseph II und Graf Ludwig Cobenzl*, *1*, 120, Cobenzl to Joseph, 19 February 1781.

57. CP Russie, *106*, Vérac to Vergennes, No. 6, 22 January/6 February 1781. Vergennes also came to share this view; see Doniol, *Histoire*, *4*, 524, Vergennes to Montmorin, 22 January 1781.

pose when he put forward the view that the British initiative was intended to "embrouiller les affaires" while Britain launched her attack on the Dutch Republic. Vérac remained convinced that the British request for a mediation had caused as much astonishment in St. Petersburg as in Versailles, and for him this was conclusive proof that the famous *insinuation verbale* made by the Russian envoys in Madrid, Versailles, and London had been identical, that no Russian offer of mediation had been intended, and that Britain, trusting in Joseph's reputed friendly feelings, had seized this opportunity to effect a diplomatic coup.[58]

Harris of course received his information from Potemkin. The Prince told him that he had never seen the Empress "more elated" than on that occasion; she entirely approved the attention Britain had shown to the Emperor, and now that she had so powerful a second Britain might expect every mark of friendship at her hands. When Harris expressed the hope that Britain might be admitted to the alliance which Potemkin had told him was about to be negotiated between Russia and Austria, the Prince assured him that this would "immediately follow the peace, if your enemies accept our offers; or we shall all then be joined in one common cause against them if these offers are refused." [59]

In the absence of direct evidence of the Empress's intentions, the character of her policy must be deduced not merely from what her various public servants said to the different envoys but from what actually happened. She had evidently been thinking of a Russian mediation when the moment seemed opportune. But it appears fairly certain that she intended to wait for an invitation and that she would prefer to be sole mediator, though with the possibility always present of using the Neutral League to enforce her terms. Moreover her mediation might well, as Stormont had surmised, turn out to be what Britain would consider hostile. What is more, the Empress did not think it worth-while for Britain to prolong the war in order to reconquer America. When she urged on Harris the necessity of making peace, at his audience in December 1780, she showed that she and Panin were in agreement on

58. CP Russie, *106*, Vérac to Vergennes, No. 10, 18 February/1 March 1781.
59. FO 65/1, Harris to Stormont, No. 9, 15/26 January 1781 (*MD, I,* 377).

the need to negotiate with the Americans and to provide some face-saving outlet for France.

Putting together the Empress's words and her policy, it seems that Panin's description of the Russian reaction to Britain's request, however biassed in form, was more correct than Potemkin's, that Cobenzl and Vérac were better informed than Harris. At any rate the Empress's first steps as regards the mediation showed no firm resolve to take things into her own hands. She brushed aside Panin's proposal to hold the congress in a Dutch town and acceded gracefully to all the Emperor's proposals: Vienna was to be the place, Kaunitz the dominant figure. Catherine even decided not to send a special plenipotentiary but to appoint her ambassador in Vienna to negotiate on her behalf in order to save trouble.[60] Indeed to Catherine, as well as to Vergennes, the *démarche* may have borne the appearance of an Anglo-Austrian plot, since the news reached her first from Vienna. There had been time for Stormont to write to Keith, and for Kaunitz's instructions to reach Cobenzl, before Simolin's courier arrived in St. Petersburg with the British reply to her *insinuation verbale*. But Catherine too desired an Austro-Russian alliance; she could not rebuff the Emperor by refusing his co-mediation.

Russia had been angling for the position of mediator for some time before the British request materialized, most probably with the interests of the Neutral League in mind. The British invitation to act with Austria came as a surprise to her. Yet it has usually been assumed that it was the Empress who offered her mediation in December 1780, and she has even been criticized for imposing her good offices on the belligerents when it would have suited Russian interests better to have allowed them to wear each other out while she matured her plans against the Porte.[61] This criticism does not take into account the fact that the success of mediation depends on the sincerity of the belligerents' desire for peace. Russia was well

60. CP Russie, *106*, Vérac to Vergennes, No. 10, 18 February/1 March 1781; FO 65/1, Harris to Stormont, No. 12, 19/30 January 1781; Beer and Fiedler, *Joseph II und Graf Ludwig Cobenzl, I*, 112, Cobenzl to Joseph, 5 February 1781, and p. 120, 19 February 1781. See also Maykov, *Pis'ma A. A. Bezborodka*, p. 72, Bezborodko to Rumyantsev, 25 January/5 February 1781.

61. See e.g. Bemis, *Diplomacy of the American Revolution*, p. 179.

aware that neither side in the war was yet prepared for serious negotiations. But the position of mediator would give her opportunities to interfere in the eventual peace settlement, possibly to impose her maritime principles on the belligerents. Moreover the mediation in the form it eventually took—with Austria—was offered to Russia precisely at the moment when the prolongation of the war in the West began to acquire significance in the light of the future Greek project. The key to this new situation is the death of Maria Theresa in November 1780. From this moment the Greek project ceased to be a dream and began to be a policy. Before the emancipation of Joseph there was no prospect of joint Russian-Austrian action against the Porte, and Prussia had already shown complete lack of understanding for Russian ambitions in that direction.[62] When Joseph's proposals for a mutual guarantee arrived and were closely followed by news of the death of the Empress-Queen, a completely new scene opened before Catherine. She was invited to make peace at the very moment when she at last began to have real hopes of profiting from the continuation of war.

Neither Harris nor Stormont could account in the autumn for the Empress's supposed intention to offer her mediation, but it never occurred to either that Harris's information could be false.[63] Having prepared himself for such an offer and having ascertained Austria's willingness to participate, Stormont and his colleagues effected a rapid coup designed to protect Britain from Russian anger at the breach with Holland. The *insinuation verbale* which

62. See above, Ch. 5, p. 122.

63. Not only Stormont was misled, but subsequent historians as well, e.g. Bemis, *Diplomacy of the American Revolution*, p. 180; Doniol, *Histoire*, *4*, 511 even goes so far as to say that "les soins de M. de Vergennes pour la [the mediation] faire venir de St. Petersbourg avaient abouti"; Arneth and Flammermont, *Correspondance*, *1*, 12, note, state also that the Empress invited Joseph to join her in the mediation on 10 January 1781, whereas it was Joseph who wrote to Catherine on that date. The correspondence between Vérac and Vergennes always refers to an English request for Russian mediation; Panin is always quoted as using the same terms; Bezborodko states "The English court had proposed to the Empress and the Emperor to mediate for peace" (Maykov, *Pis'ma A. A. Bezborodka*, p. 72, to Rumyantsev, 25 January/5 February 1781); the only mention of a Russian "offer" is in the letter from the Empress to Joseph, analysed in note 55 above. The correspondence between Keith and Stormont shows that the initiative in bringing about the mediation at this precise moment and in this form came from Britain.

the Empress had made, exhorting the belligerents to peace as leader of the Neutral League, was returned to her as an invitation to mediate together with the partner she proposed to draw into her ambitious schemes of expansion. The consequences were not entirely happy for Britain, but the mediation did at least temporarily strengthen Britain's standing by putting Russia in a position where she had to choose between acting with Austria or with the Neutral League.

Only a few days after the British cabinet had decided to invite the mediation of Russia and Austria, the first brief intimation was received from Harris that "the only cession which would induce the Empress to become our Ally, was that of Minorca." [64] The implications of Harris's report were discussed by the cabinet on 3 and 7 January 1781, when the cession of Minorca was approved in principle in exchange for "great and essential service actually performed." [65] At this point Stormont came up against an unexpected obstacle. George III utterly refused to contemplate the cession of one of his possessions as a gift, though, he added, "an unsuccessful war might, if not supported by Parliament, oblige to yield possessions conquered by the enemy on a peace." [66] In view of the King's opposition the question was for the time being dropped, but less than a week later, on 16 January 1781, Harris's vast packet arrived, with his account of his interview with the Empress and his long discussions on Minorca with Potemkin.[67] Stormont now returned to the charge. He proposed to the King that Russia should be invited "to come forth with a fair proposal of assistance, secretly engage to take part in the war unless the belligerent powers agreed to make peace upon the footing of the treaty of Paris," and that Russia should receive Minorca "in consideration of such service

64. SP 91/106, Harris to Stormont, No. 150, 24 November/5 December 1780 (endorsed "received 31 December 1780"), MD, 1, 345.

65. Fortescue, Correspondence of King George III, 5, 178. Cf. p. 181, Stormont to the King, 8 January 1781.

66. Barnes and Owen, The Sandwich Papers, 4 (1781–1782), p. 23, the King to Sandwich, 9 January 1781.

67. SP 91/106, Harris to Stormont, Nos. 157–162, 13/24 December 1780, endorsed "received on 16 January 1781."

actually performed," and unite herself to Britain in a perpetual defensive alliance.[68] This plan was, in another form, the idea which both Stormont and Harris had entertained before, namely the armed mediation of Russia, with this difference that Russia was now to be rewarded with Minorca but at the same time to tie herself down to a perpetual alliance with Britain.

George III was sufficiently shaken in his determination to attend a cabinet meeting on 19 January 1781, which devoted itself to a full examination of Russian relations with Britain. Lord Sandwich was present at the meeting and appears, according to his own account, to have taken the leading part in the discussion. His contribution explains some of the misconceptions on which British policy towards Russia was founded. Harris's dispatches (and Potemkin's glosses), with their portrayal of the Empress as likely to be driven to extreme measures unless her whims were pandered to, misled him into believing that the choice before Britain lay in having Russia fight for or against Britain. In addition, Sandwich assumed that if Britain did not cede Minorca the Bourbons would offer that same island (which they did not possess) to Russia in order to induce her to espouse their cause. Minorca would in any case be lost, whereupon, he declared, Russia would immediately promise Gibraltar to Spain and use the fleets of the Neutral League to enforce the arrangement. If Russia came out against Britain, the whole world would follow, and a defeated Britain would be dismembered, her colonies distributed, and "we shall never again figure as a leading power in Europe, but think ourselves happy if we can drag on for some years a contemptible existence as a commercial state." The alternative to this desperate picture was, with the loss solely of Minorca, to achieve with Russian support the recovery of Britain's position at the Peace of Paris of 1763 and all that it entailed— the return of the American colonies, the exclusive trade with them, and the recovery of all conquests made by the Bourbons in the present war. The cession of Minorca might even have advantages, explained the now optimistic Sandwich, for Britain would be relieved of the expense of maintaining the naval base while continuing to use it: "our power of resistance to the House of Bourbon

68. Fortescue, *Correspondence of King George III*, 5, 185, Stormont to the King, 17 January 1781.

would continue the same, or would be rather increased by such a cession," he declared. If other arguments were put forward to counter Sandwich's alternately funereal and roseate view of the future of Britain, the egregious First Lord does not record them. But apparently his eloquence won the day, for even the King, who "came to the meeting with different sentiments, was convinced and agreed to the measure." [69]

On the evening of 19 January 1781, Stormont dispatched Harris's fresh instructions. The negotiations were to be carried out in complete secrecy and were to be confined to the Empress, Potemkin, and Harris. Britain would undertake to cede Minorca to Russia; the Empress in turn should undertake to effect the restoration of peace between Britain and the Bourbons on the basis of the treaty of Paris, as modified by the conquests of the war, the present *uti possidetis* to provide the rule; the French were immediately to evacuate every part of the American continent, and no agreement should be made as regards the Americans, since "His Majesty's rebellious subjects . . . can never be suffered to treat through the medium of a foreign power." On the day the preliminaries of peace were signed, a treaty of perpetual defensive alliance between Britain and Russia would be concluded of which the cession of Minorca would form a part. But an arrangement for the eventual cession of the island could be entered into immediately though it would have to be kept absolutely secret. To forestall the danger of a sudden attack on Minorca by the Bourbons, the Russian fleet in the Mediterranean should receive orders "to be attentive to its protection." [70]

Stormont also enclosed a memorandum setting out the British peace terms as he had outlined them to Harris; it was to be delivered straight into the Empress's hands through Potemkin. Following Harris's advice to communicate to the Empress his plans for America, the King declared his desire to receive peace at the hands of the imperial mediators, his resolve to treat the colonies with clemency and to restore the situation existing before the war, with the

69. Barnes and Owen, *The Sandwich Papers*, *4*, 23 ff. Digest of speech delivered by Sandwich at a meeting of cabinet on 19 January 1781. Cf. also HMC, Knox Papers, p. 272.

70. FO 65/1, Stormont to Harris, No. 5, 19 January 1781 (*MD*, *1*, 374, wrongly dated 20 January 1781).

one concession that the colonies would tax themselves.[71] On the subject of America, no concessions to France were to be made. Nowhere in these proposals was it explicitly stated that Russia should draw the sword. But it was implicit throughout that only by a threat of force, which might lead her into war, would she be able to compel France to withdraw from America; and the suggestion that the Russian fleet should protect Minorca would probably involve it in hostilities with Spain. However disguised, what the British offer amounted to in fact was active Russian assistance in the present war in exchange for the cession of Minorca. What part Austria was to play was not so much as touched upon.

In an accompanying dispatch, designed to be read in Russia, Stormont praised the wisdom of the Empress and urged Harris to pledge himself boldly to her. "You will continue," he wrote, "to place your confidence in Prince Potemkin, who so well deserves it by the great, able and dignified part he has acted upon this occasion, and whose conduct is above all praise." Further Harris was instructed to use "as much *unction,* as much cordiality as possible" in the execution of his orders.[72] But after having thus, by precept and example, indicated to Harris the road he should follow, Stormont proceeded to rebuke him for the excesses of his language. The unfortunate Harris, who believed that a true born Briton did not know how to flatter, was now told that the compliments which he lavished on the Empress had a tendency "to raise pride and may lead the Empress to set too high a value upon any assistance she may be disposed to give this country." He had to calculate his language to a nicety to satisfy both Potemkin and Stormont! [73]

Defeat, isolation, and the new Dutch war doubtless had a depressing effect on the spirits of Britain's leading statesmen, which accounts in some measure for the confusion of British policy at that moment. They did not of course yet know whether or not the Dutch had been admitted by Russia to the Neutral League; nor did they know how the Empress had reacted to the news of the British breach with the United Provinces; nor if she had agreed to mediate

71. FO 65/1, Note for the Empress, enclosed in Stormont to Harris, No. 4, 19 January 1781.

72. FO 65/1, Stormont to Harris, No. 4, 19 January 1781.

73. FO 65/1, Stormont to Harris, No. 10, 19 January 1781.

jointly with the Emperor between Britain and France. Fear of the Neutral League, coupled with anxiety produced by Harris's description of the capriciousness and instability of Russia, led Stormont to believe that the joint mediation would not be enough to keep Russia from declaring for the Dutch Republic. And Harris's dispatches expressed such certainty that Russia would jump at the chance of securing Minorca that the opportunity perhaps seemed too good to lose. Yet if Minorca was to be sacrificed, then something more was required from Russia than her services as a strictly neutral mediator—she must become a partial, indeed an armed mediator—committed to peace terms which would certainly lead her to war with France. But British policy towards Russia was now out of step with British policy towards Austria. Keith had been instructed to find out the secret object of the Emperor's ambition. Kaunitz had already warned him off the subject of the Scheldt in September 1780, and on 30 December Keith had suggested to Stormont that Russian and Austrian ambitions could probably best be fulfilled at the expense of Turkey.[74] But he had not raised the subject of an alliance between Britain and Austria in Vienna, realizing that Austrian ties with France were too strong to be broken. Stormont evidently hoped that Austria too could be induced by the offer of the Scheldt to desert France and stand forth as an armed mediator on Britain's behalf. The day after he wrote to Harris, on 20 January 1781, he again instructed Keith to raise the subject with Kaunitz,[75] but the Chancellor, when at last Keith forced the subject upon him, would not hear of it. He could not, he declared, fly in the face of a treaty guaranteed by half the powers of Europe nor break the treaty of Munster without plunging into a war with France, Holland, and the whole of Germany.[76] Stormont, however, did not wait to hear the result of Keith's inquiries, with the result that the cabinet was inviting Russia to bind herself alone to be a

---

74. SP 80/223, Keith to Stormont, No. 125, 30 December 1780.

75. FO 7/1, Stormont to Keith, private, 20 January 1781. Stormont also hoped that Austria would agree to tolerate Protestants in the Austrian Netherlands, in which case, he believed, there was a good chance that Zeeland might desert the United Provinces for Austrian rule.

76. FO 7/1, Keith to Stormont, No. 22, secret, 7 February 1781. Stormont still attempted to argue away Kaunitz's objections but instructed Keith to drop the subject (see FO 7/1, Stormont to Keith, No. 17, 27 February 1781).

mediator secretly committed to enforce the Peace of Paris at the sword's point, without considering that this might give serious offence to Austria, joined with her in that mediation at Britain's own invitation. And was it possible for Russia (knowing nothing of the offers made by Britain to Austria) to commit herself as Britain desired, without giving her co-mediator and future ally grounds to suspect her good faith? Stormont hoped that he could bind both mediators to Britain by territorial offers. Austrian reticence frustrated this aim. But Harris's reports persuaded him that the effort to secure Russia alone was worth making.

12. Russia Refuses Minorca: The Dutch Mediation

News of the British breach with the United Provinces burst on St. Petersburg on 9 January 1781, five days after the Dutch had acceded to the Neutral League.[1] It caused a sensation. The Empress was reported to be "piquée au vif" and to have declared: "Les Anglais veulent donc la guerre avec toute l'Europe; ils m'obligeront aussi à prendre un parti, auquel j'ai répugné; mais enfin il le faudra bien." [2] The Dutch did not hesitate to ask for assistance; as early as 3/14 January the plenipotentiaries, who were still in St. Petersburg, communicated to the Empress the Dutch reply to the accusations set out in the British manifesto and demanded protection.[3] On 10 January Harris heard from Potemkin that "Her Imperial Majesty was rather disposed to believe that our conduct towards the Dutch had been a good deal influenced by their recent accession to the Armed Neutrality." He provided the Prince with sound written and verbal arguments to combat such ideas,[4] and soon after Potemkin told Harris not to be uneasy about the Dutch and to remember their secret negotiation; the Empress he declared waited with anxiety for the return of the British courier.[5] But Harris was really perturbed at the effect Britain's action might have in Russia; he tackled Bezborodko, he tackled Panin, and he implored Potemkin:

1. FO 65/1, Harris to Stormont, No. 171, 30 December 1780/10 January 1781, *MD, 1,* 372.

2. *PKFG, 45,* 208, Goertz to Frederick, 12 January 1781. As for Frederick II: "à présent je ne balance plus à loger le King George et tout son ministère à Betlam," he wrote on 1 January 1781 to the Princess of Orange (ibid., 145).

3. *Morskoy Sbornik, 44,* 379, No. 62.

4. FO 65/1, Harris to Stormont, No. 2, 1/12 January 1781.

5. FO 65/1, Harris to Stormont, No. 5, 8/19 January 1781.

"mon Prince, soutenez moi, empêchez-la [the Empress] dans un moment que les affaires se dévelopent de les embrouiller de nouveau. Persuadez la que si elle souhaite la paix il ne faut pas qu'elle fasse la mine d'après nos ennemis . . ." [6]

Indeed the Empress was now placed in a very embarrassing position. She had to decide whether the League was to abide by its obligation to defend one of its members attacked "en haine" of its membership or whether it was to reveal itself to be an empty demonstration. For the time being she temporized, under the pretext of waiting for an official communication of the British manifesto.[7] The arrival on 22 January 1781 of a courier from Vienna,[8] bearing the news that Britain had invited Austria and Russia to mediate between Britain and the Bourbons may well have presented Catherine with a solution to her problem. If once she became a mediator in that conflict, she could not very well be expected to join in the war as the ally of the Dutch. Moreover, owing to Stormont's rapidity in forcing a breach with the Dutch, Russia was left with some power of choice on the stand she could adopt. The Dutch had actually acceded after hostilities had broken out, and it could therefore be argued that they were no longer *bona fide* neutrals at the date of accession. It was also open to the Empress to accept at their face value the British reasons for the breach, notably the failure to punish those responsible for the draft treaty with America and the refusal of succours against Spain.[9] Catherine therefore chose to assume that a compromise could still be reached and that war, which would drive the Dutch into alliance with France, could still be avoided. On 13/24 January 1781 she dispatched a personal rescript to Simolin in London, instructing him to express her surprise that Britain had broken with Holland on the flimsy pretext of an offence committed by the town of Amsterdam alone and hint-

6. Letter to Potemkin enclosed in FO 65/1, Harris to Stormont, No. 7, 12/23 January 1781.

7. *PKFG, 45,* 221, Goertz to Frederick, 19 January 1781.

8. See Beer and Fiedler, *Joseph II und Graf Ludwig Cobenzl, 1,* 112, Cobenzl to Joseph, 4 February 1781.

9. It is also probable that Catherine consulted her Danish and Swedish allies, but these documents have not been printed. See FO 73/1, Wroughton to Stormont, No. 4, 16 February 1781, reporting the arrival in Stockholm on 12 February of a Russian courier bearing a letter from Panin to the effect that the Empress had not yet made up her mind what to do about the Dutch war but would consult her allies in any event.

ing broadly that it was of course possible to view the breach as having taken place as a result of the expressed Dutch intention to join the League. She went on to point out the disadvantages for Britain of taking on yet another enemy and stressed the danger that from the accidental union between the Dutch and the Bourbons a longer lasting union might be born. In the strongest terms the Empress declared that she saw "avec une sensibilité extrême, que la guerre contre la Hollande a été entreprise exactement dans le moment où la République a accédé à son plan . . . qu'elle ne s'est point attendue à des suites si desagréables de ses efforts à l'avantage de la navigation neutre." She then offered her good offices and invited Britain to let her know the terms on which she could effect a reconciliation.[10]

The Empress therefore apparently intended to see what diplomatic pressure could achieve to prevent the development of hostilities. Moreover, by half accepting the British version of the cause of the rupture—the Laurens treaty—she left herself the possibility of arguing that if she could induce the Dutch to offer suitable apologies for the misbehaviour of the pensionary of Amsterdam, then Britain must declare herself satisfied and not demand any modification of Dutch maritime privileges. The Dutch were meanwhile put off with verbal assurances that Russia intended to abide by her treaty obligations.[11]

Harris heard of course of the Empress's rescript to Simolin, but under Potemkin's influence he declared it to be of no importance and to "convey in a great many words a very little matter." Indeed Potemkin assured him that "all this neutral edifice will now fall of itself," and Harris placed so much faith in the Prince's assurances that he wrote to Stormont on 15/26 January 1781 that "on the whole . . . I think the moment I have been so long wishing for is at last arrived and that the conduct of [H.I.M.] will soon justify all I have advanced." [12] Meanwhile he issued dire warnings of the consequences for Russia of intervention on behalf of the Dutch.

10. FO 65/1, Simolin to Stormont, 19 February 1781. See also F. de Martens, *Recueil, 9*, 313–14, Rescript of Catherine to Simolin, 13/24 January 1781 (printed in part only).

11. See *AMON, 2*, 385, Vauguyon to Vergennes, 9 February 1781, reporting what the Dutch plenipotentiaries said they had been told by Panin.

12. FO 65/1, Harris to Stormont, No. 10, 15/26 January 1781 (wrongly dated December).

Potemkin was ill at the time, and Harris turned to the Empress's
secretary, Bezborodko, with whom he was now in more frequent
contact and who was rising in his estimation. He warned Bezborodko towards the end of January that should Russia take part in
the war on Dutch behalf it would put a complete stop to her trade.
"Not a ship would pass the Sound to come to Petersburg and . . .
every misfortune that could attend an Empire acting under erroneous measures would fall on Russia," he declared. Bezborodko,
who was fully alive to these issues, scarcely needed the warning
and assured Harris that the Empress had no intention of taking
the part of the Dutch.[13] Nevertheless, Harris was unable to prevent
the ratification of Dutch accession to the League, which took place
on 11 February 1781.

On 12 January 1781 the States General decided to appeal to the
members of the Neutral League, asking for their protection and
declaring themselves to have been attacked on the ground of their
accession to the Neutral League.[14] Their formal request for assistance reached Russia on 5 February and probably contributed to
move the Empress to fresh efforts. At any rate, without waiting for
a British reply to her first exhortation, at the beginning of February
the Empress sent a fresh rescript to Simolin, instructing him to
offer her formal mediation to Britain in the conflict and to concert
his measures with Galitzin at The Hague.[15] She may partly have
been moved by the desire to keep Austria out of this particular
diplomatic manoeuvre. More probably, however, she hoped that
a mediation between Britain and Holland had greater chance of
success if it did not become involved with the negotiations for
peace between Britain and the Bourbons, which were bound to run
into difficulties over America. At the same time, by offering now
her sole mediation, the Empress succeeded in keeping the other

13. FO 65/1, Harris to Stormont, No. 13, 19/30 January 1781 (*MD*, *1*, 379); No. 14,
22 January/2 February 1781.

14. Scott, *Armed Neutralities*, p. 353.

15. CP Russie, *106*, Vérac to Vergennes, No. 8, 29 January/9 February 1781. The
text of the Empress's rescript has not been printed but a note of Simolin's "représentation verbale" of 5 March 1781 is in FO 65/1, and he was evidently carrying out
instructions which must have been sent to him three or four weeks earlier. (It is
possible that the undated rescript printed in F. de Martens, *Recueil*, *9*, 301 belongs
to this date.)

members of the Neutral League out of the picture, though she could always summon them up to bring pressure to bear on a recalcitrant Britain. The Dutch appeal for assistance was directed to all three members of the League. The Empress could trust Denmark to follow her lead, but she had no certainty that Sweden would follow Russian and not French leadership. The League was after all an artificial union formed for a limited purpose. When confronted by major issues each power might well revert to its traditional alignment.[16]

Harris of course discussed the Empress's formal offer of mediation with Potemkin, and his advice to Stormont reflects the fell hand of the Prince. He wrote to warn the Secretary of State that though the Empress meant well, Panin would probably twist her intentions and make it appear that Russia condemned Britain and approved the Dutch. "Your Lordship expects," he wrote on 6 February 1781, "that Russia will tax us with hastiness, call us indiscreetly arrogant and untractable, and possibly even hint at our having broke with Holland on account of the armed neutrality; the Empress, though she never would have said this herself, will not disapprove it when [Panin] says it for her . . ." And he added, on Potemkin's authority, that even if Britain rejected the Russian offer of mediation, Russia would never give the Dutch any effective assistance. Nevertheless, Potemkin urged on Harris that Britain should accept; the Empress would be irritated if she were opposed, and, as he put it, "to obtain the primary object you must forego secondary ones." [17] The primary object was of course Minorca. Harris had still received no reply to the proposals he had made on 13/24 December 1780, but this unfinished negotiation hung over his head throughout January and February and coloured his whole attitude to the Anglo-Dutch conflict. Above all he sought to prevent Russia from committing herself in such a way to the defence of Dutch interests as to render impracticable an Anglo-Russian alliance. Hence not only did he himself view with favour the Russian

16. See for instance CP Russie, *106*, Vérac to Vergennes, No. 9, 5/16 February 1781, in which Vérac points out that the Empress was surprised at the speed with which the Dutch had demanded assistance from Denmark and Sweden. The Dutch had acceded to the Russo-Danish and the Russo-Swedish conventions at the same time as they signed the treaty with Russia (Scott, *Armed Neutralities*, p. 350).

17. FO 65/1, Harris to Stormont, No. 16, 26 January/6 February 1781.

offer to mediate in the Anglo-Dutch quarrel, but he allowed the
Russians to see that he did. In discussion with Potemkin towards
the middle of February 1781, he expressed the opinion that Britain
might agree to a settlement with the United Provinces on the basis
of the punishment of the pensionary of Amsterdam and an embassy
of apology to Great Britain.[18] Towards the end of February, speaking to the Vice Chancellor, Harris again allowed himself to be more
encouraging than prudence demanded and said that whenever the
Dutch should conform to the conditions set out in the British manifesto hostilities would cease.[19] To Bezborodko Harris spoke equally
openly, urging on him the importance of "recalling to the Empress's
mind her intentions relative to terminating this new quarrel, and
not by delay give time for new ideas to arise, or new impressions
to be made." [20] Harris in fact believed that Panin was opposed to
the plan for separate mediation between Holland and Britain, and
he had therefore all the more reason to think that he should support
it.[21] How far he had committed himself in his own mind to British
acceptance of this Russian offer is clear from his dispatch of 13/24
March 1781, in which he described the rancorous campaign
waged against him by Panin, acting in defence of Dutch interests,
and his conviction that victory would soon be his "as a very few
days must bring an answer from your Lordship to the first overture
of the Empress . . . the manner in which this overture is received
in London, and at The Hague, and that in which our answer will
be seen here, will determine the rule of conduct this court will
observe." [22]

So immersed was Harris in the politics of St. Petersburg that
he was for the moment blind to the wider issues that had moved the
British cabinet to break with the Dutch. He was so obsessed by the
secret Minorca negotiation that he took for granted that London
would immediately accept the Russian offer to make peace with
the Dutch without any reconsideration of the naval principles which

18. FO 65/1, Harris to Stormont, No. 19, 5/16 February 1781 (*MD, I*, 385, wrongly
dated 2/13 February 1781).

19. FO 65/1, Harris to Stormont, No. 28, 16/27 February 1781.

20. FO 65/2, Harris to Stormont, No. 32, 26 February/9 March 1781 (*MD, I*, 392).

21. FO 65/1, Harris to Stormont, No. 29, 19 February/2 March 1781.

22. FO 65/2, Harris to Stormont, No. 39, 13/24 March 1781 (*MD, I*, 402: extracts of
Harris's Nos. 37, 38, and 39 of the same date have been run together as one dispatch).

had been the real cause of the breach. He was encouraging Potemkin, Osterman, and Bezborodko, and through them the Empress, in a course which he hoped Stormont would follow but which would ruin the Secretary of State's policy of starving the Bourbons of naval stores.

When Potemkin had discussed the cession of Minorca in November 1780 with Harris and when the Empress had granted Harris his audience in December, Russia had been a free agent, committed in no way to either of the belligerent sides. When Stormont's instructions of 19 January 1781 finally reached St. Petersburg on 18 February the situation had changed considerably. Negotiations for a Russian alliance with France's ally Austria (however distasteful they might be for France) had progressed satisfactorily on matters of substance, though an unexpected and troublesome hitch had arisen on matters of form.[23] Russia was now bound by the Neutral League to Britain's latest enemy, the Dutch. Catherine's freedom of action was still further circumscribed by the offer of her mediation which she had made to Britain and the United Provinces and by the joint imperial mediation between Britain and the Bourbon powers which Stormont himself had conjured up.

In these somewhat inauspicious circumstances, Harris at last embarked on the negotiations which he hoped were to crown his career in Russia. The day the courier arrived, 18 February, Harris rushed straight to Potemkin and requested him "freely and candidly, to tell me, whether he felt himself sufficiently active to carry it [the negotiation] through without relaxation, whether . . . he would make it the primary object of his thoughts, and not suffer it to be driven from his mind by those many objects of dissipation that daily came in his way." Aware that Stormont might think this somewhat strong language to use to a powerful minister, Harris explained that he had already spoken frequently to the Prince "on his uncommon levity," and that he felt it necessary to issue this warning since otherwise Potemkin would not overcome the indolence which never forsook him except when his personal influence was in danger. Having received satisfactory assurances of the Prince's zeal in his service, Harris embarked on the first part of

23. See Ch. 13 for a fuller discussion.

his commission, the communication of the British peace terms, namely the Peace of Paris as modified by conquests in the war and no treating with the Americans. Potemkin took charge of communicating them to the Empress.

It is not clear from his dispatches what Harris expected the Empress to do as a result of this communication, which he seems to have made first, and quite separate from the subject of Minorca. But the Empress's reply, when it came, brought him cold comfort. After about a week Potemkin produced a memorandum written in the Empress's own hand, which he had orders to read and translate to Harris as often as he pleased but was not to leave with him. In it the Empress spoke of the satisfaction with which she had received this mark of British confidence; of her desire to see the war end on terms honourable to Britain; of her disapproval of any essential change in the balance of power. But, she explained, she did not stand single and was bound to act with her co-mediator, and "it was not in her power to be more explicit, till she was acquainted with the sentiments of her imperial colleague." [24] There was thus no sign that the Empress intended in any way to use her position to enforce these peace terms for Britain, which was perhaps what Harris had understood her to mean during his audience in December. But Potemkin, as usual, provided Harris with suitable excuses for the Empress's unaccountable behaviour. She had grown pusillanimous, he explained, and her thirst for glory had abated; though she strongly approved of Britain's peace terms, she would not draw the sword to obtain them for Britain. In his own devious way, the Prince then gave Harris a reason which in a distorted form came somewhat nearer the truth. Though the Empress had not said so, he explained very confidentially, "yet he clearly saw her pride was mortified" at having the Emperor joined to her in the mediation, and she used this as an excuse to herself for not coming up more completely to the assurances she had made to Harris.

Catherine had certainly so far shown no great interest in the joint imperial mediation, and it is more than likely that she was

----

24. FO 65/2, Harris to Stormont, No. 37, 13/24 March 1781 (*MD, 1,* 394). Harris as usual waited until the end of his negotiation to forward a full account by courier. On this occasion he was somewhat more sparing with his dates, and it is therefore impossible to establish exactly the timing of his various interviews.

displeased that Britain should have chosen to apply to the Emperor rather than to herself. But petty annoyance at having been given an adjoint in the mediation was not the cause nor even the pretext of her refusal to commit herself to assist Britain, for in spite of all Harris's assurances that Britain never wished the Empress to draw the sword, an armed mediation was almost bound to plunge Russia into the war. Moreover it was not a safe policy to embark on independently of her co-mediator, and the Empress was perfectly justified in her refusal to act without consulting him. However, Harris chose rather to believe that nothing that Britain had done could account for the Empress's change of front (as he believed it to be), and he must attribute it to "a decrease of the vigour and firmness" which had characterized her at the outset of her reign. Potemkin agreed of course entirely with this explanation, which fitted in well with his own policy of attributing every failure of his to persuade the Empress to do what Harris wanted to the Empress's declining powers. "You may assure your court," he declared to Harris, "and I will pledge myself for the veracity of what I say, that she is kept back, purely from timidity, from being degenerated, and that if she dared, she would be as strongly English in her conduct, as she is in her inclinations." And Harris, perhaps in order to justify his own previous exclusive reliance on Potemkin's interpretation of Catherine's views, added that he was confirmed in this opinion by other leading courtiers not normally in agreement with Potemkin.[25]

Harris now proceeded to the more substantial part of his negotiations. The Empress had refused to do anything for Britain for love—she might do something for Minorca. Again the negotiation was conducted with great secrecy through Potemkin, who was enormously taken with the proposals that Stormont had instructed Harris to make.[26] He carried them to the Empress and a few days

25. Ibid.
26. FO 65/2, Harris to Stormont, No. 38, 13/24 March 1781 (*MD, 1,* 398, tacked on to No. 37). Coxe, in *Memoirs of the Kings of Spain of the House of Bourbon, 3,* 448, states that the cession of Minorca was Potemkin's idea, and as a reward for his efforts he was to be "gratified" (by Britain) with the compensation allowed for the stores and artillery in the island which were valued at £2,000,000. Coxe quotes as his authority "authentic information and official documents, MSS." He undoubtedly got his information from Harris, whom he knew, and it would be interest-

later reported on the result to Harris. Never, said he, had he seen the Empress more struck. "La mariée est trop belle; on veut me tromper," she had exclaimed. But though she saw at once the advantages Russia could derive from possession of the island, she proceeded immediately to speculate on what secret and sinister British designs could be concealed behind such a noble offer. The result of her speculations in the end was that Britain wanted "to draw her into the war." In vain did Potemkin (according to his own account) endeavour to argue with her. He insisted that since the cession was not to be made until after the preliminaries of peace were signed, there could be no danger for Russia. But Catherine saw that if her fleet were to concern itself with the protection of Minorca against the Bourbons her neutrality would inevitably be endangered. When Potemkin urged her to see Harris and hear what he had to say, she refused. "I will not be led into temptation," was her reply.

For about a fortnight the Empress pondered over the British proposals, weighing the advantages and disadvantages. Finally, on 8/19 March 1781 she agreed with Potemkin on a reply which again he was instructed to translate and read to Harris.[27] With suitable expressions of gratitude for the offer made to her, the Empress declared her willingness to assist in the task of restoring peace, and should she succeed she would then with the greatest pleasure "enter into the closest connection with England and cement this union by any means likely to render it useful, sincere and lasting." But as long as she was employed as mediatrix she could not enter into an eventual convention with Britain, since the transaction could not be kept secret forever, and it would then appear at a later day that she had been influenced during the mediation by one of the parties, and her impartiality could be called in question.[28] Potem-

---

ing to know how much truth there is in the allegation that this magnificent bribe had been offered to the Prince. The anecdote does not figure in Harris's official correspondence.

27. Lebedev, *Opyt razrabotki noveyshey russkoy istorii po neizdannym istochnikam, I. Grafy Nikita i Petr Paniny*, p. 252, Catherine to Potemkin, undated, but judging by the content it must belong to this period. According to Harris the Empress's reply was in her own hand, in Russian, and with many corrections (FO 65/2, to Stormont, No. 38, 13/24 March 1781).

28. FO 65/2, Harris to Stormont, No. 38, 13/24 March 1781; Lebedev, *Opyt razrabotki*, p. 252, Draft of reply to Harris, wrongly dated 1780.

kin of course added his gloss to this answer. Though the Empress longed to have Minorca, she had not the courage to adopt the necessary means to acquire it. She was deterred by her own apprehensions and staggered by the calumnies of Britain's enemies. But he still urged Harris to believe that in the mediation with the Bourbons she would act as a true friend of Britain.[29]

Thus failed the fourth attempt made by Britain in the course of the war to induce Russia to abandon her neutrality, for whatever Harris may have said, however he may have disguised it, what Britain desired and needed was an alliance disguised as an armed mediation. This is evident from Stormont's explanation to the King of what he hoped to achieve.[30] It is also evident from the strategical situation. A mere threat from Russia could not compel France to reconsider her engagements to the Americans, the main stumbling block for a negotiated peace, when France did not despair of success in a further campaign. There was no land front on which Russia could make her manpower felt against France. Russian assistance to Britain would have to take the form of the loan of warships—possibly even of troops—to fight at a distance from Russia. The Empress had already shown reluctance at the idea of lending troops. She needed her ships to carry out the policy of the Neutral League, a policy which she would of course have to abandon were she to be drawn into the war as an armed mediator on Britain's behalf. None of these points were so much as mentioned in the course of the negotiation, but they must have occurred to the Empress. Neutrality was her policy, and nothing that she (as opposed to Potemkin) had said to Harris justified him in assuming that she was prepared to abandon it, not even at the price of Minorca. Harris, however, incited by Potemkin, remained convinced that Catherine had drawn back from a policy she had previously approved and could only lament that so great a princess "is sinking into an ordinary woman." [31]

There is no doubt that on reflection the British proposal, however tempting to the glancing genius of Potemkin, could not be entertained by the more sober Catherine. Here again she revealed

29. FO 65/2, Harris to Stormont, No. 38, 13/24 March 1781.
30. See Ch. 11, pp. 283–84 and n. 68.
31. FO 65/2, Harris to Stormont, No. 38, 13/24 March 1781.

the basic common sense which was her greatest claim to genius. Catherine realized that she could not hope to hold a naval base in the Mediterranean with British consent alone. The Bourbon fleets would have her new possession at their mercy, and Russia would be automatically drawn into the recurring bouts of Anglo-French hostility. But in addition Catherine saw the trap concealed in the British offer. From the moment she entered a secret convention with Britain, a necessary preliminary to the eventual cession and treaty of alliance (whatever vague form the convention might take), she would lose her diplomatic initiative and would be forced to follow the fortunes of British arms and the conduct of British diplomacy in reaching a settlement with her enemies. What is more, Britain would be in a position to put pressure on Russia by threatening to allow news of the secret convention to leak out. The whole carefully built edifice of neutrality would crumble overnight and, as Catherine saw, she might find herself forced into the war or at least deprived of the mediation with *éclat*.[32]

Moreover, acceptance on Catherine's part would have been an act of gross bad faith not only towards France but towards the Emperor, so recently joined with her in the mediation at Britain's request and about to become her ally. Russia would have been, unbeknown to Austria, committed to one party in a manner which could only be regarded as dishonourable when it became public.

As usual the role of Potemkin in this matter was neither straightforward nor sincere. He probably did urge acceptance of the British offers on the Empress, for the plan was one after his own heart. But he knew the real reasons for her refusal and had evidently been consulted by her when she drafted her note of rejection. When he interpreted Catherine's refusal to Harris as a sign of her declining powers, he was being disingenuous. He knew full well what the

---

32. Lebedev, *Opyt razrabotki . . . russkoy istorii*, p. 252, Catherine to Potemkin: "There is still here the danger that the moment I agree to preliminary negotiations, the one and the other power will refuse to make peace for opposing reasons, and the question of peace will come to an end, it will even slip out of my hands in an insulting manner, and then, willy-nilly we shall be dragged in to the business, or we shall be treated with less confidence . . ." (The sentence stops in the middle in the text printed by Lebedev. In *Sbornik*, 27, 273, the same sentence continues with a reference to the Duchess of Kingston; a different letter has obviously been tacked on by mistake, and the original continuation of Catherine's letter has gone astray.)

secret purpose of the new alliance with Austria was; the treaty was defensive in form but it was offensive in content. Potemkin knew and shared Catherine's ambition for expansion in the south, if he had not actually inspired it. But to excuse his failure to comply with Harris's wishes by blaming the Empress for pusillanimity was his easiest way out of a difficult situation. By dwelling on the Empress's character rather than on her policy, he provided a justification for himself which Harris was in any case predisposed to accept. And he preserved his ascendancy over Harris, because he was still free to agree with the English envoy on all aspects of Russian foreign policy and thus keep alive an illusion of identical interests.

How right the Empress had been to refuse the British offer was revealed in the following months, for while Britain was proposing to cede the island to Russia, Spain was already planning its recovery. The British relief of the besieged Gibraltar in March 1781 turned the attention of Spain to the possibility of conquering Minorca, and Floridablanca supported this course because he believed that Spain would receive more consideration from the mediators if she had a substantial acquisition to bargain with.[33] But, as might have been expected, news of the British proposal to cede the island did leak. By June 1781 it was known in Madrid, and it was generally regarded as the prime motive behind the preparations that the Spaniards were then making for an expeditionary force.[34] Both Stormont and Harris were most concerned at the news of this leakage of information, which Stormont declared could have occurred only in St. Petersburg.[35] Harris surmised that the Empress had mentioned the matter to the Emperor,[36] though no such mention occurs in their correspondence. Later he suggested that it was merely a lucky guess.[37] At any rate the Spanish expeditionary force

33. Danvila, *Historia,* 5, 163 et seq. The attack on Minorca was decided on 13 March 1781; cf. note by Floridablanca of 20 April 1781.

34. FO 27/1, Advices and Intelligences from France, which contains reports from both France and Spain. An agent wrote from Madrid on 18 June 1781 that the siege of Minorca had become necessary "puisqu'on a découvert dit-on, un traité secret entre l'Angleterre et la Russie, portant la cessation de la dite isle à cette dernière puissance."

35. FO 65/3, Stormont to Harris, No. 47, 10 July 1781.

36. FO 65/3, Harris to Stormont, No. 111, 30 July/10 August 1781.

37. FO 65/4, Harris to Stormont, No. 115, 6/17 August 1781. Harris had been told not to put anything in writing, but he did prepare a memorandum on the ad-

sailed on 22 July 1781, and in February 1782 the British troops confined to the fort in Port Mahon surrendered. The island which Britain had offered to Russia she had been unable to hold for herself.

In spite of the preparations he had made to ward off Russian anger at the British breach with the United Provinces, the news that Catherine had after all admitted them to the Neutral League came as a surprise to Stormont. She must, he believed, have been aware of the impending breach with Britain. Stormont could only understand it on the assumption that "the Empress considers this Armed Neutrality, this *Nullité Armée,* as a thing which stands quite by itself and has no connexion with her general system." [38] He soon discovered that the Empress did not intend entirely to abandon her latest ally. On 19 February 1781, Simolin delivered to him an *insinuation verbale,* based on the Empress's rescript of 13/24 January 1781.[39] In accordance with the Empress's temporizing policy Simolin spoke in such terms as to suggest that the withdrawal of ambassadors and the Order in Council authorizing reprisals at sea did not mean that war must inevitably take place. He made no formal offer of mediation but pressed the Empress's desire for a reconciliation between the two powers.[40] Warned by Harris that Panin intended to provoke Britain to an angry answer,[41] Stor-

---

vantages for Russia of holding Minorca, which was shown by Potemkin to the Empress and returned later to the British envoy. He did not destroy this memorandum which is still among the Harris Papers. It is possible that some agent did get access to it in Russia. At any rate there is no mention of the plan before June 1781 in the published correspondence of Goertz and Frederick; nor in that of Cobenzl and Joseph II; nor in the dispatches of Vérac to Vergennes. How the news leaked remains an enigma.

38. FO 65/1, Stormont to Harris, No. 7, 19 January 1781.

39. FO 65/1, Simolin to Stormont, 19 February 1781 (communication verbale, of which Stormont was allowed to take a written note). The text is not identical with that of the rescript of 13/24 January 1781 printed in F. de Martens, *Recueil 9,* 314, but is clearly based on it.

40. Simolin did speak of the war undertaken against Holland, it is true, but there was just sufficient vagueness in the terms to enable Stormont to wriggle out. See also Scott, *Armed Neutralities,* p. 375, Rescript of the Empress to Count Musin Pushkin, 1781: "We were then ignorant of the fact that hostilities were to follow immediately upon the departure of its Ambassador."

41. FO 65/1, Harris to Stormont, No. 10, 15/26 January 1781.

mont was cautious and polite but utterly refused to let himself be drawn into what he considered to be a trap. Britain did not want peace with a United Provinces entitled to the privileges and protection of membership of the Neutral League. This was of course not a policy which could be publicly proclaimed, and indeed Stormont constantly insisted that "the attempt to connect this quarrel with Holland, with the Neutral League, is a gross artifice indeed, and cannot deceive a sovereign of the Empress's great penetration." [42]

In his reply, on 26 February 1781, Stormont took advantage of the turn Simolin had given to his opening and remarked that clearly the Empress did not yet know that war had broken out. But, he declared, she would soon understand from the King's manifesto on the causes of the war the true reasons for the breach between the two countries. These were anterior in time and unconnected in substance with the Dutch accession to the Neutral League. Moreover the conventions of the Neutral League expressly stated that membership was limited to neutral powers. If the Dutch had been admitted, "c'est qu'on les regardoit alors comme une puissance neutre, ignorant qu'ils étoient dans un état d'hostilité directe avec l'Angleterre, et par conséquent aussi peu neutre que la France et l'Espagne." He concluded by suggesting that the best proof of friendship the imperial courts could offer was to restore peace, thus implying that Britain's war with the Dutch must be regarded as part of the wider war with the Bourbons and that peace must equally be treated under the auspices of the imperial mediators in the latter conflict.[43] Harris in turn was instructed to combat any idea of a separate mediation and to keep the Empress's attention fixed on the joint imperial mediation.[44] But on 5 March Simolin formally offered the Empress's sole mediation in the separate conflict with the Dutch and informed the Secretary of State that the same offer had been made to the United Provinces and that he and

42. FO 65/1, Stormont to Harris, No. 15, 15 February 1781.

43. FO 65/1, Draft of réponse verbale, 26 February 1781. Stormont believed Simolin's instructions to have been drafted before the Empress heard that she had been invited to mediate jointly with the Emperor; this was an additional reason to refuse her sole mediation. (FO 7/1, Stormont to Keith, No. 18, 27 February 1781). But the Empress had of course already heard of Britain's invitation to Austria.

44. FO 65/1, Stormont to Harris, No. 18, 27 February 1781.

Galitzin had been instructed to cooperate.[45] Stormont refused the
Russian offer outright. The war with Holland was part and parcel
of the war with France, and if peace were made with the Dutch they
would only resume their position of secret alliance with France.[46]

Though difficult to defend in public, British policy was perfectly
logical. No condign punishment of van Berckel could satisfy a
power determined to prevent by every means the supply of naval
stores to the Bourbons in Dutch bottoms. A mediation which modified or abolished the offending clauses of the Marine Treaty of
1674 might possibly have been considered. But could Russia be
trusted to propose such terms? The Empress, who took her stand
on the freedom of neutral trade, would hardly propose conditions,
let alone enforce them, which ran completely counter to the policy
she had put forward as the basis of the Neutral League. In spite of
the possibility of offending Russia by a refusal, the British reply
was in the circumstances inevitable. But in addition, by that strange
twist which all things which came from Russia now received in the
minds of British statesmen, Stormont decided that because in his
opinion a separate Russian mediation with Holland did not correspond to British interests the proposal must be the result of a
sinister plot, "planned by Count Panin, in secret concert with his
Prussian Majesty" . . . and now "held out to us with no other
view than to ensnare." The object of this plot was to turn the
Empress's attention away from the main pacification, and "it was
thought advisable here to avoid this snare without appearing to
perceive it." [47]

Harris meanwhile, obsessed with the hope of winning Russia by

45. FO 65/2, représentation verbale, Simolin to Stormont, 5 March 1781; Galitzin's
offer was made on 1 March 1781 to the States General, see *Annual Register*, 1781,
p. 310.

46. FO 65/2, Stormont to Simolin, réponse verbale, 11 March 1781.

47. FO 65/2, Stormont to Harris, No. 21, 13 March 1781. Frederick did in fact
counsel a Russian mediation to Goertz, but his advice reached Petersburg too
late for it to be said to have inspired the Empress (see *PKFG, 44, 179*, Frederick to Goertz, 13 January 1781). This may account for the report emanating
from Elliot in Berlin that the Empress had written to Frederick with her own
hand asking if Prussia would support her if she were drawn into war on behalf
of the Dutch (*MD, 1, 383–84*). I have found no trace of such a letter in the published correspondence between Frederick and Catherine, nor is it mentioned in
PKFG.

the offer of Minorca, had been encouraging the Russians to believe that Britain would accept Russian mediation in the Dutch conflict. No wonder therefore that Stormont was horrified when he saw gradually from Harris's dispatches how far the British envoy had allowed himself to approve, when speaking to Russian ministers, the plan for a separate peace. "You will have seen," he wrote on 6 April 1781, ". . . that the idea of a negotiation for a separate peace with Holland appears here in a very different light from that in which it must have struck you when you pressed the Empress's private secretary to keep her attention fixt to that project. There seem to be many objections to it upon general reasoning: But, however that may be, and in whatever light this, or any other political subject may strike you, upon a general theoretic view of it, it will be very essential . . . that you should not hazard any decided opinion, upon a subject where you have not had time to learn the sentiments of your court." [48] This, the sternest rebuke Harris ever received while he was in Russia, was perhaps justified, for he had outrun his instructions. But some blame must also attach to Stormont, who had never favoured Harris with a realistic analysis of British policy in any field and in particular had continued even in his confidential instructions to preserve the fiction that the British declaration of war on Holland had been provoked by the Dutch refusal to punish the pensionary of Amsterdam—surely an unnecessary form of deception in secret instructions to a British envoy.

By the time Stormont's reply to the Empress's first *insinuation verbale,* which Simolin had made on 19 February, reached St. Petersburg, the great Minorca negotiation was over and done with. Harris realized at once that the Empress would not be pleased at this rejection of her good offices, which he had not led her to expect, and indeed the Empress was annoyed at the suggestion that mediation between Britain and the Dutch should be left to the Emperor as well as to herself. But she still waited for the British reply to her

48. FO 65/2, Stormont to Harris, No. 28, 6 April 1781. Harris later tried to justify himself and argued that he had never let anything drop which might indicate that he was authorized to approve of the Empress's sole mediation with the Dutch, but there can be no doubt that he had been imprudent (see FO 65/2, Harris to Stormont, No. 64, 24 April/4 May 1781).

second and far more explicit approach.[49] Her patience implied no change in her policy, for to achieve the position of mediator was her only way out of an extremely awkward predicament.

In the first place a real fear was entertained that the new war would lead to a considerable disturbance of the Russian export trade and a consequent decline in the Russian revenue.[50] It was probably this aspect of the problem which led the Empress to take up the question of Prussian accession to the Neutral League. Panin had already suggested to Goertz in July 1780 that Prussia might care to join, and Frederick had agreed in principle. But he had no navy and feared that he might be expected to pay a subsidy to secure the protection of the patrolling squadrons for his merchant ships. Panin thereupon advised waiting until the Dutch had joined, when their fleet would be available, and for the time being the matter was allowed to drop.[51] These discussions may have taken place without the Empress's knowledge. But this time the initiative came from her. She may have been piqued by Harris's tactless references to Prussian desire to accede on the occasion of the private interview she granted to the British envoy in December 1780. But more probably she was influenced by the desire to increase the number of ships entitled to the protection of the League now that Dutch shipping, which played so big a part in the Russian export trade, was about to be preyed on by Britain. It is significant that Goertz mentioned to Frederick II the Russian opening made to him on the Empress's orders by Osterman, on 16 January 1781, seven days after news of the British breach with Holland reached Russia.[52] Now, when the Dutch were no longer neutrals, Frederick had two fresh reasons for acceding. In the first place, Prussian ships, if they were protected by the League, could count on capturing some, perhaps much, of the trade of the now vulnerable

49. FO 65/2, Harris to Stormont, No. 42, 13/24 March 1781. Catherine's irritation against Britain was increased at this time by news of the seizure of a Russian ship which had been taken into a Scottish port.

50. Maykov, *Pis'ma A. A. Bezborodka*, p. 72, Bezborodko to Rumyantsev, 25 January/5 February 1781. See also FO 65/3, Harris to Stormont, No. 106, 14/25 July 1781, quoting Bezborodko on the "real evils the commerce of Russia felt by the suspension of the Dutch trade."

51. See Krauel, "Preussen und die bewaffnete Neutralitaet von 1780," for the history of Prussian accession to the Neutral League.

52. *PKFG*, 45, 215, Goertz to Frederick, 16 January 1781.

Dutch shipping.[53] In the second place, towards the end of January 1781 Frederick II heard for the first time of the negotiations for an alliance between Austria and Russia. He was naturally influenced to clutch at any opening that enabled him to strengthen his connexion with Russia and appear to be deferring to the Empress's wishes.[54]

The second reason which induced the Empress to press her sole mediation so strongly was the desire to prevent the Neutral League from being drawn into the dispute. The Dutch had appealed to all the members for help,[55] and France would undoubtedly urge on Sweden that the Neutral League should come to the defence of its latest member.[56] In response to Russian soundings and Dutch appeals, both Sweden and Denmark were putting forward proposals for solving the Dutch crisis.[57] If the Empress wanted to keep matters in her own hands and to appear at the same time to be doing something for the Dutch, a prompt acceptance of her sole mediation by both sides was the simplest way out. Indeed Panin had even gone so far as to give the impression both to Wassenaer, one of the Dutch plenipotentiaries and to Vérac, that Russia meant to assist the Dutch actively, and discussions took place in St. Petersburg on the delicate question of the status of naval commanders, Russian and Dutch, should their fleets have to act in common. The Dutch were also encouraged to believe that one of the conditions which Russia would impose as mediatrix was British acceptance of the principles of the Neutral League, and of course, for them, peace on those terms was worth achieving.[58]

53. *PKFG, 45,* 226, Frederick to Thulemeier, 6 February 1781; Krauel, "Preussen und die bewaffnete Neutralitaet," pp. 119 ff.

54. Krauel, "Preussen und die bewaffnete Neutralitaet," p. 118; *PKFG, 45,* 384, Hertzberg to Frederick, 14 April 1781.

55. Scott, *Armed Neutralities,* p. 366, (Memorandum to the court of Sweden, dated 28 February 1781; also sent to Denmark and Russia).

56. CP Russie, *106,* Vergennes to Vérac, No. 8, 25 February 1781; Vergennes wished to persuade Russia and the Neutral League to interpose on Dutch behalf.

57. Scott, *Armed Neutralities,* p. 370, Memorandum of the court of Sweden, 28 February 1781; Denmark also put forward proposals but they are not exactly dated. (See Piggott and Ormond, *Documentary History,* p. 205, quoted from Goertz, *Historische und Politische Denkwürdigkeiten,* p. 227. Piggott and Ormond reject Goertz's dating, which is however correct, i.e. 1781).

58. See *AMON, 2,* 385, Vauguyon to Vergennes, 9 February 1781, quoting Panin to the Dutch envoys in St. Petersburg; p. 414, Wassenaer to the Prince of Orange,

Harris now tried to convince Stormont that the proposed mediation was Catherine's own idea, and not Panin's, and did his best
meanwhile to combat it in St. Petersburg in accordance with his
latest instructions.[59] But when the Empress received Stormont's
second and more explicit refusal of her mediation, towards the
beginning of April 1781, he heard that there was nothing but "silence and ill humour." [60] Catherine's temper did not improve
when she heard that the Dutch had accepted her mediation but
repeated their request for assistance under the terms of their treaty
of accession to the Neutral League should Britain refuse the Russian offer.[61] Harris was immediately made to feel her displeasure,
for when he paid his court to the Empress at Easter, "she bore
strong marks of discontent in her countenance" and treated him
"with a coolness and reserve she had never used before." Through
Potemkin, Harris was unable to achieve anything; relations between the Empress and the favourite were again strained, and the
disgruntled Prince used the opportunity to indulge in a diatribe
against his mistress and to express his resolve not to interfere any
more in public business until the Empress came to her senses and
turned again to him, when he would be able to make his own terms.
Harris, realizing that he had to do with "an angry sovereign, and a
discontented favourite," listened in silence and determined to
work through other channels.[62] But Bezborodko gave him cold
comfort. "He confessed to me very freely that he had never seen
his sovereign more hurt than on this occasion. That her first impressions were those of strong displeasure; and that on reflection
they became less petulant, but not less sensible. He assured me that
her intention had been to procure us a peace exactly conformable

20 March 1781; and several intercepts of Vauguyon to Vergennes, quoting assurances
said to have been made in Russia to the Dutch envoys that Russia would go to war
to defend the Republic if Britain refused the mediation, p. 434, 30 March 1781;
p. 443, 10 April 1781; p. 468, 11 May 1781. See also CP Russie, *106*, Vérac to
Vergennes, No. 10, 18 February/1 March 1781.

59. FO 65/2, Harris to Stormont, No. 46, 23 March/3 April 1781, No. 48, 26
March/6 April 1781.

60. FO 65/2, Harris to Stormont, No. 48, 26 March/6 April 1781.

61. On 12 March 1781 the States General issued their counter-manifesto on the
breach with Great Britain (Scott, *Armed Neutralities*, p. 380). On 14 March the
States General agreed to accept the Empress's mediation, (*Annual Register*, 1781,
p. 310; see also FO 65/2, Harris to Stormont, No. 55, 9/20 April 1781).

62. FO 65/2, Harris to Stormont, No. 56, 9/20 April 1781 (*MD, 1,* 410).

to the King's Manifesto, and that the whole was her own plan without having taken the advice or opinion of any of her councillors."[63] Unfortunately a peace in accordance with the terms of the King's manifesto was precisely what Britain did not want.

The Empress's irritation was all the more comprehensible in that she had already decided, in conjunction with Denmark, to take advantage of the face-saving arguments set out by Britain that the breach had not occurred "en haine" of the Neutral League. It was evidently necessary to clarify the question of whether Dutch ships were entitled to the protection of the squadrons of the Armed Neutrality. Russia at any rate had no intention of allowing her ships to be embroiled with the British navy (it must be remembered that many officers in Russian service were British), and towards the end of March the Empress had sent orders to her admiralty to the effect that, though the Dutch were members of the League, they were not to enjoy any of the privileges membership conferred.[64] The Anglo-Dutch war was thus not regarded as a *casus foederis* of the Russo-Dutch treaty. Without informing the Dutch of this decision, a courier was sent to Simolin on 30 March 1781, instructing him to make a formal communication to Stormont of Dutch accession to the League and at the same time to inform the Secretary of State that, whereas the Dutch would be accorded, as neutrals, full protection against France and Spain (scarcely a privilege, as they were now unlikely to carry any goods to British ports), they would be regarded as belligerents in relation to Britain.[65] Stormont was of course delighted to receive these assurances in mid-May 1781 and took the opportunity to stress once again British objections to a separate mediation with Holland.[66]

The decision to regard Holland as a belligerent was adopted by Denmark but not by Sweden, an omission which did not pass unperceived in Britain.[67] In a long memorandum to Russia of 17/28

63. FO 65/2, Harris to Stormont, No. 63, 20 April/1 May 1781.

64. FO 65/2, Harris to Stormont, No. 42, 13/24 March 1781.

65. FO 65/2, Harris to Stormont, No. 46, 23 March/3 April 1781. Extract of a letter from Panin to Sacken, 1781, presumably end of March or early April 1781, Scott, *Armed Neutralities*, p. 374.

66. FO 65/2, Stormont to Harris, No. 37, 25 May 1781.

67. Scott, *Armed Neutralities*, p. 374, Extract of a letter from Panin to Sacken; see also FO 65/2, Stormont to Harris, No. 37, 25 May 1781, and FO 73/1, Stormont to Wroughton, No. 14, 22 May 1781.

February, Count Scheffer, the Swedish foreign minister, had in fact analysed the situation confronting the members of the Neutral League with a good deal of realism. Scheffer had pointed out that the Northern courts were free to choose between the arguments of the British and the arguments of the Dutch on the cause of the war. But if they chose one or the other of these alternatives, they would either precipitate themselves into war on behalf of the Dutch or, if they sided with the British, exhibit "to the whole world a spectacle of utter weakness, and their absolute desertion of a State with which they fear to bind themselves by formal engagements." Scheffer proposed to take an intermediate course, namely by means of a verbal or written declaration to offer the good offices of the three crowns to effect a reconciliation and in the meantime to procure an armistice and the return to the *status quo ante*. If such a declaration were supported by the naval armaments of the three powers, Sweden believed that Britain would "reflect somewhat seriously thereon." Having thus staked a claim for armed mediation by the members of the League, Scheffer went on to express the hope that the Neutral League might, in the course of the negotiation, find an opportunity to bring together the other belligerent powers and effect a general settlement, in which the maritime principles of the League would not be forgotten.[68]

The Empress had no intention of allowing the League to take over the direction of the Dutch problem and interfere in the mediation between Britain and the Bourbons. When Britain refused her mediation, she chose rather to abandon the Dutch to their fate and accept the British demand that the Anglo-Dutch quarrel should be submitted to the imperial mediators. In her reply to the Swedish memorandum she explained that, Britain having refused her sole mediation in the Dutch conflict, Russia had agreed that it should be included in the general mediation between Britain and the Bourbons. "When that takes place," she wrote, "we shall not fail to exert our own efforts in favour of the Republic of Holland as well as to interest His Majesty the Emperor in its behalf, in order that it may be included in the general pacification." Having whisked away any prospect of mediation by the Neutral League,

68. Scott, *Armed Neutralities*, p. 370, Memorandum of the court of Sweden for the court of Russia, 17/28 February 1782.

the Empress turned to the other arguments put forward by Sweden. She agreed that the Northern courts were free to choose their course of action and agreed that, once their own neutrality was safeguarded, it was necessary to take some steps in support of the Dutch. She therefore endorsed the Swedish plan to make representations in London but objected that a common declaration might "by its very nature carry us beyond our intentions, while a mere verbal hint, expressing the same views with the same force, can bind us in no way against our will and desire." While the three courts concerted their measures and agreed on the nature of the "verbal hint," their squadrons should continue to cruise as before in order to impose respect on the belligerent powers and to protect their own trade. No mention whatsoever was made of the Swedish suggestion that the Neutral League should take over the general pacification.[69]

The impact of this inglorious policy on the Dutch can be imagined. They had constantly been assured in St. Petersburg that Russia would abide by her obligations under the treaty with them. It was with difficulty that they now extracted from Panin any information on what Russia would do. Not until 19 May 1781 did the ambassadors receive a reply to the Dutch memorial demanding the assistance of the members of the Neutral League. They were told that the United Provinces were regarded as allies "auxquels on s'intéressait beaucoup, et que l'on ferait des efforts pour tirer la République de la situation avant la pacification générale." They were in addition told that in view of the British refusal of the sole mediation, the Anglo-Dutch quarrel would also be referred to the joint mediation but that "on enverroit un plan aux cours de Suède et de Dannemark." [70] Having heard rumours of the Russian decision of 30 March 1781 not to regard the Anglo-Dutch breach as a *casus foederis* of their treaty with Russia, the Dutch ambassadors

69. Scott, *Armed Neutralities,* p. 375, Rescript of the Empress to Count Musin Pushkin (envoy to Sweden), n.d., probably April 1781.

70. See *AMON,* 2, 486, van Heeckeren to Prince of Orange, 22 May 1781; p. 258, Vauguyon to Vergennes (intercept), 26 June 1781; p. 543, Vauguyon to Vergennes (intercept), 3 July 1781; CP Russie, *106,* Vérac to Vergennes, No. 19, 30 May 1781; *PKFG, 45,* 513, Goertz to Frederick, 29 May 1781. Copies of the Russian reply were sent to Sweden and Denmark (see FO 65/3, Harris to Stormont, No. 75, 11/22 May 1781).

tried to discover from Panin and Osterman what truth there was in this report. Panin hedged and refused to reply outright; the time had not come to decide; the other courts must be consulted, he said. "Il est vrai," wrote van Heeckeren to the Prince of Orange, "que ce seroit un trait infâme de Sa Maj. après tous les assurances, auxquelles on l'aurait cru pouvoir se fier, et encore ce qu'on m'a dit à ma dernière audience." [71] But, pressed by the Russians, all the unfortunate Dutch could do was to accept to be included in the general pacification. It was a solution that satisfied Britain, France, Austria, and Russia, and the Dutch had to resign themselves to becoming the pawn of the great powers.[72]

At the end of April Harris heard rumours of the Empress's decision that the three Northern courts should make a verbal representation in Britain. But as he was now convinced that Russia did not intend to go to war for the Dutch he attached but little importance to the news [73] and assured Stormont that it would amount to nothing and was not intended to produce the smallest effect.[74] Indeed, other and more dramatic events had been taking place in St. Petersburg during the first six months of 1781, and the Dutch problem had faded for a while from Harris's horizon.

71. *AMON*, 2, 486, van Heeckeren to Prince of Orange, 22 May 1781.

72. *AMON*, 2, 543, Vauguyon to Vergennes (intercept) 3 July 1781. Vergennes disapproved of the separate Russian mediation with Holland (CP Russie, *106*, Vergennes to Vérac, No. 8, 25 February 1781) and preferred to "confondre la nouvelle guerre avec l'ancienne pour les faire terminer en même temps"; the Emperor also wished the Dutch conflict to be included in the general pacification (see *AMON*, 2, 559, Vauguyon to Vergennes, 13 July 1781 (intercept), quoting Joseph II to Vauguyon).

73. FO 65/2, Harris to Stormont, No. 61, 16/27 April 1781 (*MD, 1*, 415).

74. FO 65/3, Harris to Stormont, No. 92, 25 June/6 July 1781 (*MD, 1*, 425).

13. The Imperial Mediation Resumed

IN THE FIRST HALF OF 1781 no progress was made by the imperial mediators with the important task of peace-making. The main obstacle to joint action by Russia and Austria lay in the very nature of the unexpected hitch which had arisen in the negotiation for a treaty between the two powers. The difference had arisen on a matter of protocol, involving the prestige of both powers, and questions of prestige are notoriously the most difficult to solve.

It was a European tradition that the Holy Roman Emperor took precedence over all European sovereigns, and it was therefore customary for the Emperor to sign his name first on both copies of treaties negotiated on his behalf. In treaties between other powers the "alternative" was usual, namely one power signed first and was named first in one copy of the treaty, the other power in the second copy.[1] Catherine, a humble German princess sitting on the Russian throne, was deeply imbued with the necessity of asserting Russian prestige in all fields, and she suddenly decided that in the present negotiations Russia must insist on a status equal to that of the Emperor and therefore that the "alternative" must be a condition of the conclusion of the treaty.[2] But from the very beginning of the negotiation Joseph and Kaunitz had insisted that there should be no "alternative."[3] The Emperor saw no reason to abandon a claim sanctified by tradition, and moreover if parity in

1. See Satow, *Guide to Diplomatic Practice;* on this episode see my article, "The Secret Austro-Russian Treaty of 1781."

2. See rescript to Galitzin of 11/22 February 1781; (F. de Martens, *Recueil, 2,* 102–03).

3. Beer and Fiedler, *Joseph II und Graf Ludwig Cobenzl, 1,* 105, footnote 1. Instructions were sent to Cobenzl on 2 January 1781 and contain the terse phrase: *pas d'alternative.* Harris blamed Cobenzl for not having the character to override his instructions. (Add. MSS. 35.521, f. 117, Harris to Keith, 5/16 February 1781, ciphered).

this matter were once granted to one power there was no reason why others, and he had Prussia particularly in mind, should not demand it.[4] Thus, while agreement was fairly quickly reached between Austria and Russia on the substance of the treaty, matters reached a complete standstill on the question of form. The progress of the joint mediation was equally affected, for until the problem of precedence was settled the two courts could not put their names together to an agreed document such as preliminaries for discussion.[5]

Harris, who had as usual been kept informed by Potemkin of the progress of these negotiations, was in despair when he heard that they might fail after all.[6] At Potemkin's request, he studied his "professional books" to see if he could devise a way out of the dilemma.[7] Harris worked on Potemkin, and Potemkin worked on the Empress, but he could not persuade her to change her mind. Cobenzl argued himself to a standstill, Joseph wrote to Catherine herself, Kaunitz sent careful *en clair* compositions through the post pointing out that the Emperor could not give up his precedence without immediate repercussions throughout Germany;[8] all was of no avail. The Empress believed that Joseph needed Russian support, and her nerves were steady enough to resist all the pressure brought to bear on her and to force the Emperor to accept her terms. But she did in the end propose an original way out of the impasse: namely that the treaty should take the form of an exchange of autograph letters in which each party should set out the obligations which it undertook towards the other.[9] Joseph, out-

4. Beer, *Joseph II, Leopold II und Kaunitz*, p. 51, Kaunitz to Joseph II, 11 May 1781.

5. Beer and Fiedler, *Joseph II und Graf Ludwig Cobenzl*, 150, Cobenzl to Joseph II, 23 May 1781.

6. FO 65/3, Harris to Stormont, No. 81, 25 May/5 June 1781.

7. FO 65/1, Harris to Stormont, No. 21, 5/16 February 1781; in March Potemkin used Harris to sound Cobenzl and find out if the latter had any secret instructions to give way (FO 65/2, Harris to Stormont, No. 43, 13/24 March 1781) but Cobenzl was adamant.

8. Arneth, *Joseph II und Katharina*, p. 54, Joseph to Catherine, 6 March 1781; Beer and Fiedler, *Joseph II und Graf Ludwig Cobenzl*, *1*, p. 130, Kaunitz to Cobenzl, 7 March 1781.

9. Arneth, *Joseph II und Katharina*, p. 65, Catherine to Joseph, 6/17 April 1781; p. 67, Catherine to Joseph, 14/25 April 1781; see also F. de Martens, *Recueil*, 2, 105, Rescript of the Empress to Galitzin, 11/22 April 1781.

raged by these Russian pretensions, and "sur le point de rompre tout court avec ces grecs et de plaindre la Princesse de Zerbst . . . environnée . . . de pareils personnages," nevertheless gave in. He accepted the Empress's plan, and on 18 May 1781 copied out in his own hand and at great length the engagements he undertook towards Russia and invited the Empress to do the same.[10] But in view of the publicity which had attended the dispute over the alternative, and the necessity of avoiding speculation over the question of which power had been obliged to give way, Joseph proposed that both parties should maintain strict secrecy about the exchange of letters and should deny that any treaty had been signed.[11]

On 4 June the Emperor's courier arrived, bringing to Catherine the news of her victory. She promptly spent a whole day closeted with her secretary, engaged in her turn in the unaccustomed manual labour of copying out the terms of a treaty in her own hand, and on 9 June 1781 Cobenzl was able to inform the Emperor that this desirable agreement had at last been achieved.[12] A delightful comedy was now enacted by all concerned in St. Petersburg. Cobenzl, deliberately setting out to deceive the British envoy, looked downcast, expressed doubts of the outcome, and convinced Harris that "unless a miraculous ray of light breaks in upon the Empress and restores [her] in the critical moment, I much fear we must consider the cause as lost." Potemkin must have thoroughly enjoyed the situation. He allowed Harris to lecture him, "in the language of truth and of plain sense." Harris appealed to him not to allow the Empress to disgrace herself in such a fashion. "He heard me with attention and without any marks of displeasure, notwithstanding the strong language I made use of, my arguments made no impression on him, neither could I, from his answer, perceive any inclination or intention of assisting my colleague on this occa-

10. Beer and Fiedler, *Joseph II und Graf Ludwig Cobenzl, 1,* 148, Joseph to Cobenzl, 20 May 1781; the text of the letters is in Arneth, *Joseph II und Katharina,* pp. 67, 72, 78, dated 20 and 21 May 1781. But according to Beer and Fiedler, p. 149, note 1, Arneth's dating is incorrect, and F. de Martens, *Recueil, 2,* 106, rightly gives 18 May.

11. Beer and Fiedler, *Joseph II und Graf Ludwig Cobenzl, 1,* 148, Joseph to Cobenzl, 20 May 1781; Arneth, *Joseph II und Katharina,* p. 67, Joseph to Catherine, 20 (18?) May 1781.

12. Beer and Fiedler, *1,* 160, Cobenzl to Joseph, 9 June 1781; Arneth, pp. 81, 87, Catherine to Joseph, 24 May/4 June 1781; p. 90, 26 May/6 June 1781.

sion . . ." [13] And Potemkin knew that the agreement had been concluded! In a brief dispatch of 28 May/8 June 1781, Harris announced that the Empress had refused to give way and that the project was at an end.[14] He could not disguise his disappointment at this victory of vanity over sound policy.[15]

Less than a week after he had finally given up hope, Harris began to suspect that there was something afoot of which he was being kept in ignorance.[16] But information for once was both difficult and very expensive to procure. It was not until 6 July 1781, and at the cost of £1,600 paid over to the private secretary of Bezborodko, that Harris was able to inform Stormont that "the treaty between the two imperial courts of Petersburg and Vienna, is concluded." No one else, wrote Harris, knew anything about it except the Empress and Bezborodko, and though "I presume my friend [Potemkin] is not ignorant of the transaction, yet he does not betray to me any symptoms of his being acquainted with it." [17] All said, and all were reputed to believe, that the negotiations had been broken off. Harris himself was unable to discover the content of the treaty. But he was justified now at last in assuming that Austria and Russia would be found to be acting together in comparative harmony in the field of European diplomacy.

Harris was the only foreign envoy to penetrate the secret and Britain the only country to know that the treaty had been signed. The comedy performed by Catherine, Potemkin, Bezborodko, and Cobenzl completely deceived Vérac. On 8 June 1781, he informed Vergennes that no solution had been found for the problem of precedence and that the negotiations were over.[18] Vergennes greeted the news with relief. He had never liked the idea of this alliance, which the Emperor appeared to be negotiating without consulting France, and he feared that it might contain secret clauses

13. FO 65/3, Harris to Stormont, No. 81, 25 May/5 June 1781.
14. FO 65/3, Harris to Stormont, No. 83, 28 May/8 June 1781.
15. FO 65/3, Harris to Stormont, No. 84, 1/12 June 1781.
16. FO 65/3, Harris to Stormont, No. 88, 8/19 June 1781 (MD, 1, 424).
17. FO 65/3, Harris to Stormont, No. 94, 25 June/6 July 1781 (MD, 1, 426); cf. also private, unnumbered, 25 June/6 July 1781 (MD, 1, 430). Harris also informed Keith in Vienna directly, who otherwise might have been taken in by the comedy put on by Kaunitz (see FO 7/2, Keith to Stormont, No. 84, 4 July 1781 and No. 92, 19 July 1781).
18. CP Russie, 106, Vérac to Vergennes, No. 22, 8 June 1781.

directed against the Porte.[19] He had welcomed the hitch over the alternative and hoped that the Emperor's pretensions would disgust the Empress and make her give up the treaty.[20] In reality he found it hard to believe that the negotiations had been broken off on what appeared to be such trivial grounds.[21] But Vérac, less penetrating than Harris and perhaps less well supplied with money, continued to assert that the alternative had been the only cause which had prevented, as he believed, the conclusion of the treaty, and as late as September 1781 he was still insisting that "le traité est rompu à la vérité." [22]

The loudest sigh of relief came however from Potsdam, for it was, as may be expected, on Prussia and Panin that these negotiations had the greatest effect.[23] Relations between the Empress and Panin had been growing steadily worse since the visit of the Emperor in the spring of 1780. It is symptomatic of Catherine's attitude to Panin that she did not hesitate to conduct the negotiations over Minorca behind his back and solely through Potemkin. The arrival of the Emperor's proposals for a treaty between Austria and Russia had spelled the deathblow to Panin's influence. "Panin ne se hazarde plus à parler à sa souveraine sans y être appelé," wrote Goertz to Frederick on 19 December 1780.[24] Panin did not dare openly to oppose the Austrian proposals, since he knew the Empress to have the alliance at heart.[25] He concealed his distress at first from Goertz and even denied to him the existence of such a plan. But an emotional scene with the Grand Duke Paul, and Panin's mysterious urgings to Goertz to keep calm, aroused the Prussian envoy's suspicions.[26] Frederick at first simply refused to believe in Goertz's information. Goertz's alarm was "prématurée

19. CP Russie, *106*, Vergennes to Vérac, No. 10, 18 March 1781.

20. CP Russie, *106*, Vergennes to Vérac, No. 12, 7 April 1781.

21. CP Russie, *106*, Vergennes to Vérac, No. 18, 9 June 1781.

22. CP Russie, *107*, Vérac to Vergennes, No. 35, 10 September 1781.

23. *PKFG, 45*, 537, Goertz to Frederick, 8 June 1781; p. 547, the same to the same, 12 June 1781; p. 539, Frederick to Goertz, 23 June 1781; "Jamais nouvelle plus agréable ne pouvait me parvenir que celle de la rupture de la négociation entre les deux cours impériales . . ."

24. *PKFG, 45*, 147, Goertz to Frederick, 19 December 1780.

25. Maykov, *Pis'ma A. A. Bezborodka*, p. 72, Bezborodko to Rumyantsev, 25 January/5 February 1781.

26. *PKFG, 45*, 158, Goertz to Frederick, 22 December 1780, p. 227, the same to the same, 23 January 1781.

et outrée," he wrote: he could not credit that Catherine "se laisse embéguiner" by Austria and thought that the Grand Duke's and Panin's emotion must be due to distress at Prussia's exclusion from the mediation.[27] Little by little Frederick had to acknowledge that he might be losing his ally, and he then blamed Goertz for having failed to win over Potemkin.[28] He even agreed to the painful necessity of spending money and approved Goertz's proposal of buying, by means of a pension of up to 2,000 roubles, the secretary "du secretaire de cabinet." [29] This was possibly the same gentleman who had accepted £1,600 from Harris.

Panin's position meanwhile was becoming impossible. From January onwards he almost ceased to see the Empress though he continued to transact business on her instructions. He let it be known however that he opposed a treaty which would overthrow the existing Russian political system and that rather than put his name to it he would retire to the country.[30] To Goertz he declared, "je ne souillerai pas ma main par la signature." [31] Meanwhile the Empress was piling up grievances against her minister. In her irritation against Panin she was heard to say: "cet homme devroit sentir qu'il n'est plus bon à rien; je ne le supporte plus et il serait bien temps qu'il songeât à demander sa retraite." [32] Catherine now concentrated the business of foreign affairs in the hands of Bezborodko and Osterman, and both Harris and Vérac were convinced that she was trying to drive Panin into voluntary resignation, since she could not face as yet the task of dismissing a man who had served her for a long time.[33]

It is true that since the dawn of the Neutral League Panin had not been acting in strict loyalty to the Empress's purpose and had evidently frequently given a turn to her words and actions in his dealings with Harris, Vérac, and Goertz which the Empress may

27. Ibid., 228, Frederick to Goertz, 6 February 1781.

28. Ibid., 402, Frederick to Goertz, 21 April 1781; p. 403, to Finckenstein, 21 April 1781.

29. Ibid., 464, Frederick to Goertz, 15 May 1781; see also p. 466, note.

30. CP Russie, 106, Vérac to Vergennes, No. 15, 24 April 1781.

31. PKFG, 45, 401, Goertz to Frederick, 6 April 1781.

32. CP Russie, 106, Vérac to Vergennes, No. 15, 24 April 1781.

33. Ibid.; see also FO 65/2, Harris to Stormont, No. 41, 13/24 March 1781 (MD, 1, 405), No. 5, 23 April/4 May 1781 (MD, 1, 415).

not have intended. Moreover since autumn 1780 he had been engaged in a plot with Goertz and the Grand Duke and Grand Duchess to counter a project of the Empress to marry the sister of the Grand Duchess to the heir of Joseph II, Francis of Tuscany. Knowing nothing of these intrigues, the Empress pressed on with her plan, and by the end of April 1781 the grand-ducal couple and Panin were in a state of terror at the forthcoming inevitable revelation of their duplicity. This perhaps hastened Panin's desire to remove himself from St. Petersburg before the storm burst.[34]

In spite of his many protestations to the contrary, Harris cannot be acquitted of intriguing to the best of his ability, which was considerable, to procure the fall of Panin.[35] His letters to Potemkin,[36] his attack on Panin during his interview with the Empress, the reports which he undoubtedly circulated in St. Petersburg that Panin had provoked Bernstorff's fall, testify to the virulent campaign he waged against the minister. In his letters home he accused Panin of even more serious crimes. He had frequently accused him of taking money. He now charged Panin with sitting up at night "composing supposititious letters, calculated to hurt his enemies and serve his friends," which he then produced for the Empress's perusal as intercepts from dispatches.[37] However Harris might pro-

34. The progress of these negotiations and intrigues can be followed in *PKFG*, *44* and *45*, and in the correspondence of the Empress with Joseph, Joseph and Cobenzl, and Joseph and the Archduke Leopold.

35. For example, "I can safely say that Count Panin . . . can accuse me neither of inattention nor of uncandid opposition" (FO 65/2, Harris to Stormont, No. 41, 13/24 March 1781). See however *MD, 1*, 535, letter from Harris to Grantham, 16/27 August 1782, in which Harris accuses Panin of accusing him of setting fire to the Russian fleet, and of endeavouring to poison the grand-ducal family by means of geraniums.

36. See, for instance, when Panin denied having had any hand in thinking up the Neutral League, Harris's letter to Potemkin of May 1780: "Vous voyez mon Prince comme ce langage est insidieux et comme il est aisé, à moins que vous le prevenez, qu'il engage l'impératrice dans une démarche la plus nuisible à l'Angleterre et la plus opposée à ses premières intentions. Il travaille à cela avec une activité dont je ne le croyois pas capable, et s'applaudit de plus en plus de s'être pris d'une façon qui a trompé votre pénétration et qui détruit l'effet de votre influence" (Harris Papers).

37. FO 65/2, Harris to Stormont, No. 41, 13/24 March 1781 (*MD, 1*, 405). Harris also accuses Panin of bribing people to convince the Empress that his services were essential. See also his *en clair* letters to Keith, sent by Austrian couriers, in which he multiplied his attacks on Frederick II and on his "chief agents" in Russia, whom

test that "I never attacked him in that dark way he attacked me," it was believed by many in St. Petersburg that the British envoy belonged to the "cabale affreuse" which was supposed to have ousted Panin, a cabal led by Potemkin and supported by Bezborodko, Cobenzl, and from within the college of foreign affairs by Bakunin (who was suspected of receiving money from Harris [38]), with the aim of putting the nonentity Osterman at the head of foreign affairs.

In the hope that absence might mollify the Empress, Panin determined to withdraw from court for a while. But before retiring to his country estates, he performed one last service for Prussia by completing the negotiations for Frederick's accession to the Neutral League. Russia had fallen in with the Prussian desire to avoid naval expense and naval entanglement, and on 16 March 1781 a formal communication was made to Goertz of Russian agreement to support Prussian claims against the belligerents with her diplomacy and to protect Prussian shipping on the high seas.[39] Frederick would have been content with merely making a declaration of the principles of neutral navigation and trade, now that his ships were assured of Russian protection. But Russian pressure was brought to bear on him to become a full member, and on 23 April 1781 he addressed a fulsome letter to the Empress, expressing his intention to "profiter pour le petit commerce de ce pays de la protection que Votre Majesté Impériale daigne si généreusement lui accorder." [40] Formal negotiations began on 4 May, the convention

---

he named as among others Panin, Bakunin, and Alopeus, "and a tribe of other runners . . . whose names are unknown and who ought never to be heard of but when on the gallows" (see Add. MSS., 35.520 passim, and in particular 35.521, f. 36, Harris to Keith, 10/21 January 1781).

38. CP Russie, *106*, Vérac to Vergennes, No. 15, 24 April 1781; Beer and Fiedler, *Joseph II und Graf Ludwig Cobenzl, 1*, 150, Cobenzl to Joseph II, 23 May 1781; Harris believed Bakunin to be in the pay of France and Prussia (see FO 65/3, Harris to Stormont, No. 95, 25 June/6 July 1781).

39. *PKFG, 45*, 198, Finckenstein and Hertzberg to Frederick, 20 January 1781; see also F. de Martens, *Recueil, 6*, 109 and CP Russie, *106*, copy enclosed in Vérac to Vergennes, No. 14, 10 April 1781.

40. Krauel, "Preussen und die bewaffnete Neutralitaet," pp. 120 ff.; *Sbornik, 20*, 392. Frederick had been seeking a suitable opportunity to renew his personal correspondence with Catherine, which had lapsed for some time, but he had been wary of mentioning political topics to her. His accession to the Armed Neutrality provided him with the opening he needed, but it led nowhere. (See *PKFG, 45*, passim for his reflections on the subject.)

between Prussia and Russia was signed on 19 May 1781, and ratifi-
cations were exchanged on 29 June 1781.[41] Prussia acceded however with Russia alone and not as yet with the other members of
the League. Four days after the signature of the Russian-Prussian
convention, Panin left the capital for his estates in the country; he
did not however abandon all interest in public business, for he remained in touch with his subordinates at the college of foreign affairs.[42]

The admission of Prussia to the Armed Neutrality bewildered
Harris completely. It seemed to him incredible that at a time when
Russia was negotiating a treaty of alliance with Austria, she should
thus cement her connexion with Prussia, and, in view of the evident
impasse in May in Austro-Russian relations, he feared that this
signified a revival of Prussian influence. On a broader view, he
dreaded that Prussian ships transporting naval stores to the Bourbons would be deliberately encouraged to provoke incidents with
British ships, or would seek capture, in order to enable Frederick
to create trouble for Britain by calling on Russia and the Baltic
powers for protection.[43] He was reassured by Potemkin who, trifling
as usual with the truth, declared that "the Empress was tormented
into it by the King of Prussia's importunities; that she consented
merely to get rid of him, and now sets so little esteem on her once
favourite League that she was ready to admit even the Electors
Palatine and Saxony if they asked it of her." The Prince assured
Harris that Frederick was moved to accede by no other motive than
"to have some ostensible mark to produce of his influence not being sunk here." [44]

Potemkin in fact came much nearer than Harris to a true understanding of Frederick's motives in joining the League. His real

41. For the negotiations, see Krauel, "Preussen und die bewaffnete Neutralitaet,"
pp. 131 ff.; F. de Martens, *Recueil, 6,* 109 ff.; the text of the treaty is printed in Scott,
Armed Neutralities, p. 397. By Article 3 of the treaty Prussia claimed the right to
define contraband according to Articles 10 and 11 of the Anglo-Russian treaty of
1766. A declaration on navigation and commerce was issued by Frederick II on
30 April 1781 in which he claimed the right to apply the principles of the Neutral
League to his ships (ibid., p. 391).

42. CP Russie, *106,* Vérac to Vergennes, No. 18, 22 May 1781; *AMON, 2,* p. 486,
van Heeckeren to Prince of Orange, 22 May 1781.

43. FO 65/2, Harris to Stormont, No. 69, 30 April/11 May 1781 (*MD, 1,* 420);
No. 72, 7/18 May 1781; Harris found Potemkin's "levity" on the subject very painful.

44. FO 65/3, No. 79, 18/29 May 1781, Harris to Stormont.

anxiety at the friendship between Austria and Russia led him to clutch at any expedient to increase or simply maintain his hold on Russia. The Neutral League itself did not inspire him with much confidence, though he did not hesitate to make use of it for Prussian trade. But Russian behaviour towards the Dutch Republic confirmed him in the view that the Empress did not intend to carry its political principles into execution.[45]

Frederick II might bewail the departure of Panin; Harris welcomed it, but still believed that the Russian minister would be able to exercise his baleful influence from a distance.[46] Vergennes too was not at all happy about events in St. Petersburg. He had not welcomed the joint mediation. He positively disliked the idea of a treaty between Austria and Russia.[47] As for the Empress's offer of her sole mediation to Holland and Britain, he regarded it as "un piège tendu par l'Angleterre" to evade action by the Neutral League, as he wrote to Vérac on 25 February 1781. The news that Panin was about to withdraw from the scene filled him with apprehension. He realized that Panin was the main bulwark of France in St. Petersburg and feared that his disappearance would lead to the complete ascendancy of Austria. He expressed his forebodings to Montmorin in Spain on 14 May 1781: "La cour de Russie, désormais en proie au choc de passions d'autant plus effrénées qu'elles seront peut-être plus viles, pourra bien ne plus être qu'un théâtre de contradiction, d'injustice et d'ineptie. En voilà assés sur cette dégoutante matière." [48]

The conclusion of the agreement between Russia and Austria led to an immediate revival of the joint imperial mediation. Though the dispute over the "alternative" had rendered impossible any public *démarches* between January and May 1781 certain steps had been taken to prepare the way. Owing to the peculiar manner in which the mediation arose—an invitation extended by Britain to Austria to join in a mediation with Russia, which Russia had not in fact offered—the initiative clearly lay with Austria.

45. *PKFG, 45,* 549, Frederick to Goertz, 26 June 1781.
46. FO 65/2, Harris to Stormont, No. 65, 23 April/4 May 1781 (*MD, 1,* 415).
47. CP Russie, *106,* Vergennes to Vérac, No. 12, 7 April 1781.
48. CP Russie, *106,* Vergennes to Vérac, No. 8, 25 February 1781; Doniol, *Histoire,* 5, 9.

Kaunitz had first secured Russian agreement to Austrian participation and the consent of France to a mediation which in fact, if not in form, he was offering in the name of both powers. The King of Spain, meanwhile, had put a fresh spoke in the wheels. On 20 December 1780 Zinovyev had communicated to Floridablanca the conventions of the Neutral League and the *insinuation verbale*.[49] In his reply Floridablanca declared that Spain must use the means which Providence had placed to hand, in the shape of Richard Cumberland, to pursue direct negotiations with Britain, but should these fail he would willingly have recourse to the Empress of Russia in the hope that she might eliminate unexpected obstacles. Floridablanca probably hoped that the revelation, which was of course no news to Russia, that Britain had opened direct and secret negotiations with Spain might make Russia think twice about pursuing the idea of mediation at that moment.[50]

Stormont at once saw that Spain was putting forward the Cumberland mission, this "phantom negotiation" as he called it, as a means of evading any Russian intervention between the belligerents and blaming the evasion on Britain. "To defeat this purpose . . . ," he wrote to Harris, "the phantom will be immediately removed, and Mr. Cumberland ordered to return." [51] Harris immediately communicated to the Russians the withdrawal of the Cumberland mission, presenting it as a further mark of his royal master's confidence in the Empress's good intentions.[52] Meanwhile on 28 January 1781 Count Joseph Kaunitz, Austrian ambassador in Madrid (a son of the Chancellor), made a formal offer of the joint services of the two imperial courts.[53] On 3 February Floridablanca signified to Joseph Kaunitz Spain's acceptance of the Austro-Russian mediation; [54] by March 1781 Cumberland had left Spain, and his somewhat singular diplomatic career was over.[55]

49. Danvila, *Historia*, 5, 343.

50. Ibid., Floridablanca to Normandez, 23 December 1780.

51. FO 65/1, Stormont to Harris, No. 11, 19 January 1781.

52. FO 65/1, Harris to Stormont, No. 26, 16/27 February 1781 (*MD, 1,* 389).

53. Danvila, *Historia*, 5, 346.

54. Ibid., Floridablanca to Kaunitz, 3 February 1781.

55. Ibid., 347, Floridablanca to Aranda (Paris), 6 February 1781; to Aguilar (Vienna) of the same day. Bemis, *Hussey-Cumberland Mission*, p. 117, does not apparently realize that it was fear of jeopardizing the Austro-Russian mediation and offending Russia that led to the recall of Cumberland.

It was Stormont who had introduced Austria into the mediation in the fond hope that Kaunitz too hankered after a revival of the "old system." But any such revival was far from Joseph's thoughts and from those of his chief minister. "Je suis convaincu et assuré que nos liaisons avec la France sont naturelles, avantageuses et préférables infiniment à celle de l'Angleterre," Joseph had written to Mercy Argenteau on 5 January 1781.[56] These words were perhaps merely meant to fortify Vergennes's dubious faith in the Austrian alliance. But from the beginning Austria had shown no partiality for Britain in the mediation and above all no sympathy for British insistence that the subject of America must be excluded from the discussions.[57] Panin, who had viewed the joint mediation with disfavour from the start, took for granted that the British exclusion of America from the negotiations was proof that Stormont had simply conjured up the mediation to distract the Empress from the Armed Neutrality.[58] Both Austria and Russia now brought pressure to bear on Britain on this issue. Kaunitz's formula, that "il ne fallait se demander réciproquement que des choses faisables et que l'on croirait pouvoir accorder si l'on était à la place de l'autre," [59] by itself quite unobjectionable, was incorporated into the instructions drafted for Simolin when the Empress at last, in mid-February, acknowledged Britain's invitation to her to mediate. But in addition the Empress stressed the necessity to "ménager la dignité de la France," a clear hint that France's treaty obligations must be respected.[60] Stormont seized at once on this "extraordinary and objectionable passage" in the Russian communication, which aroused his deepest suspicions and which he believed must have been inserted by Panin with the worst intent.[61] Kaunitz in turn pointed out to Keith that though Stormont's language on the peace

56. Arneth and Flammermont, Correspondance, I, 9.

57. Beer, Joseph I, Leopold II und Kaunitz, p. 29, Kaunitz to Joseph, 9 January 1781.

58. Cf. Maykov, Pis'ma A. A. Bezborodka, p. 80, Bezborodko to Rumyantsev, 29 July/9 August 1781; Beer and Fiedler, Joseph II and Graf Ludwig Cobenzl, I, 120, Cobenzl to Joseph, 19 February 1781.

59. Cf. p. 273 above, and Arneth, Joseph II and Katharina, p. 33, Joseph to Catherine, 10 January 1781.

60. FO 65/2, Simolin to Stormont, 11 March 1781; (see also FO 65/1, Harris to Stormont, No. 24, 12/23 February 1781).

61. FO 65/2, Stormont to Harris, No. 21, 13 March 1781.

terms was perfectly proper, it was scarcely conciliatory.[62] Stormont however stuck to his guns. The peace terms between the belligerents should be the only object of the negotiations, and an essential condition of the peace was the cessation of French assistance to the rebels.[63] It was small wonder that Kaunitz began to think that it would be very difficult to draft preliminaries acceptable to both sides.[64]

In the next few months no visible progress was made, though behind the scenes Kaunitz and Galitzin agreed on a series of preliminary points to serve as a basis for negotiations. But almost as soon as Joseph had finished copying out his treaty obligations to Russia, on 18 May 1781, the mediation came to life. On 21 May Kaunitz dispatched instructions to Mercy in Versailles and to the Austrian envoy in Great Britain, Count Belgioioso, to present the preliminary bases for negotiation, in conjunction with the Russian envoys to their respective courts.[65] As a result of their joint labours, Kaunitz and Galitzin proposed four articles: (1) that all proposals put forward by the belligerents should be discussed at Vienna, without exclusion, and that parallel discussions between Britain and the American colonies should take place at the same time in Vienna but without the intervention of either the mediators or the other belligerents; (2) that the separate peace between Britain and the colonies should only be signed at the same time as the general peace, both to be guaranteed by the mediators and, if thought advisable, by the neutrals; (3) that during the negotiations there should be a general armistice based on the status quo; (4) that once the preliminary bases were agreed, negotiations should start at once.[66]

62. FO 7/1, Keith to Stormont, No. 30, 28 February 1781; FO 7/2, the same to the same, No. 50, 7 April 1781.

63. Fortescue, *Correspondence of King George III*, 5, 203, Stormont to the King, 13 March 1781; FO 7/1, Stormont to Keith, No. 25, 16 March 1781.

64. FO 7/1, Keith to Stormont, No. 44, 31 March 1781.

65. Arneth and Flammermont, *Correspondance*, *1*, 35, Kaunitz to Mercy, 21 May 1781.

66. See Flassan, *Histoire*, 7, Bk. 7, p. 315. Existing printed sources do not show whether these four preliminary bases to serve for a negotiation originated in Austria or in Russia. It was generally assumed that Kaunitz had devised them and imposed them on the malleable Galitzin. It was even believed by Harris that the Empress Catherine had not seen them at all (see FO 65/3, Harris to Stormont, No. 98, 6/17 July 1781). But a letter from Kaunitz to Cobenzl. of 25 February 1781 (Beer and

In view of the frame of mind of the belligerents and their suspicion of the motives of the mediating powers, it was not surprising
that these preliminary bases should have struck both Stormont and
Vergennes as an intrigue designed to favour the other side. Towards
the end of May, Mercy and Khotinsky submitted the four points to
Vergennes, who received them with displeasure.[67] The French Minister had from the first objected to an armistice; he feared that
Britain would use the interval thus created to break up the Neutral
League and create new continental enemies for France.[68] That such
a proposal should be made was, he believed, a sign of the victory of
Britain in the struggle to influence the mediators. "Je pense que ce
n'est pas sur ce point là que les Anglois chicanneront," he wrote to
Montmorin on 31 May 1781. "L'armistice peut leur paroitre désir-
able parce qu'ils ont beaucoup plus à espérer qu'à craindre du
bénéfice du tems et des accidens qui en sont la suite." With real
insight Vergennes pointed out that the relation of the continental
powers to France could not be expected to improve; time was on
the side of Britain, for the favour with which the French cause was
now regarded was but the result of circumstances "que l'orgueil et
l'avidité des Anglois ont fait naitre [et] n'est pas le garant de la cessation de la jalousie dont l'Europe a été si longtems travaillée
contre la maison de Bourbon." Vergennes also objected to the article concerning the Americans, which was insufficiently precise
and did not specify that they were to appear as plenipotentiaries at
the congress.[69]

But if Vergennes was astounded at what seemed to him the victory of Britain in Russia and Austria, Stormont was horrified at
what seemed to him the complete ascendancy of France. Ever since

---

Fiedler, *Joseph II und Graf Ludwig Cobenzl, 1,* 127) suggests that the preliminaries
may have originated with Panin. Kaunitz here refers to "l'idée des préliminaires
que le comte Panin a imaginée et vous a confiée." It is not clear whether this
means that Panin merely proposed that preliminary bases should be drawn up or
whether he actually suggested the substance of these preliminaries. But in view
of his many discussions with Vérac on the subject, the second alternative is the more
likely. Though Kaunitz was generally blamed, this may still in reality have been
the effect of Panin's influence exercised from behind the scenes.

67. Arneth and Flammermont, *Correspondance, 1,* 37, note 1, Mercy to Kaunitz,
1 June 1781.

68. Doniol, *Histoire, 5,* 8, Vergennes to Montmorin, 26 March 1781.

69. Ibid., 11, Vergennes to Montmorin, 31 May 1781.

he had first heard from Harris, as far back as January 1781, that the mediators intended to propose a "general suspension of arms" [70] he had opposed it as "a snare in which France constantly endeavours to entangle us." A cessation of hostilities in America was impossible until the rebels had returned to their allegiance.[71] His observations to Harris, after Simolin and Belgioioso had submitted the four points to him on 1 June 1781, are almost incoherent in their bewilderment.[72] The Empress had known of the British peace terms since March at least, when the memorandum approved by the King had been delivered to her.[73] How could she now put forward articles which would give France as great an advantage "as she could expect to draw from a long series of victory?" How had such a plan come about? Was it by agreement with France and Spain? Had the Empress seen and approved these articles before they had been dispatched? "Nothing ever was more unexpected nor more unfortunate than this proposal," continued Stormont. He instructed Harris to work on the Empress through Potemkin and persuade her of the utter impossibility of Britain accepting such a plan, which must at present be completely declined.[74] In his stress and agitation, he failed to reply to the suggestion also made by Simolin that when the Dutch applied for it they could be included in the general mediation. More painful even to Stormont than this apparent Russian betrayal was his disappointment in Kaunitz. He blamed the Austrian Chancellor for the turn the mediation had taken: there must have been a secret understanding to sacrifice Britain to France.[75] He had been so shocked, wrote Stormont to Keith, that he could no longer regard Kaunitz as a friend. Kaunitz

70. FO 65/1, Harris to Stormont, No. 9, 15/26 January 1781 (MD, I, 377).

71. FO 65/1, Stormont to Harris, No. 18, 27 February 1781; FO 7/1, Stormont to Keith, No. 19, 27 February 1781.

72. FO 65/3, Simolin and Belgioioso to Stormont, 2 June 1781 (Belgioioso seems to have submitted his papers on 1 June; Simolin's are dated 2 June). See also Fortescue, *Correspondence of King George III, 5,* Stormont to the King, 1 June 1781: "It is really surprising to me that a Minister of Pce Kaunitz's sense and experience should entertain the least expectation of such articles being agreed to"; and FO 65/3, Stormont to Harris, No. 43, 12 June 1781.

73. See Ch. 12, p. 296; the King's peace terms, it will be recalled, had been communicated to Russia in the course of the Minorca negotiation.

74. FO 65/3, Stormont to Harris, No. 43, 12 June 1781.

75. FO 7/2, Stormont to Keith, No. 48, 12 June 1781; No. 49, 12 June 1781.

had deceived him; his desire that Vienna should share in the mediation, his silence on America until after the mediation had been set in motion, his obscure hints, and his general friendliness all bore the marks of "equivocation—to give it the gentlest name." Though he still favoured the restoration of British links with Austria, it was obvious now to him that Kaunitz did not share this view. Britain must in future rely on her own vigilance and exertions to secure a fair peace.[76] He hoped the mediation would now die out and without waiting to weigh the consequences, Stormont communicated on 14 June, Britain's rejection of the preliminary bases to the Austrian envoy.[77]

The Bourbon courts delivered their concerted reply only on 16 August in Versailles—a delay which may have been inspired on the Spanish side by the desire to see the Franco-Spanish expedition which was to reconquer Minorca well on its way, in order to make clear Bourbon objections to an armistice.[78] The Bourbon reply repeated Vergennes's objections to the lack of definition of the status of the American representatives and to the armistice.[79]

The rejection of the preliminaries by both sides was received in a spirit of complete indifference by the Emperor Joseph. No power, he believed, profited more than Austria from the continuation of the war, and as far as he was concerned it could go on for a long time. Austria's right to intervene at a more promising moment had been established, and he could afford to let matters rest.[80] The Empress Catherine had more at stake.

Harris had been informed of the proposed preliminaries on 14 June 1781 by Osterman, who had seemed certain of Britain's acceptance though he expressed doubts as to the Bourbons.[81] But as

76. FO 7/2, Stormont to Keith, No. 50, 12 June 1781.

77. FO 65/3, Stormont to Belgioioso, 14 June 1781; to Simolin, 15 June 1781.

78. The preliminaries were presented on 8 June 1781 by Zinovyev and Kaunitz to Floridablanca, who replied on 11 June that the Spanish reply would be concerted with France. The Spanish text of the agreed reply is dated 7 August 1781. (Danvila, *Historia, 5,* 350 ff.) The expeditionary force sailed on 22 July 1781 (ibid., 179).

79. Doniol, *Histoire, 5,* 24; *CP Russie, 106,* Vergennes to Vérac, 16 August 1781.

80. Arneth and Flammermont, *Correspondance, 1,* 26, Joseph to Mercy, 4 March 1781; p. 43, 6 June 1781; see also Beer, *Joseph II, Leopold II und Kaunitz,* p. 80, Kaunitz to Joseph, 8 July 1781.

81. FO 65/3, Harris to Stormont, No. 86, 4/15 June 1781.

it turned out the British rejection of the preliminary bases for negotiation was far more prompt than that of France. On 12 July 1781 Harris received copies of Stormont's answer, and shortly afterwards news from Simolin himself must have reached St. Petersburg.[82] Catherine expressed no surprise at the failure of the first positive steps taken by the mediators, and Harris assumed that she treated the mediation with indifference out of injured vanity at having been given an adjoint in the task.[83] In fact the Empress did not believe that the belligerents had yet been brought to the point of preferring peace talks to the chances of the battlefield.[84]

The joint imperial mediation indeed bore every sign of unreality from the beginning. France perhaps needed peace, but not one belligerent was prepared to prefer peace to victory in spite of all their fine words. Russia had been steadily putting forward her claims to be entrusted with the task of reconciling the belligerents not with any real hope or desire of achieving peace but with the aim of forestalling any demand for assistance, fortifying her neutrality, and increasing her prestige. By the time the offer was actually made to Russia, the death of Maria Theresa, coupled with the Emperor's overtures for an alliance, opened the door to a change of policy which might render the prolongation of the war more profitable. Austria had intervened with no intention of assisting either Britain or France but merely to strengthen her ties with Russia and to keep Prussia out of an international diplomatic manoeuvre.[85] Britain had conjured up the actual mediation in December 1780, but the extent of her reliance on its effectiveness is blatantly revealed by the fact that four days after the Emperor was invited to mediate she broke with the Dutch Republic. The mediation was simply a diplomatic manoeuvre to protect her from the possible angry championship of the Dutch by the Neutral League under the leadership of Russia. France had not expected a formal mediation to be launched at the time but found it impossible to refuse

82. FO 65/3, Harris to Stormont, No. 97, 2/13 July 1781.

83. FO 65/3, Harris to Stormont, No. 103, 14/25 July 1781 (*MD, 1*, 435, tacked on to No. 102 of the same date).

84. Maykov, *Pis'ma A. A. Bezborodka*, p. 77, Bezborodko to Rumyantsev, 23 June/ 4 July 1781.

85. Arneth and Flammermont, *Correspondance, 1*, 12, Joseph to Mercy, 10 January 1781.

the offers of her Austrian ally. Spain had entered the war for Gibraltar and Minorca and would not withdraw until an attempt at least had been made to secure her objects. Though Osterman might declare that the mediators "had taken the greatest pains to conciliate the answers of England, France, and Spain; and that the preliminaries now proposed were such as seemed to meet the nearest the ideas of the three courts," [86] in fact the ideas of the three courts could not be reconciled. But the Empress intended at least to keep the mediation alive, either in correspondence through her envoys or by means of the proposed congress at Vienna. Nothing could be settled without some decisive victory of one side or the other, but once the balance of forces had been changed the stronger would the more easily compel the weaker to peace.[87] In the meantime the British rejection of the preliminary bases put forward by the imperial mediators enabled the Empress to take up again the cause of the Dutch.

When the Empress heard, in April 1781, that Britain had refused her sole mediation with the Dutch, she agreed that this new quarrel should be submitted to the joint imperial mediators. In the following months she took steps to secure the agreement of Austria and the Dutch to this new course.[88] But before such agreement could be reached—the States General accepted only on 8 August—[89] Britain had rejected the first proposals made by the mediators in the war with the Bourbons; there now appeared to be no imperial mediation to which the Dutch quarrel could be referred. In addition Catherine had involved herself in April 1781 in a plan for common action, by means of "verbal hints," with her Baltic partners in the Neutral League, to bring pressure to bear on Britain for an armistice with the United Provinces.[90] Here again it took time

86. FO 65/3, Harris to Stormont, No. 86, 4/15 June 1781.

87. Maykov, *Pis'ma A. A. Bezborodka*, p. 80, Bezborodko to Rumyantsev, 29 July/9 August 1781.

88. *AMON*, 2, 543, Vauguyon to Vergennes, 3 July 1781; p. 546, 6 July 1781; Beer and Fiedler, *Joseph II und Graf Ludwig Cobenzl*, *1*, 150, Cobenzl to Joseph, 23 May 1781; Beer, *Joseph II, Leopold II und Kaunitz*, p. 104, Kaunitz to Joseph, 12 August 1781.

89. See Coquelle, *L'alliance franco-hollandaise*, p. 249.

90. See Ch. 12, pp. 310–11.

to concert joint measures, and nothing had as yet been said or done in June 1781 when Simolin reported from London the initial failure of the joint imperial mediation. The Empress now promptly took advantage of this development which left her again with a free hand. She may have been aware of the poor figure the League was cutting in the United Provinces and of the slighting remarks her policy had provoked.[91] Russia was also in a position to bring pressure to bear on Britain, for it was becoming more and more evident that the nation was divided about the policy being pursued by North in the name of the King. The Whigs had started the year by attacking the British declaration of war on the Dutch. Since Stormont could not publicly explain the true cause of the war, his defence was weak. The Whig attacks provided Catherine with plenty of good solid arguments in favour of her policy and in particular cast ridicule on the "pretended" treaty between Mr. van Berckel and Mr. Lee.[92] Neutral observers had long ceased to share the quite unwarrantable optimism which the British ministers still showed about the recovery of America. News from America itself did not support their illusions, and there is no doubt that Catherine for instance was influenced and irritated by the apparent gap between British pretensions and the realities—a feeling in which she was no doubt fortified by the onslaught which Fox delivered on the government on 12 June 1781.[93]

At the end of July, first Osterman and then even more strongly Bezborodko took up with Harris the question of Russian mediation with the Dutch. The Secretary hinted that the Empress had been irritated by Britain's haughty rejection of the preliminaries; she doubted that Britain would ever be able to subdue America, and, if so, Britain "might in the event, end by making much worse conditions for ourselves, than those now tendered to us." Harris as usual passionately denied the aspersion on the British character and delivered himself of the quaint remark that "unfortunately

91. *PKFG, 45,* 514: "Elle ne dit pas justement aux Hollandais: 'je vous abandonne', mais elle leur dit l'équivalent. En vérité toute cette affaire de la neutralité armée ne lui fait pas grand honneur . . ." (Frederick to Goertz, 10 June 1781).

92. See Christie, *End of North's Ministry,* pp. 248–50; *Parliamentary Register, 21,* 36 ff., notably the Duke of Richmond's speech in the House of Lords, 25 January 1781.

93. Christie, *End of North's Ministry,* pp. 261 ff.; *Parliamentary Register, 20,* 511. Debate on Fox's motion to stop the American war, 12 June 1781.

the greater part of Europe were biassed." Bezborodko agreed that
the Empress was "quelquefois trop exigeante," but he nonetheless
pressed on Harris the advisability of complying with Catherine's
proposal to revive the Dutch mediation.[94]

It was now Potemkin's turn to take up the subject. "The Prince,"
wrote Harris, "sees in as strong lights as your Lordship, or any of
His Majesty's Ministers, the many inconveniencies attending a dis-
tinct negotiation with Holland, and agrees with me in the almost
impossibility of its ever being attended with success, yet he assures
me so strongly is the Empress bent on trying its effects, that he will
not be responsible for the extremities to which she may go if we
continue to decline the tender of her good offices. *'Elle s'est piquée
au jeu,'* was his expression, *'et croit son honneur intéressé à donner
la paix aux Hollandois.'* " Having thus established his position as
the one man who understood and agreed with British policy but
was unfortunately unable to persuade his mistress to see things
the same way, Potemkin proceeded in his devious way to urge on
Harris the path Britain should follow. Britain should accept the
Russian offer and put forward her terms in the form of an ultimatum admitting of no alterations. Harris went on to quote Potemkin's words: "From this . . . it will result, either that you really
will have a good peace with the Dutch, or that they will not submit
to the terms proposed, and that the refusal of the Empress's mediation will come from them, not from you. Let your acceptance . . .
be full of unction, your terms with the Dutch may then be as hard
as you please to make them, they will not be felt here." Harris
appeared really somewhat taken aback by this too frank proposal.
But Potemkin urged "the necessity of conforming to characters and
circumstances, when the end to be obtained is not dishonorable
and of such importance." The Prince entreated Harris to recommend to his superiors at least "an affectation of compliance with
the Empress's offers" and assured him that a refusal would "irritate her to excess." [95]

94. FO 65/3, Harris to Stormont, No. 101, 14/25 July 1781. See also No. 103,
14/25 July 1781 and No. 102, 14/25 July 1781 (*MD, I,* 433) in which Harris quotes
Bezborodko as saying: should the Dutch refuse the new offer of mediation "the
continuation of the war will no longer be your fault; the motives of it will remain
with them; you will have done what the Empress wishes, and she will have dis-
charged her conscience towards the Republick."

95. FO 65/3, Harris to Stormont, No. 102, 14/25 July 1781.

Potemkin's verbal disloyalty to Catherine nearly always coincided with some serious divergence of views either about national or about personal affairs. At the moment there was undoubtedly tension between the two. Potemkin made frequent references to Catherine's fear of being drawn into a war. But he was not referring to the Anglo-French conflict. The key to his discontent lies in his explosive phrase to Harris: "The greatest blessing that could befall this Empire, and the only event which could restore the Empress to a due sense of her feelings is a Turkish war." His eyes had for some time been turned towards the south of Russia, where disturbances had occurred in the Kuban and the Turks were suspected of egging the subjects of the Khan on to rebellion.[96] Harris believed that Russia might intervene to support the Khan. Both he and Stormont disapproved of a renewal of Russian interest in this quarter, not merely because it might distract Russian attention from the European scene but above all because France might again seize the occasion to be officiously friendly.[97] Stormont urged Harris to do his utmost to discover the content of the secret Austro-Russian treaty; he suspected that it concerned the Porte and that, in order to prevent France from thwarting their plans, both Catherine and Joseph were favouring France at the expense of Britain.[98]

But Catherine was evidently being prudent, and the tension between her and the Prince was caused not so much by difference of aim as by disagreement on the timing and the best means of exploiting the new Austrian alliance. The Prince therefore allowed his ill humour and his frustration to find an outlet in his talks with Harris. He accused Catherine of having become timid and narrow-minded. "In all great objects which were held out to her, she suspected some deep selfish design in him who proposes them; or if she supposed him sincere, she saw only the perils, not the glory attending the attempt." It was this pusillanimity that had prevented her from accepting Minorca at British hands.[99] Catherine, he said, had "become suspicious of his designs, and jealous of his power"; he no longer had "that influence over her he once en-

96. See *Sbornik*, 27, 191, Catherine to Potemkin, 1/12 July 1781; 11/22 August 1781; cf. Nolde, *La formation de l'Empire russe*, 2, 156 ff. and 219 ff.; FO 65/3, Harris to Stormont, No. 104, 14/25 July 1781 (*MD, 1*, 438).

97. FO 65/4, Harris to Stormont, No. 121, 17/28 August 1781.

98. Ibid., Stormont to Harris, No. 57, 7 September 1781.

99. FO 65/3, Harris to Stormont, No. 104, 14/25 July 1781 (*MD, 1*, 438).

joyed." He required no stimulus from Harris and "was not so unambitious, as to let his sloth get the better of him, in moments when his influence might be importantly employed." [100] But in spite of his irritation with Catherine's prudence, Potemkin did not cease to urge on Harris exactly the kind of conduct which would lead Britain to appear to comply with all the Empress's wishes. "Never contradict her in the instant" he said. "Affect to accept her offers, to follow her councils, and if her offers and councils are incompatible with your interests or contrary to your opinions, wait an opportunity, in the course of the business, of imperceptibly deviating from them. I am reduced," added the Prince "to give you advice, for I cannot give you assistance." Harris realized that ill humour had led the Prince to exaggerate the defects of Catherine's character, but he believed the Prince's account to be fundamentally true. He believed him "disgusted exceedingly" and began to lend credence to the idea that the Prince was planning to retire.[101]

Meanwhile news of the joint *démarche* of Russia, Denmark, and Sweden in favour of the Dutch, planned as far back as April 1781, had percolated to England and caused considerable alarm. This news coupled with the report of Prussia's accession to the Neutral League led Stormont to believe that Frederick's influence in Russia must still be very great and that it did not depend simply on Count Panin. He instructed Harris in June to sound Potemkin unofficially and find out what lay behind this rumour.[102]

Harris had already mentioned to Stormont Catherine's intention of making a verbal *démarche* jointly with the other original members of the League, and he did not attach much importance to this move. But now he felt it necessary to seek fresh information and broached the subject with Bezborodko, who was increasingly becoming the channel through whom he conducted business and who rose daily in Harris's estimation.[103] It was true, Bezborodko said, that the King of Sweden had proposed an armed mediation to

100. FO 65/3, Harris to Stormont, No. 103, 14/25 July 1781 (*MD, 1*, 435).
101. FO 65/3, Harris to Stormont, No. 104, 14/25 July 1781; see also No. 95, the same to the same, 25 June/6 July 1781.
102. FO 65/3, Stormont to Harris, No. 45, 26 June 1781.
103. See FO 65/2, Harris to Stormont, No. 61, 16/27 April 1781; No. 66, 27 April/ 8 May 1781; and FO 65/3, No. 92, 25 June/6 July 1781. On Bezborodko see e.g.

Russia. Russia had "scoff'd" at it, but, Bezborodko explained to Harris, in view of the repeated solicitations of the Dutch and because of the injury sustained by Russia as a result of the suspension of the Dutch trade the Empress had agreed to send an "exhortation amicale pour nous engager à nous accomoder avec nos anciens alliés." The measure had indeed originated in Panin's time, but orders were not to be sent to Simolin until the following week. However, if Britain accepted, as Bezborodko "ardently hoped" she would, the Empress's offer of sole mediation with Holland, the exhortation would become perfectly useless. But Harris had given Bezborodko an excellent opening, and he did not fail to make use of it. "So strenuously bent is my imperial mistress," he declared, "on inducing you to enter into a negotiation for peace with the Dutch, that I do not know how far she may go, nor whether she may not, in a moment of hastiness, subscribe to the King of Sweden's plan and you know," added he *she never retracts.*[104]

In a private dispatch to Stormont, Harris summed up his impressions and offered his recommendations. He considered the present moment as a crisis. If the British government accepted the sole mediation and it either resulted in a peace or threw the onus of a breakdown of the negotiations on the Dutch, "we certainly may fear no harm, if we can derive no good from hence." The only means of achieving this aim were "those my Friend proposed," and he believed this would satisfy the Empress. If the offer were declined for the same reasons as before, Harris was convinced that "however potent these reasons may be, however closely connected with the most essential welfare of Great Britain, that they will not be admitted as such by the Empress for . . . she will only hear her own passions and she will then enforce the *Exhortation* on a second attempt and possibly in an hour of ill humour be weak enough to subscribe to the French Swedish project." In a private letter Harris reinforced his words. He feared that Britain ran the risk, if she refused, of drawing down on her the united weight of the

FO 65/2, Harris to Stormont, No. 31, 26 February/9 March 1781: "and as I have every reason to think him well disposed, and perfectly honest and unprejudiced, I have much reliance on what he says." There are other passing tributes to Bezborodko in Harris's ciphered dispatches; they are therefore not merely meant to flatter the Secretary.

104. FO 65/3, Harris to Stormont, No. 106, 14/25 July 1781.

Neutral League. The solution was to accept the Empress's offer and then propose the only conditions on which peace could be made with the Republic.[105]

Harris had undoubtedly been under strong pressure from Osterman, Potemkin, and Bezborodko to urge acceptance of the Russian offer on his principals. Moreover the absence of Panin from the scene left him no reason to think that what he heard from three such diverse quarters was anything but the considered opinion of the Empress herself. But from the point of view of conciliating the Empress it was perhaps a mistake to suggest that the best course for all parties was to follow Potemkin's proposals and put forward terms that were tantamount to an ultimatum. Why Potemkin proposed this plan is a riddle. Was he getting tired of being constantly involved in Britain's problems? Was it just a suggestion thrown off to avoid Harris's importunities? Was it merely the result of a momentary peevishness towards the Empress? It is impossible to tell. He had certainly never shown any enthusiasm for the Neutral League and its principles. Yet at a time when Catherine was in a mood to dwell on any signs of English "roideur et froideur" it was surely tactless to submit terms on which no negotiation was to be admitted. Catherine now belonged to that majority of Europe who were unfortunately "biassed against England" as Harris put it. She believed that Britain could hold her own against the Bourbons but that America was lost. She had thought British rejection of the preliminaries put forward by the imperial mediators over hasty; the preliminaries seem to have appeared to her a fair effort at reconciling the pretensions of all parties. The Dutch mediation was much closer to her heart. Her prestige, her "conscience," and her trade were all involved. Was she likely to consent to act simply as an intermediary, imposing Britain's terms on Holland, instead of as a mediator gradually bringing both sides together?

105. FO 65/3, Harris to Stormont, No. 107, private, undated but presumably 14/25 July 1781; letter of Harris to Stormont, 14/25 July 1781, *MD, 1,* 441 (not in P.R.O.).

14. The Dutch Mediation Resumed

TOWARDS the end of August 1781 Harris's account of the renewal
of the Russian offer to mediate between Britain and Holland
reached Stormont.[1] A few days later the Russian, Danish, and
Swedish envoys in London made a joint *démarche*, as members of
the Neutral League, in favour of the United Provinces. It was not
an offer of mediation on behalf of the League, but Simolin, supported by his Danish and Swedish colleagues, urged Great Britain
"à se prêter aux intentions pacifiques que les États Généraux ont
fait connoitre tout récemment par leur consentement à entendre à
une negociation de paix." The accession of the States General to
the League made them allies of the three Northern courts, who
could not view with indifference the harmful effects of this new
quarrel on trade. If peace was also the wish of Great Britain, the
first step was to agree on a suspension of arms, since military operations were bound to hamper the progress of negotiations.[2]

Coming on top of Harris's dispatches, the *insinuation verbale*
made by Simolin seriously disturbed Stormont. He called for a
detailed examination of this new development by the cabinet,
which was summoned for 6 September 1781. Stormont feared that

1. Fortescue, *Correspondence of King George III, 5,* 367, Stormont to the King,
25 August 1781; FO 65/4, Stormont to Harris, No. 50, 28 August 1781. Harris had
sent his dispatches under flying seal via Vienna, and Keith on his own initiative
took steps to ascertain whether the Emperor would have any objection to Britain's
acceptance of the Russian sole mediation with the United Provinces, in view of the
fact that this dispute had only just been referred to the imperial mediators as well.
(See FO 7/3, Keith to Stormont, No. 101, 10 August 1781). Austrian consent was
communicated by Keith on 20 August. (Ibid., No. 107 to Stormont).

2. FO 65/4, *insinuation verbale* by Simolin, 31 August 1781; FO 22/2, ditto by
Dreyer, 31 August 1781; *Annual Register,* 1781, p. 317, ditto by Nolcken, n.d. This
démarche was also communicated to the States General by Galitzin (*AMON,* 2, 617,
Vauguyon to Vergennes, 21 August 1781).

if the Empress's offer were refused again she might draw down upon Britain the whole weight of the Neutral League. The wisest and most dignified course would be to stand by the previous refusal and accept the consequences, if Britain had strength enough to hold out against so many enemies even for one campaign. But the Northern powers could injure Britain in a vital spot by cutting off naval stores; moreover an extension of the war would probably lead to a recognition of the Americans as an independent state by the Northern powers, followed in turn by Holland and Prussia. If the mediation were accepted, such a rupture could not take place. Besides the Empress's attention would be distracted from the joint imperial mediation, from which no good could be expected.[3] Acceptance of the Russian mediation also provided a means of waving aside the *insinuations verbales* made by Russia, Sweden, and Denmark as members of the Neutral League. Not realizing how long ago this measure had originated, Stormont was excessively puzzled as to "what it is that induced the court of Petersburg to engage, I may say force the courts of Denmark and Sweden to join in an application which the Empress wished not to succeed in the shape proposed . . ." But in his view, if a separate peace was to be negotiated, "the secret offer the Empress made of her sole mediation was to be accepted in preference to the ostensible one." [4]

The cabinet followed Stormont's advice, and fresh instructions for Harris were accordingly drawn up by the Secretary of State. Stormont clearly regarded the solution arrived at as a choice between two evils and expected no good to come of it, but he was influenced by Harris and above all Potemkin. "You see that the resolution taken is such as you desired," he wrote to Harris. "The sum of your dispatches, backed by the weight of Prince Potemkin's opinion, greatly influenced the decision upon this difficult point . . . Prince Potemkin's advice is followed in communicating to the Empress our ultimatum." This compliance with Russian wishes, at a time when Britain had completely lost faith in the Empress's

3. HMC, Marquess of Abergavenny MS., John Robinson's Correspondence, No. 383, Report X, Pt. vi, p. 44, Stormont to Lord North, 2 September 1781.

4. FO 7/3, Stormont to Keith, No. 69, 14 September 1781; for Stormont's replies to Denmark and Sweden, referring them to the pacification about to be undertaken by Russia alone, see FO 22/2, Stormont to Dreyer, 17 September 1781, and *Annual Register*, 1781, p. 318, Stormont to Nolcken, 18 September 1781.

professions of good will, shows the extent of Britain's fear of Russian displeasure. As Stormont sadly commented, at the beginning of the war Britain had regarded Catherine's indifference to its outcome as an evil and endeavoured to rouse her from it; but every step she had taken had been such as tended to increase Britain's difficulties, and "happy would it have been for this country, if, like an Eastern Monarch she had slept upon her throne." [5]

The British peace terms were not put forward with any hope or intention that the Dutch would accept them. The first demand was of course satisfaction for the affront of the Laurens treaty, since this was the official cause of the quarrel. The Dutch were also to undertake to give no help to the rebels, to turn out their agents, cease their loans, and refuse admittance to American war or merchant ships. All treaties were to be renewed with the exception of the Marine Treaty of 1674 which was to be revised. The States General were to recognize the present war with France as a *casus foederis* of the Anglo-Dutch alliance and were to give compensation instead of succours. They were to carry no naval stores or munitions to the enemy. If the States General agreed to give either succours or compensation then British conquests would be returned; otherwise negotiations would be based on the *uti possidetis,* and restitution would be considered only at the general peace. The States General were also to bind themselves to expel all French troops from Dutch possessions. A suspension of arms would only take place after the signing of the preliminaries.[6] According to Stormont these peace terms were fair and moderate, and "if the Empress endeavours to draw us from that ground she will not succeed, be the consequences what they may." [7] How small was the reliance Stormont placed on the mediation is revealed by his subsequent manoeuvre. He did not communicate the British peace terms to Simolin but sent them direct to Harris with instructions to present them the moment Simolin's courier arrived, so that the Empress would not have time to think up proposals of her own.[8] And yet some tiny forlorn hope

5. See FO 65/4, Stormont to Harris, No. 54, 7 September 1781, *MD, 1,* 446, cf. Fortescue, *Correspondence of King George III, 5,* 267, Stormont to the King, 25 August 1781.

6. FO 65/4, 7 September, communication confidentielle.

7. FO 65/4, Stormont to Harris, No. 54, 7 September 1781.

8. FO 65/4, Stormont to Harris, No. 60, 7 September 1781.

still seemed to linger at the back of his mind that Russia could be induced to stand forth for Britain. If past Anglo-Dutch treaties were renewed, he wrote to Harris, the King would be justified in asking the United Provinces for succours. Could not the Empress be persuaded to press this point on the Dutch and declare that she would come to their assistance if they were attacked "en haine" of their new policy? [9] In fact would not the Empress give a military guarantee to the British ultimatum?

August and September passed before Harris could receive his fresh instructions, but time did not hang on his hands. He was absorbed in the constantly changing scene in St. Petersburg, endeavouring to analyse the sympathies and discover the allegiances as the new Austrian orientation of Russian policy gradually took shape. The first visible sign of this new orientation (it must be remembered that Harris alone of the foreign envoys in St. Petersburg knew that the Austro-Russian agreement had been concluded) was the invitation extended by the Empress to Joseph to join the Neutral League. On 3 August Cobenzl wrote to Joseph recommending that the invitation should be accepted. He feared that Prussia would now intrigue to transfer the task of mediating to the Neutral League, of which Prussia was a member. By acceding to the League, the Emperor would ensure that Catherine "ne pourroit absolument se mêler des affaires générales de l'Europe, que de concert" with the Emperor. [10] Kaunitz and Joseph both pretended to regard Austria's accession as ridiculous and useless, and they resented appearing to be dragged in in Prussia's train. [11] But in spite of his reluctance Joseph now felt himself committed to Russia, and he gave in. "Ce que femme veut, Dieu le veut," he wrote resignedly to Cobenzl on 19 August 1781 and instructed him to begin negotia-

9. FO 65/4, Stormont to Harris, No. 53, 7 September 1781; Stormont did advise Harris to press this line "discreetly."

10. Beer and Fiedler, *Joseph II und Graf Ludwig Cobenzl, 1,* 185, Cobenzl to Joseph, 3 August 1781.

11. Beer, *Joseph II, Leopold II und Kaunitz* p. 104, Kaunitz to Joseph, 12 August 1781; though Joseph spoke slightingly of the Neutral League, he could be roused to fury by British treatment of Austrian shipping. See his letter to Belgioioso of 3 July 1781: "Si elle [Great Britain] croit . . . qu'elle peut insulter mon pavillon, voler et pirater sur mer mes negocians à bon plaisir elle se trompe fort . . ." (Calvi, *Lettere dell' imperatore Giuseppe II al conte . . . di Belgiojoso,* p. 430).

tions.[12] Austrian accession formally took place on 30 October 1781; the vexed problem of the alternative was easily avoided, for Joseph acceded with Russia alone and the treaty took the form of an act of accession and an act of acceptance respectively. In addition the two powers exchanged declarations that they would, in their capacity as mediators, press for the universal adoption of the maritime principles of the League.[13]

Austrian accession to the Neutral League represented a further blow to Prussian influence in St. Petersburg, and the hopes of the Prussian party were now pinned to the return of Count Panin from the country. Harris was particularly disturbed at this prospect, for, though Potemkin assured him repeatedly that Panin would never return to power, Harris believed that the Prince, out of jealousy of the rising influence of Bezborodko, might be persuaded to support his former enemy.[14] Potemkin himself had for some time avoided political discussions with Harris. When at last the British envoy was able to pin him down and ask the cause of his apparent neglect of Britain's concerns, Potemkin assured Harris that his principles remained unchanged, but if he did not do more for England it was because he met with "a resistance and opposition I am not used to. So far from speaking too little, I am afraid I have done you harm in speaking too often." Harris at last began to doubt the value to him of Potemkin's friendship, and he feared that "some new project which he has got into his head has given him new ideas." Potemkin was in fact deeply absorbed in his new Turkish plans and in Panin's absence probably saw no reason to continue his championship of Harris.[15]

12. Beer and Fiedler, *Joseph II und Graf Ludwig Cobenzl, 1,* 196, Joseph to Cobenzl, 19 August 1781.

13. See F. de Martens, *Recueil, 2,* 120 ff. Scott, *Armed Neutralities,* p. 403, Act of Accession of the Emperor; p. 406, Act of Acceptance of the Empress; p. 409, Declaration by the Empress; p. 405, Declaration by the Emperor. The Emperor also adopted the relevant articles of the Anglo-Russian treaty of 1766.

14. FO 65/4, Harris to Stormont, No. 119, 13/24 August 1781.

15. FO 65/4, Harris to Stormont, No. 123, 24 August/4 September 1781. A vivid picture of Harris's relations with Potemkin is given by Harris in a letter to his wife of 20/31 August 1781; he had been dining with the Prince at his palace, with "that walking drunkard chevalier de la Teysonniere . . . at six a regiment was reported to be on the march through the Perspective—our breeches were put on, our nightgown put off and we all attended to inspect its passage." (Merton Papers).

In spite of the favourite's reluctance to discuss politics with him, Harris continued to urge him not to allow Panin to return to power. Potemkin refused to be drawn, and assured Harris that all would be well.[16] Indeed he was once more revealing his remarkable talent for dissimulation, for he must already have been aware of the Empress's decision in the matter. On 2/13 September 1781 Catherine sent an order to the vice-chancellor, Osterman, instructing him in future to conduct the business of the college of foreign affairs alone. The instruction was nicely timed by Catherine to coincide with Panin's return to the capital and came as a bitter blow to him. Potemkin himself affected "to disapprove the harshness of the measure," though he admitted that he thought it just. In conversation with Harris, he flattered the latter by attributing to him an important share in Panin's final disgrace. The Empress, he said, had been influenced against Panin by what Harris had told her in their second private interview, and while her mind was still wavering Potemkin had repeated to her the gist of his recent conversation with Harris.[17]

Harris's great object was now achieved; Panin was publicly disgraced and deprived of the conduct of foreign affairs. But he was not deprived of his place on Catherine's unofficial Council of State; and he enjoyed the full confidence of the Grand Duke Paul and his wife and was therefore supported by all those surrounding the young court who pinned their hopes of favour and advancement on a new reign. He was in fact to make one more desperate effort to assert his ascendancy and give Harris an opportunity to exercise to the full his not inconsiderable powers of intrigue and his love of drama. Sometime in June 1781 plans had been drawn up for the Grand Duke and his wife to undertake an extensive foreign tour. The journey had been carefully devised by Catherine in conjunction with Joseph II in order to cement their secret alliance. The couple, who were to depart in September, were

16. FO 65/4, Harris to Stormont, No. 126, 31 August/11 September 1781; Beer and Fiedler, *Joseph II und Graf Ludwig Cobenzl, I*, p. 218, Cobenzl to Joseph, 12 September 1781.

17. See Maykov, *Pis'ma A. A. Bezborodka*, p. 87, Bezborodko to Rumyantsev, 5/16 September 1781. The *ukaz* to Osterman was dated 29 August/9 September but appears to have been issued only on 2/13 September; cf. FO 65/4, Harris to Stormont, No. 131, 7/18 September 1781 (*MD, I*, 449).

to be delivered to an exclusively Austrian entourage in Vienna and Florence. Berlin was pointedly excluded from the tour.[18]

Panin of course understood clearly the purpose of the visit, and he did his best to persuade the young couple against the journey. First he inspired them with doubts about the forthcoming inoculation of their children against the smallpox. Not satisfied with unsettling the maternal feelings of the Grand Duchess, he dropped hints that the Grand Duke would not be allowed to return to Russia and that he would be disinherited. The history of the succession to the Russian throne was sufficiently highly coloured to render this prospect not improbable to the mentally unstable Paul. The young couple were so impressed that they announced to Catherine on 24 September that they would not leave until the children had recovered from their inoculation, and they refused to appoint a date. On 27 September Harris had occasion to visit Potemkin, whom he found in a state of despondency, prepared to admit that the Empress would have to allow the journey to be postponed and a visit to Berlin included in the tour. At this news Harris took fire. He was determined that this last citadel of Prussian influence should be overthrown. He urged Potemkin that to give in now would be to grant Panin his greatest triumph and would justify the young couple in the suspicions they had been entertaining. The journey must be undertaken at once, and no change in the route allowed. This was a decisive moment which would determine the extent of Potemkin's influence. Potemkin listened to Harris, pacing up and down the room in silence and without making any reply. He then went up to the Empress and returned in an hour to tell Harris that all was settled. The Grand Duke and his wife were to leave on 1 October 1781. "Having effected this," wrote Harris, he then urged on Potemkin the necessity of putting it out of Panin's power to create such a scene again.[19] But Catherine herself had already determined on the

18. Catherine's and Joseph's plans can be followed in their letters; see Arneth, *Joseph II und Katharina*, passim.

19. See Harris's account of this crisis in FO 65/4, No. 137, 17/28 September 1781, and No. 156, 21 October/1 November 1781. (*MD, 1,* 460) where almost the whole of No. 156, and parts of No. 157 of the same date have been merged by the Editor. Harris's account is confirmed by Vérac, in CP Russie, *107,* Vérac to Vergennes, No. 38, 5 October 1781, and by Cobenzl, in Beer and Fiedler, *Joseph II und Graf Lud-*

necessary steps. Out of consideration for the Grand Duke they
were kept secret until the day of his departure, but on 1 October
Panin was required to give up his secretariat and his papers, and
he was informed that his seat on the Council of State was to be
regarded as purely honorary. Nothing could now restore the fallen
minister to power. "He may consider himself as laid down on a
bed of roses," wrote Harris of the disgraced Panin; "his sentence
would have been less mild if it had been pronounced by any of
the preceding sovereigns of Russia." [20]

Though Potemkin, ably seconded by Harris, had intrigued for
many months to secure the overthrow of Panin, to a great extent
the Foreign Minister was responsible for his own fall. Since the
winter of 1780 he had been secretly countering the Empress's
policy and intriguing behind her back with Prussia. He was finally
dismissed when the Empress reached the conclusion that he could
not be trusted to follow her policy and had in fact ceased to be
her servant. But the clue to Panin's behaviour and to his almost
hysterical attachment to the Prussian system lies in the character of
the Grand Duke Paul. For Panin to abandon Prussia meant the
loss of the confidence and friendship of Paul, and who could tell
when he would mount the throne? And what vengeance might he
not wreak on those who had carried out the Empress's new policy?
Some months later, Paul revealed his innermost thoughts in an
incautious outburst to Grand Duke Leopold of Tuscany directed
at Potemkin, Bezborodko, and other members of the pro-Austrian
party in St. Petersburg: "je les ferai ausruthen et je les casserai et
chasserai . . ." [21] In such circumstances Panin's deviations from

---

wig Cobenzl, 1, 237, Cobenzl to Joseph, 30 September 1781 and p. 243, 9 October
1781. Harris however is alone in ascribing the decision of the Empress to determine
the departure of the grand-ducal couple to his influence over Potemkin. Cobenzl
attributed her decision to a letter from the Emperor.

20. FO 65/5, Harris to Stormont, No. 156, 21 October/1 November 1781. Stormont
appears to have believed that Panin was attempting something in the nature of a
coup d'état and congratulated Harris on his exertions in this "dangerous crisis." See
Fortescue, *Correspondence of King George III*, 5, 508, Stormont to the King, 30
October 1781; cf. FO 65/5, Stormont to Harris, No. 71, 30 October 1781, and letter
of same date, *MD*, 1, 456.

21. Beer and Fiedler, *Joseph II und Graf Ludwig Cobenzl*, 1, 312, Joseph to Cobenzl, 13 June 1782.

the path of honesty become more comprehensible; there was more at stake for him than the present preservation of his post.

But the disgrace of Panin, when it came, proved by no means as satisfactory an event to Harris as he had hoped for. To begin with he observed that Potemkin by no means shared his own desire to hound the fallen minister. He advised Harris to keep up appearances with Panin and to avoid any expression of triumph at his disgrace. The Prince laughed away the suggestion that he himself might be concerned to revive Panin's prestige, but Harris was not quite convinced. He began to realize that, though Potemkin had contributed to Panin's fall, "he loves Mons. Bezborodko and his set still less," and he suspected that Potemkin might one day use Panin in order to sink Bezborodko.[22] After his connexion with foreign affairs had been finally severed on 1 October, Panin fell seriously ill with the shock of his sudden disgrace. Both the Empress and Potemkin were affected.[23] When Harris continued to urge that Panin should be completely eliminated from the scene Potemkin warned him quite openly that Panin's influence was already sunk so low "that it would be wanton oppression to sink it still lower, and that anything which looked like persecution was so repugnant to the Empress's feelings" that should "the Emperor" try to persuade her in that direction "it would produce an immediate change in her sentiments for him." As for himself, added Potemkin, "no consideration should ever make him serve as the instrument of such an order." [24] Potemkin referred to the Emperor, but the remark was meant for Harris.[25] Potemkin had in fact been

22. FO 65/4, Harris to Stormont, No. 131, 7/18 September 1781; No. 157, 21 October/1 November 1781.

23. See *Vosemnadtsatyy vek, 1,* 23, A. V. Kurakin to his brother, 24 September/5 October 1781, on Catherine's attitude to Panin at this time.

24. FO 65/5, Harris to Stormont, No. 174, 16/27 November 1781 (*MD, 1,* 475). "He then observed that if the Emperor had instructed his Minister to urge a still stronger persecution of this party or to use his own words, that it should be exterminated from the face of the earth, he acted neither generously nor wisely," Harris quotes Potemkin as saying.

25. Potemkin had, however, observed that Cobenzl shared Harris's anxiety at the fact that the Prince continued to show certain attentions to the fallen and sick minister. (See Beer and Fiedler, *Joseph II und Graf Ludwig Cobenzl, 1,* 243, Cobenzl to Joseph II, 9 October 1781.)

active in preventing the Empress from dismissing Panin completely from her service and ordering him to leave St. Petersburg,
much to Harris's astonishment and concern. It is somewhat strange
to find an English envoy so perturbed at the humane treatment
meted out to a fallen minister and urging penalties which, if they
had been applied in Britain, would have caused an unbelievable
uproar. As for Potemkin's motives in thus shielding his rival, Harris believed not only that he hoped to use Panin as a make-weight
to Bezborodko but that he hoped also by these means to ingratiate
himself with the Grand Duke Paul.[26] In this he was probably correct, though it is also true that Potemkin was not vindictive and
was a good enough psychologist to know that magnanimity would
appeal more to Catherine than persecution.

With the fall of Panin the game of political intrigue in St. Petersburg changed overnight, and new combinations arose. Osterman,
the vice-chancellor, was universally regarded as a nonentity; he
lacked courage, and his mind was inelastic. Though he dealt with
the foreign envoys, his reports to the Empress went through the
Secretary.[27] Thus Bezborodko became the natural centre of a new
grouping of those who opposed Potemkin on personal grounds. In
foreign affairs the Secretary and the Prince tended to think alike.

Harris had now to steer a cautious course between these two
men. He had so long been publicly regarded as attached to the
Prince that it was difficult for him to change his allegiance without offending Potemkin. But the Prince, tired of British affairs,
had now ceased to intervene with the Empress on Harris's behalf,
provided Harris with no information, grew inattentive if Harris
discussed political matters with him, and appeared perfectly indifferent to Britain's fate. Harris however still felt bound to appear attached to him, for he realized that though Potemkin would
do little to help he could do much to injure Britain's interests, and
he would be the first to take offence at any sign of neglect. Moreover Harris's personal standing at the Russian court would immediately decline if it were suspected that he was not supported
by Potemkin. Catherine herself was now no longer so friendly to
Harris, for, as he put it, "from not suffering the intrigues of my

26. FO 65/4, Harris to Stormont, No. 157, 21 October/1 November 1781.
27. FO 65/4, Harris to Stormont, No. 119, 13/24 August 1781.

enemies to pass over unnoticed, I have acquired the reputation of *intriguant:* a reputation I should be sorry to deserve, as I know none which so ill becomes an English Minister . . ." [28]

Harris's own position in Russia had begun to grow wearisome to him. As he wrote to his sister in July 1781, "I have done all that can be done, I have brought matters to a head, and if we are brought to bed of a mouse it is not my fault. We all expected a Lion sometimes to bite us, sometimes to roar for us, but no such animal appears, and no such is to be hoped for or to be feared." [29] The departure of his wife and family for England in the summer of 1781 reduced the attractions of St. Petersburg, and in a private letter which he sent by his brother-in-law, Sir Gilbert Elliot, who had been visiting him, he urged on Stormont his desire to leave Russia.[30] But Stormont would not hear of it: it would be very difficult, he wrote, to replace Harris, and, in almost threatening tones he added: "your returning at this time would not be ending your career in the manner in which after the distinguished figure which you have made there, it ought to end." [31]

The news of Panin's disgrace caused considerable confusion in the mind of Stormont. He had ascribed Russian unfriendliness to the influence of Prussia, exercised through Panin. Panin's power however had been declining visibly for some time, and yet there was no improvement. Wildly reaching out for some *point d'appui* for Britain in Russia, he dwelt on the possible consequences of the return of the Orlov brothers to St. Petersburg. "If they could so far return to favor as to have any influence on the councils of Petersburg," an alliance would, he believed, soon be secured.[32] A more pathetic misreading of St. Petersburg politics would be difficult to find; for, in view of the essentially personal nature of the power that the Orlovs had once enjoyed and that Potemkin enjoyed at the time, there could be no question of a reconcilia-

28. FO 65/5, No. 158, 21 October/1 November 1781 (*MD*, 1, 471, tacked on to No. 156).

29. Merton Papers, Harris to Gertrude Harris, 25 June/6 July 1781.

30. This private letter has not been preserved in the P.R.O., but its tenor emerges from Stormont's reply.

31. FO 65/4, Stormont to Harris, unnumbered, private, 19 October 1781.

32. FO 65/5, Stormont to Harris, No. 73, 2 November 1781; cf. also No. 80, 28 December 1781.

tion between them. The dismissal of Panin had in fact laid bare the mechanism of the Russian court, but both Harris and Stormont were too prejudiced to see it. Neither realized that the Empress was the mainspring of Russian policy.

In the midst of the turmoil caused by the disgrace of Panin, Stormont's courier arrived, bearing the news of Britain's decision to accept Catherine's sole mediation in the Dutch conflict.[33] When Harris handed the British ultimatum to Osterman, the Vice-Chancellor took it *ad referendum;*[34] time passed, and Harris received no reply. The British envoy soon realized that the Empress intended the brunt of the negotiation to be borne by Simolin in London and that he was being pushed aside.[35] Finally, on 31 October, Osterman handed to Harris a *note verbale,* which had already been dispatched to Simolin a week earlier and was delivered to Stormont on 24 November 1781.[36] The Empress refused to accept the British terms as an ultimatum. She declared her intention first to seek the agreement of the Dutch to her sole mediation and then to be informed of their terms. "Après les avoir examiné et comparé, et pas autrement, elle pourra entamer avec quelque espérance l'affaire même."[37] But Stormont would not move from his previous position, though he agreed to the Russian proposal to hold talks in Antwerp or any other neutral town and to appoint a pleni-

---

33. FO 65/4, private letter, Harris to Benjamin Langlois, unnumbered, 21 September/2 October 1781.

34. FO 65/4, Harris to Stormont, No. 140, 24 September/5 October 1781; *note verbale,* enclosed in FO 65/5, Harris to Stormont, No. 148, 21 October/1 November 1781: "C'est l'ultimatum du Roi," wrote Harris, "et il y a cherché à rendre les conditions aussi modérées que les interêts de son peuple . . . l'ont permis . . . et c'est un ouvrage digne de sa [the Empress] sagesse et de sa puissance, de les faire goûter à Leurs Hautes Puissances . . ."

35. FO 65/4, Harris to Stormont, No. 146, 15/26 October 1781. It is noteworthy that since the arrival of Simolin in London, the Empress tended to work through him rather than through Harris. Harris's negotiations in Russia were all undertaken on British initiative. This seems to correspond with the statement made by Catherine in 1763: "I have always made it a rule to treat through my ministers stationed at foreign courts and not through foreign envoys here." (See *Sbornik, 48,* 372–73).

36. FO 65/5, Osterman to Harris, *note verbale,* 31 October 1781; cf. *insinuation verbale* pour le chevalier Harris received by Stormont on 24 November 1781 from Simolin. (See also F. de Martens, *Recueil, 9,* 301, undated rescript to Simolin, which may have accompanied the *note verbale.*)

37. FO 65/5, Note from Simolin to Stormont, 24 November 1781.

potentiary.[38] Harris in turn repeated to Osterman the arguments originally suggested by Potemkin and endorsed by Stormont: England's last word had been spoken, "and . . . if on comparing it with that of the Dutch it should appear to be widely different, it was by approaching their conditions to ours, not by endeavouring to bring ours near theirs, that the event would be successful." [39]

To Potemkin Harris also spoke with the freedom which their past association warranted and which was particularly permissible seeing that it was the Prince's advice that had been followed in Britain. But he received little help from him. Potemkin approved whole-heartedly what Britain had done and declined absolutely to intervene, asserting that an ill-timed interference on his part would do more harm than good.[40] From Bezborodko, Harris derived some solace, though this appears to have been due more to his manner than to the matter of their conversation. He assured Harris that the Empress would not insist on forcing the principles of the Neutral League into the peace but pointed out that the British demand to revise the Marine Treaty of 1674 would prove a stumbling block.[41]

These discussions led Harris to the view that the Empress did not expect the mediation to succeed, but he still considered that Britain had been right in accepting it and that Catherine had desired to serve rather than distress Britain.[42] However, it is fairly clear that Catherine's intention, when she proposed the mediation, was to serve the Dutch, in the sense that she felt it incumbent to ward off or minimize the dangers of war brought upon them by their accession to the League, without herself being forced to take action in their defence. Moreover there was a fundamental difference of view between Britain and Russia as to the ultimate purpose of the mediation. The British ultimatum implied that the Dutch were not to return to their status as neutrals, whereas the Empress

38. FO 65/5, Stormont to Harris, No. 77, 6 December 1781, enclosing "réponse à l'insinuation verbale," by a Russian courier; cf. F. de Martens, *Recueil*, 9, 316, Simolin's dispatch of 17/28 December 1781.

39. FO 65/5, Harris to Stormont, No. 148, 21 October/1 November 1781.

40. FO 65/5, Harris to Stormont, No. 149, 21 October/1 November 1781.

41. Ibid.

42. FO 65/5, Harris to Stormont, No. 150, 21 October/1 November 1781.

clearly envisaged that the United Provinces would enjoy all their past privileges, notably their freedom to act as carriers of Russian exports. Thus the question of the Armed Neutrality was bound to arise in one form or another, for this was the real issue between Britain and the Dutch. It could take one of two forms: either the inclusion of the principles of the Neutral League in the peace or the maintenance of the Marine Treaty of 1674. Both entitled the Dutch to carry Russian naval stores to Britain's enemies. The Empress was certainly likely to support one or the other of these demands since the maritime principles were her own, and from the point of view of Russia's economy it was advantageous for the Dutch to be able freely to transport naval stores.

For the moment, Russia awaited the Dutch response to her overtures. Harris, having been edged out of the negotiation, continued to argue in Russia that the open enmity of Holland was safer for Britain than the previous secret understanding with France, and, besides, an alliance between France and the Dutch would attract the attention of Europe and reveal to all that Britain was "fighting almost as much for the liberties of Europe in general, as for our own." [43] Catherine left a certain latitude in the negotiations to Simolin and appointed an adjoint, Arkady Markov,[44] to her minister at The Hague. Markov did not set out immediately for his post,[45] and Harris had time to brief him extensively. He was relieved to find him well disposed, "impartial," and "free from prejudice," [46] so much so indeed that Vérac remarked that the Empress could not have chosen a better man had she consulted Harris on whom to appoint.[47] Harris heard with satisfaction that Markov's instructions were to oppose any alliance between the Patriot party in the United Provinces and France, and he endeavoured to point out to him the inadmissibility of the Dutch

43. FO 65/6, Harris to Stormont, No. 190, 24 December/4 January 1782.

44. Arkady Markov or Morkov belonged to the Vorontsov circle. This was his first diplomatic appointment.

45. *AMON*, 2, 654, Catherine to the Prince of Orange, 20 December 1781, letters of credence, delivered in March 1782.

46. FO 65/5, Harris to Stormont, No. 172, 12/23 November 1781; FO 65/6, No. 2, 7/18 January 1782, *MD, 1*, 480.

47. CP Russie, *107*, Vérac to Vergennes, No. 41, 2 November 1781.

"foisting in" the Armed Neutrality in any shape into their terms.[48]

Meanwhile the Dutch were proving equally difficult. They had been persuaded in the course of the summer to refer the Anglo-Dutch dispute to the joint imperial mediation, much to Vergennes's satisfaction, since this seemed to guarantee that they would stay in the war until the end. He now exercised all his influence to prevent Dutch acceptance of the new Russian offer and strove to bind France and the United Provinces together by the organization of joint military operations. The lengthy procedure of consultation in the United Provinces gave full scope to the French envoy to mobilize support for French policy.[49] Not until 4 March 1782 did the States General formally accept the sole mediation which Russia had offered in August and then only "provided a free trade conformable to the principles of the armed neutrality be previously stipulated for them." At the same time they voted to concert with France military operations against Britain.[50] This was in fact a rebuff for the Empress and a victory for the pro-French party in the United Provinces.

Osterman had throughout the winter continued to press on Harris that if Britain consented to acknowledge the principles of the Neutral League, she could have peace on her own terms with the United Provinces. Harris of course rejected the argument out of hand. The problem of Dutch trade in time of war might indeed be the one outstanding obstacle to a pacification, but that could easily be solved by "a fair and candid revision of the treaty of 1674."[51] The resolution of the States General on 4 March led Russia to renew her pressure on Britain to grant free navigation to the Dutch as the price of peace. On 9 April 1782, Osterman stressed to Harris the difficulty with which even this resolution had been obtained from the Dutch; if Britain refused free navigation,

48. FO 65/5, Harris to Stormont, No. 187, 17/28 December 1781; FO 65/6, No. 2, 7/18 January 1782.

49. Coquelle, *L'alliance franco-hollandaise*, p. 249 (though both inaccurate and biassed on British policy); see also *AMON*, 2, 655, Béranger to Vergennes, 25 December 1781.

50. *Niewe Nederlandsche Jaerboeken, 1,* 1782, p. 273; FO 65/6, Harris to Stormont, No. 60, 22 March/2 April 1782; Coquelle, *L'alliance franco-hollandaise*, p. 261.

51. FO 65/6, Harris to Stormont, No. 11, 4/15 February 1782.

the Dutch would become France's allies. The Empress however was insisting that while negotiations were in progress the Dutch should not even hold *pourparlers* with the French, and she would not tolerate any Dutch demands for succours from the Neutral League.[52] But the gulf between Britain and the Dutch was too deep to be bridged by such assurances from Russia. Summing up his impressions, Harris wrote on 16 April 1782 that he believed the Empress to be displeased with the Dutch for trifling with the Americans and for acting under the impulse of France. But their demand for unlimited free navigation was too close to her own ideas for her not to think it quite admissible, and she had hinted that if Britain gave in to Russia on that point, Russia might compel the Dutch to agree to other British demands. But, cautious now where caution was soon no longer to be necessary, he added: "I confess however that I think this would be a dangerous experiment, and not to be advised till a more systematic conduct was established here." He warned Stormont not to indulge in any discussion of "the nature and extent of this free navigation," and to ground his refusal of the Dutch terms on more general issues, such as the extent of French influence. Now was the moment, thought Harris, to put an end to the separate mediation, when the Empress was beginning to see the intractability of the Dutch in its true nature.[53]

While the Empress had been concentrating mainly on the Russian mediation between Britain and Holland, Kaunitz had been devoting some attention to keeping the joint imperial mediation alive—possibly because Austria disapproved of the separate Russian mediation offered to the United Provinces.[53a] Kaunitz still hoped to gather representatives of the belligerents together under his eye at a congress in Vienna, and, after securing Russian approval of his plans,[54] he dispatched a fresh instruction in October 1781 to Mercy Argenteau in Paris and Belgioioso in London to

52. FO 65/6, Harris to Stormont, No. 34, 29 March/9 April 1782; no. 35, same date.
53. FO 65/6, Harris to Stormont, No. 37, 5/16 April 1782.
53ᵃ. See Beer, *Joseph II, Leopold II und Kaunitz*, p. 104, Kaunitz to Joseph, 12 August 1781.
54. Arneth and Flammermont, *Correspondance, 1*, 61, Kaunitz to Mercy Argenteau, 8 September 1781. The Russian and Austrian envoys acted jointly.

invite the belligerents to appoint their plenipotentiaries.[55] But the Austrian initiative was ill-timed. France was waiting on the success of the Franco-Spanish expedition against Minorca, which had already seized the island and was besieging the garrison in Fort St. Philip. Moreover, by the time Mercy received his instructions on 4 November 1781, news had reached Paris of the victory of de Grasse over the British fleet in Chesapeake Bay. Vergennes appeared so reluctant to agree to a congress, now that fortune was favouring French and American arms, that Kaunitz and the Emperor for the time abandoned the idea.[56]

In London, Simolin and Belgioioso made a similar overture on 13 November 1781;[57] the British reply evaded the issue of a congress and contrasted the "ambition démésurée" of the Bourbons with "la politique d'un souverain qui n'a jamais blessé les droits d'aucune autre puissance" in the eyes of the impartial world.[58] For the time being therefore Kaunitz's efforts to inspire life into the moribund joint mediation failed completely.

The lack of sympathy with which British concerns were regarded in Russia in the autumn of 1781 and the first few months of 1782 is largely explained by what was going on in Britain at the time. The North administration had been struggling against mounting parliamentary opposition. The violence of the Whig attacks had grown in proportion to their expectation of achieving office. But though their manoeuvres were primarily governed by considerations of domestic policy, they caused repercussions abroad and weakened the effectiveness of British foreign policy. By one of those ironical turns of fate, the Empress harboured an extravagant admiration for Charles James Fox and his spirited defence of liberty. Her admiration lasted until 1792, when Fox's attitude to the French revolution appalled the ageing autocrat, and his bust

55. Ibid., 70, Kaunitz to Mercy Argenteau, 27 October, 1781.
56. Ibid., 66, note 1, Mercy Argenteau to Kaunitz, 16 October 1781; p. 68, 23 October 1781; p. 72, 11 November 1781; p. 76, Joseph to Mercy Argenteau, 30 November 1781; p. 77, Kaunitz to Mercy Argenteau, 30 November 1781.
57. FO 65/5, Stormont to Harris, No. 74, 13 November 1781; Fortescue, Correspondence of King George III, 5, 300, Stormont to the King, 13 November 1781.
58. Réplique à la réplique des cours impériales, enclosed in FO 65/5, Stormont to Harris, No. 77, 6 December 1781 (en clair and by a Russian courier).

was removed from the gallery of notabilities which adorned the colonnade in Tsarskoye Selo. Fox in turn was one of the Empress's propagandists in Britain, believing perhaps that Catherine's philosophic enlightenment was in some way akin to his own political leanings. The Empress was not proof against the flattery that Fox at this time lavished on her: "The Empress of Russia," thundered Fox in the House of Commons, "and his present Majesty, had mounted the thrones of their respective empires, much about the same time. But how great the difference in the two reigns! Great Britain had declined with a suddenness equal to the rapidity with which Russia had arisen to her present eminence." [59]

From the very beginning of the revolt in America, Catherine had entertained a poor opinion of the North administration and had identified herself with the criticism of the Whigs. Two years before, in July 1780, the Emperor Joseph had warned Harris that the Empress was "withheld from assisting us merely because she was in opposition." [60] The Emperor's opinion was confirmed from many quarters. Aleksey Orlov, himself pro-English, told Harris that the Empress's "great misfortune was believing in Opposition, that she has received all the impressions of our government from printed speeches and newspaper trash." [61] It came as a shock to Harris when he first heard somewhat similar opinions from Potemkin himself. During the summer of 1781, Harris had been pained to hear Potemkin "hold the language of Opposition, disapproving of our conduct, and condemning our military operations." [62] The Prince appeared to be speaking jocosely, and, as others were present, Harris chose not to argue the point, but it was a disturbing sign. Later, in September 1781, Stormont made a vain effort to arouse Russian sympathy by suggesting that the Franco-Spanish attack on Minorca had been provoked by the news that the island had been offered to Russia. The leakage must have occurred in Russia, thought the Secretary of State, and little did he think when the offer was made that all the advantage Britain would draw therefrom was "the loss or at least the hazard of so

---

59. *Parliamentary Register, 18,* 370, 5 January 1781.
60. SP 91/105, Harris to Stormont, No. 82, 14/25 July 1780.
61. FO 65/2, Harris to Stormont, No. 35, 5/16 March 1781.
62. FO 65/4, Harris to Stormont, No. 126, 31 August/11 September 1781.

valuable a possession." [63] Potemkin again proved quite unsympathetic. He denied that the secret of the British offer had been betrayed in St. Petersburg; the Empress had certainly not spoken of it to anyone, and "he could be responsible for himself." He refused to transmit Harris's complaints to the Empress. Harris was so hurt by the Prince's indifference that he could not believe his words "came from the same man." Bezborodko, who had by this time been informed of the negotiations since they were public property, agreed to convey to Catherine Harris's concern at the leakage, but Harris derived scant consolation from her attitude. "It will have the fate of every other thing which passed at Petersburg, to become public," she commented coldly and refused to feel herself in any way to blame or to feel any obligation towards Britain as the result of the probable loss of Minorca.[64]

At first Harris had believed that the change in the Prince's conduct had not been due to political considerations but to problems arising out of his own personal position at court.[65] Potemkin continued to be very friendly in private with Harris, but the scales were beginning to fall from the envoy's eyes at last. It was only when he wished him to be useful as a "servant of the publick" that he perceived alteration, he wrote to Stormont on 1 November 1781, "and it is in such moments only that I set a value on his friendship." [66] Soon, however, both Harris and Cobenzl began to feel considerable alarm at rumours that Potemkin was keeping up secret connexions with the Prussian and French envoys with a view to restoring the influence of Prussia at St. Petersburg. Harris boldly tackled the Prince on the subject, but Potemkin defended himself with art and spirit against such unworthy suspicions. He

---

63. FO 65/4, Stormont to Harris, No. 56, most confidential, 7 September 1781: "It is now known, from a great variety of secret intelligence, that this discovery and this alone, determined France and Spain to the attack now made upon Minorca, so apprehensive are they of every increase of the naval strength and commerce of Russia," wrote Stormont. This was of course not true; the attack had been decided after the relief of Gibraltar in spring 1781.

64. FO 65/5, Harris to Stormont, No. 155, 21 October/1 November 1781 (*MD*, *1*, 458).

65. FO 65/5, Harris to Stormont, No. 157, 21 October/1 November 1781 (*MD*, *1*, 459, tacked on to No. 155).

66. FO 65/5, Harris to Stormont, No. 158, 21 October/1 November 1781 (*MD*, *1*, 471, tacked on to No. 156).

even succeeded in diverting Harris from more serious concerns by exercising his talent for mimicry and "counterfeited so inimitably a dialogue between himself, the French minister, and [a] French merchant that it was impossible not to lose sight for a while of the very interesting matters on which we were talking." His own policy, Potemkin explained, consisted of separating Austria and France and concluding an alliance between Britain and the two imperial courts, "a plan very advantageous to the interest of the Empire, and perfectly conformable to those of its natural friends," commented Harris. But as Potemkin's future plans started out with the necessity of subduing the Turks, it should have been clear to Harris that it was around this main theme that the variations would develop.[67] Harris was not convinced either by the Prince's arguments or by his entertainments and hastened to warn Keith in Vienna of what he believed to be a fundamental change in the views of the most powerful figure at the Russian court.[68] But indeed there was no such change, whatever the fears harboured by Harris and Cobenzl. Both Potemkin and Bezborodko were too far committed to expansion at the expense of the Porte. If anything, Potemkin's intrigues, for such they undoubtedly were, were probably connected with his growing suspicion and jealousy of the rising power of Bezborodko.[69]

It was not surprising that Harris began to find his situation in St. Petersburg most galling. He had now to struggle to maintain his spirits at a time when, after a succession of reverses, Britain suffered the major defeat of the war. By mid-December, news of the disaster of Yorktown and the surrender of Cornwallis's army reached St. Petersburg. Russian society and the diplomatic world proved most unsympathetic. "They attribute the loss we have sustained to our misconduct," wrote Harris on 7/18 December 1781,

67. FO 65/5, Harris to Stormont, No. 174, 16/27 November 1781 (*MD*, *1*, 475); see also Beer and Fiedler, *Joseph II und Graf Ludwig Cobenzl*, *1*, 243, Cobenzl to Joseph, 9 October 1781; p. 282, 18 January 1782.

68. FO 65/5, Harris to Stormont, No. 176, 23 November/4 December 1781.

69. Merton Papers, Harris to Harriet, 12/23 March 1782: "Bezborodko and his set are pushing hard for power and riches and hitherto with success. Potemkin however bears them no goodwill and I am sure meditates their destruction. They are of *no side* in politicks and tho' we are good friends I reap no advantage from their friendship." See also Beer and Fiedler, *Joseph II und Graf Ludwig Cobenzl*, *1*, 282, Cobenzl to Joseph, 18 January 1782; p. 292, 28 January 1782; p. 303, 23 March 1782.

"and instead of expressing that degree of concern and allarm . . .
they exclaim against us in the most uncandid manner." The disaster that had befallen England inspired Harris to try once more
to galvanize Potemkin into action on England's behalf. But the
Prince, though assuring Harris that his good offices would never
be found wanting, replied: "what . . . can your friends do for
you, if you do nothing for yourselves?" Harris replied with one of
his most flamboyant diatribes. "Let our friends be as attentive to
their real interests as we are to ours—it was all I required of them
. . . let them act in conformity to their own welfare and honour.
That if they did not both would soon be in danger, and it would
remain with posterity to pronounce whether the ministers who
governed this Empire, or those who direct the operations of ours,
were most entitled to censure." [70]

The surrender of Yorktown did indeed appear to the Russians
conclusive proof of the weakness and inefficiency of the North administration. Potemkin did not spare his expressions of concern,
but he "mixed them up with that great portion of illiberal blame"
that Harris kept his temper with difficulty.[71] The Empress remarked that the surrender would at least hasten the peace, and
when Harris remonstrated with Bezborodko and told him that he
hoped this meant that the Empress would now at last "put on the
character . . . of an open and expressed friend," he found him
also "tainted with a degree of those Opposition principles I had
observed so strongly to prevail in Prince Potemkin." [72] As the new
year advanced which was to see North's administration struggling
to its inglorious close, Harris saw more and more clearly how far

70. FO 65/5, Harris to Stormont, No. 182, 7/18 December 1781. (*MD, 1,* 478). The
Editor has omitted Harris's most dramatic accusations of the Prince: "I told him
. . . that it was he who would be considered in a future day as the sole Prime
Minister of the Empress and that all the false measures, incapacity, corruption or
errors her other councillors lead her into would be laid to his charge; and I begged
him to look around the throng and see whether there was amongst them any one
with whose reputation he chose to be handed down to posterity."

71. FO 65/5, Harris to Stormont, No. 182, 7/18 December 1781. (*MD, 1,* 478).

72. FO 65/5, Harris to Stormont, No. 186, 14/25 December 1781; see also Arneth,
Joseph II und Katharina, p. 115, Catherine to Joseph, 7/18 December 1781 on a
parliament "[qui] ne donne les guinées de la nation que pour faire payer à chaque
individu l'approbation des fausses mesures du ministère . . ."; and *PKFG, 46,* 419,
Goertz to Frederick, 28 December 1781, on Catherine speaking "avec le dernier
mèpris du ministère britannique."

the attacks of the opposition had undermined Britain's position in St. Petersburg. "The Empress is in Opposition," he wrote on 11/22 January 1782; "she separates the nation from the government," and the gossip of London taverns influenced her against all that he could undertake. "Those who introduced this doctrine on the Continent are the greatest enemies England ever had . . . It began by giving a dislike to our alliance; It since has alienated her friendship from us . . ." [73] It must be added that Harris himself was a Foxite Whig [74] and remained one until the secession of the Portland wing in 1794, when he too broke with Fox over his attitude to the war with France. But he was too good a diplomat and too interested in foreign service as such to allow his political opinions to colour his conduct or jeopardize his chances of employment.

There is no doubt that Russia's position in any negotiations with Britain was considerably strengthened by the attacks which the Whigs delivered in Parliament on North's foreign policy. In April 1780 the Whigs had attacked the negotiations with Russia which eventually culminated in the declaration of the Armed Neutrality by the Empress.[75] In June 1780 a further broadside was launched by Shelburne in which he accused Britain of having broken the treaty of 1674 with the Dutch "without colour or pretence." After the outbreak of the war with France, which, declared Shelburne, "we, not they commenced," the treaty of 1674 with the Dutch was "daily violated." Not content with arguing the Dutch case on neutral shipping and the French case on the origins of the war, the Whigs violently attacked the government for having alienated Russia and provoked a war with the United Provinces.[76] These parliamentary wrangles were duly reported to Cath-

73. FO 65/6, Harris to Stormont, No. 5, 11/22 January 1782.

74. See for instance Add. MSS 47.563, f. 33, Harris to Fox, 19/30 April 1782: "I must however add lest you have any doubts of my political creed, that on my return home, as well from personal attachment to you as from principle, I shall be a staunch supporter of government and my own parliamentary conduct, as well as the influence I may have over that of my friends and relations, shall all invariably tend that way." Fox was then in power.

75. *Parliamentary Register*, *15*, 218, 14 April 1780.

76. Ibid., *335*, 1 June 1780. The Whigs did not approve of the Armed Neutrality, but they attacked the government for having allowed it to happen; see also ibid., *21*, 36, 25 January 1781, and particularly p. 79, for Shelburne's onslaught on Stormont's policy towards the Dutch.

erine, and it is not to be wondered at that she was reluctant to establish a connexion with a government which could fairly be regarded as unstable and which opposed her principles, when a change of administration might lead to their acceptance. Real lack of confidence in the government, coupled with real resentment at Stormont's naval policy, restrained the Empress from any step in Britain's favour. There were other factors too, which were summed up by Bezborodko in a letter to Rumyantsev on 2/13 January 1782:

> The misfortune which has befallen Cornwallis has produced no effect here, since Britain, in spite of her unpleasant situation continues to humiliate the neutral powers not excluding Russia by seizing merchant ships, and also, in the affair of the mediation, in spite of the goodwill of both mediators, has tried to place as many obstacles in the way as the other side. The neutral powers are acting in this mediation exclusively from humanitarian motives, for they would derive more benefit from the continuation of the war; even for us, in spite of the lack of ships, the war is very profitable in the extension of direct trade to France and Spain. And moreover, all England's efforts reveal that she is still far from being crushed, and finds resources in herself and needs maybe only general agreement and a good choice of men.[77]

During this period of suspense, diplomatic activity was practically at a standstill in St. Petersburg. A crisis was also being enacted in the palace, where Potemkin was again urging on the Empress that she should get rid of her ailing favourite Lanskoy. The Empress was invisible for a fortnight, but Lanskoy remained.[78] During the standstill Harris, like a Cassandra, warned Russia in vain of the dire perils that awaited her if she continued to pursue erroneous policies; no one heeded him. "It is sufficient, intelligence

---

77. Maykov, *Pis'ma A. A. Bezborodka*, p. 95.
78. Harris to Lady Harris, 13/23 March 1782: "The Empress is going to change her favourite. Lanskoy is comme de raison become tiresome, he is worn out, but he is so good a boy that there is to be found no due reason of complaint against him, he is neither overjealous nor (?) not passionate or inconstant; he is only *ennuyeux* and HIM's delicacy is too great to think that a sufficient reason for dismissing him" (Merton Papers).

comes from me to be treated as willfull misrepresentation," he
wrote.[79] Even the British loss of Minorca was treated with general
indifference.[80] Again Harris begged to be recalled. Since Potemkin's patronage seemed to have been withdrawn from him, he had
lost his friends and dependents. He had no means of access to the
Empress and felt himself isolated and "exposed to all the malevolence of personal animosity, directed by powerful and vindictive
enemies . . . whose unfriendly dispositions towards my court are,
I am sure, increased from the ill-will they bear me." His continued
presence in Russia, Harris now believed, served Britain ill.[81] The
Empress too no longer distinguished Harris in any special way.
"She treats me very poorly," Harris wrote to his wife on 12/23
March 1782, "I am no longer her constant cardmate but confondu
dans la foule; I no longer enjoy her smile, we no longer converse
d'intelligence and I am but a degree better than Nolcken and
Sacken. Goertz and Vérac have gained ground . . ." [82] But when
news reached Russia of the debate in the House of Commons on
28 February 1782, in which North was defeated on General Con-
way's motion opposing the continuation of the war in America,
interest immediately revived. The Empress was eager to be informed and inquired through Potemkin or Osterman every post-
day if there was further news.[83] By the middle of April Harris's
own expectation was at the highest pitch. He had received no
news from London, only rumours from The Hague, but it was
clear to him and to the Russians that a new administration would
bring great changes in the conduct of British foreign policy.

79. FO 65/6, Harris to Stormont, No. 13, 8/19 February 1782 and particularly
No. 30, 22 March/2 April 1782.

80. FO 65/6, Harris to Stormont, No. 29, 18/29 March 1782.

81. FO 65/6, Harris to Stormont, No. 4, 11/22 January 1782, *MD, 1,* 482.

82. Merton Papers.

83. FO 65/6, Harris to Stormont, No. 32, 25 March/5 April 1782, *MD, 1,* 496.

15. The Effectiveness of the Armed Neutrality

THROUGHOUT 1780 and until the fall of North the problems arising out of the Armed Neutrality were an ever-present accompaniment to Harris's more dramatic diplomatic intrigues. The Empress was seriously bent on developing an export trade in Russian ships, and the war provided an excellent opportunity.[1] Having proclaimed her maritime principles and shown her intention of enforcing them, she turned to the creation of a merchant marine. It was not an easy task, for the Russians were not natural sailors, but Russia could draw on the resources of the Baltic provinces with their long tradition of seamanship and also employed seamen from other lands. Many ventures failed through the ignorance, superstition, or drunkenness of the sailors or because the ships were not sound.[2] But Catherine regarded her foreign trade, her "child" as she had called it to Harris, "with the partial affection of an overfond parent," [3] and slowly the number of Russian ships actively engaged in trade did increase. The figures speak a truer language than the somewhat jaundiced reports of Harris and Consul Shairp. In 1775 the total number of Russian ships engaged in foreign trade was seventeen; by 1780, thirty-eight Russian ships sailed from St. Petersburg alone, of which twenty-one were destined to French and Spanish ports.[4] New ships were being built in the interior,

1. For Russian policy in foreign trade, see Pokrovsky, *Vneshyaya torgovlya*, pp. 106 ff.

2. SP 91/106, Harris to Stormont, No. 160, 13/24 December 1780.

3. FO 65/2, Harris to Stormont, No. 40, 13/24 March 1781.

4. Ibid., Shairp to Stormont, 13/24 March 1781; cf. Baranovich et al, *Ocherki*, p. 128.

and the fleet was expected to number fifty in the 1781 season.[5]
Not all the ships found cargoes, and of those that did, most were
chartered to carry goods to Bourbon ports.[6] Moreover, owing to
defective seamanship, the Russians appear to have suffered heavy
losses, which Harris believed were "carefully concealed from her
[the Empress] and she is not acquainted that half of the Russian
ships which sailed last year have perished." [7] In the effort to extend Russian trade imperial frigates were even used to carry
cargoes of hemp and iron to Spain in exchange for merino wool.
Before Harris could protest at this "undignified use of the imperial navy," Potemkin, who was interested in the venture, expressed the hope that Britain would let these ships pass unhindered.[8] At least one concession however was made to British
susceptibilities on this occasion: the captains of all four frigates
were Russians and not Englishmen.[9] In spite of his indifference to
the Neutral League, Potemkin was one of the principal supporters
of the Russian merchant marine. He was actively developing trade
from South Russia through the Black Sea to France and the Mediterranean, and through a protégé of his, M. Faleyev, he maintained
an interest in trade from the Baltic. It is noteworthy that in August
1781, of ten Russian ships on which damages were in dispute be-

5. FO 65/1, Shairp to Stormont, 26 January/6 February 1781; cf. FO 65/8, Shairp
to Grantham, 15/26 August 1782.

6. In 1781, 38 or more ships left St. Petersburg of which at least 22 went to
Bourbon ports; in 1782, 21 Russian ships sailed, while 38 remained behind in
idleness. (Figures collected from: FO 65/4, Shairp to Stormont, 3 September 1781;
FO 65/5, Shairp to Stormont, 22 October 1781; 16/27 November 1781; Harris to
Stormont, No. 151, 20 October/1 November 1781; Barnes and Owen, *The Sandwich
Papers, 4*, 111, Admiral Greig to Sandwich, 14/25 October 1781; Harris Papers,
Memorandum, Ships arrived at Cronstadt in 1782.)

7. FO 65/5, Harris to Stormont, No. 151, 20 October/1 November 1781; according
to Harris, of the 21 Russian ships which sailed in 1780 to Bourbon ports only 6
reached their destination (SP 91/106 to Stormont, No. 160, 13/24 December 1780).
Shairp also mentions "a remarkable number of losses" in the autumn of 1782 (FO
65/9, to Grantham, 17 February 1783).

8. FO 65/3, Harris to Stormont, No. 93, 25 June/6 July 1781.

9. Ibid. Imperial frigates had been used, with only partial success, to develop
trade through the Dardanelles in 1775 (*Sbornik, 25*, 473, 585), and were also used
under Potemkin's direction for the same purpose during the American war (FO
65/5, Harris to Stormont, No. 171, 12/23 November 1781). The Empress herself did
not favour such practices and believed that a merchant marine should serve to
build up a navy (*Sbornik, 42*, 407, Catherine to Potemkin, n.d.).

tween Britain and Russia three belonged to Faleyev.[10] Potemkin had also frequently discussed with Corberon in 1779 the prospects of a commercial treaty with France, and he had expressed the opinion to the Empress that as long as she was "livrée aux anglais" her trade would not prosper.[11]

At first sight the Anglo-Dutch war was a substantial blow to Russia's commercial policy.[12] The number of Dutch ships passing the Sound dropped from 2,051 in 1780 to nine in 1781.[13] By October 1781 only three Dutch ships had reached St. Petersburg, and of these two were bought by Russians and sailed thereafter under Russian colours.[14] Now, however, when Dutch ships were driven out of the Baltic trade, the Neutral League began to show its value, for the Swedes, Danes, Prussians, the North German ports, and even the Austrians (from the Netherlands) stepped in to fill the gap. In spite of the absence of the Dutch, in 1781 the number of foreign ships (excluding British) to visit St. Petersburg was higher by thirty-six than the number in 1780. It is true that the number of British ships increased in that year by 182, but in 1782 the number of British ships declined, and the foreign ships outstripped them by as many as 194.[15] By the autumn of 1782 the Empress was justified in thinking that her policy of freeing her export trade from a too exclusive dependence on Britain had been successful.[16]

10. FO 65/4, State of the Russian Prize Causes, 30 August 1781.

11. CP Russie, *102*, Corberon to Vergennes, No. 18, 18 May 1779.

12. Maykov, *Pis'ma A. A. Bezborodka*, p. 72, Bezborodko to Rumyantsev, 25 January/5 February 1781.

13. Macpherson, *Annals of Commerce, Manufactures, Fisheries and Navigation*, 3, 705.

14. Barnes and Owen, *The Sandwich Papers*, 4, 111, Greig to Sandwich, 14/25 October 1781.

15. In 1779, 314 English ships and 379 foreign ships arrived in St. Petersburg; in 1780, 282 English and 301 foreign ships; in 1781, 464 English ships and 337 foreign ships; in 1782, 220 English and 414 foreign ships arrived. No French or Spanish ships arrived in 1781 (figures collected from SP 91/104, Shairp to Stormont, 15/26 February 1780; FO 65/1, 26 January/6 February 1781; 65/4, 3/14 September 1781; 65/6, 19 February/2 March 1782; 65/9, 27 December 1782/7 January 1783). St. Petersburg accounted for 60% of the Russian foreign trade (Baranovich et al, *Ocherki*, p. 128).

16. Arneth, *Joseph II und Katharina*, p. 143, Catherine to Joseph, 10/21 September 1782; cf. Maykov, *Pis'ma A. A. Bezborodka*, p. 95, Bezborodko to Rumyantsev, 2/13 January 1782.

But the elimination of the Dutch did disturb long-established trade connexions which had to be rebuilt. Moreover Britain in 1781 still took nearly three-quarters of the Russian export produce brought to the port of St. Petersburg, and this reliance on Britain disturbed the Russians. "The Empress is envious of our opulence," wrote Harris on 3/14 September 1781, "jealous of our power, and is more hurt at our having driven back the Dutch fleet than pleased with seeing her ports filled with our ships and her coffers with our money." [17] Yet in spite of the increasing number of foreign ships visiting Russian ports, the French, Spanish, and Dutch found difficulty in getting away from Russia the goods they wished to export.[18] The Danes, by the convention of 4 July 1780, had admitted that naval stores were liable to seizure by Britain and could thus not be relied on. Moreover Spain had taken action as a result of this convention and in December 1780 issued a declaration applying the definition of contraband of the convention of 4 July with Britain to Danish shipping.[19] Portuguese ships refused to take naval stores, only a few of the Swedes did so, and the Prussian ships, though willing to take any cargo, were too small to take the great masts.[20] Thus inevitably the Bourbon powers were driven to charter the unreliable Russian ships.

The suggestion that Britain should make an exception in favour of Russian ships and allow them to pass without detention and with only a superficial examination of their papers had frequently been made by Potemkin to Harris,[21] and, in the more aggressive form of a demand to respect Russian rights, by Panin. Harris himself had pressed this policy at intervals on Stormont, though he frequently undid the good his advice might have done by stressing that the Empress was "tired of her neutral plan." [22] In truth, if Britain was

17. FO 65/4, Harris to Stormont, No. 127, 3/14 September 1781.

18. FO 65/3, Harris to Stormont, No. 93, 25 June/6 July 1781.

19. Fanchille, *La diplomatie française*, p. 449.

20. In 1781, thirteen Portuguese ships visited St. Petersburg (Barnes and Owen, *The Sandwich Papers*, 4, 111, Greig to Sandwich, 14/25 October 1781); cf. also FO 65/3, Harris to Stormont, No. 93, 25 June/6 July 1781.

21. Cf. for instance SP 91/105, Harris to Stormont, No. 85, 21 July/1 August 1780, most secret: "He advised to respect no vessels but those of Russia, and make the Empress feel by this conduct, that it was not from fear but from regard that we shew'd her ships this deference."

22. Cf. FO 65/2, Harris to Stormont, No. 71, 4/15 May 1781.

really so anxious to secure a Russian alliance, it seemed scarcely worth-while to stir up so much ill feeling over Russian ships. Russia had had occasion to complain before the formation of the Neutral League; thereafter, her complaints became incessant.[23] Further to the written assurances which Harris had given to Panin on 11 January 1780 that Britain would never unjustifiably interfere with Russian navigation,[24] Harris sent in a second memorial on 6/17 March 1780, this time assuring the Russian minister that Britain would strictly observe the provisions of the Anglo-Russian treaty. But he still considered that the compulsory purchase of the naval stores on board Russian ships by the Navy Board, in fulfilment of the judgements of the admiralty courts, was in accordance with the treaty.[25] The difficulty, as Harris put it, was that "they consider as a matter of right what we grant as a matter of favour." [26] It is evident that when the Neutral League was founded Stormont certainly did not grasp that Russia was entitled by the treaty to carry naval stores to the enemy. "Free ships, free goods" was of no advantage to Russian trade, he wrote to Harris on 14 July 1780, but, if the Empress thought it was, why had she not asked for the addition of an article to the commercial treaty instead of proclaiming the principle unilaterally? [27] This confusion may well have been due to the advice of Sir James Marriott, whose judgements, according to a great legal luminary, were such as "no other person would follow." [28] Exactly when the light dawned on Stormont cannot be determined, but on 16 November 1780 Simolin lodged a further protest with him against the detention of two Russian ships and also protested against the wording of the currently valid British instructions to privateers, which allowed

23. Contrary to Bergbohm's statement (*Die bewaffnete Neutralität*, p. 144) that after 1780 there were no more complaints about Russian ships. There is no foundation either for Harris's statement that Russian ships were ignored by the admiralty courts (FO 65/5, Harris to Stormont, No. 167, 5/16 November (*MD, 1,* 472)); this is quoted by Albion, *Forests and Sea Power,* pp. 192–93 (with wrong reference) as proof of the concessions made by Britain to Russia.

24. See Ch. 6, p. 150.

25. SP 91/104, enclosed in Harris to Stormont, No. 19, 6/17 March 1780, cf. mémoire, printed in *Morskoy Sbornik, 43,* 361, No. 31.

26. FO 65/5, Harris to Stormont, No. 151, 20 October/1 November 1781.

27. SP 91/105, Stormont to Harris, No. 39, 14 July 1780.

28. *DNB.*

them to seize enemy property wherever they found it.[29] Four days later, on 20 November 1780, Britain promulgated an additional instruction to privateers, which incorporated the actual text of Articles 10 and 11 of the Anglo-Russian treaty of commerce, for the guidance of captains of privateers.[30] Stormont explained to Harris that some inconvenience had been caused by the fact that captains of privateers were "not always sufficiently acquainted with the precise nature and extent of His Majesty's engagements with the Empress of Russia," and the articles had now been inserted to prevent mistake.[31] The idea that captains of privateers, when faced with a possible prey, would trouble to look up their copy of the Anglo-Russian treaty is a charming fiction of diplomatic language. Stormont attempted to take the credit for making this decision before Simolin had lodged his latest protest—but he did not succeed.[32] Panin, to whom Harris addressed himself on the subject on 17 December 1780, was unimpressed; he demanded that Britain should not stop Russian ships at all and expose them to the lengthy procedure of the courts. He issued a stern warning to Harris: "Celui qui croit qu'aucun individu a mis dans la tête de Sa Majesté Impériale, l'idée de la Neutralité Armée se trompe; et celui qui croit qu'aucun individu est assez puissant pour la lui ôter se trompe également." [33] This was a broad hint to Harris not to place his faith in Potemkin, but it contrasts oddly with Panin's assurance to Goertz "qu'il lui avait fallu imaginer cette association maritime, pour éviter à l'Europe une guerre générale." [34]

How reluctant Britain was to admit the legal validity of the Russian stand emerges from the case of the *Huys in het Bosch,* a Russian ship (in spite of its name) laden with spars and deals from Riga to Corunna, taken into Dover in November 1780 by the privateer *Royal Henry.* The Russian consul in London, Alexander

29. See Ch. 9, pp. 233–34.

30. Text in Scott, *Armed Neutralities,* p. 328.

31. SP 91/106, Stormont to Harris, No. 66, 21 November 1780.

32. In his dispatch to Panin of 10/21 November 1780, Simolin stated that Stormont had taken his decision as a result of the protest he had made on 16 November. (Aleksandrenko, *Russkiye diplomaticheskiye agenty,* 2, 214, and SP 91/106, Stormont to Harris, No. 67, 28 November 1780).

33. SP 91/106, Harris to Stormont, No. 159, 13/24 December 1780.

34. *PKFG, 45,* 19, Goertz to Frederick, 24 October 1780.

Baxter, proposed the following solution to Stormont on 25 January 1781:

> There is little probability of settling this affair . . . to the satisfaction of all parties unless your Lordship will be pleased to give a full authority to Mr. Crespigny, [H. M. Procurator General] or some other officer of government, to undertake, and become responsible, to the captors for payment of the value of the cargo to them, upon a fair evaluation, by proper judges . . . This plan would, it is presumed, obviate any difficulty, and the ship and cargo might at once be decreed to be restored, the captors not opposing and the Russian claimants would recieve the full benefit of their claim of privilege under the treaty—without any legal decision, as to the validity of such claim . . .[35]

It was thus now admitted that the cargo of naval stores would be allowed to proceed to an enemy port; a judgement was to be evaded, and the captors were to be compensated by the government. But the clearest indication of the interpretation which was now put, though only privately, on the Anglo-Russian treaty occurs in connexion with the ship which first appears under the remarkable name of the *Vurst Potumsken,* eventually civilized into *Furst Potemkin.* The ship was captured early in 1781 and brought into Leith by the privateer *Paisley,* owned by a Mr. Elphinstone. Mr. Elphinstone was indignant to hear that he had got himself into trouble because "the articles of the treaty with Russia . . . were not given out with the other instructions when the letters of marque were issued." Moreover, said Elphinstone, when he finally heard of those new instructions, he had searched Edinburgh for two days for a copy of the treaty with Russia without finding one. He therefore expected to be indemnified for any costs incurred in the action. The ship went before the Scottish court of admiralty, and the judge released it and the cargo; but he decided that the *Paisley* had had just grounds for bringing it in to Leith and reserved judgement, apparently

35. FO 65/1, copy of affidavit, 4 November 1780; Baxter to Stormont, 25 January 1781.

sine die, on the claim for damages and costs of £2,600.[36] The
Scottish courts were of course quite independent of the English
and perhaps less amenable to direction by the government. Appeal lay to the court of session in the first place and then to the
House of Lords, but the Russians, in an effort to settle the matter
more speedily, attempted also to secure redress through diplomatic
channels. Stormont, when the Russian consul raised the matter,
realized at once that he might have difficulty with the Scottish
courts. On 20 February 1781 he wrote to Dundas, the Lord Advocate, asking him to suggest means of speeding up a decision. "The
cargo," he wrote, "under the stipulations of our treaty with Russia
(which stipulations have been published in the inclosed Additional
Instructions) cannot be condemned, and would be immediately
released in the court of Admiralty here; but if they should attempt
to try the cause in Leith, I am apprehensive of some ignorance of
or inattention to the above-mentioned instructions . . .[37] Even
more explicit is the letter of the Lord Advocate to the Crown
Agent in Scotland, of 21 February 1781: "The eleventh article of
the treaty recited in the instructions herewith sent," he wrote,
"contains an enumeration of the only goods which can be seized
in a Russian ship, and therefore the capture in this case is certainly
illegal, and every hours detention of the ship and cargo, will
subject the captor to severe pecuniary and other heavy consequences." [38] It may be added that Stormont's apprehensions were
perfectly justified; though the ship was promptly released with
cargo, the claim for costs lingered on. In 1785 it had not yet been
settled, and it led the Empress to demand tartly, in instructions to
the then ambassador in Britain, Simon Vorontsov, that if and
when the Anglo-Russian treaty were renewed it should contain
two supplementary clauses: that all privateers and cruisers should
carry a copy of the treaty and that all Russian prize cases should
go before English and not before Scottish or Irish courts.[39]

36. FO 65/1, Baxter to Under-Secretary Fraser, 20 February 1781; FO 65/7,
Simolin to Fox, 26 July 1782; FO 65/2, John Davidson to Lord Advocate, 26 February 1781.

37. FO 65/10, copy of Stormont to Lord Advocate of 20 February 1781.

38. FO 65/10, copy of Henry Dundas to Crown Agent in Scotland, 21 February
1781.

39. *AKV,* 26, 289, Catherine to Simon Vorontsov, n.d., 1785.

But though the Russian claim to "free ships, free goods" was no longer *de facto* contested after November 1780, Stormont utterly refused to make any overt concession. When Harris, as a result of his interview with Panin on 17 December, suggested to Stormont that, since "the permission of a free trade to her [the Empress's] ships is already virtually granted," privateers should be given secret instructions not to stop Russian ships, Stormont refused to consider it. "A particular exception given in formal orders is impossible, and a promise of what is so cannot be made with that good faith with which we shall ever treat," he wrote on 19 January 1781.[40] Thus, though Stormont conceded that "it is admitted on both sides that the Treaty is the law between us," [41] he refused to accept the practical implications of that concession and insisted on the necessity of bringing Russian ships into port, even if the ships and cargoes had subsequently to be released. This policy proved both unpleasant and expensive for Britain since the Russian owners demanded damages for detention, and it left Harris to continue the struggle in Russia while standing on very weak theoretical grounds.[42]

Indeed, in the summer of 1782, writing to his friend, the Whig secretary of state, Lord Grantham, Harris attributed his failures in Russia "to the very awkward manner in which we replied to

40. SP 91/106, Harris to Stormont, No. 162, 13/24 December 1780; FO 65/1, Stormont to Harris, No. 9, 19 January 1781.

41. FO 65/5, Stormont to Harris, No. 78, 6 December 1781.

42. According to Albion, *Forests and Sea Power*, p. 190, the Navy Board had by April 1779 paid more than £220,000 for the cargoes of neutrals condemned to be sold to the Navy Board, though these were valued at only £135,000. Though Sir James Marriott always insisted that the restitution of ships "without some legal proceedings . . . has in this and former wars been prohibited by the Legislature under very severe punishments" (Adm 1/3886, Marriott to the Lords of the Admiralty, 31 July 1780) nevertheless such compounding occasionally occurred. See for instance the case of an Austrian ship in which the captors, having admitted themselves in the wrong, were treating with the Austrian agent for damages to be settled by arbitration. The claimants had therefore not brought the case before the courts, and it depended on them to do so or to accept satisfaction by private agreement (FO 7/1, Keith to Stormont, No. 32, 7 March 1781; Stormont to Keith, No. 30, 23 March 1781). In the case of the Russian ship *St. Peter*, taken by a privateer into Jersey, the captor paid a large sum in damages to the captain of the ship, and had thus "empêcher que l'affaire ne fut portée devant la Haute Cour d'Amirauté" (see FO 65/7, Harris to Fraser, 29 July 1782, 65/8, Simolin to Grantham, 18 September 1782 and Grantham to Simolin, 20 September 1782).

the famous neutral declaration of February 1780." His opinion, he now stated, had been that if England could do without Russia let her reject these new-fangled doctrines, but if Britain needed Russian assistance "let it yield to the necessity of the hour, recognize them as far as they relate to Russia alone, and by a well-timed act of complaisance insure itself a powerful friend." But, added Harris, "my opinion was not received; an ambiguous and trimming answer was given; we seemed equally afraid to accept or dismiss them. I was instructed secretly to oppose but avowedly to acquiesce in them . . ." [43] To his Whig friend Harris wrote more openly and allowed himself criticisms of government policy which he was too much of a diplomat to make to Stormont. Though his dispatch bears the character of an apologia, there is truth in his statement that he repeatedly warned Stormont of the feeling aroused in Russia by Britain's maritime policy. But he was not enough of a lawyer to understand the extent to which Britain would weaken her maritime practice by creating a precedent and admitting the Russian claim to pass merely on an inspection of ship's papers.

Thus Russian ships continued to be detained and brought into British ports, evoking immediate energetic protests from Russia. On 8 January 1781 Simolin handed to Stormont a note on Russian ships on which the decisions on costs and damages were still pending, accompanied by a memorial couched in very strong language. He contrasted the behaviour of England unfavourably with that of France and Spain and repeated the Russian demand that ships should be allowed to proceed on examination of their papers alone: "Ce n'est certainement pas des loix et des decisions des cours de l'Amirauté angloise que l'Impératrice laissera jamais dependre la fortune et le sort de ses sujets." [44] Stormont was astounded to receive such angry expostulations, but he took immediate steps to investigate these particular complaints, and where there was a difference of opinion on the amount of damages to

---

43. FO 65/8, unnumbered letter, 16/27 August 1782 (*MD, 1*, 528).

44. FO 65/1, Simolin to Stormont, 8 January 1781, enclosing a note on the *Vryheit* and the *Beurs de Riga* and a further note about an attack by an allegedly British ship, the *Exeter,* on a Russian ship off Spitzbergen, when a Russian sailor was murdered and 3,000 roubles stolen.

be paid Stormont offered to submit the matter to the arbitration of the Empress—a course he was afterwards to regret.[45]

These disputes were long and unpleasant affairs, since the Russian masters invariably sought the best of both worlds. They objected to the British assessment of the value of their cargoes; they expected compensation for delays and deterioration of the cargo, for loss of freight while detained in British ports, for loss of the original return freight, even if they procured a substitute one; they demanded interest on the freight and the freight itself, even when the cargo was restored and sold to its original destination; they demanded compensation for ships' stores eaten by British prize crews, for repairs to damage incurred while in detention, and even for damage incurred after release, but which might not have happened had not the ship been seized. Sometimes the ships' owners or masters agreed to the pre-emptive purchase of the whole cargo by the Navy Board, in which case the ship went before an admiralty court which pronounced sentence accordingly. If taken by a warship, the ship and cargo were usually released immediately, without going before the courts, but this did not prevent the Russians from demanding compensation and damages for the interruption of their journey, however short.[46]

When Catherine some months later issued her judgement on the

45. FO 65/1, Stormont to Harris, No. 2, 16 January 1781.

46. These complaints are drawn from the miscellaneous memorials put in by Simolin, the complaints collected by Harris, and the correspondence between Stormont and the Lords of the Admiralty, the Advocate General, Sir James Marriott, etc. Two examples will suffice to show the kind of problem which arose: the *St. Nicolas* was taken into Lynn on 11 September 1781 and released on 15 September. On its way out of port it fell foul of a sandbank. The Russian memorial on the subject reads: "Si les Anglois ne s'étoient pas emparés de ce vaisseau en contravention du traité . . . ce navire n'auroit point eu vraisemblablement l'accident qui lui est arrivé, du moins par sur les côtes de Grande Bretagne, consequemment les suites en tombent à la charge des Anglois." (Harris Papers). The *Graf Nikita* (owned by Faleyev) arrived on 24 June 1781 at Barcelona and sailed for Ostende on 3 August. She was taken by two Mahonese privateers and on 12 August retaken by a Spanish privateer who promptly released her. The next day she was retaken by a Mahonese privateer, which in turn was seized with its Russian prize by the expeditionary force under the Duc de Crillon sailing to besiege Minorca. (Harris Papers, copy of letter from the captain to Zinovyev of 19 September 1781). Faleyev claimed compensation for the capture by Mahonese privateers, since the ship could not have been taken by the expeditionary force had it not been wrongfully seized by the privateers. (Harris Papers, n.d.)

Russian claims put forward by Simolin in January 1781 and submitted by Stormont to her arbitration, she decided in favour of
her own subjects. But Stormont was so startled by what he regarded
as new Russian pretensions that, though he declared to Simolin
that Catherine's word would be law in the cases remitted to her,
he nevertheless endeavoured to point out to her that, as he believed, she had made an error of fact.[47] Stormont thought the Empress had misunderstood the sentence of the admiralty court in
the case of one of the Russian ships. But the Empress had repeatedly stated that she did not consider herself bound by the
judgements of any admiralty courts whatsoever; she swept the sentence aside and arbitrated according to what presumably seemed
to her natural justice, which of course coincided with the interests
of her own subjects.[48] She therefore protested strongly through
Simolin when her decision was called in question, "qui par sa
nature même doit avoir la force d'une loi irrévocable, même
entre particuliers . . . et c'est moins aux décisions d'aucun tribunal qu'elle a rapporté son arbitrage, qu'aux sentimens du Roi
et à la justice de la cause." [49] The question grew to such proportions that it was not finally settled until February 1782, when
Stormont, after consultation with the King and North, gave way
and accepted Catherine's judgement.[50]

Russian feelings had been further exacerbated in the summer of
1781 by the report of an attack on a Russian bomb-ketch by a ship
flying English colours.[51] Catherine immediately ordered Simolin
to make a vigorous protest against such an attempt "parce qu'il
paroit porter ce caractère de témérité et d'insolence qui n'a rien

47. FO 65/4, Stormont to Simolin, 27 September 1781, enclosed in Stormont to
Harris, No. 67, 28 September 1781.

48. I have not been able to find a copy of Catherine's award but its substance
emerges from the dispute. Stormont argued that since the opinion of the British
government "ne pouvoit pas invalider une sentence du tribunal de l'amirauté; on
concluait naturellement de cette expression que la susdite sentence avoit reglé le
jugement de Sa Majesté Impériale sur ce point"; (FO 65/6, Stormont to Simolin,
2 February 1782).

49. FO 65/6, Simolin to Stormont, 17 January 1782 (copy in Harris Papers, n.d.).

50. On 5 February 1782 Stormont instructed the Lords of the Admiralty to pay
the Russian consul Baxter £4,161.8.1 in settlement of these claims (FO 65/6).

51. FO 65/3, Harris to Stormont, No. 110, 27 July/7 August 1781; three Russian
sailors were wounded and one killed on board the *Molniya* by a ship alleged to be
the *Plymouth*.

de sacré, et qu'il est essentiel de reprimer d'une façon exem-
plaire." [52] But the last straw, where the Empress was concerned,
was the news which reached Russia in October 1781 that a Russian
ship, the *Soeur Anne Martine,* freighted for Spain, had been taken
into Deal by a cruiser. "The Empress gave way to violent passion
on this occasion expressed in the most severe and bitter terms and
ordered Ct. Ostermann to write in the strongest manner to Monsr.
Simolin to insist on the vessel's being immediately restored . . .
She particularly added that no part of the cargo should be sold,
nor any accommodation entered into with our Admiralty," wrote
Harris on 24 October/4 November 1781. Potemkin confirmed that
he had never seen the Empress more agitated; "and that in her
gust of passion, she exclaimed in the most imbittered manner
against our proceedings." [53] Fortunately, the British authorities
decided to release the *Soeur Anne Martine* without delay, and
after a fortnight news of its release reached St. Petersburg. The
Empress thereupon toned down somewhat the acrimony of the
protest she proposed to deliver in London, but she nevertheless
demanded compensation for damage suffered by the ship and in
this case satisfaction also for the insult to her flag.[54] Osterman took
the opportunity in November to press again on Harris that "however sincere and cordial the Empress's friendship was for us, it
would not hold out against her anger if we continued to molest the
commerce of her subjects . . ." The Vice-Chancellor was very
vehement on the subject of the five principles; he declared
that "if we expected Her Imperial Majesty would give up any one

52. FO 65/4, Osterman to Harris, 11 August 1781; Stormont to Lords of the
Admiralty, 21 September 1781, enclosing memorial from Simolin. After inquiries
by the Admiralty, it was reported that the only British ship *Plymouth* had been
taken by the French before the date of the attack on the *Molniya*. This explanation
appears to have been accepted in Russia. (FO 65/5, Stormont to Simolin, 9 November 1781).

53. FO 65/5, Harris to Stormont, No. 161, 24 October/4 November 1781.

54. FO 65/5, Harris to Stormont, No. 180, 2/13 December 1781; see also Aleksandrenko, *Russkiye diplomaticheskiye agenty,* 2, 55 for what was probably the original
text of the rescript to Simolin. The *Soeur Anne Martine* flew Russian colours but
she was detained because she was Prussian built, and the master and the crew were
all Prussians, contrary to the *règlement* which Catherine had issued in May 1780 for
Russian shipping (FO 65/4, Philip Stephens to W. Fraser, 24 September 1781); see
also FO 65/6, Simolin to Stormont, 17 January 1782, and Stormont to Simolin,
Réponse verbale, 2 February 1782.

of the points she had laid down as a law in her declaration, we deceived ourselves; that she was determined to support them, at all risks; and that besides, the being convinced of their equity, her honour was engaged to maintain what she had so solemnly avowed to be her principles in the face of all Europe." [55]

It should have been clear by now that the Neutral League was the Empress's own policy and that she was determined to develop and support it. The defence of her trade in her own ships formed but a small part of the whole, and it is indeed incredible that so much ill-feeling should have been aroused, so much ink and paper wasted in correspondence between Britain and Russia over a total of seventeen detentions of ships in the course of the war.[56] But it was the treatment meted out to Russian ships which finally urged the Empress to pose the one question Britain had been avoiding all the time. Early in January 1782, she scrawled angrily in the margin of a dispatch by Simolin, in which he had again repeated Stormont's assurances that Britain abided by the droit des gens: "Lorsque Mr. Harris fera sa communication de la réponse de l'Angleterre, il sera bon de lui dire que nous serions bien aise de savoir au clair en quoi consistent les principes du droit des gens adoptés par l'Angleterre et que d'avance nous sommes persuadés que le droit de piller les vaisseaux neutres ne peut être du nombre de ces principes." [57] Harris had suspected, ever since the accession of Prussia to the Neutral League, that "the great object of our enemies, is to lead us into a further explanation here, than any we have yet given, on the manner in which we interpret the Law of Nations, *le droit des gens,* being under the certain conviction that we differ in every point from the principles of the famous *Code Primitif.*" [58] But it was in fact the inconsistency of British behaviour, the increasing gap between theory and practice, which led the Empress to press the question.

From the very beginning, when the Empress had first announced

---

55. FO 65/5, Harris to Stormont, No. 166, 5/16 November 1781.

56. It is not possible to tell the exact number of ships involved, since some names occur more than once (e.g. the *Graf Nikita* three times and the *Vryheit* twice). In four cases the cargoes were sold; in one both the ship and the cargo, the ship having been damaged.

57. F. de Martens, *Recueil, 9,* 316. Simolin's dispatch is dated 17/28 December 1781.

58. FO 65/5, Harris to Stormont, No. 152, 21 October/1 November 1781.

the five principles of the Neutral League, Britain had evaded giving a precise answer to the question and had referred vaguely to past practice, the "best authors" and treaties, where they existed, as governing British conduct. But the actual principles derived from reference to these sources had never been specified, and the admiralty courts were guided by the British declaration of October 1778 and the Acts of Parliament and Orders in Council implementing it, which authorized the compulsory acquisition of naval stores destined for the enemy, wherever found. Such a policy could be and was enforced not only by Britain but by any nation that happened to be strong at sea. But now, owing to the multiplicity of her enemies and the kind of war she was engaged in, Britain had not the strength to maintain her stand. Without relinquishing her tradition, she had gradually been forced by the pressure of neutral opinion, largely led by Russia, to modify her practice and to grant neutral trade more privileges than it had enjoyed in any previous war. Naturally enough the neutrals felt the time was opportune to force Britain to modify her theory as well, to define more clearly the system she was actually applying at the moment.

Some time in late 1781 or early 1782 an "Exposé comparatif des differens arrangemens pris par les puissances neutres et belligérentes pour la sureté du commerce et de la navigation neutres" was drawn up in Russia. It is extremely revealing of the gulf between the British and the Russian standpoints on purely legal issues. The document points out that whereas France had issued a *règlement*

> la Grande Bretagne se borna à donner de simples instructions à ses commandans de vaisseaux et armateurs qui devoient régler les formalités à observer à l'occasion des captures, et on y joignit des extraits des stipulations, qui existent entre la couronne de la Grande Bretagne et différentes puissances neutres. De cette manière l'Angleterre a éludé de s'expliquer sur ce qu'elle entend par les droits et libertés des neutres, abandonnant à ses cours d'Amirautés de décider chaque cas particulier en conformité des principes reçus dans ces tribunaux.[59]

59. *Morskoy Sbornik, 44,* 400, No. 69, n.d.

It is evident from this document that what Russia objected to was that Britain had not issued a code or written *règlement* setting out the legal principles she proposed to enforce.[60] The intricacies of the British legal system, its combination of treaties, Acts of Parliament, custom and precedent, and above all "judge-made law," were beyond the understanding of a mind trained in the logical abstractions of the "philosophes." Good laws were essential to good government, and good laws should be written down. Catherine's refusal to be bound by the judgements of the British admiralty courts is easier to understand once this fundamental difference of approach to the whole concept of law is grasped. British practice was at best unpredictable; and the fact that such principles as were proclaimed were not in fact practised, owing to Britain's weakness, only served to irritate the Empress still further. There was no point in detaining ships only to release them with damages and costs; there was no point in asserting that ships had to go before the courts, if they were released on orders from the Lords of the Admiralty or by private treaty between captor and prize.

In the circumstances it was not surprising that the Empress should have endeavoured to force Britain to define her policy towards the rights of neutrals at sea. Early in her career as legislatrix of the seas she had harboured the idea of devising a code of the rights of neutral shipping and of securing its adoption by other European nations. Whether she herself did any work on this code is not certain, but she was at one time in the summer of 1781 closeted with Admiral Greig, and it is to be presumed that she discussed with him the rules applicable to the Russian merchant navy.[61] With the accession of the Emperor to the Neutral League his opinions were invited on a Russian draft, since the joint imperial mediation might be used to force the incorporation of the proposed maritime code into the peace treaty.[62]

60. See Ch. 3, pp. 66 ff. for the mental agonies endured by Suffolk at the thought of issuing a "code."

61. FO 65/3, Harris to Stormont, No. 93, 25 June/6 July 1781: "such part of it [this work] as is done by him will certainly be very compleat." See also Beer and Fiedler, *Joseph II und Graf Ludwig Cobenzl, I*, 176, Cobenzl to Joseph, 16 July 1781.

62. FO 65/4, Harris to Stormont, No. 135, 14/25 September 1781; a Russian draft, possibly the exposé mentioned on p. 375 was handed to Cobenzl in March 1782. The

Neither Osterman acting on Harris nor Simolin in talks with Stormont was able to extract from the Secretary of State anything more precise than that the *droit des gens* as practised by Britain was to be found in the best authors and in the practice of all nations "in a position similar to that in which we stand." [63] Nevertheless this constant Russian pressure, coupled with the general activity of the members of the Neutral League and the evident failure of the policy of starving the Bourbon powers of naval stores, left its mark in Britain.

The accession of Prussia to the Neutral League in May 1781 did in fact undo, from Britain's point of view, much of the good achieved by driving the Dutch into war. In general the logical corollary of "free ships, free goods" had been "unfree ships, unfree goods"; in other words, neutral property on board an enemy ship could legitimately be condemned. The Empress's declaration of the principles of navigation had made no reference at all to this aspect of the problem, though she had in practice claimed to protect Russian property wherever seized. But the Prussian Ordonnance concerning Navigation and Maritime Commerce, dated 30 April 1781, expressed the hope, in Article 2, that the belligerents would allow Prussian non-contraband cargoes on belligerent ships to go free, thus for the first time stating the full range of privilege which neutral shipping now claimed.[64] It was to be ex-

---

Austrian comments, in the form of "Reflexions sur la liberté des mers en général . . ." were handed by Cobenzl to Osterman on 22 June 1782 (F. de Martens, *Recueil*, 2, 131–32, and 131, n. 2). This document sets forth a number of fairly controversial propositions, notably that all goods not defined as contraband are non-contraband; that neutrals shall trade freely with belligerent powers except in civil wars or to places under effective blockade; that the space occupied by a neutral at sea and within the range of its guns shall be neutral territory; that privateers should examine ships' papers only and release the ship if no suspicion is aroused, but if the ship is destined to an enemy country the privateers can examine bills of lading; that ships sailing in convoy should not be visited; that if a ship carries contraband it can be released at once on the high seas if it hands over the contraband goods to the captor; that if a ship is wrongfully detained it should claim damages from the state and not from the privateer. (A copy of these "Reflexions" was procured by Harris in 1783 and has been printed in English translation in Piggott and Omond, *Documentary History*, p. 365.)

63. See FO 65/6, Harris to Stormont, No. 10, 1/12 February 1782; F. de Martens, *Recueil*, 9, 316, Simolin to the Empress, 25 February/8 March 1782.

64. Scott, *Armed Neutralities*, p. 391.

pected that Russia would defend such claims by her own subjects and support similar Prussian claims by diplomatic means.

In spite of Frederick's spate of regulations for Prussian trade,[65] the Prussian flag was at once used to colour the trade of the Dutch who, for an oath which weighed but lightly on all consciences, transferred to the register of Emden.[66] In 1780 only 671 Prussian ships passed the Sound; in 1781 the number rose to 1507.[67] The ports of the Austrian Netherlands also flourished as a result of the process known as "ostendisiren" of ships. Flemish shipping had increased in a few years "from a state of absolute insignificancy to the possessing of upwards of three hundred sail of shipping," wrote the British envoy, Fitzherbert, on 3 August 1781.[68] Indeed, though the Emperor spoke disparagingly of the Neutral League, the Austrian envoy in London did not hesitate, after the imperial accession, to invoke the assistance of Simolin in defence of Austrian ships. The accession of Prussia and Austria thus defeated the whole purpose of the British breach with the United Provinces, and this factor certainly influenced Stormont when in September 1781 he decided to accept the Empress's renewed offer of separate mediation with Holland.[69]

When Prussian accession was formally communicated to Stormont in September 1781, he refused to admit that Prussia could adopt the definition of contraband and the rules for free trade laid down in the Anglo-Russian treaty of 1766.[70] In the same way

65. Ibid., p. 391, 30 April 1781; p. 411, 3 November 1781; p. 414, 8 December 1781.

66. Harris Papers, Elliot to Harris, 8 September 1781; see also Krauel, "Preussen und die bewaffnete Neutralitaet," pp. 141–42, and FO 65/3, Harris to Stormont, No. 105, 14/25 July 1781.

67. Krauel, "Preussen und die bewaffnete Neutralitaet," p. 141.

68. Quoted in Gorman, *America and Belguim*, p. 134. British merchant ships were not above taking advantage of the process of "ostendisiren" also; an English ship would put into Ostende, make a pretended sale of cargo and ship to a local merchant, acquire imperial papers, and trade with the enemy.

69. Fortescue, *Correspondence of King George III*, 5, 267, Stormont to the King, 25 August 1781: "The nature of the Dutch war is greatly changed by the King of Prussia's accession to the Northern League, and by his flag covering so large a number of ships that are nominally Prussian but really Dutch, in a few months the whole Dutch trade will run in that and in the Austrian channel."

70. FO 65/4, Stormont to Harris, No. 55, 7 September 1781; see also Stormont to Simolin, 15 September 1781.

Stormont refused to admit the Emperor's right to adopt Articles 10 and 11 of the Anglo-Russian treaty, when Belgioioso formally communicated Austrian accession to the Neutral League on 13 December 1781.[71]

But though Stormont still refused to concede anything orally or on paper, in practice the treatment of neutral ships by Britain became more and more lenient.[72] The change in the treatment of Prussian ships was particularly noticeable and gave some colour to the feeling harboured in Russia that Prussia was treated with more respect than Russia. In 1780, the Prussian envoy dealt with only eight ships; in the first quarter of 1781, twenty-three cases were taken up through diplomatic channels.[73] Trials were speeded

71. FO 7/3, Belgioioso to Stormont, 13 December 1781. The separate Acts in which Catherine and Joseph bound themselves to press the adoption of a maritime code at the peace were not communicated. Cf. also Stormont to Belgioioso, 27 December 1781.

72. Two Danish ships were released with costs against the captors in 1781–82 (FO 65/6, Harris to Stormont, 22 February/5 March 1782, No. 17). A Prussian ship *De Hoop* was taken into Portsmouth on 30 December 1781, with hemp and iron. The ship and the iron were restored, and the hemp, of which the ownership was doubtful, was condemned to be sold to the Navy Board, the Prussian master receiving freight and expenses. When the Russian consul claimed the hemp, he was told to prove the ownership. The explanation given to Russia was that "inasmuch as the court had never deemed hemp and iron to be contraband when claimed by the inhabitants of the country of which those commodities was the growth" it was not condemned. (FO 65/6, Stormont to Simolin, 15 February 1782). Stormont was not certain whether Russian property on board a Prussian ship could be condemned at all, and as he put it in a letter to Sandwich, "it seems to me that if the ship in question is set at liberty immediately before any complaint can be made . . . very unpleasant discussions may be avoided. If we cannot stand openly upon the ground we should wish to maintain the best expedient in my poor judgement is to avoid a formal decision which would lose the point forever." (FO 64/3, Stormont to Sandwich, 12 January 1782). The hemp was eventually restored to the Russian owner. (FO 64/3, Advocate General to Fox, 29 April 1782). In regard to the *Palmsbaum* taken on 15 May 1780, the judge released the ship, but on 7 July he condemned the hemp and tow as contraband or "as otherwise liable to confiscation" to be sold to the Navy Board. On appeal to the House of Lords on 21 January 1782, this judgement was upheld, which was not surprising since the Lords were Bathurst (Lord President of the Council), Sandwich (First Lord of the Admiralty), Stormont (Secretary of State), Loughborough (ex-Attorney General and now Chief Justice of the Common Pleas) and Clarendon (Chancellor of the Duchy of Lancaster), a clear case of the union of the executive and the judiciary. (FO 64/3, Advocate General to Fox, 29 April 1782).

73. Krauel, "Preussen und die bewaffnete Neutralitaet," p. 142.

up, and quite a number of ships did not go before the courts at all.[74] But in spite of this improvement in the British treatment of Prussian ships, they were still not in fact as favourably treated as Russian ships and cargoes, and the Prussian claim to apply the list of contraband contained in Article 11 of the Anglo-Russian treaty was not accepted.[75] The main reason for the unexpected complaisance towards Prussian shipping lay in the fear that Frederick II, who was ever seeking some ground on which to re-establish his connexion with Russia, would be enabled to make *"cause commune* with her in some point of her wild and unjust confederacy against this country." [76] But it led instead to increased irritation against Britain in Russia, for the Prussian ships began to secure higher freight charges in St. Petersburg than the Russian for the export of Russian produce. Indeed, "the Russian merchant ships have in general been sorely disappointed," wrote Consul Shairp to Stormont on 22 October/2 November 1781, "as they expected high freights and to be greatly in demand; their marine character is however so very bad that several have engaged on terms by which they must lose." [77] The preference shown to Prussian ships was due to their better seamanship, rather than to any preferential treatment by Britain since Prussia had joined the League. But the impression prevailed, and was fomented by Prussia, that Britain showed particular respect to the Prussian flag.[78]

74. FO 64/3, Lusi to Grantham, 11 November 1782, enclosing a list of 5 Prussian ships taken by British cruisers whose cargoes were restored. Of these only one had been proceeded against in the admiralty courts (the *Hoop*). The other cases had all been "privately adjusted" (FO 64/3, J. Heseltine, Doctors Commons, to George Maddison (Under-Secretary), 16 November 1782). See also Krauel, "Preussen und die bewaffnete Neutralitaet," pp. 143–44.

75. In the case of the *Vrow Maria Petronella,* Prussian, loaded with hemp and iron at St. Petersburg for Bordeaux, the cargo was condemned to be sold to the Navy Board. (FO 64/3, Lusi to Grantham, 11 November 1782, protesting against the admiralty court sentence).

76. FO 64/3, Stormont to Sandwich, 24 January 1782.

77. FO 65/4, Shairp to Stormont, 22 October/2 November 1781.

78. See e.g. Harris Papers, mémoire protesting against the detention of the *Saint Jean,* "tandisque les anglois laissent naviguer paisiblement le pavillon prussien." (November 1781). See also FO 7/3, Keith to Stormont, No. 162, 31 December 1781, quoting Kaunitz's complaints on the preferential treatment of the Prussian flag by Britain. Cf. Krauel, "Preussen und die bewaffnete Neutralitaet," p. 144.

The Neutral League was thus proving itself a sufficiently forceful political weapon to encourage the Empress to extend the network more widely. Portugal had been invited to become a member as early as March 1780, but her accession had not been encouraged by Britain. French pressure eventually forced the Queen to curtail the privileges granted to the British navy in Portugal, whereupon Vergennes in turn saw no reason why Portugal should join the Neutral League. He felt happier with Portugal dependent on France alone. The Empress thought otherwise, and eventually a convention embodying Portuguese accession was signed on 24 July 1782; Article 3 defined contraband in accordance with Articles 10 and 11 of the Anglo-Russian treaty of 1766.[79] Negotiations were also inaugurated in 1782 with the Kingdom of the Two Sicilies, but the agreement was only concluded in February 1783. Here too the relevant articles of the Anglo-Russian treaty were adopted as governing the definition of contraband.[80]

Beneath the imposing edifice of the Neutral League, the three Northern courts were also seeking to protect certain specific interests of their own. In the conventions linking the three founding members of the League, a separate article had been included to the effect that the Baltic was to be considered a closed sea.[81] No action was taken in 1780 to enforce this policy, but the outbreak of the Anglo-Dutch war led to a fear that hostilities would extend to these waters. As early as March 1781, Panin informed Harris that the Northern courts proposed to "keep this sea entirely free from privateers of every nation whatsoever."[82] On 8 May 1781, Denmark, as guardian of the Sound, took the lead in issuing a declaration stating that the King would not admit "armed vessels of the Powers at war for the purpose of committing acts of hostility against any one whatsoever."[83] France welcomed the declaration;

79. For the negotiations, see Fauchille, *La diplomatie française*, pp. 583 ff., Maykov, *Pis'ma A. A. Bezborodka*, p. 84, Bezborodko to Rumyantsev, 13/24 August 1781; FO 65/4, Harris to Stormont, No. 130, 7/18 September 1781. For the text of the treaty see Scott, *Armed Neutralities*, p. 420.

80. Scott, *Armed Neutralities*, p. 433.

81. Scott, *Armed Neutralities*, p. 299, separate Article 1, at p. 305.

82. FO 65/3, Harris to Stormont, No. 34, 9/20 March 1781 (*MD, 1*, 392).

83. Scott, *Armed Neutralities*, p. 290, wrongly dated 1780.

Britain had already anticipated it by issuing fresh instructions to privateers in April 1781, forbidding British ships to take prizes in the Baltic.[84] Catherine expressed her pleasure at this mark of consideration but immediately asked for more. On 6 June 1781, Osterman told Harris that the Empress now expressed the hope that the King "would extend the new instructions still farther, and forbid his cruizers from even coming into the Baltic." But it was limiting British freedom of action too much to agree not to allow warships into the Baltic, and for the time being the Russians did not press the point.[85] As further evidence of the seriousness of their intentions the Northern courts again sent out their squadrons on patrol. In 1781, Russia sent seventeen Russian battleships, of which a number went to the Mediterranean. From May to August, four Danish battleships were stationed in the Sound.[86] Harris was cheered to hear that the instructions to the Russian admiral were "to avoid as much as possible taking any vessel under his convoy, and to make the best of his way back." To which Harris added, "From his character (which is perfectly pacific) . . . he will . . . execute instructions very exactly." [87] In 1782, Sweden and Denmark reduced their fleets, but Russia again sent seventeen battleships and frigates out on patrol. One squadron went to the Mediterranean and indeed remained there, based on Leghorn, until September 1784. The second squadron cruised in the North Sea and returned to Cronstadt on 30 September 1782.[88]

By the spring of 1782 the Neutral League had thus succeeded in forcing Britain onto the defensive in maritime questions. Russian ships were still detained, but by paying damages for detention Britain had admitted implicitly the illegality of the seizures. Though Britain did not openly modify her stand regarding Denmark and Sweden, and unpleasant incidents still occurred, these powers too benefited from the practice of pre-emptive purchase

84. Scott, *Armed Neutralities,* p. 391, British additional instructions to privateers and warships.

85. FO 65/3, Harris to Stormont, No. 82, 28 May/8 June 1781; No. 92, 25 June/6 July 1781.

86. Anderson, *Naval Wars in the Baltic,* p. 238.

87. FO 65/3, Harris to Stormont, No. 88, 8/19 June 1781 (*MD, 1,* 424).

88. Anderson, *Naval Wars in the Baltic,* p. 239.

and from the speeding up of trials. Britain had indeed suffered a serious blow in the accession of Prussia and Austria to the Neutral League.[89] She could not afford to alienate the potentially friendly Austria and the potentially hostile Prussia, and both were prepared to take full advantage of the opportunities which the League offered for the development of their trade. The united front presented in London by the Danes, the Swedes, the Prussians, and the Austrians, supported by the irritable and powerful Russians, slowly and surely undermined Stormont's policy.[90] Whenever one of them protested about the detention of a ship, he received support from his colleagues.[91]

On the political side the Neutral League had unsuspected importance. By refusing to ally herself with Britain, and by uniting the neutrals under her wing, Russia frustrated every British effort to find allies or even temporary diplomatic support against the Bourbons. Denmark and Austria had offered the only possible hope, and both had, though for different reasons, followed in Russia's train. The League, it is true, had failed to show its teeth in defence of the Dutch. But though British treatment of Dutch navigation had in great part inspired the Empress to found the Armed Neutrality, the Dutch suffered from the weakness that they were only carriers, not producers, of naval stores. Britain could do without them, and the Northern crowns discovered in the course of 1781 that they too could dispense with their services for

89. On this point I take issue with Fauchille, who writes (*La diplomatie française*, p. 578): "L'adhésion de ces trois pays [Prussia, Austria, and the Kingdom of the Two Sicilies] dont l'importance au point de vue maritime était nulle, n'était pas en vérité pour la ligue un accroissement de puissance . . ."

90. See Aleksandrenko, *Russkiye diplomaticheskiye agenty*, 2, 219, for a rescript of 20 November/1 December 1781, to the Russian envoys in London, Madrid and The Hague, instructing them to act with their colleagues of the Neutral League on complaints regarding ships, without waiting for instructions.

91. See e.g. FO 65/5, Harris to Stormont, No. 151, 20 October/1 November 1781 enclosing a *note verbale* on a British clash with a Swedish convoy; FO 65/6, Simolin to Stormont, 4 February 1782, re the Prussian ship *De Hoop;* FO 65/7, Simolin to Fox, supporting the Austrian envoy's complaints re the *Venus* and the *Chasseur d'Ostende,* 29 June 1782; Simolin to Fox (or Shelburne), 6 July 1782, supporting Dreyer's complaint about the seizure of a Danish convoy in the West Indies; FO 65/8, Simolin to Grantham, supporting Swedish complaints about the condemnation of the *Sophia* and the *Amphitrite,* 10 October 1782, and further memorial of 28 November 1782, complaining that the previous one had remained unanswered, and of the detention of three more Swedish ships.

the export of their produce. The Baltic powers, however, particularly Russia, were in a far stronger position than the Dutch in
relation to Britain. By cutting off naval stores, and particularly
the great Riga masts, they could cripple Britain at sea and render
almost impossible the continuation of operations which depended
entirely on the possession of a powerful navy.[92] The price paid
for the neglect of the navy under Lord Sandwich's administration
was the complete dependence of Britain at a crucial moment on
supplies of naval stores from countries which insisted on their
right to supply both belligerent sides.

No adequate study has yet been made of the other aspect of the
Neutral League—the extent to which it achieved a free trade in
naval stores. But the evidence available suggests that it was far more
effective in purely economic terms than is generally admitted by
historians who have attributed the whole policy to the promptings
of Catherine's vanity. According to one authority, from November
1778 to May 1780, 96 freights of neutrals were sold to the Navy
Board whereas from May 1780 to November 1782, the number
sold was only 32.[93] But this estimate does not take into account that
from December 1780 Dutch cargoes would be condemned as enemy
and not as neutral, and they probably made up a good percentage
of the 96 freights. It is also possible that very few Dutch ships with
naval stores were captured after December 1780, since practically
no Dutch ships went to the Baltic; thus the drop of two-thirds in the
figures might simply represent the disappearance of the Dutch
merchant marine from the trade in naval stores. More conclusive
are the figures supplied by Albion. From Riga alone, 996 masts
were exported to Britain from 1778 to the end of September 1782;
in the same period 868 masts went directly to France, and 29 via
Genoa. To Holland 1,855 masts were exported, of which some 600
were not on account of the Dutch navy; 405 masts were exported
to Spain.[94] Thus the number of masts (even if of inferior quality)
reaching the French dockyards was not much less than that reaching Britain. Assuming that some of the masts exported to Holland

92. See Albion, *Forests and Sea Power*, pp. 281 ff. for a study of the effect on
British naval operations of the shortage of ships' timber, particularly masts.

93. Gerhardt, *England und der Aufstieg Russlands*, p. 136, n. 141.

94. Albion, *Forests and Sea Power*, pp. 193–94.

were re-exported to France, the French supply would have been larger than the British. These are only indications, however, and a definite conclusion could only be reached after an analysis of the number of neutrals with cargoes of naval stores reaching enemy ports before and after the accession of the neutral power concerned to the Armed Neutrality.

But whatever the objective truth, there is evidence that both in Britain and among the neutrals the League was believed at the time to be effective. The purpose of the Dutch war was defeated by the accession of Prussia and Austria to the League, as Stormont realized in September 1781. Had the Armed Neutrality not been effective, Stormont would not have been so deeply stirred by "the Empress's wild system, which, though called a neutral league, is in effect a combination against this country equally unjust in its principle, and extravagant in its aim." [95] Sandwich, in his defence of his administration of the navy, in January 1782, was more outspoken: "We have effectually blocked the port of Amsterdam during all the last summer," he declared, "and had it not been for the subterfuge of neutral colours, and from our fear of disgusting the Northern powers, not a ship could have got in or out of the Texel." [96] In August 1782, Consul Shairp reported from St. Petersburg that neutrals were loading for enemy ports quite openly, without endeavouring to conceal their destination.[97] Stormont fought a rear-guard action, grudging every inch of the way, making no open concessions; he might never have given in. The Whigs held different views. From the beginning they had attacked the government's policy towards neutral trade.[98] On the outbreak of the Anglo-Dutch war Shelburne had proclaimed in the House of Lords in January 1781 that "to the disgrace of the country, to the total dishonour of its councils, and in direct violation of all laws, whether of nations, of nature, of public honour, and private faith, the ships and cargoes are seized, not to be retained, but confiscated

95. FO 7/3, Stormont to Keith, No. 84, 28 December 1781.

96. Fortescue, *Correspondence of King George III*, 5, 342.

97. FO 65/8, Shairp to Grantham, 15/26 August 1782. Privateering had almost ceased by the end of the war since so many ships were released that the captors found no profit in it, according to Storch, *Historisch-statistisches Gemälde des russischen Reiches*, 6, 37.

98. See *Parliamentary Register*, *15*, 335, Shelburne on 1 June 1780.

for the joint advantage of the captors and the state; and what is worse than all, a commandment given to render the municipal tribunals the instrument of legalizing an act, which is equally repugnant to every law now existing in the written codes, current or of authority throughout Europe." [99] It was not therefore surprising that the Empress should have pressed so hard for Britain to define her maritime principles. The formulas that reached her through Stormont and Harris were evidently not universally acknowledged in Britain, and the "better" part of the nation contested them in even more violent language than she did. The ground was cut from under Stormont's feet in Russia by the opposition at home. Catherine's own views could not have been better expressed than by Shelburne.

Not only on political but on economic grounds as well the Whigs seemed prepared to view the maritime principles enforced by the Neutral League with more favour than the North administration. Much later, in March 1783, Grantham expressed the opinion that "with regard to the Neutral Code, it is certain that the extent of the war began to render it in some degree usefull even to ourselves, and in case of the continuation of ye war it might have been necessary to have adopted some of the principles of it." [100] The failure of Stormont's policy in fact, and their own past criticism of it, prepared the Whigs for surrender.

99. Ibid., *21*, 79, 25 January 1781.
100. FO 27/6 (France), Grantham to Fitzherbert, plenipotentiary for the negotiation of the peace treaty, No. 41, 13 March 1783.

16. Fox's Foreign Policy

By MID-DECEMBER 1781 most of the members of the North administration, including North himself, had become convinced that the struggle in America was hopeless. Not so the King. Unwilling or unable to resign, North manoeuvred for some time in the hope of maintaining the King's policy, but all efforts to reconstruct the government or to form a coalition failed, and finally, on 20 March 1782, the King accepted North's resignation.[1]

On 26 March Stormont wrote to Harris announcing the change of government.[2] He left it to his successor to reply to Harris's latest dispatches and merely stressed that as yet the King had no desire to recall him. The Whig government came to power committed to bringing the war in America to a close, and Lord Shelburne, the new secretary of state for home and colonial affairs, sent an emissary, Richard Oswald, to inaugurate discussions with Franklin in Paris. The new secretary of state for foreign affairs, Charles James Fox, had now to pick his way among the problems inherited from the previous government, namely the joint imperial mediation, the sole Russian mediation with the United Provinces, and the problems arising out of the Armed Neutrality. Fox came to power determined to reverse Stormont's policy in all fields, and he set to work at once. As foreign secretary he would have to direct peace negotiations with France, Spain, and the United Provinces, and he sent Thomas Grenville to Paris to pave the way with Vergennes.

The first stage in Fox's policy was an attempt to break the union between the United Provinces and France and to improve relations with Russia. Both objects might be achieved if Britain agreed to give up the demand to modify the Marine Treaty of 1674.

1. See Christie, *End of North's Ministry*, pp. 299 ff.
2. FO 65/6, Stormont to Harris, No. 7, 26 March 1782.

Accordingly, on 28 March 1782, the cabinet agreed to negotiate peace with the Dutch "on the footing of free navigation according to the treaty of 1674" and to an immediate cessation of hostilities.[3] On 29 March Fox communicated this decision to Simolin, who was invited in turn to inform Galitzin and Markov at The Hague. The two Russian envoys, without waiting for instructions from Russia, promptly presented a memorial to the States General on 3 April 1782, submitting the fresh British proposals.[4] The first step was thus taken in surrendering to Russian demands.

Meanwhile Harris was in complete ignorance of this great change and continued strenuously in Russia to defend the old position.[5] On 25 April he received at last the confirmation that his new chief was to be Fox, whom he knew well, and also the news that Britain had surrendered her stand on the Dutch Marine Treaty.[6] Long residence in Russia had imbued Harris with a profound belief in the importance of keeping Russia friendly, and he proceeded at once to draw the maximum advantage from Britain's new policy. He now urged on Osterman the energetic prosecution of the mediation; the Empress should act quickly and force the Dutch into submission before they got over the initial confusion caused by Britain's concession and before France had leisure to recover her influence.[7]

But the impact of the British surrender over the Marine Treaty was not so favourable in the United Provinces as Fox and the Empress might have expected. The Dutch were under very strong pressure from France not to conclude any separate treaty with Britain, nor even to negotiate separately with her. They indulged in a fresh bout of tergiversations, delaying their acceptance of Britain's conditions and generally arousing Catherine's indigna-

3. Fox, *Memorials and Correspondence, 1,* 331. There is a misprint in the text, 1764 for 1674.

4. FO 65/6, Fox to Simolin, 29 March 1782; Coquelle, *L'alliance franco-hollandaise,* p. 266.

5. FO 65/6, Harris to Stormont, No. 34, 29 March/9 April 1782.

6. FO 65/6, Harris to Fox, No. 1, 15/26 April 1782. See also Fox to Harris, No. 1, 2 April 1782, *MD, 1,* 493, which shows the friendly regard in which Fox held Harris, and his No. 2 of the same date, *MD, 1,* 494.

7. FO 65/6, Harris to Fox, No. 2, 19/30 April 1782; see Coquelle, *L'alliance franco-hollandaise,* pp. 269–70.

tion against them.[8] Indeed, Harris was so impressed that he believed that had not Potemkin "changed his system I could be responsible at this moment, that I could lead her [the Empress] into any lengths against them." [9]

Harris naturally enough took advantage of his friendship with his new chief to set some of his ideas on paper concerning the outstanding problems in Anglo-Russian relations. In a long dispatch dated 19/30 April 1782, he pointed out that the Empress was "disposed to have very great confidence in the new administration." The primary object in her mind, wrote Harris, "was the making the principles of the Armed Neutrality universal maritime law," and in this he gauged the Empress's views correctly. He expressed the belief, which he had never dared to write so openly to Stormont, that had Britain acknowledged these principles for Russia alone the Armed Neutrality would have lost its significance. But as things stood, he declared, "I am very far from thinking it is worth while gratifying Her Imperial Majesty's whim (for it is no more) at so dear a price as the acknowledging the five points of the Neutral Convention." Nothing, however, could so completely restore the Empress to Britain or be so likely to embroil her with Britain's enemies as an acknowledgement of these same principles.[10] The question to be faced was how much Britain really needed Russian friendship.

In a second dispatch of the same date, Harris pointed out that the advent of the new administration had encouraged the Empress to think of setting the joint imperial mediation in motion again. Nothing was apparently said directly to Harris in Russia on this subject, but he warned Fox that it might arise and that the Empress might bring up again those very same proposals which had been rejected out of hand by Britain in June 1781. However much ideas might have changed in Britain since then, thought Harris, it was unlikely that France's attitude would have altered. In the circumstances, he wrote, should these proposals again be brought up,

8. Cf. Coquelle, *L'alliance franco-hollandaise*, pp. 266 ff., who shows a strong nationalist French bias in his interpretation of Fox's policy and has not troubled to check the diplomatic lies of Vauguyon with British sources.

9. FO 65/7, Harris to Fox, No. 13, 3/14 May 1782.

10. FO 65/6, Harris to Fox, No. 4, 19/30 April 1782 (*MD, 1,* 501).

Britain would do well to accept them and leave the Bourbons to turn them down. Such a course might induce the two imperial courts to "speak to France and Spain, as the Empress, at this moment, does to Holland." At all events Catherine's goodwill would be won; though she had not at first been sorry to see Britain somewhat reduced from the position of superiority she had occupied after the Peace of Paris, the Empress was now unwilling to see Britain sink too low and might well prove to be a more impartial mediatrix than she was prepared to be earlier.[11]

It was true, as Harris indicated, that at the moment the Empress was more inclined to favour Britain than the Bourbons. Fox's surrender over the Marine Treaty of 1674 was a great triumph for Russia. Moreover France was countering her policy in the United Provinces, and Spain was a standing irritation. In spite of Russian and French pressure, Spain had refused to annul the order confiscating naval stores on board Danish ships, which she had issued as a reprisal for the Anglo-Danish convention of 4 July 1780. Danish shipping had been detained—even a Danish frigate—and Denmark had not failed to seek Russian support in her quarrel with Spain.[12] But Harris's advice on the revival of the joint imperial mediation suffered from the defect that he saw the matter too exclusively in terms of its impact on relations with Russia. Fox had not yet troubled to inform him of the general lines of the policy he was planning. But once peace had been decided upon, direct negotiations between France and England could clearly achieve more, and more quickly, than the mediation of two courts, neither of which could be relied upon to champion the real interests of either of the belligerents. Each would rather seek to extract for itself the maximum advantage from its position as mediator and to establish that balance of power between Britain and the Bourbons which suited it best. Moreover Harris was misled by French military successes and by their intrigues in the United Provinces into thinking that France was less likely than Britain to desire peace; he did not realize that the economic situation in

11. FO 65/6, Harris to Fox, No. 3, 19/30 April 1782 (*MD, 1,* 500).

12. See Ch. 15, p. 364 and note 19 for Spain's reprisals against Denmark. See also FO 65/6, Harris to Fox, No. 3, 19/30 April 1782 (*MD, 1,* 500) and FO 65/7, No. 11, 29 April/10 May 1782, in which he refers to instructions given to the Russian envoy in Spain to protest against the detention of a Danish frigate.

France was such that peace was a necessity and that Vergennes was simply manoeuvring in his turn to extract the utmost from the apparent defeat of Britain. Indeed, though a rapid peace was the ultimate aim of both sides, and early in May talks were begun in Paris, military operations continued in full swing. Britain was only just foiled in an attempt on the Cape of Good Hope; Spain was still determined to make one final effort to conquer Gibraltar; and Rodney had been entrusted with the defence of Jamaica against the projected invasion by the joint French and Spanish fleets under de Grasse. *Si vis pacem para bellum* was the general mood, and the fear that peace might still be long in coming guided Fox in his efforts to construct from the wreckage of the North administration some kind of foreign policy for Britain.

Apart from the first obvious steps, exploratory talks with France, carried out by Grenville, and the attempt to detach Holland from France and to renew links with Russia at the cost of Stormont's naval policy, Fox meditated a reversal of Stormont's reliance on Austria—which had indeed proved a broken reed—and the restoration of Anglo-Prussian friendship. The enmity which Frederick II harboured towards George III was well-known, and it extended to all those who could be regarded as the instruments of the King's policy. It was equally well-known that George III hated the Whigs, and most particularly Fox. Moreover since Prussia had seemingly lost ground in Russia and had not been able to break the bonds linking France and Austria, Frederick had been left somewhat isolated in Europe. He was not likely to refuse the proffered hand of friendship of Fox. Sometime in April Fox communicated with Frederick through the Prussian envoy Lusi. If one is to judge by the draft of a letter to Lusi preserved in Fox's papers, Fox spoke in terms sufficiently abject of Britain's past mistakes, which he blamed on the bad advice given to the King since the beginning of his reign, to assuage Frederick's resentment against his treatment at the hands of George III and his former first minister, Bute. In an interview with Lusi, Fox spoke in a veiled manner of his distrust of the joint imperial mediation and his hope that Prussia might be associated with the peace negotiation.[13]

13. Fox, *Memorials and Correspondence, 1*, 338, undated draft letter; cf. Conn, *Gibraltar in British Eighteenth Century Diplomacy*, p. 199, quoting Lusi to Fred-

Frederick's reply was evidently encouraging, for on 9 May 1782 Fox wrote to the Prussian envoy and laid before Frederick Britain's peace terms. Above all he raised the issue of what to do if the peace negotiations failed and hinted that whether war or peace ensued "le Roi désire également de renouer avec sa Majesté Prussienne ces liaisons d'amitié et d'alliance" which had previously united the two realms.[14] For Fox hoped to induce Prussia to intervene in some way to support the British peace terms. This was going too far and too fast for Frederick. He was willing, even eager, to intervene as a mediator, but an alliance with an exhausted Britain did not enter into his plans, which were still aimed for the time being at detaching France from Austria. Moreover, as he pointed out to his envoy in London for Fox's information, he could not ally himself with another power without Russia.[15]

Fox's initiative in reopening confidential relations with Frederick II was for the time being concealed even from the British envoy in Berlin, Hugh Elliot. Indeed Elliot, who had made himself personally obnoxious to Frederick, was shortly to be sacrificed. On 14 June 1782, Fox bluntly informed him that he was to be replaced by an envoy whose high rank in the British peerage would give proof to Frederick of the King's desire to show friendship to Prussia.[16] To Harris also Fox had made no mention of his plans but, in a very friendly dispatch of 19 April 1782, he invited Harris to give his advice on the best means to strengthen the friendship between Russia and Britain. Were any hopes to be placed on Potemkin? asked Fox. Was the court of Berlin "the certain road"? (the only clue Fox gave Harris to the ideas he entertained). And finally could anyone be effectively bribed to help?[17]

In his reply on 10/21 May 1782 Harris stressed that though

erick of 23 April 1782; Brown, *America through Prussian Eyes*, p. 24, Lusi to Frederick, 30 April 1782. There is no trace of these early talks between Fox and Lusi in the Foreign Office Papers Prussia (FO 64/3).

14. FO 64/3, Fox to Lusi, 9 May 1782.

15. FO 64/3, Lusi to Fox, quoting Frederick to Lusi, 8 June 1782. See also *PKFG*, Ergänzungsband, p. 246, Considérations sur l'état politique de l'Europe, 9 May 1782.

16. FO 64/3, Fox to Elliot, No. 4, 14 June 1782. No mention was made in this almost insulting letter of an alternative post for Elliot, which perhaps explains his later accusation that Fox had been bribed by Lord Cholmondeley with £3,000 for the post (Harris Papers, Elliot to Harris, 18 December 1782).

17. FO 65/6, Fox to Harris, No. 4, 19 April 1782, *MD, 1*, 497.

the Empress inclined by nature to Britain she had felt that for some years she had been treated with "a cool reserve and diffidence." Again he dwelt on the fact that a recognition of the principles of the Neutral League would gratify her in her "most favourite wish" and would destroy the advantage the Bourbons had now acquired at the Russian court. As for the influence of foreign courts, Harris's advice here was less soundly based. Though he alone of the foreign envoys knew of the conclusion of the secret Austro-Russian treaty, he was convinced by the apparent defection of Potemkin, his refusal to drive Panin from court, and his contacts with Goertz and the Bourbons, that Potemkin was working to overthrow the Austrian ascendancy. With his usual gift for dramatization, Harris had already warned Fox on 19/30 April that Prussia, in an effort to restore her influence, was endeavouring to gain the Prince; and the latter, resentful of the Emperor's influence over Catherine, jealous of Bezborodko, and lured by the false hope that through Panin he might preserve his titles and riches into the next reign, forsakes the cause he has set on foot, supports a man he was instrumental in oversetting and "turns his back on those who seconded him in this work," including of course Harris himself. Unfortunately Harris had always under-estimated the Prince's cunning. The moral he now drew was that joint action by Russia and Austria was unlikely.[18] Thus when Harris wrote to Fox, he estimated Prussian and Austrian influence at the Russian court as about equal, with the Prussian on the whole rising. The influence of Prussia in the past had done Britain nothing but harm. That of Austria, which he had tried to increase, had done Britain no good. At most Frederick might be persuaded to cease supporting France in Russia. At any rate no other foreign power could exercise any useful influence. As to "applications to the personal interests of individuals," Harris dismissed these out of hand as a waste of public money. Only Potemkin had any influence, "and he is so enormously rich, that nothing less than a subsidy, even supposing him venal, could purchase him." One last word of advice Harris added in his dispatch: "whatever is to be done would be better done through any other man

18. FO 65/6, Harris to Fox, No. 6, 19/30 April 1782; cf. for Cobenzl's fears, Beer and Fiedler, *Joseph II und Graf Ludwig Cobenzl*, *1*, 303, to Joseph, 23 March 1782.

than through me . . . I am *used*," he wrote. "New faces and new habits are recommendations here, and mine have been too long before their eyes." [19]

Meanwhile Harris had already been left behind by events. Britain's surrender on the Marine Treaty now led Russia to press for the adoption of the Empress's maritime principles as the groundwork of the peace with the Dutch. In a memorial of 1 May 1782 Simolin pointed out that if the British government accepted the principles of the Neutral League, "il n'est quasi pas de doute que les affaires ne prennent une tournure très avantageuse pour l'Angleterre, et que la République ne soit plongée dans le dernier embaras et compromise avec l'Impératrice qui pourroit se porter à des mesures vigoureuses. . . ." Simolin went on to point out that the five principles of the Neutral League "sont moins étendus que le traité de 1674 et les Hollandois jouiroient de moins d'avantages par ces principes que par le renouvellement du dit traité, qui par ce moyen pourroit être éludé. . . ." [20] This interesting proposal placed the acceptance of the maritime principles in a new light, for though it would guarantee to the Dutch the right to "free ships, free goods" it might leave the definition of contraband open to further discussion and enable Britain to insist on the inclusion of naval stores in the list.

In a second note of the same date, Simolin pointed out that Russia was anxious to avoid a permanent breach between Britain and the United Provinces and the conclusion of an offensive and defensive treaty between France and the Dutch. The only method to avoid such an outcome was for Britain to adopt the maritime principles of the Neutral League. The Dutch had made their acceptance of Russian mediation depend on British acceptance of these principles, and if Britain did so the Empress would be in a position to "sommer la République" to agree to the other British

19. FO 65/7, Harris to Fox, No. 17, 10/21 May 1782, confidential and secret (*MD*, *I*, 505), cf. Add. MSS. 47.563, f. 33, Harris to Fox, 19/30 April 1782: "My first wish is to return home." Harris hoped for a pension for his life and that of his eldest son, since he had spent more than £20,000 of his private fortune. He suggested that he should be appointed as one of the ministers to undertake peace negotiations with the Dutch, as a "creditable means" of withdrawing him from Russia.

20. FO 65/7, Simolin to Fox, 1 May 1782, probably a note taken in the Foreign Office of a verbal communication.

terms. Britain must prove "par une condescendance raisonnable qu'elle apprécie . . . la valeur des offices de l'impératrice." [21] This note was somewhat ambiguous, because it did not make clear whether what Simolin demanded was recognition of the principles of the Neutral League *urbi et orbi* or simply as a groundwork of the negotiation with the Dutch. Simolin probably intended to press for the former, but it was open to Fox to interpret his words as he chose. Certainly the tone of Simolin's communications, stressing as they did the Russian desire to prevent a Franco-Dutch alliance, must have been very welcome to Fox. It fitted in entirely with his own policy of driving a wedge between France and the United Provinces. Without apparently taking much time over it, Fox decided that the price was worth paying for Russian support in Holland and agreed on 4 May to Simolin's request. As far as he was concerned, by the treaty of 1674 "les principes de la neutralité armée sont établis quant aux parties contractantes dans leur plus grande étendue." Therefore Britain would accept "pour base de la paix particulière entre elle et les Etats Généraux la navigation libre selon les principes réclamés [sic] par S.M.I. dans sa déclaration du 28 fevrier 1780." [22] Thus at last Britain had been driven formally to accept the Empress's maritime principles, though so far only in relation to the Dutch.

Fox wrote at once to inform Harris of this fresh concession, and for the first time, on 6 May 1782, he touched on British foreign policy in all fields, though still with considerable reticence. As far as Russia was concerned, Britain, wrote Fox, had forestalled every demand she could make. It now remained to be seen whether France would allow the Dutch to make a separate peace. Since the new administration, Prussia, added Fox, had proved much more friendly and anxious for the conclusion of peace before Britain suffered further losses. But Fox did not mention his own initiative in the matter nor the object he had in view, namely some kind of alliance with Prussia or some form of Prussian support for the British peace terms, so that Harris remained quite in the dark on the most important aspect of Fox's foreign policy. The Secretary

21. FO 65/7, Simolin to Fox, 1 May 1782, probably also a written note of a verbal communication.
22. FO 65/7, Fox to Simolin, 4 May 1782.

of State dealt at length with the peace negotiation with France.
Harris was informed of Grenville's mission to Paris, but, wrote
Fox, supposing the negotiations failed, could Harris not sound
Russia to see whether there was some point beyond which concessions should not be made? Could some support be obtained
from Russia? Fox raised here too the question of the future of
Gibraltar. Russia was as interested as Britain, he declared, in preventing control of the Mediterranean from passing to the Bourbons. Though the loss of Minorca had been regarded with indifference in Russia, the Empress might take a more serious view of
the loss of Gibraltar. The British peace terms, wrote Fox, were
the independence of the thirteen colonies and otherwise the status
quo. If the Empress were prepared to endorse these terms, "there
would be no difficulty in order to induce her to support them, in
giving every facility in respect to the favourite point of free navigation which having been actually offered by us to the Dutch, and
being acceded to by almost all the neutral nations in Europe, is
now become rather a speculative dispute than any practical concern." Fox also brought up a further point on which he had tried
to secure the support of Prussia, namely the suggestion that the
Empress, in exchange for the acceptance of her naval principles,
might support Britain's peace terms by using her Baltic fleet to
protect British trade in the Baltic.[23]

In his long dispatch to Harris, Fox made no reference at all
to the revival of the joint mediation. Yet the mediators had made
one of their fleeting appearances on the scene when on 29 April
1782 Simolin had again invited the British government to au-
thorize its representatives in Vienna to "listen to explications." [24]
To this at the time Fox made no reply. Thus at present, without
any regard for the mediation, Russia was to be invited to support
Britain's peace terms, and the hope was expressed that she would
use her influence to keep Gibraltar for Britain and that she would
protect British trade in the Baltic against the refractory Dutch. In
exchange Fox was prepared to accept the principles of the Neutral League. But the phrase quoted above from his instructions to

23. FO 65/7, Fox to Harris, No. 5, 6 May 1782.
24. See Beer and Fiedler, *Joseph II und Graf Ludwig Cobenzl, I,* 303, Cobenzl to
Joseph, 23 March 1782, and FO 65/6, Simolin to Fox, 29 April 1782.

Harris did not specify how, and, as will appear later, Fox's colleagues were by no means as willing as he to sacrifice Britain's maritime superiority on the altar of Russia.

However it is evident that Fox had already conveyed to Simolin, in April 1782, that he was prepared to be much more yielding than Stormont on the maritime principles. Simolin had written to Russia in April recounting Fox's views on the Armed Neutrality,[25] and the Empress had expressed pleasure to hear that the new administration "rend plus de justice à ses sentimens pour la Grande Bretagne qu'on ne l'avoit fait pendant l'ancienne administration." [26] It was almost certainly Simolin's assurances which prompted the Empress to reopen in Russia and in Britain the campaign to revive the joint mediation in a more serious form and to extort from Britain a general acknowledgement of the maritime principles. On 9/20 May the Empress set out her views to the Emperor, who, it will be remembered, had committed himself, when he acceded to the Neutral League, to endeavour to impose the maritime principles on Europe in the general peace. Britain, she wrote, had agreed to negotiate with the Dutch on the basis of the maritime principles. In general the new administration had clearly shown its desire for peace. If the Bourbon powers showed an equal inclination, it would now be possible to call the peace congress together under more favourable auspices than hitherto. On her own initiative (for Fox's dispatches had not yet reached St. Petersburg) Catherine raised with the Emperor the question of the future of Gibraltar. She realized that it was the one obstacle to a negotiation where Spain was concerned, and she asked Joseph for his views on the future of a fortress of interest to all maritime powers.[27] From the tone of this letter, the Empress was clearly taking a more personal interest in the mediation than hitherto, and was moreover acting the part of spokesman of Britain, leaving it to Joseph to moderate the pretensions of France—a position which corresponded far more

25. F. de Martens, *Recueil*, 9, 320. Simolin wrote, quoting Fox: "Si la reconnaissance du système de neutralité formait encore un obstacle à l'affection et à la bienveillance de Sa Majesté Impériale pour ce pays, il pourrait être levé aisément." Martens does not make clear whether this was in Simolin's dispatch of 1/12 April 1782 or 12/23 April 1782.

26. FO 65/7, Simolin to Fox, 15 June 1782.

27. Arneth, *Joseph II und Katharina*, p. 127.

closely to the realities than previously, when France had trusted Russia, and Britain had placed her faith in Austria.

A few days after the dispatch of this letter, on 24 May 1782, Osterman addressed Harris on the same subject. His approach revealed the change in the Russian attitude towards Britain. He pointed out that now that Britain had modified her stand on America, the way was open to revive negotiations for a general peace. The preliminary projects submitted to the belligerents in 1781 might be taken up again; yet, in view of the change of policy in Britain, the Empress invited the British government to submit fresh proposals, which she was prepared to keep concealed even from the Emperor. But, added Osterman, there remained one single obstacle: the Empress considered her maritime principles just and equitable; they had been accepted by most European courts and they might even some day be useful to Britain herself. Having publicly proclaimed them, the Empress could not retract, and Osterman explained that "our not having concurred with her on this subject, had given her pain and displeasure, and . . . had furnished our enemies with the strongest and, indeed, only hold they had upon us at this court. That therefore, if we would consent to meet her ideas on this subject, and say as much, either in a *note verbale* to Mr. de Simolin, or through me here, every difficulty would be obviated . . ." The Empress would be able to take a firm stand and remove all other obstacles, and, hinted Osterman finally, though Spain must be expected to make difficulties over Gibraltar, neither Russia nor any Northern power would approve the transfer of the fortress out of British hands.[28] In a private letter to Fox, Harris, who had still been opposing British acceptance of the maritime principles tooth and nail in Russia,[29] again urged the advisability of adopting them, if it was desired to cement the friendship between Britain and Russia. It was Britain's "dubious and obscure" manner of evading Russia on this issue which had alienated Russia from the previous government.[30]

28. FO 65/7, Harris to Fox, No. 20, 14/25 May 1782.
29. FO 65/7, Harris to Fox, No. 14, 6/17 May 1782.
30. FO 65/7, Harris to Fox, 14/25 May 1782, private, unnumbered and No. 20 of the same date *en clair* and by a Russian courier. Both his No. 20 and his private letter, stated Harris, "were calculated to be read here." (Cf. No. 21, same date.)

A few days later, Harris received Fox's dispatches of 5 May 1782, which came by Simolin's courier. The Empress was thus now informed that the maritime principles had been accepted as the basis of negotiations for her mediation with Holland. But Harris called on Osterman on 29 May, since he was more alive than Fox to the necessity of explaining Grenville's presence in Paris in view of the Empress's hopes of summoning the mediating congress in Vienna. Harris stressed the exploratory nature of Grenville's mission, and Osterman, who was anything but subtle, accepted his explanations and declared that he would urge the Bourbon ministers to listen to British peace overtures and would also speak to Cobenzl to prevent the Austrians taking umbrage at this by-passing of the mediators. Harris then took up the various suggestions made by Fox. Osterman invited Harris to submit his questions in writing, and rather reluctantly, since he did not trust the security arrangements of the college of foreign affairs—with good reason— Harris drafted a letter summing up Fox's policy: peace on the basis of the independence of the thirteen colonies and the restoration of the status quo before the war; the maintenance of Gibraltar in British hands; and an invitation to Russia to support these propositions and to protect British trade in the Baltic. Finally, in view of Fox's statement that the maritime principles had become merely a speculative dispute, Harris concluded his letter with the statement that "quoique cette matière n'ait pas été traitée ministérialement à Londres, cependant je puis prendre sur moi de déclarer que les principes de la neutralité armée ne seront plus un objet de discussion entre nos deux cours; la mienne se dispose à les adopter, et je me rends responsable qu'elle facilitera, en autant qu'il dépend d'elle, leur consolidation." In his dispatch home, however, Harris toned down this phrase somewhat, thus leaving his principals unaware of the full extent of the concession which they were supposed to have made.[31]

31. Fo 65/7, Harris to Fox, No. 23, 20/31 May 1782; Harris Papers, note verbale given to the Vice-Chancellor, 18(/29) May 1782, endorsed "not in the correspondence —only extracted in my dispatch at this date." This was a justifiable precaution in order not to allow the cipher to be broken, but Harris's paraphrase in his dispatch was not quite so definite as what he had said to Osterman: "I did not hesitate to insert at the end of my letter that all disagreeable discussions relative to the principles of the Armed Neutrality were at an end, that we were no longer averse to them,

The dangers of Fox's rather casual treatment of this topic in his instructions of 5 May 1782 were here revealed. Fox had in a sense been thinking aloud, on a subject on which no firm decision had as yet been taken by the British government. Harris had acted, though he covered himself by the statement that no official communication of this decision had been made in London. Moreover Fox had made acceptance of the maritime principles conditional on Russian support of the British peace terms. In Harris's letter the conditional nature of this concession did not appear so clearly. He had therefore taken the matter further in Russia than Fox had done in England. He was no doubt influenced by his obsession that Russian friendship, and possibly a Russian promise to act, were the primary aims of British foreign policy. Indeed Fox's failure to keep his envoys abroad fully informed of his policy created unexpected problems for them. He had so far said not one word about the British attitude towards the joint imperial mediation and, by his reserve on the renewal of British friendship with Prussia, he put the British envoy in an awkward situation. Though Frederick had welcomed Fox's overtures, his purpose was to use the renewed Anglo-Prussian friendship to strengthen Prussian ties with Russia, rather than to tie himself to Britain. He had accordingly stressed that no connexion between England and Prussia could take place without Russia but had authorized his envoys abroad to cultivate their British opposite numbers, and Goertz had not hesitated to embark at once on this new course. After some preliminary skirmishing, Goertz communicated to Harris a Prussian suggestion that since the advent of the Whigs to power there was an opening for a renewed alliance between Britain and Prussia and possibly Russia as well.[32] Harris was extremely taken aback by this opening, which left him "in a state of doubt and perplexity I cannot describe." [33] Yet he answered skilfully enough, assuring Goertz that he would be happy to contribute to the formation of such a union and that the Empress would see with pleasure a *rapprochement* between Britain and Prussia. And now the two

but on the contrary were disposed to facilitate their consolidation when we were called upon to do so." The phrase "no longer averse to them" is much weaker than "se dispose à les adopter." Cf. also F. de Martens, *Recueil, 9,* 322.

32. FO 65/7, Harris to Fox, No. 29, 31 May/11 June 1782. (*MD, 1,* 509).

33. FO 65/7, Harris to Fox, No. 30, 31 May/11 June 1782.

men who had so long fought each other so ruthlessly found themselves discussing the best means of uniting their countries and inviting the Empress to join the union once she was free of her present engagements.[34] But Harris found himself awkwardly placed between Cobenzl, his open friend and secret enemy, and Goertz, his open enemy and now his secret friend.

The renewal of Anglo-Prussian contacts had not, needless to say, passed unperceived in Vienna and had driven Joseph at once into a highly critical attitude towards the Whig administration. The dispatch of Grenville to Paris led him to the conclusion that Britain intended to set aside the imperial mediation. Writing to Catherine on 1 June 1782, Joseph delivered himself of a severe diatribe against the new government, "qui ne pense derechef qu'à soi et prend seulement le parti opposé, et pour obtenir la paix, il offre, il donne, il accorde et prend tous les petits moyens . . . qui toutes démontrent son insuffisance, sa faiblesse . . ."[35] On 11 June Joseph wrote again, complaining bitterly of the moves undertaken by Britain to open direct peace negotiations and to exclude Russia and Austria "de fait et de parole de notre caractère de médiateurs." He expressed himself willing to follow the Empress in her desire to revive the mediation and suggested that the future owner of Gibraltar should be bound under the guarantee of the powers "de ne jamais mettre entraves ni difficultés quelsconques au libre passage et au commerce, soit en guerre soit en paix, des vaisseaux et bâtiments de toutes les puissances maritimes quelconques." This neutralization of the Straits would be, as Joseph pointed out, "un véritable coup d'état . . . qui rendrait la possession de Gibraltar plus indifférente."[36] As a proposal it was several centuries premature.

Harris had tried and failed to conceal from Cobenzl the new friendly relation that had been developed between Britain and

34. FO 65/7, Harris to Fox, No. 29, 31 May/11 June 1782; No. 37, 7/18 June 1782 (MD, I, 513).

35. Arneth, Joseph II und Katharina, p. 129.

36. Arneth, Joseph II und Katharina, p. 131; at the same time Joseph wrote to Cobenzl, speaking of "les démarches indécentes des Anglais vis-à-vis des médiateurs," of their "déraison" and "impudence" for it was Britain "qui nous a priés et demandés comme médiateurs." The evasion of the mediation was undertaken to please Prussia, wrote Joseph. (Beer and Fiedler, Joseph II und Graf Ludwig Cobenzl, I, 311, Joseph to Cobenzl, 11 June 1782).

Prussia and between himself and Goertz, who was indeed "as a
man of society . . . vastly preferable" to Cobenzl—though Catherine found him "pedantesco tudesco." [37] But in spite of the rain
of Austrian criticism, nothing that Britain had said or done until
then seemed to indicate to the Russians a desire to evade the imperial mediation. Harris's letter, assuring Russia that Britain intended to adopt the Russian maritime principles, seemed to indicate nothing but complaisance on the part of Britain. Indeed
Harris heard that the Empress was very pleased with his letter—
as well she might be—and he hoped even to persuade her to undertake the protection of British trade in the Baltic, as Fox had desired. But Harris warned Fox that such a proposal must be managed with the greatest delicacy, since the Empress dreaded nothing
so much as being drawn into the war.[38]

Catherine of course had no intention of undertaking anything
so dangerous as overt support of Britain with any part of her
armed forces. Her plan had been simply to extort British recognition of her maritime principles in exchange for a friendly support of Britain's peace terms at the eventual peace congress in
Vienna. Her resolution, communicated to Harris by Osterman on
1/12 June 1782, was based on the premise that Britain "should no
longer contest the five articles of the Armed Neutrality, and that in
our project for a general peace we should in all essential points
subscribe to the plan given in last summer by the two mediating
courts." In detail, Catherine's plan amounted to the following:
Osterman was to speak to both the Bourbon ministers and inform
them that their courts must listen to any fair offers of peace, not
raise their demands, and not delay the mediation; he was also to
consult the envoys of the members of the Neutral League and discuss with them the situation in general and that of England in
particular; he was to ask for their advice on what to do should the
moderate terms held out by England not be accepted by France
and, meeting Fox's point in this, consult them on whether it was

37. Merton Papers, Harris to Lady Harris, 5/16 September 1782; see *Sbornik, 23,*
261, Catherine to Grimm, 3/14 December, for the Empress's view, with which Harris
concurred: "He cannot get rid of a certain pedantick manner which would better
become a German professor than a Minister" (to Keith, 31 March/11 April 1780,
Add. MSS., 35.518, f. 218).

38. FO 65/7, Harris to Fox, No. 26, 24 May/4 June 1782.

advisable to "suffer the peace of Europe to be interrupted" in order to restore Gibraltar to Spain. Only Harris was to be told the full extent of the Empress's *démarche*. The appeal to the members of the Neutral League was to be kept from the Bourbon powers and from the Dutch, though the Emperor, as co-mediator, would be given more information.[39]

This elaborate operation could not have been what Fox had in mind when he offered up Britain's maritime principles, for it brought practically every European power into the solution of the conflict and ensured long delays before all the divergent interests could be harmonized. But Harris was given no time to express even an opinion, for, unlike Panin, Osterman acted promptly. The very next day he was able to inform Harris that he had spoken to all the envoys concerned. Vérac had taken the opening *ad referendum;* the Spaniard had rejected the argument that Spain was not justified in her claim on Gibraltar; the Dutch had complained that they wanted assistance not exhortations. As for the neutrals, Cobenzl had declared that the Emperor would readily subscribe to any course proposed by Russia; the Swede, Nolcken, would not commit himself without instructions from his court. The Danish envoy promised his court's ready cooperation, and Goertz entirely approved the plan: the King of Prussia was concerned at the situation of England, he declared, and had such confidence in the new administration that his system had changed.[40]

The two powers which acceded so readily to Catherine's plan were not moved merely by pity at England's sad plight. Denmark was extremely reluctant to see Gibraltar pass out of Britain's hands, a view in reality shared by Russia.[41] And Frederick was extremely anxious to be introduced into the mediation by hook or by crook, and his chance of success would be considerably greater if the Neutral League could take the mediation out of the hands of the joint imperial mediators.[42]

Harris, who had still received no instructions on the fate of the imperial mediation, refrained from comment on the Empress's

39. FO 65/7, Harris to Fox, No. 31, 3/14 June 1782.
40. Ibid.
41. FO 65/7, Harris to Fox, No. 37, 7/18 June 1782, quoting what Osterman had said on the subject of Gibraltar to the Danish envoy in Russia, Schumacher.
42. FO 65/7, Harris to Fox, No. 32, 3/14 June 1782, quoting his talks with Goertz.

plan to introduce the neutral powers once again into her diplomacy. But he sensed that the Russian current now flowed in Britain's favour and rose once again to heights of optimism. Fortunately the news of Rodney's victory over de Grasse at the battle of
the Saints on 12 April came in time to raise British prestige still
further, the new administration being given credit for a victory
won by an admiral who had been appointed by the old and was
already under recall when he defeated the French fleet. Potemkin,
returning from a short absence from the court, summoned Harris
to him in a brief and encouraging note: "Vive la Grande Bretagne
et Rodney; je suis arivé hier mon cher Harris, devinez qui vous
écrit et venez le voir tout de suite." [43] The Prince had only just
performed a journey of 3,000 versts in sixteen days, but so keen
was he to see Harris that he spent most of the day and the night
with him and left the British envoy the more exhausted of the two.
The heyday of their friendship seemed to Harris to have returned.
Potemkin fell in with all Harris's suggestions and constantly assured him of the warm regard the Empress felt for Britain. Harris
in turn resumed his old campaign, endeavoured to pique the
Prince's ambition and to "point out to him at how cheap a rate
he might purchase glory and immortal honour." [44]

What Harris now had in mind was a revival of the plan for an
armed mediation which he had first launched in the summer of
1779. "Would she join her fleet to that of Denmark, and appear in
the North Sea or Mediterranean with thirty or forty ships of the
line, she might command peace," he wrote to Fox on 7/18 June
1782.[45] Shortly afterwards, he discovered what he believed to be
a dead secret, that the Empress had apparently cancelled the
orders to her fleet to sail to the Mediterranean and the North Sea
(in pursuance of the general policy of the Neutral League); that
she had ordered every ship fit for service to be got ready and
was determined, should the Dutch continue to refuse her offers, to support her mediation "by a formidable armament."

43. FO 65/7, Harris to Fox, No. 39, 10/21 June 1782 (*MD, 1,* 514, tacked on to
No. 40 of the same date). *MD, 1,* 517, facsimile.

44. Ibid. See also *AKV, 13,* 26, Bezborodko to Simon Vorontsov, undated, but May
1782 is suggested by the editor. The date can be narrowed to late June 1782 by a
reference to the return of Potemkin from a journey.

45. FO 65/7, Harris to Fox, No. 37, 7/18 June 1782.

The resolution had been taken, he declared, as a result of his talks with Potemkin and Bezborodko. It was a false report in fact, and the fleet sailed away on 2 July.[46] But for the moment it appeared to Harris as though the culminating point of his long mission had at last arrived. Unfortunately the British envoy had not yet grasped the significance of an item of news which he had reported to London but a fortnight before. The Kuban Tartars had invaded the Crimea; the Khan, Shaguin Girey, had been driven from his throne and had appealed to the Empress for assistance.[47] Rodney's victory had been welcomed in Russia but not for love of Britain. "If the English raise their heads a little the war will go on and give us time to deal with the Tartars and the Turks, who are more our affair," wrote Bezborodko to Simon Vorontsov in June 1782.[48] Faced with this new development, Russian policy was about to change overnight.

Meanwhile the arrival in London of Harris's dispatches of 19/30 April at last woke Fox up to the necessity of giving his envoy in Russia some sort of guidance on the British attitude to the joint imperial mediation. It did not, unfortunately, lead Fox to tell Harris the truth, namely that he would prefer to evade it, and, if it must take place, to have Prussia added to the mediators. He simply informed Harris that Grenville had been given full powers to negotiate a treaty with France on the basis of the independence of the thirteen colonies and the treaty of Paris. But, he added, the King had taken no step in this matter without fully informing the court of Russia, and he expressed the hope that the Empress would not consider Grenville's mission "as any mark of disrespect to the mediation of Their Imperial Majesties," but rather "as an additional proof of the sincerity with which he [the King] wishes to second the benevolent and pacific intentions of the two high mediating powers." [49]

Meanwhile Simolin in London carried on with the Empress's campaign to extort British recognition of the maritime principles

46. FO 65/7, Harris to Fox, No. 40, 10/21 June 1782 (*MD, 1,* 513); No. 46, 24 June/5 July 1782 (*MD, 1,* 518).
47. FO 65/7, Harris to Fox, No. 40, 10/21 June 1782.
48. *AKV, 13,* 26.
49. FO 65/7, Fox to Harris, No. 8, 21 May 1782, *MD, 1,* 507.

in exchange for her benevolent mediation. On 15 June 1782, in a *note verbale* to Fox, he repeated the proposal which Osterman had already made to Harris, that recognition should take the form of a *note verbale* addressed to him. The Empress was determined to secure universal adoption of her maritime code, added Simolin, "aussi ne contractera-t-elle jamais des engagemens qui ne reposent sur cette base." As a further argument, Simolin pointed out that Britain had in practice released almost all the ships loaded with naval stores, paying damages for loss of time and for legal costs. "Les jugemens de ses cours d'amirauté," he wrote, "ont donc été calqués sur des principes prisés dans le droit des gens, sur ces mêmes principes qu'établit la declaration de 1780, et dont l'observation auroit épargné à la Grande Bretagne force de dépenses et d'embarras." As regards the mediation, Simolin appeared in every way desirous of complying with British wishes. The Empress was urging France to make peace; Spain appeared obstinate as regards Gibraltar: would the King consider offering some alternative? And he invited Fox again to submit Britain's fresh peace terms, which would be kept secret even from the Emperor.[50]

Though Sir James Marriott might disagree with Simolin's description of the admiralty court's judgements, Britain's naval policy had now failed, and her stand might well be reconsidered. The issue was of considerable importance, and it was not one on which Fox could act without consulting his colleagues, whatever he might have written to Harris more than a month before. Moreover there was one person who did not approve of Fox's "adoption of all the wild ideas of Russia concerning the Neutral League," and that was the King.[51] Harris's private letter to Fox of 14/25 May 1782, in which he had again stressed that nothing could be so effective in winning over Russia as the recognition of the maritime principles, was shown to George III, and he pointedly reminded Fox to lay it before the cabinet.[52] Fox saw the implied rebuke and answered that he would never take any decision on so important a subject as recognizing the principles of the Armed Neu-

50. FO 65/7, Simolin to Fox, 15 June 1782.

51. Fortescue, *Correspondence of King George III, 6,* the King to Shelburne, 7 May 1782.

52. See above, note 41; see also Fortescue, *Correspondence of King George III, 6,* 56, Fox to the King, 15 June 1782, and the King to Fox of the same date.

trality without consulting his colleagues.[53] In complete ignorance of the fact that, acting on Fox's incautious instructions, Harris had already admitted in Russia that Britain was preparing to adopt these principles, the cabinet proceeded to debate the matter. The minute of the meeting on 26 June 1782 gives no indication of the division of opinion within the cabinet, but the result shows that Fox was overruled. The recognition of the maritime principles was agreed to, but only as the basis of a treaty of alliance between Britain and Russia.[54]

Meanwhile Simolin had been sufficiently encouraged by Fox's reception of his overtures to write home on 18 June that Fox was prepared to sacrifice anything to recover the Empress's goodwill. Instead, on 28 June 1782, Fox communicated to him the decision taken by the cabinet. Taking advantage of the sentence included in Simolin's overture, to the effect that the Empress would not undertake any engagements unless they were based on the maritime principles, Fox proceeded to interpret these words as an offer of alliance contingent on acceptance of the maritime principles. Stressing the tremendous sacrifice Britain was making in giving up her traditional attitude in maritime affairs, Fox declared that Britain "souhaite l'alliance de Sa Majesté l'Impératrice et n'hésite pas à accepter et admettre ses principes et son système dans toute son etendüe comme base de cette alliance." Regarding the mediation, Fox was now more precise about Britain's peace terms. There was nothing to be said about the Dutch, since they appeared, under French guidance, to be about to refuse Russia's proposals. In relation to the Bourbons, Britain accepted the independence of America and the restitution of all conquests, which would not exclude exchanges and equivalents. But the King did not think himself justified in ceding anything else, notably Gibraltar.[55]

The attempt to tie recognition of the maritime principles into

53. Ibid., 62, Fox to the King, 17 June 1782.
54. Ibid., 67, Minute of Cabinet, 26 June 1782.
55. F. de Martens, *Recueil*, 9, 322, Simolin to Catherine, 7/18 June 1782; p. 323, Simolin to Catherine, 17/28 June 1782; FO 65/7, Fox to Simolin, 28 June 1782. Fox again urged that in view of the way the Dutch trifled with Russia, the Empress might use her fleet to protect British trade in the Baltic; and also to threaten the Dutch into giving up their plan for concerting military operations with the French.

an alliance with Russia was not unreasonable. As Fox pointed out, His Majesty "passe par dessus bien des préjugés, elle ferme les yeux peut-être sur quelques principes assez solides . . ." Therefore such a concession should only be made if Britain could rely on the permanence of Russian feelings towards her.[56] But there is no doubt that Fox himself was prepared to adopt the maritime principles without an alliance, as Harris had proposed. In a private letter to Harris, accompanying his official instructions, he wrote on 29 June 1782: "I return you many thanks for your private letter, which perfectly convinced me, but unfortunately not others, so that the answer is as you will see . . . I hope you will endeavour to represent it as like a complete complaisance as the thing will bear . . ." [57]

Yet it was a strange moment to choose to bind Britain's fortune to Russia. Fox himself may of course have held with Harris that accepting the maritime principles would be the best way of neutralizing them. A Russian alliance might have strengthened Britain's position in the peace negotiations—were Russia not hampered from taking too active a course by her position as mediator in both the Anglo-Dutch and the Anglo-Bourbon wars—but above all it does not seem as though the British cabinet had combined its policy towards Russia and its policy towards Prussia into any coherent system. Fox was still pressing hard for a triple alliance between Russia, Prussia, and Great Britain. Trusting in the existence of the alliance between Russia and Prussia, he was inviting Frederick II to pave the way in Russia for this union of the three powers.[58] He may have been misled by Harris's assurances that Austrian influence was in decline in St. Petersburg. Or he may simply not have appreciated that the Austro-Russian secret treaty effectively annulled the Russian-Prussian alliance. It is even possible

56. FO 65/7, Fox to Simolin, 28 June 1782.

57. Fox, *Memorials and Correspondence*, *1*, 333, Fox to Harris, 29 June 1782. Cf. p. 334, Harris's views in his letter to Fox of July 1782.

58. FO 64/3, Fox to Lusi, 16 June 1782: "L'alliance qui subsiste actuellement entre les cours de Petersbourg et de Berlin, bien loin de faire naître des difficultés seroit une raison de plus pour faire désirer à l'Angleterre celle de Sa Majesté Prussienne . . . Une triple alliance entre la Russie, la Prusse et la Grande Bretagne seroit indubitablement celle qui conviendroit le mieux aux circonstances actuelles de l'Europe."

that he hoped that Russia would refuse the alliance and leave Britain with her maritime principles intact.

Long before Fox's new instructions could reach Harris, fate had intervened to give a fresh turn to the wheel. The Khan of Crimea's appeal to the Empress for protection and assistance against his rebellious subjects did not go unheard. The Empress was entitled to intervene, in order to enforce the terms of the treaty of Kutschuk-Kainardji and the convention of Ainalikawak. But the possibility of war with the Porte could not be excluded if such an active policy were followed, and caution was indicated at first.[59] The Empress wrote immediately to the Emperor, on 14/25 June 1782, claiming his support by virtue of the secret treaty of 1781.[60] Meanwhile the Emperor's distrust of Fox had continued to deepen steadily, and Cobenzl was constantly urging on Osterman and Bezborodko that Grenville's mission to Paris was intended to evade the mediation.[61] Harris, who still did not know whether Britain intended to escape from the net of the mediation or, after Grenville had explored the ground, agree to the summoning of a congress, temporized. In any case he believed that Austrian influence was sinking, that the Emperor had let slip his opportunity, and that he "never will recover." [62] He was at the same time unaware that Cobenzl had pierced the secret of his links with Goertz.[63] The strong Austrian pressure drove Harris

59. See *Imperatritsa Yekaterina II i Knyaz' Potemkin Tavricheskiy, Podlinnaya ikh perepiska. Russkaya starina, 16,* 33, Catherine to Potemkin, 3/14 June 1782: "Cette affaire me parait délicate par ce qu'elle peut avoir de suites qu'il seroit bon d'éviter encore quelque temps."

60. Arneth, *Joseph II und Katharina,* p. 134.

61. FO 65/7, Harris to Fox, No. 34, 7/18 June 1782; for Joseph's opinion of the British government, see his letter of 14 August 1782 to Belgioioso: "J'admire il bel coraggio du Roi qui voit marqué de honte son règne . . . sans en faire un enfant de moins à sa femme" (Calvi, *Lettere dell'imperatore . . . al conte . . . Belgioioso,* p. 438).

62. FO 65/7, Harris to Fox, No. 38, 10/21 June 1782.

63. FO 65/7, Harris to Fox, No. 37, 7/18 June 1782, in which Harris declared that Cobenzl had no knowledge "that I am intimate with his rival" (*MD, 1,* 513). But see Beer and Fiedler, *Joseph II und Graf Ludwig Cobenzl, 1,* 318, Cobenzl to Joseph, 18 July 1782: "J'avois déja remarqué depuis quelques tems . . . que Goertz et Harris commençoient à se repatrier malgres les procédés qui étoient tels, qu'un galant-homme n'auroit pu se les permettre même contre le ministre d'une puissance avec laquelle sa cour seroit en guerre."

to commit himself further, and he repeatedly declared, in accordance with Fox's instructions of 21 May 1782, that the mission of Grenville was only intended to further the Empress's own humane intentions and not "to take the salutary work out of their [the mediators'] hands." These assurances were welcomed naturally enough by Osterman, Potemkin, and Bezborodko, who in turn advised Harris to take steps to do away with Austrian doubts; otherwise the Empress would be subjected to endless complaints from the Emperor.[64]

Evidently Britain's attitude was becoming a bone of contention between Austria and Russia. Joseph's diatribes were not enough to shake the Empress's conviction that Harris's explanations were to be preferred.[65] Nevertheless, having appealed to the Emperor for support in the event of trouble arising out of the revolt in the Crimea, the Empress now found it necessary to pay a little more attention to his complaints against Britain. On 2/13 July 1782 she wrote again to the Emperor, stressing that she had frequently insisted in her communications with Britain that Grenville's mission could have no other object than to "accélérer la paix, en avançant la médiation au point qu'elle puisse être conclue au congrès de Vienne par l'entremise des deux cours impériales." She could not conceive, she wrote, that after all the efforts of the mediators, "la paix pût être conclue à leur insu." She had warned London that she had spoken in these terms to the Emperor and had hinted that any action running counter to her words would not be in conformity with the good intelligence reigning between Russia and Britain. Thus, to some extent, the Empress was now guaranteeing to the Emperor that Britain would not evade the mediation. But she was not prepared to sacrifice Britain entirely. She did not fail to point out that a separate peace without participation of the mediators could only take place with the consent of both belligerent sides, "en quel cas les cours de Bourbon, ayant une fois accepté la médiation, ne montreraient pas moins d'inconsidération pour nos offices." An insinuation in these terms on the

64. FO 65/7, Harris to Fox, No. 42, 17/28 June 1782.

65. Ibid.; see also Beer and Fiedler, *Joseph II und Graf Ludwig Cobenzl, I,* 318, Cobenzl to Joseph, 18 July 1782: "on s'est entièrement reposé sur toutes les assurances donnés par Mr. Harris que jamais la paix ne se feroit que par la médiation des deux cours imples."

part of the Emperor to the Bourbon courts would have beneficial effects, concluded Catherine.[66]

By the beginning of July, when Harris heard that the Empress had appealed to the Emperor in connexion with the Crimean revolt, he understood that Russia was at the parting of the ways. If the Emperor supported Catherine, the alliance between them would be confirmed; if Joseph trifled with her, the alliance would dissolve. He wrote at once to Fox, advising him that the moment was a decisive one and that Britain should not be too precipitate; she should not engage herself too far or form any connexions from which she could not retract. A Turkish war would necessarily leave Britain the choice of a system on the continent. If Russia and Austria were connected in the war, France and Prussia would unite against them. If Russia and Prussia acted together, Austria and France would naturally oppose them. "In both cases we shall be sure of Russia, and one of the great German powers," wrote Harris. For the moment, he suggested that, should it prove that the Tartar rebellion was fomented by either France or Turkey, Britain should make the gesture of offering her ports to the Russian fleet, and her political influence to be employed in Russia's favour. If it turned out to be merely a local revolt, then Britain should show more reserve, for fear of offending the Empress.[67]

Thus, as so often before, the instructions of Britain's foreign secretary were out of date before they could reach Russia. But in any case, the proposal for a Russian alliance at the cost of Britain's naval practice was Fox's swan-song. On 2 July 1782 Lord Rockingham, the Whig leader, died. The serious differences which existed in the cabinet between the Fox faction and the Shelburne group came into the open when the King, ignoring the request of the Rockingham party to send for the Duke of Portland, appointed Shelburne First Lord of the Treasury. Fox, who had already quarrelled with Shelburne and threatened to leave office before the death of Rockingham, now resigned the seals. He had been foreign secretary for fifteen weeks and in this brief period had galvanized

66. Arneth, *Joseph II und Katharina,* p. 137. (Vergennes, incidentally, was only too willing to evade the mediation; see Arneth and Flammermont, *Correspondance, I,* 92, note 1, quoting Vergennes to Montmorin, of 16 March 1782).

67. FO 65/7, Harris to Fox, No. 45, most secret, 21 June/1 July 1782.

British foreign policy into new life. Russian friendship had been
to a great extent recovered by Fox's acceptance of Russian mediation with Holland on the basis of the principles of the Neutral
League. His too frank avowals to Simolin of his willingness in
general to adopt these principles had done even more. He had
placed British relations with Prussia on a better footing, at the
cost of alienating the never really friendly Austria. How the proposed Anglo-Russian alliance could combine with the existing
system of alliances on the continent had not entered into Fox's
calculations. As Bezborodko commented acidly on 5/16 July 1782:
"England's fate, apparently, is that her rulers should know no
measure in anything; the previous ministers would agree to nothing; the present ministers give way on everything, even without
being asked, and when no one will accept anything from them.
The previous ministers held away from all alliances without dis-
crimination; the present ministers are glad to form connexions
with everyone." [68] Fox had indeed launched out like a Catherine
wheel in all directions, but no consistent policy had emerged.
Under his successor it was scarcely likely to do so.

68. Maykov, *Pis'ma A. A. Bezborodka,* p. 97, Bezborodko to Rumyantsev, 5/16 July
1782. Cf. also Grantham to Harris, 24 July 1782: "My predecessor with most
splendid abilities . . . opened . . . a new field of expectation. Perhaps he was
precipitate and his concessions everywhere and to everybody were dealt out too
liberally" (Harris Papers).

17. The End of a Mission

As JULY advanced Harris became more and more convinced that the time was quite inappropriate to tie Britain's fortunes to Russia. The Empress waited for the neutrals to respond to her latest effort to use them to enforce peace and continued absorbed in the affairs of the Crimea.[1] Meanwhile Harris was constantly being pressed by Goertz, who saw that a war with Turkey would cement the entente between Russia and Austria.[2] This Prussian pressure placed Harris in an extremely awkward position, for he had still not been let into the secret of Fox's talks with the Prussian envoy in London. He therefore did not know, in the event of any action being undertaken by Russia on Britain's behalf, whether Austria or Prussia was the desirable partner from Britain's point of view. Until Austria replied to the Russian request for support in the event of a war with Turkey, the question was in the balance in St. Petersburg as well. Harris urgently demanded instructions, but when they came, by 19 July, they cast no light whatsoever on British relations with Prussia. Moreover nothing could be further from Harris's own ideas than Fox's proposal to accept the Russian maritime principles in exchange for an alliance.[3] In addition Harris was aware that Britain's conditional acceptance of the maritime principles was not what the Empress had been led to expect by Fox or by himself, and it "had raised in her mind a temporary gust of ill-humour." The Empress began to suspect that there was some substance in the constant Austrian complaints that Britain intended to evade the mediation.[4]

1. FO 65/7, Harris to Fox, No. 50, 5/16 July 1782; No. 51, same date.
2. FO 65/7, Harris to Fox, No. 53, 8/19 July 1782 (*MD, I*, 521).
3. On 19 July Harris received copies of Fox's correspondence with Simolin, cf. Ch. 16, pp. 405–07.
4. FO 65/7, Harris to Fox, No. 54, 12/23 July 1782.

Though what he said might differ from what Fox had indicated to Simolin, Harris determined to give himself a certain latitude, and in his talks with Potemkin and Bezborodko he used the fiction of talking "as from himself" in order to make it possible for Britain to withdraw or modify her proposals when his own dispatches of 21 June/1 July 1782, reporting the consequences of the flare-up in the Crimea, should reach London.[5] To Bezborodko Harris proposed that, as a condition of Britain's acknowledgement of the maritime principles, a quadruple alliance should be formed between Britain, Russia, Denmark, and one of the German powers, leaving the choice of this latter to Russia—though he hinted that he was aware that Russia would probably find Austria the most useful. Bezborodko's reply was extremely reserved. He pointed out that the Empress had always refused to enter into any alliances with the belligerents as long as the war lasted, since such alliances could not be concealed.[6] Harris stressed in turn the magnitude of the sacrifice demanded from Britain and the dangers of making such a concession without some compensation. But he did no more than pave the way for a future alliance. Meanwhile he asked, hinted at, and demanded the further instructions he declared had been promised him and explained to Fox that: "I have given some latitude to my instructions, but if I have departed from their letter, I hope I have not mistaken their spirit."[7]

A few days after his interview with Bezborodko Harris received his formal reply from Osterman. It showed the extent to which Russia was turning away from the war in the West and absorbing herself in the conflict on her southern border. The Empress had hoped, declared Osterman, after Fox's unreserved declarations to Simolin in London, that Britain, by her free adherence to the principles of the Armed Neutrality, would enable her to draw the members of the League into her plan of intervening on Britain's behalf. Now, however, the Empress would drop the whole plan without waiting to hear what replies she received from her fellow

5. *AKV, 13,* 28, Bezborodko to S. Vorontsov. The editor assumed this undated letter to belong to 1781, but judging from a reference to the recent death of Rockingham it clearly belongs to late July 1782.

6. Ibid. See also FO 65/7, Harris to Fox, No. 54, 12/23 July 1782.

7. FO 65/7, Harris to Fox, No. 54, 12/23 July 1782.

neutrals.[8] She would wait to see what the imperial mediation and the separate Dutch mediation could achieve before taking any further step, before even stating whether she considered an alliance with Britain advisable or not. Osterman stressed again the Empress's reluctance to enter into any engagements with either belligerent during the war, since such treaties could not remain secret and might entangle her in hostilities. For the same reason Russia utterly refused to take steps to protect British trade in the Baltic.[9] In general Harris believed that the Russian ministers on the whole favoured the projected alliance. The only obstacle was the Empress herself, who, he thought, could not yet choose between Prussia and Austria. Consistency in her policy could not be expected of her until a decision was forced on her.[10]

In assuming that all Catherine's ministers favoured this new policy Harris was mistaken. He had been misled by a remarkable change that had come over Osterman, who had escaped from Panin's influence and was now on good terms with him. Bezborodko thought it too soon to take on obligations towards Britain, though there was no harm in exploring the ground. But it was better, he thought, to leave matters to be settled between the Emperor and the Empress and meanwhile "to put Mr. Harris off with compliments and words, but in a better manner than the answers he used

8. Seeing that this plan was dropped, it is only necessary to mention briefly that the Danes in a reply which reached St. Petersburg about 11 August 1782 declared themselves ready to agree to any plan of Catherine's but proposed waiting to see if the change of ministry in England (after the death of Rockingham) led to a change of policy. (FO 65/7, Harris to Fox, No. 60, 2/13 August 1782). The King of Sweden's reply, printed in Scott, *Armed Neutralities,* p. 423, is dated 7 August 1782 and proposes that a congress of all the members of the Neutral League (including Prussia) should be summoned at the same time and place as a meeting of the plenipotentiaries of the belligerents (including the United States). The neutrals would supervise the peace-making and establish the maritime laws "with that splendour and all that security, with which those of the German Empire were fixed by the treaty of Westphalia." Seeing that the Empress had by now abandoned the whole plan, her reply to this "piece of presumption" (FO 65/8, Harris to Grantham, 23 August/9 September 1782) swept the King of Sweden's proposals aside almost with contempt. (Scott, *Armed Neutralities,* p. 429, Reply of the Empress of Russia, 7(?18) September 1782).

9. FO 65/7, Harris to Fox, No. 56, 15/26 July 1782.

10. Ibid. See also F. de Martens, *Recueil,* 9, 323–24, procès verbal of a conference of Harris and Osterman, 13/(24) July 1782.

to get from Count Nikita Ivanovich [Panin]." [11] As for the Empress herself, all hesitation (if there ever was any) was soon driven from her mind. At the same time all hope of a rift between Russia and Austria from which Britain might draw profit disappeared. For towards the end of July, Joseph's reply to the Empress's appeal of 14/25 June 1782, invoking his support in view of the Crimean disturbances, arrived in St. Petersburg. "Recevoir la lettre . . . que V.M.I. a bien voulu m'écrire," Joseph had written on 12 July, "et y répondre dans les mêmes vingt-quatre heures, n'ont été qu'un même sentiment et une même action en moi. Il ne me faut ni délibération ni combinaison, ni calcul, quand mon coeur sent et il s'agit de servir, j'ose dire, mon Impératrice, mon amie, mon alliée, mon héroïne. Oui, je suis prêt toujours et de quelconque façon de m'entendre avec V.M.I. sur tous les évènements possibles, que les troubles de la Crimée dont je reçois par elle la première nouvelle, pourraient occasionner." [12] Joseph's hour had struck at last, and the alliance, from which Russia was to derive so much more profit than Austria, was about to be consummated.

Meanwhile in London a new secretary of state for foreign affairs had been appointed, this time Lord Grantham, who had been ambassador in Madrid at the outbreak of the war and was said to be "a very agreeable pleasing man," who "possessed solid, though not eminent parts." [13] He was in addition an old and close friend of Harris. The government crisis in Britain had of course been reflected in the conduct of foreign affairs, and from 29 June to 27 July 1782 not one dispatch was sent to Harris other than a circular announcing Grantham's appointment.[14] On 27 July 1782 Grantham wrote his first instruction on policy to Harris. Unfortunately Harris's dispatches forecasting a breach between Russia and the Porte and recommending the postponement of an offer of alliance had not yet reached Grantham. The new foreign secretary therefore contented himself with remarking that the change in the government was one of persons and not of policy and that he could

11. *AKV, 13,* 28, Bezborodko to S. Vorontsov, n.d., presumably July 1782.

12. Arneth, *Joseph II und Katharina,* p. 136.

13. *DNB,* quoting Walpole and Wraxall.

14. FO 65/7, No. 10, circular of 19 July 1782. (Grantham's dispatches continue to be numbered in the series begun by Fox.)

not "add anything to Mr. Fox's letter to Mr. Simolin of the 28th of June last, in which the King's readiness to cooperate with the Empress in her great and extensive plans keeps pace with the project of forming the strictest connection." [15] The scantiness of Grantham's official dispatches was made up for by the extent and volubility of his private letters to his old friend. He was flustered and bewildered by the suddenness with which he had been summoned to high office from his retirement in Yorkshire, and, as he wrote himself "I have been so little used, and I am afraid to say so little earnest, in public transactions, that, notwithstanding all my supposed qualifications, my situation is as new to me as the Eastern languages." [16] He too hoped for a Russian alliance, made during the war, as a means of hastening a satisfactory peace.[17] But there was no mention either in his official instructions or in his private letters of the attitude of Britain to the possible consequences of the rising in the Crimea.[18]

At last however Harris was treated to an exposé of British policy towards Prussia.[19] The Prussian envoy in London had not been idle; he was aware that on 2 July 1782, Simolin and Belgioioso, the Austrian envoy, had again presented an *insinuation verbale* urging the belligerents to send full powers to their representatives in Vienna to enable the mediating congress to meet and start its labours.[20] The death of Rockingham and the cabinet crisis that followed prevented for the time being any reply from being made. Lusi now staked a claim for Prussia to be admitted to the media-

15. FO 65/7, Grantham to Harris, No. 11, 27 July 1782.

16. Grantham to Harris, private letter, 28 July 1782, *MD, 1,* 524.

17. Harris Papers, Grantham to Harris, 24 July 1782, enclosed in his letter of 28 July as Grantham had previously mislaid it; FO 65/7 Grantham to Harris, No. 13, 27 July 1782.

18. Harris's dispatch reporting the rising had already been received in London when Grantham wrote, though not his No. 45 in which he outlined the possible consequences for Russia.

19. See Fortescue, *Correspondence of King George III, 6,* 68, Fox to the King, 29 June 1782; Fox had realized that Harris must be informed of his talks with Lusi.

20. FO 65/7, Simolin to (?), 2 July 1782. Since Fox had resigned there was no one to address the *insinuation verbale* to. A similar *insinuation verbale* was addressed to Versailles at about the same time. Mercy Argenteau reported to Kaunitz on 5 July 1782 that, according to Vergennes, the initiative for separate peace talks had come from Britain, and he could not jeopardize their success (Arneth and Flammermont, *Correspondance, 1,* 117, note).

tion and recalled that, in the event of a congress meeting in Vienna, Fox had promised to invite the King of Prussia to intervene as a mediator. He suggested that before a reply was delivered to the imperial mediators, he, Lusi, should be consulted.[21]

This imbroglio was quite beyond Grantham's capacities. He remained wedded to the idea, inherited from Fox, of choosing Prussia as Britain's partner on the continent. But Frederick II had made it clear that he would contemplate no alliance with Britain that did not include Russia. "You see therefore," wrote Grantham, "how necessary it is that Her Imperial Majesty should, if possible, be encouraged . . . to confirm her friendly disposi- tions, by adopting the idea of a tripple or quadruple alliance be- tween us, herself, Prussia and Denmark"; if the idea could come from the Empress herself, it would be even better than if Britain solicited it.[22] Finally, Grantham invited Harris to "labour the point of trying if your court will admit Prussia to the mediation. It is much desired here, and in fact Fox promised it to him, whether of his own accord or by ye insinuation of ye Prussian Minister I can- not tell." [23]

This instruction to Harris to seek the approval of the Empress for the introduction of Prussia into the mediation was dispatched when for the first time the British government was facing the issue that it intended to evade the mediation. The first categorical

21. FO 64/3, Lusi to Fraser, 5 June 1782 (but from the content clearly July: "Je vous prie aussi de faire souvenir à Monsieur Fox de mettre au fait son successeur de ce qui s'est passé entre nous . . ."); Lusi to Shelburne, 6 July 1782.

22. FO 65/7, Grantham to Harris, No. 13, 27 July 1782. In common with Stormont, Grantham also proposed that Russia should attack Spain: "As I am persuaded that nothing would be more agreeable to the Empress, than an extension of her Empire; it has occurred to me to suggest to you a hint which you may perhaps be able to employ with advantage," he wrote to Harris. Several plans had been "offered" for expeditions to Spanish South America. "Might not her Imp. Majesty be tempted to acquire possessions of this kind, which we know are a favorite object of her ambition. The assistance she might give, on this occasion, would be liberally rewarded in a participation of the advantages to be obtained." The utterly hare-brained na- ture of such proposals must have struck Harris forcibly. But he replied politely that he would not lose sight of this "important" proposal and would produce it when he saw a fair opening. But "I must again repeat that, at this moment, nothing can find a way to the Empress's ear, that does not bear an immediate reference to the troubles in the Crimea" (FO 65/8, Harris to Grantham, No. 5, 16/27 August 1782).

23. FO 65/7, Grantham to Harris, No. 13, 27 July 1782. Harris Papers, Grantham to Harris, private, 28 July 1782, *MD, 1*, 524.

statement to this effect was in fact made to Harris by Lord Shelburne, in a letter of 27 July answering one from Harris in which the latter had endeavoured to ensure that his services to the North administration should not be counted against him now that his friends the Whigs were in power.[24] After reassuring Harris on this point, Shelburne recalled that his principles had "uniformly" led him to "everything respectful to the court of Russia." But, he wrote, "we wish to avoid the mediation, because we have no confidence in the court of Vienna, and are ignorant of the private connexion which appears to have taken place between the imperial courts."[25]

Meanwhile, at his first conference with Grantham at the end of July, Simolin, with the support of the Austrian envoy, again pressed the imperial mediators' desire to inaugurate a congress and required an answer to their *insinuation* of 2 July. It now became exceedingly difficult, as Grantham wrote to Harris, when negotiations were being carried on in Paris, to accede to the mediators' request. "Yet how was it to be avoided without giving room to misrepresentation, and affording our enemies the pretence of asserting that we were averse to a mediation?"[26] How in fact was Britain to set aside the mediation without enabling her enemies to assert that she was doing so? Grantham was driven into a corner, and the solution he found was intricate indeed. On the one hand, full details of the negotiations then carrying on in Paris, where Alleyne Fitzherbert[27] was to replace Grenville, were to be supplied to Harris for Catherine's information. On the other hand Grantham was to concert with Simolin "how to comply or not, at this juncture, with the request of the insinuation verbale." He stressed the necessity for Britain to answer Vergennes's rejoinder to Grenville's first overtures, and explained that he was authorized "for the purpose of removing all possible idea of inattention to the mediating powers, to consult him upon so delicate a point, as

24. Harris had written via his brother-in-law, Sir Gilbert Elliot. As he explained to his wife, he considered himself entitled to a pension without any conditions attached. "It is neither bassesse nor servility to urge it repeatedly . . . it is a recompense for the past, not des arrhes to tye up my future conduct" (Merton Papers, Harris to Lady Harris, 15/26 August 1782).

25. Shelburne to Harris, 27 July 1782, *MD, 1,* 522.

26. FO 65/7, Grantham to Harris, No. 12, 27 July 1782.

27. Fitzherbert had been minister in Brussels and eventually replaced Harris in Russia.

not answering the insinuation at this moment." [28] Simolin apparently agreed that a reply to France might be misrepresented as
"an intention to elude the mediators," and he consented to communicate to St. Petersburg his own personal approval of a formula
devised by Grantham to avoid replying to the joint Austro-Russian
insinuation verbale first made on 2 July 1782. This was to the effect
that *"the reason of an answer not being at this instant formally
made to the insinuation verbale was that this court waited for
some éclaircissement upon certain points of importance."* However, as this formula was drawn up to the accompaniment of many
assurances by Grantham that "neither the King nor his confidential servants could entertain any the least thought of abandoning
the mediation," [29] it is not surprising that Simolin misunderstood
its ultimate purpose. He showed his dispatch to Grantham before
sending it, and Grantham hastened to comment in a private letter
to Harris that though it was very fair, yet Simolin "rather heightens
the expressions which I made use of to him with regard to resuming the mediation or doing it soon. I was very guarded in my
expressions to him and said that the continuation of the business
at Paris did not affect the reliance on ye mediation, but I did not
give any assurances of the time when and the period in which it
ought to be had recourse to. I say this because if perchance anything should go on so rapidly at Paris as to make ye mediation unnecessary it would be well to strike while the iron's hot." [30] Thus
at the cost of fresh misunderstandings the issue was again postponed.

Meanwhile, during July and August, Harris had been reduced
to the position of an observer at the Russian court. He could do
nothing until he received fresh instructions from London. The
almost indecent haste with which the Empress had seized on the
pretext of Britain's conditional acceptance of the maritime principles to escape from her own plan to mobilize the Neutral League
in Britain's favour proved that she did not want to be involved in
Western concerns, at a time when she could not foresee into what

28. FO 65/7, Grantham to Harris, No. 12, 27 July 1782.
29. Ibid.
30. Harris Papers, Grantham to Harris, 28 July 1782, private.

complications the Crimea would lead her. From the Russian point of view there was certainly no purpose in alienating France, the traditional protector of Turkey, by entering into a secret alliance with Britain. Harris of course believed that France was behind the troubles in the Crimea; he also believed that the Empress was wrong in thinking that a war with Turkey could be conducted independently of the war in the West.[31] As so often before, Harris under-estimated the diplomatic shrewdness of the Empress, and his strictures were to some extent inspired by her evident indifference to the imperial mediation, the Dutch mediation, and the British offer of an alliance.[32] But Catherine realized that as long as the maritime war continued only Prussia could be a danger. Prussia was the connecting link which, by intervening against Austria, might unite the two theatres of war, the East and the West. France could clearly not come to Turkey's active assistance alone when she was barely able to survive the conflict with Britain. And joint action by France and Prussia would mean the end of the Franco-Austrian alliance, a revolution which Catherine trusted Joseph to prevent. Britain, as the Russians well knew, would take no action unless France did. The problem therefore as both Joseph and Catherine saw it, and as Joseph put it, was to ward off the evil designs "du puissant et mauvais voisin que nous avons à dos." [33]

Rumours of the changes in the administration had of course reached Harris, and he was by no means pleased at the news: "I am most heartily tired of eternally shifting my chief, it retards business and throws impediments in the way not to be surmounted. Things begin to smile here after much," he wrote to his wife on 2 August 1782. He expressed the hope that Fox would remain at his post: "He did too well not to be missed." [34] Not till 15 August did Harris receive confirmation that Grantham had been appointed foreign secretary, and on the same day a courier arrived with Grantham's instructions of 27 July 1782.[35] They provided him with no fresh guidance on the vexed question of an Anglo-

31. FO 65/8, Harris to Fox, No. 58, 22 July/2 August 1782.
32. FO 65/8, Harris to Fox, No. 59, 26 July/6 August 1782.
33. Arneth, *Joseph II und Katharina*, p. 136, Joseph to Catherine, 12 July 1782.
34. Merton Papers, Harris to Lady Harris, 22 July/2 August 1782.
35. FO 65/8, Harris to Grantham, No. 1 (new series), 5/16 August 1782.

Russian alliance, and Harris wrote at once to warn Grantham that there were no hopes of forming this alliance, and he asked to be approved for having rather prepared Russia "for an alliance than actually proposed one." [36] At the same time Harris stressed the difficulty of persuading the Empress in the present circumstances to agree to an alliance with Prussia and Denmark and to the admission of Prussia to the mediation.[37] A week later he wrote again to explain why he thought direct proposals would at the moment be ill-timed. The situation of Russia was critical: the Empress was secretly allied to the Emperor, openly to Prussia; it was impossible to see how this contradictory system would work until events forced it on. Would the Emperor support Russia at the expense of a possible breach with France? The conduct of Prussia would be regulated not by the treaty with Russia but by hatred of Austria, wrote Harris. "In this state of uncertainty, when it is dangerous to venture even a conjecture, either on what will be the position of this court when you receive this letter, or of that in which the two German powers who, at this moment, hold the balance of Europe, may find themselves, your Lordship will, I am sure, agree with me in thinking it a very unfit moment for making direct propositions for an alliance, and that the formation of one, at this conjuncture, would be impracticable." [38]

Relying on his old friendship with Grantham, Harris did not hesitate not only to depart from his instructions but to offer his advice. His first proposal was that, if Britain really wished to conciliate the Empress, some notice must be taken of her Turkish policy. He repeated his earlier suggestion that the use of British ports should be offered to the Russian fleet in the event of war with the Porte. His second proposal was based on the assumption that the Empress desired a Turkish war, and that the Emperor would support her. In those circumstances Harris felt it essential for Britain to have some sort of footing in Russia, and the only hope in his view of prevailing on the Empress to agree to any British proposals was to hold out to her "that we are ready to acknowledge *immediately* and universally the principles of her

36. FO 65/8, Harris to Grantham, No. 2, 9/20 August 1782.
37. FO 65/8, Harris to Grantham, No. 5, 16/27 August 1782.
38. FO 65/8, Harris to Grantham, No. 7, 16/27 August 1782.

Neutral Convention, provided she will sign *immediately* a treaty of defensive alliance with us, but which is not to be considered as valid till either at the conclusion of the present war, or until it entirely changes its nature." [39] The novelty in Harris's proposal was that it took account of what he believed to be the impending war between Russia and Turkey and the, to him, equally inevitable junction of this war with the maritime war.

In a private letter to Grantham, Harris expressed his pleasure at having a chief "with whom *j'ose m'épancher*" and promised to "decorate" his instructions with "proper flourishings." But he also hinted at a further obstacle to a closer connexion with Russia. The Empress had not been impressed by the disintegration of the first Whig government; she harboured doubts as to its stability and suspected that further changes might take place. Harris contemptuously explained that "in common with all other foreigners, [she] has not an idea what is meant by Opposition and Resignations: to explain it to them would be explaining snow to an African prince." [40] Again he was guilty of under-estimating the intelligence opposed to his own; Catherine might not grasp the subtle reasoning on which Fox based his resignation of the seals; yet she was justified in having little faith in the stability of an administration which had passed through one major crisis in barely four months of office. But Harris could not rid himself of his prejudices. In a long apologia for his mission, he gave Grantham a highly biassed account of his various negotiations at the Russian court. At the root of his bias lay his conception of "the inseparable interests of Great Britain and Russia." Any Russian ministers who did not agree with this assumption were in Harris's interpretation guilty of ignorance or of indifference to the welfare of Russia. This dispatch, which was intended to save his chief the labour of reading Harris's voluminous correspondence, would have misled a more penetrating mind than Grantham's. It ended however on one familiar note: again Harris begged to be recalled. He was worn out, *"usé,"* he wrote. "A new face, new manners, new flatterers, are necessary here." The methods he had been compelled to use had created too many animosities, and he realized that "in all

39. Ibid.
40. *MD, 1,* 535.

essential points" he had become "absolutely disqualified" for the post.[41]

Meanwhile, having for the moment postponed on his own responsibility any further pursuit of the Anglo-Russian alliance, Harris turned his attention to making the best of the muddle which had arisen over the imperial mediation. The replies of the Bourbon courts to the *insinuations verbales* made by the mediators in July 1782 reached Russia in mid-August. Vergennes had wriggled out of the difficulty by declaring that the initiative lay with England. Spain objected to the fact that no mention had been made of Gibraltar.[42] Harris in turn, acting on Grantham's instructions, argued that if the congress had not yet met it was the fault of Britain's enemies—a statement which did not gain with Osterman "all the credit I could have wished"; and that in any case the proposals for direct negotiations between the belligerents had originated from France.[43] Osterman who, be it remembered, was not a subtle man (he "does not rightly understand in his reports to the Empress what should be said, and what should be kept back; what expressed with energy, and what only slightly touched upon") summed up what he understood Harris to mean, namely that "before we saw the event of Mr. Fitzherbert's negotiation, we could not give a formal answer to the mediating courts. But that whether Mr. Fitzherbert's mission should be successful or not, that we did not mean to set aside the mediation and should ultimately, in all cases, have recourse to it. This, he said was what was expressed in Mr. Simolin's dispatches . . ." Harris was "rather puzzled for a reply" to this direct question and tried to evade it. Osterman however pressed him to be more precise, and Harris, alarmed at the Vice-Chancellor's inability to take a hint, rushed off to Bezborodko to continue his explanations. Bezborodko had succeeded in raising the belief in Harris that he could speak to him as a "private

41. *MD, 1,* 528. Harris to Grantham, 16/27 August 1782. This letter should most emphatically not be taken as an accurate description either of the Russian court or of Harris's mission.

42. FO 65/8, Harris to Fox, No. 60, 2/13 August 1782.

43. FO 65/8, Harris to Grantham, No. 4, 16/27 August 1782. Already under North an unofficial emissary had been sent to France (Bemis, *Diplomacy of the American Revolution,* p. 191).

friend" who knew how to distinguish between what was said to him officially and what was entrusted to him from motives of personal regard and confidence. Harris therefore abandoned the pretence that Britain had no intention of setting aside the mediation and approached the subject openly, counting on the Empress's pro-British sentiments to make her enter into Britain's position. Britain wanted peace; so did the Empress. She would not therefore try to deprive Britain of the advantage of direct negotiations. Paris was near, quick, and easy. The Empress would surely be less susceptible than the Emperor and would connive at such means of procuring a peace "tho' perhaps they were not strictly consistent with the idea of our having put the whole transaction into the hands of the mediation." Again Harris blamed France's extravagant demands for the delay in calling a congress, but Bezborodko was not convinced by his arguments. France might indeed have behaved with duplicity, but he nevertheless advised Harris that Britain should not evade the mediation, after the assurances she had made, "since it certainly would have a bad effect here."

Seeing the Bezborodko proved unresponsive, Harris turned to Potemkin to whom he could speak even more freely. He recalled "how Vienna came to be tacked on to the mediation" and in a most involved argument endeavoured to prove that in reality Count Panin was to blame, if not Potemkin himself, for having failed to procure Harris's second private audience with the Empress sooner. Potemkin listened with his usual attentiveness and good humour to this account of the origin of the joint mediation, of the inaccuracy of which he was no doubt aware. The Emperor, by insisting on calling a congress was prolonging the war, said Harris, and if she followed him, Catherine would prolong the calamities of England. It might not be noticed now, but "the pens of posterity" would record it as a blemish on her reign. After much badgering Potemkin finally agreed to speak to the Empress and assured Harris that "objects very different from those we were discussing occupied her whole thoughts, and left room in her mind for nothing else." [44]

44. Ibid. All these interviews took place on 4/15 or 5/16 August.

Indeed the mediation was rapidly degenerating into a farce. The separate Russian mediation between Britain and the United Provinces petered out in July.[45] The States General finally decided on 1 July 1782 that they could not, in the course of the present campaign, listen to any proposals for an armistice or a separate peace without France.[46] French diplomacy had won the day in the United Provinces, and without anyone realizing it yet the only chance of introducing the maritime principles into the peace treaty was lost.

As for the imperial mediation, though the Empress did not want to hasten the peace, she could continue to make things awkward for Britain by taking Grantham's assurances to Simolin at their face value. On 9/20 August, Osterman explained to Harris that Catherine was satisfied with Britain's reasons for postponing for the time being a reply to the mediators and understood that the final negotiations would not be transferred to Paris. On her orders he had explained to Cobenzl that this delay was by no means "likely to impede the business of their joint mediation, to which we had assured the Empress we should in the end resort." What is more, Osterman had given the Bourbon envoys in St. Petersburg to understand that, from what Britain had said, "it would be *their* fault, not *ours,* if the mediation did not immediately take place." And the innocent Osterman expected Harris to be pleased! [47]

Harris was horrified to find Britain thus committed not only with the Emperor but with the Bourbons. The Empress, he explained, appeared to have taken Grantham's talks with Simolin as an actual reply to the mediators' *insinuation verbale,* whereas it was only an explanation intended for Catherine's private ear "of why we did not actually give this answer." The negotiations carried on in Paris "might, in fact, force us to give an answer con-

45. In the course of April, May, and June, Simolin and Fox had exchanged various notes on the Dutch mediation, in which Simolin showed himself very understanding of the British point of view once the Russian request to base the negotiations on the maritime principles had been accepted. It is not worth going into these exchanges in detail, since nothing ever came of them (see FO 65/6 and 7, passim).

46. Coquelle, *L'alliance franco-hollandaise,* pp. 271 ff. France succeeded in having the Dutch included in the peace negotiations in Paris, and a Dutch plenipotentiary turned up in the course of the summer.

47. FO 65/8, Harris to Grantham, No. 4, 16/27 August 1782.

trary to the assertions he had made." Harris found himself thus obliged to put into plain words what he had all along avoided saying officially to Osterman, though he had not hesitated to confide in Bezborodko and Potemkin. He left Osterman soured, blaming Britain for not being more explicit.[48]

Catherine's policy at this time and her general view of the European situation are perfectly summed up in a letter she wrote to the Emperor on 10/21 September 1782. Though doubtless she was not perfectly frank with her imperial friend, nevertheless, when they were on the eve of embarking on an enterprise that might lead them both into war, it was incumbent on her to lay before the Emperor the real problems which confronted them. Of the possible trouble-makers, Sweden could only be expected to act if incited to do so by a major power, and it was Joseph's business to see to it that no such incitement should be given by his ally France. As regards Britain, the Empress pointed out with conscious or unconscious irony that Austria's neutrality and her good offices must have been appreciated there. Guided by the same principle of neutrality the Empress had done all she could to promote the peace which Britain so badly needed, and moreover Britain had "outre celà des intérêts de commerce très essentiels à ménager avec mon Empire." Besides, the Neutral League "met les intérêts du commerce de l'Angleterre dans une sorte de dépendence de la Russie, puisque nous pouvons nous passer de sa navigation marchande pour l'exportation des produits de mon Empire, dont l'Angleterre a cependant un si pressant besoin." Prussia, in the Empress's opinion, was the main problem, but Frederick was old and it seemed unlikely that he would act alone or that either France or England, exhausted as they both were by a long war, would wish to incur fresh expenses in a cause which did not concern them directly by supporting him. If, as the Empress assumed, the Emperor had no designs in Germany, it should not be impossible to mobilize a number of princes of the Empire to paralyse

48. Ibid. Simolin incidentally had also raised the issue again in London. Grantham wrote to Harris on 20 August 1782, that Simolin seemed to have gone further in stating a time for the congress, and proposing its transfer to Paris from Vienna, than was warranted by their conversation (FO 65/8, Grantham to Harris, No. 14, 20 August 1782).

any action by Frederick—a clear hint that Catherine intended to use the Austro-Russian alliance for her aggressive purposes against Turkey but was not going to allow Joseph to indulge in any adventures in Germany and thus overthrow the balance recently established by the treaty of Teschen. The longer the maritime war continued, the better for the imperial plans, added Catherine. All the major powers would find themselves unable to interfere.[49]

The parts which the Emperor and she herself were to play are clearly stated in Catherine's letter. The mediation was to be allowed to slide, though the Neutral League was to be maintained and used to bring pressure on Britain by economic means. As long as the war lasted Britain was dependent on the Baltic powers, and particularly Russia, for naval stores. She could not afford to break with Russia, whereas there was now visible evidence that the Russian export trade could be carried on in the ships of members of the Neutral League. Nevertheless, British friendship might prove valuable should the Bourbon powers prove hostile to Russian plans against the Porte and attempt to close the Mediterranean to the Russian fleet. Hence it was up to Joseph to control France, his ally, and Russia would maintain friendly relations with Britain, bearing in mind that the need for a closer connexion might arise.[50]

It is noteworthy that the Empress's letter to Joseph did not mention the Crimea. Nevertheless, Russian troops entered the peninsula during the summer to restore the puppet Khan to his throne, and soon afterward the rumour spread in St. Petersburg that the Empress intended to annex the peninsula.[51] In the circumstances the renewal of pressure by Osterman on Harris for Britain formally to bind herself not to evade the mediation was merely an academic exercise.[52] The real requirements of Russian policy were hinted by Potemkin when he proposed to Harris what Harris had already suggested to London some two months before:

49. Arneth, *Joseph II und Katharina*, p. 143.

50. Ibid. Joseph, be it noted, did not share the Empress's confidence in the incapacitating effect of age on Frederick II or in French gratitude for the efforts of the mediators. See his letter of 13 November 1782, ibid., p. 169.

51. FO 65/8, Harris to Grantham, No. 23, 23 September/4 October 1782.

52. FO 65/8, Harris to Grantham, No. 17, 13/24 September 1782.

that Britain should offer to place her ports at the disposal of the Russian navy in the event of a squadron being sent again to the Mediterranean.[53]

For a while the peace negotiations in Paris, in which the United Provinces were now joining, hung fire. All eyes were turned, some with hope, others with fear, on the final grand assault launched by the joint Franco-Spanish forces under the Duc de Crillon on Gibraltar. Early in October, news arrived in Russia of the destruction of the floating batteries in the harbour and of the failure of the attempt to storm the fortress. The way was now open for a resumption of the direct peace negotiations between France and Britain.[54]

Grantham had finally acceded to Harris's repeated request that some sort of notice should be taken of the Empress's Turkish projects. On 15 October 1782, in an *en clair* dispatch, he flattered Catherine by asserting that she would be sure to overcome the troubles in the Crimea very easily, but that "every instance and proof of friendship which this court can shew may be depended upon." Grantham still hoped that the Emperor would not follow Catherine in her projects and that in her disappointment with him the Empress would turn again to Prussia. Thus the burden of his instructions to Harris in the cipher portion of this dispatch was to work for a real union between the Northern courts and to be discreet in his professions of assistance to Russia in her Turkish projects, about which too little was really known to warrant that Britain, in her present parlous condition, should commit herself.[55]

Harris did not share Grantham's hopes. He saw that the Empress was far too deeply absorbed in her oriental schemes, and he was more aware than Grantham appeared to be of the strength of the Austro-Russian connexion. He was throughout the autumn of 1782 prevented by illness from taking an active part in the life of the court, but he continued in touch with events owing to the genuine kindness of Potemkin who visited him frequently and

53. FO 65/8, Harris to Grantham, No. 12, 30 August/10 September 1782.

54. FO 65/8, Harris to Grantham, No. 28, 11/22 October 1782. See Bemis, *Diplomacy of the American Revolution*, pp. 220 ff. and Doniol, *Histoire, 5*, passim, for these peace negotiations.

55. FO 65/8, Grantham to Harris, No. 22, 15 October 1782.

wrote or sent to him with even greater frequency.[56] This contact served only to convince Harris more than ever that the point of his mission was over. Britain and Russia were at the parting of the ways; their interests diverged, and there was at present no prospect of joint action.

During October and November the peace negotiations went forward in Paris and London. The Emperor continued his carping letters, complaining of the lack of attention shown by Britain to the august mediators. The Empress paid him back in kind, stressing that it was Vergennes "qui s'est gardé l'échappatoire d'une paix précipitée par les évènements." [57] Neither took the mediation seriously, but each extended the veil of charity over the misdeeds of the party to which their interests linked them most closely. Not till December 1782 did the Austrian chargé d'affaires in London, Kageneck, approach Grantham again for an answer to the *insinuation verbale* of 2 July 1782, which the foreign secretary had evaded answering in the summer. Grantham could now afford to be more frank in the knowledge that the preliminaries of peace were reaching completion, and he expressed the hope that the mediators would not be offended at peace being reached without them.[58]

Partly in order to ward off the ill humour which Harris feared the Empress might feel at the news of the impending peace, accomplished without the mediators, the British envoy had hinted in mid-December to Potemkin, on one of the Prince's visits to his sick bed, that Britain would be as friendly as materially possible in her present situation should Russia's Crimean troubles spread.[59] On Potemkin's insistence he even gave this assurance in writing, though he safeguarded himself by prefacing his note with the declaration that he was not speaking ministerially but merely describing His Majesty's principles.[60] Potemkin's pressure was not

56. FO 65/8, Harris to Grantham, No. 31, 25 October/5 November 1782; No. 47, 2/13 December 1782.

57. Arneth, *Joseph II und Katharina*, p. 159, Joseph to Catherine, 5 October, 1782; p. 166, Catherine to Joseph, 18/29 October 1782.

58. FO 65/8, Grantham to Harris, No. 25, 10 December 1782.

59. FO 65/8, Harris to Grantham, No. 47, 2/13 December 1782.

60. FO 65/8, Harris to Grantham, No. 48, 6/17 December 1782; No. 51 of the same date.

surprising, and Harris's assurances may have influenced the Empress when, on 14/25 December 1782, she at last put her name to a rescript charging the Prince with the task of annexing part if not the whole of the Crimea.[61]

In the circumstances the Empress did not propose to make an issue of British evasion of the mediation. Early in January 1783 Harris was able to present himself at court for the first time since his illness in the autumn and assured the disgruntled Osterman that as soon as the negotiations were advanced enough they would be communicated to Russia.[62] Catherine and Joseph continued to blame France and Britain respectively for the lack of respect shown to the mediators,[63] but when the Empress saw Harris she maintained a complete silence on the subject. Only Potemkin showed himself anxious to know the "system" Britain would follow once peace was achieved.[64] The dearth of activity in St. Petersburg, coupled with his own ill health, led Harris to demand his recall all the more insistently.[65]

The preliminaries of peace between Britain, on the one hand, and France and Spain, on the other, were signed in Versailles on 20 January 1783. The news reached Russia on 7 February, and Harris was immediately surrounded and congratulated. But behind the polite phrases he discerned that neither the Empress nor her ministers viewed the occasion with any great pleasure.[66] Britain and France were now to some extent recovering their freedom of action in relation to the forthcoming annexation of the Crimea, an event which was generally talked about though not as yet officially proclaimed. However from the Russian point of view much might happen between the signature of the preliminaries and the conclusion of the definitive treaties. But the apparent indifference with which the subject was treated in Russia led Harris to hope

61. Sbornik, 27, pp. 221 ff.

62. FO 65/9, Harris to Grantham, No. 1, 3/14 January 1783.

63. Arneth, Joseph II und Katharina, p. 178, Catherine to Joseph, 14/25 December 1782; p. 180, Joseph to Catherine, 11 January 1783.

64. FO 65/9, Harris to Grantham, No. 14, 3/14 February 1783.

65. See particularly his letter of 1/12 November 1782, in MD, 2, 8, where it appears tacked on to extracts from Nos. 32 and 33 of the same date.

66. Letter from Harris to Grantham, 27 January/7 February 1783, MD, 2, 29; FO 65/9, Harris to Grantham, No. 13, 31 January/11 February 1783, MD, 2, 29.

that he had heard the end of both the joint mediation and the Armed Neutrality.[67] He was wrong.

Early in January 1783 Vergennes had raised with the British envoy in Paris, Fitzherbert, the question of how to introduce a reference to the august mediators into the negotiations. He suggested not only that a complimentary declaration acknowledging the imperial good offices should be made on presenting the preliminaries but also that the mediators should be invited to take a formal part in drawing up the definitive treaty. His ulterior motive, which he revealed to Fitzherbert, was the hope that by insinuating Austria and Russia into these negotiations a handle would be given to France and Britain to intervene in the impending troubles in the East.[68] Grantham was above all anxious that the role of the mediators should be purely ceremonial and that they should have no opportunity to introduce extraneous matter, such as the maritime principles, in the negotiations. He accordingly proposed certain amendments to Vergennes's draft, which Vergennes accepted, but did not trouble to produce one himself.[69] On 9 February he wrote again to Fitzherbert, suggesting that now that the preliminaries had been signed some notice might be taken of the mediators.[70] But Vergennes had not waited for Britain to act, and on 12 February the French invitation to Russia to resume her functions as a mediator had been dispatched. Fitzherbert assumed, or chose to assume, that Grantham had already issued a similar invitation, but he took the precaution of writing directly to Keith and to Harris to inform them that such a measure had been approved of in principle in London so that they might counter the Bourbon efforts to take to themselves all the merit of appearing more attentive than the court of St. James.[71] Grantham also hastened to issue the expected invitations and communicated the decision to Simolin and the Austrian chargé d'affaires, Kageneck, in the form of a reply to the *insinuation verbale* to which he

67. FO 65/9, Harris to Grantham, No. 13, 31 January/11 February 1783.
68. FO 27/5, Fitzherbert to Grantham, No. 2, 5 January 1782; No. 7, 19 January 1783.
69. Ibid., Grantham to Fitzherbert, No. 10, 14 January 1782.
70. FO 27/5, Grantham to Fitzherbert, No. 24, 9 February 1783.
71. Ibid., Fitzherbert to Grantham, No. 21, 11 February 1783 and enclosure.

had so strenuously evaded replying in the summer of 1782.[72]

As Fitzherbert had suspected, Vérac took full advantage in Russia of being the first to propose the revival of the imperial mediation, but this diplomatic trick had little effect, since Harris acted on Fitzherbert's warning without waiting for instructions from London.[73] The Empress received the informal British invitation, followed by the official one, with pleasure, he reported, and Markov, who until then had been kicking his heels at The Hague, was to be instructed to join Baryatinsky in Paris, which would replace Vienna as the centre of the so-called mediation.[74]

Meanwhile Harris had discovered that the Empress had not abandoned all hope of introducing her maritime principles into the peace settlement,[75] and he warned Grantham and Fitzherbert what to expect.[76] Shortly afterwards Osterman was instructed to communicate to the envoys of the members of the Neutral League that the mediation had been revived and that the imperial mediators intended pressing for the adoption of their maritime principles. The decision to draft a comprehensive code for neutral trade had probably not been implemented, and it appears that early in 1783 matters had not progressed further than the "Reflexions sur la liberté des mers en général . . ." which Cobenzl had produced in June 1782. The argument now put forward was that it would take too long to study and discuss a comprehensive code in the course of the peace negotiations. Hence Catherine proposed simply that the four main points of the declaration should be taken over bodily, leaving the discussion of a code for a later date.[77] Meanwhile instructions were sent to Russian representatives in the allied countries to invite these countries to mobilize their envoys in Paris to press for acceptance of the maritime principles. But the limitations which the Empress set on her plan are revealed by a

72. FO 65/9, Grantham to Harris, No. 6, 22 February 1783, and No. 7 of the same date.

73. FO 65/9, Harris to Grantham, No. 21, 28 February/11 March 1783.

74. FO 65/9, Harris to Grantham, No. 26, 10/21 March 1783. The formal invitation to mediate was made some ten days later by Britain than by France.

75. FO 65/9, Harris to Grantham, No. 18, 10/21 February 1783; No. 23, 3/14 March 1783; No. 26, 10/21 March 1783.

76. FO 65/9, Harris to Grantham, No. 26, 10/21 March 1783.

77. FO 65/9, Harris to Grantham, No. 28, 24 March/4 April 1783; No. 34, 23 April/4 May 1783.

phrase in the instructions to Galitzin in Vienna to the effect that "si il est reconnu que cette proposition sera declinée par les belligerants, ou par l'Angleterre seule, il serait préférable de s'en abstenir." [78]

Grantham did at one point admit that, had the war continued, Britain might have found some use for the principles of the Neutral League, though he would have found it "painful" to see the naval stores of Britain's enemies sail down the Channel unhindered.[79] But he was not called upon to deal with the problem. For the preliminaries of the peace signed on 20 January 1783 had led to a parliamentary outcry in Britain, and the government fell before the combined onslaught of Fox and North. From 24 February to 2 April the country was without any fixed government. Finally the two who had fought each other so ardently during the American war joined forces to form an administration. North became home secretary, and Fox returned to his previous office as secretary of state for foreign affairs.[80]

Now that the preliminaries of peace had been concluded, and now that Russia might be in a situation to need Britain, Fox no longer saw any need to sacrifice Britain's maritime practice, and his instructions to the Duke of Manchester, who was to take over from Fitzherbert in Paris, were quite categorical.[81] Moreover the Empress's own interest in forcing her maritime code into universal

78. See F. de Martens, *Recueil*, *13–14*, 157, for the instructions to Galitzin; ibid., *6*, 119, Osterman to Dolgoruky in Berlin, 15 March 1783.

79. FO 27/6, Grantham to Fitzherbert, No. 41, 13 March 1783; Grantham was disturbed at the incursion of the mediators into the peace before the preliminaries with the Dutch had been signed. He feared that the mediators might support Dutch demands to include the maritime principles in their peace and instructed Fitzherbert to reject any such demands. See FO 27/5, Fitzherbert to the Dutch plenipotentiaries, 31 December 1782, pointing out that Fox had admitted the maritime principles only as the basis of negotiation in the separate Russian mediation; Grantham to Fitzherbert, No. 6, 9 January 1783, instructing him to take special care that no mention should be made of the Neutral Code in the Dutch negotiation, and Fitzherbert to Grantham, No. 1, 5 January 1783, in which Fitzherbert suggests that Vergennes was not prepared to support the Dutch demand for the inclusion of the maritime principles. See also Grantham to Fitzherbert, No. 27, 14 February 1783.

80. Grantham informed Harris on 22 February 1783 that Fox would probably be his new chief (Harris Papers), but Fox issued a circular announcing his appointment only on 4 April 1783 (FO 65/9, No. 8).

81. FO 27/6, Fox to Manchester, No. 43, 18 April 1783; No. 5 (new series), 30 April 1783.

acceptance was subordinated to much more pressing considerations. On 8/19 April 1783 she signed a manifesto proclaiming the annexation by Russia of the Crimea, the Kuban, and the Taman peninsula.[82] The Empress had every reason to suppose that France would oppose her by diplomatic means, possibly even by stronger means. Hence she had no desire to alienate Britain by pressing her unpopular principles. The instructions to Markov in Paris, echoing what had been said to Galitzin, allowed him to drop the attempt to introduce the maritime code into the peace if it met with strong resistance.[83] Meanwhile Harris, who still believed that war between Russia and the Porte was inevitable, seized every opportunity to portray Britain as Russia's friend and, except for the vexed question of the maritime principles, relations between the two powers once again reached a high degree of intimacy. Harris deliberately took the risk of being disavowed and assured the Empress that Britain would assist Russia in so far as was compatible with her own interests and with her paramount need of peace, a declaration which was heartily welcomed in Russia.[84] In addition he had to fight against a French attempt to make it appear that Britain would join with France in endeavouring to secure a solution of the Russo-Turkish conflict more favourable to the Porte. Such a policy had been inaugurated by Vergennes, apparently on a hint from Shelburne, but whatever hopes he might have entertained of British support proved vain when Fox took over. For Fox harboured the classical view that Britain had only one enemy—France. Thus the policy followed by Harris on his own initiative met with Fox's hearty approval.[85]

There was however a difference of opinion between Harris and Fox on the policy to be pursued towards Russia. Fox still clung to his old idea of an alliance between Britain, Russia, and Prussia. Harris knew only too well that to introduce Prussia into such an

82. For the diplomatic consequences of the Russian annexation of the Crimea, see Anderson, "The Great Powers and the Russian Annexation of the Crimea, 1783–4," and see my article, "The Secret Austro-Russian Treaty of 1781."

83. FO 65/9, Harris to Grantham, No. 29, 28 March/8 April 1783.

84. FO 65/9, Harris to Fox, No. 35, 23 April/4 May 1783.

85. FO 65/9, Harris to Grantham, No. 26, 10/21 March 1783. Vérac had insinuated that Britain would oppose Russian policy towards Turkey, reported Harris. For Fox's approval of Harris's conduct, see FO 65/9, No. 12, 4 July 1783; No. 13, 27 July 1783, and private letter, 27 July 1783 in MD, 2, 50.

alliance was impossible, but he also believed that it was unwise for Britain to commit herself to an alliance with Russia at all at that moment. By waiting until Russia was thoroughly committed in Turkey, Britain would be in a position to make better terms.[86] Nevertheless he carried out Fox's instructions faithfully and assured Osterman of the pleasure Fox would feel at establishing closer connexions with Russia.[87]

Vergennes too had his reasons for not wanting to press the adoption of the maritime principles at this juncture. He did not wish anything to delay the conclusion of the peace in view of the threatening situation in the East, and he did not wish to alienate Britain, since he still hoped to draw her into joint action in support of the Porte.[88] Thus the Russian attempt, when it came, was half-hearted and easy to parry. On 20 May, Markov and Baryatinsky raised the question with Manchester, who insisted that the peace should not be delayed by the introduction of extraneous matter. An attempt by Vergennes to place the blame for France's refusal to accept the maritime code on Britain, by stressing the latter's well-known aversion to the Empress's principles, was foiled by Fitzherbert. Though Mercy Argenteau seconded the efforts of the Russians, he did so but feebly, and the envoys of the other members of the Neutral League seem to have done nothing at all.[89]

In the circumstances it no longer mattered. Towards the end of June the Empress heard from her envoys in Paris that her proposals had been turned down. Not a word was said to Harris on the subject, and indeed for the rest of his stay it was never mentioned again. Thus the great hope of guaranteeing the safety of neutral navigation in time of war faded away before the more

86. For Harris's own views, see his private letter to Grantham of 18/29 January 1783, *MD*, 2, 23.

87. FO 65/9, Harris to Fox, No. 41, private, 5/16 May 1783 (*MD*, 2, 44); No. 40, 2/13 May 1783; No. 45, 12/23 May 1783. On Fox's preference for Prussia see his letter of 27 July 1783 in *MD*, 2, 50.

88. Vergennes dreaded a Turkish war and told Manchester that France would take no action in the Russo-Turkish conflict without first informing Britain; see FO 27/6, Manchester to Fox, No. 14, 18 June 1783.

89. FO 27/9, Manchester to Fox, No. 8, 23 May 1783; Harris Papers, Fitzherbert to Harris, 28 May 1783; F. de Martens, *Recueil, 13–14,* 158, cf. Krauel, "Preussen und die bewaffnete Neutralitaet," pp. 152 ff. for Frederick's indifference. This disposes of Bergbohm's suggestion that Russia and Austria had probably not even proposed the adoption of the maritime principles at the peace (*Die bewaffnete Neutralität*, p. 209, note 24).

thrilling realities of conquering for Russia a strong base on the Black Sea and of continuing the traditional Russian policy of expansion in the South.

The return of Fox to power led Harris once again to beg for his recall. He no longer felt such a distaste for St. Petersburg, since his wife and sister had heroically undertaken the long journey back to join him on hearing of his protracted illnesses. Moreover a new scene was opening out before him, centring on Russia's Turkish policy, and he "heartily loved the rocking of the battlements." [90] He foresaw a period in which Britain might recover much of her ascendancy in Russia, but his health had been so seriously impaired that he could not contemplate staying to enjoy it. Finally on 16 May 1783 Fox wrote to Harris to inform him that he would be recalled and that Fitzherbert, who was anxious to leave Paris, where the Duke of Manchester had been appointed over his head, would replace him in Russia. [91]

During the last few months of Harris's stay the problems which had been created by the Anglo-American war solved themselves or were quietly shelved. Harris played a small part in the diplomatic flutter to which the Russian annexation of the Crimea gave rise. France was too exhausted, and Britain was unwilling, to oppose it. Fox's policy of punctiliously communicating France's every overture for joint action to Russia won golden opinions in St. Petersburg, and Harris basked in the reflected glow. The Empress was even inspired to communicate confidentially to Fox, through Simolin, the existence of an agreement between herself and Austria, which was of course until then officially unknown. Simolin expressed the hope that Britain would not enter into engagements which might prevent the eventual achievement of an alliance— a broad hint to steer clear of Prussia. [92] No alliance emerged from this happy state of affairs; Fox still hoped for Prussia; Prussia still hankered after France; [93] France was still bound to Austria, and Austria to Russia. And Catherine did not at the time wish for the conclusion of an alliance with Britain, though friendly relations

90. Harris to Lord Mountstuart (Turin), 14/25 October 1782, *MD*, 2, 1.

91. FO 65/9, Fox to Harris, No. 10, 16 May 1783, *MD*, 2, 45.

92. FO 65/10, Simolin to Fox, 24 August 1783; see also my article, "The Secret Austro-Russian Treaty of 1781." The existence of a secret treaty was communicated for the first time by Russia to Prussia and by Austria to France in June 1783.

93. FO 65/10, Fox to Harris, No. 13, 27 July 1783.

had to be maintained as long as she was uncertain of getting her own way with the Porte.[94] By the summer of 1783 she knew that neither the Porte nor France would fight. For the time being, all the powers could sit back, lick their wounds, and digest their acquisitions. The war was over.

On 31 August 1783 Harris was received by the Empress in his farewell audience. Catherine expressed herself very warmly towards Britain and was her old kind and gracious self to Harris. She presented him with her portrait surrounded by diamonds and made gifts of jewels to Lady Harris and to Harris's sister Gertrude. The scene had greatly changed since Harris first set foot in St. Petersburg at the end of 1777. Potemkin, with whom he had indulged in such high flown intrigue, had left the capital on 17 April 1783 to take command of the troops which were to annex the Crimea. Throughout the winter he too had been an ardent champion of Russia's pro-British orientation. His very last communication with Harris was a message sent to the British envoy through an aide-de-camp from the Crimea to the effect that he had written to the Empress recommending the conclusion of an alliance with Britain.[95] Panin, with whom Harris had fought so bitterly, had died on 11 April 1783. He had never recovered from his disgrace, and, whatever the secret of the mysterious contacts which Potemkin had maintained with him since his dismissal in October 1781, foreign policy had been in the hands of the Empress herself, ably assisted by the rising Bezborodko.

The Grand Duke and his consort had returned from their European trip in December 1782, but in spite of all the efforts of the Emperor, his brother the Grand Duke of Tuscany, and his sister, the Queen of France, he remained as hostile to Austria as before. But he lacked any influence whatsoever and, with the death of Panin, he ceased even to have any importance as the potential leader of a party. The scene had been cleared for the second phase of Catherine's reign. The stage was set for the opening of the attempt to realize the famous Greek project, the cast was drawn up and waiting, and the curtain had risen in the Crimea.

94. FO 65/10, Simolin to Fox, 24 August 1783: "cet état d'incertitude [about the Crimea] empêche de prendre quelque parti relativement à vos ouvertures . . ."
95. FO 65/10, Harris to Fox, No. 71, 28 July/8 August 1783.

18. Conclusion

THE FIVE YEARS of Harris's mission in St. Petersburg were not an outstanding success in British foreign relations. The fault was only partly Harris's. He and his superiors in London were heirs to a tradition which regarded Russia as the "natural ally" of Great Britain. Yet in the first phase of the war relations with Britain were by no means the most important aspect of Russian foreign policy. British statesmen were strangely reluctant to recognize that at this time German and Turkish problems were of more vital concern to Russia than the war in the West. Russia was not anti-British; indeed Panin counted on an English alliance in the event of a European war. But the policy of pacifying the continent, which Vergennes so skilfully pursued, inevitably increased the distance between Britain and Russia and drew Russia closer to France.

Russia emerged from the crisis of the War of the Bavarian Succession with her prestige enhanced and her power undiminished. She held the balance of power in Europe between the great powers and was looked up to as the possible leader of the small powers. The temptation to exploit this opportunity was one to which Catherine could not but yield. The foundation of the Armed Neutrality placed her at the head of the maritime neutral powers and in a position from which she could hope to impose her mediation on the belligerents. Meanwhile the secret alliance with Austria altered the very foundation of her foreign policy, but since the alliance remained secret until June 1783 Russia retained to the full her diplomatic initiative. There is no evidence that the Empress sought to exploit the Austro-Russian alliance at once for an attack on the Porte, but she was secretly ready should the occasion arise. Meanwhile Russia continued to be wooed by the great powers and was offered by Britain the mediation which she had previously sought

439

for herself. For a while it seemed possible to exploit the mediation in the interests of the Neutral League by introducing the maritime principles into the final peace treaty. But the moment a serious revolt broke out in the Crimea, in June 1782, the Empress lost all interest in procuring a peace. She made no move to be invited to resume her functions as a mediator after the preliminaries had been signed, and it was Vergennes who took the initiative in this respect, hoping to be given an opportunity to interfere on behalf of the Porte in Russia. By the end of the maritime war Russian annexation of the Crimea was a *fait accompli*. The Empress had been lucky, but she had also been skilful, for the annexation was achieved when France and Britain were too near peace to wish to involve themselves in another war, and yet too near war to be able to act together.

The Armed Neutrality was by far the most important event in Anglo-Russian relations. Basically the Armed Neutrality developed from a number of factors: the Russian desire to crown the achievement of the peace of Teschen with the further triumph of mediating in the conflict between the two great Western powers; the favourable conditions for the expansion of Russian trade provided by a maritime war; the opportunities provided by the war for the neutral trading nations: the acrimonious disputes between a weakened Britain, on the one hand, and the Baltic powers and the Dutch, on the other; similar disputes between Spain and the neutrals; the diplomacy of Vergennes, who had pacified the continent and nursed the neutrals; the traditions of Russia and the Baltic states; and, last but not least, the Empress Catherine's ambition, which led her to respond to the appeals made to her from many quarters to use her influence with both Britain and Spain. Thus, though the form which the Armed Neutrality ultimately took may have flashed suddenly into the Empress's brain, the elements of which it was composed had been maturing for some time.

The first efforts of Russia to secure an invitation to mediate were frustrated by the entry of Spain into the war. But Vergennes was skilful enough to conciliate Russia by maintaining a pretence of talks on the subject. Britain's attitude to these same overtures was more off-hand, partly because the King would listen to no peace talks unless France broke with America, partly because Britain still hoped to secure a Russian alliance and the use of the Russian navy. Yet it was perhaps Harris himself who put into the Empress's head the idea from which the Armed Neutrality may have eventually evolved. This was the proposal for armed mediation which he discussed with the Empress and Potemkin in the summer of 1779 and which the Empress rejected in September. In a slightly modified form, it was the basis of the proposals put forward by Stormont, which occupied Harris in December 1779 and January 1780. The Empress's offers of strictly impartial good offices twice returned to her from Britain in the form of a request to enforce the British peace terms at the sword's point.

But neutrality was the keyword in Russian policy. The *rapprochement* with France was a reality, and the only way to keep Russia out of the war and yet be entrusted with the mediation was to refrain from action that might alienate France. Hence the refusal of the British offers, so incomprehensible to Harris. Hence also the idea that union with the neutrals, notably the Dutch, a naval power, might provide Russia with sufficient support to launch an armed mediation that really was neutral. It was a short step from this plan to the proclamation of the maritime principles and the formation of the Armed Neutrality. The idea of an armed mediation sank into the background, since the Dutch, the first maritime power to be approached, were the last to accede. But Russia, independently of the Neutral League yet acting as its leader, continued ever more strongly throughout 1780 to press her good offices on the belligerents, culminating in the *insinuation verbale* of December 1780. For whatever may have been the Empress's intentions when she founded the Neutral League, she never allowed any of its members to take any independent political initiative in its name and kept the direction of its policy firmly in her hands. It was an instrument she could use or not as she chose, and one behind which she could shelter when it suited her.

The Armed Neutrality has frequently been under-estimated as a political and economic weapon because of a tendency prevalent at the time—and predominant since in many quarters—to consider vanity as the mainspring of the Empress's actions. The reason for this tendency is easy to understand. The sudden eminence Russia acquired during these years, her capacity to play off Prussia against

Austria, Britain against France, provoked a good deal of resentment. The Empress did not hesitate to exploit to the full the opportunities offered by the rivalry of the four great powers, and the
depth of feeling which her presumption aroused is revealed repeatedly in the correspondence of Joseph and Frederick with their
ministers and envoys. In both cases their supercilious attitude was
the expression of resentment at the dominant position which a
parvenu power like Russia had fortuitously acquired; they suffered
from their dependence on the Empress and chose to portray themselves as deferring to her vanity when they were in fact deferring
to her power. The same attitude is revealed by Stormont and Vergennes and by the French and British envoys in Russia. Thus they
all depicted the Neutral League as yet one more example of the
Empress's injudicious meddling in matters of no concern to Russia;
her efforts to protect and expand the Russian export trade were
regarded as vain pretensions to become a universal legislatrix in a
field of no possible consequence to a non-maritime power. Vanity
did indeed play a big part in Catherine's policy, but it was a national as well as a personal vanity, founded on her high estimate of
Russia's place in Europe. She is not to be blamed if others did not
share her view. To ascribe her actions to vanity alone may have
assuaged the wounded feelings of Joseph and Frederick, and indeed of Stormont, but the historian is in duty bound to take account
of the bias of her detractors.

Previous histories of the diplomacy of this period have devoted
little if any space to the ideas on economics and trade underlying
the Russian maritime principles.[1] Only a brief attempt has been
made here to sketch in the background, but it is necessary to stress
that the place of the Armed Neutrality in Russian history will never
be understood unless it is seen in the light of the economic ideas

1. Not one of the standard histories of the diplomacy of this period or of the
Neutral League touches upon the organization of Russian foreign trade in connexion with it. They make the point that the Empress intended to develop trade
under her own flag but do not see the significance of the protection extended to
other neutrals. Gerhardt, *England und der Aufstieg Russlands*, pp. 130 ff. gives a
brief analysis of the place of the Neutral League in Russian economic history.
Fauchille, *La diplomatie française*, pp. 192 ff. notes the interest of Russia in the
Anglo-Dutch dispute but does not develop the idea of any community of commercial interests between the two countries.

current at the time. Granted that the predominant position which Britain occupied in Russian foreign trade had begun to be seen as a restriction on the free development of that trade, it was inevitable that Russian interests should lead her to make common cause with the neutrals. It was the extent and above all the nature of the Dutch dispute with Britain that led Russia to take up the idea first of an armed mediation and then of the Neutral League. With perhaps the exception of Vergennes, contemporaries, who saw Russia as a land power with a minute merchant navy, seldom grasped what advantages she obtained from the Armed Neutrality. But if Dutch shipping could maintain its privileged neutral status it could considerably raise total Russian exports by supplying the increased needs of the Bourbon powers during the war. By claiming the same privileged status for other neutrals, Russia was able to keep this trade going even after the Dutch were driven out of it by the outbreak of the Anglo-Dutch war. From the strictly national point of view the opportunity to develop trade in Russian bottoms was excellent and, even though after the war the demand for Russian shipping declined, by 1787 the number of Russian ships engaged in Russian foreign trade was more than eight times greater than in 1775.[2]

The theory that the defence of the maritime privileges of the Dutch was one of the main motives for the formation of the Neutral League is not disproved by the subsequent Russian failure to mobilize the League in Dutch defence. First, it never occurred to the Empress that Britain would go to war. Secondly, she never had the slightest intention of abandoning her neutrality. And thirdly, the League was fundamentally too weak an instrument and the political interests of its members were too divergent to constitute an efficient instrument for military action. Yet the Empress was far more determined in pressing her mediation between Britain and the Dutch than between Britain and the Bourbons and showed a constant interest in recovering for the Dutch their status as neu-

2. FO 65/10, Shairp to Fox, 23 August/2 September 1783; Russian ships found no cargo as long as others were available, reported Shairp. But see Baranovich et al, *Ocherki*, p. 128: in 1775, 414 ships were engaged in foreign trade of which 17 were Russian and 236 British; in 1787, 2,015 ships were engaged in foreign trade, of which 141 were Russian and 767 were British. The total number of ships had increased by roughly five times, the number of British ships by a little over three.

trals. But she was less than ever inclined to go to war for them when she discovered that the other neutrals could so adequately replace them in the Russian export trade.

A further reason for the bad press from which the Armed Neutrality has suffered is that its final failure overshadowed its early success. The betrayal of the Dutch in 1781 and the fact that the maritime principles were not introduced into the peace treaty in September 1783 led informed opinion in general to regard the Neutral League as merely a piece of Russian self-advertisement. The Dutch, understandably, had nothing but contempt for it. The Austrians and the Prussians soon forgot the temporary benefits their shipping had derived from membership. For a long time it was not known for certain that Russia had raised the question of the inclusion of the maritime principles at the peace negotiations at all.

This suggestion of a lack of seriousness in Russia in pressing for the adoption of the maritime principles derives from a number of sources: first and foremost, the betrayal of the Dutch, and secondly the Empress's mysterious reference in her interview with Harris in December 1780 to a "nullité armée." Though in the same interview she declared "je soutiendrai mon projet, je le crois salutaire," the catch-phrase "nullité armée" has echoed down the ages, contributing to the impression that the Empress attached no great importance to the substance of her policy but only to its appearance. Furthermore the history of the Neutral League has been written so far on the basis of French sources and on the incomplete excerpts printed in the *Malmesbury Diaries*. But France accepted the Russian maritime principles; hence the subject occupied but little space in the correspondence of its envoys in Russia. On the other hand, Harris's only too frequent references to the Empress's failure to understand what she was doing have overshadowed his equally frequent references to her demand that free passage should be granted to her ships. It is in the unpublished correspondence of Harris that evidence of Russian persistence in enforcing the maritime code can be found. The numerous memorials put in by the Russian envoys, both before and after the foundation of the Neutral League, illustrate the extent of Russia's vigilance. From January 1781 to the fall of North, Anglo-Russian relations were governed primarily by disputes over the detention of Russian ships and by the Anglo-Dutch war, itself a consequence of Russian maritime policy. Stormont was driven to abandon one position after another either secretly, as in the case of the treatment of neutral ships, or openly, as in his acceptance of Russian mediation with the Dutch in September 1781. Before him lay the constant threat that the Empress might mobilize the Neutral League against Britain and that the Baltic partnership might cut off Britain's supplies of naval stores. Thus the Neutral League gave the Empress the whip-hand over Britain in her hour of need. But it is quite true that Russia sacrificed the neutral code to the annexation of the Crimea. She could not afford to antagonize a potentially friendly Britain until the seal of great power approval had been finally placed on her new acquisition. Had Russia not been diverted by the Crimea she might well have driven Austria into supporting a much stronger intervention in defence of neutral trade in the course of the Paris peace negotiations.

Moreover the Empress must not bear all the blame for the fact that the adoption of her maritime principles was postponed until the Peace of Paris of 1856. Some of the blame must fall on France and on the United Provinces. Had the Dutch accepted the Empress's mediation in May 1782, when Britain agreed to negotiate on the basis of the maritime principles, their hand and that of Russia would have been immeasurably strengthened at the final peace. Once negotiations with the Dutch had actually begun, Britain would have been committed to acceptance of the maritime principles, and once these principles had been included in a treaty with Britain's principal naval rival the pressure to adopt them *urbi et orbi* would have been very strong. The Dutch had every reason to distrust Russia, but it is likely that the Empress would have secured a better peace for them in 1782–83 than the one they obtained in 1784.

The Neutral League presents certain interesting features which should not be overlooked in the twentieth century. It was not the first Armed Neutrality, but it was the first to proclaim principles of international law (whether rightly or wrongly formulated) and to endeavour to enforce them. In the long series of attempts at peaceful collective action which have since punctuated the history of Europe, it was one of the first to lay down certain principles of international behaviour by agreement between a group of powers. It was not surprising that the Empress should have compared her plan to the Utopian "projet de paix perpetuelle" of the Abbé de St. Pierre.[3]

In a general way the Neutral League played a bigger part in the diplomacy of this period than has usually been admitted. It provided a system into which the neutral nations could fit, a kind of third force in Europe. Neutrality became an active policy, linking together powers which had nothing in common but their neutrality. Moreover by uniting the Baltic powers, and subsequently Austria and Prussia as well, into one loosely knit group, the Armed Neutrality frustrated every British effort at finding allies or even friends on the continent. It would not have been easy for Britain to do so in any event, but the combination of existing alliances—the Franco-Austrian, the Russo-Prussian, the secret Austro-Russian, and the conventions of the Neutral League—rendered it impossible.

Coming after Potemkin's constant assurances of the Empress's affection for Britain and after Harris's extremely optimistic portrayal of the Empress as only too anxious to "stand forth" on Britain's behalf, the Armed Neutrality led to a wave of revulsion

---

3. *Sbornik*, 23, 171, Catherine to Grimm, 2/13 February 1780. The subsequent fate of the maritime principles may be briefly noted here. The period 1780 to 1790 saw the conclusion of a considerable number of commercial treaties not one of which was based on the Consullat del Mar (Bergbohm, *Die bewaffnete Neutralität*, p. 250). But the Empress sacrificed her principles in the ideological war against revolutionary France. The Anglo-Russian treaty of 1793 bound both sides to forbid any trade in any goods with France. Paul I, at the end of 1800, made a fresh effort to establish an Armed Neutrality in the north, and conventions were signed between Russia and Sweden and Denmark. But by March 1801 Paul was dead, and Alexander I reversed his father's policy. A new convention was signed between Britain and Russia on 17 June 1801; Art. 2 stated that enemy goods on board a neutral were liable to confiscation; Art. 3 established that naval stores were not contraband, but if loaded on French account on board a Russian ship they would be liable to seizure under Art. 2. Britain had triumphed. During the war between Britain and Napoleonic Europe, the rights of neutrals at sea practically disappeared. After the war the question became less acute. During the Crimean War the belligerents agreed to abandon privateering, and the Peace of Paris of 1856 finally consecrated the Empress's maritime principles. In practice they have now been superseded. (See Bergbohm, *Die bewaffnete Neutralität*, pp. 248 ff., and Phillips, *Neutrality, Its History, Economics and Law;* for relevant documents see Scott, *Armed Neutralities*, pp. 672 ff.)

against Russia in Britain. Her renewed offers of mediation, stemming not only from Panin but from Potemkin, were waved aside with scant attention. Russia had revealed herself as unpredictable and untrustworthy. The two countries were driven further and further apart by Russian pressure on the Dutch to accede to the Armed Neutrality and by British determination to force a breach if they did so. Thus the Armed Neutrality led directly to the Anglo-Dutch war and indirectly to the joint imperial mediation which Stormont brought about to paralyse Russia at a critical moment.

With the advent of Fox, committed to winding up the war in America, the intrinsic importance of relations between Russia and Britain diminished. The opening of direct negotiations with France, Spain, and America and the renewal of British contacts with Prussia gave far more flexibility to Britain's foreign policy, and she was enabled to emerge from the position of virtual paralysis which had afflicted her in the last months of North's administration. Moreover the opening of the Eastern Question reduced Russia's invulnerability to pressure and intrigue. The Empress still hoped to use the joint imperial mediation to introduce the maritime principles into the peace—it could serve as a useful red herring. But now that France and Britain were rapidly resuming their freedom of action as the negotiations advanced, Russia had to calculate in terms of neutralizing possible French action in support of the Porte. Though no bargain between Britain and Russia was ever proposed or struck, the abandonment of the maritime principles was a *quid pro quo* for Fox's refusal to contemplate the joint action with France which Shelburne had vaguely hinted at. The divergent interests of Austria and Prussia, the too recent memories of Anglo-French hostility, and Prussian preference for France rather than Britain as an ally prevented any combination forming to hold Catherine in check.

Turning now to the actual conduct of foreign policy and to the methods employed by Britain and Russia, certain conclusions suggest themselves. The role of the Whig opposition in Britain in undermining the effectiveness of British foreign policy has not perhaps been sufficiently appreciated. From the foundation of the Neutral League in March 1780, the Whig attacks on the government constantly played into Russian hands. Whig criticism of

North's policy led opinion on the continent to expect that a Whig government would bring the war with America to an end. It led Russia to expect that the Whigs would be more lenient to neutral trade and even that they might adopt the Russian maritime principles. Russia had therefore no desire to fortify North's government with a diplomatic success and could well afford to wait until its inevitable fall. Rarely has the paralysing effect of a divided parliament on foreign policy been so strikingly revealed.

A further weakness in the British position was the lack of a professional approach to the problems involved, notably under Suffolk, that "Arch-Pecksniff" of diplomacy, in the words of Professor Temperley. At no point does one find a realistic appraisal, as a Russian might have made it—and as Vergennes made it—of Russian national interests. Suffolk, Stormont, Grantham, and Harris clothe their thought in out-of-date assumptions, and well-worn clichés flow mellifluously from their pens. Only in the case of Fox does one catch a glimmer of a fresh approach to the realities of Britain's situation—and even Fox was unable to free himself from the obsession with the "natural alliance" between Britain and Russia. It was this amateurish approach to their task which explained Stormont's proposal of a Russian attack on Majorca in spring 1780 and Grantham's really preposterous idea that Russia should seek an establishment in South America at a time when she was meditating the seizure of the Crimea.

A further misconception seriously affected British policy in Russia at this time—namely that British aims could be achieved by corruption, by the use of money to influence the statesmen surrounding the Empress. Such methods had achieved some success when the Empress Elizabeth sat on the throne. For some reason it was assumed that the presence of a woman again on the throne rendered the corruption of her servants a particularly apt method of diplomacy. The Empress Catherine, however, was not of the same cast of character as her predecessor.

From the beginning of his mission, Harris was authorized to promise lavish monetary rewards for the successful conclusion of a treaty. "Never go to the North without the purse in your hand," wrote Yorke to Harris on 12 November 1779,[4] and it was of course

4. Harris Papers.

assumed that all the powers indulged in these practices in Russia—hence the accusations of bribery so frequently bandied about in the dispatches of all the envoys.[5] Harris himself soon discovered that money could buy information but not influence policy. But he still firmly believed that Russian foreign policy resolved itself into the question of who exercised most influence over the mind of the Empress: Panin or Potemkin. His conception was based on a complete misunderstanding of the character of the Empress. Harris refers only too often to her vanity, her fickleness, her "passions," her declining powers, the effect of unbridled sensuality on her will, courage, and ability. These defects of character were supposed to render her vulnerable in a manner from which her masculine fellow-sovereigns were preserved. But not least in her variegated love-life Catherine showed many masculine traits, and her emotions but seldom overruled her judgement.

Incapable of discerning that Panin's opposition to an alliance with Britain stemmed from genuine conviction that it was not in Russia's interests at the time, Harris as early as March 1779 saw in him merely an agent of the King of Prussia—which he had then not yet become. The British envoy's attitude to Potemkin in the first phase of their association illustrates the extent to which he

5. It is probable that Harris was by far the most lavish distributor of largesse in St. Petersburg, though what he spent never amounted to what he was accused of spending by others. From the end of 1777 to August 1782, he spent £19,450 on the purchase of information; from August 1782 to August 1783 he spent a further £10,000 (see my article, "The Use of British Secret Funds in St. Petersburg, 1777–1782," and FO 65/9, Harris to Grantham, No. 3, 3/14 January 1783; No. 37, 23 April/4 May 1783, and FO 65/10, unnumbered, 14/25 August 1783, a final payment to keep his agents going until Fitzherbert arrived). See also Add. MSS. 47.563, Fitzherbert to Fox, 26 October 1783, on Harris's contacts: "The only two persons he said, from whom he used to obtain intelligence of that sort, were Count Woronzow [S. R. Vorontsov] and one of P. Potemkin's nieces, the Grande Generale de Branicki [Alexandra Engelhardt] . . . it would have been very difficult" added Fitzherbert, "not to say impossible, considering their high quality and station, to have transferred to me their connection with Sir J. Harris." (Cf. Harris to Lady Harris, 20 October/1 November 1782: Count Simon Vorontsov "is of great and real use to me." Merton Papers). Harris confirmed to Fitzherbert that he had never been able to bribe P. Bakunin or Alopeus, Osterman's secretary. Vergennes's correspondence does not reveal any secret service expenditure except on the very lowest scale, and Frederick's letters reveal him as reluctant to spend the meanest sum. It is possible however that pensions were paid to Russians without going through the French and Prussian envoys in Russia.

believed all Russian ministers to be moved only by appeals to their self-interest. He believed that Potemkin had refrained from supporting his proposals for an armed mediation in September 1779 because he had been seduced by Prussian offers of a duchy and a wife. Again, in May 1780, when he feared that the Prince might succumb to Prussian wiles, he contemplated bribing him on a magnificent scale.

Meanwhile Potemkin saw in the eager Harris the perfect instrument for the undermining of Panin's credit as foreign minister. In order that Harris should remain tied to his leading strings, he confirmed him in all his prejudices. He portrayed the Empress as weak and vacillating, driven by passion and vanity. He exaggerated the extent of Panin's hostility and impressed Harris with the fact that only through him, Potemkin, could Britain achieve anything. With the gradual growth of Potemkin's ascendancy over Harris, the British envoy ceased to believe him venal, but he came to believe that Potemkin was committed to the defence of British interests at the Russian court. From the spring of 1780 he saw everything through Potemkin's eyes. The Prince fed him a judicious mixture of truths, half-truths, and lies, aimed invariably at getting Britain to do exactly what the Empress wanted or what he wanted. When Harris believed he was using the Prince, the Prince was using him. Every single defeat of Harris's was explained away by the Prince, either on the grounds of the Empress's pusillanimity or because the baleful influence of Panin had been exercised once again. Harris in turn did his best to serve Potemkin by promoting the Austro-Russian *rapprochement* and eventually the alliance, which he of course believed would be in the interests of Britain too. At the same time he pursued a campaign designed to drive Panin from office once and for all.

Predisposed to believe that the Empress would respond to appeals to her vanity, Harris was led to recommend and pursue strangely irrelevant tactics. Such manoeuvres as the letter which George III was persuaded to write in November 1779 and the ostensible "panegyrick" on Potemkin which Stormont wrote with his own hand are shown up as pathetic and ineffective tricks. Even more pitiful seems Harris's advice to Keith to persuade Kaunitz to persuade the Emperor to include some expressions of esteem for "our worthy principal" in one of his letters to the Empress, in the hope that she would feel more kindly disposed towards Stormont as the result of the Emperor's praise.[6] Again, in his efforts to discredit Frederick II, Harris could think of nothing better than to write in an *en clair* letter sent by an Austrian courier that the King of Prussia rated the Dowager Queen Juliana of Denmark above the Empress Catherine.[7] The offer of Minorca must ultimately be seen in the same light, as an appeal to the Empress's vanity and as an affort to bribe her. This time Potemkin fell into the trap, but the Empress did not—proof, if proof were needed, that Potemkin's influence over her mind was less than over her heart. "Why this project failed I am still at a loss to learn," wrote Harris in August 1782; never had the Empress seemed more taken with any proposal, "nor was I ever more astonished than when I found her shrink from her purpose."[8] Neither he nor Stormont understood that the Empress's rejection of Minorca was conclusive evidence of the uselessness of diplomacy by personal intrigue.

It was Harris who, by attaching himself to Potemkin, turned Panin's neutrality into active hostility towards the British envoy and hence towards Britain. The more Harris tried to woo Russia through Potemkin, the more violently Panin opposed him. But he certainly never dreamt of provoking a breach between the two countries, since above all he wished to keep Russia out of the war. Harris's support of the new Austrian orientation of Russia contributed further to poison relations between the two men. Though the Empress no longer listened to his advice, Panin was still the instrument through which the day-to-day conduct of foreign affairs was carried out. It was he who drafted the Empress's instructions to her envoys and carried on the talks concerning Russian mediation.

By cutting himself off from confidential contact with Panin, Harris lost touch with the realities of Russian policy. Though the Empress consulted Potemkin about most things, he concerned himself mainly with the grand designs. He was not particularly experienced in foreign affairs, and he was in many respects igno-

6. Add. MSS. 35.521, f. 167, Harris to Keith, 19 February/2 March 1781.
7. Ibid., f. 36, Harris to Keith, 10/21 January 1781.
8. *MD, I,* 528.

rant of the details of the Empress's activities. It is quite possible for instance that when the Empress showed him her plan for the Armed Neutrality, he did not quite understand the international implications of her policy. Certainly throughout the period of their association, though Potemkin always advised Harris to persuade Britain to give way on this issue, he attached but little importance to the League itself and spoke of it with impatience and even with contempt, echoing the currently accepted version that the Empress had been misled by Panin and by her own vanity. It was a policy that did not interest him.

How sterile was Harris's plan of attaching himself so exclusively to the Prince is revealed by what happened after Panin's fall. Now that according to Harris's calculations Potemkin should have been all-powerful, Anglo-Russian relations remained tense. The latent Russian disdain for the government of North came increasingly into the open, and the Empress pressed ever more strongly for Britain to clarify her stand on neutral trade. Potemkin and Bezborodko echoed each other in the pressure they brought to bear on Harris, and behind them stood the Empress whose policy remained unchanged despite the disgrace of Panin. Thus the value of Potemkin proved illusory: he used Harris as long as he needed him to undermine Panin. Once Panin had fallen he ceased to take any interest in British concerns. Bezborodko later provided a penetrating comment on Harris's fate in Russia. When the young Comte de Ségur appeared in St. Petersburg in 1785 as minister of France, the Secretary wrote to Simon Vorontsov, then minister in Britain: "He is beginning to fall into the same confusions and vexations which I believe befell our friend Harris. Accustomed to recognize a certain person as all-powerful, he frequently interprets his silence or his encouragement as something achieved . . . and then he is surprised when the ministry gives him a decisive answer in a different sense." [9]

The elegance, fullness, and vividness of Harris's dispatches have won him a great reputation as a diplomat. He was able, witty, shrewd, arrogant, and a born intriguer. His subsequent extremely successful mission to The Hague, where he helped the Orange family to overthrow the Patriot party, shows him in his real ele-

9. *AKV, 13*, 92, 24 October/4 November 1785.

ment.[10] Yet a less positive character might have served Britain better at the time in Russia. Harris was too deeply impressed with the importance of his mission, too anxious to achieve a resounding success. By taking a leading part in the campaign to oust Panin, he subordinated the fate of Anglo-Russian relations to the outcome of a court intrigue. Despite his protestations, intrigue was the breath of life to him, and he was far happier conducting his secret plots with Potemkin than pursuing difficult negotiations requiring great tact with Panin. It is even permissible to doubt whether his dispatches convey a true picture of his conspiracies with Potemkin; there are times when one senses an effort on his part to take over the direction of British policy towards Russia and to impose it from St. Petersburg on his principals. The full truth will probably never be known.

As a man Harris made many friends in Russia; he was popular at court and appears to have been one of the ornaments of Catherine's salon for a considerable time. The duration of Potemkin's friendship for him is a striking tribute to his powers of entertainment and the charm of his society. But, perhaps because the man was too deeply absorbed in the task, the charm wore off with the passage of time. He was remembered in Russia as a master of intrigue. Potemkin spoke of Harris contemptuously in 1785 as a "lying and cunning man of by no means laudable qualities"— a bad case of the pot and the kettle.[11] In 1787 the Empress, writing to Grimm, referred to Harris as "un brouillon et un intrigant . . . quand il ne peut ni brouillonner ni intriguer, il prend la jaunisse; c'est ce qui lui est arrivé ici." [12] Some of the ill will expressed in these remarks must be discounted since it was due to resentment of the policy of alliance with Prussia which Britain was pursuing at the time and which Harris was engaged in implementing. Nevertheless Harris's mission to Russia was not an outstanding success for British diplomacy, and it is not on a par with his later mission to The Hague.

But if British policy was in many respects ill conceived and founded on a distorted image of Russian realities, Russian per-

10. See Cobban, *Ambassadors and Secret Agents*.
11. *AKV, 13*, 92, Bezborodko to A. Vorontsov, 8/19 July 1785.
12. *Sbornik, 23*, 429, 29 November/10 December 1787.

sonalities, and Russian power, it was pursued with vigour. One
cannot but admire Harris's energy, resourcefulness, audacity, and
tenacity. His dispatches are masterly—if very long. In the bal-
anced prose of the Augustan age he penned his vivid descriptions
of dialogues with the Empress, with Potemkin, with Panin, his
disdainful, irreverent, or censorious comments on the Russian
court. Because they were the first dispatches of that period to be
published they have exercised a powerful influence on the history
of Catherine's reign and on the study of her character and court.
In this respect it is opportune to issue a warning against too implicit a reliance on them. Scarcely one of Harris's interpretations
is objectively valid, and the hand of Potemkin, who had his own
purposes in mind, too often guided his pen.

With the passing of time Harris too lost all remaining consideration for Russia and the Russians, and he never shed his prejudices.
"I have not a grain of opinion left for Catherine—would that she
had her Petruchio again," he wrote on 2 February 1785.[13] Both in
Russia and later he remained convinced that "she is actuated in all
her public conduct by motives of vanity alone." [14] On Potemkin he
was silent, and in his printed correspondence there is not even a
mention of the death of his quondam friend in 1791. Indeed it is
unlikely that Harris could have retained any admiration for a man
who was so alien in every respect to an eighteenth-century English
gentleman and who had so thoroughly deceived him; for Harris
was a typical product of England at the height of her power,
imbued with an unbounded confidence in the superiority of everything British and full of that moral arrogance which was in many
ways the greatest barrier to understanding. As he wrote to his sister
in 1781: "All you say relative to our behaviour about foreigners is
perfectly true but it is an ill without a cure. We are an odd people,
never are rightly understood but by those who are as odd as ourselves and who possess as good intellects—this is rarely the case
as many foreigners are odd but few are odd and clever." [15]

Russian foreign policy in this period seems to have suffered from
one great miscalculation and from a good deal of over-elaboration.

13. *MD*, 2, 101, to Carmarthen.
14. *MD*, 2, 414, to Carmarthen, 5 February 1788.
15. Merton Papers, 13/24 March 1781 to Gertrude Harris.

The miscalculation arose over the British breach with the United Provinces. The Empress under-estimated the importance of economic warfare in British eyes, and thus, in January 1781, she was suddenly faced with the situation which she had all along endeavoured to avoid, namely a treaty commitment with one of the powers at war. Her betrayal of the Dutch was perhaps inevitable in the circumstances. Not one member of the League wished to draw the sword in defence of Dutch trade. Russia wanted to preserve her neutrality. Denmark and Sweden hoped to profit from the disappearance of Dutch shipping to increase their own trade.

The Empress's efforts to get out of this embarrassing situation are marked by her awareness of the ridicule the League was incurring. She was driven to take up one expedient after another. She offered her good offices, she offered her mediation, she recognized Dutch belligerency, she withdrew her mediation and referred the Dutch to the joint imperial mediation, she took part in a common *démarche* with Sweden and Denmark and at the same time pressed her own single mediation again. These various moves were almost all made without awaiting the results of the previous ones, often without consulting her allies. They led to a great deal of confusion about Russian intentions and a great deal of irritation at the Empress's general meddlesomeness. The Dutch were not conciliated by her endeavours. Once they had refused Fox's offers in spring 1782, they were abandoned to their fate. But they were as much the victims of Russia as of Britain.

The Neutral League itself, the most successful of the Russian improvisations during the war, suffered from the defects of over-elaboration and over-ambitiousness. The union of the neutrals to defend their trade did not take sufficiently into account the basic rivalry among the several powers. It grouped together powers with divergent political interests, and lack of trust between the members paralysed it as an instrument for positive action such as an armed mediation. The same over-elaborate activity can be seen in the plan put forward by Osterman in summer 1782, in answer to Fox's overtures, to mobilize the Neutral League in Britain's favour. Fortunately perhaps for Britain, the Empress did not even wait to receive replies from her allies. The revolt in the Crimea turned her away with almost bewildering speed from any policy likely to hamper her freedom of action in the East.

If, in spite of these weaknesses, Russian policy showed throughout a consistent grasp of Russian interests, it nevertheless suffered
in its execution from the system prevailing at the Russian court.
Though the Empress and her ministers were unmoved by appeals
to their passions or their pockets, the orientation of policy still
tended to become associated with personalities. Panin was the ex-
ponent of the Prussian system, Potemkin the architect of the Greek
project. Their inability to work together meant that a change of
policy had to be accompanied by a change of ministers. The methods which Panin used to preserve his power and his policy cannot
be defended, not merely in relation to Harris but with regard to
the Empress herself. The deliberate evasions and deceptions of
Panin, his secret plottings with the Bourbon envoys and with
Goertz, the language he used to and about Harris, make sorry
reading. Inevitably his behaviour gave rise to false impressions of
the opinions of the Empress by perverting the manner if not the
matter of her policy. Potemkin was not much better. He seems to
have confined his grosser charges against Panin to Harris; he does
not appear to have spoken with such freedom to other envoys. He
identified himself more closely with the Empress's policy, for in
the long run his advice to Harris always amounted to urging on
Britain compliance with her wishes. On matters of real importance
to him, such as Russian policy towards the Porte and the Austro-
Russian alliance, he maintained an impenetrable secrecy. Yet
he was ready to blacken the Empress's character over and over
again in the process of maintaining his ascendancy over Harris and
in his struggle to overthrow Panin. The Empress's policy, in the
case of Panin, and her character, in the case of Potemkin, were
betrayed in pursuit of their personal rivalry by those whose task
it should have been to defend her. Unnecessary complications
were also introduced into Russian foreign relations by the merci-
less duel between the two men. After the fall of Panin the atmosphere became clearer. Bezborodko showed himself in this respect
more worthy of the confidence reposed in him, and though Potemkin had no love for him the two men were at least in agreement on the foreign policy pursued by the Empress.

The battle between Panin and Potemkin explains many of the
difficulties of the foreign envoys in Russia and adds piquancy to

their dispatches. It also tends to make their reports unreliable, for so much depended on their source of information. Only by checking one source against another and against the Empress's own instructions can some of the distortion be corrected. The last word will only be said when the publication of Catherine's diplomatic correspondence is resumed and when every scrap emanating directly from her is made available for examination by scholars.

In spite of the revulsion in Britain against Russia, provoked mainly by the Armed Neutrality, Fox remained wedded to the idea of a Russian alliance, and, indeed, immediately after the war it was Russia who tended to evade the British offers.[16] With the arrival of Pitt, however, new ideas gradually replaced the traditional assumptions of British foreign policy. Almost at once, without any open breach, relations between Britain and Russia became more distant as a result of Britain's support of the Prussian-led *Fürstenbund* in the interests of Hanover.

The Empress's unpopular maritime principles reappeared as an obstacle in Anglo-Russian relations when, in the mid 1780s, negotiations were started to renew the Anglo-Russian commercial treaty which was due to expire in 1786. The Empress insisted on the inclusion of her code in the treaty. As she wrote later, in 1789, she saw no reason why Britain should not grant to Russia what had been granted to France in the Auckland treaty of 1786.[17] The negotiations failed, and the treaty was not renewed. A few years later the Armed Neutrality reared its head in good earnest in the so-called Ochakov crisis, which culminated in 1791. It provided a useful rallying cry for those who saw in Russia a potentially dangerous and hostile country. But the memory of the harm it had done was not enough to overcome the prejudices of two generations, and the combination of powerful Whig attacks and a hostile public opinion frustrated Pitt's anti-Russian policy. It was the first attempt to break with tradition, and it failed.[18]

Catherine's victory in the Ochakov crisis served to increase

16. See e.g. *AKV, 31, 438*, A. Vorontsov to S. Vorontsov, n.d., 1784.

17. On these negotiations see Gerhardt, *England und der Aufstieg Russlands*, pp. 150 ff.; cf. *AKV*, Catherine to S. Vorontsov, 28 February/11 March 1789.

18. For the Ochakov crisis, see Anderson, *Britain's Discovery of Russia, 1553–1815*, pp. 143 ff., and Gerhardt, *England und der Aufstieg Russlands*, pp. 275 ff.

awareness in Britain of Russia's growing might. Subsequent
Anglo-Russian relations were conditioned by a host of new factors,
and were complicated by the outbreak of the French revolution
and the fresh partitions of Poland. As the war against France
moved into the forefront of Anglo-Russian relations, the Armed
Neutrality became only a bad memory. It flickered into brief life
again in 1800 and was finally laid to rest in the Anglo-Russian
treaty of 17 June 1801.

Looking back from the present it is possible to observe that the
period 1777–83 had a more profound influence on the British outlook on Russia than on the Russian attitude towards Britain. Russian attachment to Britain had always been tinged with resentment
at the subordinate position which she felt herself to occupy in
British foreign policy. Hence the period of the war of American
independence saw the continuation of Russia's march to great-
power status at an increased pace. Though Russia might occasionally trifle with France, not once was an alliance seriously considered. Britain remained the pivot of Russian policy in the West:
it was Pitt, not Catherine, who would create the tension in 1791.
But the Armed Neutrality represented Russia's complete political
emancipation and was at the same time a strenuous effort at economic emancipation from Britain. Having freed her diplomacy
from British assumptions of inferior status, Russia proceeded to
exploit to the full her newly acquired diplomatic eminence. Britain, having spent five years in the humiliating position of a sup-
pliant to Russia and having received only the rebuff of the Armed
Neutrality, was eventually led to the realization that Russia had
grown up into a full member of the circle of great powers in Europe. Though she might be considered barbarous and uncivilized
in the domestic sphere, in the international sphere she was at last
recognized as a power potentially as dangerous as any other. Never
again did Britain take Russia for granted.

Appendix

The Origin of the Armed Neutrality in Historical Literature

THE HISTORY of the Armed Neutrality of 1780 has suffered from the very beginning from the intrigues that surrounded its birth, and it has since aroused passionate controversy. When the anti-British nature of the League became apparent, Panin's version of its origin, as told to Goertz and repeated by him, naturally gained credit. Harris himself, though his dispatches reveal that he knew better at first, rapidly adopted—under Potemkin's influence —the interpretation put about by Panin through Goertz, in preference to what Panin told him personally. Indeed he must have come to believe quite genuinely that this version was true; otherwise he would scarcely have dared to say to the Empress herself, in December 1780, that she was reported to have adopted "le projet des françois et que le votre étoit très différent" (*MD*, *1*, 355). The current opinion in England throughout the later 1780s was that the Neutral League had originated either with France or with Prussia.

The first account to appear in print by one of the diplomats accredited to the Russian court at the time was that of Goertz, which appeared anonymously and without his authority in London, in 1792, under the title *The Secret History of the Armed Neutrality*. A later, authenticated edition appeared in Bâle in 1801, as *Mémoire ou précis historique sur la neutralité armée et son origine, suivi de pièces justificatives*, by Johann Eustache von Goertz. In the meantime Baron d'Albedyhll published in 1798 his *Recueil de mémoires et autres pièces authentiques . . .*

459

which, however, does not add much to our knowledge of the origins of the Neutral League. Goertz's account therefore held the day, and it was taken up by C. Dohm (who knew Goertz) in his *Denkwürdigkeiten meiner Zeit . . . 1778–1806*, published in 1814–19. A cursory glance at Goertz's history reveals the extent of his errors. He states (p. 19 of the 1801 edition) that Britain, in 1779, encouraged Russia in her plans at Turkey's expense as the *quid pro quo* of an alliance; that Catherine had proposed to Britain an armed mediation in Britain's favour (p. 26 ff.); that Harris and Potemkin persuaded the Empress to sign the order to arm the fleet; and that Harris even secured a secret promise that if Spain did not change her tune the Russian ships would be used to force her to do so (p. 30 ff.). Harris's dispatches reveal how completely false this picture is.

The next important documentary source to appear in print, Harris's own dispatches, selected and edited by his grandson and published in 1844, served to strengthen the Panin-Goertz-Dohm version of the origins of the League, since Harris had been converted to the view that the Empress did not understand what she was doing when she proclaimed her maritime principles. In 1859 a selection of the most important Russian documents concerned with the foundation of the Neutral League was printed in the *Morskoy Sbornik,* and serious study of the problem at last became possible.

Historians of the Neutral League have inevitably taken sides on the question whether or not the Empress knew what she was doing. The first to write after the publication of the Russian documents in the *Morskoy Sbornik,* D. Katchenowsky, in his *Prize Law* (English translation, 1867), makes a sensible summary (p. 70) in favour of the argument that the Empress understood her maritime principles. His arguments are developed at more length by O. Eichelmann in "Der bewaffnete Neutralitätsbund Russlands vom Jahre 1780" (*Russische Revue,* 1880). C. Berg-bohm, in his *Die bewaffnete Neutralität 1780–1783* (1884), follows the Panin-Goertz version and condemns Katchenowsky outright; he is grossly unfair to Eichelmann (see his critical bibliography, pp. 28–29). He is in turn criticized by V. A. Bil'basov in "Rossiya i Angliya v XVIII veke" (*Russkaya Starina, 80,* 19 ff.).

Among non-Russian historians, Paul Fauchille, in his *La diplomatie française et la Ligue des Neutres* (1893), credits the Empress with understanding her principles but quite unjustifiably credits Vergennes with the idea of the League. I cannot accept his statement (pp. 353 ff.): "Ne sont-ce pas en définitive les refus répétés de l'Angleterre d'accepter la médiation moscovite qui suggérèrent l'idée de former, de concert avec la Hollande, une ligue commerciale des neutres?" This simplifies the issue beyond recognition. The Russian mediation policy had not yet advanced far enough for it to suffer from Britain's refusal to listen to overtures. Up to that time, for example, no mention of the subject had been made to Spain. Fauchille produces the frankly fantastic explanation for Panin's performance that the Empress, knowing him to be lazy, deliberately let him believe that the order to arm the fleet had been made at Harris's instigation, in order to provoke him to immediate activity designed to defeat Harris and Potemkin. Believing himself to be the victim of their plot, Panin then used the Empress's plan to restore his fallen credit with the Prussian and French envoys (pp. 336–41).

R. Krauel, in his "Preussen und die bewaffnete Neutralitaet" (1908), repeats the Panin-Goertz-Dohm version, and so does F. Edler in *The Dutch Republic and the American Revolution* (1911). C. F. Carusi and C. D. Kojouharoff, in "The First Armed Neutrality" (1929), acknowledge that Catherine knew what she was doing, but their bias against Britain is so strong that they distort the picture of her policy. S. F. Bemis, in his *The Diplomacy of the American Revolution* (1935), does not go into detail on this particular issue but seems to assume (pp. 153–54) that while the Empress ordered a declaration of principles to be made it was Panin who actually thought of incorporating the basically anti-British principle of "free ships, free goods" into the Russian declaration.

The most solid of the works dealing exclusively with the Armed Neutrality of 1780 is the monograph by C. Bergbohm. Yet on the question of the origins of the Neutral League I find myself in complete disagreement with him, and I have therefore summarized here my arguments against his theory. Bergbohm worked entirely on printed documents and therefore knew noth-

ing of the vital Russian *insinuation verbale* of 20/31 December
1778, protesting to Britain against Suffolk's declaration of 19
October 1778. He thus did not realize how early or how constant
was Russian interest in the theoretical, legal side of the dispute
over neutral trade. Moreover Bergbohm relied on Goertz's
Memoire ou précis historique of 1801, and he never saw Goertz's
actual dispatches from St. Petersburg. He also relied too much
on those of Harris's dispatches which show him converted to the
Panin version of the origin of the League and ignores the many
occasions when Panin told Harris that the Empress had conceived the whole idea. Only once does he query Harris's account,
when he makes the somewhat unworthy suggestion (p. 236, n. 8)
that Harris's report of 25 February/7 March 1780 (No. 17 bis)
was printed only in part in *MD, 1,* 284, in order to safeguard the
British envoy's reputation. Bergbohm also does not mention, and
possibly does not consider relevant, the British attack on the
Dutch convoy in December 1779; of Galitzin's approaches to the
Prince of Orange at the end of January 1780 he knew nothing—
indeed the archives of the House of Orange have not been used
by any previous historian of this problem. Nor does Bergbohm
see the point of Catherine's rescript to Galitzin of 14/25 February
1780. Indeed he does not relate his account to specific incidents
in the war at sea other than the Spanish detentions of Russian
ships and property. Finally he is influenced by a sentimental desire to acquit Catherine of "Treulosigkeit" towards Britain.

Bergbohm, however, forgets that when Bernstorff first proposed
his five points in favour of neutral trade to Russia, in his note
to Sacken of 18/29 September 1778, he made it perfectly clear
that his object was to force *Britain* to adopt new and milder
principles towards neutral trade. This same Note by Bernstorff is
referred to twice in the Empress's rescript of 9 March 1780 addressed to the Russian envoy in Denmark proposing the formation of the Neutral League. There is ample evidence that the
Empress read all dispatches and official documents; it is incon-
ceivable that with Bernstorff's Note before her she should have
failed to understand that these principles were opposed to British
practice.

That the principles proposed were those of Bernstorff, with

minor modifications, is a tribute not to Panin's ingenuity but to his laziness. Whether Catherine actually enclosed a draft of the maritime principles she wished to proclaim in her rescript to Panin of 14/25 February 1780 remains uncertain. No such draft is printed with her rescript in *Morskoy Sbornik*. On the other hand Harris in May 1780 was told that "the five points required were in the rough draft she sent to Count Panin and this Minister had added nothing material of his own . . ." This information was purchased by Harris from a man whom he described as secretary to the Empress and to Potemkin. This informant added that he did not know what had put these ideas into the Empress's head, "but as she had, for several months past, seen frequently Mr St Paul (her agent at Hamburgh) and Count Woronzow at the head of the Commission of Commerce, he believed she had collected them from conversation" (*MD, 1*, 307). Perhaps the Empress did discuss her plans with St. Paul and Vorontsov, but certainly the five points came from Bernstorff. According to Simon Vorontsov (younger brother of the president of the college of commerce), it was P. Bakunin who actually drafted the declaration of maritime principles (*AKV, 9*, 133, to Alexander Vorontsov, 19/30 August 1788) and not Panin. It will be remembered that according to the Empress it was also Bakunin who opened Panin's eyes to the merits of her maritime policy (see above, p. 74).

If one collates what Panin told Goertz with what Panin told Harris (as opposed to what Harris later chose to believe), it is evident that Panin lied either to the one or to the other. Previous historians have refrained from putting this inescapable conclusion into words. But putting together all the evidence on the origins of the Neutral League, such as the Empress's own instructions, the actions of her envoys abroad, letters from courtiers unconnected with the struggle between Panin and Potemkin, and even what Panin told Harris, a consistent story emerges. Only what was told by Panin to Goertz contradicts the evidence of the documents. In the circumstances the Goertz version, as echoed by Bergbohm, should, unless new Russian material is discovered to support it, finally be abandoned.

Bibliography

THE STARTING POINT in the study of the diplomacy of the
period 1777–1783 is *The Diplomacy of the American Revolution*
by Samuel Flagg Bemis, which contains a valuable bibliographical
survey. The most complete modern bibliography for the legal
issues involved in the Armed Neutrality is to be found in *The
Armed Neutralities of 1780 and 1800,* edited by James Brown
Scott. A wider selection of Russian sources is given by C. F. Carusi
and C. D. Kojouharoff in their article "The First Armed Neutrality" (*National University Law Review*). C. Bergbohm's *Die
bewaffnete Neutralität* includes a thorough critical bibliography
and is otherwise invaluable for the analysis of the legal issues,
though the interpretation of both British and Russian foreign
policy suffers from too narrow a selection of diplomatic documents.

The general diplomacy of the period I have reconstructed from
a number of sources. On the English side I have been able to
use the official correspondence between London and the major
European courts, deposited in the Public Record Office, including the dispatches of Sir James Harris from St. Petersburg. A
selection of extracts from these dispatches was published in 1844,
edited by Harris's grandson (herein cited as *MD*). I have checked
these printed versions in every case against the originals, and in
view of the many slight variations in the texts, I have decided
invariably to quote from the text in the Public Record Office,
indicating however when a dispatch is also printed. If only an
extract of a dispatch is printed the reference is enclosed in
brackets. I have also consulted Harris's private correspondence
with his friends and colleagues in the Auckland, Hardwicke, and
Fox Papers in the British Museum.

I have been extremely fortunate in being allowed to examine some of Harris's papers in the possession of the Earl of Malmesbury who most kindly placed them at my disposal (herein cited as Harris Papers). I had hoped to find some traces of Harris's personal relations with Potemkin, perhaps some letters from the Prince, but these do not seem to have been preserved, if they ever existed. However I found extremely useful the letters to Harris from British envoys at other courts (Keith in Vienna, Yorke at The Hague, Elliot and Liston in Berlin, Alleyne Fitzherbert in Paris). There are also a number of conference papers which supplement those in the Public Record Office.

I have also been allowed by kind permission of the Warden and Fellows of Merton College to examine the Harris papers deposited there (herein cited as Merton Papers). The relevant papers consist of letters from Harris to his wife, Harriet, and to his sister, Gertrude, during the period of their absence in England. They provide some amusing sidelights on the Russian scene but add nothing substantial to our knowledge. Harris's letters to Lady Harris show him to have been a fond husband, though a pious hand has deleted most of his affectionate messages.

As regards published letters, memoirs, and biographies, I have confined my selection to those works which throw light on the character, thoughts, and actions of only those people actually involved in my story.

La Diplomatie française et la Ligue des Neutres by P. Fauchille provides a most comprehensive study of French relations with Russia and with members of the Neutral League, but it is too one-sidedly based on French archives and is marred by a strong nationalist bias. Fauchille's quotations are moreover frequently unreliable: he paraphrases, runs two dispatches together, or fails to indicate dates clearly. I have therefore consulted the original correspondence between Vergennes and Corberon and Vérac in St. Petersburg, and my quotations are from the archives in their case, though I have occasionally used Fauchille for French correspondence with other courts at the time.

Austrian diplomacy is extensively documented in print. Particularly valuable are the published correspondence between Catherine II and Joseph II, and Joseph II and Count Ludwig

Cobenzl, Austrian envoy to St. Petersburg. For the Prussian point of view I have drawn on the printed correspondence of Frederick II who was to all intents and purposes his own foreign minister. Unfortunately this edition publishes only Frederick's own letters in full. Goertz's dispatches from St. Petersburg are printed only in part and one cannot judge of the importance of what has been left out. Nevertheless the broad outlines of Prussian diplomacy can be reconstructed from this correspondence, though it should not be used without some caution. I have found Frederick II surprisingly ill-informed of what was going on and an adept at launching various *canards* throughout Europe.

In Russia the Armed Neutrality has been the object of some study in isolation or as part of the history of the development of international maritime law. But there exists no single study of Russian foreign policy as a whole during the period of the American war which, from the Russian point of view, represents merely a breathing space between the two Russo-Turkish wars. The great history of Solov'yev comes to an end in the 1770s. A supplementary volume has been added which sketches briefly and inaccurately the diplomatic history of 1778–80, but the documents quoted are frequently dated wrongly or not at all. I have had to rely on printed documents for lack of access to Russian archives, but these are fortunately numerous, though very scattered. The many volumes of the *Sbornik imperatorskago russkago istoricheskago obshchestva* and the *Arkhiv Knyazya Vorontsova* contain much useful material, and I have consulted the other major Russian historical collections and journals. Russian diplomacy and particularly the early period of the Armed Neutrality is considerably illuminated by the published Archives of the House of Orange. The archives contain letters exchanged by the Prince of Orange and the Grand Pensionary, and there are also reports from the Dutch ambassadors in St. Petersburg and many intercepts from the correspondence of some of the foreign envoys at The Hague with their courts.

Unpublished Documents

Admiralty Papers (Public Record Office, London)
  Letters from Doctors' Commons, Adm 1/3886
  Letters from Secretaries of State, Adm 1/4140–44
  Secretary's Department. In-Letters from Port Admirals, Adm 1/663
Auckland Papers (British Museum, London)
  Letters from James Harris to W. Eden, Add. MSS. 34.414–16.
Correspondance Politique (Archives des Affaires Étrangères, Paris)
  Correspondance Politique, Russie, vols. *101–107*
Foreign Entry Books (Public Record Office)
  Miscellaneous Letter-Book, 1778, SP 104/236
Foreign Office Papers (Public Record Office)
  Austria, FO 7/1–5
  Denmark, FO 22/1–2
  France, FO 27/1, 5–9
  Prussia, FO 64/3–5
  Russia, FO 65/1–10
  Sweden, FO 73/1
Fox Papers (British Museum)
  Letters from James Harris and Alleyne Fitzherbert to C. J. Fox, Add.
    MSS. 47.653
Hardwicke Papers (British Museum)
  Letters from James Harris to Sir Robert Murray Keith, Add. MSS.
    35.513–27
  Copies of Sir Joseph Yorke's letters to James Harris, Add. MSS.
    35.434
Harris Papers (in the possession of the Earl of Malmesbury)
  Original letters of Sir Joseph Yorke to James Harris and letters from
    Sir Robert Murray Keith, Hugh Elliot, Robert Liston, Alleyne
    Fitzherbert, and others.
Haus-, Hof- und Staatsarchiv (Wiener Staatsarchiv, Vienna)
  Several documents dated early 1780
Merton Papers (at Merton College, Oxford)
  Letters from James Harris to his wife and to Gertrude Harris
State Papers (Foreign) (Public Record Office)
  Austria, SP 80/221–23
  Bavaria, SP 81/113
  Denmark, SP 75/134–36
  Holland, SP 84/561–2; 565–66; 569–73

Prussia, SP 90/102
Russia, SP 91/101–106
Sweden, SP 95/129–30
Treaty Papers, Russia, 1762–80, SP 103/63
Turkey, SP 97/55

PUBLISHED DOCUMENTS

d'Albedyhll, Baron G., *Recueil de mémoires et autres pièces authentiques, relatives aux affaires de l'Europe, et particulièrement celles du Nord, pendant la dernière partie du 18e siècle*, Stockholm, 1798.

Albemarle, Earl of, *Memoirs of the Marquis of Rockingham and his Contemporaries*, 2 vols., London, 1852.

Archives ou correspondance inédite de la Maison d'Orange-Nassau, 5e série, *1* (1766–79), *2* (1779–82), *3* (1782–89), Leyden, 1910, 1913, 1915.

Arkhiv gosudarstvennogo soveta, *1*, Sovet v tsarstvovaniye Imperatritsy Yekateriny II (1768–98), ed. I. A. Chistovich, St. Petersburg, 1869.

Arkhiv Knyazya Vorontsova, ed. P. Bartenev, 40 vols., Moscow, 1870–95.

    9, Letters from Count S. R. Vorontsov to his brother, Count A. R. Vorontsov; letters to Count A. A. Bezborodko.

    13, Letters of Prince A. A. Bezborodko.

    16, Letters of Count S. R. Vorontsov to Count A. A. Bezborodko.

    28, Letters, rescripts, and ukazes from the Empress Catherine II to Count S. R. Vorontsov.

    31, Letters of Count A. R. Vorontsov to his brother, S. R. Vorontsov, 1783–85.

    34, Miscellaneous papers.

Arneth, A. von, *Joseph II und Katharina von Russland: Ihr Briefwechsel*, Vienna, 1869.

—— *Maria Theresia und Joseph II: Ihre Correspondenz*, 2 (1773–78), 3 (1778–80), Vienna, 1867.

—— and Flammermont, J., *Correspondance secrète du Comte de Mercy Argenteau avec l'Empereur Joseph II et le Prince de Kaunitz*, 2 vols., Paris, 1889.

Authentic memoirs of the life and reign of Catherine II, Empress of all the Russias, Collected from authentic MS's, translations etc. of the King of Sweden, Right Hon. Lord Montmorres, Lord Malmesbury and other indisputable authorities, London, 1797.

A Vindication of the Convention lately concluded between Great Britain and Russia in Six Letters addressed to—, London, 1801.

Barnes, G. R. and Owen, J. H., *The Sandwich Papers, 1771–1782*, Publications of the Navy Records Society, *69, 71, 75, 78*, 1932–38.

Beer, A., *Joseph II, Leopold II und Kaunitz: Ihr Briefwechsel*, Vienna, 1873.

—— and Fiedler, J., eds., *Joseph II und Graf Ludwig Cobenzl: Ihr Briefwechsel—Fontes Rerum Austriacarum, 53*, Vienna, 1901.

Bodham Dunne, W., ed., *The Correspondence of George III with Lord North from 1768 to 1783*, 2 vols., London, 1867.

British Diplomatic Instructions, 1689–1789.

    3, Denmark, ed. J. F. Chance, Camden Society, *36*, London, 1926.

    5, Sweden, ed. J. F. Chance, Camden Society, *39*, London, 1928.

    7, France, Pt. 4, 1745–89, ed. L. G. Wickham Legg, Camden Society, *49*, London, 1934.

Brown, Marvin L., *American Independence through Prussian Eyes*, Durham, N. Carolina, Duke University Press, 1959.

Buckingham, Duke of, *Memoirs of the Court and Cabinets of George III*, 2 vols., London, 1853.

Chalmers, G., *A Collection of Treaties between Great Britain and other Powers*, 2 vols., London, 1790.

Chteniya v imperatorskom obshchestve istorii i drevnostey rossiyskikh, 2, Pt. 2, Pis'ma i zapiski imperatritsy Yekateriny II k grafu Nikite Ivanovichu Paninu, Moscow, 1863.

Clausen, H. F. C., *Recueil de tous les traités . . . de Danemark, 1766–1794*, n.p., 1796.

de Clercq, A. J. H., *Recueil des traités de la France (1713–1906)*, 23 vols., Paris, 1861–1919.

Collection of Publick Acts and Papers relating to the Principles of Armed Neutrality brought forward in the years 1780 & 1781, London, 1801.

Corberon, Marie-Daniel Bourrée, Chevalier de, *Journal Intime: Un diplomate français à la cour de Catherine II, 1775–1780*, 2 vols., Paris, 1901.

Danske Tractater 1751–1800, Copenhagen, 1882.

Dobrynin, G. I., *Istinnoye povestvovaniye ili zhizn' Gavrila Ivanovicha Dobrynina im samim pisannaya*, ed. A. P. Storozhenko and L. N. Antropov, *Russkaya Starina, 3* (St. Petersburg, 1871), 119, 247, 395, 562, 651; *4*, 1, 97, 177, 305.

Dumont, J., *Corps universel du droit des gens*, 8 vols. in 11, Amsterdam and The Hague, 1726–31.

Eggers, C. U. D. von, *Denkwürdigkeiten aus dem Leben Andreas Petrus Grafen von Bernstorff*, Copenhagen, 1800.

Fortescue, Sir John, *The Correspondence of King George III from 1760 to December 1783*, 5 vols., London, Macmillan, 1927–28.

Frederick II, *Mémoires depuis la paix de Hubertsbourg jusqu'à la paix de Teschen (Oeuvres, 6)*, Berlin, 1847.

Fruin, R. and Colenbrander, H. T., eds., *Depêches van Thulemeier, 1763–88*, Historisch genootschap, Utrecht, derde serie, No. 30, Amsterdam, 1912.

Garden, Comte de., *Histoire générale des traités de paix*, 15 vols., Paris, 1848–87.

Gillespie Smyth, Mrs. [Amelia], *Memoirs and Correspondence of Sir Robert Murray Keith*, 2 vols., London, 1849.

Goertz, J. E. von, *Historische und Politische Denkwürdigkeiten*, 2 parts, Stuttgart and Tübingen, 1827–28.

—— *Mémoire ou précis historique sur la Neutralité Armée et son origine suivi de pièces justificatives*, Basle, 1801.

d'Hangest, Baron D. M. D'Yvoy, *Frankrijks invloed op de buitenlandsche aangelegenheden der voormalige Nederlandsche Republiek*, Arnhem, 1858.

Hennings, August, *Sammlung von Staatschriften welche die Freiheit des Handels und der Schiffahrt in dem Seekriege von 1776 bis 1783 betreffen, und von den Kriegführenden sowohl als den neutralen Mächte öffentlich bekannt gemacht worden sind. Nebst einer Abhandlung über die Neutralität und Ihre Rechte*, 2 vols. in 1, Hamburg, 1792.

Hertzberg, Comte de., *Recueil de déductions, manifestes etc.*, rédigés et publiés . . . par le comte de Hertzberg, 2 vols., 1756–78, 1778–79, Berlin, 1789.

Historical Manuscripts Commission, Report 3, pp. 125 ff.; Report 5, pp. 215 ff.; Marquess of Lansdowne Papers.

—— Report 10, Pt. 6, Marquess of Abergavenny MSS, John Robinson's Correspondence, No. 383.

—— Miscellaneous Collection, 6, Papers of H. V. Knox.

Imperatritsa Yekaterina II i knyaz' Potemkin-Tavricheskiy—Podlinnaya ikh perepiska, 1782–1788: Russkaya Starina, 16 (St. Petersburg, 1876), 33, 329, 441, 571.

Jenkinson, C., *A Collection of all the Treaties of Peace, Alliance and Commerce between Great Britain and other Powers . . .* To which is prefixed a discourse on the conduct of the government of Great Britain in respect to Neutral Nations, 3 vols., London, 1785.

Khrapovitsky, A. V., *Dnevnik za 1782–1793*, ed. N. Barsukov, St. Petersburg, 1874.

Lettere del' imperatore dei romani eletto Giuseppe II° di Absburgo-Lorena al tenente maresciallo conte Lodovico Antonio di Belgiojoso-Este: 1774–1787. Curiositá storiche e diplomatiche del secolo decimottavo, ed. F. Calvi (Milan, 1878), pp. 419–513.

Letters of Sulpicius on the Northern Confederacy, with an Appendix containing the Treaty of Armed Neutrality together with other documents relative to the subject, London, 1801.

Malmesbury, Earl of, ed., *A Series of Letters of the First Earl of Malmesbury, his family and friends, from 1745 to 1820,* 2 vols., London, 1870.

—— *Diaries and Correspondence of James Harris, First Earl of Malmesbury,* 4 vols., London, 1844.

Martens, F. de, *Recueil des traités et conventions conclus par la Russie avec les puissances étrangères; 2,* l'Autriche; *6,* l'Allemagne; *9,* l'Angleterre; *13–14,* la France, St. Petersburg, 1874–1909.

Martens, G. F. de, *Recueil des traités,* 2nd ed., Göttingen, 1817.

—— *Supplément au recueil des principaux traités . . . conclus par les puissances d'Europe,* Göttingen, 1807.

Maykov, P. M., ed., *Pis'ma A. A. Bezborodka i P. V. Zavadovskago k grafu P. A. Rumyantsovu, 1775–1793,* St. Petersburg, 1900.

Memorials and Correspondence of Charles James Fox, ed. Lord John Russell, 4 vols., London, Richard Bentley, 1853.

Minto, Countess of, *Life and Letters of Sir Gilbert Elliot from 1751 to 1806,* 3 vols., London, 1874.

O vooruzhennom morskom neytralitete (Introduction and documents), ed. P. A. Obolensky, *Morskoy Sbornik, 43, 44, 45,* St. Petersburg, 1859.

Parliamentary Register or History of the Proceedings and Debates of the House of Commons, 1774–80 (*16* and *17*), 1780–81 (*18, 19,* and *20*).

Parliamentary Register or History of the Proceedings and Debates of the House of Lords, 1774–80 (*15*), 1780–81 (*21*).

Piggott, F. T. and Omond, G. W. T., *Documentary History of the Armed Neutralities,* London, University of London Press, 1919.

Politische Korrespondenz Friedrichs des Grossen, 41–46, Berlin, 1929–39, Ergänzungsband, 1920.

Polnoye sobraniye zakonov, 45 vols., St. Petersburg, 1830.

Recueil des instructions données aux ambassadeurs de France, 9, Russie, 1749–89, Paris, 1890.

Reddaway, W. F., ed., *Documents of Catherine the Great,* The Correspondence with Voltaire and the *Instruction* of 1767 in the English text of 1768, Cambridge University Press, 1931.

Sbornik imperatorskago russkago istoricheskago obshchestva, St. Petersburg, 1867–1916.

1, Reskripty i pis'ma imp. Yekateriny II na imya grafa A. G. Orlova, 1–114; Reskripty i instruktsii imeyushchiye otnosheniye k arkhipelagskoy ekspeditsii, 115–68; Pis'ma imp. Yekateriny II k g-zhe Geoffrin, 253–90.

19, Diplomaticheskaya perepiska angliyskikh poslov i poslannikov pri russkom dvore.

20, Perepiska imperatritsy Yekateriny II s korolem Fridrikhom II.

23, Pis'ma imperatritsy Yekateriny II baronu Mel'khioru Grimmu.

26 and *29,* Grigorovich, N., Kantsler knyaz' A. A. Bezborodko v svyazi s sobytiyami yego vremeni.

27, Bumagi imp. Yekateriny II khranyashchiyesya v gosudarstvennom arkhive ministerstva inostrannykh del s 1774 po 1778.

33, Pis'ma barona Mel'khiora Grimma k imperatritse Yekaterine II.

42, Bumagi imp. Yekateriny II khranyashchiyesya v gosudarstvennom arkhive ministerstva inostrannykh del s 1788 po 1796.

48, Diplomaticheskaya perepiska imperatritsy Yekateriny II za 1762–1764 g.

65, Diplomaticheskiye akty iz arkhiva knyazya N. V. Repnina otnosyashchiyesya do Teshenskago kongressa 1779 g.

87, Diplomaticheskaya perepiska imperatritsy Yekateriny II s 1768–1769.

145, Diplomaticheskaya perepiska imperatritsy Yekateriny II za 1776 i 1777 gg.

Scott, James Brown, ed., *The Armed Neutralities of 1780 and 1800,* London and New York, Oxford University Press, Carnegie Endowment for International Peace, 1918.

Shchelkunov, I. Ya., ed., *Pis'ma imperatritsy Yekateriny II k datskoy koroleve Yuliane Marii,* Copenhagen, 1914.

Vosemnadtsatyy vek, Istoricheskiy sbornik, izdavayemyy po bumagam famil'nago arkhiva knyazem Fedorom Alekseyevichem Kurakinym, ed. V. N. Smol'yaninov, *1* (Moscow, 1904), 2 (1905).

Walpole, H., *The Last Journals of Horace Walpole during the reign of George III from 1771–1783,* ed. A. Francis Steuart, 2 vols., London, John Lane, The Bodley Head, 1910.

Wraxall, Nathaniel W., *Historical Memoirs of my Own Time,* 2nd ed., London, 1815.

CONTEMPORARY MAGAZINES

Annual Register, London, 1778–83.
Niewe Nederlandsche Jaerboekken, Amsterdam, 1779–82.
The Gentleman's Magazine, London, 1778.

SECONDARY WORKS

Adamczyk, Theresa, *Fürst G. A. Potemkin,* Emsdetten, Verlags-Anstalt
Heinr. und J. Lechte, 1936.
Agramonte, Marques de., *Friedrich der Grosse,* Die letzten Lebensjahre
nach bisher unveröffentlichten Dokumenten aus den spanischen,
französischen Archiven, deutsche Bearbeitung von Alfred Semran,
Berlin, 1928.
Albion, R. G., *Forests and Sea Power,* Harvard Economic Studies,
Cambridge, Mass., 1926.
Aleksandrenko, V. N., *Beiträge zur Geschichte der diplomatischen
Verhandlungen zwischen Russland und England im XVIII Jahr-
hunderte,* Sonderabdrück aus dem Jahrbuch der Internationalen
Vereinigung, Berlin, 1898.
────── *Russkiye diplomaticheskiye agenty v Londone v XVIII v.,*
2 vols., Warsaw, 1897.
Aleksandrov, P. A., *Severnaya sistema,* Moscow, 1914.
Anderson, M. S., *Britain's Discovery of Russia, 1553–1815,* London,
Macmillan, 1959.
Anderson, R. C., *Naval Wars in the Baltic during the Sailing-ship
Epoch, 1522–1850, London,* C. Gilbert Wood, 1910.
Arneth, A. von, *Maria Theresias letzte Regierungszeit, 1763–1780,* 4
vols., Vienna, 1879.
Bancroft. *See* Circourt.
Bantych-Kamensky, N. N., *Obzor vneshnikh snosheniy Rossii s derzh-
avami inostrannymi,* 2 vols., Moscow, 1894–1902.
Baranovich, A. I., Kafengauz, B. B., Alefirenko, P. K., Klokman, Yu. P.,
and Kusheva, E. N., *Ocherki istorii SSSR—Period feodalizma—Ros-
siya vo vtoroy polovine XVIII v.,* Moscow, Academy of Sciences of
the USSR, 1956.
Beer, A., *Die Orientalische Politik Österreichs seit 1774,* Prague, 1883.
Bemis, S. F., ed., *The American Secretaries of State and Their Diplomacy,* 10 vols., New York, Knopf, 1927–29; *1,* Historical Introduction
by J. B. Scott.

——— *The Diplomacy of the American Revolution*, New York and London, Appleton-Century, 1935.

——— *The Hussey-Cumberland Mission and American Independence*, Princeton University Press, 1931.

Bergbohm, C., *Die bewaffnete Neutralität 1780–1783*, Berlin, 1884.

Bil'basov, V. A., *Istoriya Yekateriny vtoroy*, 4 vols., London, 1895.

Bindoff, S. T., *The Scheldt Question to 1839*, London, Allen and Unwin, 1945.

Boye, T., *De vaebnede Neutralitetsforbund et avsnit av Folkerettens Historie*, Christiania, 1912 (translated extracts printed in Scott, *Armed Neutralities*, q.v.).

Brückner, A., *Katharina die Zweite*, Berlin, 1883.

——— *Potemkin*, St. Petersburg, 1891.

Butterfield, H., *George III, Lord North and the People, 1779–80*, London, G. Bell and Sons, 1949.

Castéra, Jean Henri de, *Vie de Catherine II de Russie*, 2 vols., Paris, 1797.

[Cérenville, J. E. de], *Vie du Prince Potemkin rédigée d'après les meilleurs ouvrages allemands et français*, 2nd ed., Paris, 1808.

Chechulin, N. D., *Vneshnyaya politika Rossii v nachale tsarstvovaniya Yekateriny II, 1762–1774*, St. Petersburg, 1896.

Christie, I. R., *The End of North's Ministry, 1780–1782*, London, Macmillan, 1958.

Chulkov, M. D., *Istoricheskoye opisaniye rossiyskoy kommertsii*, 7 vols., Moscow, 1781–88.

Circourt, A. de, *Histoire de l'action commune de la France et de l'Amérique pour l'indépendence des États Unis*, 3 vols., Paris, 1876. Translation of the *History of the United States* by G. Bancroft. Vol. 3 contains additional documents not in Bancroft.

Clark, G. N., *The Dutch Alliance and the War against French Trade, 1688–1697*, Manchester University Press, 1923.

Cobban, A., *Ambassadors and Secret Agents: The Diplomacy of the First Earl of Malmesbury at The Hague*, London, Jonathan Cape, 1954.

Colenbrander, H. T., *De Patriotentijd*, 3 vols., The Hague, 1899.

Colombos, C. J., *A Treatise of the Law of Prize*, Grotius Society Publications, 2nd ed., London, 1940.

Conn, Stetson, *Gibraltar in British Diplomacy in the Eighteenth Century*, Yale Historical Publications, New Haven, Conn., 1942.

Coquelle, P., *L'alliance franco-hollandaise contre l'Angleterre, 1735–1788*, Paris, 1902.

Coxe, W., *History of the House of Austria*, 3 vols., London, 1807.

—————— *Memoirs of the Kings of Spain of the House of Bourbon*, 3 vols., London, 1813.

—————— *Travels into Poland, Russia, Sweden and Denmark*, 2 vols., London, 1794; supplementary Vol. *3*, London, 1790.

Danvila y Collado, M., *Historia del reinado de Carlos III*, 5 vols., Madrid, 1888.

Denkwürdigkeiten und Geheime Geschichte des Peterburger Hofes, Leipzig, 1845.

Dohm, C. W. von, *Denkwürdigkeiten meiner Zeit oder Beiträge zur Geschichte vom letzten Viertel des achtzehnten und vom Anfang des neunzehnten Jahrhunderts, 1778 bis 1806*, 5 vols., Lemgo-Hanover, 1814–19.

Doniol, H., *Histoire de la participation de la France à l'établissement des États Unis d'Amérique*, 5 vols., Paris, 1884–92.

Druzhinina, E., *Kyuchuk-Kaynardzhiyskiy mir 1774 goda*, Moscow, Academy of Sciences of the USSR, 1955.

—————— *Severnoye Prichernomor'ye, 1775–1800*, Moscow, Academy of Sciences, 1959.

Edler, F., *The Dutch Republic and the American Revolution*, Johns Hopkins University Studies in Historical and Political Science, Baltimore, 1911.

Fauchille, P., *La diplomatie française et la Ligue des Neutres de 1780*, Paris, 1893.

Fernan Nuñez, Carlos José Gutierrez de los Ríos, Conde de., *Vida de Carlos III*, ed. A. Morel Fatio and A. Paz y Melia, 2 vols., Madrid, 1898.

Ferrer del Río, A., ed., *Obras originales del Conde de Floridablanca*, Biblioteca de autores españoles, *59*, Madrid, 1867.

Firsov, N. I., *Pravitel'stvo i obshchestvo v ikh otnosheniyakh k vneshney torgovle Rossii v tsarstvovaniye Imperatritsy Yekateriny II*, Kazan', 1902.

Fitzmaurice, Lord, *Life of William Earl of Shelburne afterwards First Marquess of Lansdowne with Extracts from his Papers and Correspondence*, 2nd rev. ed., 2 vols., London, Macmillan, 1912.

Flammermont, Jules, *Les Correspondances des Agents Diplomatiques Étrangers en France avant la Révolution*, Paris, 1896.

Flassan, R. de, *Histoire générale et raisonée de la diplomatie française*, 7 vols., Paris, 1811.

Fogdall, J. M. P., *Danish-American Diplomacy 1776–1920*, University of Iowa Studies in the Social Sciences, *7*, No. 2, Iowa, 1922.

Fonvizin, D. I., *Zhizn' grafa Nikity Ivanovicha Panina,* printed in *Polnoye sobraniye sochineniy* (St. Petersburg, 1893), p. 165.

Fulton, T. W., *The Sovereignty of the Sea,* Edinburgh and London, Blackwood, 1911.

Geffroy, A., *Gustave III et la cour de France,* Paris, 1867.

Gerhardt, D., *England und der Aufstieg Russlands,* Munich and Berlin, 1933.

Germiny, M. de, *Les Brigandages Maritimes de l'Angleterre,* 3 vols., Paris, 1925.

Gorman, T. K., *America and Belgium,* London, Fisher Unwin, 1925.

Gribovsky, A. P., *Zapiski o Yekaterine Velikoy,* Moscow, 1847.

Hammer, J. de, *Histoire de l'Empire Ottoman depuis son origine jusqu'à nos jours,* traduit de l'allemand par J. J. Hellert, *16,* Paris, 1839.

Helbig, G. A. W. von, *Russische Günstlinge,* edited and annotated by M. Bauer and Georg Muller, Munich and Berlin, 1917.

Herrmann, E., *Geschichte des russischen Staates,* 7 vols., Gotha, 1860.

Hertz, G. B., *British Imperialism in the Eighteenth Century,* London, Constable, 1908.

Hildt, J. C., *Early U.S. Diplomatic Negotiations with Russia,* Johns Hopkins University Studies in History and Political Science, Baltimore, 1906.

Holdsworth, W. S., *A History of English Law,* 3rd ed., London, Methuen, 1922.

Holm, E., *Om Danmarks Deeltagelse i Forhandlingerne om en vaebnet Neutralitet fra 1778–1780 (Historisk Tidsskrift,* Tredie Raekke, udgivet af den danske historiske Forennig, pp. 1–164), Copenhagen, 1866.

Horn, D. B., *British Diplomatic Representatives 1689–1789,* Royal Historical Society, Camden Third Series, *46,* London, 1932.

Hübner, Martin, *De la saisie des bâtiments neutres ou du droit qu'ont les Nations belligérantes d'arrêter les navires des peuples amis,* The Hague, 1759.

Istoriya russkoy armii i flota, 7 and *8,* Moscow, 1912.

Jessup, P. C. and Deak, F., *Neutrality, Its History, Economics and Law, 1,* Columbia University, Council for Research in the Social Sciences, New York, 1935.

Katchenowsky, D., *Prize Law,* translated from the Russian by F. T. Pratt, London, 1867.

Kulsrud, Carl J., *Maritime Neutrality to 1780,* Boston, Little, Brown, 1936.

Laird Clowes, W., *The Royal Navy—A History from the Earliest Times to the Present*, 6 vols., London, 1899.

Lebedev, P., *Opyt razrabotki noveyshey russkoy istorii po neizdannym istochnikam. I. Grafy Nikita i Pyotr Paniny*, St. Petersburg, 1863.

Lecky, W. E. H., *A History of England in the Eighteenth Century, 4, 5,* and *6*, London, 1923.

Leeds, Duke of, *Political Memoranda*, ed. O. Browning, Camden Society, new series, *34*, London, 1884.

Lodge, Sir Richard, *Great Britain and Prussia in the Eighteenth Century*, Oxford, Clarendon Press, 1923.

Lyashchenko, P. I., *Istoriya narodnogo khozyaystva SSSR, 1*, Moscow-Leningrad, Gosudarstvennoye izdatel'stvo politicheskoy literatury, 1947.

Macpherson, D., *Annals of Commerce, Manufactures, Fisheries and Navigation*, 4 vols., London, 1805.

Mahan, A. T., *The Influence of Sea Power upon History, 1660–1783*, London, Sampson Low, Marston, Searle and Rivington, 1890.

—— *The Major Operations of the Navies in the War of American Independence*, London, Sampson Low, Marston, 1913.

Mahon, Lord, *History of England from the Peace of Utrecht to the Peace of Versailles, 1713–1783*, 3rd ed., 7 vols., London, 1854.

Makogonenko, G., *Nikolay Novikov i russkoye prosveshcheniye XVIII veka*, Moscow-Leningrad, Gosudarstvennoye izdatel'stvo khudozhestvennoy literatury, 1951.

Marbault, A., *Essai sur le commerce de la Russie avec l'histoire de ses découvertes*, Amsterdam, 1777.

Martens, C. de, *Causes célèbres du droit des gens*, deuxième édition, revue, corrigée et augmentée par l'auteur, Leipzig, 1861.

—— *Nouvelles causes célèbres du droit des gens*, Leipzig, Paris, 1843.

Matzen, H., *Forelaesninger over den Positive Folkeret*, extracts printed in translation in Scott, *Armed Neutralities*, q.v.

Meng, John J., *The Comte de Vergennes—European Phases of His American Diplomacy, 1774–1780*, Washington, 1923.

Minot, G., ed., *Decisions of the High Court of Admiralty during the Time of Sir George Hay and of Sir James Marriott, 1*, 1776–79, Boston, Little, Brown and Co., 1853.

Mintslov, S. P., *Obzor zapisok, dnevnikov, vospominaniy, pisem i puteshestviy otnosyashchikhsya k istorii Rossii i napechatannykh na russkom yazyke*, Novgorod, 1911.

Mitchell, Mairin, *Russian Maritime History, 848–1948*, London, Sidgwick and Jackson, 1949.

Morley, Charles, *Guide to Research in Russian History*, Syracuse University Press, 1951.

Namier, L. B., *England in the Age of the American Revolution*, London, Macmillan, 1930.

—— *Additions and Corrections to Sir John Fortescue's Edition of the Correspondence of King George III*, Manchester University Press, 1937.

Nolde, B., *La formation de l'Empire russe: Études, Notes et Documents*, 2 vols., Paris, Institut d'études slaves, 1952.

Oddy, J. J., *European Commerce*, London, 1805.

Oursel, P., *La diplomatie française sous Louis XVI: Succession de Bavière et paix de Teschen*, Paris, 1921.

Pares, R., *Colonial Blockade und Neutral Rights, 1739–1763*, Oxford, Clarendon Press, 1938.

—— *King George III and the Politicians*, Oxford, Clarendon Press, 1953.

—— *War and Trade in the West Indies, 1739–1763*, Oxford, Clarendon Press, 1936.

Pargellis, S. and Medley, D. J., eds., *Bibliography of British History: The Eighteenth Century, 1714–1789*, issued under the direction of the American Historical Association and the Royal Historical Society of Great Britain, Oxford, 1951.

Peters, E., *Die Orientpolitik Friedrichs des Grossen nach dem Frieden von Teschen, 1779–1786*, in *Historische Studien*, ed. R. Fester, Halle, 1914.

Phillips, W. A., *Neutrality, Its History, Economics and Law, 2*, Columbia University, Council for Research in the Social Sciences, New York, 1936.

Pokrovsky, S. A., *Vneshnyaya torgovlya i vneshnyaya torgovaya politika Rossii*, Moscow, 1947.

Potemkin, V. P., *Istoriya diplomatii, 1*, Moscow, Gosudarstvennoye sotsial'no-ekonomicheskoye izdatel'stvo, 1941.

Ranke, L. von, *Die deutsche Mächte und der Fürstenbund*, 2 vols., Leipzig, 1871.

Raumer, F. von, *Beiträge zur neueren Geschichte aus dem britischen und französischen Reichsarchive*, 5 parts, Leipzig, 1836–39.

Reading, Douglas K., *The Anglo-Russian Commercial Treaty of 1734*, Yale Historical Publications, New Haven, Conn., 1938.

Reimann, E., *Geschichte des Bairischen Erbfolgkrieges*, Leipzig, 1869.

Renaut, Francis P., *L'Espionnage naval au XVIII siècle: Le secret service de l'Amirauté britannique, 1776–1783*, Paris, 1936.

────── *Les Provinces Unies et la Guerre d'Amerique (1775–1784): 1, De la neutralité à la belligérence (1775–1780)*, Paris, 1924; *2, La propagande insurgente: C. W. F. Dumas (1775–1780)*, Paris, 1925; *3, La Marine Hollandaise*, Paris, 1932.

────── *Les relations diplomatiques entre la Russie et les États Unis 1776–1823: 1, Catherine II et les insurgents—La Mission Dana 1776–1783*, Paris, 1923.

Ritcheson, Charles R., *British Politics and the American Revolution*, Norman, Okla., University of Oklahoma Press, 1954.

Roscoe, E. D., *A History of the English Prize Court*, London, Lloyds, 1924.

────── ed., *Reports of Prize Cases determined in the High Court of Admiralty, 1745–1859*, London, Steven, 1905.

Salomon, R., *La politique orientale de Vergennes, 1780–1784*, Paris, 1935.

Satow, Sir Ernest, *A Guide to Diplomatic Practice*, 2 vols., London, Longmans Green, 1922.

────── *The Silesian Loan and Frederick the Great*, Oxford, Clarendon Press, 1915.

Schérer, J.-B., *Histoire raisonnée du commerce de la Russie*, 2 vols., Paris, 1787.

Ségur, L. P., *Politique de tous les cabinets de l'Europe pendant les règnes de Louis XV et de Louis XVI*, 2nd ed., 3 vols., Paris, 1801.

Soloveytchik, G., *Potemkin*, London, Thornton Butterworth, 1938.

Solov'yev, S. M., *Istoriya Rossii s drevneyshikh vremen*, 6 vols., St. Petersburg [1911].

Sorel, A., *La question d'Orient au dixhuitième siècle*, Paris, 1878.

Soulavie, J. L. Giraud, *Mémoires historiques et politiques du règne de Louis XVI*, 6 vols., Paris, 1801.

Steven Watson, J., *The Reign of George III, 1760–1815*, Oxford History of England, Oxford, Clarendon Press, 1960.

Storch, H., *Historisch-statistisches Gemälde des russischen Reichs am Ende des achtzehnten Jahrhunderts*, 6 vols., Leipzig and Riga, 1797–1802.

Tarle, Ye. V., *Chesmenskiy boy i pervaya russkaya ekspeditsiya v Arkhipelag, 1769–1774*, Moscow, 1945.

Taube, Baron M., *Le statut juridique de la mer baltique jusqu'au début du XIX siècle*, Académie de Droit International, Recueil des Cours, 53, The Hague, 1935.

Temperley, H. V., *Frederick the Great and Kaiser Joseph*, London, Duckworth, 1915.

Tereshchenko, A., *Opyt obozreniya zhizni sanovnikov upravlyavshikh inostrannymi delami v Rossii,* St. Petersburg, 1837.

Thomson, M. A., *The Secretaries of State, 1681–1782,* Oxford, Clarendon Press, 1932.

Tooke, W., *View of the Russian Empire during the reign of Catherine II and to the close of the eighteenth century,* 2nd ed., 3 vols., London, 1800.

Traité des prises ou principes de la jurisprudence françoise, La Rochelle, 1743.

Uebersberger, H., *Russlands Orientpolitik in den letzten zwei Jahrhunderten,* Vienna, Gesellschaft für neuere Geschichte Österreichs, 1910.

Ulyanitsky, V. A., *Russkiye konsul'stva za granitsey v XVIII v.,* Moscow, 1899.

Unzer, A., *Der Friede von Teschen,* Kiel, 1903.

Urtasún, V., *Historia diplomática de América,* Primera parte, *La emancipación de las colonias británicas,* Tomo 1, *La alianza francesa,* 2 vols., Pamplona, 1920 and 1924.

Ustryalov, N., *Russkaya istoriya,* St. Petersburg, 1855.

Weydemeyer, A., *Dvor i zamechatel'nyye lyudi v Rossii,* St. Petersburg, 1846.

Wood, A. C., *A History of the Levant Company,* London, Oxford University Press, 1935.

Yela Utrilla, J. F., *España ante la independencia de los Estados Unidos,* 2 vols., Lérida, 1925.

Zhizn' grafa Nikity Ivanovicha Panina, St. Petersburg, 1787.

Zhizn' knyazya fel'dmarshala G. A. Potemkina Tavricheskago, 2 parts, St. Petersburg, 1811.

Zhizn' knyazya G. A. Potemkina Tavricheskago, Moscow, 1812.

Zinkeisen, J. W., *Geschichte des osmanischen Reiches in Europa,* 7 vols., 6 (1774–1802), Gotha, 1859.

ARTICLES

Anderson, M. S., "Great Britain and the Russo-Turkish War of 1768–74," *English Historical Review,* January 1954, pp. 39–58.

—— "The Great Powers and the Russian Annexation of the Crimea, 1783–4," *Slavonic and East European Review, 37,* No. 88 (1958), 17.

Bak, I. S., "Dmitriy Alekseyevich Golitsyn," *Istoricheskiye Zapiski,* No. 26 (Moscow, 1948), p. 258.

Bil'basov, V. A., "Rossiya i Angliya v XVIII veke," *Russkaya Starina, 80,* (St. Petersburg, 1893), 1 ff.

Brückner, A., "Vskrytiye chuzhikh pisem i depesh pri Yekaterine II," *Russkaya Starina, 7* (1873), 75 ff.

Carusi, C. F. and Kojouharoff, C. D., "The First Armed Neutrality," *National University Law Review,* No. 9 (1929), pp. 3–69.

Dmitryshin, B., "The Economic Content of the 1767 Nakaz of Catherine II," *American Slavic and East European Review, 19,* No. 1 (February 1960), 1–9.

Eichelmann, O., "Der bewaffnete Neutralitätsbund Russlands vom Jahre 1780," *Russische Revue, 16* (St. Petersburg, 1880), 197.

Fagniez, G., "La politique de Vergennes et la diplomatie de Breteuil, 1774–1787," *Revue historique, 140* (Paris, 1922), 1–25, 161–207.

Fedosov, A., "Voprosy torgovli i promyshlennosti v publitsistike M. P. Shcherbatova," *Uchenyye zapiski,* vypusk 167 kafedry istorii SSSR (Moscow, 1954), p. 99.

Golder, F., "Catherine II and the American Revolution," *American Historical Review, 21* (1915), 92–96.

Guttridge, G. H., "The Whig Opposition in England during the American Revolution," *Journal of Modern History, 6,* No. 1 (1934), 1–13.

Krauel, R., "Preussen und die bewaffnete Neutralitaet von 1780," *Forschungen zur Brandenburgischen und Preussischen Geschichte, 21* (Leipzig, 1908), 435–99.

Lodge, Sir Richard, "The First Anglo-Russian Treaty, 1739–1742," *English Historical Review, 43* (1928), 354.

Madariaga, Isabel de, "The Secret Austro-Russian Treaty of 1781," *Slavonic and East European Review, 38,* No. 90 (London, 1959), 114–45.

———— "The Use of British Secret Funds at St. Petersburg, 1777–1782," *Slavonic and East European Review, 32,* No. 79 (London, 1954), 464–74.

Miller, Margaret, "The Spy Activities of Dr. E. Bancroft," *Journal of American History, 22* (New Haven, Conn., 1928), 70–77, 157–70.

"Obozreniye traktatov o morskom torgovom neytralitete" (anon.) *Morskoy Sbornik, 12* (1854), 173.

Rahbek Schmidt, K., "The Treaty of Commerce between Great Britain and Russia, 1766: A Study in the Development of Count Panin's Northern System," *Scandoslavica, 1* (Copenhagen, 1954), 115–34.

Reddaway, W., "Macartney in Russia 1765–1767," *Cambridge Historical Journal, 3,* No. 3 (Cambridge, 1931), 271.

Rubinshteyn, N. L., "Vneshnyaya torgovlya Rossii i russkoye kupe-chestvo vo vtoroy polovine XVIII v.," *Istoricheskiye zapiski,* No. 54 (Moscow, 1955), pp. 343–61.

Sanchez Diana, J. M., "España y la política exterior de Federico II de Prusia (1740–1786)," *Hispania,* t. *15,* No. lix (Madrid, 1955), p. 590.

———— "Relaciones diplomáticas entre Rusia y España en el siglo XVIII," *Hispania,* t. *12,* No. xlix (Madrid, 1952), p. 590.

Spencer, F., "Lord Sandwich, Russian Masts and American Independ-ence," *The Mariner's Mirror, 44,* No. 2 (1958), 116–27.

Tratschewsky, A., "Das russisch-österreichische Bündniss vom Jahre 1781," *Historische Zeitschrift, 43* (Munich, 1875), 361.

Winter, E., "Grundlinien der österreichischen Russlandpolitik am Ende des 18 Jahrhunderts," *Zeitschrift für Slawistik, 4,* Heft 1 (Ber-lin, 1959), 94.

Index

Admiralty courts, 58, 62, 64, 68, 69 and n.44, 70 and nn.45 and 46, 88, 93, 149, 150 and n.36, 154 nn.41 and 46, 187 and n.50, 198, 199 and n.15, 269 n.18, 372 and n.48, 375–76, 379 n.72, 406; in West Indies, 15 and n.23; ships released without trial, 369 n.42, 371, 380 n.74; Scottish courts, 367–68
Alexander I, Emperor of Russia, 446 n.3
Almodóvar, Pedro Lugán Jimenez de Góngora, Marques de, 100
Alopeus, M. M., 319 n.37, 449 n.5
American colonies, 5, 9–10, 12, 22, 33, 109 and n.37, 110 and n.38, 134 n.31, 223–24, 225 and n.35, 229, 235–36, 245, 253, 255, 257, 273–74, 280, 284–86, 292, 325–28, 331, 338, 399, 405, 440. *See also* United States of America
Amherst, Jeffrey, Lord, 271 n.23
Amphitrite, 383 n.91
Amsterdam, 143, 168, 237, 290
Anna, Empress of Russia, 113 n.48
Archipelago, 6, 45–46
Arethusa (HMS), 37, 39, 58
Armed Neutrality, 111, 140, 240, 245, 252, 255–56, 260, 263, 271, 284, 293, 295, 299, 326, 358, 361, 389, 393, 432, 452, 457–58; origins of, 151–52, 156–57, 170–71, 178–81; launched by Russia, 158–60, 166–67; negotiations with Sweden, 190–91 and n.62, 211, 212 and n.46, 222; negotiations with Denmark, 185–89, 190 n.62, 211, 212 and n.46, 222; conventions, 190–91, 212 and n.46, 246, 249, 266, 268, 269 and n.18; negotiations with Portugal, 191–92, 381; accession of Kingdom of Two Sicilies, 381; accession of Prussia, 252, 320 ff., 334,

374, 377–78; accession of Austria, 340–41, 376, 379 n.71; negotiations with United Provinces, 152–53, 192–93, 195–96, 230–32, 234–37; accession of United Provinces, 219, 238, 244, 249, 263–64, 286, 289, 293 n.16, 302–03, 309, 311–12, 349–50, ratified, 292;

policy to United Provinces after outbreak of Anglo-Dutch war, 290–91, 309–12, 330, 334–36, 337–38, 383, 443–44, 455; and France, 184, 274, 275 n.39, 276; and Spain, 184–85, 226 and n.36, 323; and Britain, 195–98, 202; British reply, 198–99, 203–04, 269 n.18; maritime principles, 172–74, 304, 307, 341, 349–51, 373–76, 398, 405–06, 422–23, 432, 435–37, 446 n.3; as basis of British peace with United Provinces, 394–95, 434 n.79; Austrian draft code, 376 n.62, 433; Russian draft code, 375–76; to be introduced in the final peace negotiations, 340, 379 n.71, 397, 433, 436; and n.89; failure to do so, 426, 445; and mediation of Russia, 223, 280–83, 337–38; and joint imperial mediation, 376, 379 n.71, 402–03, 413, 415 n.8; effectiveness of, 307, 363, 382, 383 and nn.90 and 91, 384–85; significance, 439–47; disappearance of privateering, 385 n.97; closing of Baltic, 381–82. *See also* Catherine II; Panin; *under individual countries*
Armed Neutrality of *1800*, 446 n.3, 458
Augustus III, Elector of Saxony, 7
Austria, 13, 23, 26, 29, 33–34, 39, 43, 48, 82, 90, 105, 114 n.50, 115, 218–19, 411, 422; policy in Bavarian war, 24, 27, 41–42, 47, 51 and n.87; relations with